Children's Literature Review

Guide to Gale Literary Criticism Series

For criticism on	Consult these Gale series
Authors now living or who died after December 31, 1999	*CONTEMPORARY LITERARY CRITICISM (CLC)*
Authors who died between 1900 and 1999	*TWENTIETH-CENTURY LITERARY CRITICISM (TCLC)*
Authors who died between 1800 and 1899	*NINETEENTH-CENTURY LITERATURE CRITICISM (NCLC)*
Authors who died between 1400 and 1799	*LITERATURE CRITICISM FROM 1400 TO 1800 (LC)* *SHAKESPEAREAN CRITICISM (SC)*
Authors who died before 1400	*CLASSICAL AND MEDIEVAL LITERATURE CRITICISM (CMLC)*
Authors of books for children and young adults	*CHILDREN'S LITERATURE REVIEW (CLR)*
Dramatists	*DRAMA CRITICISM (DC)*
Poets	*POETRY CRITICISM (PC)*
Short story writers	*SHORT STORY CRITICISM (SSC)*
Literary topics and movements	*HARLEM RENAISSANCE: A GALE CRITICAL COMPANION (HR)* *THE BEAT GENERATION: A GALE CRITICAL COMPANION (BG)* *FEMINISM IN LITERATURE: A GALE CRITICAL COMPANION (FL)* *GOTHIC LITERATURE: A GALE CRITICAL COMPANION (GL)*
Asian American writers of the last two hundred years	*ASIAN AMERICAN LITERATURE (AAL)*
Black writers of the past two hundred years	*BLACK LITERATURE CRITICISM (BLC)* *BLACK LITERATURE CRITICISM SUPPLEMENT (BLCS)* *BLACK LITERATURE CRITICISM: CLASSIC AND EMERGING AUTHORS SINCE 1950 (BLC-2)*
Hispanic writers of the late nineteenth and twentieth centuries	*HISPANIC LITERATURE CRITICISM (HLC)* *HISPANIC LITERATURE CRITICISM SUPPLEMENT (HLCS)*
Native North American writers and orators of the eighteenth, nineteenth, and twentieth centuries	*NATIVE NORTH AMERICAN LITERATURE (NNAL)*
Major authors from the Renaissance to the present	*WORLD LITERATURE CRITICISM, 1500 TO THE PRESENT (WLC)* *WORLD LITERATURE CRITICISM SUPPLEMENT (WLCS)*

ISSN: 0362-4145

volume 272

Children's Literature Review

Reviews, Criticism, and Commentary on Books for Children and Young People

Carol A. Schwartz
Editor

Produced in association with
Layman Poupard Publishing

Children's Literature Review, Vol. 272

Layman Poupard Publishing, LLC

Editorial Director: Richard Layman

Production Managers: Katherine Macedon, Cindi Barton

Permissions Manager: Jayne Stevens

Senior Editors:
Dennis Poupard, Eric Bargeron, Hollis Beach

Editors: DeAnna Ellis, Kevin C. Kyzer

Editorial Associates: Giesela Patrick, Joanna Burch, Anna Copeland

Content Conversion, Data Coding, Composition: Apex CoVantage, LLC

Volume Advisors:
Patrick K. Dooley, St. Bonaventure University (for "Stephen Crane")
Roberta Seelinger Trites, Illinois State University (for "E. B. White")

© 2024 Gale, part of Cengage Group

ALL RIGHTS RESERVED. No part of this work covered by the copyright herein may be reproduced or distributed in any form or by any means, except as permitted by U.S. copyright law, without the prior written permission of the copyright owner.

This publication is a creative work fully protected by all applicable copyright laws, as well as by misappropriation, trade secret, unfair competition, and other applicable laws. The authors and editors of this work have added value to the underlying factual material herein through one or more of the following: unique and original selection, coordination, expression, arrangement, and classification of the information.

For product information and technology assistance, contact us at
Gale Customer Support, 1-800-877-4253.
For permission to use material from this text or product, submit all requests online at **www.cengage.com/permissions.**
Further permissions questions can be emailed to
permissionrequest@cengage.com

While every effort has been made to ensure the reliability of the information presented in this publication, Gale, part of Cengage Group, does not guarantee the accuracy of the data contained herein. Gale accepts no payment for listing; and inclusion in the publication of any organization, agency, institution, publication, service, or individual does not imply endorsement of the editors or publisher. Errors brought to the attention of the publisher and verified to the satisfaction of the publisher will be corrected in future editions.

Gale
27555 Executive Dr., Ste. 270
Farmington Hills, MI, 48331-3551

LIBRARY OF CONGRESS CATALOG CARD NUMBER 76-46132

ISBN-13: 978-1-5358-7755-8

ISSN: 0362-4145

Print Number: 1 Print Year: 2024
Printed in Mexico

Contents

Preface vii

Acknowledgments xi

Stephen Crane 1871-1900 1
    Entry devoted to the novel The Red Badge of Courage *(1895)*

E. B. White 1899-1985 121
    Entry devoted to the novel Charlotte's Web *(1952)*

CLR Cumulative Author Index 177

Literary Criticism Series Cumulative Topic Index 205

CLR Cumulative Nationality Index 229

CLR-272 Title Index 235

Preface

Literature for children and young adults has evolved into both a respected branch of creative writing and a successful industry. Currently, books for young readers are considered among the most popular segments of publishing. Criticism of juvenile literature is instrumental in recording the literary or artistic development of the creators of children's books as well as the trends and controversies that result from changing values or attitudes about young people and their literature. Designed to provide a permanent, accessible record of this ongoing scholarship, *Children's Literature Review* (*CLR*) presents parents, teachers, and librarians—those responsible for bringing children and books together—with the opportunity to make informed choices when selecting reading materials for the young. In addition, *CLR* provides researchers of children's literature with easy access to a wide variety of critical information from English-language sources in the field. Users will find balanced overviews of the careers of the authors and illustrators of the books that children and young adults are reading; these entries, which reprint reviews and criticism from books and periodicals, assist users by suggesting ideas for papers and assignments as well as supplementary and classroom reading. Ann L. Kalkhoff, president and editor of *Children's Book Review Service, Inc.*, writes that "*CLR* has filled a gap in the field of children's books, and it is one series that will never lose its validity or importance."

Scope of the Series

Each volume of *CLR* profiles the careers of a selection of authors and illustrators of books for children and young adults from preschool through high school. The series also features entries on notable single works by an author, as well as entries on topics of significance in children's literature. Entry lists in each volume reflect:

- an international scope

- representation of authors of all eras

- the variety of genres covered by children's and/or YA literature: picture books, fiction, nonfiction, poetry, folklore, and drama

Authors new to *CLR* are an important focus of the series and entries on older authors will be updated periodically.

Organization of the Book

A *CLR* entry consists of the following elements:

- The **Author Heading** cites the name under which the author most commonly wrote, followed by birth and death dates. If the author wrote consistently under a pseudonym, the pseudonym will be listed in the author heading and the author's actual name given in parentheses on the first line of the biographical and critical introduction. Also located here are any name variations under which an author wrote, including transliterated forms for authors whose native languages use nonroman alphabets. Uncertain birth or death dates are indicated by question marks. Single-work entries are preceded by a heading that consists of the most common form of the title in English translation (if applicable) and the author's name (if applicable).

- The **Introduction** contains background information that introduces the reader to the author, work, or topic that is the subject of the entry.

- The list of **Principal Works** is ordered by age-level headings, beginning with titles for the youngest readers (such as picture books and early readers) and proceeding through young-adult books. Under each heading, the most important works by the author are organized chronologically. Series by the author are listed in chronological order under an additional heading in the appropriate age-level category. An **Other Major Works** heading lists works produced for an adult audience, if applicable. The genre and publication information of each work is given. In the case of works not published in English, a translation of the title is provided as an aid to the reader; the translation is a published translated title or a free translation provided by the compiler of the entry. As a further aid to the reader, a list of **Principal English Translations** is provided for authors who did not publish in English; the list focuses primarily on those works most commonly considered the best by critics. Unless otherwise indicated, plays are dated by first performance, not first publication, and the location of the first performance is given, if known. Lists of **Representative Works** discussed in the entry appear with topic entries.

- **Criticism** is located in three sections: **Author Commentary** (when available), **General Commentary** (when available), and **Title Commentary** (commentary on specific titles).

    The **Author Commentary** presents background material written by the author or by an interviewer. This commentary may cover a specific work or several works.

    The **General Commentary** consists of criticism that considers more than one work by the author or illustrator being profiled. When appropriate, a selection of reviews is included to supplement the general commentary.

    The **Title Commentary** begins with the title entry headings, each of which provides the title and original publication date of the work being reviewed. The title heading lists the title of the work as it appeared in its first English-language edition. When a work is written by an individual other than the one being profiled, such as an illustrator, the parenthetical material following the title cites the author of the work before listing its publication date.

Reprinted criticism is arranged chronologically in each section to provide a useful perspective on changes in critical evaluation over time. The critic's name and the date of composition or publication of the critical work are given at the beginning of each piece of criticism. Unsigned criticism is preceded by the title of the source in which it appeared. All titles by the author that are listed in Principal Works or Representative Works are printed in boldface type. Footnotes are reprinted at the end of each essay or excerpt. In the case of excerpted criticism, only those footnotes that pertain to the excerpted texts are included.

Entries devoted to an individual title include essays arranged chronologically in a general **Criticism** section. Topic entries include essays arranged chronologically under subject headings.

- A complete **Bibliographical Citation** of the original essay or book precedes each piece of criticism. Citations conform to recommendations set forth in the Modern Language Association of America's *MLA Handbook,* 9th ed., 2021.

- Critical essays are prefaced by brief **Annotations** describing each piece.

- An annotated bibliography of **Further Reading** appears at the end of each entry and suggests resources for additional study. In some cases, significant essays for which the editors could not obtain reprint rights are included here. Boxed material following the further reading list provides references to other biographical and critical sources on the author in series published by Gale.

Special Features: Entries on Illustrators

Entries on authors who are also illustrators will occasionally feature commentary on selected works illustrated but not written by the author being profiled. These works are strongly associated with the illustrator and have received critical acclaim for their art. By including critical comment on works of this type, the editors wish to provide a more complete representation of the artist's career. Criticism on these works has been chosen to stress artistic, rather than literary, contributions. Title entry headings for works illustrated by the author being profiled are arranged chronologically within the entry by date of publication and include notes identifying the author of the illustrated work. In order to provide easier access for users, all titles illustrated by the subject of the entry are boldfaced.

CLR also includes entries on prominent illustrators who have contributed to the field of children's literature. These entries are designed to represent the development of the illustrator as an artist. The illustrator's section is organized like that of an author, with two exceptions: the introduction presents an overview of the illustrator's styles and techniques, and the commentary written by the illustrator on his or her works is called "Illustrator Commentary" rather than "Author Commentary." All titles of books containing illustrations by the artist being profiled are highlighted in boldface type.

Indexes

A **Cumulative Author Index** lists all of the authors who have appeared in *CLR* with cross-references to the biographical, autobiographical, and literary criticism series published by Gale. A complete list of these sources is found facing the first page of the Author Index. The index also includes birth and death dates and cross-references between pseudonyms and actual names.

A **Cumulative Topic Index** lists the literary themes and topics treated in the series as well as in *Classical and Medieval Literature Criticism, Literature Criticism from 1400 to 1800, Nineteenth-Century Literature Criticism, Twentieth-Century Literary Criticism, Contemporary Literary Criticism, Drama Criticism, Poetry Criticism,* and *Short Story Criticism.*

A **Cumulative Nationality Index** lists all authors featured in *CLR* by nationality, followed by the number of the *CLR* volume in which their entries appear.

A **Title Index** lists all author titles covered in that volume of *CLR*. Each title is followed by the author's name and corresponding volume and page numbers where commentary on the work is located. All titles reviewed in *CLR* and in the other Literary Criticism Series can be found online in the *Gale Literary Index.*

Citing *Children's Literature Review*

When citing criticism reprinted in the Literary Criticism Series, students should provide complete bibliographic information so that the cited essay can be located in the original print or electronic source. Students who quote directly from reprinted criticism may use any accepted bibliographic format, such as Modern Language Association (MLA) style or University of Chicago Press style. Both the MLA and the University of Chicago formats are acceptable and recognized as being the current standards for citations. It is important, however, to choose one format for all citations; do not mix the two formats within a list of citations.

The examples below follow recommendations for preparing a works cited list set forth in the Modern Language Association of America's *MLA Handbook,* 9th ed., 2021. The first example pertains to material drawn from periodicals, the second to material reprinted from books:

Wolf, Virginia L. "Readers of *Alice*: My Children, Meg Murry, and Harriet M. Welsch." *Children's Literature Association Quarterly,* vol. 13, no. 3, 1988, pp. 135-37. *Children's Literature Review,* edited by Lawrence J. Trudeau, vol. 187, Gale, 2013, pp. 3-6.

Morris, Linda A. "Beneath the Veil: Gender Play in *Pudd'nhead Wilson.*" *Gender Play in Mark Twain: Cross-Dressing and Transgression,* U of Missouri P, 2007, pp. 59-88. *Children's Literature Review,* edited by Lawrence J. Trudeau, vol. 187, Gale, 2013, pp. 176-89.

The examples below follow recommendations for preparing a works cited list set forth in *The Chicago Manual of Style,* 17th ed., 2017. The first example pertains to material drawn from periodicals, the second to material reprinted from books:

Wolf, Virginia L. "Readers of *Alice*: My Children, Meg Murry, and Harriet M. Welsch." *Children's Literature Association Quarterly* 13, no. 3 (Fall 1988): 135-37. Reprinted in *Children's Literature Review.* Vol. 187, edited by Lawrence J. Trudeau, 3-6. Detroit: Gale, 2013.

Morris, Linda A. "Beneath the Veil: Gender Play in *Pudd'nhead Wilson.*" In *Gender Play in Mark Twain: Cross-Dressing and Transgression,* 59-88. Columbia: University of Missouri Press, 2007. Reprinted in *Children's Literature Review.* Vol. 187, edited by Lawrence J. Trudeau, 176-89. Detroit: Gale, 2013.

Suggestions Are Welcome

In response to various suggestions, several features have been added to *CLR* since the beginning of the series, including author entries on retellers of traditional literature as well as on those who have been the first to record oral tales and other folklore; entries on prominent illustrators featuring commentary on their styles and techniques; entries on authors whose works are considered controversial; entries devoted to criticism on a single work or a series of works; sections in author introductions that list major works by and about the author or illustrator being profiled; explanatory notes that provide information on the critic or work of criticism to enhance the usefulness of the essay; a cumulative nationality index for easy access to authors by nationality; and occasional guest essays written specifically for *CLR* by prominent critics on subjects of their choice.

Readers who wish to suggest new features, topics, or authors to appear in future volumes, or who have other suggestions or comments, are cordially invited to write the Product Manager:

Product Manager, Literary Criticism Series
Gale, part of Cengage Group
27555 Executive Dr., Ste. 270
Farmington Hills, MI 48331-3551
gale.customersuccess@cengage.com

Acknowledgments

The editors wish to thank the copyright holders of the criticism included in this volume and the permissions managers of many book and magazine publishing companies for assisting us in securing reproduction rights. Following is a list of reprinted essays included in this volume of *CLR*. Licensors of copyrighted material are noted. Every effort has been made to trace copyright, but if omissions have been made, please let us know.

MATERIAL IN *CLR*, VOLUME 272, WAS REPRODUCED FROM THE FOLLOWING PERIODICALS:

American Literary Realism, vol. 40, no. 3, 2008. Copyright © 2008 *American Literary Realism*. Reproduced by permission of the publisher.—*American Literature,* vol. 11, no. 1, 1939; vol. 11, no. 3, 1939.—*Children's Literature Association Quarterly,* vol. 10, no. 4, 1986. Copyright © 1986 Children's Literature Association. Reproduced by permission of the publisher. —*CLA Journal,* vol. 40, no. 1, 1996. Copyright © 1996 *CLA Journal*. Reproduced by permission of the publisher.—*Journal of Juvenilia Studies,* vol. 2, no. 1, 2019 for "White's Wilbur and Whiteley's Peter Paul Rubens" by Juliet McMaster. Copyright © 2019 Juliet McMaster. Reproduced by permission of the author.—*The Lion and the Unicorn,* vol. 15, no. 2, 1991; vol. 38, no. 3, 2014. Copyright © 1991, 2014 *The Lion and The Unicorn*. Both reproduced by permission of the publisher. —*Midwest Quarterly,* vol. 59, no. 1, 2017. Copyright © 2017 *Midwest Quarterly*. Reproduced by permission of the publisher.—*Modern Fiction Studies,* vol. 5, no. 3, 1959.—*The New Review,* vol. 14, no. 80, 1896.—*School Library Journal,* vol. 22, no. 3, 1975. Copyright © 1975 Library Journals LLC. Reproduced by permission of the publisher.—*South Atlantic Review,* vol. 52, no. 1, 1987. Copyright © 1987 *South Atlantic Review*. Reproduced by permission of the publisher.—*Studies in the Novel,* vol. 10, no. 1, 1978. Copyright © 1978 *Studies in the Novel*. Reproduced by permission of the publisher.—*The University of Kansas City Review,* vol. 19, no. 4, 1953.—*War, Literature, and the Arts,* vol. 18, nos. 1-2, 2006; vol. 21, nos. 1-2, 2009. Copyright © 2006, 2009 *War, Literature, and the Arts*. Both reproduced by permission of the publisher.

MATERIAL IN *CLR*, VOLUME 272, WAS REPRODUCED FROM THE FOLLOWING BOOKS:

Conrad, Joseph. From *Stephen Crane: A Study in American Letters,* by Thomas Beer, William Heinemann, 1924.—Crane, Stephen. From *Stephen Crane: Prose and Poetry,* Library of America, 1984.—Crisp, Thomas. From *Crossing Textual Boundaries in International Children's Literature,* edited by Lance Weldy, Newcastle upon Tyne, Cambridge Scholars Publishing, 2011. Copyright © 2011 Cambridge Scholars Publishing. Reproduced by permission of the publisher.—Hergesheimer, Joseph. From *The Work of Stephen Crane,* vol. 1, edited by Wilson Follett, Alfred A. Knopf, 1924.—Martin, Cathlena. From *Adaptation in Contemporary Culture: Textual Infidelities,* edited by Rachel Carroll, London, Continuum International Publishing, 2009. Copyright © 2009 Bloomsbury Publishing. Reproduced by permission of the publisher.—Weisberger, Bernard. From *Twelve Original Essays on Great American Novels,* edited by Charles Shapiro, Wayne State University Press, 1958. —White, E. B. From *Charlotte's Web,* Harper and Row, 1952.

The Red Badge of Courage
Stephen Crane

(Full name Stephen Townley Crane; also wrote under the pseudonym Johnston Smith) American short-story writer, novelist, poet, and journalist.

The following entry provides criticism of Crane's novel *The Red Badge of Courage* (1895). For additional information about the novel, see *CLR,* Volume 132.

INTRODUCTION

In *The Red Badge of Courage,* Stephen Crane (1871-1900) offers a vivid portrait of American Civil War combat through an account of a young Union soldier's first days on the battlefield. Embraced as a hallmark of American literature, the novel is a study of heroism and the complex psychology of the common foot soldier during wartime. Remarkably, Crane's knowledge of the Civil War was culled solely from historical texts and autobiographical accounts, as he had not witnessed military action prior to writing the work. *The Red Badge of Courage* is commonly approached from two different critical perspectives. One school views it as an essentially realist text documenting an unromanticized account of warfare and a soldier's maturation; proponents of the naturalist school, on the other hand, focus on the social, biological, and psychological forces that shape the youth's experiences. Other critics have examined the novel within the context of several major literary trends of the nineteenth century. A meditation on pride, fear, bravery, humility, and mortality, *The Red Badge of Courage* is widely regarded as Crane's masterpiece. Given its accessible length, relatable narrative voice, and applicable themes about identity, violence, and the amorphous definition of courage, Crane's novel remains a fixture on school reading lists, enabling Crane's literary influence to affect large segments of adolescent readers.

PLOT AND MAJOR CHARACTERS

The Red Badge of Courage presents a series of episodes that trace the experiences and conflicting emotions of a new Civil War Union Army recruit, Private Henry Fleming, who is referred to as "the youth" throughout the narrative. As the novel opens, the young soldier's regiment is camped along a riverbank, where they have been awaiting orders for several weeks. The narrator describes the young soldier's reminiscences about his departure from home. Though the youth had felt daring and confident upon enlisting, he worries about remaining courageous during his first engagement. Marching orders eventually arrive, and the young soldier's regiment advances to the front line. As the Confederate Army charges toward him, Fleming readies himself and manages to fire a shot as rival troops rush by in pursuit. Yet, when the enemy reappears unexpectedly for another skirmish, Fleming is overtaken with fear and runs away. He thinks his fellow soldiers foolish for not having retreated until he overhears a Union general declare that the enemy has been repulsed. Fleming feels angry and cheated out of his opportunity for valor. He decides to flee into the woods, imagining Nature as a protective goddess. While rationalizing his continued retreat, he stumbles upon the rotting corpse of a Union soldier. Shrieking, he runs back toward the front. Fleming falls in with a group of wounded soldiers and encounters "the tattered man," a mortally wounded compatriot who questions Fleming about his nonexistent injury. Deeply ashamed of his cowardice, Fleming escapes from the tattered man and drifts into the crowd of injured men. Fleming is embarrassed and envious of their wounds and wishes for his own "red badge of courage." Among the crowd, Fleming recognizes his friend, Jim Conklin, "the tall soldier," who is near death. With the help of the tattered man, Fleming carries Conklin to a nearby field where he can rest without being trampled by the artillery. The youth and the tattered man watch as Conklin dies. Enraged by what he has witnessed and agitated by the tattered man's inquiries, Fleming leaves the dying tattered man wandering aimlessly in the field. Contemplating whether to rejoin his regiment, Fleming notices groups of Union infantry retreating in mass confusion from combat. One of the fleeing soldiers hits Fleming on the head with his rifle. Dazed and bleeding, Fleming is led back to his regiment by an anonymous soldier. The youth's injury is misidentified as a battle wound, which his companions interpret as the reason for his absence. Fleming's comrade, Wilson, who early in the novel is the belligerent "loud soldier," dresses his wound.

The next day, Fleming demonstrates the skills of a fine, upstanding soldier, fighting bravely alongside Wilson and rescuing the regimental flag. Displaying camaraderie and leadership, Fleming wins the praise of officers. In the final battle charge, Fleming accompanies Wilson as he captures the enemy flag, which signals the regiment's victory. The novel concludes with Fleming's reflections on the past days' events. Though haunted by his abandonment of the tattered man, he is proud of his accomplishments in battle and celebrates his entrance into manhood.

MAJOR THEMES

The Red Badge of Courage explores notions of bravery and cowardice through the thoughts and actions of an inexperienced soldier on the verge of maturity. The novel contemplates the definition of heroism, illustrating how Fleming's romantic conception of courage evolves into a mature, complex assessment as he transitions from adolescence to adulthood. Coming-of-age themes in the novel are underscored by the symbolic function of Conklin and Wilson—both of whom exhibit self-assurance and leadership, as well as vulnerability—as authentic representations of masculinity. Crane incorporates motifs of noise and silence to signal the maturity of his characters. The sounds of artillery and male bravado that permeate the early chapters turn to quiet reflection at the novel's end. Crane also utilizes irony to demonstrate the complicated nature of heroism, as evidenced by Fleming's so-called red badge of courage, which he receives when a retreating Union soldier strikes him on the head with his weapon. In addition to themes concerning valor and maturation, the novel addresses the power and indifference of Nature, emphasizing the relative insignificance of man. By referring to his characters as "the youth," "the loud soldier," "the tattered man," and "the tall soldier," Crane imbues the narrative with allegorical significance reminiscent of the everyman parable. Religious imagery in the book includes the gathering of foliage that Fleming designates as a "chapel" during his respite in the woods. Fleming's sense of sanctuary, however, is quickly shattered by the discovery of the decomposing Union soldier, which suggests a fatalistic counterpoint to the character's inarticulate spirituality. Other significant motifs include the symbolic use of color, such as Crane's description of the sun at the time of Conklin's death as "a fierce red wafer," and the use of mechanical imagery to depict combat.

CRITICAL RECEPTION

The Red Badge of Courage was a bestseller on both sides of the Atlantic when it was first published. The novel rapidly gained an iconic, then canonical, status and has never gone out of print. Four versions of the novel have been published: a shortened, syndicated newspaper version from December 1894; the 1895 Appleton version, generally regarded as the standard edition, since Crane himself prepared and proofread it; a hybrid University of Virginia version edited by Fredson Bowers in 1975; and a final version published in 1978 by Harry Binder, who reinserted words, phrases, and full paragraphs that Crane had excised, along with an abandoned chapter. Scholars have placed lower priority on the 1894 and 1975 editions. In the essay "*The Red Badge of Courage* Nobody Knows" (1978), Binder portrayed Crane as a poor, pliable, and hungry writer who succumbed to the wishes of Appleton's overbearing editor, Ripley Hitchcock. Seeking to undo the purported pressures that Crane received from Hitchcock, the expanded Binder edition substantially alters the novel's ending by rendering the irony and uncertainty of the final state of Henry Fleming unequivocal. The end of the Appleton version, however, retains a teasing ambiguity, inspiring scholars to debate how much irony to factor into the narrator's final comments about Henry: "He saw that he was good"; "He felt a quiet manhood, nonassertive but . . ."; "He was a man."

Critics have debated the value of *The Red Badge of Courage* as a war novel, examining its portrayal of fear, frenzy, courage, heroism, and other complex ethical concerns. Scholars have also examined Crane's portrayal of race, gender, and class in the novel, as well as his inclusion of religious themes and symbols. The novel's impact on other late nineteenth- and early twentieth-century American and British authors has received regular attention. Its compact length has made it ideal for high school and college classes. The novel's stylistic firepower and energy have made it both student friendly and a compelling read for a broad audience.

Adapted from *The Red Badge of Courage* entry in *CLR,* Vol. 132

Academic Advisor: Patrick K. Dooley

Patrick K. Dooley is Distinguished Board of Trustees Professor of Philosophy, emeritus at St. Bonaventure University. He is the author of *The Pluralistic Philosophy of Stephen Crane* (1993) and *Stephen Crane: An Annotated Bibliography of Secondary Scholarship* (1992). He has published numerous essays tracing philosophical themes in the works of the American Literary Realists and Naturalists, notably works by John Steinbeck, William Dean Howells, Harold Frederic, Frank Norris, Willa Cather, Jack London, and Norman Maclean.

PRINCIPAL WORKS

Maggie: A Girl of the Streets. As Johnston Smith. Privately printed, 1893. Rev. ed. As Stephen Crane. D. Appleton, 1896. Print. (Novel)

The Black Riders and Other Lines. Copeland and Day, 1895. Print. (Poetry)

*The Red Badge of Courage: An Episode of the American Civil War. D. Appleton, 1895. Print. (Novel)

George's Mother. E. Arnold, 1896. Print. (Novel)

The Little Regiment and Other Episodes of the American Civil War. D. Appleton, 1896. Print. (Short stories)

The Third Violet. D. Appleton, 1897. Print. (Novel)

The Open Boat and Other Stories. London, William Heinemann, 1898. Rev. ed. *The Open Boat and Other Tales of Adventure.* Doubleday and McClure, 1898. Print. (Short stories)

Active Service. Frederick A. Stokes, 1899. Print. (Novel)

The Monster and Other Stories. Harper and Brothers, 1899. Expanded ed. London, Harper and Brothers, 1901. Print. (Novella and short stories)

War Is Kind. Frederick A. Stokes, 1899. Print. (Poetry)

Whilomville Stories. Harper and Brothers, 1900. Print. (Short stories)

Wounds in the Rain: War Stories. Frederick A. Stokes, 1900. Published as *Wounds in the Rain: A Collection of Stories Relating to the Spanish-American War of 1898.* London, Methuen, 1900. Print. (Short stories)

Great Battles of the World. J. B. Lippincott, 1901. Print. (History)

Last Words. London, Digby, Long, 1902. Print. (Short stories)

The O'Ruddy: A Romance. With Robert Barr. Frederick A. Stokes, 1903. Print. (Novel)

The Works of Stephen Crane. Edited by Wilson Follett. Alfred A. Knopf, 1925-26. 12 vols. Print. (Nonfiction, novels, poetry, and short stories)

The Collected Poems of Stephen Crane. Edited by Follett. Alfred A. Knopf, 1930. Print. (Poetry)

Stephen Crane: Letters. Edited by R. W. Stallman and Lillian Gilkes. New York UP, 1960. Print. (Letters)

The Complete Short Stories and Sketches of Stephen Crane. Edited by Thomas A. Gullason. Doubleday, 1963. Print. (Short stories)

Stephen Crane: Uncollected Writings. Edited by Olov W. Fryckstedt. University of Uppsala, 1963. Print. (Nonfiction and sketches)

The War Dispatches of Stephen Crane. Edited by Stallman and E. R. Hagemann. New York UP, 1964. Print. (Journalism)

The New York City Sketches of Stephen Crane, and Related Pieces. Edited by Stallman and Hagemann. New York UP, 1966. Print. (Short stories)

The Poems of Stephen Crane. Edited by Joseph Katz. Cooper Square Publishers, 1966. Print. (Poetry)

Sullivan County Tales and Sketches. Edited by Stallman. Iowa State UP, 1968. Print. (Short stories)

The Notebook of Stephen Crane. Edited by Donald J. Greiner and Ellen B. Greiner. Kingsport Press, 1969. Print. (Notebook)

†*The Works of Stephen Crane.* Edited by Fredson Bowers. UP of Virginia, 1969-76. 10 vols. Print. (Nonfiction, novels, poetry, and short stories)

Stephen Crane in the West and Mexico. Edited by Katz. Kent State UP, 1970. Print. (Journalism)

The Red Badge of Courage: A Facsimile Edition of the Manuscript. Edited by Bowers. Bruccoli Clark/Microcard Editions, 1972. 2 vols. Print. (Novel)

The Western Writings of Stephen Crane. Edited by Frank Bergon. New American Library, 1979. Print. (Short stories)

Stephen Crane: Prose and Poetry. Edited by J. C. Levenson. Library of America, 1984. Print. (Nonfiction, novels, poetry, and short stories)

The Correspondence of Stephen Crane. Edited by Stanley Wertheim and Paul Sorrentino. Columbia UP, 1988. 2 vols. Print. (Letters)

The Red Badge of Courage and Other Stories. Edited by Pascal Covici, Jr. Penguin Books, 1991. Print. (Novel and short stories)

*An abridged version of *The Red Badge of Courage* was syndicated by Bacheller & Johnson Newspaper Syndicate in December 1894.

†*The Red Badge of Courage* was volume 2 of the Virginia Edition, published in 1975.

CRITICISM

PRIMARY SOURCE: *The Red Badge of Courage* **(novel date 1895)**

SOURCE: Crane, Stephen. "The Red Badge of Courage." *Stephen Crane: Prose and Poetry,* Library of America, 1984, pp. 179-88.

[*In the following excerpt, Crane creates a memorable portrayal of battlefield frenzy.*]

It seemed to the youth that he saw everything. Each blade of the green grass was bold and clear. He thought that he was aware of every change in the thin, transparent vapor that floated idly in sheets. The brown or gray trunks of the trees showed each roughness of their surfaces. And the men of the regiment, with their starting eyes and sweating faces, running madly, or falling, as if thrown headlong, to queer, heaped-up corpses—all were comprehended. His mind took a mechanical but firm impression, so that afterward everything was pictured and explained to him, save why he himself was there.

But there was a frenzy made from this furious rush. The men, pitching forward insanely, had burst into cheerings, moblike and barbaric, but tuned in strange keys that can arouse the dullard and the stoic. It made a mad enthusiasm that, it seemed, would be incapable of checking itself before granite and brass. There was the delirium that encounters despair and death, and is heedless and blind to the odds. It is a temporary but sublime absence of selfishness. And because it was of this order was the reason, perhaps, why the youth wondered, afterward, what reasons he could have had for being there.

Presently the straining pace ate up the energies of the men. As if by agreement, the leaders began to slacken their speed. The volleys directed against them had had a seeming windlike effect. The regiment snorted and blew. Among some stolid trees it began to falter and hesitate. The men, staring intently, began to wait for some of the distant walls of smoke to move and disclose to them the scene. Since much of their strength and their breath had vanished, they returned to caution. They were become men again.

The youth had a vague belief that he had run miles, and he thought, in a way, that he was now in some new and unknown land.

The moment the regiment ceased its advance the protesting splutter of musketry became a steadied roar. Long and accurate fringes of smoke spread out. From the top of a small hill came level belchings of yellow flame that caused an inhuman whistling in the air.

The men, halted, had opportunity to see some of their comrades dropping with moans and shrieks. A few lay under foot, still or wailing. And now for an instant the men stood, their rifles slack in their hands, and watched the regiment dwindle. They appeared dazed and stupid. This spectacle seemed to paralyze them, overcome them with a fatal fascination. They stared woodenly at the sights, and, lowering their eyes, looked from face to face. It was a strange pause, and a strange silence.

George Wyndham (essay date 1896)

SOURCE: Wyndham, George. "A Remarkable Book." *The New Review*, vol. 14, no. 80, 1896, pp. 30-40.

[*In the following essay, Wyndham stresses the differences between combat narratives written by officers and those by recruits. He explains that instead of including battle details and strategy Crane restricts himself to Henry Fleming's impressions, "minute to minute, during two days of heavy fighting."*]

All men are aware of antagonism and desire, or at the least are conscious, even in the nursery, that their hearts are the destined theatres of these emotions; all have felt or heard of their violence; all know that, unlike other emotions, these must often be translated into the glittering drama of decisive speech and deed; all, in short, expect to be lovers, and peer at the possibility of fighting. And yet how hard it is for the tried to compare notes, for the untried to anticipate experience! Love and war have been the themes of song and story in every language since the beginning of the world, love-making and fighting the supreme romances of most men and most nations; but any one man knows little enough of either beyond the remembered record of his own chances and achievements, and knows still less whither to turn in order to learn more. We resent this ignorance as a slur on our manhood, and snatch at every chance of dispelling it. And at first, in the scientific "climate" of our time, we are disposed to ask for documents: for love-letters, and letters written from the field of battle. These we imagine, if collected and classified, might supply the evidence for an induction. But, on second thoughts, we remember that such love-letters as have been published are, for the most part, not nearer to life than romantic literature, but further removed from it by many stages: that they are feeble echoes of conventional art—not immediate reflections, but blurred impressions of used plates carelessly copied from meretricious paintings. And so it is with the evidence at first hand upon war. The letters and journals of soldiers and subordinate officers in the field are often of a more pathetic interest than most love-letters; but to the searcher after truth they are still disappointing, for they deal almost exclusively with matters beyond the possibilities of the writer's acquaintance. They are all of surmises—of what dear ones are doing at home, or of the enemy's intentions and the general's plans for outwitting him: they reflect the writer's love and professional ambition, but hardly ever the new things he has heard and seen and felt. And when they attempt these things they sink to the level of the love-letters, and become mere repetitions of accepted forms.

I can remember one letter from an English private, describing an engagement in which some eighty men were killed and wounded out of a force of eight thousand: he wrote of comrades in his own battalion "falling like sheep," and gave no clue to the country in which he served. It might have been in Siberia or the Sahara, against savages or civilised troops; you could glean nothing except that he had listened to patriotic songs in music halls at home. Perhaps the most intimate love-letters and battle-letters never get printed at all. But, as it is, you cannot generalise from collections of documents as you can from collections of ferns and beetles: there is not, and there never can be, a science of the perceptions and emotions which thrill young lovers and recruits. The modern soldier is a little less laconic than his mediæval forbear. Indeed he could hardly surpass the tantalising reserve of, say, Thomas Denyes, a gentleman who fights at Towton, and sums up the carnage of thirty-eight thousand men in a single sentence:—"Oure Soveraign Lord hath wonne the feld."[1] But it is astonishing to note how little even the modern soldier manages to say. He receives rude and swift answers in the field to the questions that haunted his boyish dreams, but he keeps the secret with masonic self-possession.

Marbot's *Memoirs* and, in a lesser degree, Tomkinson's *Diary of a Cavalry Officer* are both admirable as personal accounts of the Peninsular Campaign, but the warfare they describe is almost as obsolete as that of the Roses, and, even if it were not so, they scarcely attempt the recreation of intense moments by the revelation of their imprint on the minds that endured them. And, on the score of art and of reticence, one is glad that they do not. Their authors were gallant soldiers waging war in fact, and not artists reproducing it in fiction. They satisfy the special curiosity of men interested in strategy and tactics, not the universal curiosity of Man the potential Combatant. He is fascinated by the picturesque and emotional aspects of battle, and the experts tell him little of either. To gratify that curiosity you must turn from the Soldier to the Artist, who is trained both to see and tell, or inspired, even without seeing, to divine what things have been and must be. Some may rebel against accepting his evidence, since it is impossible to prove the truth of his report. But it is equally impossible to prove the beauty of his accomplishment. Yet both are patent to every one capable of accepting truth or beauty, and by a surer warrant than any chance coincidence of individual experience and taste.

Mr. Stephen Crane, the author of *The Red Badge of Courage* (London: Heinemann), is a great artist, with something new to say, and consequently, with a new way of saying it. His theme, indeed, is an old one, but old themes re-handled anew in the light of novel experience, are the stuff out of which masterpieces are made, and in *The Red Badge of Courage* Mr. Crane has surely contrived a masterpiece. He writes of war—the ominous and alluring possibility for every man, since the heir of all the ages has won and must keep his inheritance by secular combat. The conditions of the age-long contention have changed and will change, but its certainty is coeval with progress: so long as there are things worth fighting for fighting will last, and the fashion of fighting will change under the reciprocal stresses of rival inventions. Hence its double interest of abiding necessity and ceaseless variation. Of all these variations the most marked has followed, within the memory of most of us, upon the adoption of long-range weapons of precision, and continues to develop, under our eyes, with the development of rapidity in firing. And yet, with the exception of Zola's *la Débâcle,* no considerable attempt has been made to pourtray war under its new conditions. The old stories are less trustworthy than ever as guides to the experiences which a man may expect in battle and to the emotions which those experiences are likely to arouse. No doubt the prime factors in the personal problem—the chances of death and mutilation—continue to be about the same. In these respects it matters little whether you are pierced by a bullet at two thousand yards or stabbed at hands' play with a dagger. We know that the most appalling death-rolls of recent campaigns have been more than equalled in ancient warfare; and, apart from history, it is clear that, unless one side runs away, neither can win save by the infliction of decisive losses. But although these personal risks continue to be essentially the same, the picturesque and emotional aspects of war are completely altered by every change in the shape and circumstance of imminent death. And these are the fit materials for literature—the things which even dull men remember with the undying imagination of poets, but which, for lack of the writer's art, they cannot communicate. The sights flashed indelibly on the retina of the eye; the sounds that after long silences suddenly cypher; the stenches that sicken in after-life at any chance allusion to decay; or, stirred by these, the storms of passions that force yells of defiance out of inarticulate clowns; the winds of fear that sweep by night along prostrate ranks, with the acceleration of trains and the noise as of a whole town waking from nightmare with stertorous, indrawn gasps—these colossal facts of the senses and the soul are the only colours in which the very image of war can be painted. Mr. Crane has composed his palette with these colours, and has painted a picture that challenges comparison with the most vivid scenes of Tolstoï's *la Guerre et la Paix* or of Zola's *la Débâcle.* This is unstinted praise, but I feel bound to give it after reading the book twice and comparing it with Zola's Sédan and Tolstoï's account of Rostow's squadron for the first time under fire. Indeed, I think that Mr. Crane's picture of war is more complete than Tolstoï's, more true than Zola's. Rostow's sensations are conveyed by Tolstoï with touches more subtle than any to be found even in his *Sébastopol,* but they make but a brief passage in a long book, much else of which is devoted to the theory that Napoleon and his marshals were mere waifs on a tide of humanity or to the analysis of divers characters exposed to civilian experiences. Zola, on the other hand, compiles an accurate catalogue of almost all that is terrible and nauseating in war; but it is his own catalogue of facts made in cold blood, and not the procession of flashing images shot through the senses into one brain and fluctuating there with its rhythm of exaltation and fatigue. *La Débâcle* gives the whole truth, the truth of science, as it is observed by a shrewd intellect, but not the truth of experience as it is felt in fragments magnified or diminished in accordance with the patient's mood. The terrible things in war are not always terrible; the nauseating things do not always sicken. On the contrary, it is even these which sometimes lift the soul to heights from which they become invisible. And, again, at other times, it is the little miseries of most ignoble insignificance which fret through the last fibres of endurance.

Mr. Crane, for his distinction, has hit on a new device, or at least on one which has never been used before with such consistency and effect. In order to show the features of modern war, he takes a subject—a youth with a peculiar temperament, capable of exaltation and yet morbidly sensitive. Then he traces the successive impressions made on such a temperament, from minute to minute, during two days of heavy fighting. He stages the drama of war, so to speak, within the mind of one man, and then admits you as to a theatre. You may, if you please, object that this youth is unlike most other young men who serve in the ranks, and that the same events would have impressed the average man differently; but you are convinced that this man's soul is truly drawn, and that the impressions made in it are faithfully rendered. The youth's temperament is merely the medium which the artist has chosen: that it is exceptionally plastic makes but for the deeper incision of his work. It follows from Mr. Crane's method that he creates by his art even such a first-hand report of war as we seek in vain among the journals and letters of soldiers. But the book is not written in the form of an autobiography: the author narrates. He is therefore at liberty to give scenery and action, down to the slightest gestures and outward signs of inward elation or suffering, and he does this with the vigour and terseness of a master. Had he put his descriptions of scenery and his atmospheric effects, or his reports of overheard conversations, into the mouth of his youth, their very excellence would have belied all likelihood. Yet in all his descriptions and all his reports he confines himself only to such things as that youth heard and saw, and, of these, only to such as influenced his emotions. By this compromise he combines the strength and truth of a monodrama with the directness and colour of the best narrative prose. The monodrama suffices for the lyrical emotion of Tennyson's *Maud;* but in Browning's *Martin Relf* you feel the constraint of a form which in his *Ring and the Book* entails repetition often intolerable.

Mr. Crane discovers his youth, Henry Fleming, in a phase of disillusion. It is some monotonous months since boyish "visions of broken-bladed glory" impelled him to enlist in the Northern Army towards the middle of the American war. That impulse is admirably given:—"One night as he lay in bed, the winds had carried to him the clangouring of the church bells, as some enthusiast jerked the rope frantically to tell the twisted news of a great battle. This voice of the people rejoicing in the night had made him shiver in a prolonged ecstasy of excitement. Later he had gone down to his mother's room, and had spoken thus: 'Ma, I'm going to enlist.' 'Henry, don't you be a fool,' his mother had replied. She had then covered her face with the quilt. There was an end to the matter for that night." But the next morning he enlists. He is impatient of the homely injunctions given him in place of the heroic speech he expects in accordance with a tawdry convention, and so departs, with a "vague feeling of relief." But, looking back from the gate, he sees his mother "kneeling among the potato parings. Her brown face upraised and stained with tears, her spare form quivering." Since then the army has done "little but sit still and try to keep warm" till he has "grown to regard himself merely as a part of a vast blue demonstration." In the sick langour of this waiting, he begins to suspect his courage and lies awake by night through hours of morbid introspection. He tries "to prove to himself mathematically that he would not run from a battle"; he constantly leads the conversation round to the problem of courage in order to gauge the confidence of his messmates.

> "How do you know you won't run when the time comes?" asked the youth. "Run?" said the loud one, "run?—of course not!" He laughed. "Well," continued the youth, "lots of good-a-'nough men have thought they was going to do great things before the fight, but when the time come they skedaddled." "Oh, that's all true, I s'pose," replied the other, "but I'm not going to skedaddle. The man that bets on my running will lose his money, that's all." He nodded confidently.

The youth is a "mental outcast" among his comrades, "wrestling with his personal problem," and sweating as he listens to the muttered scoring of a card game, his eyes fixed on the "red, shivering reflection of a fire." Every day they drill; every night they watch the red camp-fires of the enemy on the far shore of a river, eating their hearts out. At last they march:—"In the gloom before the break of the day their uniforms glowed a deep purple blue. From across the river the red eyes were still peering. In the eastern sky there was a yellow patch, like a rug laid for the feet of the coming sun; and against it, black and pattern-like, loomed the gigantic figure of the colonel on a gigantic horse." The book is full of such vivid impressions, half of sense and half of imagination:—The columns as they marched "were like two serpents crawling from the cavern of night." But the march, which, in his boyish imagination, should have led forthwith into melodramatic action is but the precursor of other marches. After days of weariness and nights of discomfort, at last, as in life, without preface, and in a lull of the mind's anxiety, the long-dreaded and long-expected is suddenly and smoothly in process of accomplishment:—"One grey morning he was kicked on the leg by the tall soldier, and then, before he was entirely awake, he found himself running down a wood road in the midst of men who were panting with the first effects of speed. His canteen banged rhythmically upon his thigh, and his haversack bobbed softly. His musket bounced a trifle from his shoulder at each stride and made his cap feel uncertain upon his head." From this moment, reached on the thirtieth page, the drama races through another hundred and sixty pages to the end of the book, and to read those pages is in itself an experience of breathless, lambent, detonating life. So brilliant and detached are the images evoked that, like illuminated bodies actually seen, they leave their fever-bright phantasms floating before the brain. You may shut the book, but you still see the battle-flags "jerked about madly in the smoke," or sinking with "dying gestures of despair," the men "dropping here and there like bundles"; the captain shot dead with "an astonished and sorrowful look as if he thought some friend had done him an ill-turn"; and the litter of corpses, "twisted in fantastic contortions," as if "they had fallen from some great height, dumped out upon the ground from the sky." The book is full of sensuous impressions that leap out from the picture: of gestures, attitudes, grimaces, that flash into portentous definition, like faces from the climbing clouds of nightmare. It leaves the imagination bounded with a "dense wall of smoke, furiously slit and slashed by the knife-like fire from the rifles." It leaves, in short, such indelible traces as are left by the actual experience of war. The picture shows grisly shadows and vermilion splashes, but, as in the vast drama it reflects so truly, these features, though insistent, are small in size, and are lost in the immensity of the theatre. The tranquil forest stands around; the "fairy-blue of the sky" is over it all. And, as in the actual experience of war, the impressions which these startling features inflict, though acute, are localised and not too deep: are as it were mere pin-pricks, or, at worst, clean cuts from a lancet in a body thrilled with currents of physical excitement and sopped with anæsthetics of emotion. Here is the author's description of a forlorn hope:—

> As the regiment swung from its position out into a cleared space the woods and thickets before it awakened. Yellow flames leaped toward it from many directions. The line swung straight for a moment. Then the right wing swung forward; it in turn was surpassed by the left. Afterward the centre careered to the front until the regiment was a wedge-shaped mass . . . the men, pitching forward insanely, had burst into cheerings, mob-like and barbaric, but tuned in strange keys that can arouse the dullard and the stoic. . . . There was the delirium that encounters despair and death, and is heedless and blind to odds. . . . Presently the straining pace ate up the energies of the men. As if by agreement, the leaders began to slacken their speed. The volleys directed against them had a seeming wind-like effect. The regiment snorted and blew. Among some stolid trees it began to falter and hesitate. . . . The youth had a vague belief that he had run miles, and he thought, in a way, that he was now in some new and unknown land. . . .

The charge withers away, and the lieutenant, the youth, and his friend run forward to rally the regiment.

> In front of the colours three men began to bawl, "Come on! Come on!" They danced and gyrated like tortured savages. The flag, obedient to these appeals, bended its glittering form and swept toward them. The men wavered in indecision for a moment, and then with a long wailful cry the dilapidated regiment surged forward and began its new journey. Over the field went the scurrying mass. It was a handful of men splattered into the faces of the enemy. Toward it instantly sprang the yellow tongues. A vast quantity of blue smoke hung before them. A mighty banging made ears valueless. The youth ran like a madman to reach the woods before a bullet could discover him. He ducked his head low, like a football player. In his haste his eyes almost closed, and the scene was a wild blur. Pulsating saliva stood at the corner of his mouth. Within him, as he hurled forward, was born a love, a despairing fondness for this flag that was near him. It was a creation of beauty and invulnerability. It was a goddess radiant, that bended its form with an imperious gesture to him. It was a woman, red and white, hating and loving, that called him with the voice of his hopes. Because no harm could come to it he endowed it with power. He kept near, as if it could be a saver of lives, and an imploring cry went from his mind.

This passage directly challenges comparison with Zola's scene, in which the lieutenant and the old tradition, of an invincible Frenchman over-running the world "between his bottle and his girl," expire together among the morsels of a bullet-eaten flag. Mr. Crane has probably read *la Débâcle,* and wittingly threw down his glove. One can only say that he is justified of his courage.

Mr. Crane's method, when dealing with things seen and heard, is akin to Zola's: he omits nothing and extenuates nothing, save the actual blasphemy and obscenity of a soldier's oaths. These he indicates, sufficiently for any purpose of art, by brief allusions to their vigour and variety. Even Zola has rarely surpassed the appalling realism of Jim Conklin's death in Chapter X. Indeed, there is little to criticise in Mr. Crane's observation, except an undue subordination of the shrill cry of bullets to the sharp crashing of rifles. He omits the long chromatic whine defining its invisible arc in the air, and the fretful snatch a few feet from the listener's head. In addition to this gift of observation, Mr. Crane has at command the imaginative phrase. The firing follows a retreat as with "yellings of eager metallic hounds"; the men at their mechanic loading and firing are like "fiends jigging heavily in the smoke"; in a lull before the attack "there passed slowly the intense moments that precede the tempest"; then, after single shots, "the battle roar settled to a rolling thunder, which was a single long explosion." And, as I have said, when Mr. Crane deals with things felt he gives a truer report than Zola. He postulates his hero's temperament—a day-dreamer given over to morbid self-analysis who enlists, not from any deep-seated belief in the holiness of fighting for his country, but in hasty pursuit of a vanishing ambition. This choice enables Mr. Crane to double his picturesque advantage with an ethical advantage equally great. Not only is his youth, like the sufferer in *The Fall of the House of Usher,* super-sensitive to every pin-prick of sensation: he is also a delicate meter of emotion and fancy. In such a nature the waves of feeling take exaggerated curves, and hallucination haunts the brain. Thus, when awaiting the first attack, his mind is thronged with vivid images of a circus he had seen as a boy: it is there in definite detail, even as the Apothecary's shop usurps Romeo's mind at the crisis of his fate. And thus also, like Herodotus' Aristodemus, he vacillates between cowardice and heroism. Nothing could well be more subtle than his self-deception and that sudden enlightenment which leads him to "throw aside his mental pamphlets on the philosophy of the retreated and rules for the guidance of the damned." His soul is of that kind which, "sick with self-love," can only be saved "so as by fire"; and it is saved when the battle-bond of brotherhood is born within it, and is found plainly of deeper import than the cause for which he and his comrades fight, even as that cause is loftier than his personal ambition. By his choice of a hero Mr. Crane displays in the same work a pageant of the senses and a tragedy of the soul.

But he does not obtrude his moral. The "tall soldier" and the lieutenant are brave and content throughout, the one by custom as a veteran, the other by constitution as a hero. But the two boys, the youth and his friend, "the loud soldier," are at first querulous braggarts, but at the last they are transmuted by danger until either might truly say:—

> We have proved we have hearts in a cause, we are noble still,
> And myself have awaked, as it seems, to the better mind;
> It is better to fight for the good than to rail at the ill;
> I have felt with my native land, I am one with my kind,
> I embrace the purpose of God, and the doom assigned.

Let no man cast a stone of contempt at these two lads during their earlier weakness until he has fully gauged the jarring discordance of battle. To be jostled on a platform when you have lost your luggage and missed your train on an errand of vital importance gives a truer pre-taste of war than any field-day; yet many a well-disciplined man will denounce the universe upon slighter provocation. It is enough that these two were boys and that they became men.

Yet must it be said that this youth's emotional experience was singular. In a battle there are a few physical cowards, abjects born with defective circulations, who literally turn blue at the approach of danger, and a few on whom danger acts like the keen, rare atmosphere of snow-clad peaks. But between these extremes come many to whom danger is as strong wine, with the multitude which gladly accepts the "iron laws of tradition" and finds welcome support in "a moving box." To this youth, as the cool dawn of his first day's fighting changed by infinitesimal gradations to a feverish noon, the whole evolution pointed to "a trap"; but I have seen another youth under like circumstances toss a pumpkin into the air and spit it on his sword. To this youth the very landscape was filled with "the stealthy approach of death." You are convinced by the author's art that it was so to this man. But to others, as the clamour increases, it is as if the serenity of the morning had taken refuge in their brains. This man "stumbles over the stones as he runs breathlessly forward"; another realises for the first time how right it is to be adroit even in running. The movement of his body becomes an art, which is not self-conscious, since its whole intention is to impress others within the limits of a modest decorum. We know that both love and courage teach this mastery over the details of living. You can tell from the way one woman, out of all the myriads, walks down Piccadilly, that she is at last aware of love. And you can tell from the way a man enters a surgery or runs toward a firing-line that he, too, realises how wholly the justification of any one life lies in its perfect adjustment to others. The woman in love, the man in battle, may each say, for their moment, with the artist, "I was made perfect too." They also are of the few to whom "God whispers in the ear."

But had Mr. Crane taken an average man he would have written an ordinary story, whereas he has written one which is certain to last. It is glorious to see his youth discover courage in the bed-rock of primeval antagonism after the collapse of his tinsel bravado; it is something higher to see him raise upon that rock the temple of resignation. Mr. Crane, as an artist, achieves by his singleness of purpose a truer and completer picture of war than either Tolstoï, bent also upon proving the insignificance of heroes, or Zola, bent also upon prophesying the regeneration of France. That is much; but it is more that his work of art, when completed, chimes with the universal experience of mankind; that his heroes find in their extreme danger, if not confidence in their leaders and conviction in their cause, at least the conviction that most men do what they can or, at most, what they must. We have few good accounts of battles—many of shipwrecks; and we know that, just as the storm rises, so does the commonplace captain show as a god, and the hysterical passenger as a cheerful heroine.

It is but a further step to recognise all life for a battle and this earth for a vessel lost in space. We may then infer that virtues easy in moments of distress may be useful also in everyday experience.

Note

1. Review of the Paston Letters, *Saturday Review,* November 30th, 1895.

Joseph Conrad (essay date 1924)

SOURCE: Conrad, Joseph. "Introduction." *Stephen Crane: A Study in American Letters,* by Thomas Beer, London, William Heinemann, 1924, pp. 1-35.

[*In the following essay, Conrad discusses his friendship with Crane, with passing references to* The Red Badge of Courage *(1895).*]

On a rainy day of March of the year 1923, listening to the author of this biography telling me of his earnest labours for the memory of a man who was certainly unique in his generation, I exclaimed to myself with wonder: "And so it has come to pass after all—this thing which I did not expect to see!" In truth I had never expected the biography of Stephen Crane to appear in my lifetime. My immense pleasure was affected by the devastating touch of time which like a muddy flood covers under a mass of daily trivialities things of value: moments of affectionate communion with kindred spirits, words spoken with the careless freedom of perfect confidence, the deepest emotions of joy and sorrow—together with such things of merely historical importance as the recollection of dates, for instance. After hearing from Mr. Beer of his difficulties in fixing certain dates in the history of Stephen Crane's life, I discovered that I was unable to remember with any kind of precision the initial date of our friendship. Indeed life is but a dream—especially for those of us who have never kept a diary or possessed a note-book in their lives.

In this extremity I had recourse to another friend of Stephen Crane, who had appreciated him intuitively almost as soon as I did myself and who is a woman of excellent memory. My wife's recollection is that Crane and I met in London in October 1897, and that he came to see us for the first time in our Essex home in the following November.

I have mentioned in a short paper written two years ago that it was Mr. S. S. Pawling, partner in the publishing firm of Mr. Heinemann, who brought us together. It was done at Stephen Crane's own desire.

I was told by Mr. Pawling that when asked whom he wanted to meet Crane mentioned two names, of which one was of a notable journalist (who had written some novels) whom he knew in America, I believe, and the other was mine. At that time the only facts we knew about each other were that we both had the same publisher in England. The only other fact I knew about Stephen Crane was that he was quite a young man. I had, of course, read his ***Red Badge of Courage,*** of which people were writing and talking at that time. I certainly did not know that he had the slightest notion of my existence, or that he had seen a single line (there were not many of them then) of my writing. I can safely say that I earned this precious friendship by something like ten months of strenuous work with my pen. It took me just that time to write *The Nigger of the Narcissus,* working at what I always considered a very high pressure. It was on the ground of the authorship of that book that Crane wanted to meet me. Nothing could have been more flattering than to discover that the author of ***The Red Badge of Courage*** appreciated my effort to present a group of men held together by a common loyalty and a common perplexity in a struggle not with human enemies, but with the hostile conditions testing their faithfulness to the conditions of their own calling.

Apart from the imaginative analysis of his own temperament tried by the emotions of a battlefield, Stephen Crane dealt in his book with the psychology of the mass—the army; while I—in mine—had been dealing with the same subject on a much smaller scale and in more specialized conditions—the crew of a merchant ship, brought to the test of what I may venture to call the moral problem of conduct. This may be thought a very remote connection between these two works and the idea may seem too far-fetched to be mentioned here; but that was my undoubted feeling at the time. It is a fact that I considered Crane, by virtue of his creative experience with *The Red Badge of Courage,* as eminently fit to pronounce a judgement on my first consciously planned attempt to render the truth of a phase of life in the terms of my own temperament with all the sincerity of which I was capable.

I had, of course, my own opinion as to what I had done; but I doubted whether anything of my ambitiously comprehensive aim would be understood. I was wrong there; but my doubt was excusable, since I myself would have been hard put to it if requested to give my complex intentions the form of a concise and definite statement. In that period of misgivings which so often follows an accomplished task I would often ask myself, who in the world could be interested in such a thing? It was after reading *The Red Badge,* which came into my hands directly after its publication in England, that I said to myself: "Here's a man who may understand—if he ever sees the book; though of course that would not mean that he would like it." I do not mean to say that I looked towards the author of *The Red Badge* as the only man in the world. It would have been stupid and ungrateful. I had the moral support of one or two intimate friends and the solid fact of Mr. W. E. Henley's acceptance of my tale for serial publication in the *New Review* to give me confidence, while I awaited the larger verdict.

It seems to me that in trying to recall my memories of Stephen Crane I have been talking so far only about myself; but that is unavoidable, since this Introduction, which I am privileged to write, can only trace what is left on earth of our personal intercourse, which was even more short and fleeting than it may appear from the record of dates. October 1897—May 1900. And out of that beggarly tale of months must be deducted the time of his absence from England during the Spanish-American war, and of his visit to the United States shortly before the beginning of his last illness. Even when he was in England our intercourse was not so close and frequent as the warmth of our friendship would have wished it to be. We both lived in the country and, though not very far from each other, in different counties. I had my work to do, always in conditions which made it a matter of urgency. He had his own tasks and his own visions to attend to. I do not think that he had more friendships to claim him than I, but he certainly had more acquaintances and more calls on his time.

This was only natural. It must be remembered that as an author he was my senior, as I used to remind him now and then with affected humility which always provoked his smiles. He had a quiet smile that charmed and frightened one. It made you pause by something revelatory it cast over his whole physiognomy, not like a ray but like a shadow. I often asked myself what it could be, that quality that checked one's care-free mood, and now I think I have had my answer. It was the smile of a man who knows that his time will not be long on this earth.

I would not for a moment wish to convey the impression of melancholy in connection with my memories of Stephen Crane. I saw his smile first over the table-cloth in a restaurant. We shook hands with intense gravity and a direct stare at each other, after the manner of two children told to make friends. It was under the encouraging gaze of Sydney Pawling, who, a much bigger man than either of us and possessed of a deep voice, looked like a grown-up person entertaining two strange small boys—protecting and slightly anxious as to the experiment. He knew very little of either of us. I was a new author and Crane was a new arrival. It was the meeting of *The Red Badge* and *The Nigger* in the presence of their publisher; but as far as our personalities went we were three strangers breaking bread together for the first time. Yet it was as pleasantly easy a meal as any I can remember. Crane talked in his characteristic deliberate manner about Greece, at war. I had already sensed the man's intense earnestness underlying his quiet surface. Every time he raised his eyes that secret quality (for his voice was careless) of his soul was betrayed in a clear flash. Most of the true Stephen Crane was in his eyes, most of his strength at any rate, though it was apparent also in his other features, as for instance in the structure of his forehead, the deep solid arches under the fair eyebrows.

Some people saw traces of weakness in the lower part of his face. What I could see there was a hint of the delicacy of sentiment, of the inborn fineness of nature which this man, whose life had been anything but a stroll through a rose-garden, had managed to preserve like a sacred heritage. I say heritage, not acquisition, for it was not and could not have been acquired. One could depend on it on all occasions; whereas the cultivated kind is apt to show ugly gaps under very slight provocation. The coarseness of the professedly delicate must be very amusing to the misanthrope. But Crane was no enemy of his kind. That sort of thing did not amuse him. As to his own temper it was proof against anger and scorn, as I can testify, having seen him both angry and scornful, always quietly, on fitting occasions. Contempt and indignation never broke the surface of his moderation, simply because he had no surface. He was all through of the same material, incapable of affectation of any kind, of any pitiful failure of generosity for the sake of personal advantage, or even from sheer exasperation which must find its relief.

Many people imagined him a fiery individuality. Certainly he was not cold-blooded. But his was an equable glow, morally and temperamentally. I would have said the same of his creative power (I have seen him sit down before a blank sheet of paper, dip his pen, write the first line at once and go on without haste and without pause for a couple of hours), had he not confided to me that his mentality did flag at times. I do not think it was anything more than every writer is familiar with at times. Another man would have talked of his "failing inspiration." It is very characteristic of Crane that I have never heard him use that word when talking about his work.

His phraseology was generally of a very modest cast. That unique and exquisite faculty, which Edward Garnett, another of his friends, found in his writing—"of disclosing an individual scene by an odd simile"—was not apparent in his conversation. It was interesting, of course, but its charm consisted mainly in the freshness of his impressions, set off by an acute simplicity of view and expressed with an amusing deliberation. Superabundance of words was not his failing when communing with those whom he liked and felt he could trust. With the other kind of "friends" he followed the method of a sort of suspended silence. On a certain occasion (it was at Brede Place), after two amazingly conceited idiots had gone away, I said to him, "Stevie, you brood like a distant thunder-cloud." He had retired early to the other end of the room, and from there had sent out, now and then, a few words, more like the heavy drops of rain that precede the storm than growls of thunder. Poor Crane, if he could look black enough at times, never thundered; though I have no doubt he could have been dangerous if he had liked. There always seemed to be something (not timidity) which restrained him, not from within but, I could not help fancying, from outside, with an effect as of a whispered *memento mori* in the ear of a reveller not lost to the sense of grace.

That of course was a later impression. It must be stated clearly that I know very little of Stephen Crane's life. We did not feel the need to tell each other formally the story of our lives. That did not prevent us from being very intimate and also very open with each other from the first. Our affection would have been "everlasting," as he himself qualified it, had not the jealous death intervened with her cruel capriciousness by striking down the younger man. Our intimacy was really too close to admit of indiscretions; not that he did not speak amusingly of his experiences and of his hardships, and warmly of the men that helped him in his early days, like Mr. Hamlin Garland for instance, or men kindly encouraging to him, like Mr. Howells. Many other names he used to utter lovingly have been forgotten by me after so many years.

It is a fact that I heard more of his adventures than of his trials, privations, and difficulties. I know he had many. He was the least recriminatory of men (though one of the most sensitive, I should say), but, in any case, nothing I could have learned would have shaken the independent judgement I had formed for myself of his trustworthiness as a man and a friend. Though the word is discredited now and may sound pretentious, I will say that there was in Crane a strain of chivalry which made him safe to trust with one's life. To be recognizably a man of honour carries no immunity against human weaknesses, but comports more rigid limitations in personal relations than the status of an "honourable man," however recognizable that too may be. Some men are "honourable" by courtesy, others by the office they hold, or simply by belonging to some popular assembly, the election to which is not generally secured by a dignified accuracy of statement and a scrupulous regard for the feelings of others. Many remain honourable (because of their great circumspection in the conduct of their affairs) without holding within themselves any of these restraints which are inherent in the character of a man of honour, however weak or luckless he may be.

I do not know everything about the strength of Crane's circumspection, but I am not afraid of what the biography which follows may disclose to us; though I am convinced that it will be free from hypocritical reservations. I think I have understood Stephen Crane, and from my too short acquaintance with his biographer I am confident he will receive the most humane and sympathetic treatment. What I discovered very early in our acquaintance was that Crane had not the face of a lucky man. That certitude came to me at our first meeting while I sat opposite him listening to his simple tales of Greece, while S. S. Pawling presided at the initiatory feast—friendly and debonair, looking solidly anchored in the stream of life, and very reassuring, like a big, prosperous ship to the sides of which we two in our tossing little barks could hook on for safety. He was interested in the tales too; and the best proof of it is that when he looked at his watch and jumped up, saying, "I must leave you two now," it was very near four o'clock. Nearly a whole afternoon wasted, for an English business man.

No such consideration of waste or duty agitated Crane and myself. The sympathy that, even in regard of the very few years allotted to our friendship, may be said to have sprung up instantaneously between us, was the most undemonstrative case of that sort in the last century. We not only did not tell each other of it (which would have been missish), but even without entering formally into a previous agreement to remain together, we went out and began to walk side by side in the manner of two tramps without home, occupation, or care for the next night's shelter. We certainly paid no heed to direction. The first thing I noticed were the Green Park railings, when to my remark that he had seen no war before he went to Greece, Crane made answer: "No. But *The Red Badge* is all right." I assured him that I never had doubted it; and, since the title of the work had been pronounced for the first time, feeling I must do something to show I had read it, I said shyly: "I like your General." He knew at once what I was alluding to, but said not a word. Nothing could have been more tramp-like than our silent pacing, elbow to elbow, till, after we had left Hyde Park Corner behind us, Crane uttered with his quiet earnestness the words: "I like your young man—I can just see him." Nothing could have been more characteristic of the depth of our three-hour-old intimacy than that each of us should have selected for praise the merest by-the-way vignette of a minor character.

This was positively the only allusion we made that afternoon to our immortal works. Indeed we talked very little of them at any time, and then always selecting some minor point for particular mention; which, after all, is not a bad way of showing an affectionate appreciation of a piece of work done by a friend. A stranger would have expected more, but, in a manner of speaking, Crane and I had never been strangers. We took each other's work for granted from the very first, I mean from the moment we had exchanged those laudatory remarks alongside the Green Park railings. Henceforth mutual recognition kept to that standard. It consisted often of an approving grunt, sometimes of the mention of some picked-out paragraph, or of a line or only of a few words that had caught our fancy and would, for a time, be applied more or less aptly to the turns of our careless, or even serious, talks.

Thus, for instance, there was a time when I persecuted poor Crane with the words "barbarously abrupt." They occur in that marvellous story "The Open Boat" and are applied by him to the waves of the sea (as seen by men tossing in a small dinghy) with an inspired audacity of epithet which was one of Crane's gifts that gave me most delight. How amazingly apt these words are where they stand, anybody can see by looking at that story, which is altogether a big thing, and has remained an object of my confirmed admiration. I was always telling Crane that this or that was "barbarously abrupt," or begging him not to be so "barbarously abrupt" himself, with a keen enjoyment of the incongruity; for no human being could be less abrupt than Crane. As to his humanity (in contra-distinction to barbarity) it was a shining thing without a flaw. It is possible that he may have grown at length weary of my little joke, but he invariably received it with a smile, thus proving his consistent humanity toward his kind. But, after all, he too liked that story of his, of four men in a very small boat, which by the deep and simple humanity of presentation seems somehow to illustrate the essentials of life itself, like a symbolic tale. It opens with a phrase that anybody could have uttered, but which, in relation to what is to follow, acquires the poignancy of a meaning almost universal. Once, much later in our acquaintance, I made use of it to him. He came on a flying visit to Pent Farm where we were living then. I noticed that he looked harassed. I, too, was feeling for the moment as if things were getting too much for me. He lay on the couch and I sat on a chair opposite. After a longish silence in which we both could have felt how uncertain was the issue of life envisaged as a deadly adventure in which we were both engaged like two men trying to keep afloat in a small boat, I said suddenly across the width of the mantelpiece:

"None of them knew the colour of the sky."

He raised himself sharply. The words had struck him as familiar, though I believe he failed to place them at first. "Don't you know that quotation?" I asked. (These words form the opening sentence of his tale.) The startled expression passed off his face. "Oh, yes," he said quietly, and lay down again. Truth to say, it was a time when neither he nor I had the leisure to look up idly at the sky. The waves just then were too "barbarously abrupt."

I do not mean to say that it was always so. Now and then we were permitted to snatch a glance at the colour of the sky. But it is a fact that in the history of our essentially undemonstrative friendship (which is nearly as difficult to recapture as a dream) that first long afternoon is the most care-free instant, and the only one that had a character of enchantment about it. It was spread out over a large portion of central London. After the Green Park the next thing I remember are the Kensington Gardens, where under the lofty and historical trees I was vouchsafed a glimpse of the low mesquit bush overspreading the plum-coloured infinities of the great Texas plains. Then after a long tramp amongst an orderly multitude of grimy brick houses—from which the only things I carried off were the impressions of the coloured rocks of Mexico (or was it Arizona?), and my first knowledge of a locality called the Painted Desert—there came suddenly Oxford Street. I don't know whether the inhabitants of London were keeping indoors or had gone into the country that afternoon, but I don't remember seeing any people in the streets except for a figure, now and then, unreal, flitting by, obviously negligible. The wheeled traffic, too, was stopped; yet, it seems, not entirely, because I remember Crane seizing my arm and jerking me back on the pavement with the calm remark: "You will get run over." I love to think that the dear fellow had saved my life and that it seemed to amuse him. As to London's enormous volume of business all I know is that one A.B.C. shop had remained open. We went through the depressing ceremony of having tea there; but our interest in each other mitigated its inherent horrors and gave me a good idea of Crane's stoicism. At least I suppose we had tea, otherwise they would not have let us sit there so long. To be left alone was all we wanted. Neither of us had then a club to entertain the other in. It will give a good notion of our indomitable optimism (on that afternoon) when I say that it was there, in those dismal surroundings, we reached the conclusion that though the world had grown old and weary, yet the scheme of creation remained as obscure as ever, and (from our own particular point of view) there was still much that was interesting to expect from gods and men.

As if intoxicated by this draught of hope we rolled out of that A.B.C. shop, but I kept my head sufficiently to guess what was coming and to send a warning telegram to my wife in our Essex home. Crane then was, I believe, staying temporarily in London. But he seemed to have no care in the world; and so we resumed our tramping—east and north and south again, steering through uncharted mazes the streets, forgetting to think of dinner but taking a rest here and there, till we found ourselves, standing in the middle of Piccadilly Circus, blinking at the lights like two authentic night-birds. By that time we had been (in Tottenham Court Road) joined by Balzac. How he came in I have no idea. Crane was not given to literary curiosities of that kind. Somebody he knew, or something he had read, must have attracted lately his attention to Balzac. And now suddenly at ten o'clock in the evening he demanded insistently to be told in particular detail all about the *Comédie Humaine*, its contents, its scope, its plan, and its general significance, together with a critical description of Balzac's style. I told him hastily that it was just black on white; and for the rest, I said, he would have to wait till we got across to Monico and had eaten some supper. I hoped he would forget Balzac and his *Comédie*. But not a bit of it; and I had no option but to hold forth over the remnants of a meal, in the rush of hundreds of waiters and the clatter of tons of crockery, caring not what I said (for what could Stephen want with Balzac?), in the comfortable assurance that the Monstrous Shade, even if led by some strange caprice to haunt the long room of Monico's, did not know enough English to understand a single word I said. I wonder what Crane made of it all. He did not look bored, and it was eleven o'clock before we parted at the foot of that monumentally heavy abode of frivolity, the Pavilion, with just a hand-shake and a good-night—no more—without making any arrangements for meeting again, as though we had lived in the same town from childhood and were sure to run across each other next day.

It struck me directly I left him that we had not even exchanged addresses; but I was not uneasy. Sure enough, before the month was out there arrived a post card (from Ravensbrook) asking whether he might come to see us. He came, was received as an old friend, and before the end of the day conquered my wife's sympathy, as undemonstrative and sincere as his own quiet friendliness. The friendship that sprang up between them was confirmed by the interest Crane displayed in our first child, a boy who came on the scene not quite two months afterwards. How strong was that interest on the part of Stephen Crane and his wife in the boy is evidenced by the fact that at the age of six weeks he was invited to come for a long visit to Ravensbrook. He was in fact impatiently expected there. He arrived in state, bringing with him not only his parents but also a young aunt, and was welcomed like a prince. This visit, during which I suffered from a sense of temporary extinction, is commemorated by a group photograph taken by an artist summoned with his engine (regardless of expense) to Ravensbrook. Though the likenesses are not bad, it is a very awful thing. Nobody looks like him or herself in it. The best yet are the Crane dogs, a very important part of the establishment and quite conscious of it, belonging apparently to some order of outlandish poodles, amazingly sedate, and yet the most restless animals I have ever met. They pervaded, populated, and filled the whole house. Whichever way one looked at any time, down the passage, up the stairs, into the drawing-room, there was always a dog in sight. Had I been asked on the first day how many there were I would have guessed about thirty. As a matter of fact there were only three, but I think they never sat down, except in Crane's study, where they had their *entrée* at all hours.

A scratching would be heard at the door, Crane would drop his pen with alacrity to throw it open—and the dogs would enter sedately in single file, taking a lot of time about it, too. Then the room would resound for a while with grunts, sniffs, yawns, heavy flops, followed by as much perhaps as three whole minutes of silence. Then the dogs would get up, one after another, never all together, and direct their footsteps to the door in an impressive and ominous manner. The first arrival waited considerately for the others before trying to attract attention by means of scratching on the bottom panel. Then, never before, Crane would raise his head, go meekly to the door—and the procession would file out at the slowest possible pace. The recurrent sedateness of the proceedings, the utter unconsciousness of the dogs, dear Stephen's absurd gravity while playing his part in those ceremonies, without ever a muscle of his face moving, were irresistibly, exasperatingly funny. I tried to preserve my gravity (or at least to keep calm), with fair success. Only one afternoon on the fifth or sixth repetition I could not help bursting into a loud interminable laugh, and then the dear fellow asked me in all innocence what was the matter. I managed to conceal my nervous irritation from him, and he never learned the secret of that laugh in which there was a beginning of hysteria.

If the definition that man is a laughing animal be true, then Crane was neither one nor the other; indeed he was but a hurried visitor on this earth on which he had so little reason to be joyous. I might say that I never heard him laugh, except in connection with the baby. He loved children; but his friendship with our child was of the kind that put our mutual sentiment, by comparison, somewhere within the arctic region. The two could not be compared; at least I have never detected Crane stretched full length and sustained on his elbows on a grass plot, in order to gaze at me; on the other hand, this was his usual attitude of communion with the small child—with him who was called *the Boy*, and whose destiny it was to see more war before he came of age than the author of **The Red Badge** had time to see in all the allotted days of his life. In the gravity of its disposition the baby came quite up to Crane; yet those two would sometimes find something to laugh at in each other. Then there would be silence, and glancing out of the low window of my room I would see them, very still, staring at each other with a solemn understanding that needed no words, or perhaps was beyond words altogether. I could not object on any ground to their profound intimacy, but I do not see why Crane should have developed such an unreasonable suspicion as to my paternal efficiency. He seemed to be everlastingly taking the boy's part. I could not see that the baby was being oppressed, hectored over, or in any way deprived of its rights, or ever wounded in its feelings by me; but Crane seemed always to nurse some vague unexpressed grievance as to my conduct. I was inconsiderate. For instance—why could I not get a dog for the boy? One day he made me quite a scene about it. He seemed to imply I should drop everything and go look for a dog. I sat under the storm and said nothing. At last he cried, "Hang it all, a boy ought to have a dog." It was an appeal to first principles, but for an answer I pointed at the window and said: "Behold the boy." ... He was sitting on a rug spread on the grass, with his little red stocking-cap very much over one eye (a fact of which he seemed unaware), and propped round with many pillows on account of his propensity to roll over on his side helplessly. My answer was irresistible. This is one of the few occasions on which I heard Stephen Crane laugh outright. He dropped his preaching on the dog theme and went out to the boy while I went on with my work. But he was strangely incorrigible. When he came back after an hour or so, his first words were, "Joseph, I will teach your boy to ride." I closed with the offer at once—but it was not to be. He was not given the time.

The happiest mental picture my wife and I preserve of Crane is on the occasion of our first visit to Brede Place when he rode to meet us at the Park gate. He looked at his best on horseback. On that day he must have been feeling well. As usual, he was happy in the saddle. As he went on trotting by the side of the open trap I said to him: "If you give the boy your seat I will be perfectly satisfied." I knew this would please him; and indeed his face remained wreathed in smiles all the way to the front door. He looked about him at that bit of the world, down the green slopes and up the brown fields, with an appreciative serenity and the confident bearing of a man who is feeling very sure of the present and of the future. All because he was looking at life from the saddle, with a good morning's work behind him. Nothing more is needed to give a man a blessed moment of illusion. The more I think of that morning the more I believe it was just that; that it had really been given me to see Crane perfectly happy for a couple of hours; and that it was under this spell that directly we arrived he led me impatiently to the room in which he worked when at Brede. After we got there he said to me, "Joseph, I will give you something." I had no idea what it would be, till I saw him sit down to write an inscription in a very slim volume. He presented it to me with averted head. It was **The Black Riders**. He had never spoken to me of his verse before. It was while holding the book in my hand that I learned that they were written years before in America. I expressed my appreciation of them that afternoon in the usual half-a-dozen, or dozen, words which we allowed ourselves when completely pleased with each other's work. When the pleasure was not so complete the words would be many. And that was a great waste of breath and time. I must confess that we were no critics, I mean temperamentally. Crane was even less of a critic than myself. Criticism is very much a matter of a vocabulary, very consciously used; with us it was the intonation that mattered. The tone of a grunt could convey an infinity of meaning between us.

The articulate literary conscience at our elbow was Edward Garnett. He, of course, was worth listening to. His analytical appreciation (or appreciative analysis) of Crane's art, in the London *Academy* of 17th Dec. 1898,[1] goes to the root of the matter with Edward's almost uncanny insight, and a well-balanced sympathy with the blind, pathetic striving of the artist towards a complete realization of his individual gift. How highly Edward Garnett rated Crane's gift is recorded in the conclusions of that admirable and, within the limits of its space, masterly article of some two columns, where at the end are set down such affirmative phrases as: "The chief impressionist of the age." ... "Mr. Crane's talent is unique" ... and where he hails him as "the creator of fresh rhythms and phrases," while the very last words state confidently that: "Undoubtedly, of the young school it is Mr. Crane who is the genius—the others have their talents."

* * *

My part here being not that of critic but of private friend, all I will say is that I agreed warmly at the time with that article, which from the quoted phrases might be supposed a merely enthusiastic pronouncement, but on reading will be found to be based on that calm sagacity which Edward Garnett, for all his fiery zeal in the cause of letters, could always summon for the judgement of matters emotional—as all response to the various forms of art must be in the main. I had occasion to re-read it last year in its expanded form in a collection of literary essays of great, now almost historical, interest in the record of American and English imaginative literature. I found there a passage or two, not bearing precisely on Crane's work but giving a view of his temperament, on which of course his art was based; and of the conditions moral and material under which he had to put forth his creative faculties and his power of steady composition. On those matters, as a man who had the opportunity to look at Crane's life in England, I wish to offer a few remarks before closing my contribution to the memory of my friend.

I do not know that he was ever dunned for money and had to work under a threat of legal proceedings. I don't think he was ever dunned in the sense in which such a phrase is used about a spendthrift unscrupulous in incurring debts. No doubt he was sometimes pressed for money. He lived by his pen, and the prices he obtained were not great. Personally he was not extravagant; and I will not quarrel with him for not choosing to live in a garret. The tenancy of Brede Place was held by him at a nominal rent. That glorious old place was not restored then, and the greatest part of it was uninhabitable. The Cranes had furnished in a modest way six or seven of the least dilapidated rooms, which even then looked bare and half empty. Certainly there was a horse, and at one time even two, but that luxury was not so very expensive at that time. One man looked after them. Riding was the only exercise open to Crane; and if he did work so hard, surely he was entitled to some relaxation, if only for the preservation of his unique talent.

His greatest extravagance was hospitality, of which I, too, had my share; often in the company, I am sorry to say, of men who after sitting at his board chose to speak of him and of his wife slightingly. Having some rudimentary sense of decency, their behaviour while actually under the Cranes' roof often produced on me a disagreeable impression. Once I ventured to say to him, "You are too good-natured, Stephen." He gave me one of his quiet smiles, that seemed to hint so poignantly at the vanity of all things, and after a period of silence remarked: "I am glad those Indians are gone." He was surrounded by men who, secretly envious, hostile to the real quality of his genius (and a little afraid of it), were also in antagonism with the essential fineness of his nature. But enough of them. *Pulvis et umbra sunt.* I mean even those that may be alive yet. They were ever hardly anything else; one would have forgotten them if it were not for the legend (if one may dignify perfidious and contemptible gossip by that name) they created in order to satisfy that same obscure instinct of base humanity, which in the past would often bring against any exceptional man the charge of consorting with the devil. It was just as vague, just as senseless, and in its implications just as lying as the mediaeval kind. I have heard one of these "friends" hint before several other Philistines that Crane could not write his tales without getting drunk!

Putting aside the gross palpable stupidity of such a statement—which the creature gave out as an instance of the artistic temperament—I am in a position to disclose what may have been the foundation of this piece of gossip. I have seen repeatedly Crane at work. A small jug of still smaller ale would be brought into the study at about ten o'clock; Crane would pour out some of it into a glass and settle himself at the long table at which he used to write in Brede Place. I would take a book and settle myself at the other end of the same table, with my back to him; and for two hours or so not a sound would be heard in that room. At the end of that time Crane would say suddenly: "I won't do any more now, Joseph." He would have covered three of his large sheets with his regular, legible, perfectly controlled handwriting, with no more than half-a-dozen erasures—mostly single words—in the whole lot. It seemed to me always a perfect miracle in the way of mastery over material and expression. Most of the ale would be still in the glass, and how flat by that time I don't like to think! The most amusing part was to see Crane, as if moved by some obscure sense of duty, drain the last drop of that untempting remnant before we left the room to stroll to and fro in front of the house while waiting for lunch. Such is the origin of some of these gleeful whispers making up the Crane legend of "unrestrained temperament." I have known various sorts of temperaments—some perfidious and some lying—but "unrestrained temperament" is mere parrot talk. It has no meaning. But it was suggestive. It was founded on Crane's visits to town, during which I more than once met him there. We used to spend afternoons and evenings together, and I did not see any of his supposed revels in progress; nor yet have I ever detected any after effects of them on any occasion. Neither have I ever seen anybody who would own to having been a partner in those excesses—if only to the extent of standing by charitably—which would have been a noble part to play. I daresay all those "excesses" amounted to very little more than the one in which he asked me to join him in the following letter. It is the only note I have kept from the very few which we exchanged. The reader will see why it is one of my most carefully preserved possessions.

RAVENSBROOK, OXTED,
March 17 (1899).

My dear Conrad: I am enclosing you a bit of MS. under the supposition that you might like to keep it in remembrance of my warm and endless friendship for you. I am still hoping that you will consent to Stokes' invitation to come to the Savage on Saturday night. Cannot you endure it? Give my affectionate remembrances to Mrs. Conrad and my love to the boy.

Yours always,
STEPHEN CRANE.

P.S. You must accept says Cora—and I—our invitation to come home with me on Sat. night.

I joined him. We had a very amusing time with the Savages. Afterwards Crane refused to go home till the last train. Evidence of what somebody has called his "unrestrained temperament," no doubt. So we went and sat at Gatti's, I believe—unless it was in a Bodega which existed then in that neighbourhood—and talked. I have a vivid memory of this awful debauch because it was on that evening that Crane told me of a subject for a story—a very exceptional thing for him to do. He called it "The Predecessor." I could not recall now by what capricious turns and odd associations of thought he reached the enthusiastic conclusion that it would make a good play, and that we must do it together. He wanted me to share in a certain success—"a dead sure thing," he said. His was an unrestrainedly generous temperament. But let that pass. I must have been specially predisposed, because I caught the infection at once. There and then we began to build up the masterpiece, interrupting each other eagerly, for, I don't know how it was, the air around us had suddenly grown thick with felicitous suggestions. We carried on this collaboration as far as the railway time-table would let us, and then made a break for the last train. Afterwards we did talk of our collaboration now and then, but no attempt at it was ever made. Crane had other stories to write; I was immersed deeply in *Lord Jim*, of which I had to keep up the instalments in *Blackwood*; difficulties in presenting the subject on the stage rose one after another before our experience. The general subject consisted in a man personating his "predecessor" (who had died) in the hope of winning a girl's heart. The scenes were to include a ranch at the foot of the Rocky Mountains, I remember, and the action, I fear, would have been frankly melodramatic. Crane insisted that one of the situations should present the man and the girl on a boundless plain standing by their dead ponies after a furious ride (a truly Crane touch). I made some objections. A boundless plain in the light of a sunset could be got into a back-cloth, I admitted; but I doubted whether we could induce the management of any London theatre to deposit two stuffed horses on its stage.

Recalling now those earnestly fantastic discussions, it occurs to me that Crane and I must have been unconsciously penetrated by a prophetic sense of the technique and of the very spirit of film-plays, of which even the name was unknown then to the world. But if gifted with prophetic sense, we must have been strangely ignorant of ourselves, since it must be obvious to any one who has read a page of our writings that a collaboration between us two could never come to anything in the end—could never even have been begun. The project was merely the expression of our affection for each other. We were fascinated for a moment by the will-of-the-wisp of close artistic communion. It would in no case have led us into a bog. I flatter myself we both had too much regard for each other's gifts not to be clear-eyed about them. We would not have followed the lure very far. At the same time it cannot be denied that there were profound, if not extensive, similitudes in our temperaments which could create for a moment that fascinating illusion. It is not to be regretted, for it had, at any rate, given us some of the most light-hearted moments in the clear but sober atmosphere of our intimacy. From the force of circumstances there could not be much sunshine in it. "None of them saw the colour of the sky!" And alas, it stood already written that it was the younger man who would fail to make a landing through the surf. So I am glad to have that episode to remember, a brotherly serio-comic interlude, played under the shadow of coming events. But I would not have alluded to it at all if it had not come out in the course of my most interesting talk with the author of this biography, that Crane had thought it worth while to mention it in his correspondence, whether seriously or humorously, I know not. So here it is without the charm which it had for me, but which cannot be reproduced in the mere relation of its outward characteristics: a clear gleam on us two, succeeded by the Spanish-American war into which Crane disappeared like a wilful man walking away into the depths of an ominous twilight.

The cloudy afternoon when we two went rushing all over London together was for him the beginning of the end. The problem was to find £60 that day, before the sun set, before dinner, before the "six-forty" train to Oxted, at once, that instant—lest peace should be declared and the opportunity of seeing a war be missed. I had not £60 to lend him. Sixty shillings was nearer my mark. We tried various offices but had no luck, or rather we had the usual luck of money-hunting enterprises. The man was either gone out to see about a dog, or would take no interest in the Spanish-American war. In one place the man wanted to know what was the hurry? He would have liked to have forty-eight hours to think the matter over. As we came downstairs Crane's white-faced excitement frightened me. Finally it occurred to me to take him to Messrs. William Blackwood & Sons' London office. There he was received in a most friendly way. Presently I escorted him to Charing Cross, where he took the train for home with the assurance that he would have the means to start "for the war" next day. That is the reason I cannot to this day read his tale *The Price of the Harness* without a pang. It has done nothing more deadly than pay his debt to Messrs. Blackwood; yet now and then I feel as though that afternoon I had led him by the hand to his doom. But, indeed, I was only the blind agent of the fate that had him in her grip! Nothing could have held him back. He was ready to swim the ocean.

* * *

Thirteen years afterwards I made use, half consciously, of the shadow of the primary idea of the "Predecessor," in one of my short tales which were serialized in the *Metropolitan Magazine*. But in that tale the dead man in the background is not a Predecessor but merely an assistant on a lonely plantation; and instead of the ranch, the mountains, and the plains, there is a cloud-capped island, a bird-haunted reef, and the sea. All this the mere distorted shadow of what we two used to talk about in a fantastic mood; but now and then, as I wrote, I had the feeling that he had the right to come and look over my shoulder. But he never came. I received no suggestions from him, subtly conveyed without words. There will never be any collaboration for us now. But I wonder, were he alive, whether he would be pleased with the tale. I don't know. Perhaps not. Or, perhaps, after picking up the volume with that detached air I remember so well, and turning over page after page in silence, he would suddenly read aloud a line or two and then, looking straight into my eyes as was his wont on such occasions, say with all the intense earnestness of affection that was in him: "I—like—that, Joseph."

Note

1. Extended and republished in the volume *Friday Nights.*

Joseph Hergesheimer (essay date 1924)

SOURCE: Hergesheimer, Joseph. "Introduction." *The Work of Stephen Crane,* vol. 1, edited by Wilson Follett, Alfred A. Knopf, 1924, pp. ix-xviii.

[*In the following essay, Hergesheimer praises* The Red Badge of Courage *(1895) as the story of a boy's growing "knowledge of himself and of self-command ... the fixed pattern of maturity," related with "directness and candour" and conveying the soldiers' words in the "flexible" manner of "the new language of a new land."*]

It is one of the minor treacheries of time that twenty-nine years have vanished almost—as more than a quarter of a century—unnoticed since I first read THE RED BADGE OF COURAGE. I was, then, fifteen years old, and beyond all doubt a better reader than I am now. I had an enormous enthusiasm for the books I liked, a private and unquestioned and passionate allegiance to them long ago diluted by my own experience and difficulties, and by the inevitable development of considerations not always admirable. I do not mean that I wouldn't, to-day, if I were reading it for the first time, completely surrender myself to Stephen Crane's young private of the Civil War; I would, of course; for his is a created story of inescapable fineness. But in the present I would regard it, in part at least, as a deliberate accomplishment in composed periods; while at fifteen it was a great and personal experience.

I read it at once upon its publication—books have a habit of reaching their specially right readers—and I was deeply engaged even before I had opened the straw-coloured buckram, printed in black and red and gold, of its binding. It had come to me widely heralded, borne on the excitement, the derision and praise and curiosity, its appearance had instantly upraised. I have no way of knowing what, at that day, made a large sale; it may be that the interest in THE RED BADGE OF COURAGE was limited to a changelessly small superior public. It may be, but it isn't in my memory that it was; trying to recall those circumstances it seems to me that Crane's novel of battle brought out a very general, and heated, warfare in itself.

You see, it was everywhere regarded as fantastically modern, and one sentence in it, a paragraph, really, became particularly celebrated:

"The red sun was pasted in the sky like a wafer."

That phrase, actually, was made into the standard, the flag —like the flag the youth himself twisted from a dying standard-bearer and carried forward—about which the climax of the action revolved. It was regarded in one camp as a superb piece of imagery, a line which invested one of the oldest of observations with a new and living freshness and vigour; and by the other as a strained and artificial figure. When I reached it I hadn't, for that single instance, an entirely virgin attention; already the struggle had given it an exaggerated importance; and I was appropriately amazed. I thought of an actual red wafer, such as druggists fixed to their bottles; it had a definite, a limited, size for me, an established clear vermilion colour.

I thought of it, for the moment, constantly, repeating it for the benefit of any who could be persuaded to listen; I was, in a minute way, part of the noise that made it notable. But there was no doubt about my opinion of such a remarkable, and modern, paragraph—I was convinced that it was marvellous. The sun itself was diminished, in the sky like a wafer, a wafer of glazed vermilion paper with a regularly serrated edge. For the rest, I felt, together with my enthusiasm, an impatience at what, then, appeared to be a large lack of story; I had no recognition of an underlying structure and ordered whole.

* * *

It was, however, a slight compensation for the passage of so many swift years that I could, now, grasp that: the order and progression, the singleness of purpose, were exact ... and not entirely modern, even in 1895. It was the story of the birth, in a boy, of a knowledge of himself and of self-command; the beginning, in short, of the fixed pattern of maturity. And, as was usual in such forms, it was a birth out of a tragic agony and doubt, a success scarcely won from the edge of eternal defeat.

What, I realized, had worried me at fifteen was that THE RED BADGE OF COURAGE was not at all the story of the practically nameless youth of whom, apparently, it was written; Crane's interest in him, as an individual, was small—he was present for what, as universally as possible, he represented. This coldness to the boy himself, this aloofness from a specific sympathy—from, in reality, sentimentality—left me, too, the implicated reader, more than a little cold. It was the true, the singular, mark of an authentic classical accomplishment; but at fifteen I wasn't aware of so much.

I was perfectly merged with the subject of the book, he was a vessel carrying me over a threatening sea; his undignified cowardice, the temporary spiritual meanness of flight, were mine; when he ran I ran, when he skulked I skulked; when, in the wavering line of the retreating wounded, he was asked where he had been hit, my acute shame was his. Even the eventual firmness and triumph did not, completely, restore me to a necessary warm glow of reassurance. I had, it seemed, been studied by an essentially wise but, where I was intimately concerned, a detached intellect. Stephen Crane might have been a doctor exploring me, to my ultimate good, with frigid and unerring fingers.

I didn't then, and then I was abjectly synonymous with what is called the reading public, want to be so justly regarded, so unsparingly valued; what I did want was to be filled with praise, to hum with a beautiful valour rewarded by all material good; I wanted to be decorated before all the files of men alive, and before the loveliest lady imaginable. This Stephen Crane would not allow; and so my enthusiasm was a little subdued; privately I was even slightly bored; yet, in spite of that, THE RED BADGE OF COURAGE had my devoted, if youngly uncritical, support.

I was not then, naturally, separately conscious of its words, they had to be indicated to me; I discovered no pleasure in them as accomplishments and ends; but I was highly responsive to their effects. Two novels, in that past, made clearer than all others what might, perhaps, be called scenes in nature—THE RED BADGE OF COURAGE and JANE EYRE. The battle-fields and wooded hills, the ruined peace of little valleys, of the first, shrouded in the smoke of guns, were as vivid as the headlong action. The men dead and dying, their sounds and pallors and last rigidity, held a fearful reality which came from the perfection of Stephen Crane's visualization, a quality not alone optical:

He saw them emotionally, in the mystery of creative perception, and put them down in a simplicity of words that cast back, like the reflection in a clear mirror, every leaf and hurt that passed through his imagination. The transition from his conception to its formal expression was as instantaneous, as untroubled, as the flight of a bar of music to a receptive brain and heart.

* * *

The whole form of THE RED BADGE OF COURAGE is amazing for, as much as anything, its directness and candour. That was not, merely, the result of an æsthetic sophistication—simplicity usually is—but the effect on the entire book of the character of the pictured youth. He is singularly candid; and all the sentences, all the pages, have an air of coming from him. Even the lyrical beauty of the objective descriptions, impossible for him to formulate, take the shape and fervour of his inherited reactions to them. When, with his fellows, he moves across a field, the field and the youth are seen together; he walks or desperately charges and the grass is beaten down by his passage; he marches over the roads in loose formation or is momentarily soothed by the peace of casual meadows ... the shuffling tramp of feet accompanies him or he is set in a calm with idly floating butterflies.

And, through it all, the army, the soldiers, talk; they talk in a dialect which seems hopelessly arbitrary, a mere scrambling of disjointed syllables; but actually it is as easy to read, its intent is as plain, as the wording on a sign-board. It's the actual living American language, or, rather, the language that was American—the talk of multitudes of small towns and farming districts. It isn't so much a dialect as it is the flexible and successful record of what promised to be the new language of a new land. This, in the sequel, it did not become; a new land, for reasons inherent in the fatality of humanity, failed to appear; but its pastoral speech, as valid and charming as the rustic measures in Theocritus, has been saved in THE RED BADGE OF COURAGE.

There is, too—a part of Stephen Crane's accomplishment here—a strong sense of humour behind everything said; there isn't a breath, a suspicion, of satire; the spirit of the ludicrous, ungainly like the soldiers themselves, permeates their heated or philosophical or rebellious phrases. The men are eternally complaining or arguing or predicting; they are always beginning bitter quarrels that fade into diminishing curses in turn obliterated by the roll of the cannon. It is possible that no book had ever been written with so much and such a literal transcription of general and particularized talk.

That, the humour investing the things said, was a result of the detached attitude of which, at fifteen, I was critical. Crane was not his youth, the voice of one was not the voice of the other; no, the writer was a completely understanding listener. An unfailing sense of proportion—the heart of humour—gave each uttered sound its true place in the harmony of the whole, no one was covered with decorative ribbons in the face of a silent and respectful masculine world, under the tender gaze of an appealing loveliness. The tumult of the world was not stopped in order to let one voice dominate fate and the law of physics ... in the character of the youth I was slovenly in speech and often hysterical in expression. I had a small habit of mumbling to myself; and it was evident that a great deal I said was humiliating nonsense. Yes, it was funny! The difference between what I was and what I thought and said of myself was made too easily discoverable for my pleasure.

* * *

The controversy over what was referred to as the extremely modern form of THE RED BADGE OF COURAGE has, naturally and long ago, died; and what, on that plane, remains is the realization that it is neither modern nor conservative. There is literally nothing in its treatment which suggests the period that saw it produced; its underlying spirit belongs to no current fashion. Its situations and development were seen not in relation to what else was then being written—it wasn't, in that sense, a piece of the time—but as independent and unliterary facts. Being, in a very fine sense indeed, literature it wasn't concerned with literary values at all. It must have fallen into its period with the effect of a shell from a heavy mortar. The result was as final—thereafter all novels about war must be different; the old pretentious attack was for ever obliterated.

Novels such as, at fifteen, I demanded would continue to satisfy the private vanity of the public; and quite admirable they were; but they had no part in the engagement that held Stephen Crane. They came and went; but here, after twenty-nine years, I was writing a preface to a book that had survived death—the story of a boy who went to war, who fell a victim to fear, and who recovered. That pattern would not have been sufficient for the writers of current successes; in it they could not have discovered a pattern at all. No romance! Nothing prepared at the beginning and no more solved at the end. Yes, and profane ... at the expense of God, pronounced Gawd, and the dignity of men. Where, in all THE RED BADGE OF COURAGE, was the nobility of a cause even hinted at? Where was Lincoln bearing his benevolence like a tendered pardon to fault? Where was Grant with his half-consumed cigar? Where, above everything, was General Lee?

The truth is that they were absent for the reason that they weren't needed; they could have added nothing to Crane's narrative of the Civil War. In writing, so late, the word narrative, which is supposed to carry a different meaning from the word novel, I realize that I am inviting the patronage of the learned. A narrative is not a novel. But in such a confusion of definitions I was, at least, deliberate. THE RED BADGE OF COURAGE is both a novel and a narrative; since the difference between realism and romance has never been defined it may, as well, be both romantic and realistic. At once, I mean. I have an idea, too, that it is poetry, lyrical as well as epic; no one, certainly, can deny that it is completely classic in its movement, its pace and return.

It is all these things, and, in addition, it is life; and it can no more be neatly fitted into a definition than can the mystery of birth. As a child it disturbed and excited and challenged me; and as a man—it would be more precise to say as a writer—it satisfies me. A tranquil countryside is torn for a little by human strife, the stillness is broken by a hideous clamour of explosions and cries, and then the quiet comes back with evening. The dead are removed, the trees are healed, the brooks are again softly audible. Wars are unimportant; individuals are unimportant—actually there are no individuals, but only connected and momentary activities, one fading into the other in a march from dark to dark. That is the burden of THE RED BADGE OF COURAGE, it is the meaning of its title, since courage is not a means but an end. Its incentives are chimeras.

Lyndon Upson Pratt (essay date 1939)

SOURCE: Pratt, Lyndon Upson. "A Possible Source of *The Red Badge of Courage*." *American Literature*, vol. 11, no. 1, 1939, pp. 1-10.

[*In the following essay, Pratt discusses the influence of General John Bullock Van Petten on Crane when he was in school and an officer in his school's "military."*]

Before entering upon a discussion of new material concerning **The Red Badge of Courage,** it is necessary to review the old. Information relating to sources and origins of the novel has always been meager. It is commonly said that the book was undertaken because of a dare which Crane accepted to surpass Zola's depiction of war, *Le Débâcle*, which he read one afternoon during the winter of 1892-1893.[1] Shortly thereafter, he is known to have spent some time searching through old magazines and poring over the stiffly pictured heroics of the *Century's* "Battles and Leaders of the Civil War."[2] Mr. Beer has also shown that, during Crane's boyhood, realistic war reminiscences had impressed him, such as the fatuousness of burying the regimental dead with canteens of whiskey still upon them.[3] Other Crane authorities, notably Mr. Follett, have mentioned the existence of a relative whose war stories Crane listened to during the years at Port Jervis.[4] Finally there is the statement that Stephen's older brother William was considered an expert in the strategy of Chancellorsville and Gettysburg.[5] But fragments as scarce as these are suggestive rather than illuminating.

Mr. Beer was apparently led to believe that, while at Claverack, Crane sensed much the same irony in the presence of military pomp that he later wrote into "War Is Kind."[6] Evidence that this view is inadequate has already been offered.[7] The record of Crane's activity in the school battalion as shown by his repeated promotions can hardly be construed as evincing either lack of interest or deficiency of skill. When one considers that military drill was compulsory for the boys at Claverack, and that the masculine part of the school's enrollment stood in 1890 at about one hundred,[8] Crane's acting as the Colonel's adjutant seems no less remarkable than his being singled out in June for one of the next year's captaincies.[9] Finally it should not be forgotten that the company of which he was then lieutenant won the Washington's Birthday "prize-drill," earning by the precision of its manoeuvres the praise of the judges and the smiles of the young ladies.[10] It seems probable, in fact, that Crane's success in the school battalion would, in itself, have tended toward keeping pleasantly alive his boyish interest in war. There is little reason to doubt that Crane's memories of Claverack were in his mind as he drew the picture of Henry Fleming's farewell to his schoolmates at the "seminary."[11]

But there is another possible connection between Claverack and **The Red Badge of Courage** of considerably greater potential importance. One of the judges of the "prize-drill" which Crane's company won was General John Bullock Van Petten, professor of history and elocution at Claverack.[12] It seems altogether possible that **The Red Badge of Courage** owes more to General Van Petten than to any other single source of influence.

While at Claverack Crane had ample opportunity to become acquainted with the General. The relatively small size of the institution meant, in fact, that everyone knew everyone else, and the custom of commemorating the various holidays throughout the year brought students and faculty together in assemblies as well. The more elaborate of such exercises took the form of banquets, after which toasts and speeches were given.[13] At the conclusion of the dinner on Thanksgiving, 1889, one of the toasts, delivered by Captain Puzey of Company D of the battalion, was reprinted in the *Vidette* as follows:

> I would today present to you a member of the Grand Army of the Republic; an organization whose name implies patriotism, bravery, and indomitable energy. ... The member whom I would toast is one of its most honored and respected. One who has bravely endured the hardships of war as well as enjoyed the pleasures of peace. One who, in the service of his country, has stood before the cannon's mouth, and in the service of his God appeared in the pulpit to instruct and enlighten his fellow-men, and now in his old age is imparting to the young, knowledge of incalculable worth,—a brave soldier, a true Christian, and an enlightened scholar. The Rev. General Van Petten, Ph. D., LL. D.[14]

The *Vidette's* next sentence reads: "This toast was received in a manner showing the estimation in which the worthy General is held, alike by pupils and teachers."

On the same occasion the General himself was called upon to speak. The *Vidette* further reports that "Prof. McAfee next introduced General Van Petten, from whom we are always glad to hear." From this and other references equally cordial in tenor, the inference is clear that the General was a genuinely popular as well as a prominent figure in school life. At the Washington's Birthday devotions, he "very appropriately had charge of the Service" and chose the hymns.[15] Later in the year, when spring came, the condition of his garden received attention by the *Vidette*.[16] And before the summer vacation, his plans were announced as follows: "Gen. and Mrs. Van Petten will attend the National Grand Army Encampment at Boston. The General's class will also meet at Wesleyan [Conn.] for the 40th Anniversary, with which he will meet."[17]

In the natural course of Crane's schoolwork, contact with the General was inevitable. Declamation was required of each student during his stay at the institution,[18] and the *Vidette* for the month following the occasion reported that the exercises preceding the Christmas, 1889, recess included orations by the members of the fourth form, "under the tutorship of Gen'l Van Petten." As has been indicated, the General also taught classes in Roman, English, and American history, although the first two were optional. In addition, the General's wife, listed in the catalog as Mrs. M. B. Van Petten, A.M., taught French, and Crane, by his own admission, studied French while at Claverack.[19]

Since General Van Petten's career forms a considerable basis of what follows, a biographical summary[20] is here inserted for convenience:

> Van Petten, John B., educator; *b*. in Sterling, N. Y., June 19, 1827; *s*. Peter and Lydia (Bullock) V.; grad. Wesleyan Univ., Conn., 1850; completed conf. course in divinity, 1856 (Ph.D., Syracuse Univ., 1888); *m*. Aug. 10, 1850, Mary B. Mason. Prin. Fairfield (N. Y.) Sem., 1855-61 and 1866-9. Was clergyman, M. E. Ch., chaplain 34th N. Y. inf., June 15, 1861, to Sept. 22, 1862; lt.-col. 160th N. Y. inf., Sept. 25, 1862, to Jan. 20, 1865; in permanent command of regiment over 2 yrs.; comd. 2d brigade of 1st div., 19th corps, at Pt. Hudson, June 14, 1863; severely wounded at battle of Opequan, Sept. 19, 1864; complimented in gen. orders by Gen. Sheridan for conspicuous gallantry; col. 193d N. Y. inf. and bvt. brig.-gen. U. S. V., comdg. dist. of Cumberland in W. Va., June, 1865, to Jan., 1866; State senator, 1868-9. Prin. Sedalia, Mo., Sem., 1877-82; prof. Latin and history, Claverack Coll., N. Y., 1885-1900.

Doubtless the reader will have noted one singularity in Van Petten's war record: his commission as lieutenant-colonel of the 160th infantry followed with peculiar suddenness his discharge as chaplain of the 34th regiment. Attention is thus naturally directed to the circumstances surrounding such an immediate change in his status, and the search for a possible explanation leads to the history of his regiment during the latter part of September, 1862.

The 34th New York Volunteers, or Herkimer regiment,[21] had served in the Peninsular campaign during 1862, participating in the battles of Williamsburg, Fair Oaks, Allen's Farm, White Oak Swamp, Malvern Hill, and the Second Bull Run.[22] At the beginning of September, Pope's unsuccessful army of Virginia being amalgamated with the army of the Potomac, and the whole command reverting to McClellan, the 34th New York constituted one of the many regimental units of the Second Corps under General Sumner. Within the Second Corps, Sedgwick commanded the Second Division, in the first brigade of which, that of General Gorman, was the 34th New York regiment under Colonel Suiter.[23]

After Lee's invasion of Maryland had been partly checked at South Mountain, the two armies faced each other on September 16 along a line extending north from the village of Sharpsburg, Maryland. That evening McClellan advanced his right wing to the attack, Hooker and Mansfield crossing Antietam Creek and occupying a position to the north of the Confederate left wing. The next morning they advanced southward to the attack, and fought a severe but indecisive engagement until they were in need of reinforcements. General Sumner's Second Corps marched to their relief late in the forenoon of the seventeenth, the General himself accompanying Sedgwick's 2nd Division which led the attack. "Shortly after nine, Sedgwick's three brigades in three columns emerged from the belt of woods east of the Hagerstown turnpike, deployed, and in three lines, facing west, crossed the cornfield and the turnpike, passing Greene's troops who heartily cheered them, and, leaving the Dunker Church on their left, entered the woods which lay west of the turnpike."[24] The line of Gorman's leading brigade, however, somehow became over-extended, and the regiment on the extreme left, while under severe enemy fire, lost touch with the other regiments of its brigade.[25] This unfortunate regiment was the 34th New York Volunteers.[26] The Confederates, sensing their advantage, advanced at this time, and were thus in a position to deliver a fire upon the flank of the 34th as well as in front.[27]

At this difficult juncture of events, an attempt was made by the 34th New York to extend its own front perhaps in order to reestablish contact with Union forces next to it.[28]

> ... The manoeuvre was attempted under a fire of the greatest intensity, and the regiment broke. At the same moment the enemy perceiving their advantage, came round on that

flank. Crawford was obliged to give way on the right, and his troops pouring in confusion through the ranks of Sedgwick's advance brigade, threw it into disorder and back on the second and third lines. The enemy advanced their fire increasing.

> General Sedgwick was three times wounded, in the shoulder, leg, and wrist, but he persisted in remaining in the field as long as there was a chance of saving it. ... Lieutenant Howe, of General Sedgwick's staff, endeavored to rally the Thirty-Fourth New York. They were badly cut up and would not stand. Half their officers were killed or wounded, their colors shot to pieces, the color-sergeant killed, every one of the color-guard wounded.[29]

Other less hysterical sources, while varying in detail, corroborate the essential features. The brigade-commander, General Gorman, reported:

> The Thirty-fourth New York, being upon the extreme left in the front line of battle, after having withstood a most terrific fire, and having lost nearly one-half of the entire regiment in killed and wounded, was ordered by Major General Sedgwick, as will be seen by Colonel Suiter's official report, to retire and take up a new position behind a battery to the right and rear. Immediately ordered them to reform on the left of the brigade, which they did.[30]

Colonel Suiter's report, naturally, pays less attention to the details of his regiment's rout than to the bravery of certain individuals under the galling circumstances of the battle.

> Of my color-sergeant [Colonel Suiter writes] I cannot speak in too high terms. He had carried the banner through all of the battles in which we have been engaged while on the Peninsular without receiving a wound. Here it was his fate to be struck five times, and when he was compelled to drop his colors he called upon his comrades to seize them and not to let them fall into the hands of the enemy. This was done by Corporal G. S. Haskins, who nobly bore them from the field.[31]

The casualties suffered by the unfortunate 34th, while actually less than the *Tribune* account would lead one to expect, were however considerable. The regiment lost in all 4 officers and 150 men, or about forty per cent of its total strength, although of this aggregate only ten were ultimately reported missing.[32] In other words, despite the heavy casualties suffered, and the probability that during the flight many of the men became separated from the regiment, these men sought out their command and returned to it, until all but ten were accounted for. Of these ten it is likely that several were among the unknown dead on the battlefield.[33]

Such was the course of events that so closely preceded Van Petten's transfer and promotion, although it is not the purpose of this study to infer any causal relationship between these happenings. The significance for the present purpose surely lies in the fact that Van Petten's regiment was forced into flight at the Battle of Antietam, and that he in all probability was an eyewitness to the scenes described. If this was indeed the case, it is unlikely that even his subsequent responsibilities and honors would have wholly obliterated from his mind the memory of his regiment's rout.[34]

It is reasonable to expect that General Van Petten's public utterances would have contained no mention of the 34th at Antietam. Certainly his Thanksgiving speech at Claverack in 1889 is filled with conventional patriotic fervor.[35] But not all of his contacts with the students were formal, and the tone of the *Vidette's* paragraphs concerning him surely indicates that he possessed a compelling, human side. He even used to lend his choice sword to a favored student to wear on dress parades.[36]

At Claverack the custom obtained of having faculty members preside over the tables in the dining hall. General Van Petten had charge of one such table, and thus, three times a day, a small group of students would be gathered around him under circumstances which, while assuredly polite, were to a certain degree informal. Under such conditions as these it is not impossible to conceive of the General remembering Antietam. A feminine student of the time was able to recall the following: "While at Claverack I was at General Van Petten's table for one year and he often recounted some of his war experiences. I can not now recall them, of course, but he became much excited as he lived over the old days."[37]

The aim of the foregoing pages has been to establish a sequence of likelihood, not to claim a factual necessity. It has already been shown that Crane, fond of war from boyhood, became while at Claverack still more interested in military matters. Furthermore, it seems certain that the elderly Van Petten, who had real war anecdotes to tell, was exactly the sort of man to whom Crane would have been responsive. Under these circumstances, then, Crane would surely have disregarded no opportunity to absorb further the lore of the battlefield from this veteran whose eyes had witnessed the scenes he so eloquently described.

It would be useless, of course, for anyone to seek in ***The Red Badge of Courage*** a transliteration of the Battle of Antietam. Numerous details of the story, such as the references to the pontoon-bridges,[38] the plank road,[39] and the Rappahannock,[40] obviously support the traditional view that Crane had Chancellorsville in mind.[41] But in other respects the story more closely resembles certain aspects of Antietam than coincidence would seem to dictate.[42] As a result, the novel may rather be regarded as a synthesis of more than one battle than an historical portrayal of a single engagement. In all probability, some elements were drawn from one source, and some from another. If this principle is accepted, the higher reality of the story is made more credible by broadening the basis in fact even from one battle to two. Thus, if Chancellorsville contributed the general setting and rough plan of the novel, Antietam may well have provided at least two additional elements: the idea of Henry's panic and flight,[43] and the heroism of the wounded color-bearer.[44]

Of these two elements, the latter is admittedly the sort of incident that is traditional in war, and Crane might have found his inspiration in a score of other sources as well. But the former element, that of Henry's flight, seems clearly otherwise, for honest treatments of such disasters do not abound either in pictures or in writings dealing with the Civil War. It should be especially recalled, moreover, that Crane's unheroic treatment of the panic-stricken youth has been largely responsible for the notable position of *The Red Badge of Courage* among war novels.

From this viewpoint, a corresponding importance accrues to the various possible springs of Crane's thinking. Realisms of war remembered since boyhood, as well as unrecorded presumptive conversations with William Crane, are in this sense consequential, since their reflection at least is to be found in *The Red Badge of Courage*. But the weakness of attaching an exclusive momentousness to such origins as the war tales of Crane's "grandfather," for example, as Mr. Follett appears to do, seems apparent in the fact that to annotate *The Red Badge of Courage* Mr. Follett offers only "The Veteran."[45] The latter tale, it should be noted, first appeared in August, 1896,[46] and thus might conceivably have been even a fictitious, though convincing, completion of the story of Henry Fleming, perhaps deriving its very existence from the success of Fleming's earlier appearance. The fact remains, however, that in the rout of Van Petten's 34th New York regiment, one finds for the first time a definite episode basically analogous to the story of Henry Fleming's 304th New York regiment, and one which in all probability Crane had heard told. If this be so, Crane had only to invest the characters of the actual drama with his own thoughts and emotions, which has always been the way of the creative artist.

Notes

1. Thomas Beer, *Stephen Crane: A Study in American Letters* (New York, 1924), p. 97.
2. *Ibid.*, p. 98.
3. *Ibid.*, p. 46.
4. Wilson Follett, "The Second Twenty-Eight Years," *Bookman*, LXVIII, 532-537 (Jan., 1929).
5. Beer, *op. cit.*, p. 47.
6. *The Collected Poems of Stephen Crane*, ed. Wilson Follett (New York, 1930), pp. 77-78.
7. Lyndon U. Pratt, "The Formal Education of Stephen Crane," *American Literature*, X, 460-471 (Jan., 1939).
8. *Claverack Catalog* (1890), p. 25. Of course, some of the boys would have been too young to serve as officers.
9. Pratt, *op. cit.*, p. 465.
10. *Ibid.*
11. "The Red Badge of Courage," *The Work of Stephen Crane* (hereinafter referred to as *Work*) (New York, 1925-1926), I, 28.
12. *Claverack Catalog* (1890), p. 2. See also Pratt, *op. cit.*, p. 464.
13. *Vidette* (the Claverack school magazine), I, 4 (Dec., 1890).
14. *Ibid.*, p. 8. Mr. Beer (*op. cit.*, p. 162) notes Crane's fondness for elderly people.
15. *Ibid.*, I, 2 (March, 1890).
16. *Ibid.*, I, 10 (April, 1890).
17. *Ibid.*, I, 13 (June, 1890).
18. *Claverack Catalog* (1890), p. 16. The curriculum is reprinted by Pratt, *op. cit.*, pp. 462-463.
19. *Claverack Catalog* (1890), p. 2. See also Beer, *op. cit.*, p. 53.
20. *Who's Who in America*, 1903-1909.
21. Frederick H. Dyer, *Compendium of the War of the Rebellion* (Des Moines, 1908), p. 1416.
22. Louis N. Chapin, *A Brief History of the Thirty-fourth Regiment N. Y. S. V.* (New York, 1903), *passim*.
23. Frederick Phisterer (comp.), *New York in the War of the Rebellion, 1861-1865* (3d ed., Albany, 1912), III, 2125-2137, *passim*.
24. John C. Ropes, *The Story of the Civil War* (New York, 1898), Pt. II, p. 363.
25. Colonel Suiter, in his official report, says: "From some cause to me unknown, I had become detached from my brigade, the One Hundred and Twenty-fifth Regiment Pennsylvania Volunteers being on my right ..." (*The War of the Rebellion: A Compilation of the Official Records of the Union and Confederate Armies*, Washington, 1901, XIX, Pt. 1, p. 316. Hereinafter called *War Records*.)

26. *War Records,* XIX, Pt. 1, p. 312.

27. William A. Crafts, *The Southern Rebellion* (Boston, 1870), II, 243.

28. The (New York) *Tribune,* Sept. 20, 1862, p. 5. The account was written by George N. Smalley, the *Tribune's* special correspondent, from the "battlefield, near Sharpsburg," Wednesday evening, Sept. 17, 1862. This *Tribune* account is also printed in *Rebellion Records,* ed. Frank Moore (New York, 1863), V, 469.

29. *Ibid.* There seems to be disagreement among the sources as to the origin of the order.

30. *War Records,* XIX, Pt. 1, p. 312.

31. *Ibid.,* XIX, Pt. 1, p. 316.

32. *Ibid.,* XIX, Pt. 1, p. 192.

33. The 34th Regiment enjoyed an excellent record throughout the war. Except for the disaster at Antietam, no regiment of Sumner's corps lost a gun or a flag up until May 10, 1864, and was, in fact, "the only corps in the army which could make that proud claim" (Francis W. Palfrey, *The Antietam and Fredericksburg,* New York, 1897, pp. 81-82).

34. It should be here admitted that no specific mention of Van Petten's presence at Antietam has been found. There are even discrepancies in the sources concerning the date of his discharge. However, besides the entry in *Who's Who in America* already cited, the records of the 34th regiment filed with the Adjutant General of the State of New York specify September 20. (This information was furnished by Mr. William A. Saxton, Chief, Bureau of War Records, State of New York, in a letter dated Feb. 19, 1937, to the present writer.) September 20 is also given by Frederick Phisterer, *op. cit.,* III, 2136. Finally in Van Petten's Declaration for Original Invalid Pension, dated Nov. 17, 1888, now on file in the office of the Adjutant General of the War Department in Washington, he himself states that he served as Chaplain of the 34th "to about 25 Sept. 1862." (This information is taken from a letter dated April 30, 1937, written by Mr. Nelson Vance Russell, Chief, Division of Reference, The National Archives.)

It is in the statements Van Petten made during later years that discrepancies occur which are quite irreconcilable. But the earlier mentions seem reasonably consistent, and a New York State Senator who was also a Brevet Brigadier General, and had been cited for gallantry in action, certainly cannot be considered remiss, because of a slight inexactitude in dates. Finally, probability of Van Petten's presence at Antietam becomes almost a certainty when the fact is noted that he was a trustee of the National Cemetery at Antietam (*Who's Who in New York City and State,* rev. ed., New York, 1905, p. 914).

35. *Vidette,* I, 5 (Dec., 1889).

36. Letter of Aug. 10, 1936, to the writer from the late Rev. Robert W. Courtney, who attended Claverack between 1891 and 1894.

37. Letter to the writer dated Feb. 5, 1937, written by Mrs. Bertha Holmes Courtney.

38. *Work,* I, 46; and Abner Doubleday, *Chancellorsville and Gettysburg* (New York, 1912), p. 9.

39. *Work,* I, 113; and Doubleday, *op. cit.,* pp. 44 ff.

40. *Work,* I, 140; and Doubleday, *op. cit., passim.*

41. Ripley Hitchcock, in his introduction to the second edition of *The Red Badge of Courage* (New York, 1900) has written: "... the battle which he [Crane] had in mind more than any other was that of Chancellorsville." But the very phrase "more than any other" clearly implies plurality, and, since Hitchcock had himself been the book's purchaser for Appleton's in 1894, his information should have been correct. See also Beer, *op. cit.,* p. 125.

42. Note, for example, the number assigned to Fleming's mythical regiment, the 304th New York (*Work,* I, 57). Since there was no actual 304th regiment among the New York contingent ("Bibliography of State Participation in the Civil War," *United States War Department Library,* 3d ed., Washington, 1913, p. 546), it seems, to say the least, uncanny that Crane should have happened by chance upon a fictitious number so similar to that of Van Petten's 34th New York Volunteers.

Other details in the novel are worth noting. When the 304th is sent into the line as a relief regiment (p. 52; this and the following page numbers refer to the *Work,* Vol. I), the men march westward to their assignment (p. 39). The battle itself is commenced by the brigade on their right (p. 56), and their division occupies a position in the center of the line of battle (p. 59). After the first day's fighting, the number of men "missing" gradually dwindles from half the enrollment of the regiment to a mere handful as the stragglers make their way back (p. 133). When the 304th is itself relieved, the men are marched to the rear, past a battery of artillery, and across the same stream over which they had come to the battle field (p. 196). Although these details are by no means uniquely true of the Battle of Antietam, they more nearly describe the rout of Sedgwick's brigade in that engagement than they do the destruction of Howard's corps at Chancellorsville, for example (Palfrey, *op. cit.*, pp. 81-88, and Doubleday, *op. cit.*, pp. 25-40; also Ropes, *op. cit.*, pp. 363-365, and Pt. III, Book I, pp. 161-165). In opposition, however, such statements cannot be ignored as that the 304th was an inexperienced regiment (p. 33), and that it awaited an attack instead of delivering one (p. 62).

43. *Work,* I, 74 ff.

44. *Ibid.,* pp. 164-165.

45. Follett, *loc. cit.*

46. Claude E. Jones, "Stephen Crane: A Bibliography of His Short Stories and Essays," *Bulletin of Bibliography,* XV, 170 (Jan.-April, 1936).

H. T. Webster (essay date 1939)

SOURCE: Webster, H. T. "Wilbur F. Hinman's *Corporal Si Klegg* and Stephen Crane's *The Red Badge of Courage.*" *American Literature,* vol. 11, no. 3, 1939, pp. 285-93.

[*In the following essay, Webster examines the influence of Hinman's fictional "reminiscences"* Corporal Si Klegg and His "Pard" *(1887) on* The Red Badge of Courage *(1895).*]

In 1887, Wilbur F. Hinman, late lieutenant colonel of the 65th regiment, Ohio volunteer infantry, published a volume of Civil War reminiscences entitled *Corporal Si Klegg and His "Pard." Corporal Si Klegg* is written in a manner which is often engaging, and evidently it enjoyed a fair popularity, for the second edition of 1890 carried it through twenty-six thousand copies and another was forthcoming in 1898. Probably the sale was largely confined to Civil War veterans. In his preface Colonel Hinman has the following to say of the nature of his book:

> There is no end of histories—of campaigns and battles and regiments—and lives of prominent generals; but these do not portray the everyday life of the soldier. To do this, and this only, has been the aim of the author in *Corporal Si Klegg and his "Pard."*

> This volume is not a history, nor is it a "story," in the usual acceptation of the word. "Si Klegg" and "Shorty," his "Pard," are imaginary characters—though their prototypes were in every regiment—and Company Q, 200th Indiana, to which they belonged, is of course, fictitious. Their haps and mishaps while undergoing the process of transformation that made them soldiers ... were those that entered directly into the daily life or observation of all the soldiers. ... The author has made no attempt at literary embroidery, but has rather chosen the "free and easy" form of language that marked the intercourse of the soldiers, and therefore seemed most appropriate to the theme.

Colonel Hinman's seven-hundred-odd pages of text were supplemented by the pencil of George Y. Coffin, who gave the book one hundred and ninety-three illustrations which are not without a grotesque realism.

Unless chance violates probability, Stephen Crane was much more intimately indebted to both the text and illustrations of *Corporal Si Klegg* for his **Red Badge of Courage** than he was to *Battles and Leaders of the Civil War* or to the conversations with veterans such as General Petten.[1] Indeed, Crane's extreme youth at the time he wrote **The Red Badge of Courage** supports the belief that there is a single written source to which the work is mainly indebted; for youth does not have a multitude of impressions to fuse together. The following pages, then, attempt to demonstrate that nearly everything that makes up **The Red Badge of Courage** exists at least in germ in *Corporal Si Klegg*.

Colonel Hinman's preface alone very pointedly suggests two familiar ingredients of **The Red Badge of Courage**: the hero who has his "prototype in every regiment," and the extensive use of American dialect. And if we recognize a general coincidence of aim in the separate works, their parallelism of general imaginative conception is even more striking. Each story tells of the development of a raw recruit into an experienced soldier, constantly emphasizing the thesis and investing it with a quasi-philosophical significance. It is impossible to read very far in either text without becoming aware of this basic similarity in the interpretation of the characters and their adventures. The protagonists who embody the "development" theme, Hinman's Si Klegg and Crane's Henry Fleming, are both farm boys much given to self-dramatization. Moved by patriotism and romantic imaginings of military glory, they enlist in the Union army against the wishes of their parents,[2] and each boy comes home to a touching domestic scene. There is some description in both books of the kit that the mother gives to the departing soldier. After joining his regiment, each boy goes through a period of training and delay which very largely dispels his romantic notions of war. When the first battle finally impends, Si and Henry each lies awake at night and doubts his courage,[3] but each later distinguishes himself in the conflict, seizing the flag from the falling standard bearer to lead a charge,[4] and learning from hearsay afterwards that he has been noticed and praised by the colonel.[5]

In addition, it should be remarked that both Stephen Crane and Colonel Hinman tend to see their characters symbolically in the moment of battle. On Hinman's part, this symbolism is quite explicit. Si Klegg "pictured what it was that conquered the great rebellion. See in those flashing eyes and firmly-set lips the spirit of courage, of unyielding determination, and of patriotic devotion, even to the supreme sacrifice if need be, of life itself."[6] That is the way Colonel Hinman is likely to put things in moments of fervor, which are fortunately rare. Stephen Crane, on the other hand, lets the reader guess for himself what Henry Fleming represents, but the task is not difficult, though the description is less formal and stylized. Henry Fleming, like Si Klegg before him, loads and fires his musket with a blind intensity, but his lips instead of being "firmly set" are contorted into a "cur-like snarl," and when the enemy seemed to give way, "he went instantly forward, like a dog who, seeing his foes lagging, turns and insists on being pursued."[7] Pretty clearly, Henry here symbolizes the spirit of conflict, and a slightly Kiplingesque reversion to the latent savagery in civilized man.

In addition to these parallels of imaginative conception, many details confirm the impression that Stephen Crane had *Corporal Si Klegg* in mind when he wrote ***The Red Badge of Courage***. When Henry Fleming comes home after enlisting, he finds his mother "milking the brindle cow."[8] It is Si's sister, not his mother, who is milking. She drops the pail in surprise at seeing Si in uniform and Si himself takes over the chore patting the cow and calling her "old Brindle."[9] Henry Fleming is given eight pairs of socks and some blackberry jam when he leaves for the army;[10] for Si Klegg, the jam is cranberry; the socks number only three pairs![11] When Henry and Si join their regiments, they each meet a tall soldier of considerable sang-froid: Jim Conklin in ***The Red Badge of Courage***, and Si's "pard," Shorty, in the Hinman book. A good deal is made of the way Si gets rid of his superfluous kit during the first long march.[12] Henry Fleming and his companions simply throw their knapsacks away completely in the same circumstances.[13] When, in his first battle, Si feels "a smart rap on his head," and says to his pard: "Did ye bump me with yer gun, Shorty?"[14] he finds that he has been grazed by a bullet. It will be remembered that during his panic Henry Fleming is hit over the head by the gun of another fleeing soldier, and is thus enabled to tell his comrades that he has been shot during the battle. "Yeh've been grazed by a ball. It's raised a queer lump jest as if some feller had lammed yeh on the head with a club,"[15] says the companion who examines him. Incidentally, a procession of wounded like that which Henry Fleming joins during his flight[16] is seen by Si as he goes into action, and is also represented for the reader by Coffin's pencil.[17]

It is possible to cite other incidents of this sort which these two books have in common, but those already mentioned are the least open to question, and perhaps they are sufficient. They illustrate the fact that Stephen Crane frequently parallels details which are found in *Corporal Si Klegg*. There are, in addition, some passages which are remarkably similar in content. Four examples of these are here cited:

1. From *Corporal Si Klegg:*

> As we have seen in the experience of the 200th Indiana, full regiments on taking the field were rapidly decimated by the ravages of disease and bullets. Scarcely more than half of the men enlisted proved to be physically able to "stand the service," and battles fast thinned the ranks. New organizations were constantly going to the front, but a "veteran" regiment having three hundred men was a large one. ...[18]

From ***The Red Badge of Courage***:

> But the regiment was not yet veteranlike in appearance. Veteran regiments in the army were likely to be very small aggregations of men. Once, when the command had first come to the field, some perambulating veterans, noting the length of their column, had accosted them thus: "Hey, fellers, what brigade is that?" And when the men had replied that they formed a regiment and not a brigade, the older soldiers had laughed, and said, "O Gawd!"[19]

2. From *Corporal Si Klegg:*

> The single hour's experience on the road had served to remove the scales from the eyes of a goodly number of the members of Company Q. They began to foresee the inevitable, and at the first halt they made a small beginning in the labor of getting themselves down to light marching orders—a process of sacrifice which a year later had accomplished its perfect work, when each man took nothing in the way of baggage save what he could roll up in a blanket and toss over his shoulder.[20]

From ***The Red Badge of Courage***:

> The men had begun to count the miles upon their fingers, and they grew tired. "Sore feet an' damned short rations, that's all," said the loud soldier. There was perspiration and grumblings. After a time they began to shed their knapsacks. Some tossed them unconcernedly down; others hid them carefully, asserting their plans to return for them at some convenient time. Men extricated themselves from thick shirts. Presently few carried anything but their necessary clothing, blankets, haversacks, canteens, and arms and ammunition. ...[21]

3. From *Corporal Si Klegg:*

> The officers had ordered the men to lie down, that they might be less exposed to the enemy's fire. But Si will not lie down. ... This feeling was common to new troops in their first fight. In their minds there was an odium connected with the idea of seeking cover. It was too much like

showing the white feather. But in the fullness of time they all got over this foolish notion.[22]

From *The Red Badge of Courage*:

During this halt many men in the regiment began erecting tiny hills in front of them.... This procedure caused a discussion among the men. Some wished to fight like duelists, believing it to be correct to stand erect and be, from their feet to their foreheads, a mark. They said they scorned the devices of the cautious. But the others scoffed in reply, and pointed to the veterans on the flanks who were digging at the ground like terriers.[23]

4. From *Corporal Si Klegg:*

Pretty soon he struck a veteran regiment from Illinois, the members of which were sitting and lying in all the picturesque and indescribable attitudes which the old soldiers found gave them the greatest comfort during a "rest." Then the fun commenced....

"What rijiment is this?" asked Si, timidly.

"Same old rijiment!" was the answer from half a dozen at once. A single glance told the swarthy veterans that the fresh-looking youth who asked this conundrum belonged to one of the new regiments, and they immediately opened their batteries upon him:

"Left—Left—Left!" ...

"Ye'd better shed that knapsack, or it'll be the death of ye!"

"I say, there, how's all the folks to home?"

"How d'ye like it's fur's ye've got, anyway?"

Si had never been under so hot a fire before. He stood it as long as he could, and then stopped.

"Halt!" shouted a chorus of voices. "Shoulder—Arms! Order—Arms!"

By this time Si's wrath was at the boiling point. Casting around him a look of defiance, he exclaimed:

"Ye cowardly blaggards. I kin jest lick any two of ye, an' I'll dare ye to come on. Ef the 200th Injianny was here we'd clean out the hull pack of ye quicker'n ye kin say scat!"[24]

From *The Red Badge of Courage*:

As they approached their own lines there was some sarcasm exhibited on the part of a gaunt and bronzed regiment that lay resting in the shade of trees. Questions were wafted to them.

"Where th' hell yeh been?"

"What yeh comin' back fer?"

"Why didn't yeh stay there?"

"Was it warm out there, sonny?"

"Goin' home now, boys?"

One shouted in taunting mimicry: "Oh, mother, come quick an' look at th' sojers!"

There was no reply from the bruised and battered regiment, save that one man made broadcast challenges to fist fights. ...[25]

The writer believes that the repetition of matter and essential situation in the preceding passages establishes beyond serious doubt that Stephen Crane drew extensively from *Corporal Si Klegg* for his own war novel. This belief raises the question of the precise use he made of his source. Clearly Crane's narrative style is quite unaffected by that of Hinman. This, one would take for granted. Three of the parallel passages, moreover, occur in totally different contexts, though in the passages where the new recruits show reluctance to shelter themselves from the bullets, the context is the same in each text. This juxtaposition of material is characteristic of the way in which Crane handles his source. While most of the detail in *The Red Badge of Courage* can be paralleled in *Corporal Si Klegg,* little of it is given exactly the same application. The much withered condition of example four as it appears in *The Red Badge of Courage* is interesting and illustrative. Hinman revels in incident and authorial comment for its own sake. In no sense an imitator of Dickens, he nevertheless gives the impression that he knew his Dickens intimately, and that he almost intuitively followed the rambling Dickensian pattern in his war book. Crane, on the other hand, subordinates detail to the whole of his conception, and passages which cover pages in *Corporal Si Klegg* offer merely a minor suggestion to the author of *The Red Badge of Courage.* Thus, for example, Henry Fleming's conversation with a Confederate picket[26] recalls to the present writer a much longer passage of the sort in the Hinman book,[27] while the veteran's comment to Henry on the conversation suggests several similar remarks in *Corporal Si Klegg*.[28] The only material which Crane duplicates and greatly expands is the theme of the hero's fright before and during battle. Si Klegg runs away in momentary panic several times in his career, but these incidents are brief and comic. For the most part Hinman keeps his hero hyperconventionally heroic.

In conclusion, it seems appropriate to attempt a summary of what Stephen Crane does and does not owe to Colonel Hinman, if the likelihood of the debt is accepted by the reader. It should be emphasized at once that the total effects of the two books are dissimilar, in spite of their many common details. Hinman's book is much longer than *The Red Badge of Courage,* and a substantial part of the difference in length is taken up with comic incident and comment. The author, indeed, has a flair for drollery, while in passages of purported seriousness he is likely to pull out all the stops on the organ of Victorian rhetoric with results which have already been illustrated. Thus *Corporal Si Klegg* by the intention and talent of its creator, remains a comic book. **The Red Badge of Courage** is hardly that. But evidently, Crane got his conception of a commonplace, unromantic hero from Hinman, together with the theme of this raw recruit's development into the capable veteran. The development theme is much emphasized in both stories, and if Crane looked into a copy of *Corporal Si Klegg*, he could hardly have remained unaware of its existence there, for Coffin's pencil assists the reader with a double frontispiece delineating how Si went away to war, and how he came back. In addition to this, Crane apparently adapted a good deal of the essential structure of his narrative from Hinman, as well as many incidents and details of army life.

It is difficult to say how far Crane may have been influenced by Hinman in his use of dialect. Very probably, the influence is slight. The flavor of the speech is noticeably different, and certainly indicates an attempt on the part of each author to capture the regionalisms familiar to him.[29] Hinman's dialect has a certain raciness which hardly belongs in the scope of Crane's book, and it is set in a less mannered narrative style which gives it a certain advantage as far as naturalness is concerned, but Crane impresses the present writer as being the more accurate transcriber of actual speech. It would seem plausible to believe that Hinman was the source of Crane's army slang, but the correspondence between the expressions actually used is not great. One then gets the impression that Crane was relying mainly on his ear in his reproduction of the soldiers' speech, for certainly army slang and dialect were available to him from many sources.

Crane's narrative style and his descriptive passages are, of course, not suggested by Hinman, and his psychologizing is developed from his model's barest hints. To be sure, Si Klegg, like Henry Fleming, is endowed with a considerable degree of self-consciousness, and a tendency to self-dramatization, but what he thinks and feels is entirely conventional and obvious. Hinman shows no desire to deal with more than the externals of army life. He mitigates the serious and seamy side of war with bursts of Victorian rhetoric, on the one hand, and comedy on the other. Thus, Crane is entirely original when he reconciles meanness and self-sacrifice, panic and heroism in Henry Fleming and his comrades.

Notes

1. Mr. Lyndon Upson Pratt suggests this possibility in *American Literature*, XI, 1-10 (March, 1939).

2. Wilbur F. Hinman, *Corporal Si Klegg and His "Pard"* (Cleveland: N. G. Hamilton and Co., 1890), pp. 4, 15. This edition is not listed in the Library of Congress catalogue, but two other editions are, one printed by the Williams Publishing Company, Cleveland, 1887, and the other issued by N. G. Hamilton and Company, 1898. *The Red Badge of Courage*, ed. Max J. Herzberg (New York: D. Appleton and Co., 1926), pp. 6-8.

3. *Corporal Si Klegg*, pp. 394-395. *The Red Badge of Courage*, pp. 30-31.

4. *Corporal Si Klegg*, pp. 483-484; also illustration facing p. 484. *The Red Badge of Courage*, p. 182.

5. *Corporal Si Klegg*, pp. 494-495. *The Red Badge of Courage*, pp. 206-207.

6. *Corporal Si Klegg*, p. 407.

7. *The Red Badge of Courage*, pp. 164, 167.

8. *The Red Badge of Courage*, p. 7.

9. *Corporal Si Klegg*, pp. 20-21.

10. *The Red Badge of Courage*, pp. 8-9.

11. *Corporal Si Klegg*, pp. 31-32.

12. *Corporal Si Klegg*, pp. 156-161.

13. *The Red Badge of Courage*, p. 33.

14. *Corporal Si Klegg*, p. 410.

15. *The Red Badge of Courage*, p. 133.

16. *The Red Badge of Courage*, p. 85.

17. *Corporal Si Klegg*, p. 402.

18. *Corporal Si Klegg*, p. 696.

19. *The Red Badge of Courage*, pp. 33-34.

20. *Corporal Si Klegg*, p. 158.

21. *The Red Badge of Courage*, p. 33.

22. *Corporal Si Klegg*, p. 409.

23. *The Red Badge of Courage*, p. 41.

24. *Corporal Si Klegg*, pp. 192-193.

25. *The Red Badge of Courage*, p. 200.

26. *The Red Badge of Courage*, pp. 11-12.

27. *Corporal Si Klegg*, pp. 466-469.

28. *Corporal Si Klegg*, p. 133.

29. Perhaps examples will be of interest here. The writer submits for comparison two dialect passages of similar content:

The Red Badge of Courage, pp. 206-207:

"Yeh jest oughta hear!" repeated the other, and he arranged himself to tell his tidings. The others made an excited circle. "Well, sir, th' colonel met your lieutenant right by us—it was the damnedest thing I ever heard—an' he ses: 'Ahem! ahem!' he ses. 'Mr. Hasbrouck!' he ses, 'by th' way, who was that lad what carried th' flag?' he ses, an' th' lieutenant, he speaks up right away: 'That's Flemin', an' he's a jimhickey,' he ses, right away. What? I say he did. 'A jimhickey,' he ses—those'r his words. He did, too. I say he did. If you kin tell this story better than I kin, go ahead an' tell it. Well, then, keep yer mouth shet. Th' lieutenant, he ses: 'He's a jimhickey,' an th' colonel, he ses: 'Ahem! ahem! he is, indeed, a very good man t' have, ahem! He kep' th' flag 'way t' th' front. I saw 'im. He's a good un,' ses th' colonel. . . ."

Corporal Si Klegg, pp. 494-495:

"I axed the cap'n 'f I mout hunt ye up, 'n' he said he didn't have no 'bjections pervidin' the colonel was willin'. I made bold to ax him 'cause I knowed he allus had a warm side fer ye, 'n' I didn't b'lieve he'd think any less on ye fer carryin' the flag o' the old 200th Injianny up to the top o' that blazin' ridge. Jest' soon' I told him what I wanted he said right away, the colonel did: 'Certingly, my man, 'n' when ye git back' says he, come straight ter my tent 'n' tell me how badly Corp'ral Klegg's wounded. He's a brave fellow, is Klegg.' . . ."

John E. Hart (essay date 1953)

SOURCE: Hart, John E. "*The Red Badge of Courage* as Myth and Symbol." *The University of Kansas City Review,* vol. 19, no. 4, 1953, pp. 249-56.

[*In the following essay, Hart explores how Henry Fleming is reborn by analyzing a cluster of redemptive moments he undergoes and symbols he encounters.*]

When Stephen Crane published ***The Red Badge of Courage*** in 1895, the book created an almost immediate sensation. Crane had had no experience in war, but in portraying the reactions of a young soldier in battle, he had written with amazing accuracy. As one way of re-examining ***The Red Badge of Courage,*** we would want to read it as myth and symbolic action. Clearly, the construction of the story, its moral and meaning, its reliance on symbol follow in detail the traditional formula of myth.[1] Crane's main theme is the discovery of self, that unconscious self, which, when identified with the inexhaustible energies of the group, enables man to understand the "deep forces that have shaped man's destiny."[2] The progressive movement of the hero, as in all myth, is that of separation, initiation, and return.[3] Within this general framework, Crane plots his story with individual variation. Henry Fleming, a Youth, ventures forth from his known environment into a region of naturalistic, if not super-naturalistic wonder; he encounters the monstrous forces of war and death; he is transformed through a series of rites and revelations into a hero; he returns to identify his new self with the deeper communal forces of the group and to bestow the blessings of his findings on his fellow comrades.

Whatever its "realistic" style, much of the novel's meaning is revealed through the use of metaphor and symbol. The names of characters, for example, suggest both particular attributes and general qualities: the Tall Soldier, whose courage and confidence enable him to measure up to the vicissitudes of war and life; the Loud Soldier, the braggart, the over-confident, whose personality is, like Henry's, transformed in war; the Tattered Soldier, whose clothes signify his lowly and exhausted plight; the Cheery Man, whose keenness and valor prevent his falling into despair. Likewise, the use of color helps to clarify and extend the meaning. Red, traditionally associated with blood and fire, suggests courage, flag, life-energy, desire, ambition. Black, traditionally associated with death, implies "great unknown," darkness, forests, and, by extension, entombment and psychological death. The whole paraphernalia of myth-religious and sacrificial rites—the ceremonial dancing, the dragons with fiery eyes, the menacing landscape, the entombment, the sudden appearance of a guide, those symbols so profoundly familiar to the unconscious and so frightening to the conscious personality—give new dimensions of meaning to the novel.

What prompts Henry to leave his known environment is his unconscious longing to become a hero. In a state of conscious reflection, he looks on war with distrust. Battles belonged to the past. Had not "secular and religious education" effaced the "throat grappling instinct" and "firm finance" "held in check the passions"? But in dreams, he has thrilled to the "sweep and fire" of "vague and bloody conflicts"; he has "imagined people secure in the shadow of his eagle-eyed prowess." As the wind brings the noise of the ringing church bells, he listens to their summons as a proclamation from the "voice of the people." Shivering in his bed in a "prolonged ecstasy of excitement," he determines to enlist. If the call has come in an unconscious dream-like state where the associations of wind, church bells, ecstasy, heroism, glory are identied with the "voice" of the "group," Henry, fully "awake," insists on his decision. Although his mother, motivated apparently by "deep conviction" and impregnable ethical motives, tries to dissuade his ardor, she actually helps him in the initial step of his journey. She prepares his equipment: "eight pairs of socks," "yer best shirts," "a cup of blackberry jam." She advises him to watch the company he keeps and to do as he is told. Underlining the very nature of the problem, she warns that he will be "jest one little fellow amongst a hull lot of others."

It is this conflict between unconscious desire and conscious fear that prevents Henry from coming to terms with his new environments. Consciously concerned with thoughts of rumored battle, he crawls into his hut "through an intricate hole that served it as a door," where he can be "alone with some new thoughts that had lately come to him." Although his apparent concern is over fear of battle, his real anxiety is that of his individuation. As far as his relationship to war is concerned, he knows "nothing of himself." He has always "taken certain things for granted, never challenging his belief in ultimate success, and bothering little about means and roads." Now, he is an "unknown quantity." If his problems merge into that of whether he will or will not run from an "environment" that threatens to "swallow" his very identity, he sees that it cannot be solved by "mental slate and pencil." Action—"blaze, blood, and danger"—is the only test.

In giving artistic conception to Henry's conflict, Crane relies on a pattern of darkness and light, but adapts such traditional machinery to his particular purpose. As we have seen, Henry achieves courage and strength in the "darkness" of his tent, where his unconscious mind faces the problems of his new surroundings openly and bravely. As he peers into the "ominous distance" and ponders "upon the mystic gloom" in the morning twilight, he is eager to settle his "great problem" with the "red eyes across the river"—eyes like "orbs of a row of dragons advancing." Coming from the darkness towards the dawn, he watches "the gigantic figure of the colonel on a gigantic horse." They loom "black and pattern like" against the yellow sky. As the "black rider," the messenger of death lifts "his gigantic arm and calmly stroke[s] his mustache," Henry can hardly breathe. Then, with the hazy light of day, he feels the consciousness of growing fear. It seems ironic that his comrades, especially the Tall Soldier, should be filled with ardor, even song—just as he was in the darkness of his room at home. With the "developing day," the "two long, thin, black columns" have become "two serpents crawling from the cavern of night." These columns, monsters themselves, move from darkness to light with little fear, for they move, not as so many individuals, but as group units. Clearly, if Henry is to achieve his ambitions, he must "see" and "face" the enemy in the light of day without fear, as well as "perceive" his relationship to the group, which is, in a sense, a "monster" itself.

Henry's growing concern is not for his comrades, but for himself. Although he must march along with them, he feels caught "by the iron laws of tradition." He considers himself "separated from the others." At night, when the campfires dot the landscape "like red peculiar blossoms (as communal fires which impregnate the landscape with "life" and "vitality," they suggest the life energy of the group), Henry remains a "few paces in the gloom," a "mental outcast." He is "alone in space," where only the "mood of darkness" seems to sympathize with him. He concludes that no other person is "wrestling with such a terrific personal problem." But even in the darkness of his tent he cannot escape: the "red, shivering reflection of a fire" shines through the canvas. He sees "visions of a thousand-tongued fear that would babble at his back and cause him to flee." His "fine mind" can no more face the monster war than it can cope with the "brute minds" of his comrades.

Next day as Henry, with sudden "impulse of curiosity," stares at the "woven red" against the "soft greens and browns," the harmony of landscape is broken when the line of men stumble onto a dead soldier in their path. Henry pauses and tries to "read in the dead eyes the answer to the Question." What irony it is that the ranks open "to avoid the corpse," as if, invulnerable, death forces a way itself. He notes that the wind strokes the dead man's beard, just as the black rider had stroked his mustache. Probing his sensations, he feels no ardor for battle. His soldier's clothes do not fit, for he is not a "real" soldier. His "fine mind" enables him to see what the "brute minds" of his comrades do not: the landscape threatens to engulf them. Their ardor is not heroism. They are merely going to a sacrifice, going "to look at war, the red animal—war the blood-swollen god." Even if he warned them, they would not listen. Misunderstood, he can only "look to the grave for comprehension." His feeling is prophetic, for it anticipates the death and transformation of personality that is about to occur.

Before he actually runs from battle, Henry experiences a moment of true realization. Impatient to know whether he is a "man of traditional courage," he suddenly loses "concern for himself," and becomes "not a man but a member." "Welded into a common personality" and "dominated by a single desire," he feels the "red rage" and "battle brotherhood"—that "mysterious fraternity born of the smoke and danger of death." He is carried along in a kind of "battle sleep." He rushes at the "black phantoms" like a "pestered animal." Then, awakening to the awareness of a second attack, he feels weak and bloodless. "Like the man who lost his legs at the approach of the red and green monster," he seems "to shut his eyes and wait to be gobbled." He has a revelation. Throwing down his gun, he flees like a "blind man." His vision of "selflessness" disappears; in this "blindness" his fears are magnified. "Death about to thrust him between the shoulder blades [is] far more dreadful than death about to smite him between the eyes." Impotent and blind (without gun and "vision"), he runs into the forest "as if resolved to bury himself." He is both physically and psychologically isolated from the group and hence from the very source of food and energy, both material and spiritual, that impels heroic achievement.

In the language of myth Henry's inability to face the monsters of battle in the "light," to identify himself with his comrades (both acts are, in a sense, identical), and thus to give up his individual self, which is sustained only in "darkness and in isolation, so that his full self can be realized in the light of communal identification symbolize a loss of spiritual, moral, and physical power, which only a rebirth of identity can solve. Only by being reborn can he come to understand that man's courage springs from the self-realization that he must participate harmoniously as a member of the group. Only then can he understand the "deep forces" from which his individual energy and vitality spring. Thus, Henry's entombment in the forest is only preliminary to the resurrection that will follow. Without his full powers, his transformation cannot be effected by himself, but requires the necessity of ritualistic lessons and the aid of outside forces or agents. His own attempts to expiate his feeling of guilt by logic only leave him lost and confused in the labyrinth of his limitations.

After the burial of himself in the forest, it is his unconscious awareness of the nature of death that restores the strength and energy he had felt in his dreams at home. As he pushes on, going from "obscurity into promises of a greater obscurity," he comes face to face with the very "act" from which he is running. It is a dead soldier covered with "black" ants. As he recoils in terror, the branches of the forest hold him firm. In a moment of blind fear, he imagines that "some strange voice ... from the dead throat" will squawk after him in "horrible menaces," but he hears, almost unconsciously, only a soft wind, which sings a "hymn of twilight." This aura of tranquility, produced in a "religious half light"—the boughs are arched like a chapel—transfixes Henry. He hears a "terrific medley of all noises." It is ironic that he should be fleeing from the black rider only to encounter death and "black ants." His ego is deflated. Did he ever imagine that he and his comrades could decide the war as if they were "cutting the letters of their names deep into everlasting tablets of brass?" Actually, the "affair" would receive only a "meek and immaterial title." With this thought and the song of the wind comes a certain faith. "Pictures of stupendous conflicts" pass through his mind. As he hears the "red cheers" of marching men, he is determined: he runs in the direction of the "crimson roar" of battle.

Although Henry's old fears have not been completely overcome, his meeting with the Tattered Man clarifies the need and method of atoning for his guilt. Having joined the marching soldiers, Henry is envious of this mob of "bleeding men." He walks beside the twice-wounded Tattered Man, whose face is "suffused with a light of love for the army which [is] to him all things beautiful and powerful." Moving in the "light of love," the Man speaks in a voice as "gentle as a girl's." "Where yeh hit?" he repeatedly asks Henry. "Letters of guilt" burn on the Youth's brow. How can he defend himself against an agency which so pitilessly reveals man's secrets? How can he atone for his guilt? His wish that "he, too, had a wound, a red badge of courage" is only preliminary to the fulfillment of atonement, just as in the rites of some primitive tribes or as in Christ's crucifixion on the cross, "blood" plays an essential part in the act of atonement and in the process of transformation.

If the Tattered Man's questioning reveals the need and nature of atonement, meeting the Tall Soldier shows the quality of character needed to make the sacrifice. Justifying the "tall" of his name by his "supreme unconcern" for battle, Conklin accepts his role as part of the group with coolness and humility. Because he realizes the insignificance of self, he has no fear of a threatening landscape. Sleeping, eating, and drinking afford him greatest satisfaction. During meal time, he is "quiet and contented," as if his spirit were "communing with viands." Now, fatally wounded, he is at his rendezvous with death; his actions are ceremonial, "rite-like." He moves with "mysterious purpose," like "the devotee of a mad religion, blood-sucking, muscle-wrenching, bone-crushing." His chest heaves "as if an animal was within," his "arms beat wildly," "his tall figure [stretches] itself to its full height" and falls to the ground—dead. His side looks "as if it had been chewed by wolves," as if the monster war had eaten him and then swallowed his life. This "ceremony at the place of meeting," this sacrificial ritual of placating the monster has enabled him to find the ultimate answer to the Question, but it has consumed its victim in the process.

It is the receiving of the wound, a kind of "magic" touch, whatever its irony of being false, that actually enables Henry to effect atonement. As the army itself retreats, he is truly "at one" with the group ("at one" and atone have similar functions as the very words imply), for both are running from battle. Actually, Henry is not "conscious" of what has happened. Clutching boldly at a retreating man's arm, he begs for an answer. Desperate at being restrained, the man strikes the Youth with his rifle. Henry falls. His legs seem "to die." In a ritual not unlike that of Conklin's dying (it is Henry's "youth," his immature self dying), he grabs at the grass, he twists and lurches, he fights "an intense battle with his body." Then, he goes "tall soldier fashion." In his exaltation, he is afraid to touch his head lest he disturb his "red badge of courage." He relishes "the cool, liquid feeling," which evokes the memory of "certain meals his mother had cooked," "the bank of a shaded pool," "the melody in the wind of youthful summer." The association of blood with that of food suggests the identical function of each. Just as food is nourishment to the body, so blood is nourishment to his spiritual and moral self. Because the monster has "eaten" of him and thus destroyed his fears, he has achieved a moral and spiritual maturity, even, as his going "tall" implies, sexual potency. He feels the tranquility and harmony that has always characterized his dream state. But his wound is an actual fact, and the achieved atonement is not quite the same as in a "pure" dream state. Yet it is still achieved under the ægis of "dusk," and can only be fully realized in the full "light" of group identification.

Henry is further assisted in his transformation by an "unseen guide." Wandering in the darkness, he is overtaken by the Cheery Man, whose voice, possessing a "wand of a magic kind," guides him to his regiment. Thinking of him later, Henry recalls that "he had not once seen his face."

It is important to note here what part food and eating play in Henry's atonement and rebirth. As we have seen, food has both physical and spiritual significance. From the first, Henry has observed that "eating" was of greatest importance to the soldiers. After the Tall Soldier's death, he has speculated on "what those men had eaten that they could be in such haste to force their way to grim chances of death." Now, he discovers that he has "a scorching thirst," a hunger that is "more powerful than a direct hunger." He is desperately tired. He cannot see distinctly. He feels the need "of food and rest, at whatever cost." On seeing his comrades again, he goes directly towards the "red light"—symbol of group energy. They fuss over his wound and give him a canteen of coffee. As he swallows the "delicious draught," the mixture feels as cool to him as did the wound. He feels like an "exhausted soldier after a feast of war." He has tasted of and been eaten by the great monster. By the wound (the being eaten), he has atoned for his guilt with blood. In eating and drinking with his comrades (the communal feasting), he has achieved both literal and spiritual identification with the group. Through his initiation, he has returned as a "member," not an isolated individual. By "swallowing or being swallowed," he has, through atonement and rebirth, come to be master of himself and, henceforth, to be master of others. The Loud Soldier gives up his blankets, and Henry is, in sleep, soon "like his comrades."

In the language of myth, Henry has become a hero. When he awakes next morning from a "thousand years'" sleep, he finds, like Rip Van Winkle, a new "unexpected world." What he discovers has happened to the Loud Soldier is actually the same change that has come over him. For the first time Henry is aware that others have been wrestling with problems not unlike his own. If the Loud Soldier is now a man of reliance, a man of "purpose and abilities," Henry perceives in imagery that recalls the "blossoming campfires" of his comrades that

> a faith in himself had secretly blossomed. There was a little flower of confidence growing within him. He was a man of experience.

Again like the Loud Soldier, he has at last

> overcome obstacles which he admitted to be mountainous. They had fallen like paper peaks, and he was now what he called a hero. He had not been aware of the process. He had slept and, awakening, found himself a knight.

Having overcome the obstacle of self, Henry has at last discovered that the dragon war is, after all, only a gigantic guard of the great death.

If the hero is to fulfill the total requirements of his role, he must bring back into the normal world of day the wisdom that he has acquired during his transformation. Like the "knight" that he is, Henry is now able to face the red and black dragons on the "clear" field of battle. He performs like a "pagan who defends his religion," a "barbarian," "a beast." As the regiment moves forward, Henry is "unconsciously in advance." Although many men shield their eyes, he looks squarely ahead. What he sees "in the new appearance of the landscape" is like "a revelation." There is both a clarity of vision and of perception: the darkness of the landscape has vanished; the blindness of his mental insight has passed. As with the wound and the coffee, he feels the "delirium that encounters despair and death." He has, perhaps, in this "temporary but sublime absence of selfishness," found the reason for being there after all. As the pace quickly "eats up the energies of the men," they dance and gyrate "like savages." Without regard for self, Henry spurs them forward towards the colors.

In the language of myth, it is woman who represents the totality of what can be known. As "life," she embodies both love and hate. To accept her is to be king, the incarnate god, of her created world. As knower (one who recognizes her), the hero is master. Meeting the goddess and winning her is the final test of the hero's talent. Curiously, it is the flag that occupies the position of goddess in the story. The flag is the lure, the beautiful maiden of the configuration, whose capture is necessary if Henry is to fulfill his role as hero. Crane writes:

With [Henry], as he hurled himself forward, was born a love, a despairing fondness of this flag which was near him. It was a creation of beauty and invulnerability. It was a goddess, radiant, that bended its form with an imperious gesture to him. It was a woman, red and white, hating and loving, that called him with the voice of his hope. Because no harm could come to it he endowed it with power. He kept near, as if it could be a saver of lives, and an imploring cry went from his mind.

As Henry and his comrade wrench the pole from the dead bearer, they both acquire an invincible wand of hope and power. Taking it roughly from his friend, Henry has, indeed, reached heroic proportions.

In his role as hero, Henry stands "erect and tranquil" in face of the great monster. Having "rid himself of the red sickness of battle," having overcome his fear of losing individual identity, he now despises the "brass and bombast of his earlier gospels." Because he is at-one with his comrades, he has acquired their "daring spirit of a savage religion-mad," their "brute" strength to endure the violence of a violent world, the "red of blood and black of passion." His individual strength is their collective strength, that strength of the totality which the flag symbolizes. As Crane says:

> He felt a quiet manhood, nonassertive but of sturdy and strong blood. He knew that he would no more quail before his guides wherever they should point. He had been to touch the great death, and found that, after all, it was but the great death. He was a man.

At last he has put the "somber phantom" of his desertion at a distance. Having emerged into the "golden ray of sun," Henry feels a "store of assurance."

Following the general pattern of myth with peculiar individual variations, Crane has shown how the moral and spiritual strength of the individual springs from the group, and how, through the identification of self with group, the individual can be "reborn in identity with the whole meaning of the universe." Just as his would-be hero was able to overcome his fears and achieve a new moral and spiritual existence, so all men can come to face life, face it as calmly and as coolly as one faces the terrors, the odd beings, the deluding images of dreams. If it is, as Campbell points out, the "unconscious" which supplies the "keys that open the whole realm of the desired and feared adventures of the discovery of self," then man, to discover self, must translate his dreams into actuality. To say that Henry accomplishes his purpose is not to imply that Crane himself achieved the same kind of integration. Whatever the final irony implied, he certainly saw that the discovery of self was essential to building the "bolder, cleaner, more spacious, and fully human life."

Notes

1. See Joseph Campbell, *The Hero with a Thousand Faces* (New York, 1949), p. 3. Campbell defines myth as "the secret opening through which the inexhaustible energies of the cosmos pour into human cultural manifestation."

2. *Ibid.*, p. 256.

3. *Ibid.*, p. 30.

Bernard Weisberger (essay date 1958)

SOURCE: Weisberger, Bernard. "*The Red Badge of Courage*: Crane, 1895." *Twelve Original Essays on Great American Novels,* edited by Charles Shapiro, Wayne State UP, 1958, pp. 96-123.

[*In the following essay, Weisberger notes that* The Red Badge of Courage *(1895), a modern realist masterpiece, was concocted wholly in Crane's imagination, and portrays "a successful search for identity" in a wartime setting.*]

The year 1893 was hardly the moment for an American literary event. The United States was painfully preoccupied with a simmering political rebellion in its Mid-west and with a nationwide economic collapse. The social problems swept under the carpet in the Gilded Age were about to explode into new violence. A culture still staggering under the impact of the age of steam was confidently, but somewhat groggily, preparing to grapple with the consequences of electricity and internal combustion. It seemed unlikely that a small artistic revolution could attract much attention.

Creativity, however, has a way of choosing its own auspices. In that year's summer, a twenty-one year old native of Newark, New Jersey, the son of a minister with a solid American ancestry two and one half centuries long, covered one hundred and seventy-six sheets of blue, ruled paper with a novelette. He called it *The Red Badge of Courage: An Episode of the American Civil War.* Its theme of courage was timeless. Its setting was a nineteenth-century war, already haloed with erroneous romance. Its technique and conception were uncompromisingly modern, unshakably identifying it with the literature of the century ahead. To these apparently unrelated parts, Stephen Crane added the intangible element of his talent and the sum of them was a kind of greatness. The book was, and is, a brief classic.

It had overwhelming consequences for Crane; in fact, it stamped out the pattern for the remainder of his life. Published first in a newspaper and then in hard covers, it was a sensational success. Because of it, he was able in 1896 to bring out *Maggie, A Girl of the Streets* under his own name. Because *Maggie* dealt with slum life in a way that was then considered too sordid for propriety, it had first seen print anonymously. With two widely read novels to his credit, Crane could now select his own writing assignments from a variety of offers. His choice led him into an existence which was a study in irony. He hungered for a broader experience of life than the New Jersey parsonages of his childhood had given him. He elected, therefore, to become a roving newspaper correspondent. In 1896 he went out to the Far West. There he looked among the ghosts of mining camp, Indian war and cattle trail, hoping to find some violence left in them. But the West was already freezing into maturity. The next year Crane headed for Cuba, where a native insurrection against the Spanish was blazing. His ship was wrecked off the coast, and he spent nearly two days at sea in an open boat. Later he translated that horror into a famous short story. His compulsive curiosity for "experience" was still unsatisfied. He went to Greece before the year was out, and covered a Greco-Turkish war. In 1898 he was in Cuba again to report on the American campaign against Spain. The irony was most apparent here. Stephen Crane, the writer of *The Red Badge of Courage,* should have turned a searchlight on that fustian adventure and exposed it for the shabby thing it was. Instead, Stephen Crane, the man, could not get too close to the "glory" of the front. He was cited in dispatches for bravery under fire. The next year he went to England to rest up and meditate new undertakings. But his health was wrecked by his Cuban exposures. In June of 1900, still only twenty-eight years old, he died of consumption on the continent.

Out of this untimely cutting-off rose a paradox. Crane was a pioneer in "realism," and *The Red Badge of Courage* should have done to heroic epics of the Civil War what *Don Quixote* is supposed to have done to romances of chivalry. Moreover Crane was a hard-working literary man, who published enough in eight years to fill twelve volumes of collected works. And Crane was successful and recognized and well paid for his endeavors from the time he brought out his second novel. His newspaper career and early death veiled these facts, however. In his manner of living and dying he emerged as a stereotype of popular fiction—an amalgam of Richard Harding Davis and Lord Byron, who dared all, drank deeply of life and died while yet a boy, unfulfilled. As an artist, Stephen Crane would sharply have rejected anything so palpably phony as his own legend.

What is more, no man ever dealt so cruel a blow to his own favorite literary theory. It was Crane's feeling that the author must be as close as possible to the experience which he crystallized in words; that one could do nothing good aesthetically unless it had once meant something important to him. Yet his two most lasting novels, *Maggie* and *The Red Badge of Courage* were spun out of imagination, during unagitated afternoons in small-town family residences. Nothing could better illustrate the fallacy of believing that the "slice of life" offered by a realistic author need be in any way a slice of his own exterior history.

* * *

The fact is that *The Red Badge of Courage* is both realistic and modern precisely because of its masterly handling of interior action. This is the first of its claims to be ranked with the best fiction of the present. It is a story with movement and with crises, but the movements are of images within the mind, and the crises are crises of soul. For the story, taken merely as a story, is a lean one. Briefly, it is the history of a member of a fictitious regiment, fighting a nameless Civil War battle. The hero is a youthful soldier, whom we first meet, beset by fears, as the regiment is moving into action. He wonders if he can stand the naked shock of battle, and he makes fumbling and frustrated efforts to shore up his nerve by seeking out others as frightened as himself. But he cannot break through the defensive wall with which each man is invisibly surrounding himself, and his turmoil increases as they get nearer to the fighting. The troops line up and repulse one attack, but when the second wave of the enemy hurtles through the smoke, the boy bolts and runs away—or rather, gallops away in the blind, terrible, unreasoned thrashing of animal terror. Soon he is mingling with a motley crowd of couriers, teamsters, other skulkers and walking wounded, the normal refuse of the front line. He meets a wounded man who torments him by solicitously asking where he has been hurt. He finds a friend from his own company who, in the final agonies of a mortal injury, dies before his eyes. Then he meets another cluster of retreating soldiers. When he tries to stop one of the frenzied men to get some information, he is clubbed with a rifle butt. Stumbling and jerking about in a daze, he is discovered by a cheerful trooper who leads him back to his outfit. There, to his vast relief, it is assumed merely that he got lost during the action and suffered a head wound.

Next day there is more fighting, but this time the youth plays his part well. In one charge he advances the flag with a recklessness that wins the regimental commander's notice. After a day of confused motion, the regiment is ordered away from its new position, with the usual pointlessness of war from the private's unillusioned point of view. As they leave the place of "blood and wrath," the soul of Henry Fleming changes. He has been to touch the great death and found that, after all, it is but the great death. He is a man. And so, he "came from hot ploughshares to prospects of clover tranquilly, and it was as if hot ploughshares were not. Scars faded as flowers."

This is hardly a story with a sweeping focus. In form, it is compressed. Its foreground is never wider than the view taken in by the single pair of eyes belonging to the hero. Its action is not of a kind for satisfactory dispatches and six-column headlines. Yet *behind* these eyes there is continuous and detailed motion, adding up to development. The book is really a rich and complete story of a successful search for identity. It is, in fact, significant that the full name of Henry Fleming is not revealed until well along in the tale. What is most important, there are no pauses in this action, no suspended moments between charges and bombardments, or halts by the roadside. Every impression, every word, every shape, color, sound and smell is in some direct way related to the emotional experience of the boy. So tight is the construction, and so continuous the flow of impression and mental reaction, that the book could easily be re-written as a monologue by Fleming in stream-of-consciousness style.

There is no character in these pages except for the frightened soldier. Almost immediately, we are introduced to the "youthful private." Within another few paragraphs we learn of the fictitious image of himself that he created before his enlistment and during his early days of service. He saw war as a series of "large pictures extravagant in color, lurid with breathless deeds," and in the first weeks of strutting in uniform, he had "believed that he must be a hero." In the following months of drill and encampment, that original image has been lost, and he has sunk into the anonymity of the army; he is "part of a vast blue demonstration." Now, confronted by action, he is aware of himself again. In a sense the other soldiers, loud and swaggering or stubbornly refusing to speculate on the impalpable tomorrow, are personifications of the various protective attitudes which he himself has adopted. But the question abides. He can no longer find rest in military depersonalization. "Now, with the newborn question in his mind, he was compelled to sink back into his old place as part of a blue demonstration." Compelled to do what was previously voluntary, he is unsatisfied. And so he continually tries "to measure himself by his comrades."

Yet his aloneness continues to be overwhelming. As they move up towards the line he is suddenly obsessed with the idea that they are headed for a trap, and that he alone knows it. "He thought that he must break from the ranks and harangue his comrades. . . . There was but one pair of eyes in the corps. He would step forth and make a speech."

But of course he does not. In the first fighting he finds temporary reassurance in being a part of the regiment, "welded into a common personality which was dominated by a single desire." But then the rage of battle sweeps around him, cutting him off from the others. He is dazed and suffocated—sensations like those of being buried alive, cut off from the living earth. The words of another soldier ring in his mind: "I didn't come here to fight the hull damned rebel army." The vision of himself alone against the gray lines is all too intense. When he finally breaks and runs, he loses his sense of direction. There is no longer any comfort in the thought of others at his side, or support troops behind. Rather, "destruction threatened him *from all points*." He is in the direct center of the stage.

In his odyssey through the rear area, this is made even more clear. The tattered soldier whom Henry meets, wounded in the head and the arm, can easily be taken for the romantic hero parading through those large and colorful pictures of war in Henry's mind as a raw recruit. There is a hint of this in the fact that the tattered soldier is first encountered gawking, his mouth "agape in yokel fashion," at a bearded sergeant who is telling a story. This is a flashback to the wide-eyed greenhorn that Henry has been. But now this pristine and virginal personage is tattered, fouled with blood and powder stains, and, wounded in the *head* and *arm,* unable to think or act sensibly. From this ghost of himself the boy hears an insistent question that racks him with shame. "Where yeh hit, ol' boy?" The answer which he cannot give, of course, is "in his manhood."

Henry escapes from this inquisitor, and meets the wounded "tall soldier," mumbling and lurching toward his death spasm, minutes away. Jim Conklin is not described as an older man, but it is clear earlier in the book that Fleming looks up to him and leans on him for reassurance. He seems to represent the consolations and supports of those who are respected in youth—parents, elders, teachers, and ministers. Now he dies, with horrible contortions, leaving Henry with a childish desire "to screech out his grief." One more refuge is gone. The tattered soldier then reappears. This time, he has become partly identified with Conklin, since he hints that he is an older man, with children. He is visibly getting weaker from his own hurts. He begins to babble and to confuse Henry with one of his own friends, highlighting Henry's further alienation from his past and from others who have shaped him. Remorselessly, the tattered man presses his question, until Henry snaps, "Oh, don't bother me!" and leaves him. But this is a fresh crime to add to cowardice. He is deserting a wounded comrade, and further deserting both his idealized self and the standards set for him before he put on the blue.

A climax is approaching. Henry is buffeted by emotions. He wishes that the army would lose the battle and share his disgrace. Then he recoils from the idea, because his need to believe in certain success for "that mighty blue machine" is overwhelming. A man cannot hide his own failure by pulling the universe down around his ears; the will to order is too strong. Next, he wishes to die. Suddenly, he is agonized by a fantasy in which the whole regiment is discussing his cowardice. In a sense, he is going through the crisis of guilt felt by the "convicted" sinner of a revival. He is thinking of "rules for the guidance of the damned," in Crane's own phrase. And the fact is that he is about to be, in the words of a Christian, "born again."

There is going to be a rebirth, indeed, but not a supernatural one. What happens, rather, is that he meets another panicky refugee, with livid face and rolling eyes. When he tries to intercept this flying fragment of an organization, the man smashes his rifle across Henry's head. This is a turning point. For the frightened soldier is precisely what Henry was himself in the moment when he began to speed toward the rear "in great leaps." Up to now the boy has angrily turned aside the tattered man's question, refusing to recognize the reality of his act. Now he is face to face with his own image at last, and what happens? Clubbed over the skull, he has at last received a wound—a "red badge of courage." From that very moment, the direction of the story changes. The trek *back* to the front begins. The wound is a first stage in redemption, and for all practical purposes, it is self-inflicted.

The next redemptive step comes soon. Henry wanders aimlessly, deliriously thinking of home. He remembers days as a schoolboy, swimming in a favorite pool. He can feel "the swash of the fragrant water upon his body." This is his baptism, and the redeemer is at hand. A cheery voice at the boy's shoulder hails him, his arm is firmly taken, and he is walked along in the darkness towards his regiment. The man with him is a tower of strength, threading the mazes of the tangled forest, avoiding guards and patrols, beating "ways and means out of sullen things," steadily guiding them both on the road back to the campfire—to light, and most of all, to companionship. All the while he is delivering a long, rambling monologue, the whole point of which is that it says nothing coherent. The core of it is in a sentence that spells out the pointlessness of battle.

> ... By dad, I give myself up fer dead any number 'a times. There was shootin' here an' shootin' there, an' hollerin' here an' hollerin' there, in th' damn darkness, until I couldn't tell t' save m' soul which side I was on.

What a shock the Reverend J. T. Crane would have experienced, had he lived to read and understand these lines by his son. *"I couldn't tell t' save m' soul which side I was on."* The gospel that saves Henry Fleming is no assurance of purpose and ultimate salvation in an ordered universe, where good and evil are definable. No; it is the statement of the fact that there *is* no fathomable purpose, that the souls, wandering and crying in the damned darkness, never know their own side. Here is a negation of the Christian conversion, in which one sees the light and is enrolled among the saints. Yet from this negation, the boy will take strength. A man is courageous, at last, because he must be. He has no prop but himself. But let him prove himself once, and then he can never be betrayed.

And who offers this counsel of iron? No prophet, no saint, no elder—in effect nobody. For there is one enormously important detail. Once Henry has found his old outfit, the voice disappears in the darkness. And suddenly the youth realizes that not once has he seen his benefactor's face. His journey has been one of *self*-discovery. His injury has come from his own hand. Either the cure for it has come from the same place, or else from nothingness. There is no saviour to whom he can offer a prayer of thanks, just as there was no devil to blame for his wound.

One final step remains. He hesitates about going back to the campfire, trembling at the thought of the "barbed missiles of ridicule" which will be aimed his way. But he finds that he does not need to invent a story. His friends assume that he was misplaced in action, and they make a satisfying to-do about nursing his bruise, which they assume is from a bullet-graze. So he makes a final connection. He had been alone, true. But there is compensation for the isolation. Weakness, if it goes unnoticed, makes no more of a ripple in society or the universe than unseen courage. "He had performed his mistakes in the dark, so he was still a man." At first he had created a false hero-image of himself, tailored to meet false standards. The image and the standards are now as dead as Jim Conklin. The facts of the situation are plain. There is man, and there is impersonal fate. If fate is kind, the favor is accepted gratefully. If not, a man does the best he can. In neither case is there much purpose in looking further.

> In the present, he declared to himself that it was only the doomed and the damned who roared with sincerity at circumstance. Few but they ever did it. A man with a full stomach and the respect of his fellows had no business to scold about anything that he might think to be wrong in the ways of the universe, or even with the ways of society. Let the unfortunates rail; the others may play marbles.

He does not have to worry any longer about future battles. "It was not essential that he should plan his ways in regard to them. He had been taught that many obligations of a life were easily avoided." So much for the responsibilities of the "saved." Freed from fear, he knows that the necessary evil will come when it will come. Meanwhile he can sink again into the anonymity of the company, moved aimlessly here and there, and perform heroically.

His conversion has led him to a kind of traditional religion in reverse. He can take his loss of identity in battle, because he is reconciled to his own character. If he has no control over his fate, neither has anyone else. He can be a conventional warrior, because he knows that the conventions of fictitious war do not really exist, and cannot make impossible demands. So the goal of an essentially psychological story is reached. The rest of the book is merely to prove the change in Henry.

* * *

Crane's story is one of the first robins of a literary spring, in which hundreds of bewildered young men will hunt for bearings in a world they never made and are not hopeful about mending. But there is a second seal of the contemporary age stamped into the narrative, by the very manner of its telling. Crane constructed the tale with devices which were to become the badges of several schools of modern fiction. For one thing, the careful descriptions of scenery and climate are intended to create a tone matching that of the hero's mind at any given moment. In this kind of environmental symbolism, the ideas will be implicit in the action and the setting. They will not be lifted out by the intervening hand of the writer, and examined. The communication from the invented character to the reader will be direct, but carried on through suggestions.

The very start of the book—the cold, passing "reluctantly from the earth"—immediately establishes a chill, foreboding atmosphere; a sense of 3 A. M., when the muscles are torpid, the body's juices congealed, and every prospect vile. And when, in the final sentence, a golden ray of sun bursts through "hosts of leaden rain clouds," it is almost too pat, too much of a celluloid bromide. In between, this parallel construction of mood and setting reappears again and again. When the regiment is hurrying into action, it is during the "rushing yellow of the developing day." But even as the sun "strikes mellowingly" on the earth, two columns of soldiers moving across a hill look like "two serpents crawling from the cavern of the night." Readers will not be allowed to forget that encroaching darkness. As the troops make a crossing of the river by night, a fire gives to its waters a winelike tint. But the tint of wine is also that of blood, suggesting the kind of river that is going to run through the action of the next day. It is well to notice again the occurrence of two images from the evangelical literature of conversion—the river which must be crossed for salvation, and the blood in which the sinner must be washed. When the regiment has managed to meet the first charges bravely, the boy notices that "the sky is blue and pure, and the sun gleaming." But when he is running away, as the crisis of darkness draws on, the same sun is emitting "slanted bronze rays," and when Jim Conklin dies, it is red and "pasted in the sky like a wafer."

Another development in "new" writing at this time was the effort to break down barriers between art forms and fuse different sensory images of experience. It was especially notable in symbolist poetry, where words were used for their musical effects rather than their meaning, in some cases, and certain sounds were identified with particular colors and the emotions which they evoked. *The Red Badge of Courage* is in step with this trend because in good part it is a painting.

Crane uses colors almost compulsively. In the very first paragraph the sun rises and turns the landscape from brown to green. An amber-tinted river purls at the army's feet, and at night hostile campfires gleam like red eyes. We learn later that when Henry had his first dreams of martial glory, his mother discouraged him, throwing "a yellow light" on his ambitions. The army is a "blue demonstration." But the most effective use of color is in the scene when Henry stumbles on a decaying corpse in the woods. The overarching boughs make a little chapel of the place, entered through "green doors," with a "gentle brown carpet" of pine needles. In this cloister-like atmosphere of warm browns and greens, the boy is paralyzed with terror when he discovers a long-dead soldier. The uniform has faded to a melancholy, sick green—not the fresh hue of the grass. The eyes are the color of a dead fish. The mouth has turned yellow; black ants parade hungrily over the gray skin of the face. This abrupt precipitation into violent greens, yellows, blacks and grays burns the symbol of rejection of conventional religious supports—the "church" containing only a moldering carcass—deeply into the consciousness. Towards the end of the book, when Henry is exhilarated and bold in the final fighting, pieces of the battleground are fought over as if they were "gold thrones or pearl bedsteads"—colors again taken from the popular impression of the heavenly city—and the battle flags fly "like crimson foam," setting the triumphant tone of final salvation.

A third brand identifies *The Red Badge of Courage* with writing styles that were breaking down the conventions of the novel as the nineteenth century ended. Crane is included by critics among the "naturalists" of that period—writers who made man something of a cipher in a world ruled by a "nature" which had no respect for his purposes, and which as often as not crushed him in its blind movements. *The Red Badge of Courage* seems entitled to the label. Certainly, Henry is carried, in his personal retreat, towards the conclusion that the cosmos is not interested in him. The theme is presented most directly when he stumbles into a wood, "as if resolved to bury himself" in nature, the great consoler of so many romantics. But this is not the benign nature of Transcendentalism. As Henry forces his way along, vines cling to his legs and branches shout his secret shame. He cannot "conciliate the forest." He pushes further, looking for "dark and intricate places" and it needs no profound acquaintance with psychoanalysis to guess what they are. Suddenly there is a flash of false hope. He shies a pine cone at a squirrel, which sensibly runs away and does not remain to "die with an upward glance at the sympathetic heavens." This is cheering. Here is nature supporting his own craven action with a demonstration of instinct at work. "She re-enforced his arguments with proofs that lived where the sun shone."

But immediately he blunders into a swamp, where a small animal is observed, pouncing into some *black* water, and emerging with a fish. It is a quite conventional reminder of the cruelty of the struggle for life. The thickets get deeper, but then there is a second illusion of hope. He reaches the little chapel in the forest, with the "high, arching boughs" through which a "religious half-light" is falling. Here is another conventional scene. The groves, after all, were God's first temples. The stage is set for the formal rite of purification and prayer. And what leaps out as the branches are pulled aside? The ant-eaten corpse! The shock underlines the sardonic joke, like the grin of a skull suddenly discovered. Henry runs for his life. Nature may not take the trouble to be an enemy, but she is no friend.

Crane also hammers repeatedly on the theme of the frustration of the individual will in the collective personality of the regiment. The military units are *things*—sometimes living organisms, sometimes machines. A column of stragglers and wounded is "a flow of blood from the torn body of the brigade." After one action, the regiment lies "heaving from its hot exertions." A battle in the distance is a contest between beings who strike savagely and powerfully at each other." But on the other hand, mechanistic images are frequent. The boy imagines that the charging Confederates are "machines of steel." He never quite loses his faith in the final victory of his "mighty blue machine." His company, tired out by repeated charges, is "a machine run down." Most of these similes are pedestrian, but occasionally Crane is capable of greater polish in his imagery, as when he describes bullets which "buff" into men with "serene regularity, as if controlled by a schedule."

The soldiers sense their helplessness and frustration. "The slaves toiling in the temple of this god began to feel rebellion at his harsh tasks," Crane says in one of his more awkward and inexperienced passages. Later, he returns to his proper technique of letting feelings escape in the words and deeds of his characters. (His writing is worst when he is untrue to the style he is creating.) Rebellion simmers effectively in Henry's outburst:

> 'Good Gawd,' the youth grumbled, 'we're always being chased around like rats! It makes me sick. Nobody seems to know where we go or why we go. We just get fired around from pillar to post and get licked here and get licked there, and nobody knows what it's done for. It makes a man feel like a damn' kitten in a bag.'

This is Thomas Hardy or Omar Khayyam, flavored with the American countryside. The lieutenant gives the proper naturalistic answer. "'You boys shut right up! There no need 'a your wastin' your breath in long-winded arguments about this an' that an' th' other.'" In the end, frustration is dominant. After a successful charge, the regiment is reproached by the commanding general, who knows it only as a number, for not having gone far enough. It is as senseless as the rebuke of God for alleged sins, committed in ignorance. And what is more, when all is over, the regiment goes back across the river, presumably to its starting point. Yet there is victory of a kind, but the victory of these veterans is in their acceptance of this real war in place of the fraudulent heroic illusion towards which they bravely marched two days before. They are disenchanted but not beaten. And the moral is plain that man does not choose his destination. He cannot even hold on to the scarred bit of ground which he has won at the price of his youth.

A final hallmark of the book is its "realism." Here, Crane was something less of an innovator. Symbolism and naturalism were somewhat new in 1893. But the pedigree of the novel's fidelity to detail goes back to the "local color" tradition which Crane inherited from the writers who were forging their fame during his childhood—Mark Twain, George Cable, Sarah Orne Jewett, and their like. These authors differed considerably from each other, but they were all trying to re-create accurately the dialects and mannerisms of certain sections and classes of the country. Crane and others were to marry this technique to a more liverish view of life than the seventies and eighties had thought fashionable. They helped to link realism with what was, in the stock phrase, "hard-boiled," and they laid down a road which some have followed all the way to Erskine Caldwell and James T. Farrell.

However, the "ash-can" school of writing was not necessarily implicit in the "realistic" writing of Crane's day. The modern thinker recognizes many "realities." Crane and his contemporaries were after a kind of "realism" which was particular and had boundaries. Sometimes it was called "copyistic," sometimes "veritistic," and sometimes more simply, "photographic." Its aim was to copy objective surroundings as faithfully as possible, and as impersonally as a wet plate. The impact was made on the audience by making the external resemblance between fact and fiction so exact, that the original sensations of an actual event were rekindled. It did not intend to shock deliberately, but it did not flinch from whatever was necessary to complete the sensation of a genuine experience, verifiable by life. One recent edition of *The Red Badge,* in fact, is illustrated by some of Matthew Brady's photographs, and no love-match of text and illustration could be happier.

Crane's method of achieving this special kind of realism was to record his soldier talk in what he considered a reproduction of Eastern rural speech. It is hard to tell whether or not the longer spoken passages accomplished his mission. After a time, such words as "sech," "hull," and "dumbed," and the persistent omission of final sounds, as in "t'" and "an'" become rather stylized themselves. Stenographic accuracy has a way of dating with appalling quickness. The dialogue is a weak link.

But the language of gesture and expletive, on the other hand, is timeless. There is a sense of imminence and closeness in some of Crane's prose because of what his characters do and say in their more terse moments. When we first meet the troops, they are in an argument with the tall soldier, who has picked up a rumor of impending movement, while in the unheroic act of washing his shirt. When Henry leaves his mother to rally to freedom's starry flag, she furnishes counterpoint to his fantasies by making her parting remarks to him as she peels potatoes. When he is lying in his tent, seeing visions of a "thousand-tongued fear" that will betray him the next day, the voices of his fellows are heard in a card game.

Even these homey touches can, by themselves, fade quickly into picturesque, Norman-Rockwell-like effects. Crane avoids this by contrasting them with the crashing events around them, thus making them powerful. The thunder of battle reinforces the intensely human quality of the trivial action. The flyspeck of detail underscores the solemnity of an entire scene. We are all conscious of this contrast in life between the sublime occasion and the ridiculous human animals taking part in it. Crane digs out the full dramatic value hidden in such linked opposites as the sneeze at the funeral, the nervous banality at the scene of an accident, or the drop of perspiration on the upper lip of the great orator.

These antitheses are superbly used. When the first Confederates come charging across the fields, a soldier is seen knotting a red handkerchief about his throat, giving "exquisite attention to its position." Even better, when the second wave comes over, a cry goes up: "Here they come ag'in!" Upon this, one soldier leaps to his feet and utters a simple, single word. He says, "Gosh!" It is a conversational two-cent piece, but standing out alone, it has the impact of a shout. When Jim Conklin feels his life draining away through a side which looks as if it had been chewed by wolves, he can only murmur: "An', b'jiminey, I got shot—I got shot. Yes, b'jiminey, I got shot." To deglamorize war further, Crane has the generals, in their occasional appearances, talk in the same rural patois as the men, which is historically correct as well as artistically satisfying. And as a last example of this, one of the more potent speeches in the book is made by Henry's lieutenant when a new order for a charge is carried to the exhausted and thoroughly bloodied regiment. "Charge?" he says. "Well, b'Gawd!"

* * *

Oddly, it is this kind of detail which spells out the really remarkable feat of the boy Crane's imagination. He himself might well have undergone the central struggle of his hero to find manhood. Certainly the book's moral is a rejection of his own upbringing. The fight for emancipation needed no special setting. But it is remarkable that the imagined backdrop is so convincing.

It is tempting to wonder what his sources were. There was some realistic war writing for him to draw on, but not much, and it is hard to know what he had gotten hold of. John W. De Forest had printed some vivid letters describing infantry combat, which were buried in bound volumes of *Harper's.* He had also, soon after the war, published *Miss Ravenel's Conversion From Secession to Loyalty,* a superb and unsparing (and mostly unsold) novel of the high and low levels of military life. Walt Whitman had put out *Specimen Days,* which treated, without gloves, the horrors of military hospitals. There were some good reporters in the war, and one of them, George A. Townsend, had, in 1866, written *Campaigns of a Non-Combatant,* which set forth the fevers, the plundering, the filth and the pain of parts of the war in unsparing terms. Brady's photographs were widely known. And there were the veterans—men only in their forties, then—who might have given an unlacquered account of camp and battle to a wide-eyed little boy in Port Jervis, or Newark, or Asbury Park, assuming that they chose to.

But the point is that even if we could isolate Crane's raw material, we must still credit him with amazing discernment, for he would have to weigh his truth against a mass of more conventional military reminiscence which dominated the market. There was far more of this than of useful material, for it was the age of formal military portraiture, in high collars and well-combed beards. The style of most non-fictional war writing was being set by the "Battles and Leaders" series of generals' memoirs appearing in the *Century Magazine,* where the war was fought over bloodlessly and with dignity ninety per cent of the time. (The other ten per cent was fine.) The fiction was mostly of the kind typified by the boys' histories emitted from the pen of Charles Carleton Coffin, a saintly Bostonian newspaperman, whose style was considered admirably suited to the task of embalming the nation's past, thus:

> The men throw aside everything which will hinder them, fix their bayonets, and prepare for the work. Their blood is up. They know that it is to be a desperate struggle. But it is not death they are thinking of, but victory.

Crane would normally acquire tons of this kind of forget-me-not kind of romance to every ounce of genuine depiction he found. He had to do an enormous job of sifting. Then he had to break up what he had sifted, and re-fuse it in the heat of his imagination to make it a fit vehicle for his central struggle. This is the really astounding part of his youthful achievement. It still stands amazingly free of minor flaws. If **The Red Badge of Courage** is read and laid alongside a really good non-fictional memoir of the war, such as De Forest's, it matches up amazingly well.

* * *

There is no doubt that the credit for this achievement goes to Crane's genius. It is no ordinary thing to create a small masterpiece of imagination first, and wait for experience to validate it later—a little like digesting first and eating afterwards. Even more impressive is the universality of a book by a writer of such limited attendance at the school of life. **The Red Badge of Courage** rises above the times both of Henry Fleming and Stephen Crane. It paints the experience of all young men who go into battle, familiar with fright but strangers to themselves, and who come out of it touched with sin but somehow stronger. Its baptism in war might have taken place anywhere between the Trojan plain and Pork Chop Hill. Sometimes it almost seems as if it could do altogether without the background of war. The real story is in the emotional storm which divides maturity from innocence.

Yet even if we grant the truth of this, no creative work can be sliced entirely out of its context. Crane is a writer of his times, and he did not invent symbolism, or naturalism, or copyism, however much of them he unearthed on his own. But more than this, **The Red Badge of Courage** tells a story which marks a new approach to the literary treatment of the Civil War. It is a special landmark in the history of our taste, the placement of which raises some absorbing questions. And in addition, the story of Henry Fleming is not in free flight, entirely independent of its setting in the Union army of the sixties. The book is great in part just *because* it takes place when and where it does.

The first of these points is of special interest to history. **The Red Badge of Courage** is the first novel to scrub the war of moonbeams and still find wide acceptance in the market place. It is the first widely accepted work in which a writer who sees life in its rank and primal conditions sees the war in the same light as a part of the whole of that life.

As we have seen, there were a few books which did expose the ugly realities of a fighting man's life, written by men who had taken part in the Civil War. These books died on the sales counters. Twenty years after the peace of 1865, there were realists like Garland, Howells, Ed Howe, Joseph Kirkland and others who did not hesitate to point out the defects of postwar society and to paint the unpleasant features of victorious materialism and sordid politics leering over the American scene. (The Gilded Age, after all, got its name from a novel by Mark Twain and Charles Dudley Warner.) Yet the two streams of realism do not run together. There is no single school of writers to take the two contrasting opposites—the idealism of the war for freedom and the Union and the corruption of national reconstruction—and push them up to confront each other.

There were men who could face the basic unpleasantness of combat without blinking. Yet such men cling to the idealism with which they enlisted. Oliver Wendell Holmes, Jr., of the 20th Massachusetts Infantry, survived the worst fighting of the war and three severe wounds. In his old age, however, he could still recall the experience as one which touched his heart with fire. At the opposite end of the social scale is Private Ben Falls, of the 19th Massachusetts. He re-enlisted in 1864, commenting simply: "Well, if new men won't finish the job, old men must, and as long as Uncle Sam wants a man, here is Ben Falls." It did not occur to him that a job which cost so much in human agony might simply not be worth finishing. Nor does any veteran, looking around him in later years at what happened, announce publicly that the job might as well not have been done in the first place.

On the other hand, the writers who lash out at the grinding of the poor and the preening of respectable plutocracy in the eighties and nineties do not argue that the betrayal of American democracy and idealism began with the war itself. They accept the official valuation. There is almost a mutual agreement that the war will stay encased in a moment of time, forever different from what follows it. There was the war, with its lights and shadows; there is the acknowledged evil in what follows; but in the popular mind neither will be allowed to tarnish the other.

There is the sharpest kind of contrast between this literary situation and that of the twenties. The writers like Cummings, Hemingway, Dos Passos and their kin (to mention only the Americans involved), who found American society vulgar, craven, fraudulent or hollow in their day, also wrote books which debunked the war as a trick played upon them by their elders. The sell-out of what they were taught to believe in as children began when they put on their uniforms, not after they had laid them in mothballs, to judge by much of their writing. But the Civil War itself does not fall victim to this kind of hostile recollection by its veterans, or even by their children. No one says that the war itself is the tree which has borne the bitter fruit.

The Red Badge of Courage changed all this only slightly. It is not a "debunking" book in any sense. It does not deride courage as the false coinage of a propaganda machine. Rather, it simply says that courage, like the fear which it overcomes, has animal reasons for being. Yet Crane's book is free of the conventional posturing of the war fiction then current. The reader of 1895 could not really accept the death of Jim Conklin and simultaneously believe in the fairy-tale heroes in blue who expired with eyes heavenward and a dying message to Mother on their lips. Crane had made a small breach in the wall of myth surrounding the war.

The question is, Why could readers of 1895 accept even that breach? Was it merely because nothing central in the myth was sacrificed? Or did the war already seem safely remote from anything in which they were concerned—a fight between Greeks and Trojans, in which bones could splinter and bowels spill without impropriety? Had the legend done enough work in the politics of justifying the *status quo* to be safely trimmed at the edges? Or was the world of Hanna and McKinley simply too busy to care one way or another? For that matter, why does our own age still enshrine the era of Lee and Grant with legend, when it has learned long since that the years of 1861 to 1865 were as bloody, brutal and stupid as any other war years?

These questions are merely variations on a basic inquiry—what is the effect of culture on literature? The fact remains that a fundamental national experience such as war itself is translated into different kinds of art under different conditions. What circumstances must be ripe to produce "real" wars, and "useless" wars and "noble" wars in fiction? In the case of *The Red Badge of Courage,* it took twenty-eight years for a popular market to be ready for a work which said that the Civil War could be, for the common soldier, a cruel and purposeless war at times. The timing of the book gives it the status of a special problem in the sociology of art.

* * *

There is one other way in which the story receives a special impact from its Civil War setting. If it is the story of innocence transformed into maturity, then it means more because the boy soldiers of the sixties were especially innocent in a way that our world cannot entirely re-create. The teen-ager of a century ago, especially in the farm world, lived in unimaginable isolation. He was a realist about many things—pain, hard work, death. But his *vicarious* experiences were limited. He read little. He had to find types of humanity by digging them out from behind the masks worn by his few immediate kinfolk and neighbors. He did not see movies, hear programs or read articles describing the lives and labors of statesmen, safe-crackers, cowboys, spies, evangelists, mountain climbers and confidence men.

This put him under a handicap. The self which he would discover in the tragedy of war was somewhat cramped imaginatively. The rural boy of that time could not play the game of identifying himself with characters of fiction, and trying on their supposed attitudes for size, which is one way for an adolescent to learn something of life. If he read much about war, it was in popular romance which said simply that a young man in battle should be chivalrous and fearless. It was precisely this image which he would try to force over his own craven and stubbornly resisting body, and his failure to get a good fit would terrify him.

By the time of the first and second World Wars, however, the situation had changed. In 1917 the early movies and the popular magazines had helped to create roles for boys to practice imaginatively—the wise guy, the tough mug, the strong and silent type and the others in the gallery of cheap fiction. And by 1941, the new soldiers were drenched with vicarious experience. Many of them lived in a world shaped entirely by comics, radio and movies. The more literate ones had read the realistic portraits of the war of Woodrow Wilson's day. The depression had brought its own disillusionments to their childhood. Popular psychoanalysis told them of unsuspected deeps in their souls. Comics, radio and the movies had inured them to violence from babyhood. The government thoughtfully provided them with canned and cellophane-wrapped entertainment, mostly freshly exported comics, radio programs and movies, to distract them up to the moment of combat from thinking any thoughts of their own.

Their problem, in fact, was the reverse of Henry Fleming's. Henry and his comrades did not know of the many forms which the self might take. The soldiers of MacArthur and

Eisenhower had tried on so many imaginative suits that they were unable, in some cases, to decide among them. Their personalities were more deeply buried under layers of pretense, borrowed from the world of popular entertainment which rarely left them alone. The world was too much with them, just as it was too little with the soldiers of *The Red Badge of Courage.*

In the end, the essential experience may have been the same. War peeled the layers of pseudo-sophistication from the armed children of the nineteen-forties with as much finality as it stripped the posed romantic valor from youngsters in blue and gray. But it is still significant that innocence and maturity were not so badly confused by Private Fleming's generation. Fleming was more alone because, in battle, he had fewer stylized responses, fewer *learned* attitudes to adopt. And yet, on the other hand, perhaps he was more tough-minded in the long run. Was the boy bred close to the earth more aware of the permanence under the flux? More habituated to tragedy? Was he readier to examine his experiences more deeply and realistically under pressure, simply because they were fewer? Was his "self" more accessible and more resilient than the complex and many-faceted ego of the soldier who followed him into war eighty years later?

These questions are raised when the hero of Crane's novel is transferred from a universal setting and seen as the simple fighting man of a pastoral republic in 1861. Soldier and republic alike are entering battle full of strong and simple notions. Neither of them has yet any awareness of the catastrophe which will overwhelm those notions. It may be a classic of war anywhere and anytime, to be sure, but *The Red Badge of Courage* has the additional distinction of being specifically an epic of America's national tragedy, the Civil War.

James Trammell Cox (essay date 1959)

SOURCE: Cox, James Trammell. "The Imagery of *The Red Badge of Courage*." *Modern Fiction Studies,* vol. 5, no. 3, 1959, pp. 209-19.

[*In the following essay, Cox argues that the "initiation story" of Henry Fleming in* The Red Badge of Courage *(1895), is "symbolically presented to the reader through the imagery," suggested by "a pervasive dramatic irony" that highlights Fleming's "slow discovery" of maturity.*]

"The red sun . . . pasted in the sky like a wafer" of Stephen Crane's *The Red Badge of Courage* continues to generate more critical heat than light. Since the publication in 1951 of R. W. Stallman's much-debated introduction to the Modern Library edition of the novel and his later expansions of this reading, contemporary criticism has been sharply divided on at least three issues: the significance of the religious imagery, the closely related problem of Henry Fleming's development or lack of it, and the question of Crane's fictional method, naturalist or symbolist. Seldom however are these fundamental points of disagreement recognized as such; all too frequently they are obscured or simply avoided in a dispute over critical method. If the imagery gets re-examined, the examination is likely to limit itself to this single image in isolation. Only a single article is devoted primarily to a study of the imagery as a whole.[1] Another look is urgently needed.

Of what has been done, the best on the significance of the religious imagery is Bernard Weisbarger's recent suggestion that "There is going to be rebirth, indeed, but not a supernatural one. Here is a negation of the Christian conversion."[2] This obvious obverse significance of the Christian symbolism, noted but misinterpreted by Stallman and quite consistent with Henry Fleming's naturalistic re-education, seems to have occurred to no one but Mr. Weisbarger. On the problem of Henry Fleming's development, more specifically on its significance in the naturalistic universe depicted in the novel, Stanley B. Greenfield's summation is thoughtful and valuable, especially to the extent that it reconciles what seems a discrepancy between Crane's determinism and the manifest value he attaches to individual insight and moral behavior:

> Crane's magnum opus shows up the nature and value of courage. The heroic ideal is not what it has been claimed to be: so largely is it the product of instinctive responses to biological and traditional forces. But man does have will, and he has the ability to reflect, and though these do not guarantee that he can effect his own destiny they do enable him to become responsible to some degree for the honesty of his personal vision.[3]

Closer textual analysis—a method Mr. Greenfield inconsistently ridicules and utilizes at will—reveals a need for considerable qualification of the cheerful indifference of Nature and of the "decided growth in moral behavior"[4] he finds in Henry Fleming's development. For the imagery suggests that this cheerful appearance of Nature is a part of its treacherous hostility. As Crane expresses the idea in an expunged passage from an earlier manuscript version, "It [Nature] could deck a hideous creature in enticing apparel."[5] The imagery also insists upon the irony of Henry's discovery of unselfishness and courage through the wounded vanity of egocentrism, so that the decided growth toward moral manhood posited by Greenfield ignores this basic irony, as well as its chief philosophical implication: that man's relationship to his universe is paradoxical. He becomes least an animal when most an animal. On the question of Crane's fictional method, Stallman is still significantly right in his recognition of the extent to which "Crane puts language to poetic uses, which is to use it reflexively and symbolically."[6] And it is past time that this fundamental question be considered apart from any given interpretation, for a full understanding and appreciation of the better works of Stephen Crane are absolutely dependent upon an awareness of this method.

What makes this awareness so very important, in particular, to a reading of *The Red Badge of Courage* is that the novel is an initiation story, the account of a young man's discovery of the nature of reality, and the definition of this reality, symbolically presented to the reader through the imagery, provides Henry Fleming's slow discovery with a pervasive dramatic irony as essential to a full appreciation of the work as, for example, a foreknowledge of Oedipus' origin is in *Oedipus Rex*.

Briefly paraphrased, the definition Crane provides us with is largely the same naturalism to be found in "The Blue Hotel." The earth and all life on it originated from the fierce fire of the sun, which continues ultimately to determine both life and death on the earth in the dependence of all life here upon its warmth and light for existence. It is this condition of things, further, which requires that all life—specifically man, animal, and plant, as enumerated by Crane—must alike struggle to survive. Whatever the decking or coloration for the plant or animal, whatever the disguises for man—which would include all the myths of man's mind that obscure this conception of himself and his universe, notably his pretense to honor and glory, his romantic concept of nature, and his belief in eternal life—all are engaged in an endless struggle to survive that necessitates a conflict relation to environment. For this reason the inner nature of all life is hostile. Its battles are for existence, and the essence, in fact, of existence is a battle. This being true, all attempts either to escape or to deny this conflict are doomed to meaninglessness. For meaning, man's only recourse in such a universe is to heed the general's exhortation, "t' go in—everlastingly—like blazes—anything"; that is, to embrace life as conflict. In so doing, man achieves a paradoxical harmony with his hostile universe that allows him, like the regiment, to proceed "superior to circumstances until its blazing vitality fades." It also allows him to know, for a moment, "a temporary but sublime absence of selfishness" and the undeceived brotherhood which his nature, his condition, and his disguises otherwise preclude. And with full knowledge comes, finally, a certain dignity, nothing more.

What is of further interest in the imagery as a whole is that Crane employs here the same images for the same symbolic purposes he later uses in "The Blue Hotel." To symbolize life as an eternal conflict, he uses a battle in the novel as a "way that seemed eternal" and two fights in the short story, one of which is also described as "eternal to his [the Easterner's] sense." To suggest the deterministic inevitability of this conflict and its destructive power, he uses machine images in both, while its ferocity and its limited grandeur are compared to a firework display. To equate man with other forms of life in the identity of their struggle for survival, he relies heavily upon comparisons to animals. To call attention to the timelessness and also the brutality of this struggle, comparisons to primitive warriors are abundant. To make a mockery of man's chief delusion, which is Christianity with its promise of eternal life, Stephen Crane—no matter whose son he is—compares the victims of both conflicts to Jesus Christ. Inferno images abound for roughly the same purpose. To define the essence of reality as treacherous in that its facade conceals the inner hostility which emerges only when existence is threatened, Crane employs a blue exterior with a fire or simply red within in both works. To suggest that death is an inevitable consequence of this fire within, actually differing from life only as colors on the spectrum differ—in degree, not in kind—yellow is used to symbolize death in both. To represent miseducation, particularly in regard to Nature, green and brown have identical functions in both. To symbolize fear, white is used in both, though white in the novel is also linked with stoic calm or love—all three of which associations possess commonality in being opposites to the red of hostility and anger. Only black shows change: in the novel it is the equivalent of red, while in the story it is the oblivion of death, grey in the novel assuming approximately this significance. The two works, in fact, are companion pieces: studies of fear and courage and awareness in a naturalistic universe.

Consistently overlooked, even by Edward Stone,[7] in the long wrangle over the wafer image is the central role of the sun, metaphorically and philosophically, in the novel as a whole. It is set up in the beginning of the novel in the account of Henry's misconceptions as a youth: "There was a portion of the world's history which he had regarded as the time of wars, but it, he *thought,* had been *long gone over the horizon* and had disappeared forever" (6).[8] To this Crane adds, "He had long despaired of witnessing a Greek-like struggle. Such would be no more. Men were better, or more timid. Secular and religious education had effaced the throat-grappling instinct, or else firm finance held in check the passions." Furthermore, this whole idea, with the last two sentences verbatim, is repeated on page 13. Consequently, it cannot be without significance and irony that the general who is in charge of the fighting that Henry has deserted on the first day of battle is described first as "much harassed" with the appearance "of a business man whose market is swinging up and down" (84), secondly, as having in his eyes "a desire to chant a paean" (86), and thirdly as one who "beamed upon the earth like a sun" (86).

Here is ample evidence, indeed, manifest in the action and explained in the imagery, that the time of wars is anything but "long gone over the horizon." As a Greek, an ironically unfirm representative of firm finance, and a sun, this general as the immediate cause of the conflict that ensues is still very much on Henry Fleming's horizon. The explanation provided by the imagery is first of all that finance is neither firm nor capable of holding in check men's passions. Further, in their common identity through metaphor, the imagery also calls attention to the common relation both the general and the sun have to the conflict which follows: it is causal, the general immediate and the sun ultimate. This is again the chief significance and the chief irony in the timely reappearance of the "red sun ... pasted in the sky like a wafer" (115) when Henry has just observed in Jim Conklin's fall that his "side looked as if it had been chewed by wolves." The time of wars has still to go over the horizon because religious education has also failed to efface "the throat grappling instinct."

The lieutenant is thus ironically profounder than he knows when he observes, "'I was willin' t' bet they'd attack as soon as th' sun got fairly up'" (184). This role of ultimate responsibility would also seem to be the implication of the abrupt appearance of the sun in this picture of the dead soldiers: "A dead soldier was stretched with his face hidden in his arm. Farther off there was a group of four or five corpses keeping mournful company. A hot sun had blazed upon the spot" (98). Other corpses are described as "dumped out upon the ground from the sky" (71) or as "stricken by bolts from the sky" (245). The din of this battle is indeed, as Crane tells us, "fitted to the universe" (242), and the sun, though capable of appearing "bright and gay in the blue, enameled sky," is ultimately red and responsible, as the "cloud of dark smoke, as from smoldering ruins" (196), which goes up toward it, reveals like an accusing finger.

The red badge that Henry Fleming wears is seed and sign of this same sun. For in the necessity imposed by the sun on all life to struggle for survival, man retains within a fiery hostility as revealed in the description of his hut, where it is not surprising that we find a fire in a "flimsy chimney of clay and sticks [that] made endless threats to set ablaze the whole establishment" (5). Philosophically, it is the same fire. It is the same fire that disturbed Henry when he "burned to enlist" (6). In the heat of battle, with existence threatened, it is this fire that has now emerged upon Henry's "red and inflamed features" (207) and upon the general's face, "aflame with excitement" (85). The regiment itself is a "firework that, once ignited proceeds superior to circumstances until its blazing vitality fades" (65).

Of course fiery hostility is not the only reaction Henry and the regiment show to this conflict threatening existence. Fear is common and is invariably denoted with expressions suggesting the emergence of white upon the features instead of fire or red, as when Henry "blanched" before turning to run. For fear, like hostility, is a constituent part of the make-up of the inner man as again he is defined in his quarters, with the suggestion that it is from his environment or the outside that his fear derives: "A small window shot an oblique square of whiter light upon the cluttered floor" (5).

Confirming the determining role of the sun as overhanging or providing the conditions under which man, so defined, exists, the sun appears here too: "The sunlight, without, beating upon it [the folded tent which serves as a roof] made it glow a light yellow shade" (5). Thus besides giving the fire necessary to existence, it demands finally as a consequence of this fire death. For yellow is consistently associated with death. The first corpse Henry sees is dressed in a suit of "yellowish brown" (43), and the mouth of the corpse in the chapel of the trees has changed from red "to an appalling yellow" (92). And overhanging the battle area Henry flees from exactly as it overhangs his quarters is "a yellow fog [that] lay wallowing on the treetops" (87). Though the exterior of this hut is brown, careful readers of "The Blue Hotel" cannot fail to note the astonishing similarity between these quarters and the "proper temple" of the short story.

A further aspect of man's nature is symbolically revealed in this interior: his tendency, deriving from his hostility, to screen from himself his inner nature, wreathing it in constructs of belief and value which only obscure the truth, as the smoke from the fire here "at times neglected the clay chimney and wreathed into the room" (5), obscuring this fire as the smoke of battle so often obscures the flames of the enemy guns, making it "difficult for the regiment to proceed with intelligence" (212). A part of this tendency is laziness and ignorance, qualities frequently associated with smoke: "some lazy and ignorant smoke curled slowly. The men, hiding from the bullets, waited anxiously for it to lift and disclose the plight of the regiment" (224). Primarily however it is the fear of death which leads man to construct his own smokescreens, as suggested in the frequent linkage of smoke with the color gray. For the face or prospect of death is gray in each of the deaths that Henry has occasion to observe closely: in the "ashen face" (44) of the first, in "the gray skin of the face" (92) of the corpse in the chapel of the trees, and in "the gray appalling face" (106) of Jim Conklin. Also revealing is its identification with phantom: "Smoke clouds went slowly and insolently across the fields like observant phantoms" (52). For both Jim Conklin and the guilt Henry feels over his desertion of Jim are repeatedly referred to as a "specter" or "somber phantom." The implication of the linkage would seem to be that the guilt Henry feels is a part of the "clogged clouds," from which Henry's brain must emerge before his eyes are opened to new ways and the old sympathies are defeated. It derives from those systems of false belief and value which only obscure from man the fiery essence of the naturalistically conceived universe finally recognized and accepted by Henry Fleming. As such, this "sin" may be put "at a distance" by Henry with somewhat less callousness.

Aside from the false concept of heroism and the emptiness of its values, honor and glory, which it is the obvious purpose of the story to expose as so much smoke obscuring the true nature of man and his conflicts, a romantic concept of Nature, as a part of Henry's secular education, must also be included in this smoke. This romanticism is especially apparent in the sentimental pantheism which leads him to see in the landscape he comes to in his flight "a religion of peace" (90), where the arching boughs in a grove of trees "made a chapel" (92), with the sunlight in them providing "a religious half light" (92) and the wind "a hymn of twilight" (95). The low branches are "green doors" (92) to this chapel and the pine needles "a gentle brown carpet" (92). But exactly as the sentimentality of his earlier reaction to "the gentle fabric of softened greens and browns" which "looked to be a wrong place for a battlefield" (43) is revealed when it becomes the scene of the holocaust he flees, so here are his illusions shattered: within these green doors, resting on this gentle brown carpet is a rottening corpse, its uniform, once blue, now faded to a "melancholy shade of green" (92). However gentle green and brown may seem to the miseducated Henry Fleming, Crane makes it shockingly clear to the reader here and elsewhere that green and brown are the colors of the earth which requires death and decay for its fertility.

In the further relation of image to incident, Crane tells us a great deal more about Nature in this particular passage. The eyes have the "dull hue to be seen on the side of a dead fish" (92), linking the corpse to the frequently noted fish devoured previously by the small animal. The corpse, in other words, is like the fish in its failure to survive. What is not so frequently noted is that on five other occasions we are reminded of this resemblance. Henry, for example is a "'Fresh fish!'" (15) and the courageous Lieutenant Hasbrouck "a whale" (265). Also war is twice a "red animal" (46 and 137) and more than twenty times either war or the enemy is a monster about to devour the men, whose frequent fear is "'We'll git swallowed'" (205). Thus through its connection with this meal of the small animal and the corpse, the conflict that takes place on the battlefield becomes itself a symbol of the struggle for survival. And the connection is repeated, emphasizing that all life is involved in this struggle, in the detail of the ant on the lip "trundling some sort of bundle" (92), for again through simile and metaphor Crane elsewhere identifies this bundle as the soldiers being devoured by the red animal, war: they are "Grunting bundles of blue" (247) that drop here and there "like bundles" (69). Henry himself is "a parcel" (154).

Also significant in this passage is the threat of the branches "to throw him over upon it [the corpse]" (93), symbolizing Henry's involvement in the natural order which demands ultimately a return to the earth like that of the corpse. Furthermore this involvement is carefully elaborated through the tree symbolism. Not only are Henry and the men frequently entangled in Nature's trees or her "brambles [which] formed chains and tried to hold him back" (97), but they are repeatedly likened to a tree to reveal the identity of their mutual struggle, as in the song of the soldiers:

> A dog, a woman, an' a walnut tree,
> Th' more yeh beat 'em th' better they be
>
> (96)

If they survive, that is. The tattered soldier, whose wounded arm dangles "like a broken bough" (102) and Jim, whose body swings forward as he goes down "in the manner of a falling tree" (114), can hardly be described as "better." To indicate that this bit of homely naturalism is to be taken seriously, incidentally, Crane frequently repeats the beating or thrashing imagery like this picture of Henry, who sprawls in battle "like a man who had been thrashed" (193), and compares the soldiers also to women and dogs.

The idea of entanglement is also carried over into the machine imagery, which is used more than fifteen times to describe the battle, suggesting both the deterministic inevitability of this struggle and its destructive power. For instance, as Henry joins the column of the wounded: "The torn bodies expressed the awful machinery in which the men had been entangled" (101). And this machinery is not only the battle but the fixed processes of the natural order demanding conflict and death: "The battle was like the grinding of an immense and terrible machine to him. Its complexities and powers, its grim processes, fascinated him. He must go close and see it produce corpses" (98). A flood is also used on several occasions for the same symbolic purpose. The meaninglessness of this conflict, morally speaking, is apparent in Crane's mention only once of the causes over which the Civil War was fought and then as less important than "the subtle battle brotherhood" of the men, and it is symbolically stated in comparisons of the battle to a circus or carnival and to sporting events. Jim Conklin, for example, gestures toward the battle and says, "'An, Lord, what a circus!'" (108). Over seventy comparisons of the men to animals contribute to this significance of the battle, and in this line, its immediate source is defined as the animal-like hostility of the inner man: "A dull animal-like rebellion against his fellows, war in the abstract, and fate grew within him" (89). To suggest that man is as helpless as a babe in the grinding machinery of the natural order and his fury against it as foolish as that of a child, there are over twenty-five comparisons like these of the men to infants and children: An officer displays "infantile features black with rage" (211) and another "the furious anger of a spoiled child" (59), while Henry before his first battle feels "in the face of his great trial like a babe" (41). This is Nature as it really is—hardly the "woman with a deep aversion to tragedy" (91) Henry Fleming conceived it to be.

Nature's processes are not simply grim however. It is a part of its essence to conceal its inner violence behind a bright facade of blue or blue and gold, so that Nature on occasion parades a gleaming sun in a "blue, pure sky" (73) even as the recruits strut in the "blue and brass" of their new uniforms. Previous to contact with that which threatens existence, man knows only this facade, and Henry on the march to the front sees the sky as a "fairy blue" (28) and does not see "The rushing yellow of the developing day [that] went on behind their backs" (27). Before the march the men themselves are still but a part of this facade, being referred to four times as only a "blue demonstration." And because isolation from the known breeds fear, the same linkage of blue and white is used here that appears in the short story: Wilson tells Henry, "'You're getting blue, my boy. You're looking thundering peaked'" (32). But note what happens to both this fairly blue sky and this blue uniform when Jim Conklin falls: "As the flap of the blue jacket fell away from the body" it exposes Conklin's side, which "looked as if it had been chewed by wolves" (115)—in other words a red and bloody side. And then as a repetition on the cosmic level temporally of the same exposure we have just observed spatially Crane reveals a "red sun" in what was a bright, blue sky. All nature is alike. This is its double essence—the red of violence within the blue of innocence. Innocence in the sense both of inexperience and of beguiling beauty. This spatial relation of blue and red is even preserved in the movement of the troops from their "eternal camp," where they are only a "blue demonstration." For as they prepare to move off toward the front "their uniforms glowed a deep purple" (25), and when they arrive in the battle area "these battalions with their commotions were woven red and startling into the gentle fabric of softened greens and browns" (43).

As a further aspect of the miseducation which obscures from Henry Fleming the fiery essence of his naturalistic universe, his religious education is also responsible. It too is a part of the "clogged clouds" and the old sympathies, as revealed not only in the imagery depicting Jim Conklin's death but also in the inferno imagery and in the imagery of the primitive warrior-worshiper. In the ironic resemblances of Conklin to Christ, Crane is perhaps naively, but clearly and powerfully saying that in this red world Jesus Christ is a grim joke. It is to this climatic conclusion that Crane builds in this crucial chapter exactly as he built up to the shattering revelation of the corpse in the trees. Only here it is the reader who gets the shock instead of Henry, for to have had Henry consciously perceive the resemblance would have been both too obvious and too implausible.

The resemblances are manifestly here however. Since Stallman has noted many of them, I would call attention only to the principal resemblance he's missed: when Jim Conklin falls, his "body seemed to bounce a little way from the earth" (114-15). Here, the point of this carefully and subtly prepared resemblance to Christ, with eight preceding hints, becomes clear. We know why, as Henry rushes to the fallen body, he discovers that "the teeth showed in a laugh" (115). It is because this death, which is all too real, makes of the other a palpable absurdity with its Ascension to the right hand of God. The only ascension here is a grotesque bounce "a little way from the earth." And when then the ultimate source and seal of this grimly naturalistic death appears in the sky in the shape—of all things—of a wafer, the irony is devastating and the significance no less: this *red* wafer symbolizes that there will be *no* miraculous transubstantiation from this mangled and meaningless corpse. Rather, it is a reminder of what we have seen of another corpse: the "red animal, war" and the ants will be the unholy communicants that devour this quite untransubstantiated and unrisen body which is left "laughing there in the grass" (118)—laughing at the appalling joke Henry Fleming's religious education has perpetrated upon him in its promise of eternal life.

What has confused some readers in this resemblance is that Crane does the same thing with his religious imagery here that he does in the short story, where Scully is at one moment God and Satan the next. Jim Conklin is *also* compared to the imps of hell in his "hideous hornpipe," his arms flailing about "in expression of implike enthusiasm" (114), and the "'God!'" that the tattered soldier exclaims upon the fall is starkly changed to "'Hell—'" (115). The significance of this apparent inconsistency is simply that all of heaven and hell man will ever know is here on earth, the product of his own efforts to obscure from himself the truth of his hostile nature in a hostile universe. And inferno imagery, like this line linking Jim to these imps, abounds throughout the text: "The black forms of men, passing to and fro before the crimson rays made weird and satanic effects" (31). They dodge "implike around the fires" (32). War, like life, is hell.

It is in the interesting sense in which Crane uses "enthusiasm" that the religious imagery becomes most revealing, for this enthusiasm is "the daring spirit of a savage religion mad" (251). Again it may be traced from the very beginning of the novel in the "enthusiast" (8) who rings the church bell with news of battle. In Henry too we see it on the march where for a moment "The thrill of his enthusiasm made him ... fiery in his belief in success" (33-34). Finally, it is this religious enthusiasm of the pagan worshiper and warrior that defines the state of mind necessary for the performance of unselfish or heroic deeds:

> The men, pitching forward insanely, had burst into cheerings, moblike and barbaric.... It made a mad enthusiasm.... There was the delirium that encounters despair and death, and is heedless and blind to the odds. It is a temporary but sublime absence of selfishness.
>
> (209)

In a sense Crane seems to be saying that the Dionysiac fury of the pagan worshiper, who at least recognized his universe as hostile, was closer to a valid view of man and his universe than the Christian is with his humanistic veneer and false promise of eternal life. If the general, who gives us the central thematic statement of the novel—"t' go in—everlastingly—like blazes"—were to chant his paean, it would with more validity be addressed to the red sun than to the Heavenly Father.

This pattern is further revealing if we examine the source of this enthusiasm more closely. For it is in the flames of man's inner egotism, stirred up through wounded vanity to a pitch of hatred that is repeatedly described as "a dream" (191), a "delirium" (209), and a "state of frenzy" (251), precluding the consciousness necessary to will. As Crane tells us on the occasion of Henry's first experience of it, from which he awakes a knight or hero, "he lost sense of everything but his hate, his desire to smash into pulp the glittering smile of victory which he could feel upon the faces of his enemies" (191). And it is not only his enemies: "his greater hatred was riveted upon the man, who, not knowing him, had called him a mule driver" (220). The friendly jeers of the veterans produce the same reaction, the praise of the lieutenant an infantile swelling of the same vanity. Before the final charge of the enemy it is again the recollection of being called mud diggers that determines the men to hold and again "some arrows of scorn" (246) that generate "the strange and unspeakable hatred" in Henry, who desires nothing so much as "retaliation upon the officer who had said 'mule drivers' and later 'mud diggers'" (246). To see in this childish hatred with its subsequent "enthusiasm of unselfishness" (250) a "decided growth in moral behavior" is a misreading quite as mistaken as a Christian redemption. Both interpretations miss the point of the paradox Crane *labors* throughout the latter half of the book: that the selfless behavior of heroism paradoxically emerges only from the grossest, most infantile, animalistic, fiery hatred born of the vanity of egocentrism. Though in his non-conscious "enthusiasm" he may be temporarily a man (see 227), it is only after Henry Fleming's "eyes seemed to open to some new ways" (265) that he feels "a quiet manhood" (266). Awareness—the ability to perceive truthfully the nature of this symbolically revealed, hostile universe—alone confers this new quiet, this new dignity.

Notes

1. John E. Hart, "*The Red Badge of Courage* as Myth and Symbol," *University of Kansas City Review*, XIX (Summer 1953), 249-257. The value of Mr. Hart's analysis is limited by his purpose, which is to compare Henry Fleming to the mythic hero, thus reflecting more the anthropological interests of 20th century criticism than the naturalism of late 19th century fiction.

2. Bernard Weisbarger, "*The Red Badge of Courage*," *Twelve Original Essays on Great American Novels*, ed. by Charles Shapiro (Detroit, 1958), pp. 104-105.

3. Stanley B. Greenfield, "The Unmistakable Stephen Crane," *PMLA*, LXXIII (December 1958), 572.

4. *Ibid.*, 569.

5. R. W. Stallman, *Stephen Crane: An Omnibus* (New York, 1952), p. 292.

6. *Ibid.*, xlv.

7. Edward Stone, "The Many Suns of *The Red Badge of Courage*," *American Literature*, XXIX (November 1957), 322-326.

8. Italics mine. All text references are to the Modern Library edition.

Eric Solomon (essay date 1959)

SOURCE: Solomon, Eric. "The Structure of *The Red Badge of Courage*." *Modern Fiction Studies*, vol. 5, no. 3, 1959, pp. 220-34.

[*In the following essay, Solomon argues that* The Red Badge of Courage *(1895) shows the same cycle carried out three times: "the psychological journey of Henry Fleming from a foolish romantic pride, through the depths of fear, the first qualms of conscience, and a realization of his place in the military scheme."*]

I

In spite of the abundance of war novels produced by two world conflicts, *The Red Badge of Courage* is still the masterwork of war fiction. Stephen Crane's novel is the first work in English fiction of any length purely dedicated to an artistic reproduction of war, and it has rarely been approached in scope or intensity since it was published in 1895.

Any judgment of the influence of *The Red Badge of Courage* on later war fiction would of necessity be conjectural. The circumstance that Ford Madox Ford and Ernest Hemingway worshipped at the Crane shrine does not in itself prove that *No More Parades* or *A Farewell to Arms* was directly affected by Crane's book. But the novel became part of the literary heritage of the twentieth century, and whether or not a war writer consciously recalls Crane's performance, the fact remains that *The Red Badge of Courage* is a touchstone for modern war fiction. Stephen Crane gave the war novel its classic form.

Crane, however, made no great innovation in style or subject matter. Realism, irony, detail, the emotional impact of combat—all these had appeared somewhere in earlier war fiction. The contribution of Stephen Crane to the genre of war fiction was twofold. First, he defined the form in his novel that deals with war and its effect upon the sensitive individual who is inextricably involved; war is treated as neither journalism nor autobiography nor dashing romance, but as a test of mind and spirit in a situation of great tension. Crane also constructed a book that still stands as the technical masterpiece in the field.

Crane accomplishes in the longer form of the novel what Ambrose Bierce attains in the short story. *The Red Badge of Courage* creates a single world, a unique atmosphere where war is the background and the foreground. Without resorting to the props of counter-plots dealing with romance and intrigue employed by every novelist who wrote of war from Scott to Kipling (with the possible exception of the Tolstoy of *Sevastopol*), Crane works within a tightly restricted area. Like the painters of the Italian Renaissance who conceived the *tondo,* a form that forced the artist to choose and manipulate his subject matter to fit a small, circular canvas, Crane chooses to restrict his novel to war and its impact upon his hero. There is no mention of the causes or motives of the war or of any battle; Crane's war is universal, extricated from any specific historical situation. We may gain an impression of how a literary artist makes war his *tondo* by an analysis of the structure of *The Red Badge of Courage.* For Crane approached the subject of war as an artist, picking his materials for their fictional value. He was not reliving an experience, but creating one.

Two recent interpreters of Crane have given the novel intensive readings. Maxwell Geismar[1] sees the novel as a psychiatric case study that reflects Crane's childhood traumas and has mythopoeic overtones of pagan ritual and tribal law. Robert Wooster Stallman, in addition to his invaluable edition of *The Red Badge of Courage*[2] that restores all the variant passages from Crane's manuscript and the first edition, supplies a reading that understands the novel largely in terms of Christian allegory, as an expression of redemption through confession and absolution.[3] In this study we shall examine *The Red Badge of Courage* as a war novel and concentrate on the form and techniques employed to recapture the essentials of war in a work of fiction.

Even the most sympathetic critics have been unable to call the book a unified whole. It has usually been passed off as an impressionistic novel. Edward Garnett speaks of the book as "a series of episodic scenes ... it was not constructed in any sense of the word";[4] H. L. Mencken thinks Crane "lacked the pedestrian talent for linking one situation to another."[5]

It is true that many of Crane's effects are gained by recourse to an impressionistic method a technique used by previous war writers to convey the sense of a vast battle scene. His combat descriptions are swiftly shifting impressions of action. Furthermore, he shows the influence of the impressionists in his dependence on color, the contrasts of light and shade. And his characters have a certain anonymity. Although Crane shows many of the realities of war, there is not as much careful detail in his novel as in De Forest's *Miss Ravenel's Conversion*. It is possible to apply the term impressionistic to one aspect of *The Red Badge of Courage*; certainly intensity and expressiveness are stressed—but not necessarily at the expense of symmetry and neatness. For an example of a fully impressionistic war novel, we need only consider Andreief's *The Red Laugh*, where disjointed and blurred fragments of combat are joined together to give a vast vision of horror.

It is equally an oversimplification to think of Crane's book merely in terms of naturalistic fiction. There are, to be sure, certain naturalistic doctrines that Crane follows. Some details appear to be chosen for their shock effect, like the corpse Henry finds in the forest—a sight that makes the dead bodies in Bierce seem pleasant by comparison. But the presence of the corpse is not arbitrary. It fits into the youth-to-experience theme, teaching Henry to understand death as something ghastly—not noble. Henry's salvation comes from a newfound sense of dedication to life and beauty after he has understood the ugliness of death. When he finally risks his life in battle, after having viewed the disgusting corpse, he knows what death involves.

One aspect of naturalism that had already appeared in the war fiction of Bierce and Rudyard Kipling is the double process of animation of mechanical objects and depersonalization of human beings. Crane's novel is packed with parallels between the animal and human worlds. His picture of war shows the iron and steel weapons in the role of flesh-and-blood inhabitants of the combat world. Even the battle flag, normally a symbol, takes on a more human dimension here. The flag struggles to free itself from an agony and finally falls with a gesture of despair (257).

The machines are humanized, and an abstraction like war itself is described as a red animal. Men, for their part, become either animals or machines. It is interesting to note how consistently Crane avoids physical descriptions of his characters and uses animal imagery to tell how men look in war. The regiment seems like "one of those moving monsters" or "crawling reptiles" (240); men are pigs, worms, cows, rats, kittens, etc. Fear makes Henry look like "a jaded horse" (267), "a craven loon" (295). War seems so brutally deterministic to Crane that it robs man of the free will and intelligence that differentiate him from the animals. For this reason the use of animal imagery is fitting for the naturalistic interpretation of war. The images reflect the belief that combat is the most savage pattern of human existence.

Crane's vision is basically ironic, perhaps not as sardonic as that of Bierce, but certainly bitter. He understands war in the naturalistic sense of involving the loss of individual initiative and motivation. The fatalism of war seems for a time to crush Henry. He compares himself to a squirrel who automatically must run away from danger in order to obey the law of survival of the fittest (275). Nature is apparently allied with the superior, intangible force that rules the world of war. One of the most illuminating passages that Crane cut out of the final version of the novel represents war in naturalistic terminology. "From his pinnacle of wisdom, he regarded the armies as large collections of dupes. Nature's dupes who were killing each other to carry out some great scheme of life" (291). But when Henry succeeds in war, nature shines upon him benignly, and the book closes with a lyric description of the sun breaking through the clouds. Neither impressionism nor naturalism is the dominant mode for dealing with the world of war. We shall see that Henry's actions are those of a free individual.

Perhaps *The Red Badge of Courage* should be called an impressionistic-naturalistic novel—or vice-versa. Certainly Crane uses both manners throughout. The combination of a vivid, swift montage of combat impressions with a harsh, overwhelming, naturalistic picture of the individuals trapped in the war machine is Crane's method of fitting the combat world into fiction. The seminal quality of Crane's novel is more evident when one considers that Barbusse and Remarque, in writing of the incredible butchery of World War I, turn to a similar joining of impressionism for the overall battle picture and naturalism for the detail and characterization.

II

Robert Wooster Stallman comes closest to understanding the nature of the novel's structure. He describes *The Red Badge of Courage* as a series of fluctuations between hope and despair, a group of withdrawals and engagements.[6] This is accurate, and we shall notice how Crane follows war's own pattern in his alterations between action and inaction.

There is evidence of much tighter control in Crane's war novel, however. Like the careful symmetry of *The Scarlet Letter*—which has scenes on the scaffold in chapters one, twelve, and twenty-four—so in the twenty-four chapters of *The Red Badge of Courage* there is a careful unfolding of plot; in the latter work there is a triple development.

The first section of the novel shows the dilemma of the youthful hero who feels, and then actually becomes, isolated from the group in war. Crane portrays the psychological journey of Henry Fleming from a foolish romantic pride, through the depths of fear, the first qualms of conscience, and a realization of his place in the military scheme—marked by his return to the regiment following the climactic wound he received in Chapter Twelve.

The same cycle is repeated, once he has rejoined his comrades. Now he interacts with the group as the regiment undergoes *its* test of fear and the recapture of confidence in combat. Finally, the regiment and Henry act as veterans in a successful skirmish. The *Bildungsroman* ends, on the scaffold, as it were, with the young man from the provinces altered and matured by war but still an ambiguous figure who has come to terms with the realities of the world through which he has made his picaresque way to knowledge. Like a lesser Melville, Crane deals with the ambiguities of character, and the battlefield, instead of a ship, is his world.

Henry Fleming's progression, on the most obvious level, is from fear to courage. Crane also extends the meaning of war and its impact upon the hero to a more involved moral nexus. Before he joins the army, Henry is a romantic dreamer, inspired by visions of a chivalric type of warfare in which he becomes a mighty hero. The immediate shock of training destroys any Homeric view of war, but Crane shows, in the book's only flashback out of the immediate war situation, the pre-war dreams of the youth. Like the child in Bierce's "Chickamauga," Henry has been brought up on books and pictures of battle. Crane fixes the pattern of the esthetic young man off to the wars—a figure that was to become a stereotype in the fiction of two world conflicts. Henry enlists in a haze of glorious aspiration that is undercut only by his mother's sober, sad advice. Through Henry's posturing, his ability to conjure a vague smile from a female student into an idealized vision of the girl he left behind him, Crane establishes the character of a sensitive, highly imaginative youth. As Herman Melville wrote, "All wars are boyish and are fought by boys." It is to be expected that Henry's illusions will die hard.

When the rumor of impending action reaches the waiting army, Henry withdraws to worry about the necessity of proving his courage, since he knows nothing about himself as far as war is concerned. He must prove himself in the heat of combat, in the destructive element. Just before the first engagement, Henry gives way to pure hysteria, believing that he is in a trap and being led to certain death. His feeling of persecution is replaced by a wild, animal rage, once the actual combat commences; when the first lull comes, Henry believes he has passed his test. The mercurial youth is in an ecstasy of self-satisfaction. "So it was all over at last! The supreme trial had been passed. The red, formidable difficulties of war had been vanquished" (265).

The author, however, equates war to life, and the reality of battle is made to parallel the reality of human existence where the mere passing of one test does not remove the possibility of other tests being imposed. In war the process is speeded up. Under the shock of the enemy's second attack, Henry protests, gives in to panic, and finally flees in fear. He reaches his low point of cowardice here. From this point on his emotional movement is forward, to a rebirth of courage.

After his communion with nature in the forest, Henry starts back towards the holocaust, fully realizing the irony involved in such a return to danger. He still retains his vague dreams of leading heroic charges, but once he has come back to his regiment—half way through the novel—the fear motif of *The Red Badge of Courage* is completed. For the remainder of the book the hero is sure of himself, even overconfident; and by the end of the story he has become a war devil, exulting in action, capturing a flag, and receiving praise from his superiors. Taken as simply a "psychological portrayal of fear,"[7] the novel is not only ironic, it is amoral. The successful hero has only learned that he is not particularly cowardly. Incisive as his probing of the hero's neurotic fright is, Stephen Crane has much more to say about the influence of combat upon the inexperienced participant.

III

The essential quality of Crane's novel cannot be derived from the study of one man's response to war. War has presented, among other things, a highly developed social problem ever since the days of individual combat were over. The gradation of the army system and its rigid chain of command combine with the massive troop movements of modern warfare to make combat a reflection of a special society with its own precise rules of conformity. And as Mark Schorer has pointed out, any novel must find a form that will encompass both the individual and social experiences.[8]

It may not be immediately obvious that *The Red Badge of Courage* is more than the story of the young soldier who is Crane's hero and point-of-view character. The author does not try to describe his individuals fully. We do not even know the youth's whole name until Chapter Twelve. Taking Crane's novel on its own terms, we need not expect rounded figures, logically described, having past histories; neither should we overlook Henry Fleming's comrades in the war situation.

Henry comes into close contact with five other soldiers in his passage from apprenticeship to mastery. Of these, the tall soldier, Jim Conklin, is most important. Henry identifies with Conklin's calm attitude when faced with combat and attempts to accept his steadying advice. The death of Conklin has particular meaning to the hero; just as in Crane's story, "The Open Boat," the stronger personality does not survive the test. The loud soldier, Wilson, a foil to Henry's fears at the start, undergoes a similar, and even more rapid, growth to manhood through the ordeal. The attitude of the somewhat anonymous lieutenant, Hasbrouck, reflects the hero's place in the military society. When Henry is a coward, the officer strikes at him with a sword, but when the youth is fighting well, he and the lieutenant are filled with mutual admiration.

Two more figures, shadowy ones to be sure, but still vividly realized, provide a commentary on the soldier's progress. Direct opposites, the tattered soldier whom Henry leaves wandering blindly in a field, and the cheery stranger who guides Henry back to his regiment, signify respectively betrayal and comradeship. The interaction of the hero with these five characters and the regiment as a whole furnishes the fundamental theme of *The Red Badge of Courage*. The standards by which Henry's development is measured are those of group loyalty rather than fear and courage. Although the secondary characters are typed, and meant to be so, and not sharply individualized, they are still effectively presented.

The novel opens on the large picture of the entire fighting force. "The cold passed reluctantly from the earth and the retiring fogs revealed an army stretched out on the hills, resting" (226). As in a motion-picture opening, the scene gradually focuses on a particular group of soldiers—Conklin doing his washing, Wilson arguing violently, and then on Henry in a solitude of self-mistrust.

The key to Henry's development, and the essential meaning of war for him, comes in the flashback to his farewell from his mother. The importance of this scene is not in his mother's adjuration to do his duty bravely, nor in the general anti-romantic atmosphere of cows and socks, but in her words that remind the youth of his own insignificance in the larger scheme. "'Yer jest one little feller amongst a hull lot of others, and yeh've got to keep quiet an' do what they tell yeh. I know how you are, Henry'" (231). She knows, but he must learn in battle what kind of a man he is.

Henry's vanity does not allow him to be a little fellow among a whole lot of others except in the rare moments of rationalization when he comforts himself with the consideration that he is part of a vast blue demonstration. Because abstract judgment fails him in his fear, he is isolated. Crane stresses Henry's feeling of solitude. He has no one with whom to compare suspicions; he is different, "alone in space," "a mental outcast" (245). Both the calm competence of the tall soldier and the brash assurance of the loud soldier convince Henry that his is a unique weakness.

When the regiment advances for its baptism of fire, Henry is a part of the group, albeit unwillingly. He feels himself carried along by a mob. The image Crane uses to signify Henry's attitude of helplessness is important. "... there were iron laws of tradition and law [sic] on four sides. He was in a moving box" (248). He is doing exactly what his mother warned him against, considering himself an important individual. He hates the lieutenant and believes that only he, Henry, knows that the entire regiment is being betrayed. In other words, the youth revolts against the iron laws of the war world, the traditions of obedience and humility in the ranks. Crane plays off Henry's condition of rage against Jim Conklin's faithful acceptance of the new environment. The other soldiers are shadowy figures in Henry's mind, since his ego has denied him the comforts of military friendships. He is too wrapped up in himself to realize that others are in the same condition of doubt and fear.

A sudden shift in emphasis takes place when the battle starts, as Henry rapidly adjusts to reality. Losing concern with himself for the moment, he becomes "not a man but a member," a part of a "common personality," a "mysterious fraternity" (261). Whereas in his isolation and doubt he was trapped in a moving box, now, by sinking his personality into the larger personality of the group, he regains control of himself. Crane describes Henry's combat activity with the same box image as before, but there is one important difference. Henry is now in charge. "He was like a carpenter who has made many boxes, making still another box. ..." (261).

Crane transfers the point of view from Henry to the regiment at this juncture. In the impressionistic battle scene, the focus is on "the men," "they," "a soldier" (263) while the regiment goes about its grim business. An integral part of Henry's development is the realization that even the regiment is not the only important participant in the battle. He understands that the fighting involves many regiments and momentarily grasps the idea of his own relative unimportance. But Crane is too acute a psychologist to conceive such a rapid character change and have Henry learn the soldier's hardest lesson easily. When the break in the combat comes, Henry reverts to his pride and considers his rather petty action to have been magnificent. He must undergo a more serious test before he can reap the full benefits of his war experience.

The second attack is too much for him. Henry cannot comprehend the rules of war that are so irrational as to impose another test so soon. He deserts the group, and by this act he breaks all the rigid rules of war. The sight of the lieutenant, angrily dabbing at him with his sword, symbolizes for Henry his new role as an outcast. The youth is no longer, in the Conradian sense, one of them. He asks himself, "What manner of men were they anyhow?" (270), those fools who stayed behind to meet certain death.

The novel is not merely a portrait of fear; it is the portrait of a mind that learns to come to terms with itself and to live down an act of cowardice. Henry Fleming must become a man according to the rules war sets forth. Therefore, he must cast off the egoism that made him run, and gain a true perspective on his importance.

The book is often ironic, since his growth is neither particularly moral nor is it without fluctuations. Henry's failures and successes in war are those of a hero *manqué,* if we are to measure them by the usual Christian ethic. But ***The Red Badge of Courage*** is a war novel, and Henry Fleming should be judged by the ideals of a war world. The lesson Henry has to learn is basic to combat. The individual cannot depend on his personal reasoning powers. Henry's mind has seen the danger and he has fled, while his stupid comrades have stayed and shown courage. The beginning of wisdom comes with the comprehension that his own judgment is insufficient. He is in the position of a criminal because of his enlightened intellect. Henry feels the bitterness and rage of an outcast, a sensitive dreamer who, trapped between romance and reality, can make the best of neither world. Caught in a box of his own making, Henry faces the age-old problem of the individual at odds with society. He has not only indulged in an act of self-betrayal, he has thrown over his responsibilities to and for the others. He does not yet understand that his own salvation (physical and spiritual) must be the product of his dedication to universal salvation. Henry's story is not tragic, because, unlike Lord Jim, the young soldier manages to compensate for his anti-social action and work his way back to the fellowship of men which, in the world of war, is represented by the regiment. But the road back is not easy.

After his dark night of the soul passed in the forest where nature appears to second war's cruelty, Henry commences his return to the battle—to life or death. The physical isolation of the youth ends when he meets a line of wounded soldiers staggering towards the rear, soldiers coming out of the active world from which Henry had fled. Henry joins the crowd, but he remains an outsider, for he has no wound. Crane reverses the symbolism of Hawthorne's *The Scarlet Letter* or "The Minister's Black Veil." Henry is distinguished by his *lack* of any mark. "He was continually casting sidelong glances to see if the men were contemplating the letters of guilt he felt burned into his brow. ... He wished that he, too, had a wound, a red badge of courage" (282). Ironically enough, he desires to be marked by the red death he had feared. Honor, or the appearance of honor, is his new goal.

As if to emphasize his sin, Henry remains with the denizens of the strange world of wounded. He meets the tattered man, one of Crane's most brilliant portraits of a nameless figure. We know nothing about the tattered man except that he is wounded, and that he is a rather naïve and gentle soul. He is the antithesis of the young soldier in every way. The tattered man has been hit; he talks proudly of his regiment and its performance; he is humble and loves the army. In other words, he stands for the simple man who has done his duty and received his mark of honor. The tattered man represents society, and to the conscience-stricken Henry the wounded soldier is a reminder of guilt. Henry cannot remain with the tattered man when he asks the probing question, "'Where yeh hit, ol' boy?'" (281), that emphasizes the youth's isolation.

A greater shock is in store for Henry Fleming. After he leaves his tattered companion behind, he meets the spectral soldier—the tall soldier, Jim Conklin—transformed by a fatal wound. Henry's feeble wish for a little wound pales into the realm of bathos in comparison to Conklin's passion. The dying man's expression of sympathy and concern for Henry adds to the acute discomfort of the youth's position. In his walk through the valley of the shadow of death at Conklin's side, Henry's education advances. Conklin's death brings home to Henry the true nature of war, brutal and forbidding, more than the sight of an unknown corpse in the forest could do. The body of his friend stretched out before him, Henry curses the universe that allows such things to be. He shakes his fist at the battlefield and swears, but his insignificance in the larger scheme is indicated by Crane's most famous line, "The red sun was pasted in the sky like a wafer" (287).

Despite his genuine grief at Conklin's death, Henry is unable to accept responsibility for the tattered man, who has returned to pry at Henry's guilty secret, the crime "concealed in his bosom" (290). He deserts the tattered man a second time, and in denying him the young soldier commits his real sin. He breaks both a Christian and a military ethical rule ("Greater love hath no man. ..."). Like his original act of cowardice, this desertion goes unpunished. If we are to read the novel as a study in irony, there is no confusion; Henry is a sinner who succeeds in war without ever changing his ways. Crane's attitude towards his hero is ambiguous throughout the novel, however, and the betrayal of the tattered man is essential to Henry's growth to maturity. Although the tattered man himself says that "'a man's first allegiance is to number one'" (287), Henry realizes what he has done. His later heroism is a successful attempt to wipe out his cowardice. While he eventually rationalizes his betrayal, the memory of the tattered man blocks any real return to the egocentric immaturity that marked his character at the outset of the novel.

He heads back to the "furnace" (292) of combat, since the heat of that purgatory is clearly more desirable than the icy chill of solitude. His progress is halting. Henry is unable to throw off his romantic visions; he imagines his new self in a picturesque and sublime role as a leader of lurid charges. Once again the reality of war breaks his dreams apart, reality in the forms of physical exhaustion, thirst, and the memory of his cowardice. No longer a visionary, Henry can now make his way through the war world.

Crane's bitterness comes to the surface in this part of the novel. Henry is really worried about appearance. How can he pretend to be something he is not—a hero? It is when the self-centered youth is concerned with the difficulty of fabricating a lie effective enough to account for his disappearance that his full name is given for the first time by the author. The young soldier mentions it in apprehension of the name, "Henry Fleming," becoming a synonym for coward. Names and appearances are his only concern.

Henry Fleming's actions must be judged by the standards of war. While he is planning his lie (a sin, from a normal ethical viewpoint), fate, in the form of a hysterical soldier who clubs Henry out of the way, provides the wound that not only preserves the appearance of his integrity but also opens the way for his attainment of genuine honor. It is ironic, even cynical, for war to help Henry after he has broken the rules, and for the coward to pass as a hero. Two other points must be kept in mind, however. Crane constantly refers to his hero as "the youth," and despite his transgressions, Henry is still an innocent fumbling for the correct path, not a hardened sinner. Furthermore, he does not receive his wound in flight, but in the performance of an act of courage! Henry is struck down (by a coward) while inarticulately striving "to make a rallying speech, to sing a battle hymn" (300). He is in a position to suffer such a wound because he has originally fled from his regiment, but he is going against the current of retreating infantry, *towards* the battle, when he gains the red badge. The wound, then, may be seen as the result of heroism, not cowardice, and the irony is vitiated. Henry has escaped from his nightmare of weakness before he is wounded. His own efforts have proved him not completely unworthy of the saving grace granted him by the fate of war.

The wounded Henry is again part of the fellowship of armed men. "The owner of the cheery voice" (304), who plays Mr. Strongheart in Henry's progress, guides the dazed youth through the forest wasteland back to the regiment. The gratuitous support of the cheery man is in direct contrast to Henry's earlier refusal to accompany the tattered man. The first twelve chapters of the novel come to an end with Henry outlined in the reflection of his regiment's campfires. The return to the company, which in war fiction has stood for homecoming from Kipling's "The Man Who Was" to Jones's *From Here to Eternity*, marks the completion of Henry Fleming's isolation and the start of the conquest of glory for himself and the regiment.

The hero of Crane's war novel has not yet learned what the author is in a later story to call "virtue in war." His relief at the arrival back into the "low-arched hall" (310) of the forest (a suggestion perhaps of the mead hall of the Old English epics, the symbol of the fellowship of strong warriors) is intense. He views the sleeping company with complacency because to all appearances he is one of them, since he performed his mistakes in the dark. In the second part of the novel Henry will come to understand war and his own nature. For the present, it is enough to go to sleep with his fellows. "He gave a long sigh, snuggled down into his blanket, and in a moment was like his comrades" (312).

IV

Only Joseph Conrad, of the multitude of Crane's critics, grasps the essential duality of *The Red Badge of Courage*. Conrad seems to realize that Henry Fleming *and* the regiment are in the same position. "In order that the revelation should be complete, the young soldier has to be deprived of the moral support which he would have found in a tried body of men matured in achievement to the consciousness of its worth."[9] Conrad pinpoints the idea that the maturation process does not affect the hero alone. "Apart from the imaginative analysis of his own temperament tried by the emotions of a battlefield, Stephen Crane dealt in his book with the psychology of the mass . . ."[10] The remainder of the novel treats the group that Henry has rejoined.

Although Crane's narrative technique still enforces the use of Henry as the point-of-view character, the youth is attentive to others as well as himself. Wilson, the former loud soldier, has been altered by his day of combat from a blatant, self-confident boy to a calm, quietly self-reliant soldier who is proud of the regiment. In order to perfect his relationship with Wilson and the other soldiers, Henry must try to understand their sources of fear and courage.

When the regiment goes into action on the second day, Crane focuses on the whole body, giving equal space to anonymous soldiers' complaints, the lieutenant's anger, and the serious determination of Wilson and Henry. The young soldier sinks himself completely into the business of battle and transfers his doubts and dreams into a savage hate of the enemy. If Crane indicated the importance of Henry's wound by giving his full name for the first time, here he emphasizes the youth's continuing growth as a human being by describing him physically. As Henry thinks less of himself, he becomes more of an individual in the pages of the novel. He fights well in this battle and becomes a hero in the eyes of his regiment.

The personal insignificance that Henry discovered applied to himself in the first section of the novel, now appears to fit the regiment which Crane describes in terms similar to those he earlier utilized for the young soldier. "The world was fully interested in other matters. Apparently, the regiment had its small affair to itself" (337).

Henry and the regiment undergo another severe exposure to fire in their first charge. Crane describes the mass movement brilliantly, transferring the attention from the youth to the men, and back. The crucial episode is the same for all of them, "a temporary but sublime absence of selfishness" (339).

The regiment falters in the confusion of the attack; the men go through Henry's former mental turmoil. "Here, crouching and cowering behind some trees, the men clung with desperation . . . the whole affair seemed incomprehensible to many of them" (340-341). The advance is saved by the courage and leadership of three men: the lieutenant, Wilson, and Henry. They lead the regiment forward, and symbolically Henry takes over as flag-bearer, participating in the combat in the absolute center of the group, the one position that more than any other represents the mass spirit. When the regiment is forced to retreat, Henry feels *their* shame as acutely as he felt *his* earlier. (Formerly he was selfish enough to pray for the army's defeat so his cowardice might go unnoticed). He harangues his comrades, striving to save the regiment's reputation.

The regiment turns and drives the enemy back; it passes its test. Henry is free from doubt and fear because he has committed himself to the larger unit. By losing himself in the mass, he has found himself. To the same extent, the regiment has conquered its panic and irresolution. "The impetus of enthusiasm was theirs again. They gazed about them with looks of uplifted pride, feeling new trust in the grim, always confident, weapons in their hands. And they were men" (348).

The final stage of development in war for Henry and the regiment involves the learning of the veterans' virtues—calmness and workmanlike efficiency. The young soldier is an observer in the last attack, a tiny player in a huge, impressionistic drama. Before, as a coward, he was the god-like center of a tiny stage; now, as a good soldier, he is absorbed into the regimental chorus. Henry loses all sense of individuality. "He did not know that he breathed; that the flag hung silently over him, so absorbed was he" (357).

Crane makes much of the fact that when the regiment is pinned down by enemy fire, Henry—the veteran—knows that the only thing to do is to return to the attack. To hang back would mean annihilation; to retreat would build up the enemy's spirit. Henry has assimilated the rules of war. Now his thoughts and emotional responses are the proper ones, forgetful of self in the face of duty. His companions, too, respond automatically to the necessities of battle, the facts of military life. The climax of *The Red Badge of Courage* comes as the regiment and its flag-bearer, without regard to vanities, charge once more and victoriously overrun the enemy's position. They have all passed the test.

The last chapter of the novel is an artfully contrived anti-climax. The regiment marches on; the author's attention is again directed to his hero. Henry has proved his courage; he has even been singled out for praise by the colonel. "He had dwelt in a land of strange, squalling upheavals and had come forth. He had been where there was red of blood and black of passion, and he was escaped" (365). Were the novel to end here on this note of rejoicing and pride, an ironic reading of the book would be justified. Henry would be a mock hero, a Jonathan Wild. Henry cannot forget the tattered soldier, however, whom Crane characterizes in lyrically sentimental language, ". . . he who, gored by bullets and faint for blood, had fretted concerning an imagined wound in another . . . he who, blind with weariness and pain, had been deserted in the field" (367). Again Henry considers himself a moral leper. He is filled with concern lest his comrades realize his secret sin.

Crane cancelled the passage that explains Henry's final rationalization of the betrayal, but these omitted words help to explain the moral construction of the book. "At last, he concluded that he saw in it quaint uses. He exclaimed that its importance in the aftertime would be great to him if it even succeeded in hindering the workings of his egotism. . . . He would have upon him often the consciousness of a great mistake. And he would be taught to deal gently and with care. He would be a man" (369).

These last words, a repetition of those applied earlier to the regiment, show that Henry has matured as an individual and a member of society. Henry has learned the nature of fear and battle. "He had been to touch the great death, and found that, after all, it was but the great death" (369). More important, he has learned the essence of man's duty to man, as well as the fact that life (like war) is not a romantic dream but a matter of compromises. Perhaps there is an element of irony, since he has not become a "good" man, but he has done a "good" act—in the terms of the war world—by displaying courage and self-abnegation in the final skirmish. At least war has shown the young soldier his real self, and the acquisition of self-knowledge is no small accomplishment. Henry has become a new man who views life in a fresh framework, aimed not towards glory but a job to be done. Glory is pleasant but irrelevant. In the final scenes of *The Red Badge of Courage,* Henry takes full responsibility for his life; he is no longer an automaton. His properly disciplined ego comprehends the nature of obedience and action. And the development of his inner life is paralleled by that of the regiment.

The novel ends with a sweeping peroration, hailing Henry as a part of the procession of weary soldiers, a part of the regiment that has proved itself worthy of the army just as he has proved himself an individual worthy of inclusion in the group. They have all succeeded in the war which telescopes such a tremendous amount of experience into a brief moment. "Over the river a golden ray of sun came through the hosts of leaden rain clouds" (370).

Notes

1. Maxwell Geismar, "Stephen Crane: Halfway House," *Rebels and Ancestors* (Cambridge, Mass., 1953), pp. 69-136.

2. Stephen Crane, *The Red Badge of Courage* in *Stephen Crane: An Omnibus,* ed. Robert Wooster Stallman (New York, 1952), pp. 225-372. All subsequent references to this edition will appear in the text.

3. There are many attractive aspects to this theory. It does not seem reasonable, however, to go as far as Mr. Stallman does in reading the novel as a religious work. Where he rejoices to discover many religious connotations in passages Crane expurgated from his final manuscript, a differently oriented critic could hold that these passages were omitted precisely because Crane did not want to stress religion heavily in the final version. It is more difficult to accept Mr. Stallman's view of Jim Conklin as a Christ figure. Conklin's initials, his passion, and his death are part of the book's context, to be sure. But so are his violent cursing, his fist fight, his voracious appetite, and, most significant, his terror of death. Would a Christ figure (even one as perverted as Faulkner's Joe Christmas) be so afraid of what might happen to his body after his death? The inconsistency of Crane's religious symbolism which mixes Biblical and pagan phrases without any apparent order would seem to vitiate a theory of a controlled religious structure. It would be safer to say that there are religious overtones to Crane's novel.

4. Edward Garnett, "Stephen Crane and His Work," *Friday Nights* (New York, 1922), p. 208.

5. Henry L. Mencken, "Introduction," *The Work of Stephen Crane,* ed. Wilson Follett (New York, 1926), X, xii.

6. Robert Wooster Stallman, "Stephen Crane: A Revaluation," *Critiques and Essays on Modern Fiction,* selected by John W. Aldridge (New York, 1952), pp. 263-265.

7. Stephen Crane, "Letter to John N. Hilliard," *The Academy,* LIX (August 11, 1900), 116.

8. Mark Schorer, "Foreword," *Critiques and Essays on Modern Fiction* (New York, 1952), p. xviii.

9. Joseph Conrad, "His War Book," *Tales of Hearsay and Last Essays* (London, 1955), p. 121.

10. Joseph Conrad, "Introduction," Thomas Beer, *Stephen Crane* (New York, 1923), p. 3.

Henry Binder (essay date 1978)

SOURCE: Binder, Henry. "The *Red Badge of Courage* Nobody Knows." *Studies in the Novel,* vol. 10, no. 1, 1978, pp. 9-47.

[*In the following essay, Binder examines the first draft of* The Red Badge of Courage *(1895) and sees the source of critical confusion about whether the work is a story of maturation in the first draft's persistent irony, with no sense of personal growth by the young soldier. Binder compares it to the revised novel and finds that the final draft retained but confused the irony, "reduced the psychological complexity of Henry Fleming," and "left the text incoherent at several places."*]

This essay celebrates an unknown novel by Stephen Crane entitled *The Red Badge of Courage,* a novel that only a few of Crane's friends and early editors ever had a chance to read, a *Red Badge of Courage* that existed only in Crane's manuscript, not in any published version of the story. In the manuscript, the novel is longer and much different from the *Red Badge* that was first issued as a book by D. Appleton & Co. of New York in October, 1895. The Appleton edition pleased the contemporary audience and has become a classic of American literature, but it is not what Crane conceived the story to be. Most contemporary readers found the Appleton *Red Badge* to be an account of a young man's growth from confused youth to resolute manhood; but ever since the first close readings appeared in the 1940s, modern critics have argued inconclusively as to whether or not this growth takes place; and still others have said that ***Red Badge*** is a flawed work which cannot be satisfactorily explicated.[1] What happened is that Crane wrote an ironic story in the manuscript, a story in which the central character does not undergo any positive growth; and then apparently in response to editorial suggestions at Appleton, made or allowed two series of deletions in the novel just prior to publication. These deletions confused the original irony; reduced the psychological complexity of Henry Fleming, the main character; also obscured the function of Wilson and the tattered man; and left the text incoherent at several places, in particular the final chapter. The critical disagreements about ***Red Badge*** arise mainly because of the problematic state of the text Appleton published, a text which, owing to the cuts, no longer embodied Crane's intentions.

As things stand now, Crane's masterpiece is an unread work. And because some pages are missing from the manuscript as a result of the deletions, certain details of the original ***Red Badge*** may never be known, and we may never be able to read the story in its full richness. Nevertheless, by restoring passages legible in manuscript but not included in the Appleton edition, and by using passages from Crane's early draft to supply closely equivalent text for some of the missing pages, the manuscript can be reconstructed to provide a satisfactory reading text, one in which the author's original conception is available in all essentials.[2]

Crane's dealings with his Appleton editor, Ripley Hitchcock, began in late 1892 or early 1893 when Crane offered and had the editor reject his first novel, ***Maggie, A Girl of the Streets,*** which Crane later had privately printed.[3] Approximately two years afterward, following a successful newspaper serialization of ***Red Badge,*** Hitchcock accepted the war story for Appleton. Then, on the strength of the surprising success of ***Red Badge*** as a book, Hitchcock set Crane to work revising ***Maggie*** for Appleton publication. With Crane an instant celebrity, ***Maggie*** could be redeemed; but in the months between Hitchcock's acceptance of ***Red Badge*** and its publication, Crane had no celebrity and no power. He was anxious for publication and had reason to be cynical about the literary climate of his time; and he was apparently willing to abide by extensive suggestions for revision from Hitchcock before ***Red Badge*** was published. Editorial requests, with Crane taking only a limited interest in carrying them out, are the only explanation for the kinds of cuts that were made in the story. In arguing, then, that the manuscript not the Appleton version is the ***Red Badge*** that Crane wrote, it is necessary to distinguish between revisions brought about by an author's wish to improve his work and revisions that are the consequence of an editor's stipulations, in this case revisions performed largely by Crane himself though required by the publisher.

My intention in this essay is to reopen the case of ***The Red Badge of Courage*** by presenting all of the pertinent evidence which argues, in various ways, for reading the story as Crane had it in manuscript. In the first section, I simply describe the material cut from the novel and submit apparent reasons why this material was removed. The next section relates the story of the Appleton publication, indicating the deletions were made in response to editorial suggestions. The third section shows why the final chapter of the Appleton text is so problematic and then offers a contrasting critical analysis of this chapter as it stands in the manuscript. The final section is a new reading of the story based on the manuscript.

I

THE NATURE OF THE CUTS

Red Badge has an intricate textual history. The most important extant document is the bound manuscript which survives in the Stephen Crane Collection in the Clifton Waller Barrett Library at the University of Virginia Library. Four of six leaves removed from this manuscript when the original chapter twelve was deleted are scattered among the Butler Library at Columbia, the Houghton Library at Harvard, and the Berg Collection in the New York Public Library.[4] On the versos of many manuscript leaves appear portions of an early draft of the story (Crane was conserving paper as he copied and revised from the draft to the final manuscript). Before the novel was issued in book form by Appleton, a much-shortened version (reduced from 55,000 to 18,000 words) was issued by the Bacheller & Johnson syndicate and appeared in several newspapers in December, 1894 and belatedly in July, 1895.[5] In August, 1895 a prepublication excerpt from chapter four was printed in a New York journal, *Current Literature*.[6] The Appleton edition appeared in early October. There were at least two typescripts made of the novel, but neither survives: one was used by the syndicate for typesetting; the other by Appleton. The first section of this essay describes the extensive cuts made in ***Red Badge*** prior to publication by Appleton, and shows that the deleted material comprised, for the most part, thoughts by Henry Fleming which were intended to expose him as a uniquely problematic character. These cuts were performed in two separate stages, partially in the manuscript and partially in the Appleton typescript or proofs.

The first stage of excisions was made in Crane's manuscript by pencil deletion on pages which were retained and by the removal of whole pages. These first-stage cuts comprised the deletion of an entire chapter (the original chapter twelve) and the endings of chapters seven, ten, and fifteen (this last in Crane's original numbering before chapter twelve was removed). Since chapter twelve was deleted in toto, all six of its pages were removed from the manuscript. Crane shortened chapters seven, ten, and fifteen by deleting the lower portions of pages 65, 85, and 125 in pencil and then removing subsequent pages to the end of each chapter. He then indicated the gaps left by the missing pages with a "bridge" notation (e.g., "66-67") at the top of the first page following each of these cuts.

Because these first-stage cuts involved the deletion of several contiguous paragraphs or pages, they were the boldest of the cuts made before Appleton publication. A similarity existed between all of these passages: the material in chapter twelve and in the excised endings of chapters seven and ten comprised interior monologues by Henry Fleming, and the ending to chapter fifteen consisted, in part, of his evaluation of these monologues. In the monologues (rendered in third-person paraphrase with none of the more modern strategy of dispensing with conventional syntax or punctuation), Henry rebels against or bitterly accepts a variously named cosmic agency—"nature," "the powers of fate," "the source of things," "a God," "the Great Responsibility"—as the ultimate cause of his own actions. Each of the monologues in chapters seven, ten, and twelve occurs after Henry has run from battle; each is an escape into self-justification, self-pity, or anger that begins when he comes to a point of despair and frustration over his failure to meet traditional standards of manhood.

In the deleted conclusion to chapter seven, seeing that nature's laws will not justify his flight, Henry decides that nature is universally malevolent. Repeating this thought in an angrier mood at the close of chapter ten, he concludes that nature must have created glory in order to entice men to war "because ordinary processes could not furnish deaths enough" (p. 85). The original chapter twelve presents a climax in this philosophizing, with Henry envisioning himself the "growing prophet of a world-reconstruction," the spiritual founder of a "new world modelled by the pain of his life," prepared to show men the folly of their tradition-founded illusions (p. 99). All of these monologues are empty rationalizations which Henry later refers to as his "rebellions." His strategy in rebelling is to envision his behavior as determined by a universal causality and then assume a vain stance of contempt for the race of human beings who, unlike him, are unable to recognize the deterministic state of affairs he sees. At the close of the original chapter fifteen, Henry has returned to his regiment and feels relatively secure that he will not be discovered as a coward, but when he learns from Wilson that other men were separated from the regiment he is angered that the previous day's "experiences" which occasioned his rebellions are no proof of his uniqueness among men; he retrospectively feels a contempt for "all his grapplings and tuggings with fate and the universe" (p. 125).

These first-deleted passages in which Henry questions cosmic justice may have struck the Appleton editor, Ripley Hitchcock, as the most obviously unacceptable material in the original story, and Crane's consent to these large deletions was probably crucial to Appleton publication. After the author made the cuts, Hitchcock apparently ordered a typescript and then negotiated further revisions. The typescript was made by midsummer 1895, for Crane had the manuscript to do with as he pleased in August. Neither this typescript nor the Appleton proofs survive, and so there is no visual evidence for the process of the later, second-stage deletions which removed material that is still intact in the manuscript but does not appear in the first edition.[7] An obvious distinction between the longer, first-stage, cuts and the second-stage deletions is that the latter involved a more specific excision of short paragraphs, sentences, brief passages, and single words, not extended passages. The second-stage cuts, then, appear to be a finalization of the process begun by the cuts made in the manuscript that would have required a closer scrutiny of the text in order to isolate the material to be excised.

Most of the second-stage deletions were made in chapter sixteen and in chapter twenty-five (the final chapter in the original numbering before chapter twelve was removed). In Crane's plotting of the original *Red Badge,* these two chapters contained markedly parallel material that provided an ironic frame for Henry Fleming's combat successes in the intervening chapters, seventeen through twenty-four. The cuts made in these chapters can be seen as of a piece with the first-stage excisions in that references to Henry's earlier and already deleted rebellions against nature were removed, and, again, interior monologues in which he explained his behavior and his "fate" as cosmically decided were cut. Also deleted was material that specifically laid bare Henry's enduring meanness and vanity.

In the manuscript text of both chapters sixteen and twenty-five, Henry finds peace of mind by fantastical and selfish rationalizations. In both chapters he scorns his earlier rebellions against an indifferent or malevolent nature and decides that he is, after all, of special consequence to a benign cosmic order: "He saw plainly that he was the chosen of some gods" (ch. 16, p. 130); "He beheld that he was tiny but not inconsequent to the sun" (ch. 25, p. 192). In both chapters he thinks of himself as a "man," but in each case this appears as a spurious notion in the light of a thought that precedes it: "He had performed his mistakes in the dark, so he was still a man" (ch. 16, p. 128); "death ... was for others. He was a man" (ch. 25, p. 192). And in both chapters, he thinks that he has avoided death because of his uniqueness: "how could they kill him who was the chosen of gods and doomed to greatness" (ch. 16, p. 131); "He had been to touch the great death and found that, after all, it was but the great death and was for others" (ch. 25, p. 192). In chapter sixteen he predicts that "by fearful and wonderful roads" he will "be led to a crown" (p. 130); then in the final chapter he deems this prediction fulfilled: "He saw that he was good. He re-called with a thrill of joy the respectful comments of his fellows upon his conduct. He said to himself again the sentence of the insane lieutenant: 'If I had ten thousand wildcats like you, I could tear th' stomach outa this war in less'n a week.' It was a little coronation" (p. 188). Finally, in both chapters, Henry is contrasted with Wilson in poignant and dramatic scenes which are designed to reveal him as hopelessly self-concerned. In chapter sixteen Wilson asks Henry to return some letters he gave him before the first battle, but Henry is reluctant, wanting to keep them as insurance against Wilson's possible questioning his whereabouts at the battle the previous day; in the final chapter, the indictment is much more subtle when Wilson's concern over the death of a fellow soldier, Jimmie Rogers, appears side by side with Henry's blithe self-absorption.

Much of the parallel material was removed from these two chapters with the result that the reader could progress through the final chapter without ever being reminded of chapter sixteen. Chapter twenty-five provided the final evidence about Henry that was more crucial to the story, and it was more heavily cut.

When the cuts were made, mentions of Henry's rebellions against nature (which had already been excised) were removed. In chapter sixteen Henry's thought that he is "the chosen of some gods" was deleted with the removal of a long passage, although a subsequent echo of this idea in the same chapter was allowed to stand, perhaps inadvertently, as part of his notion that fate has prevented his death in battle. In chapter twenty-five his corresponding thought that he is "tiny but not inconsequent to the sun" was cut as well as his notion that death is "for others." In both chapters his conclusion that he is a "man" was allowed to stand, with the preceding ironic thought remaining in chapter sixteen but not in chapter twenty-five. The image of the crown in chapter sixteen and the mention of Henry's "coronation" in the final chapter, originally intended as an important symbol in his mental posturing, were both cut (Henry thinks of heroism in terms of a "crown" beginning in the first chapter when his romantic concept of war is linked "with his thought-images of heavy crowns and high castles"). Also in chapter sixteen, Henry's repudiation of "some poets" and "their songs about black landscapes" (pp. 129-30) was removed.[8] And in the final chapter his "plan for the utilization of a sin" (p. 191) to justify his desertion of the tattered man was cut.[9] The scene in which Wilson asks Henry to return his letters in chapter sixteen was left intact for the Appleton edition, but the parallel scene, the much more damning report of Jimmie Rogers's death and Wilson's response, was deleted entirely from the final chapter.

A distinction between the first-stage and the second-stage deletions is necessary to describe the chronological order of the excisions. But the second-stage deletions made in chapters sixteen and twenty-five were apparently an extension of the first-stage cuts: the cumulative effect of both stages of excision being to change Henry Fleming from a youth who rebels against the "powers of fate" and chronically employs specious rationalizing to justify himself to a youth who undergoes a change of character in battle. The first-stage cuts removed the most blatant of Henry's offbeat, near-blasphemous tergiversations concerning cosmic determinism. The second-stage cuts weeded out references to passages already excised, removed minor instances of Henry's "fraternizing with nature," and deleted specific clues that indicated his moral intransigence. Since the consultations between Hitchcock and Crane regarding **Red Badge** apparently took place in the Appleton offices, and since the Appleton typescript (which would provide the best evidence about the second-stage cuts) does not survive, we will probably never know the exact nature or extent of the editor's suggestions. But we do know their outcome. If these revisions were intended to offer the public a conventional war-story protagonist, one who ends as a hero and a man as in the successful newspaper serialization, then the excisions were the quickest way to obtain this. The editor would have known that a psychologically complex character, whose thought revealed a vain cynicism concerning God, country, and all humanity, might needlessly unsettle or confuse a wide range of the often finicky readership of the eighteen-nineties.

In addition to the material deleted from chapters sixteen and twenty-five, all of which had a direct bearing on the characterization of Henry Fleming, a motley array of other cuts, some that were related to his characterization and others that were not, were made at various points in the story. In chapter one the farewell speech by Henry's mother was reduced by the omission of her repetitious admonishment for Henry to avoid bad company and send his clothing home for repair as well as the mention of a bible she gives him to take to war. It is difficult to say why her speech was shortened; the dialogue may have seemed artlessly repetitive and sentimental, especially since she appears later only in Henry's passing thoughts. In chapter four a sizeable portion of the soldiers' rumors that originally comprised the opening half of the chapter was not used by Appleton. Again, it is difficult to say for certain why this cut was made. The excision begins at the point where a soldier reports the colonel as saying "he'll shoot th' first man what'll turn an' run" (p. 40). Various comments by the men follow. The rumor was unpleasantly realistic; however, it originally served, along with Henry's early interrogation of Conklin and Wilson in regard to running from battle and the description of the soldier whose flight is arrested by Lieutenant Hasbrouck in chapter five, as a preparation for Henry's own flight. In chapter seven, perhaps the most curious of all these cuts was made in a sentence that fused Henry's guilt and vanity: "When he looked loweringly up, quivering at each sound, his eyes had the expression of those of a criminal who thinks his guilt little and his punishment great and knows that he can find no words; who, through his suffering, thinks that he peers into the core of things and see [sic] that the judgment of man is thistle-down in wind" (p. 62). In the Appleton edition the part of this sentence after "he can find no words" was not printed. The deleted clause contains one of the most remarkable metaphors that Crane wrote in *Red Badge*. Because it is a mention of insight by virtue of suffering, it seems the image was intended to be linked with Henry's dream of "a new world modelled by the pain of his life" (p. 99) in the deleted chapter twelve, and with his passing feeling of kinship for poets who "had wandered in paths of pain" (p. 129) which was also deleted.

In the ninth chapter, two important instances occur where single words were excised. At the outset of the chapter in the manuscript, Henry wishes for "a little red badge of courage"; but in the Appleton edition "little" did not appear. And the concluding sentence to this chapter appears in the manuscript as "The red sun was pasted in the sky like a fierce wafer"; but Appleton did not print "fierce." The obtrusive irony of a "little" red badge was removed, no doubt, because of the changed tenor of the story after the large-scale Appleton excisions were made. Concerning the excision of "fierce," any number of scruples might have required the excision of an adjective intended to characterize "the powers of fate" at one of the most extreme moments of Henry's rebellious anger.

In chapters ten, fifteen, and twenty-five, some conspicuous details were deleted. In chapter ten the tattered soldier recalls his friend, Tom Jamison, as telling him, "'Yer shot, yeh blamed, infernal, tooty-tooty-tooty-too,' (he swear horrible)" which appeared, somewhat illogically, in the Appleton text with the adjective "infernal" but without "tooty-tooty-tooty-too" (p. 82).[10] In the original chapter fifteen, a description of the awakening troops read, "The corpse-hued faces were hidden behind fists that twisted slowly in eye-sockets. It was the soldier's bath" (p. 120); but Appleton did not print the second of these sentences. (This sentence was also cut from the newspaper version: we can guess that to any responsible editor of the time, baths, even for soldiers in battle, were an issue not to be dealt with irreverently.) Then in the final chapter a description was cut of "the contorted body of the color-bearer in grey whose flag the youth's friend was now bearing away"; and a few sentences later, a related one-sentence paragraph was removed: "As they passed near other cammands [sic], men of the delapidated [sic] regiment procured the captured flag from Wilson and, tossing it high into the air cheered tumultuously as it turned, with apparent reluctance, slowly over and over" (p. 186). Whatever the reason for this cut, with the loss of the paragraph, there remained no moment in which the men of Henry's regiment parade their battle victory before the eyes of other commands, no resolution to the mockery and degradation they incur first from the catcalls of the veterans and then from the dressing-down the general's staff officer gives their colonel. In sum, these scattered cuts consisted of what, for the time, would have been considered "realistic" details that could be classified as vulgar or shocking, the cuts being made without any apparent concern for damage to the story.

Two small additions to *Red Badge* also appeared for the first time in the Appleton edition. One was appended to a humorous incident in chapter two: "A rather fat soldier attempted to pilfer a horse from a door-yard. He planned to load his knapsack upon it. He was escaping with his prize when a young girl rushed from the house and grabbed the animal's mane. There followed, a wrangle" (p. 23). In the Appleton text, a sentence was added at the close of the paragraph: "The young girl, with pink cheeks and shining eyes, stood like a dauntless statue." The addition was probably required to prevent any reader from imagining that the wrangle included physical contact between the soldier and the heroic girl. Then in the final chapter, a one-sentence paragraph was tagged on to the end of the story: "Over the river a golden ray of sun came through the hosts of leaden rain clouds." This new image was almost certainly meant to assure the reader that Henry Fleming had indeed "emerged from his struggles" a changed man. As John T. Winterich remarked in 1951, this sentence "bears the unmistakable spoor of the editor" and "sounds like a concession to the send-the-audience-home-feeling-good school."[11] Apparently, when this new ending was added, no thought was given to the fact that several times (in passages that were retained in the Appleton text) the "sky" had been presented as utterly indifferent to the men and the battle.

What Appleton offered the contemporary reader, then, was a seriously reduced version of Crane's carefully constructed and pointedly ironic psychological novel. It is difficult if not impossible to regard these cuts as Crane's final polishings of the story, or careful redraftings to perfect his original intention or embody a new one. Instead, the excisions were perfunctorily made by a process of cutting out large or small pieces and splicing loose ends together with almost no attempt at rephrasing places where the deletions left the text obscure or incomplete. Realistic details that risked an affront to genteel taste were removed, and the pseudo-intellectual fanfare of Henry's desperate rebellions against nature or illusory embracing of it were cut in the attempt to recast him as a youth who finds courage and self-possession, instead of one who, if he changes at all, becomes at the end even more egotistical and obtuse than he is at the beginning.[12]

II

Accounting for the Cuts

A basic difficulty has existed for scholars wanting to account for the differences between the manuscript and the Appleton edition of *Red Badge*: the manuscript text has become available in published form only little by little and in a manner that has hindered anyone from reading the story as Crane originally wrote it. In 1951 most of what was cut in the second-stage deletions was bracketed in the text proper of an edition edited by John T. Winterich for the Folio Society, but no mention of the much more sweeping first-stage deletions was made. After this, in *Stephen Crane: An Omnibus* (1952), R. W. Stallman included much more of the deleted material, bracketing the second-stage cuts in the text as Winterich had done, and footnoting passages that were marked out in the manuscript as part of the first-stage deletions.[13] But the *Omnibus* did not include the text of any of the four surviving pages from the deleted chapter twelve, although in a footnote the text of three early draft pages from this chapter was set out as a way of suggesting its probable content. Stallman mentioned the two pages from this chapter at the Houghton Library (one of these is a false start of page 98, not a final manuscript page), but apparently he had not discovered their whereabouts in time to include them in the *Omnibus*. In a 1955 bibliographical note Stallman printed and compared the text of the first page of chapter twelve in the manuscript (page 98 in the Berg Collection at the New York Public Library) and the text of the false start of that page in the Houghton.[14] And in the Signet paperback edition of *Red Badge* (1960) Stallman printed passages marked out in the manuscript, this time in an appendix, including all four of the pages known to survive from chapter twelve in addition to the draft pages from this chapter and the false start of page 98. Repeating the format of the Folio Society edition and the *Omnibus,* Stallman bracketed second-stage deletions in the text of the Signet edition. Then in 1972, Fredson Bowers edited a facsimile edition of the *Red Badge* manuscript which makes available by photographic reproduction the text of the bound pages in the Barrett Library, followed by the four surviving pages of chapter twelve, other pages which contain false starts, and the early draft pages.

Editions of *Red Badge* that have appeared since the Folio Society edition have, in most cases, not printed any of the passages that were marked out in the manuscript or the deleted pages of chapter twelve; but some have copied Winterich's bracketing format for including second-stage cuts; and others have set out some of the second-stage deletions in an appendix. By printing only the second-stage deletions, or, in the case of Stallman's *Omnibus* and the Signet edition, by printing the first-stage deletions in footnotes or an appendix to the story, editors have, unconsciously and by implication, promulgated the notion that the later cuts have a greater degree of authority and critical relevance to *Red Badge.* But this notion is based on the distinction that arises only from the appearance of the manuscript which contains some passages marked out in pencil during the first-stage deletions, but which contains, intact, the material later cut from the Appleton typescript or proofs during the second-stage deletions. The fact is that Crane *finished* the story as he wanted it before *any* of the cuts was made. The excisions—both first-stage and second-stage—were made at a distant remove in time and intention from the story Crane completed in the manuscript and have no relation to the process by which that story came about. Even in the photographic *Facsimile,* the pages of chapter twelve are reproduced separately—after all the pages of the bound manuscript appear in sequence—so that their integral place in Crane's original novel is tacitly abjured. There is no edition of *Red Badge,* then, that has ever respected what Crane wrote.

Knowing that Crane allowed the novel to be published in its Appleton form, and having no evidence that he ever disavowed the Appleton text in any way, many critics and scholars have assumed that Crane made the cuts as part of the process of bringing the story to the form he desired.[15] But a few others have not been satisfied with simply calling the cuts authorial improvements. John T. Winterich, the first editor to include any of the excised material in an edition of *Red Badge,* saw immediately that the cuts did not have the appearance of authorial revision (although he did not consider the deletions a loss to the story): "One can only say that portions of the handwritten draft failed to survive into the printed text. Crane may have killed these passages in his final revision of the typescript. His editor may have killed them. More likely still, the slaughter was conspiratorial, with Crane and his editor each having a hand in it."[16] And in the *Omnibus,* R. W. Stallman judged some of the cuts, specifically the deletion of chapter twelve, as improvements, but his more general assessment came closer to describing the true effect:

> Many of the passages that Crane expunged from the typescript or canceled in the manuscripts during the process of revision contribute additional symbolic overtones, reinforce the dominant patterns of imagery and meaning; they help toward illuminating what the book is really all about. Their omission is therefore a distinct loss not only to the imaginative scheme of relationships but also to the directional line of the author's concealed intention. A few of these expunged passages are furthermore a loss to the picturesqueness of the style.[17]

Several years later in his biography of Crane, having meanwhile edited the letters from Crane to Ripley Hitchcock and published a study of important variants between the privately-printed *Maggie* and the expurgated Appleton edition, Stallman was willing to submit, without elaboration, that Crane "resented Hitchcock's tampering with *Maggie,* as he had done before with *The Red Badge.*"[18]

Neither Winterich's early intuition of editorial intervention or Stallman's praise for the value of the excised passages prompted a textual scrutiny that took the story Crane had in his manuscript as a separate work. Subsequent editors either agreed or disagreed as to the suitability of printing some of the deleted material in an edition, but all held (and often militantly so) that Crane wanted the text cut, and that the Appleton edition represented his final intention concerning *Red Badge.*[19]

In 1968 Donald B. Gibson saw a distinction "between the novel Crane actually wrote and the one he *wished* to present to the public. Clearly they are not the same." But thinking that "we will never know exactly why Crane chose to make public the one novel but not the other," Gibson did not pursue the topic.[20] Joseph Katz stated in 1969 that to include the deleted material in an edition "is to ask a reader to absorb a work that was never meant to exist." But Katz later qualified this pronouncement (although only concerning the second-stage deletions), saying "of course some of the passages left uncanceled in the manuscript may not have appeared in the first edition through the tampering of an editor, not because of Crane's shifts in thinking about what he had written."[21] Then in 1976, in a review of both the *Facsimile* of the manuscript and the University of Virginia edition of *Red Badge,* Hershel Parker asked, "did Crane yield halfheartedly first to one advisor then another, gradually losing his sense of the work as an aesthetic unity and relinquishing his practical control of it in order to get it into print, however maimed?"[22] Parker submitted that a text of *Red Badge* which would truly serve critics could be satisfactorily reconstructed from surviving manuscript and rough draft pages. He observed that "the Appleton text . . . reached its final form as the result of omissions so hasty and ill-conceived that several passages still depend for their meaning upon passages which were excised." After examining the evidence of the texts and Crane's letters to Ripley Hitchcock, Parker, like Stallman, saw that the Appleton edition owed not to aesthetic revisions, but to "various outside pressures." Stallman and Parker went so far as to relate *Red Badge* and *Maggie,* because Hitchcock was in charge of the publication of both works, and because the Appleton editions of both works are clearly products of a process of reducing by excision what Crane originally wrote. But there still remained the task of bringing together the available biographical details surrounding the publication of *Red Badge.*

* * *

No evidence whatsoever exists to suggest that Crane conceived the cuts made in *Red Badge* of his own volition. But there is much evidence to the contrary. Close to a year and a half intervened between the time he completed the manuscript, probably early in 1894, and the time the Appleton revisions were made in the summer of 1895. It was time enough for a writer to want to take a second look at an old manuscript, but Crane was notoriously not a reviser; he endured a number of problems with publishers during this period and would have wanted to see the story in print as soon as possible. His first collection of poems, published as *The Black Riders and Other Lines,* was accepted by Copeland and Day of Boston sometime in August or September of 1894. But the acceptance was accompanied by a demand that certain poems be excluded. And Crane wrote a sharp letter of protest on 9 September, outlining what he valued most in what they deemed objectionable:

> I should absolutely refuse to have my poems printed without many of those which you just as absolutely mark "No." It seems to me that you cut all the ethical sense out of the book. All the anarchy, perhaps. It is the anarchy which I particularly insist upon. From the poems which you keep you could produce what might be termed a "nice little volume of verse by Stephen Crane," but for me there would be no satisfaction. The ones which refer to God, I believe you condemn altogether. I am obliged to have them in when my book is printed.[23]

It is understandable that Crane wanted to be sincere in his first book to have a house imprint, but in spite of the staunchness in his protest he must have found that the publisher could be equally firm, for he compromised concerning the selection for *Black Riders,* apparently conceding the final say to the editors.[24]

Copeland and Day was not the only publisher who disappointed Crane at this time. *Red Badge* was tied up by S. S. McClure for several months, much to the author's chagrin. On 15 November 1894, after the story had been accepted by Bacheller & Johnson, he wrote to Hamlin Garland: "I have just crawled out of the fifty-third ditch into which I have been cast and I now feel that I can write you a letter that wont make you ill. McClure was a Beast about the war-novel and that has been the thing that put me in one of the ditches. He kept it for six months until I was near mad. Oh, yes, he was going to use it, but—Finally I took it to Bacheller's."[25] In this same letter he informed Garland that he had "just completed a New York book," which must have been *George's Mother.* Crane could be relieved if not happy about the newspaper serialization of *Red Badge,* even though this was yet another instance of having what he had written issued without any of the original "ethical sense." But as things stood in December of 1894, he had three complete novels with no publisher for any of them. There can be little doubt that he was more than anxious for a change in his fortunes as an author.

Just after the serialized *Red Badge* appeared (9 December 1894) in the New York *Press,* Crane took some stories to the Appleton offices, and when Hitchcock asked if he had something that was long enough to make a book,[26] he sent clippings of the serialization to the editor with a laconic disclaimer: "This is the war story in it's syndicate form—that is to say, much smaller and to my mind much worse than its original form."[27] Ironically, this is the only surviving mention by Crane of the "original form" of *Red Badge*—made in a letter to the editor who was to cause that form to be much altered before the book was published. Crane probably sent the clippings to Hitchcock with the understanding that, if the editor liked the serialized version of *Red Badge* well enough, he would read the full manuscript. Soon afterward, Crane did leave the manuscript at Appleton, then departed on an extended correspondence trip for Bacheller & Johnson in the South and West. In February, Hitchcock wrote him, accepting *Red Badge,* and on 25 February mailed the manuscript to Crane in New Orleans for revision.[28] Crane returned it in early March, remarking that he had "made a great number of small corrections."[29] After this, Crane's itinerary took him to Mexico. He returned to New York in May, and signed the Appleton contract for *Red Badge* on 17 June.[30] A single letter to Hitchcock during the summer shows him approving the title-page-proof in August.[31] The book was issued in early October.

In his preface to a 1900 memorial printing of *Red Badge,* Hitchcock twice recalled the "delay in the proof reading" of the novel so that "the book was not issued until the autumn of 1895."[32] Although he claimed that the postponement was due to "Mr. Crane's absence in the South and West," it would have taken very little time to proofread, in any normal sense of the word, a small book like *Red Badge.* As it happened, the "proofreading" required the entire summer. From a letter that Hitchcock sent Crane in January, 1896, accepting *The Third Violet,*[33] it seems that "proofreading" was a term the editor used to cover all operations he found necessary between the time a book was accepted and the time the final type was set—including the negotiating and carrying out of his own suggestions for revision. The stages in the revision of *Red Badge,* and especially the selectivity of the second-stage deletions, would have required more than one conference between author and editor. Crane would hardly have made the extensive cuts in the story while he was in New Orleans and then returned the manuscript to Hitchcock, referring to what he had done as "small corrections." This evidence, although not conclusive by itself, suggests very strongly that the delays Hitchcock recollected in 1900 owed, in part, to his editorial call for alterations and to Crane's making the cuts—a process which Hitchcock had postponed until Crane returned from his correspondence trip and he could confront the author in person.

While the story of the Appleton *Red Badge* from acceptance to first printing is revealed only superficially by surviving documents, a picture of the working relationship between Crane and Hitchcock can be shown from letters that concern two of Crane's other Appleton books, *The Third Violet* and *Maggie.* On 6 January 1896, three months after the Appleton *Red Badge* was issued, Hitchcock accepted *The Third Violet.* But in his letter he worried that the main characters were "slangy in their conversation," and he thought the heroine might be "a little more distinct." He also mentioned that he wanted to see Crane in person to "talk over the story." His tone was deferential, but Crane knew the meeting was not to be denied. A few days after receiving Hitchcock's letter, he wrote to Nellie Crouse: "I have a new novel coming out in the spring and I am ... obliged to confer with the Appleton's about that."[34]

In order to allow "plenty of time for the proof reading," Hitchcock set March or April as the projected month for publication of *The Third Violet.* But publication was put aside for over a year. Apparently in search of a more likely sequel to the successful ***Red Badge,*** the editor set Crane to work revising ***Maggie,*** which Crane had paid to have printed privately almost three years before. Many extant letters document the process of revisions. In February Crane wrote to the editor: "I am working at ***Maggie.*** She will be down to you in a few days. I have dispensed with a goodly number of damns";[35] and later that month: "I will send you ***Maggie*** by detail. I have carefully plugged at the words which hurt";[36] and in still another letter: "I send you under two covers six edited chapters of Maggie to see if they suit."[37] These letters, and others, show that Hitchcock was requiring a cleaning up of the Bowery story before he would allow it to become an Appleton book; and they show that Crane—even with the new leverage of his ***Red Badge*** success—was revising to suit the editor's stipulations, probably somewhat surprised at being able to look forward to publication of a story which he told Nellie Crouse was "the worst—or the most unconventional" of himself.[38]

When Crane sent clippings of ***Red Badge*** to Hitchcock, his hopes for seeing one of his novels issued by a major house were undoubtedly high. After ***Maggie*** had been rejected by such powerful New York editors as Richard Watson Gilder and Hitchcock himself,[39] and after his experiences with Copeland and Day, Crane would have understandably become cynical about the exigencies of publication enforced by the moralistic literary climate of his time. He was impoverished and anxious for publication. Despite serious disappointments, he continued to write by virtue of fierce resolution and the encouragement of William Dean Howells and Hamlin Garland. When he took ***Red Badge*** to Appleton, Crane knew that no major house would issue a book it felt was "unsafe"—a book that chanced adverse reviews because it contained passages which could be considered distasteful or immoral or in any way seemed too unconventionally risky. When Hitchcock called for revisions of ***Red Badge*** more than a year after the story had been completed and months after it had been drastically condensed for newspaper serialization, Crane probably felt that acquiescence to the editor's suggestions was the only way he was likely to see the novel printed in anything that approached its "original form."

III

THE APPLETON FINAL CHAPTER AND
THE MANUSCRIPT FINAL CHAPTER

The basic interpretive disagreements about ***Red Badge*** in modern criticism arise mainly over the final chapter which Crane originally intended as a quiet but sharply ironic coda demonstrating Henry Fleming's continuing proclivity for vainglorious egotism and self-delusion. Since in the Appleton edition the final chapter was left especially confusing and incoherent by the second-stage deletions, it is natural that critics have found that chapter difficult or impossible to explicate. A recent essay (1974) by Robert Rechnitz opens with the observation that, "Studies of ***The Red Badge of Courage*** continue to question whether the intention of the novel's final paragraphs is literal or ironic";[40] Rechnitz himself concludes that "it is impossible to take the final four paragraphs as either intentionally straightforward or ironic in tone"; and he agrees with Richard Chase that, ultimately, "these paragraphs reflect Crane's embarrassment 'about the necessity of pointing a moral.'"[41] Rechnitz is correct in observing that the final paragraphs of the Appleton text are obscure. But Chase's hypothesis proceeds from the assumption that the Appleton version of the final chapter represents Crane's intentions for ending the novel. Even if Crane was "embarrassed" about moralizing, this would have no bearing on the textual problems in the final chapter, for they exist solely because of the excisions. To agree with Chase and others who have said that Crane failed as an artist, that he could not write a satisfactory final chapter to ***Red Badge,*** is to deny the existence of the chapter he *did* write, the one which ends ***Red Badge*** in the manuscript.

In fact, the final chapter of the Appleton edition was so altered that it was left problematic in much more than the last four paragraphs, and much more than the "tone" was rendered ambiguous. By offering in this section a demonstration of why the Appleton text does *not* make sense, followed by an interpretive reading of the same chapter as it stands in the manuscript, I hope to show how different these two versions of the ending are; and as a by-product of this demonstration, make clear why critics have had such difficulty in explicating the story.

Crane's original design in the final chapter was to have Henry Fleming recall from the first day of battle those experiences about which he is still ashamed, and then have him contrive justifications and excuses to resolve his shame. The experiences in question are his flight from battle (which lost most of its sting after his success on the second day), his denunciations of the cosmos, and his desertion of the tattered man. But in the Appleton edition Henry could not reflect on his rebellions against the heavens because they had already been deleted in the manuscript. Nor could he offer his highly questionable "plan for the utilization of a sin" to justify his desertion of the tattered man if he was to be pushed toward the character of a morally changed hero. In the Appleton final chapter, Henry's guilt over these experiences is still evoked, but only shreds of the original justifications appear. With these justifications deleted along with other material, the chapter is erratic and confusing and terminates on an inappropriate note, the bright promise of "Over the river a golden ray of sun came through the hosts of leaden rain clouds." In short, the ambiguity in the final Appleton paragraphs that Rechnitz and others have noted exists for one reason: *because things are missing*.[42]

About midway in the Appleton chapter Henry has his first guilty thoughts: "Nevertheless, the ghost of his flight from the first engagement appeared to him and danced. There were small shoutings in his brain about these matters" (p. 229). The Appleton text reads "these matters," but there is only one "matter" present, because the appropriate revision was not made at the time of the excision of the other matter which appeared after "danced" ("Echoes of his terrible combat with the arrayed forces of the universe came to his ears"). In the Appleton edition, Henry has a passing response to "these matters": "For a moment he blushed, and the light of his soul flickered with shame"; but it is passing indeed, for the next paragraphs which contained Henry's "explanation" and "apology" for his rebellions were cut. The following paragraph in the Appleton text opens with Henry's immediate conjuring of a different problem from the previous day: "A specter of reproach came to him. There loomed the dogging memory of the tattered soldier" (p. 230). Henry's thoughts about his desertion of the tattered man continue, interrupted at one point by a snatch of dialogue from the soldiers near him, until the matter is closed by a sentence that begins the fifth-to-last paragraph: "Yet gradually he mustered force to put the sin at a distance" (pp. 231-32). But the reader never learns about the nature of Henry's "force" or what kind of "distance" is involved, because—except for this sentence—the Appleton edition deleted all of a two-paragraph description of how Henry transforms his "sin" into a usable voice in his moral conscience. The sentence beginning "Yet gradually" originally served to introduce this description; in the Appleton text, however, the sentence was spliced onto the paragraph that *followed* Henry's rationalizing process. A short phrase—"And at last"—was added at the beginning of the next sentence to imply the duration of the excised process of distancing and ease the transition to Henry's final thoughts on his rebellions: "Yet gradually he mustered force to put the sin at a distance. And at last his eyes seemed to open to some new ways. He found that he could look back upon the brass and bombast of his earlier gospels and see them truly. He was gleeful when he discovered that he now despised them" (p. 232). Henry may well be both gleeful and despising here all at once, but the careful reader of the Appleton text can only be confused, wondering if he has not forgotten something, namely the "earlier gospels." None of their brass and bombast was any longer in the story.

Having the apparent notion that either glee or despisal or both taken together are convictive, the narrator seems to proceed positively and unhesitatingly in the next Appleton paragraph: "With this conviction came a store of assurance. He felt a quiet manhood, nonassertive but of sturdy and strong blood. He knew that he would no more quail before his guides wherever they should point. He had been to touch the great death, and found that, after all, it was but the great death. He was a man" (p. 232). The reader, however, has reason to be less than convinced by Henry's "store of assurance," for there is no "conviction" left: deletion of the two paragraphs which originally preceded its mention having removed the "conviction" on which Henry's assurance is founded—his sense that he is "tiny but not inconsequent to the sun." The reader of the Appleton text is also left to wonder who Henry's "guides" might be in this paragraph, since they were lost as a consequence of the excisions.

The next, third-to-last, paragraph in the Appleton edition begins, as it does in the manuscript, in high biblical style: "So it came to pass that as he trudged from the place of blood and wrath his soul changed" (p. 232). Then there is a paraphrase of Henry's thoughts which includes a biblical allusion: "He came from hot plowshares to prospects of clover tranquilly, and it was as if hot plowshares were not. Scars faded as flowers." The ironic tone of this allusion to Isaiah 11:4 ("They shall beat their swords into ploughshares") is clear in the manuscript when preceding it in one of the deleted passages appears the sentence, "It had been necessary for him to swallow swords that he might have a better throat for grapes"—a highly ironic echo of Revelation 19:15.[43] But without this foregoing irony, Henry's transposition from hot ploughshares to clover seems intended literally and in concert with "his soul changed." And the two final Appleton paragraphs seem to support the idea that Henry has changed as he turns "with a lover's thirst to images of tranquil skies, fresh meadows, cool brooks—an existence of soft and eternal peace"; finally, nature herself smiles overhead, dramatically parting the clouds at just the right moment.

The heavy-handed cutting that went into the preparation of **Red Badge** for Appleton publication concerned itself only with the removal of certain pieces of the story, not at all with recasting what remained into an intelligible form. As a consequence, the final and, in some ways, most important chapter was rendered incoherent; and critics like Rechnitz and Chase have been left with the job of explicating an impossible text.

In the final chapter as it appears in the manuscript, Henry moves through a series of moods: self-congratulation, lingering shame, whimsical ratiocination, guilty fear, utter self-delusion, and finally dreamy tranquility. As already mentioned, several parallels exist between this chapter and chapter sixteen in the manuscript; but in the final chapter, Henry turns over new leaves of self-delusion and moves even deeper into the empty regress of his vanity. He awakens from his battle-sleep to "study his deeds—his failures and his achievements," and by exonerating himself of the former and exulting in the latter he can conclude that he is "not inconsequent to the sun." Henry's most delusive thought follows from this, that death is "for others," but equally crucial to his final portrayal is Crane's use of Wilson's response to the report of Jimmie Rogers's death which closes a sequence of incidents that begins in chapter fifteen.

As if Crane were inviting us to think that the youth will learn by the example of his friend, it is Henry who in chapter fifteen notes the "remarkable change" in Wilson:[44] "He seemed no more to be continually regarding the proportions of his personal prowess. . . . There was about him now a fine reliance. He showed a quiet belief in his purposes and his abilities. And this inward confidence evidently enabled him to be indifferent to little words of other men aimed at him" (pp. 121-22). Shortly after this recognition, Wilson, in his new character, interferes when three soldiers of his company, including one Jimmie Rogers, seem about to fight among themselves. Wilson prevents the fight, but reports an unexpected consequence to Henry: "'Jimmie Rogers ses I'll have t' fight him after th' battle t'-day,' announced the friend as he again seated himself. 'He's [sic] ses he don't allow no interferin' in his business. I hate t' see th' boys fightin' 'mong themselves'" (p. 124). Rogers is next mentioned at the opening of chapter nineteen, after the first fighting of the day has taken place; this time he is badly wounded, "thrashing about in the grass, twisting his shuddering body into many strange postures" (p. 146). Again in his new character, Wilson volunteers help: "The youth's friend had a geographical illusion concerning a stream and he obtained permission to go for some water. Immediately, canteens were showered upon him. 'Fill mine, will yeh?' 'Bring me some, too.' 'And me, too.' He departed, ladened. The youth went with his friend, feeling a desire to throw his heated body into the stream and, soaking there, drink quarts" (p. 146). No water is found, but we can see that Wilson is thinking and acting with compassion; the other soldiers only want their canteens filled; and Henry is dreaming of a soak in the cool water.

These two brief mentions of Rogers are designed to build toward a climactic scene in the final chapter in which his death comes as an unexpected report. (Since the culminating scene did not appear in the Appleton text, the other mentions were left dangling.)[45] Coming to the final chapter, the reader has good reason to think that Henry and Wilson are equals by virtue of their similar heroism in the regimental charge. But when Rogers's death is told, their disparate responses show them to be much different. As they walk along together after the battle, Henry begins "to study his deeds," but is temporarily interrupted:

> His friend, too, seemed engaged with some retrospection for he suddenly gestured and said: "Good Lord!"
>
> "What?" asked the youth.
>
> "Good Lord!" repeated his friend. "Yeh know Jimmie Rogers? Well, he—gosh, when he was hurt I started t' git some water fer 'im an', thunder, I aint seen 'im from that time 'til this. I clean forgot what I—say, has anybody seen Jimmie Rogers?"
>
> "Seen 'im? No! He's dead," they told him.
>
> His friend swore.
>
> But the youth, regarding his procession of memory, felt gleeful and unregretting, for, in it, his public deeds were paraded in great and shining prominence. Those performances which had been witnessed by his fellows marched now in wide purple and gold, hiding various deflections. They went gaily, with music. It was pleasure to watch these things. He spent delightful minutes viewing the gilded images of memory.
>
> (p. 187)

Crane makes an obtrusive show of Henry's self-congratulation with all of the narrative irony balanced neatly on the "But" which follows "His friend swore." Unlike Wilson, Henry has not exchanged his youthful egotism for a mature humility and regard for his fellow man. This is the second of the moments in **Red Badge** in which Wilson is informed that another soldier has been killed; the first is when he learns of Jim Conklin's death from Henry in chapter fifteen and is regretful. In both cases there is the poignancy that these soldiers have been Wilson's antagonists, although under different circumstances—Conklin before Wilson's change in character when he is still an argumentative "loud soldier" and Rogers after Wilson has changed and attempts to be a peacemaker among the men.

Crane seems to have contrived Henry's thoughts in the next paragraph just as ironically in relation to another earlier scene: "He said to himself again the sentence of the insane lieutenant: 'If I had ten thousand wild-cats like you, I could tear th' stomach outa this war in less'n a week.' It was a little coronation" (p. 188). The lieutenant makes this remark in chapter eighteen after Henry has continued to fire at the battlefield without noticing that the enemy has retreated and his fellows have stopped firing. Much more of a "coronation" for Henry to recall would be the reported statement of the colonel in chapter twenty-two that Henry and Wilson "deserve t' be major-generals" for their part in the charge. But in his vanity Henry imagines a scene in which only he has been congratulated.

Henry's train of egotistical reflection halts when he remembers "his flight from the first engagement" and "his terrible combat with the arrayed forces of the universe." It remains, at this point, to be seen whether his proclivity for self-justification has abated. Obviously it has not, for his explanation and apology for his flight and rebellions are that

> those tempestuous moments were of the wild mistakes and ravings of a novice who did not comprehend. . . . It had been necessary for him to swallow swords that he might have a better throat for grapes. Fate had in truth, been kind to him; she had stabbed him with benign purpose and diligently cudgeled him for his own sake . . . now that he stood safe, with no lack of blood, it was suddenly clear to him that he had been wrong not to kiss the knife and bow to the cudgel.
>
> (p. 188)

This is not far from the reflective conclusion that Henry arrives at in chapter sixteen when he feels certain his cowardice will not be discovered: "in all his red speeches he had been ridiculously mistaken. Nature was a fine thing moving with a magnificent justice" (p. 129). Crane never intended that Henry's concept of the heavens be of serious philosophical importance; the importance lies in his characterization of Henry as repeatedly extending his feelings to a vision of his "place" in the universe relative to a deterministic and judicial supernatural power.

As soon as Henry is able to explain away his rebellions, "the dogging memory of the tattered soldier" looms before him. Henry's cowardice is of much less concern now that he has fought well on the second day of battle, but his betrayal of the tattered man haunts him as a sin more serious than his violation of conventional codes of heroism. His guilt is severe enough to make him withdraw into silence as he thinks, for a moment, that his error may "stand before him all of his life." But he improvises an ingenious escape:

> Yet gradually he mustered force to put the sin at a distance. And then he regarded it with what he thought to be great calmness. At last, he concluded that he saw in it quaint uses. He exclaimed that it's importance in the aftertime would be great to him if it even succeeded in hindering the workings of his egotism. It would make a sobering balance. It would become a good part of him. He would have upon him often the consciousness of a great mistake. And he would be taught to deal gently and with care. He would be a man.
>
> (p. 191)

Henry has the correct formula for manhood here, as that formula has been defined by Jim Conklin, by the cheery voiced stranger who returns Henry to his regiment in chapter thirteen, and by the changed Wilson. But the narrator's ironic labeling of Henry's scheme as a "plan for the utilization of a sin" which Henry must combine with "his successes, or public deeds" before he is fully content, suggests that Crane was showing, in Henry, the same psychological irony described by one of Pascal's *Pensées*: "When someone realizes that he has said or done something silly, he always thinks it will be the last time. Far from concluding that he will do many more silly things, he concludes that this one will prevent him from doing so."[46] That is, we are being given a highly ironic indication that "the workings of his egotism" are not lessened and that, unlike Wilson, Henry has not been changed by experience.

After this "plan for the utilization of a sin" restores Henry's composure to some extent, he once again becomes an amateur theologian with a generous new conception of the cosmos and his own modest but not unremarked place in it:

> He was emerged from his struggles, with a large sympathy for the machinery of the universe. With his new eyes, he could see that the secret and open blows which were being dealt about the world with such heavenly lavishness were in truth blessings. It was a deity laying about him with the bludgeon of correction.
>
> His loud mouth against these things had been lost as the storm ceased. He would no more stand upon places high and false, and denounce the distant planets. He beheld that he was tiny but not inconsequent to the sun. In the space-wide whirl of events no grain like him would be lost.
>
> (pp. 191-92)

These two paragraphs are those which contain the "conviction" that brings Henry's "store of assurance" in the next paragraph. Here, as in chapter sixteen, when he is self-satisfied Henry concludes, with cosmic vanity, that he is noticed by the heavens (thinking of himself as if he were considering a universal state of affairs); in the earlier "rebellious" passages, when he feels guilty he concludes, with the same vanity inverted, that a universal law, blind to his individual situation, is entirely responsible.

His conviction concerning his place in the universe leads, in the following paragraph, to the notion that "He had been to touch the great death and found that, after all, it was but the great death and was for others." As Mordecai Marcus has observed, the last four words of this sentence—which were deleted in the Appleton text—reveal "a Henry who completely misses the most important thing he could have learned."[47]

The chapter ends quietly. Henry is self-satisfied and thinks, much as he did in the opening of chapter six after he has stood and fought in his first engagement, that war is somehow behind him: "He had rid himself of the red sickness of battle" (p. 192). And so he turns "with a lover's thirst, to images of tranquil skies, fresh meadows, cool brooks; an existence of soft and eternal peace." None of which, from a literal point of view, he will find on the next day; none of which, from Crane's point of view, he has earned on this day.

IV

The "Red Badge of Courage" Nobody Knows

In his fiction, Crane was dedicated to illuminating the subtleties of human psychology and the deterministic forces of social machinery. An undercurrent often existed in his stories: an indistinct code, implying duty toward others, "a comprehension of the man at one's shoulder," as he might have termed it.[48] In the original *Red Badge,* the workings of Henry's mind constitute a sustained examination of conflict in a single character. And behind Henry's various battles with the universe, his persisting egotism, and his failure to gain humanity from his experiences—in effect, his never coming to comprehend the man at his shoulder—lay some of the most specifically documented of Crane's psychological interests and philosophies.

One state of mind that interested Crane involved the moments when a person's anger is directed against the entire "world." Closing a letter to his friend, Willis Brooks Hawkins, just after *Red Badge* had been published, Crane told an anecdote of striking obstruction after obstruction on a day of sailing:

> I lost my temper to-day—fully—absolutely—for the first time in a good many years. I sailed the cat-boat up the lake today in the stiffest breeze we've had in moons. When I got near to the head of the lake, the boat was scudding before the wind in a manner to make your heart leap. Then we got striking snags—hidden stumps, floating logs, sunken brush, more stumps,—you might have thought ex-Senator Holman of Indiana was there. Anything that could obstruct, promptly and gracefully obstructed. Up to the 5th stump I had not lost my philosophy but at the 22d I was swearing like cracked ice. And at the appearance of the 164th, I perched on the rail, a wild and gibbering maniac. It is all true. I cant remember when I was so furiously and ferociously angry. Never before, I think.
>
> Teddie has a Belton setter named Judge. When the girls run Judge out of the kitchen, his soul becomes so filled with hate of the world, that outside, he pounces on the first dog he meets. . . . This is the way I felt up the pond. But there was nobody there.[49]

Refined into a highly ironic fictional context, a related state of anger appears as Henry's rebellions against nature in *Red Badge.* The impetus is always a loss of personal dignity which is then displaced by the false dignity of a revolt against the "universe," wherein Henry never accepts the real source of his frustration, his own insignificance to nature.

Scattered throughout his long letters to Nellie Crouse, Crane revealed as much of a personal philosophy as he was ever to do.[50] In the first letter of this exchange (which occurred between 31 December 1895 and 18 March 1896), he seemed concerned with the question of his own public identity, remarking, "I go through the world unexplained." And in his next letter he confessed: "Anyhow, it is a very comfortable and manful occupation to trample upon one's own egotism. When I reached twenty-one years and first really scanned my personal egotism I was fairly dazzled by the size of it. The Matterhorn could be no more than a tenpin to it. Perhaps I have succeeded in lowering it a trifle."[51] When these letters were written success was coming rapidly to Crane in the form of increasing *Red Badge* sales and laudatory reviews of the novel, both English and American. Miss Crouse seems to have been someone to whom Crane could talk plainly at a time when he had good reason to examine himself and his beliefs in light of his new fortune as a widely acclaimed writer. In his next letter to her he offered, after an oblique introduction, an enigmatic view on wisdom and human kindness:

> For my own part, I am minded to die in my thirty-fifth year. I think that is all I care to stand. I don't like to make wise remarks on the aspect of life but I will say that it doesn't strike me as particularly worth the trouble. The final wall of the wise man's thought however is Human Kindness of course. If the road of disappointment, grief, pessimism, is followed far enough, it will arrive there. Pessimism itself is only a little, little way, and moreover it is ridiculously cheap. The cynical mind is an uneducated thing.[52]

This is a melancholy passage for a writer espousing human kindness. Crane had obviously been peering into the core of things and, in juggling metaphors to link kindness and wisdom, pessimism and actuality, he saw the two "roads" of life, one of thought and the other of felt experience, with a "final wall" at which they reach the same lesson.

* * *

I do not intend my reading of *Red Badge* that follows here as a response to past critical interpretations. The great divergence of opinion about the Appleton text exists not because of critical subjectivity, but owing to the incomplete nature of the text critics have read. In *Red Badge,* as he wrote it in manuscript, Crane tied together Henry's ambivalent conclusions about his place in the universe, his desertion of the tattered soldier, his continuing egotism, his failure to change in battle, and the very different matters of Conklin's blindly fated death, the cheery-voiced stranger's courageous optimism and kindness, and Wilson's step toward manhood and understanding. In Crane's original conception, all of these matters worked in close concert. But with the rebellious passages deleted, Henry's extreme rationalizing was no longer the focus of his characterization in the novel. And with the final mention of Jimmie Rogers cut, Wilson's function as Henry's foil was blurred. Also the importance of Henry's promise to remain with the dying Conklin and the significance of his immediately subsequent desertion of the tattered man was obscured when Henry's justification for the desertion was deleted from the final chapter. Which is all to say that, after the cuts were made, the most marked clues to Crane's intentions in the story were gone.

As in other works that he wrote both before and after *Red Badge*, Crane preferred to conclude the central action and then continue with a final scene in which one or more of the characters "interprets" the action by a backward glance. The realistically "distant" narrative stance in this kind of after-the-fact closure provides an intense dramatic irony: a scene on which the reader can look down judgmentally and understand the character's "interpretation" to be misconceived or very limited. Such scenes include Mrs. Johnson's "Oh, yes, I'll fergive her! I'll fergive her!" at the close of *Maggie,* and the easterner's remarks at the end of "The Blue Hotel" which point to but hardly solve the riddle of causality.

The plot of *Red Badge* can be seen as comprising two significant actions: Henry's wandering behind the battle lines in chapters six through thirteen, and his successful soldiering with the regiment on the next day. The conclusion to the novel is his "interpretation" of these experiences in the final chapter. In what may be taken as transitional scenes between these two actions, Henry is "wounded," the cheery-voiced man appears to guide him back to camp, and, most important to the second half of the story, we find that Wilson has undergone a profound change in character.

The scenes behind the battle lines in which Henry is separated from his duty as a soldier and his regiment offer the fullest gamut of dramatic action in *Red Badge,* including, as they do, Conklin's death and Henry's rebellions against the universe. After overhearing at the close of chapter six that his regiment has successfully held its position without him, he wanders in the vicinity of the battle throughout the next seven chapters, thinking that he is "more sinned against than sinning," questioning and denouncing the gods, encountering the grotesque and heart-rending sights of other unfortunates, until he is safely returned to his fellows, those he feels will most reject him. In his experiences behind the lines, Henry is not in the state of "battle-sleep" in which he fights during the moments of actual combat, both earlier and later. We would expect him to be affected and changed by these experiences, but he takes all that he sees—the dead soldier in the forest, the procession of the wounded, the death of Jim Conklin, and the helpless tattered man—as if they were commissioned by the "powers of fate" to mock his earlier cowardice or probe his conscience. His ultimate reaction is to rage against the heavens and to explain that these experiences are his because he has been especially selected for them, or that, at least, he is uniquely insightful in understanding the injustice of circumstance, and somehow deserves fairer treatment.

In chapter seven, after throwing a pine cone at a squirrel, he watches it escape and then concludes that "Nature had given him a sign" to justify his flight from battle. But shortly he discovers the dead Union soldier in the green "chapel" of arching boughs and is "for moments, turned to stone." When he finally runs, he is "pursued by a sight of the black ants swarming greedily upon the grey face and venturing horribly near to the eyes" (p. 65). It is an image that manifests the indifference of life's processes to human dignity, but Henry takes the encounter personally as a sign of the insolent malice of natural law, "all life existing upon death, eating ravenously, stuffing itself with the hopes of the dead" (p. 65).

Fascinated by the sounds of war he hears at a guilty distance, Henry is drawn toward the battle in the next chapter: "he must go close and see it produce corpses." He comes upon a grotesque procession of wounded men, including one who has a "shoeful of blood" and hops "like a school boy in a game"; he hears another, who is "marching with an air imitative of some sublime drum-major," "his features . . . an unholy mixture of merriment and agony," sing a sardonic nursery tune of resignation and death:

> "Sing a song 'a vic'try"
> "A pocketful 'a bullets"
> "Five an' twenty dead men"
> "Baked in a—pie."

(p. 70)

The war realism in *Red Badge* is intensely focused in these images of the wounded. What Henry finds here is ample reason to see the fighting as a bitter and immediate process for the individual man, a "pitiless monotony of conflicts," not "one of those great affairs of the earth" that proceed according to romantic myth or heroic tradition.

The most ghastly episode is foreshadowed in this same scene by the mention of one of these wounded who has "the grey seal of death already upon his face" with "his eyes burning with the power of a stare into the unknown." The "tattered man" here attaches himself to Henry, but, in a preenactment of the desertion in chapter ten, the youth slips away from him, being unnerved by his question, "Where yeh hit, ol' boy?" Goaded by this question and recognizing that he is "amid wounds," Henry self-pityingly wishes at the outset of the next chapter "that he, too, had a wound, a little red badge of courage" (p. 74). But this wish vanishes when he discovers, suddenly, the identity of the soldier with the grey face whose eyes are "still fixed in a stare into the unknown":

> "Gawd! Jim Conklin!"
>
> The tall soldier made a little common-place smile. "Hello, Flem," he said.
>
> The youth swayed on his legs and glared strangely. He stuttered and stammered. "Oh, Jim—oh, Jim—oh, Jim—"
>
> The tall soldier held out his gory hand. There was a curious, red and black combination of new blood and old blood upon it. "Where yeh been, Flem?" he asked. He continued in a monotonous voice. "I thought mebbe yeh got keeled over. There's been thunder t' pay t' day. I was worryin' about it a good deal."
>
> (p. 75)

Conklin's worry about Henry links him with the cheery-voiced stranger and Wilson who both act with a selfless concern. Henry and the tattered man, who has rejoined him, watch Conklin's crazed flight into the fields and then see him in a dance of death: "For a moment, the tremor of his legs caused him to dance a sort of hideous horn-pipe. His arms beat wildly about his head in expression of imp-like enthusiasm" (p. 79). Conklin's death suggests some macabre ritual and comes as the culmination of incidents that begin in chapter three when Henry looks "keenly" at the first dead soldier he sees with "the impulse of the living to try to read in dead eyes the answer to the Question" (p. 32); then in chapter seven he is surprised by the dead soldier seated against a tree in the woods and feels "a subtle suggestion to touch the corpse" (p. 65). Watching Conklin die, he is bluntly forced to confront the "unknown" his dying friend's eyes have been fixed on. Before the battle, Conklin is portrayed as a "tall soldier" with both courage and self-possession; in this scene Henry can discover that fate is indifferent to such qualities—the race is not to the swift, nor the battle to the strong. He should be humbled by what he witnesses, and afterward be ready to take nothing for granted about his own destiny. But his immediate reaction is angrily rhetorical; he shakes his fist at the battlefield and seems "about to deliver a phillipic," but no words come out except "Hell—." It is significant that his rage over the death of Jim Conklin is earth-bound, directed at the battlefield in contrast to the rebellions he wages against the universe when he feels personally wronged.

The tattered man who is with Henry throughout this scene is brilliantly drawn: a yokel whose stupidity and abject humility provide a contrast to Henry's rationalizing and vanity. Indeed, the tattered soldier's entire life seems to be told in the few speeches that Crane gives him. He serves, at Conklin's death, to share Henry's horror and grief but also to give the youth's feelings substance by taking part in his experience of the strange ritual. The tattered man has run from battle also (after being shot); helpless and wounded though he is, he proves most threatening to the youth's desperate need to hide his shame. After he and Henry walk away from Conklin, the tattered man rambles about himself and admonishes Henry to care for his "hurt" ("It don't do t' let sech things go") until Henry abandons him even while seeing "that he, too, like that other one, was beginning to act dumb and animal-like" (p. 84).

When Henry looks back to see the man he has just deserted "wandering about helplessly in the fields," he laments only for himself: "The simple questions of the tattered man ... asserted a society that probes pitilessly at secrets until all is apparent." Characteristically, his frustration leads to anger against nature and a scorn of mankind:

> Nature was miraculously skilful in concocting excuses, he thought, with a heavy, theatrical contempt. It could deck a hideous creature in enticing apparel.
>
> When he saw how she, as a women [sic] beckons, had cozened him out of his home and hoodwinked him into wielding a rifle, he went into a rage.
>
> He turned in tupenny fury upon the high, tranquil sky. He would have like to have splashed it with a derisive paint.
>
> And he was bitter that among all men, he should be the only one sufficiently wise to understand these things.
>
> (Early Draft, p. 76)

Henry's is a "tupenny" fury because it is pessimistic and cynical, involving a bitterly "cheap" separation of himself from the rest of mankind. Here, as elsewhere in **Red Badge,** the heavens Henry addresses, for which the "sky" is always emblematic, are omnipotent and beyond appeal. When he is guilty and fearful, he rebels against this force; when he is self-satisfied and feels secure, he is much at home with the same distant agency. Justice hangs balanced or imbalanced depending on his changeable moods.

In chapter eleven, Henry considers different ways in which he might be redeemed. Watching a fresh regiment advance eagerly toward the battleground, he imagines himself fighting heroically, "a blue desperate figure leading lurid charges with one knee forward and a broken blade high." He considers returning to battle, but immediately thinks of various objections that deter him. His thoughts then change direction completely, and he wishes that his own forces will be defeated so that "there would be a roundabout vindication of himself. ... A serious prophet, upon predicting a flood, should be the first man to climb a tree" (p. 95). But when he reflects on this wish, he denounces himself as "the most unutterably selfish man in existence." At the close of the chapter an even more painful presentiment occurs to him as he imagines what seems inevitable: his return to camp, the contempt of the other soldiers, and his own derision. In the eyes of all, he will be a "slang-phrase."

Chapter twelve—the original chapter twelve—is Henry's longest and most complex rebellion. Like the passages at the ends of chapters seven, ten, and fifteen, it begins at a moment when he is cornered in his own thoughts by fear of social condemnation—in this case the scene of his rejoining the regiment which he imagines at the close of the previous chapter. And like the ending of chapter ten, this rebellion contains a climax in Henry's various battles: his egotism and his irrational scheming are raised to their highest power. Henry has changed his mind about the heavens to some extent, thinking that there is "no malice in the vast breasts of his space-filling foes" (p. 98). And so he mulls over traditional codes of conduct and conceives of himself as a reformer of mankind, preventing men from carrying on according to a "universal adoration of the past" especially where standards of courage are concerned:

> He thought for a time of piercing orations starting multitudes and of books wrung from his heart. In the gloom of his misery, his eyesight proclaimed that mankind were bowing to wrong and ridiculous idols. He said that if some all-powerful joker should take them away in the night, and leave only manufactured shadows falling upon the bended heads, mankind would go on counting the hollow beads of their progress until the shriveling of the fingers. He was a-blaze with desire to change. He saw himself, a sun-lit figure upon a peak, pointing with true and unchangeable gesture. "There!" And all men could see and no man would falter.
>
> (Early Draft, p. 86)

Henry's egotism reaches its zenith here as he imagines changing what he cannot change, human society; and, a few paragraphs later, of avoiding what he cannot avoid, his own fate. He does not, at this point, consider a change in himself. But, predictably, he abandons "the world to it's devices," giving up his dreams of world-reconstruction, and sinks into despair, conceiving that he measures "with his falling heart, tossed in like a pebble by his supreme and awful foe, the most profound depths of pain" (p. 102). Following this comes his most irrational plan in which he bathetically regresses:

> Admitting that he was powerless and at the will of law, he yet planned to escape; menaced by fatality he schemed to avoid it. He thought of various places in the world where he imagined that he would be safe. He remembered hiding once in an empty flour-barrel that sat in his mother's pantry. His playmates, hunting the bandit-chief, had thundered on the barrel with their fierce sticks but he had lain snug and undetected. They had searched the house. He now created in thought a secure spot where an all-powerful eye would fail to percieve [sic] him; where an all-powerful stick would fail to bruise his life.
>
> (p. 102)

Paradoxically, although he recognizes the arrayed forces of the universe are omniscient and omnipotent, Henry hopes to avoid their power. He thinks that there is "in him a creed of freedom which no contemplation of inexorable law could destroy" (p. 102); but the prison that prevents his own freedom is just such illusory thinking. "Freedom" would be to share what courage he does have as selflessly as possible with others; but he seems to be little inclined to this—he recollects his flour-barrel escape with the same smug content that he apparently felt while hiding from his playmates. If there is a lesson here, it is in the extremeness of Henry's psychological position: that he cannot recognize the difference between the self he is becoming both publicly and in his own thoughts, and a purely imagined unique self in the "scheme of things" which he conceives to be decided by an "inexorable law." The "final wall of the wise man's thought" lies on another path and at some remove from such illusions.

The cheery-voiced stranger who appears only in the next chapter, after Henry has been "wounded" by another Union soldier, interrupts the mood that has pervaded the story up to this time, a mood of the oppressiveness of war, and the consequent despair and terse resignation of the men. Like Henry, this stranger has become separated from his regiment in the confusion of the day, and only hours before has seen a friend die that he "thought th' world an' all of." But, unlike Henry, he has the strength of his cheerful attitude and is able to "beat ways and means out of sullen things" to help the hurt and exhausted youth find his camp. The cheery man has the cardinal virtues in **Red Badge**: self-possession, optimism, and courage for selfless action. In more ways than the reader can understand at the close of chapter thirteen, Henry does not see the face of the cheery man, for he takes no step, then or later, toward becoming like him. The cheery man provides both a fleeting but important touchstone in the story and an interface between the previous scenes in which Henry has wandered in cynical despair and the remainder of the novel in which he is closely aligned with Wilson.

Wilson functions as Henry's foil and as the index of his failure to change. Less memorably characterized than Jim Conklin, the tattered man, or the cheery man, he is closer to Henry's youthful, unformed character than any of the other soldiers in **Red Badge**. And, like Henry, he is seriously frightened before the first battle. Apparently acting the part of a "loud soldier" in the opening scenes to hide his own doubts and apprehension, Wilson predicts in chapter three that he is going to be killed and hands Henry a packet of letters with a "quavering sob of pity for himself." After giving Henry these letters, Wilson does not reappear in the story until the opening of chapter fourteen when Henry is returned to camp by the cheery man. Wilson welcomes Henry back to camp with "husky emotion in his voice," and the youth humbly accepts the coffee and blankets Wilson offers him, only to awaken the next day, feisty and complaining, bragging about what he had "seen over on th' right" during the previous day's battle. On the same morning, Henry notices the change in Wilson's character (the process of this change is left a mystery); and immediately after this recognition the initial scene with Jimmie Rogers takes place.

The scenes in the first half of the novel in which we find Henry behind the battle lines after he has run comprise the most forcible experiences from which Henry could learn the lessons that Wilson has learned. But no such learning occurs for him. Despite his key part in the latter half of the story, Wilson never knows of these earlier episodes. And, consequently, the experiences remain a shared secret between Henry and the reader: the youth cannot divulge his flight from battle or his desertion of the tattered man to Wilson, nor can he discuss in any detail the death of Jim Conklin and how he happened to witness it. He can only accept Wilson's friendship in a continuing state of furtiveness and potential shame, most sharply dramatized when he is reluctant to return Wilson's letters in chapter sixteen, preferring to retain the packet as "a small weapon with which he could prostrate his comrade at the first signs of a cross-examination." This plan does restore his self-confidence, however, and he becomes delusively reflective: "Indeed, when he remembered his fortunes of yesterday, and looked at them from a distance he began to see something fine there. He had license to be pompous and veteran-like" (p. 128). At the close of this chapter, after more fantasizing by Henry (including his recollection that he had fled from the battle "with discretion and dignity"), Wilson has the letters, and Henry is dreaming on—this time of "his mother and the young lady at the seminary" listening to his stories of "brave deeds on the field of battle."

The closing chapters of **Red Badge** are concerned with presenting actual "brave deeds" in warfare as mysterious in several ways. In the heat of the battle, the soldiers fight in a psychologically numbed state of "battle-sleep" during which the ego is obviated, the individual is not "a man but a member" who is "welded into a common personality . . . dominated by a single desire" (p. 47). (Cowardice—as in the case of Henry's flight on the first day—occurs when the imagination takes over, when normal consciousness is displaced by panic, when the "odds" appear disproportionately overwhelming.) In these concluding chapters when Henry actually does perform heroically, he is often in the state of "battle-madness" with no time for contemplation. After we see the wounded Rogers in chapter nineteen, Henry and Wilson go in search of water; they overhear a staff-general report to the division commander that their regiment fights "like a lot 'a mule-drivers." This same general then volunteers the regiment for a charge, and there is the commander's grim augury: "I don't believe many of your mule-drivers will get back" (p. 148). The prediction does not seem to cause either Henry or Wilson any heightened apprehension, and both of them perform heroically in the charge. The key to this paradox appears to be given in a passage in chapter eighteen that concerns Henry: "He had not deemed it possible that his army could that day succeed and, from this, he felt the ability to fight harder" (p. 142). In a last battlefield scene, Crane offers yet another comment on the mystery of heroism using the "grim and obdurate group" of Confederate soldiers in chapter twenty-four as a way of showing that bravery is sometimes irrational and foolhardy; even when their fellows are running away and death or capture is inevitable, these soldiers obstinately stay and fight.

In the final chapter Henry reflects on his experiences during both days of battle with the intention to appraise himself. As many critics have pointed out, Henry, from the beginning of the story, goes to war in search of a mature identity, to discover what kind of man he might be. He has had the usual youth's abiding faith in his destiny, "never challenging his belief in ultimate success and bothering little about means and roads" (p. 12). Aroused in the first chapter by Jim Conklin's rumor of an impending engagement, he becomes introspective and discovers that "as far as war was concerned he knew nothing of himself" (p. 13). The Henry who sets off to war looks forward to becoming a "man of traditional courage." But after he runs from the first battle, he needs, more desperately, a reassurance of dignity, even a false one, and pursues this not by examining his own thoughts and motives but in raging against the "universe." Conklin's death compounds his despair; and when he deserts the tattered soldier, he moves into an even more dangerous sidetrack of psychological and social cowardice by betraying a seriously wounded man. In the twelfth chapter, he expends himself in a waste of illusions about world-reconstruction. But for all this, "fate" rewards him with the kindness and help of the cheery-voiced soldier and the friendship of Wilson. In the next chapters, his traditional manhood is established in the eyes of all, and it seems his earlier cowardice will not be discovered; but in the concluding scenes, he has no fleeting thought for the dead Jimmie Rogers; and, never seeming to comprehend the man at his shoulder—a "duty" more fundamental and more difficult than heroism or friendship—his "interpretation" of battle is that "death is for others."

The *Red Badge of Courage* as Stephen Crane wrote it is the story of an episode in the life of Henry Fleming. The final mystery of heroism in this episode is that Henry finds no real identity or selfhood in battle; and his notions of "fate" remain justifications for his own errors, reinforcements for his youthful vanity. The intricacies of each character's thoughts and feelings in the continuum of the war press along their own paths, perhaps breaching final walls, perhaps not. Conklin is a man before he goes to battle; Wilson becomes one; Henry does not change. From the first, we sense the advancing edge of Henry's expectations for himself; but as the story proceeds, in the no-man's land between his wavering self-image and his intermittent scorn and eagerness concerning bravery, there is no footing for a real change to prevail, never an awakening in him to what manhood is, only the confusion of his delusive explanations.

Notes

1. Appropriately enough, these first close readings appeared in *The Explicator*: R. B. Sewall, "Crane's *The Red Badge of Courage*," *Explicator,* 3 (May 1945), item 55; Winifred Lynskey, "Crane's *The Red Badge of Courage*," *Explicator,* 8 (Dec. 1949), item 18. As R. W. Stallman has observed in *Stephen Crane: A Critical Bibliography* (Ames: Iowa State Univ. Press, 1972), p. 365: "With Sewall's article and Lynskey's rejoinder the critical warfare about *The Red Badge of Courage* begins." Sewall and Lynskey were divided about whether Henry Fleming comes to a "moral victory" or an "undeserved reward" in the final chapter. See Steven Mailloux, "*The Red Badge of Courage* and Interpretive Conventions: Critical Response to a Maimed Text," in this issue of *Studies in the Novel.* Mailloux provides an overview of *Red Badge* criticism and a discussion of the various conventions that critics have employed in interpreting the Appleton text.

2. I gratefully acknowledge the help of Hershel Parker who in the fall of 1975 suggested that I be the one to reconstruct the manuscript of *Red Badge* as fully as possible, then read what Crane had written. My interpretive comments on what I will refer to as "the original *Red Badge*" or "the *Red Badge* as Crane wrote it" are based on my subsequent reconstruction of the text in which deleted but legible passages are restored, the four surviving pages of the original chapter twelve are restored, and in which early draft pages are used at the close of chapter ten and in chapter twelve to supply some of the text for pages of the manuscript that are presumed lost. Fredson Bowers has edited *The Red Badge of Courage: A Facsimile Edition of the Manuscript,* 2 vols. (Washington, D.C.: NCR/Microcard, 1972 and 1973), which makes available by photographic reproduction all of the manuscript pages from which I will be quoting in this essay. References to "the original *Red Badge*" will appear parenthetically in the text and are keyed to Crane's manuscript pagination. In the two instances when an early draft page is quoted, I indicate the fact by specifying "Early Draft" in the page notation. W. W. Norton will soon be issuing an edition of *Red Badge* based on my reconstruction of the manuscript. This text will also appear in full in the forthcoming *Norton Anthology of American Literature.*

3. The source for Hitchcock's early rejection of *Maggie* is a memoir by Willis Fletcher Johnson, "The Launching of Stephen Crane," *Literary Digest International Book Review,* 4 (April 1926), 288-90. Donald Pizer, in his introduction to a facsimile of the privately printed *Maggie* (San Francisco: Chandler, 1968), p. xiv, has rightly pointed out that some of Johnson's dating is awry and that he borrows from Thomas Beer's biography of Crane rather than writing wholly from personal recollection. But the recollections, although they contain errors, are clearly an attempt to get the true story on record, and Johnson and Hitchcock had indeed been colleagues on the New York *Tribune.* There is more corroborative support for Johnson's assertion in that when Hitchcock suggested a revised version of *Maggie* for Appleton publication, he did not have a copy of the *Maggie* which Crane had privately printed in 1893; therefore he must have made his recommendation based on an earlier reading of the story. (See Crane to Hitchcock, 4-6 Feb. 1896 in *Stephen Crane: Letters,* ed. R. W.

Stallman and Lillian Gilkes [New York: New York Univ. Press, 1960], p. 112.) Lastly, Crane apparently did not offer either *Maggie* or his other Bowery novel, *George's Mother,* to Hitchcock after the success of the Appleton *Red Badge* which is more understandable if the editor had already turned down *Maggie.*

4. My thanks to Michael J. Plunkett, Assistant Curator of Manuscripts, and the staff at the University of Virginia Library for very encouraging help while I was examining the manuscript and other Crane materials in the summer of 1976; to Kenneth A. Lohf, Librarian for Rare Books and Manuscripts, at the Butler Library at Columbia for allowing me access to the original manuscript pages; and to the librarians at the Houghton Library and the New York Public Library.

5. The newspaper version is available in facsimile: *"The Red Badge of Courage" by Stephen Crane: A Facsimile Reproduction of the New York "Press" Appearance of December 9, 1894,* introd. Joseph Katz (Gainesville, Florida: Scholars' Facsimiles & Reprints, 1967). Also see the bibliographical description of the six newspaper appearances in *The Red Badge of Courage,* ed. Bowers, introd. J. C. Levenson (Charlottesville: Univ. Press of Virginia, 1975), pp. 249-52.

6. The excerpt was titled "In the Heat of the Battle," *Current Literature,* 18 (Aug. 1895), 142-43.

7. Both Stallman in *Stephen Crane: Letters,* p. 51, n. 49, and William L. Howarth in *"The Red Badge of Courage* Manuscript: New Evidence for a Critical Edition," *Studies in Bibliography,* 18 (1965), 245, agree that Crane left the manuscript which survives in the Clifton Waller Barrett Library at the University of Virginia with Ripley Hitchcock at the Appleton offices in January, 1895 before he departed on a correspondence trip for the next five months; and that whatever changes he made in *Red Badge* before an Appleton typescript was made, he made in this manuscript. In February, Hitchcock sent the story to Crane for revision while the author was in New Orleans. Crane returned it in early March, remarking that he had "made a great number of small corrections" (Crane to Hitchcock, 8 March 1895, *Letters,* p. 53). In his letters to Hitchcock at this time, Crane explicitly mentions "the Mss," "the manuscript," and "the Ms"; and Hitchcock's note at the top of one of these letters reads "Ms sent by express Feb. 25." Bowers, however, has recently conjectured an elaborate theory about typescripts and their carbon copies (none of which survives) that presupposes the long cuts in the manuscript were made before Crane took *Red Badge* to the Bacheller & Johnson syndicate in 1894, that he made his revisions for Appleton in a carbon copy of the typescript that was made for the syndicate typesetting, and that Appleton set from this marked up carbon copy.

Bowers's hypothesizing begins in his introduction to the *Facsimile* of the manuscript (pp. 47-51), but it is more explicitly spelled out in the University of Virginia edition of *Red Badge*: "A typescript for the book made independently of the typescript for Bacheller, both stemming from the Barrett MS, is an impossible hypothesis: both the newspaper version and the book repeat common departures from the MS that can be identified as typist's errors" (p. 207). The upshot is that Bowers calls the most reasonable assumption—that Appleton had their own typescript made of *Red Badge*—an "impossible hypothesis"; but he reaches this conclusion on meagre evidence that indicates no such thing.

Bowers's list of "common departures"—where the newspaper text agrees with the Appleton text, but the manuscript is different—other than those he himself ascribes to "fortuitous agreement," number only three. (There are well over 100 instances where the Appleton edition and the manuscript agree and the newspaper version departs markedly.) Bowers concludes his setting out of this evidence with an even more implausible assertion that reverses his own line of argument by claiming that since the newspaper text and the Appleton edition *differ* in one instance *this time* it is because both the syndicate compositors and the Appleton compositors were reacting to the same "typist's errors" which appeared in the Bacheller typescript, but not in the manuscript. Such confusing and inadequate evidence inhibits serious reply by requiring that it deal polemically with minutiae. (See in the present issue of *Studies in the Novel* David J. Nordloh's attempt to suggest some of the problems with Bowers's presentation of the evidence about setting copy for *Red Badge.*) Here I will briefly present facts (some of which Bowers overlooks) that very strongly tend to date the excisions made in the manuscript as occurring after the syndicate version was set, which means they were part of the preparation of the story for Appleton publication.

The variant readings between the newspaper version of *Red Badge* and the Appleton edition show that Crane was in the middle of making at least one kind of consistent revision when the newspaper text was set—that of changing the names, Fleming, Wilson, and Conklin, to "the youth," "the loud soldier" or "his friend," and "the tall soldier." In the newspaper version these often appear simply as "he" or "him" and in one instance as "the tall private" and "the loud young one" (referring to Conklin and Wilson); but in the Appleton edition they appear consistently as "the youth," "the loud soldier," and "the tall soldier." The point is that when the syndicate text was set, Crane was apparently still hesitant about these changes, but while he was preparing the story for, Appleton he knew exactly what he wanted, and in almost every case in the manuscript the final readings are corrected to exactly the way they appear in the Appleton edition. (See 3.28-29, 4.28, and 10.24-25 in the "Historical Collation" of the Virginia *Red Badge* where the variant readings are given.) This evidence indicates that these changes are made *after* the newspaper serialization, and that Crane was, indeed, revising the manuscript for Appleton publication.

In addition to this evidence, a crucial textual document was overlooked by Bowers when he conjectured regarding the typescripts of *Red Badge*. This is the prepublication excerpt from chapter four which was printed in *Current Literature*. Apparently, in the summer of 1895 Crane took the four pages now missing from chapter four in the manuscript to the editor of this journal for the typesetting of the excerpt. This shows that Crane did have the Barrett manuscript in New York in the summer of 1895 when the cuts in *Red Badge* were almost certainly made. (Bowers thinks the four pages were removed as part of an authorial revision.) See Henry Binder, "Unwinding the Riddle of Four Pages Missing from the *Red Badge of Courage* Manuscript," *Publications of the Bibliographical Society of America,* 72 (1978), 100-106.

The greatest problem with Bowers's hypothesis is that if what he says were true then the first-stage deletions and the second-stage deletions were made months apart. But this is difficult to imagine since much of what was cut in the second-stage deletions referred to the monologues cut in the first-stage deletions and also removed shorter monologues that were much of a piece with the passages cut in the manuscript. Bowers does see that the second-stage cuts were made for Appleton, and he does recognize that these cuts contained "the introspective examination of the youth's states of mind" (Virginia edition, p. 229), but he apparently thinks that Crane made the second-stage cuts in chapters sixteen and twenty-five in New Orleans in February-March, 1895 while on his correspondence trip. Bowers never refers to these cuts explicitly, but only mentions the removal of "about 1,250 words" that "had an important effect on the shape of the latter part of the book" (Virginia edition, p. 229). Effect they had indeed; but it is impossible to think that Crane drastically and illogically changed a novel that had just been accepted and then referred to the changes as "small corrections" when he mailed the manuscript back to the publisher! The basic problem with Bowers's hypothesis is that it concerns itself with and relies on documents that do not survive—and in the case of the "carbon" of the Bacheller typescript, a document that may never have existed—instead of relying on the documents that do survive, the draft and the final manuscript of *Red Badge* and Crane's letters.

8. No previous mention of these poets appears on any surviving manuscript or early draft page; they may well have been mentioned on one of the pages lost when chapter ten or chapter twelve was cut.

9. In the passage deleted at the close of chapter fifteen Henry probably recalled his desertion of the tattered man for the first time. It would seem that Crane was working too carefully to wait until the final chapter to introduce Henry's recollection of his most serious sin.

10. There was also one bit of recasting in chapter ten that occurred at some point between the completion of the manuscript and the printing of the Appleton edition. In the manuscript, just before he deserts the tattered man, Henry wonders, "Was his companion ever to play such an intolerable part? Was he ever going to up-raise the ghost of shame on the stick of his curiosity?" (pp. 83-84). In the Appleton edition, these sentences were changed to read, "His companions seemed ever to play intolerable parts. They were ever upraising the ghost of shame on the stick of their curiosity" (p. 104). When Crane made this revision he may have had in mind Henry's other two companions who later question him innocently and call up his guilt: Wilson in chapter fifteen and the sarcastic man in chapter seventeen.

11. *The Red Badge of Courage,* ed. John T. Winterich (London: The Folio Society, 1951), p. 25.

12. Although my argument is that what Appleton printed was a watered-down story, *Red Badge* as published retained enough of the essential Crane to evoke several comments from contemporaries concerning its innovativeness and liberating influence. A reviewer for the *National Observer,* 15 (11 Jan. 1896), 272,

wrote, "Some of Mr. Crane's descriptions both of scenery and mental phases are very happy, and in the death of 'the tall soldier' he is really powerful. Many readers will not like the book the less for its entire lack of feminine interest and character. We are beginning to hope from a like lack in several other works of fiction we have met lately that ladies are really getting a little less fashionable at last." And Robert Bridges, writing in *Life,* 27 (5 March 1896), 176-77, commented that, "the 'woman problem' has become a pale and unsubstantial phantom in fiction; and one may be glad that it has been shelved even if it took a baptism of blood to do it. Americans can rejoice that while England sent us in the pestilence of the new-woman novel and play, we have furnished England with the most potent antidote for the poison yet found in Stephen Crane's surprisingly vivid story *The Red Badge of Courage.*" After *Red Badge* had become successful, Elbert Hubbard claimed that if Crane "never produces another thing, he has done enough to save the fag-end of the century from literary disgrace," *Roycroft Quarterly,* 1 (May 1896), 26. In a letter to Max J. Herzberg, 19 October 1921, Ellis Parker Butler recalled: "It was not until Stephen Crane, standing on the bank, tossed the 'Red Badge' into the stream that any real writers dared start across from the safe old-style literature toward the realistic goal on the other side of the stream. The 'Red Badge' was undoubtedly the first permanent stepping stone from the real literature of our early days to the real literature of tomorrow. Its instant popularity made it 'safe'—in the sense of approval by the reading public—and the reading public began to believe that other realistic fiction might be 'safe.' Having put a foot on the 'Red Badge' and found it bore a man's weight we were encouraged to take another step and try another stepping stone." (This typed letter is bound in *Stephen Crane—A Chorus of Tributes* in the Stephen Crane Collection in the Clifton Waller Barrett Library at the University of Virginia Library.)

13. *Stephen Crane: An Omnibus,* ed. Stallman (New York: Alfred A. Knopf, 1952).

14. Stallman, "'The Red Badge of Courage': A Collation of Two Pages of Manuscript Expunged from Chapter XII," *Publications of the Bibliographical Society of America,* 49 (1955), 273-77.

15. The conclusions drawn by these critics and scholars are generally formulated in an impressionistic sentence or two without evidence and simply extend their own critical judgments on the Appleton *Red Badge.* These conclusions fall into four categories, either holding that Crane wanted to have less "irony" in the story, that he wanted a quicker narrative "pace" or a more "condensed" narrative, that he changed his thinking about the story (at some unspecified time) and decided to remove some ideas or "themes" he had begun with, or that he decided to change Henry Fleming as a character. For arguments on removal of irony see Stanley B. Greenfield, "The Unmistakable Stephen Crane," *PMLA,* 73 (1958), 571; and Mordecai Marcus, "The Unity of *The Red Badge of Courage,*" in *The Red Badge of Courage, Text and Criticism,* ed. Richard Lettis et al. (New York: Harcourt, Brace & World, 1960), p. 195: "It is obvious that Crane has vastly improved his conclusion by his excisions. Without these excisions the final chapter would be quite ambiguous and would suggest that Crane regarded Henry ironically to the very end." For arguments based on "pace" or a happy condensing of the story see Winterich, Folio Society edition, p. 25; Thomas A. Gullason, *The Complete Novels of Stephen Crane* (Garden City, N.Y.: Doubleday, 1967), p. 801; Bowers, "The Text: History and Analysis," in the Virginia *Red Badge,* p. 229; and Richard Chase, "A Note on the Text" in *The Red Badge of Courage* (Boston: Houghton Mifflin, 1960), p. xxi: "I have thought it best not to restore what Crane himself wanted left out (not of great bulk, in any case), because, as it seems to me, every passage he expunged, without exception, is inferior to the whole, being either inept, sententious, thematically misleading, or merely superfluous (in a story which the author himself was correct in thinking a little too long for its subject)." For arguments concerning theme or philosophy see Olov W. Fryckstedt, "Henry Fleming's Tupenny Fury: Cosmic Pessimism in Stephen Crane's *The Red Badge of Courage,*" *Studia Neophilologica,* 33 (1961), 277; Edwin H. Cady, *Stephen Crane* (New York: Twayne, 1962), p. 126; Levenson, Introduction to the Virginia *Red Badge,* pp. lv-lvi; and James B. Colvert, "Stephen Crane's Magic Mountain," in *Stephen Crane: A Collection of Critical Essays,* ed. Maurice Bassan (Englewood Cliffs, N.J.: Prentice-Hall, 1967,) pp. 97-98: "In effect, Crane was attempting to eliminate the emphasis on Henry's struggle against a hostile Nature and the issue of the hero's sentimental misreading of Nature's meaning. . . . In short, the moral issue which Crane raises in his treatment of Nature in the novel is abandoned—or rather Crane attempts to abandon it." Finally, for arguments that Crane wanted to change Henry Fleming (and, indeed, Henry's characterization

was changed when the cuts were made) see William L. Howarth, "*The Red Badge of Courage* Manuscript: New Evidence for a Critical Edition," *Studies in Bibliography* 18 (1965), 241; Pizer, *The Red Badge of Courage,* A Norton Critical Edition, 2nd ed. (New York: W. W. Norton, 1976), p. 112; and Frederick C. Crews, "A Note on the Text," in *The Red Badge of Courage* (Indianapolis: Bobbs-Merrill, 1964), pp. xxx-xxxi: "The omitted passages consist of minor variations of phrasing, prolix extensions of dialogue, and ponderously ironical commentary on the progress of Henry Fleming's soul. These latter passages are suggestive, to be sure, but they reveal a heavy-handed, sarcastic treatment of Henry that Crane had the good sense to modify."

16. Folio Society edition, p. 23.

17. *Omnibus,* p. 217.

18. Stallman, *Stephen Crane, A Biography* (New York: Braziller, 1968), p. 199.

19. The question this study will raise for many critics and scholars is that of what is to be used as evidence for determining an author's final intention. The most ready answer in the case of *Red Badge* is to accept the Appleton text as Crane's intention, because it is the version that was printed. But the unsatisfactory state of that text requires explanation. The simplest explanation, which is supported by all the factual evidence that has come to light, is that Crane's intention for the story he completed in manuscript was one thing; but his intention in making the cuts before Appleton publication was quite another, being neither an extension of his original intention, nor a matter of aesthetic revision.

20. Donald B. Gibson, *The Fiction of Stephen Crane* (Carbondale and Edwardsville: Southern Illinois Univ. Press, 1968), p. 68.

21. Katz, "Editor's Note" to *The Portable Stephen Crane* (New York: Viking Press, 1969), p. xxii; Katz, "Practical Editions: *The Red Badge of Courage*," *Proof,* 2 (1972), 306.

22. Hershel Parker, rev. of *The Red Badge of Courage: A Facsimile Edition of the Manuscript,* ed. Bowers and *The Red Badge of Courage: An Episode of the American Civil War,* ed. Bowers, introd. Levenson, *Nineteenth-Century Fiction,* 30 (1976), 562.

23. Crane to Copeland and Day, 9 Sept. 1894. *Letters,* pp. 39-40.

24. I am indebted to Katz's telling of the story of the negotiations between Crane and Copeland and Day in his introduction to *The Complete Poems of Stephen Crane* (Ithaca: Cornell Univ. Press, 1972). Other details are added to this story by Bowers in *Poems and Literary Remains,* ed. Bowers, introd. Colvert (Charlottesville: Univ. Press of Virginia, 1975), pp. 193-201.

25. Crane to Hamlin Garland, 15 Nov. 1894, *Letters,* p. 41.

26. This account of Crane's visit to the Appleton offices is given by Ripley Hitchcock in his preface to *The Red Badge of Courage* (New York: D. Appleton & Co., 1900), pp. v-vi.

27. Crane to Hitchcock, 18 Dec. 1894, *Letters,* p. 46.

28. See Crane to Hitchcock, 12 Feb. 1895, *Letters,* p. 51; and Crane to Hitchcock, 20 Feb. 1895, *Letters,* p. 53.

29. Crane to Hitchcock, 8 March 1895, *Letters,* p. 53.

30. The Appleton contract for *Red Badge* is reproduced in the *Stephen Crane Newsletter,* 2 (Summer 1968), 5-10.

31. Crane to Hitchcock, 26 Aug. 1895, *Letters,* p. 62.

32. Hitchcock, pp. vi, ix.

33. This typed letter signed by Hitchcock is printed here for the first time. It is the only known letter of acceptance for any of Crane's Appleton books. The letter is tipped in a first edition of *The Third Violet* in the Dartmouth College Library and is reproduced here by courtesy of the library. Walter W. Wright, Chief of Special Collections at Dartmouth, gave me very welcome assistance. The letter is described in Herbert Faulkner West *A Stephen Crane Collection* (Hanover, N.H.: Dartmouth College Library, 1948), p. 8. It is on the stationery of D. Appleton & Co., 75 Fifth Avenue, New York:

January 6th, 1896

Stephen Crane, Esq.,
Hartwood, N. Y.

Dear Mr. Crane:

We shall be happy to publish "The Third Violet" and I enclose agreements for your signature. I hardly know yet how we shall issue the book. It is rather short for the Town and Country Library and rather long for the 75 cent series. Perhaps we shall publish it at $1, but I can determine that better after obtaining an exact estimate of length from the printer.

I wish you were here in the city for I should like to talk over the story with you. I should make any suggestions with the greatest difference, for your pictures of summer life and contrasting types and your glimpses of studio life are so singularly vivid and clear. I have found myself wishing that Hawker and Hollended [*sic*] were a trifle less slangy in their conversation, and that the young lady who plays the part of the heroine was a little more distinct. You will pardon these comments I am sure, for I think you know my appreciation of your work and the value that I set upon the original flavor of your writing. Sometime, perhaps, we can talk the matter over. It will probably not be desirable to publish before March or April so that there will be plenty of time for the proof reading. I will let you know as soon as the style of the book is settled.

Very sincerely yours,
Ripley Hitchcock [signed]

34. Crane to Nellie Crouse, 12 Jan., 1896, *Letters,* p. 100.

35. Crane to Hitchcock, 4-6? Feb. 1896, *Letters,* p. 112.

36. Crane to Hitchcock, 10 Feb. 1896, *Letters,* p. 113.

37. Crane to Hitchcock, 15 Feb. 1896, *Letters,* p. 117.

38. Crane to Nellie Crouse, 5 Feb. 1896, *Letters,* p. 112.

39. See Thomas Beer, *Stephen Crane, A Study in American Letters* (New York: Alfred A. Knopf, 1923), pp. 83-86, for the account of Crane's taking the manuscript of *Maggie* with a note of introduction from his brother, Townley, to Gilder at the offices of *The Century* in March of 1892, and Gilder's rejection of the story because it was "too honest" in an interview with Crane on the following day.

40. Robert Rechnitz, "Depersonalization and the Dream in *The Red Badge of Courage,*" *Studies in the Novel,* 6 (1974), 76, 86.

41. Chase's comments appear in his introduction to the Riverside edition of *Red Badge,* p. xiii. Others who have felt that *Red Badge* demonstrates a failure on Crane's part to handle his material are Colvert, "Stephen Crane's Magic Mountain"; Levenson in the Virginia *Red Badge,* pp. lv-lxxvi; and Stallman, *Bibliography,* pp. 533-34.

42. In the following three paragraphs which discuss the Appleton final chapter, page notations that appear parenthetically in the text are keyed to a first printing of *The Red Badge of Courage* (New York: D. Appleton & Co., 1895) in the American Literature Collection at the University of Southern California Library.

43. The passage echoed is: "And out of his mouth goeth a sharp sword, that with it he should smite the nations: and he shall rule them with a rod of iron: and he treadeth the winepress of the fierceness and wrath of Almighty God."

44. In making a study of the manuscript, Howarth raised the question, Why was Crane "so careful to make his hero the only 'youth' in the book?" (Howarth, p. 239). He answered the question insightfully by noting that Wilson's character change was first described in the manuscript by a sentence that read, "He was not a youth," but that when Crane decided to refer to Fleming consistently as "the youth," he changed this sentence to "He was no more a loud young soldier." Howarth went on to say, "On the battle-field that is the world of *The Red Badge,* a man's character is measured by his ability to profit from experience. Wilson moves toward a maturity that Fleming will never grasp, and Crane chose to indicate his hero's pathetic inadequacy by labeling him the only 'youth' in a company of men" (p. 240).

45. To my knowledge, the only critic who has ever mentioned Jimmie Rogers is Wayne Charles Miller, *An Armed America, Its Face in Fiction: A History of the American Military Novel* (New York: New York Univ. Press, 1970), p. 79.

46. Pascal, *Pensées,* trans. A. J. Krailsheimer (London: Penguin, 1966), p. 358.

47. Marcus, p. 194.

48. Crane to Willis Brooks Hawkins, about 5 Nov. 1895, *Letters,* pp. 69-70. The passage reads: "We in the east are overcome a good deal by a detestable superficial culture which I think is the real barbarism. Culture in it's true sense, I take it, is a comprehension of the man at one's shoulder. It has nothing to do with an adoration for effete jugs and old kettles. This latter is merely an amusement and we live for amusement in the east."

49. Crane to Willis Brooks Hawkins, 19 Nov. 1895, *Letters,* pp. 76-77. Crane also made use of a state of anger against the "world" in "The Open Boat": "When it occurs to a man that nature does not regard him as important, and that she feels she would not maim the universe by disposing of him, he at first wishes to throw bricks at the temple, and he hates deeply the fact that there are no bricks and no temples. Any visible expression of nature would surely be pelleted with his jeers" (*The Open Boat And Other Tales of Adventure* [New York: Doubleday & McClure, 1898], p. 44). Crane's own conviction about the

indifference of God and nature to man is explicit in poems such as "God Fashioned the Ship of the World Carefully" or "A Man Said to the Universe." In his stories, a character often awakens to this "truth" while under pressure—either dramatized as in the case of Henry Fleming's rebellions, or offered in a narrator's comment as in "The Open Boat."

50. Valuable comments on these letters are made by Cady and Lester G. Wells in *Stephen Crane's Love Letters to Nellie Crouse* (Syracuse: Syracuse Univ. Press, 1954).

51. Crane to Nellie Crouse, 6 Jan. 1896, *Letters,* p. 98.

52. Crane to Nellie Crouse, 12 Jan. 1896, *Letters,* p. 99.

Kirk M. Reynolds (essay date 1987)

SOURCE: Reynolds, Kirk M. "*The Red Badge of Courage*: Private Henry's Mind as Sole Point of View." *South Atlantic Review,* vol. 52, no. 1, 1987, pp. 59-69.

[*In the following essay, Reynolds closely scrutinizes the full range of Crane's ironic statements throughout the novel, with attention to Henry Fleming's tenuous hold on reality and his faulty self-awareness. He concludes that when Crane writes "in the last paragraphs that Henry Fleming has become a man" this is Crane's fully ironic, negative verdict on Henry.*]

Since its first publication in book form in 1895, Stephen Crane's *The Red Badge of Courage,* now available in the authoritative edition by Bradley and others, has elicited a spectrum of interpretations that invariably are seeking a coherent structure that will adequately account for the ending of the novel.[1] When we read in the last paragraphs that Henry Fleming has become a man, "his soul changed," can we believe it? When we reach the last sentence of the novel, whose observation about the appearance of sunshine on that rainy day do we read? And what does such a final sentence indicate about the meaning of the novel? The critics have argued inconclusively that the ending is affirmative, ironic, ambiguous, or, because the problems seem irresolvable, that Crane's work is flawed.[2] Robert Rechnitz concludes that "it is impossible to take the final four paragraphs as either intentionally straight-forward or ironic in tone" (86). Henry Binder agrees that the published text, the Appleton text, "does not make sense" and that this text "terminates on an inappropriate note." Binder argues, therefore, that "the ambiguity in the final Appleton paragraphs ... exists for one reason: because things are missing" (24-25).

Rejecting Binder's reconstruction that too neatly supplies the so-called missing emendations,[3] I offer here an alternative interpetation that finds coherent sense in the published novel and in its ending, simply by reexamining its point of view. Heretofore, all criticisms suggest that Crane's novel has a dual point of view: the reader sees through both Henry Fleming's eyes and those of an outside observer-narrator; in other words, the novel has a limited omniscient viewpoint. I will demonstrate that instead Crane has created a piece of fiction in which the observer-narrator is actually an illusion.

James Nagel's recent study (1980) provides the most thorough analysis of Crane's uses of the limited omniscient viewpoint—"the natural expression of Literary Impressionism"—really a dual viewpoint that Nagel defines as follows:

> The point of view Crane employed in *The Red Badge* is basically that of a limited third-person narrator whose access to data is restricted to the mind of the protagonist, Henry Fleming. ... Although there are a few passages with an intrusive narrative presence, and a few other complicating devices involving temporal dislocations, the central device of the novel is the rendering of action and thought as they occur in Henry's mind, revealing not the whole of the battle, nor even the broad significance of it, but rather the meaning of this experience to him.
>
> (52-53)

With this view of the narrator, Nagel points to Henry's "epiphany" in chapter 18, and, by finding that after Henry's epiphany "narrative irony ceases" (61), he represents those critics who find the ending of the novel straightforward and indicative of moral growth in the young soldier. However, such a subtle narrative method as that described above by Nagel offers no clear explanation of just how one determines which sentences one will read as only accurate renderings of thoughts in Henry's mind and which sentences as including narrative commentary. For example, when Nagel reads in chapter 18, "New eyes were given to him," and in chapter 24, "And at last his eyes seemed to open to some new ways," how does Nagel know to read these sentences (or any sentence in all twenty-four chapters) as both Henry's thought and narrative observation instead of as only the narrator's comment or as only the boy's thought? Why should we readers be more inclined to read these sentences as epiphany rather than irony, or as irony rather than ambiguity, or as ambiguity rather than a flaw? The dual viewpoint promoted by Nagel and all other critics of *Red Badge* leads us either to rather arbitrary decisions about meaning or to observations similar to Rechnitz's puzzlement about the ending.

Because all previous interpretations, all of which suggest the dual viewpoint, fail to resolve the problems of the ending, I propose that, before we write off the work as flawed, we reevaluate Crane's novel as one in which the reader sees *only* through Henry's eyes and mind. There is not someone else watching. The novel merely seems to have an outside narrator until the subjective ending surprisingly redefines the previous point of view to be only Henry's. The ending indicates not the novel's ambiguity but its point of view. **Red Badge** is an interior monologue.

To define the prose technique that I suggest Crane employed, let us look at a more recognizable example of the same technique, which may be found in Ambrose Bierce's short story "An Occurrence at Owl Creek Bridge," a story that has three distinct sections.

In his first section, Bierce presents through an objective third-person point of view the last-minute preparations for the military hanging of a planter, Peyton Farquhar, from a railroad bridge. Towards the end of this section, the point of view shifts subtly into the mind of the man who, with noose already around his neck, awaits hanging and looks at the stream beneath his feet, and the movement into his thoughts is evident. But at the end of the section, the point of view becomes objective again: "As these thoughts ... were flashed into the doomed man's brain rather than evolved from it the captain nodded to the sergeant. The sergeant stepped aside." Because the sergeant's weight is all that prevents the plank upon which the planter stands from falling, this last sentence indicates sure death. Clearly, in section one Bierce has established a distinct dual point of view.

In section two, Bierce presents an entirely objective flashback to the incident that causes the planter to be in the predicament of execution. It would seem at the end of section two that little remains for discussion or observation except a dead planter.

Bierce provides, however, a third section that begins with the following:

> As Peyton Farquhar fell straight downward through the bridge he lost consciousness and was as one already dead. From this state he was awakened—ages later, it seemed to him—by the pain of a sharp pressure upon his throat, followed by a sense of suffocation. ... These sensations were unaccompanied by thought. ... Then all at once, with a terrible suddenness, the light about him shot upward with the noise of a loud plash; a frightful roaring was in his ears, and all was cold and dark. The power of thought was restored; he knew that the rope had broken and he had fallen into the stream.
>
> (13)

In this paragraph, after the first objective observation, Bierce seduces the reader into reentering the mind of the man who, by all rights, should be dead at this point, and Bierce seduces the reader into assuming that the man's perceptions of the actual situation are reliable. In this section, Bierce seems to use the subtle dual point of view that Nagel ascribes to **Red Badge**.

Bierce maintains this apparent duality in describing Farquhar's successful escape and return to his home, and the reader believes the distorted, blurred details and confusion of action to be a logical result of Farquhar's traumatic experience. The subtle dual point of view seems to remain intact as it continues to provide narrative of this dreamlike journey which eventually leads Farquhar to his home and wife.

At the end, however, Bierce shocks the reader with his last two sentences. The first of the two is apparently a continuation of the action and the dual point of view: "As he is about to clasp her [his wife] he feels a stunning blow upon the back of his neck; a blinding white light blazes all about him with a sound like the shock of a cannon—then all is darkness and silence!" Abruptly, the next sentence resumes the objective viewpoint seen in sections one and two: "Peyton Farquhar was dead; his body, with a broken neck, swung gently from side to side beneath the timbers of the Owl Creek bridge" (18). The effect of this last sentence is to startle the reader into realizing that he has been duped. All of the third section of the story between the first sentence and the last is an expression of the mind of Peyton Farquhar as he dies—there is not objective reality behind any action in this dream. Suddenly, we recognize that what we thought was actually happening was instead a projection of what Farquhar desires most in his last brief moment. Bierce creates the illusion of the dual viewpoint and then uses his last sentence to reveal the true point of view in the preceding narrative.

I propose that Crane's technique in **Red Badge** is similar to Farquhar's dream in the last section of Bierce's "An Occurrence at Owl Creek Bridge"; however, unlike Bierce, Crane provides no objective outside framework to enclose this interior point of view. All of Crane's story from beginning to end comes from Henry's mind and perception, but Crane uses a trick similar in effect to Bierce's in order to clarify his technique: his ending, with ironic surprise, redefines the point of view in the preceding story.

To test this interpretation, we must see if the subjectivity of the last few paragraphs of **Red Badge** can redefine the point of view to be that of the boy Henry alone—an uncomfortable consideration for the reader. In such a case, upon reaching the novel's ending and supposing himself at comfortable objective distance, the reader, who has been amused watching the immature youth be victimized by dramatic irony, becomes also the victim of irony: he has been seduced into misreading the novel.

Let us look at the story before Crane's ending. Because many sentences throughout the novel include guide-verbs, such as "seemed," "thought," "felt," and "wished," that clearly indicate the subjective view of Henry, other passages that do not contain such guides must also be interpretable as purely subjective—or else the dual point of view exists.

The opening paragraph of the novel provides a combination of apparently objective details and subjective impressions:

> The cold passed reluctantly from the earth, and the retiring fogs revealed an army stretched out on the hills, resting. As the landscape changed from brown to green, the army awakened, and began to tremble with eagerness at the noise of rumors. It cast its eyes upon the roads, which were growing from long troughs of liquid mud to proper thoroughfares. A river, amber-tinted in the shadow of its banks, purled at the army's feet; and at night, when the stream had become of a sorrowful blackness, one could see across it the red, eyelike gleam of hostile campfires set in the low brows of distant hills.
>
> (5)

At first glance, the reader assumes the final metaphor, which expresses a demon in the dark, is the impression of the observer-narrator. A few paragraphs later this narrator seems to display omniscience into Henry's mind: "He [Henry] wished to be alone with some new thoughts that had lately come to him" (6). However, among the thoughts that the boy considers is the troubling sentence: "He could not accept with assurance an omen that he was about to mingle in one of those great affairs of the earth" (7). In seeking the referent for "omen," the reader must admit three possibilities. One ready possibility is that Henry refers to Jim Conklin's "rumor" of imminent troop movement. But the presentation of this rumor, discussed by the men, seems an unlikely omen even for a naive boy, because we assume from the early paragraphs that such a rumor is typical of the many buzzing through the camp. Another possible referent for "omen" is the apparent bad luck of a corporal whose new "costly board floor" (6) will be useless if the camp moves. But this detail seems to be nothing more than an indication of the extreme length of time the men have been encamped.

For a member of this long-positioned, impatient, and rumor-filled camp, a more likely "omen" would be something of larger significance, and prior to the point of reference, the only paragraph offering promise of change for the entire scene is the first paragraph, cited above. The seasons are changing, fruition is becoming evident, and vision is clearing. If this sense of change is the "omen," then the indication in this first chapter is that the outside narrator's "objective" commentary merges with Henry's later subjective thought to suggest that only one mind presents both.

This view of the first paragraph of chapter 1 is further supported in two paragraphs in the next chapter, before the regiment leaves the camp and moves off to battle. The eleventh paragraph in chapter 2 repeats the "red eyes" metaphor from the beginning of chapter 1: "One morning, however, he found himself in the ranks of his prepared regiment. The men were whispering speculations and recounting the old rumors. In the gloom before the break of the day their uniforms glowed a deep purple hue. From across the river the red eyes were still peering" (15). Taken alone, the sentence containing the "red eyes" metaphor might seem to be entirely from the outside narrator's viewpoint. However, examining the context, one will note that, after an initial topic sentence, this paragraph enumerates what Henry is observing. And the word "still" connects this observation with the only previous "red eyes" metaphor in the first paragraph of chapter 1. Two paragraphs later, another use of the "red eyes" metaphor occurs: "As he looked all about him and pondered upon the mystic gloom, he began to believe that at any moment the ominous distance might be aflare, and the rolling crashes of an engagement come to his ears. Staring once at the red eyes across the river, he conceived them to be growing larger, as the orbs of a row of dragons advancing" (15). Because in the second sentence "red eyes" best fills the role of antecedent for "them," we notice again that Henry's metaphorical view here is the same one that is presented in the first paragraph of chapter 1. If we assume an omniscient separate voice, a dual point of view, then we must wonder when a character expresses impressions that are identical to those expressed earlier by the supposed "outside" viewpoint. Because in such a case the character is looking into the narrator's mind instead of vice versa, nothing separates Henry's view from that of the apparent omniscient narrator. Without separation, the dual view is no more; only Henry's view remains.

If the point of view is entirely from Henry's mind, each sentence need not blatantly remind the reader of this viewpoint. Subtlety cannot exist otherwise. Many sentences exist in this story that, if taken out of context, do seem entirely objective. An example of such sentences is the first mentioning of Henry in the early paragraphs of chapter 1: "There was a youthful private who listened with eager ears to the words of the tall soldier and to the varied comments of his comrades" (6). Even in its immediate context such a sentence seems an objective comment by an outside observer. But taken in context of the few subtle indicators in chapters 1 and 2 mentioned above, this sentence could also represent a subjective mind observing its own persona, in this case a mildly egotistical and, for all we know, accurate perception.

To further this argument, I suggest that we consider scenes in the novel from a position that Edwin H. Cady defines: "He [Crane] handles point of view more like a movie camera than perhaps any predecessor had done. The reader stands to see somewhere back of Fleming's eyes. Sometimes the reader gets the long 'panning' shot, sometimes the view only Henry could see, sometimes an interior view..." (120). Although Cady is trying to define a dual point of view, he hits upon exactly the right explanation of the single viewpoint. Just as any one mind has moments of external "panning" for action and details, moments of internal reflection, and other moments of mixed detail and interpretation, so does the mind of Henry Fleming.

Most important to this argument for a single point of view is evidence that Henry's mind and physical presence coexist reasonably with all "objective" observations in each scene. Otherwise, his perception could not be the only point of view. Two examples of the relationship of camera-like views to Henry's presence can be found in the extremes of the novel. At the beginning, when "a youthful private" is first mentioned, the point of view follows him as "he went to his hut. . . . He wished to be alone . . ." (6). Once inside the hut, the boy lies on his cot, and the reader receives apparently "objective" descriptions of details. But the arrangement of the details is in an order that might be best seen by the boy's eyes "panning" the room from his position on the cot at one end of the room.

Turning to the crucial last chapter, we find that another example of this relationship between viewpoint and Henry's presence also ends the novel. In the last two sentences of the novel, we learn: "He turned now with a lover's thirst to images of tranquil skies, fresh meadows, cool brooks—an existence of soft and eternal peace. Over the river a golden ray of sun came through the hosts of leaden rain clouds" (109). Taken out of context, the last sentence could be an objective observation. "Golden" and "leaden" could be descriptions of color. However, the preceding sentence is clearly a subjective view through Henry's imaginings, and the movement from the one sentence to the other suggests that the last sentence is also subjective: either entirely a metaphor for the boy's perspective or a subjective view of the literal sky in front of Henry as he looks up—subjective in the sense that the primary emphasis is on "a golden ray of sun" instead of the subordinated "leaden rain clouds," a priority of detail that matches perfectly the idealized view of nature in the preceding sentence. Upon reaching the ending, we realize these examples indicate that, in spite of the apparent dual perspective throughout, the viewpoint is Henry's from beginning to end. This indication holds true for every sentence of apparent objectivity in the novel because we see only when Henry sees. When Henry sleeps and his perception and mind are inactive at the end of chapters 1 and 13, the action and commentary break off and do not resume until he is awake at the beginning of the next chapter. Because of so many apparent objective observations throughout, the reader tends to disregard the subtle clues suggesting a single viewpoint and assumes the presence of the observer-narrator. However, by ironically confirming Henry's viewpoint, the final sentences force the surprised reader to reconsider the preceding tale.

What kind of mind presents or dreams this tale of soldiering? As other critics have accurately noted,[4] the tale indicates that Henry is childish and does not change. He is an egotistical brat whose thoughts and actions move in circles and only mimic the behavior of any nearby group. When confronted with any situation requiring personal integrity or individual responsibility, Henry escapes by becoming involved in a group and forgetting the troubling previous situation.

Because all comes from Henry's mind and because such a novel depends on the reader's mature perceptions to make distinct Henry's immaturity by providing an external frame of reference, Henry's perception is the theme of the novel. We have no way of clearly defining anything else through Henry's distorted vision except Henry's perception. Nature and other themes exist in this novel much like the "rumors" in chapter 1. Possibly, there is no objective reality behind any of this story; it may all be a dream. Therefore, the novel is not naturalistic in any sense and only realistic in a psychological sense. The whole work consists of impressions of a childish consciousness that cannot perceive its own lack of maturity. But from this journey inside Henry's mind, the reader infers a clear message: any individual or group must overcome egotistical perception to some extent, to any extent, in order to mature and coexist with the rest of the universe. Otherwise, the mind ironically imprisons itself, as does Henry's mind. His military rank is appropriate but eerie: "Private" Henry Fleming. The ironic ending is even more horrifying than that in Bierce's "An Occurrence at Owl Creek Bridge."

Finally, as additional but secondary support for my suggestion of a connection between the Crane and the Bierce stories, biographical information reveals the possibility that Crane specifically used "An Occurrence at Owl Creek Bridge" as a model for his technique in **Red Badge.** Bierce's tale first appeared in serial form in the *San Francisco Examiner* of 13 July 1890 (12) and in 1892 in *Tales of Soldiers and Civilians* (Grenander 175), that is, more than two years before **Red Badge** was published as a novel. In the context of this chronology, the following anecdote, related by Robert H. Davis, could be significant. In 1896, while working for the *New York Journal,* Davis, who had known Bierce when he worked in San Francisco before coming to New York, sought an introduction to Stephen Crane in order that Davis might relay to Crane Bierce's favorable reaction to **Red Badge.** After failing to gain an interview, Davis happened to see Crane late at night on the street in New York and invited Crane to accompany him to the nearby bar of the Imperial Hotel. About this encounter Davis writes:

> It was there, jostled by all sorts and conditions of laymen, that I told Crane what Bierce had said of him. He made no comment whatever but seemed content to slide his glass of whisky up and down a wet spot that glistened on the walnut bar.
>
> In one corner of the room there was a group of rubber plants in tubs.
>
> "If we were in Cuba now," observed Crane, "there would be five murderers with drawn machetes behind those Brooklyn palms. Two of them would be candidates for office."
>
> His glass continued to glide up and down the bar while his mind shifted back to an earlier subject.
>
> "Read Bierce's 'Occurrence at Owl Creek Bridge'!"
>
> I informed him that I had.
>
> "Nothing better exists. That story contains everything."
>
> (xix-xx)

In light of the present study of **Red Badge,** we must wonder if, with these words, Crane was offering Davis a clue.

Notes

1. For impressionistic views, see Overland and Wyndham; for naturalistic views, see Walcutt 75-82 and Pizer, "Late"; for a psychological view, see Vanderbilt; for symbolic views, see Hart and Stallman; for structural views, see Solomon, LaFrance, Klotz, and Free.

2. For interpretations that find affirmation, see Hart, Stallman, Solomon, LaFrance, Fraser, and Colvert, "Structure"; for one that finds irony, see Walcutt 75-82; for those that find ambiguity, see Marcus and Berryman; for one that finds flaws, see Colvert, "Magic."

3. See Binder's edition of *Red Badge*; for a rejection of Binder's text and argument see Pizer, "Rejoinder."

4. See Walcutt 81-82, Rechnitz 76-87, and Lorch 229.

Works Cited

Berryman, John. "Stephen Crane: *The Red Badge of Courage.*" *The American Novel: From James Fenimore Cooper to William Faulkner.* Ed. Wallace Stegner. New York: Basic Books, 1965. 86-96.

Bierce, Ambrose. "An Occurrence at Owl Creek Bridge." *The Collected Writings of Ambrose Bierce.* New York: Citadel, 1946. 9-18.

Binder, Henry. "*The Red Badge of Courage* Nobody Knows." *Studies in the Novel* 10 (1978): 9-47.

Cady, Edwin H. "The Red Badge of Courage." *Stephen Crane.* New York: Twayne, 1962. 115-144.

Colvert, James B. "Stephen Crane's Magic Mountain." *Stephen Crane: A Collection of Critical Essays.* Ed. Maurice Bassan. Englewood Cliffs, NJ: Prentice-Hall, 1967. 95-105.

———. "Structure and Theme in Stephen Crane's Fiction." *Modern Fiction Studies* 5 (Autumn 1959): 204-5.

Crane, Stephen. *The Red Badge of Courage.* Ed. Henry Binder. New York: Avon, 1983.

———. *The Red Badge of Courage: An Authoritative Text, Backgrounds and Sources, Criticism.* Ed. Sculley Bradley et al. New York: Norton, 1976. 1-119.

Davis, Robert H. "Introduction." Vol. 2 of *The Work of Stephen Crane.* Ed. Wilson Follett. 11 vols. New York: Knopf, 1925. ix-xxiv.

Free, William Joseph. "Smoke Imagery in *The Red Badge of Courage.*" *College Language Association Journal* 7 (December 1963): 148-52.

Grenander, M. E. *Ambrose Bierce.* New York: Twayne, 1971.

Hart, John E. "*The Red Badge of Courage* as Myth and Symbol." *University of Kansas City Review* 19 (Summer 1953): 249-56.

Klotz, Marvin. "Romance or Realism?: Plot, Theme, and Character in *The Red Badge of Courage.*" *College Language Association Journal* 6 (December 1962): 98-99.

LaFrance, Marston. "Private Fleming: His Various Battles." *A Reading of Stephen Crane.* New York: Oxford UP, 1971. 98-124.

Lorch, Thomas M. "The Cyclical Structure of *The Red Badge of Courage*." *College Language Association Journal* 10 (March 1967): 229-38.

Marcus, Mordecai. "The Unity of *The Red Badge of Courage*." *The Red Badge of Courage: Text and Criticism*. Ed. Richard Lettis et al. New York: Harcourt, 1960. 189-95.

Nagel, James. *Stephen Crane and Literary Impressionism*. University Park: Pennsylvania State UP, 1980.

Overland, Orm. "The Impressionism of Stephen Crane." Vol. 1 of *Americana Norvegica*. Ed. Sigmund Skard and Henry H. Wasser. 2 vols. to date. Philadelphia: U of Pennsylvania P, 1966.

Pizer, Donald. "'*The Red Badge of Courage* Nobody Knows': A Brief Rejoinder." *Studies in the Novel* 11 (Spring 1979): 77-81.

———. "Late Nineteenth-Century American Naturalism." *Realism and Naturalism in Nineteenth-Century American Literature*. Carbondale: Southern Illinois UP, 1966. 11-36.

Rechnitz, Robert M. "Depersonalization and the Dream in *The Red Badge of Courage*." *Studies in the Novel* 6 (Spring 1974): 76-87.

Solomon, Eric. "The Structure of *The Red Badge of Courage*." *Modern Fiction Studies* 5 (Autumn 1959): 220-34.

Stallman, R. W. "Introduction." *The Red Badge of Courage*, by Stephen Crane. New York: Modern Library, 1951. v-xxxvii.

Vanderbilt, Kermit, and Daniel Weiss. "From Rifleman to Flagbearer: Henry Fleming's Separate Peace in *The Red Badge of Courage*." *Modern Fiction Studies* 11 (Winter 1965-66): 371-80.

Walcutt, Charles C. "Stephen Crane: Naturalist and Impressionist." *American Literary Naturalism, A Divided Stream*. Minneapolis: U of Minnesota P, 1956. 66-86.

Wyndham, George. "A Remarkable Book." *New Review* 14 (January 1896): 30-32.

Verner D. Mitchell (essay date 1996)

SOURCE: Mitchell, Verner D. "Reading 'Race' and 'Gender' in Crane's *The Red Badge of Courage*." *CLA Journal*, vol. 40, no. 1, 1996, pp. 60-71.

[*In the following essay, Mitchell observes that "signs of 'gender' and 'race' in Crane's fiction have gone largely uninterrogated," providing a textual examination of both.*]

Taking my cue primarily from Nobel Laureate Toni Morrison's "Unspeakable Things Unspoken: The Afro-American Presence in American Literature" (1989) and *Playing in The Dark: Whiteness and the Literary Imagination* (1993), I want to offer, in this brief paper, what I trust will be a relatively new look at Stephen Crane's classic civil war novel, ***The Red Badge of Courage***. In a 1992 review of Melville scholarship, critic Andrew Delbanco writes that Morrison's "Unspeakable Things Unspoken"[1] "opens new entrances into Melville in ways that earlier estimable works ... had not quite managed to do. It will be a long time," he adds, "before these entrances are closed."[2] Morrison's critical work offers, I would contend, an equally fortuitous opening into Crane. For with the exception of criticism on ***George's Mother*** and ***Maggie***, and on "The Monster," signs of "gender" and "race" in Crane's fiction have gone largely uninterrogated—or, in Morrison's language, they have been unspeakable and unspoken. The foregrounding of constructions of "gender" and "race" therefore promises to offer new openings into ***The Red Badge*** and, perhaps more importantly, suggests that in his most successful work Crane challenges and in some instances subverts categories which controlled much of nineteenth-century Euro-American thought.

Ralph Ellison in his 1986 work *Going to the Territory* notes perceptively that ***The Red Badge of Courage*** "is about the Civil War, but only one black person appears, and then only briefly."[3] After zooming in on his character, however, Ellison, like most other critics, seems at a loss concerning exactly what to make of the novel's unnamed black man. That they would have such difficulty is not at all surprising, given that the black man drops in (seemingly out of nowhere) for all of two sentences, and then he disappears, just as abruptly, never to be heard from again. The novel's opening scene shows Jim Conklin rushing back from washing a shirt in order to broadcast excitedly, though erroneously, that the regiment will attack the following day. "To his attentive audience," reports the narrator, Conklin

> drew a loud and elaborate plan of a very brilliant campaign. When he had finished, the blue-clothed men scattered into small arguing groups between the rows of squat brown huts. A negro [sic] teamster who had been dancing upon a cracker box with the hilarious encouragement of two-score soldiers was deserted. He sat mournfully down.[4]

I want to linger, for just a moment, on the variously dancing and mournful character.

At its most basic level, the description is simply one of a black man dancing, in typical minstrel fashion, so as to entertain a group of white men.[5] This dancing black man and his amused audience, especially with the rows of "squat brown huts" as backdrop, would appear to be more at home in postbellum, romanticized defenses of slavery. Even so, the three-sentence side show, when situated within the era's typical portraits of African Americans, would not be particularly noteworthy were it not for the fact, as Ralph Ellison reminds us, that Crane's is a novel of the Civil War. Yet precisely because the American Civil War is the novel's subject,[6] this fleeting portrait of black-white interaction actually drives to the very heart of *The Red Badge.* Why do Henry and his colleagues enlist? Why are they fighting, risking and all too often losing their lives? On this crucial point, even the characters themselves remain unclear. By means of their "hilarious encouragement" of the teamster and even more so their rudely abrupt departure, they do signal, however, that for them their black colleague is of little, if any, consequence. As a result, although we cannot determine exactly why they are fighting, we can see rather clearly that abolition, Negro freedom, and black uplift are far from the top of their agenda.

Amy Kaplan offers a more sympathetic reading. In a probing, subtly-nuanced analysis, she maintains that in an effort to map new arenas for warfare and for imaginative literature, Crane divorces both the Civil War from its historical context and his novel from generic narrative conventions.[7] Hence the opening scene, rather than an endorsement, is actually a rejection of minstrelsy. She explains that "[i]n the 1880s, tales of chivalric exploits ... superseded the older narrative of emancipation." Crane, therefore, by divorcing his own narrative from these "former stories about freeing the slaves" actually "calls attention to the process whereby the history of emancipation has been reduced to a form of entertainment." The novel's sympathy, then, in Kaplan's view, rests not with the laughing two-score soldiers, but with the "deserted" teamster who "sits 'mournfully down' to lament his loss of an audience and his own passing as a figure for the subject of emancipation."[8]

Kaplan's reading, while not altogether convincing, is especially helpful to the extent that it locates the teamster center stage, rescuing him, at last, from the textual and critical margins. In so doing, she retards what Morrison has referred to as long-standing acts of "willful critical blindness,"[9] Nonetheless, any number of critics continue to argue, as does Daniel Aaron, that Crane's soldiers ... have no antecedents to speak of, no politics, no prejudices. Negroes and Lincoln and hospitals and prisons," he maintains, "are not to be found in Crane's theater; these and other matters were irrelevant to his main concern—the nature of war and what happens to people who engage in it.[10] Here we are told that Crane focuses on people and that Negroes and other similar irrelevances are not to be found in his theater. Such readings so marginalize the novel's black man (and his interests) that he is all but pushed out of *The Red Badge* and rendered invisible. In contrast, the novel's young protagonist, Private Henry Fleming, finds it much more difficult to escape such matters as politics and prejudices, hospitals and Negroes.

Since my own analysis thus far has focused on how the laughing soldiers view the teamster, I also think it important, like Kaplan, to examine how he views them and even more importantly, how he views himself. As the twoscore soldiers depart, does the teamster actually sit mournfully down to lament his passing as a figure for the subject of emancipation, or does he merely lament his loss of an audience? If the latter is true, and I suspect that it is, then the teamster sees himself (or at least the novel would have us believe that he sees himself) as a subservient appendage to a group of other men. Rather than utter a healthy sigh of relief at their departure, he apparently prefers that they remain and continue their "hilarious encouragement." He thus measures his self-worth, as Du Bois would phrase it, through the eyes of those who "look on in amused contempt."[11] Notice, too, that the only visible role that the novel permits him is as entertainer for the dominant culture and according to the dominant culture's limited expectations. As a result, in this, the novel's opening scene, Crane has materfully constructed a rigid, racialized hierarchy, one which dates back in American literature at least to Jefferson's *Notes on the State of Virginia* (1787). Simply put, Crane's dancing black man boosts the white soldiers' egos and their sense of self-worth, and in so doing he serves as a convenient device for cementing both his and their God-ordained place on the Great Racial Chain of Being.

As we flip to page two, the teamster is figuratively buried, never to be heard from again. In his place surfaces a more abstract, less concrete figuration of darkness, one which Morrison in a somewhat different context has labeled a "disrupting darkness."[12] What we might term "the great unseen presence in the text," therefore, persists. Chapter 16, for example, finds Henry reveling in his recently received red badge of courage. The narrator notes, somewhat derisively, that Henry "had performed his mistakes in the dark, so he was still a man. Indeed," he continues, "when he remembered his fortunes of yesterday, and looked at these from a distance he began to see something fine there. He had license to be pompous and veteran-like" (79). Here darkness is presented as a positive and perhaps even benevolent force. In keeping concealed the fact that Henry's wound, his bandage of courage, occurred as a consequence of his throwing down his rifle and running "like a rabbit"

(35), the darkness enables his manhood to remain intact. Of course the darkness does not blind Henry to the circumstances of his wound nor, by extension, to the substance of what he considers his "manhood." Hence in this scene we can begin to understand his ambivalence toward darkness, or what I prefer to call his love-hate relationship with blackness.

In the chapter's succeeding paragraphs, Henry undertakes a more sustained meditation on blackness. He is now a man of experience, an authentic hero, and he accordingly struts about and looks with scorn upon lesser men. To capture the passage's essence, I need quote at length:

> Some poets ... had wandered in paths of pain and they had made pictures of the black landscape that others might enjoy it with them. He had, at that time, been sure that their wise, contemplating spirits had been in sympathy with him, had shed tears from the clouds. ...
>
> But he was now, in a measure, a successful man and he could no longer tolerate in himself a spirit of fellowship with poets. He abandoned them. Their songs about black landscapes were of no importance to him since his new eyes said that his landscape was not black. People who called landscapes black were idiots. He achieved a mighty scorn for such a snivelling race.
>
> (80)

The antecedent of "snivelling race," I would argue, is intentionally vague. Does "snivelling race," for instance, refer to the poet race or, just as likely, to the black race? Here, as elsewhere throughout the novel, the passage is sufficiently complex to accommodate multiple readings. What seems indisputable, however, and what for me is the more salient point, is that within the passage, "blackness" takes on for Henry (as it does throughout Western civilization) a clear and unrelentingly negative connotation. What is equally clear is that the scene's biting irony renders Henry's judgment vain at worst and naive at best. Therefore, where the portrait of the teamster reinforces myopic conceptions of blackness and whiteness, Henry's ironized "scorn for such a snivelling race" challenges, perhaps unintentionally, all such constructions.

A later meeting between Henry and two members of the army's elite brings the novel's evolving depiction of "race" into even sharper focus. In chapter 19, Henry and another "foot-soldier" happen to overhear two officers insulting their regiment, the 304th. In this scene, we as readers are positioned with the foot soldiers, and we accordingly must similarly stand back and listen, unseen, and afterwards interpret the officers' conversation:

> The officer who rode like a cow-boy reflected for an instant. "Well," he said, "I had to order in th' 12th to help th' 76th an' I haven't really got any. But there's th' 304th. They fight like a lot 'a mule-drivers. I can spare them best of any." The youth and his friend exchanged glances of astonishment. The general spoke sharply. "Get 'em ready then. ..." As the other officer tossed his fingers toward his cap and, wheeling his horse, started away, the general called out to him in a sober voice: "I don't believe many of your mule-drivers will get back."
>
> (92-93)

The uncomplimentary label "mule-drivers" bridges the color divide by figuratively linking Henry and his regimental brothers to the Negro teamster, who is literally a mule-driver. Once again, Morrison aids our interpretation. She writes in *Sula* of "old women who worried about such things as bad blood mixtures and knew that the origins of a mule and a mulatto were one and the same."[13] Indeed, an attentive examination of Henry's "glance of astonishment" reveals that he understands that which Morrison's old women understand, and like them he fears being collapsed into an arena of mules and other "mixed" beings, and thus placed on the bottom rung of humankind's evolutionary ladder. To be sure, Henry's gender and race set him above and apart from Morrison's old women. His race and phenotype do the same vis-á-vis the Negro teamster/mule-driver. Yet viewed through the general's eyes, they are all, at bottom, much the same. Crane's narrator reports that in listening to the officers "the most startling thing [for Henry] was to learn suddenly that he was very insignificant" (93). Henry certainly realizes, then, that the officers see him as mere cannon fodder, as one whose class renders him little better than Negroes and mules and such.

At first glance, Henry's romanticized encounter with a "dark girl," just prior to his leaving for the war, seems to further problematize stereotypic notions of blackness and whiteness. So, too, does the opening chapter's description of Henry's mother's "brown face" (6). Before turning to Henry and his brown-faced mother, whose extended conversation will shortly bring this paper to a close, I want to comment first on his encounter with the dark girl. We certainly need not look far into the canon of American literature to find synecdochial signifiers of race, more often than not ones mapped onto and played out by means of the female body. Let me offer three specific examples. In Cooper's *The Last of the Mohicans* (1826), Alice and Cora Munro brave a gauntlet of dangers to visit their father, a British officer fighting against the French in hostile Indian territory. During the course of their journey, dark-haired Cora, whose mother is West Indian,[14] is killed; her golden-haired, blue-eyed half-sister, Alice,[15] in contrast, lives and can thus marry and propagate the race in her own image. Hawthorne's *The Blithedale Romance* (1852) makes use of a similar pattern. Zenobia, a dark-haired woman drawn to recall and mock the pioneering feminist Margaret Fuller, drowns herself after being rejected by Hollingsworth.[16] Hollingsworth chooses, instead, "fair" Priscilla, who is painted as "perfectly modest, delicate, and virginlike."[17] Moreover, in the novel's famous last sentence, the narrator discloses that he, too, prefers Priscilla: "I—I myself—was in love—with—Priscilla!"[18] Even in Alcott's *Little Women* (1868), which like **The Red Badge** is set during the Civil War, it is a dark-haired sister, Beth, who catches scarlet fever and dies.[19] And it is her sister Amy, described as "A regular snow maiden with blue eyes, and yellow hair," who lives, eventually marrying the man whom Beth had fallen in love with and giving birth to a "golden-haired" baby girl.[20] Rather than cite additional instances of what eventually became a staple in nineteenth-century American literature, suffice it to say that Henry's longing for a dark girl stands this pattern on its head. Not only does he dismiss, rather decisively, a light-haired girl, and she him, but he finds (or at least he thinks that he does) in the dark girl his potential soul mate:

> From his home, he had gone to the seminary to bid adieu to many schoolmates. They had thronged about him with wonder and admiration. ... A certain lighthaired girl had made vivacious fun at his martial-spirit but there was another and darker girl whom he had gazed at steadfastly and he thought she grew demure and sad at the sight of his blue and brass. As he had walked down the path between the rows of oaks, he had turned his head and detected her at a window watching his departure.
>
> (6)

The above description of Henry desiring a dark girl rather than the unattractive, stereotypical blonde-haired beauty challenges and arguably subverts common turn-of-the-century constructions of race and gender. Henry's relationship with his brown-faced mother, however, is less clear-cut. Henry's mother, similar to his light-haired female schoolmate, "look[s] with some contempt upon the quality of his war-ardor and patriotism" (3). When he tells her that he has decided to enlist, she replies succinctly and bluntly, "Henry, don't you be a fool" (4). The ensuing verbal give-and-take between Henry and his mother, which is at bottom little more than a duel or a gendered battle,[21] draws to a close when Henry enlists. As he views it, "he had made firm rebellion against this yellow light thrown upon the color of his ambitions" (4).

Nonetheless, a short while later Henry finds himself wishing, without reserve, that he had needed his mother's advice. In this rare moment, for him, of clear thought, the yellow light personifies safety, courage, and insight, while brass buttons and red badges are merely the unfortunate by-products of a hyper and misguided masculine ethos. Feeling sorry for himself,

> [h]e wishe[s] without reserve that he was at home again, making the endless rounds, from the house to the barn, from the barn to the fields, from the fields to the barn, from the barn to the house. He remembered he had often cursed the brindle-cow and her mates, and had sometimes flung milking-stools. But from his present point of view, there was a halo of happiness about each of their heads and he would have sacrificed all the brass buttons on the continent to have been enabled to return to them.
>
> (15)

This picture of a frustrated Henry milking cows, of him in fact as a milkmaid, captures compellingly the domestic realm which he had made firm rebellion against. But now, only a short while after having charged forth to become "a man," he would all too willingly retrace his steps. Indeed, he wishes with all his heart that he could step back over that dividing line which he had erroneously come to see as separating men from women, bulls from cows.

Unfortunately, this moment of lucidity does not last. A few chapters later he is again neck-deep in dreams of heroism and valor, of bloody battles and brass buttons. To cite one brief instance, toward the end of chapter sixteen he pictures himself back home

> in a room of warm tints telling tales to listeners. ... He saw his gaping audience picturing him as the central figure in blazing scenes. And he imagined the consternation and the ejaculations of his mother and the young lady at the seminary as they drank his recitals. Their vague feminine formula for beloved ones doing brave deeds on the field of battle without risk of life, would be destroyed.
>
> (82)

Of course the irony here is too apparent to be missed. This vague feminine formula for beloved ones doing brave deeds on the field of battle which Henry details is neither his mother's nor his female classmate's. Instead, Henry is actually describing his own mistaken masculine formula, and it is the two women who have tried valiantly, though unsuccessful, to destroy it. Recall that when young Henry initially boasts of his forthcoming martial exploits, his mother cries out, in disgust, "Henry, don't . . . be a fool." Likewise, to the extent that the young woman at the seminary grows demure and sad at his departure, she, too, in all likelihood sees what he even by novel's end cannot see. The novel, therefore, in this and similar scenes, forcefully exposes and explodes what I earlier labeled Henry's misguided masculine ethos.

Hence for Henry to recognize and afterwards construct a more wholesome definition of manhood, he must first embrace his mother's teachings and thus collapse his flawed notions of the feminine and the masculine. No less important, constructing a healthier definition of personhood requires that he also move beyond hierarchical, dichotomous notions of race. Likely the novel's great message, then, for Henry and his critics alike, is that they look to the margins: to his dark-skinned potential lover, his African-American brother in arms, and his wise, though generally ignored, brown-faced mother.

Notes

Author's note: I wish to thank Professors Donald B. Gibson and John Clendenning for their help with this essay.

1. See Toni Morrison, "Unspeakable Things Unspoken: The Afro-American Presence in American Literature," *Michigan Quarterly Review* 28.1 (Winter 1989): 1-34.

2. Andrew Delbanco, "Melville in the '80's," *American Literary History* 4.4 (Winter 1992): 722.

3. Ralph Ellison, *Going to the Territory* (New York: Vintage: 1987) 237.

4. Stephen Crane, *The Red Badge of Courage* (1895; New York: Avon, 1982) 1. Hereafter cited parenthetically in the text by page reference only.

5. For an excellent analysis of minstrelsy, see Eric Lott, *Love and Theft: Blackface Minstrelsy and the American Working Class* (New York: Oxford UP, 1993).

6. The novel's full title is *The Red Badge of Courage: An Episode of the American Civil War.*

7. Amy Kaplan, "The Spectacle of War in Crane's Revision of History," in *New Essays on The Red Badge of Courage*, ed. Lee Clark Mitchell (New York: Cambridge UP, 1986) 78.

8. Kaplan 85.

9. Toni Morrison, *Playing in the Dark: Whiteness and the Literary Imagination* (New York: Vintage, 1993) 18.

10. Daniel Aaron, *The Unwritten War* (Madison, U of Wisconsin P, 1987) 214-15.

11. W. E. B. Du Bois, *The Souls of Black Folk* (1903; New York: Vintage, 1990) 8.

12. Morrison 91.

13. Toni Morrison, *Sula* (New York: Plume, 1973) 52.

14. James Fenimore Cooper, *The Last of the Mohicans* (1826; New York: Signet, 1980) 118, 187.

15. Cooper 20.

16. Nathaniel Hawthorne, *The Blithsdale Romance* (1852; New York: Oxford UP, 1991) 15, 47.

17. Hawthorne 77.

18. Hawthorne 274; emphasis Hawthorne's.

19. Louisa May Alcott, *Little Women* (1868; New York: Penguin, 1989) 177, 183, 419.

20. Alcott 4, 489.

21. Chapter two contains another gendered battle. In this contest, the male is again found lacking and a young, pink-cheeked female proves his superior: "A rather fat soldier attempted to pilfer a horse from a dooryard. He planned to load his knapsack upon it. He was escaping with his prize when a young girl rushed from the house and grabbed the animal's mane. There followed a wrangle. The young girl, with pink cheeks and shining eyes, stood like a dauntless statue. ... The regiment rejoiced at his downfall. Loud and vociferous congratulations were showered upon the maiden, who stood panting and regarding the troops with defiance" (14).

Michael Schaefer (essay date 2006)

SOURCE: Schaefer, Michael. "'Heroes Had No Shame in Their Lives': Manhood, Heroics, and Compassion in *The Red Badge of Courage* and 'A Mystery of Heroism.'" *War, Literature, and the Arts,* vol. 18, nos. 1-2, 2006, pp. 104-13.

[*In the following essay, Schaefer contends that since Fleming is arguably less mature and actually more self-deluded at the end of the novel, Crane's remark, "he was a man," should be taken ironically.*]

The Civil War, the bloodiest conflict ever conducted on American soil, raged for four years. Far longer, though fortunately less bloody, at least in literal terms, has been the conflict over the meaning of the greatest novel of that war, Stephen Crane's **The Red Badge of Courage.** The central issue in this debate is whether Crane intends for the reader to take the protagonist's final assessment of himself straightforwardly or ironically. On his first day of battle, Henry Fleming flees in terror and endures various physical and mental agonies as a result, including being clubbed in the head by another panic-stricken man and fearing that his cowardice will be revealed to all, to his undying shame. However, upon returning to his unit that evening, Fleming finds his comrades willing to accept his lie that he was "separated" from them during the fighting and that his head wound was caused by enemy fire. Realizing that he "had performed his mistakes in the dark, so he was still a man" (86), Fleming fights fiercely the next day, winning praise from his officers and fellow soldiers. With these plaudits ringing in his ears, he concludes that he is "now what he called a hero" (97) and, indeed, as he had concluded earlier, "a man" (135). John J. McDermott is representative of the critics who argue that Crane wishes for the reader likewise to call Henry a hero and a man, discerning in Henry's deeds on the second day "a final pattern of courageous action" and thus "genuine heroics" (330). Weihong Julia Zhu, on the other hand, offers one of the most recent statements of the opposing view, asserting that Henry's courage is "absurd" on several counts.[1] My own view, based on a close reading of *The Red Badge* that synthesizes the separate insights of a number of other critics, and on the depiction of heroics and manhood that Crane offers in "A Mystery of Heroism," the first Civil War story he wrote after this novel, is that the ironic interpretation is accurate but no single critic has probed the full depths of Crane's interrogation of these subjects.

Most of the negative critiques of Henry's self-assessment examine the nature of the courage he displays. Howard Horsford argues that Henry's supposed bravery on the second day is finally no different from his flight on the first in that neither behavior stems from "conscious, willed intention"; his flight results from fear, while his courage results from an equally involuntary upwelling of the opposite emotion, rage (123). As John Clendenning more elaborately explains, "Henry's shameful cowardice, his archaic dependence on motherly solicitation—the specter of a primitive female identification—his fear, in short, that he is not a real man and others know it, turns to furious hatred" on the second day. He "now wants to destroy the enemy whom he perceives as somehow to be blamed for his impotence. His rage—or what self psychologist Heinz Kohut calls 'narcissistic rage'—is his revenge against everyone and everything that insults his grandiose, exhibitionist self" (31). Picking up on the note of narcissism, Zhu rates Henry's courage as absurd partly on the grounds that it "derives from vanity"—from his desire to gain the praise of his peers and superiors—rather than from the "righteous inducement" of true mental or moral force (3-4).

Support for these views is widespread in Crane's depiction of Henry's second day of battle. That Henry operates out of vanity, judging himself only on the basis of what others can see rather than his own moral sense, is clear both before and after the fighting. Early in the morning, while Henry is waiting for marching orders, we are told that "since [he knew that] nothing could now be discovered" about his cowardice, he "did not shrink from the eyes of judges, and allowed no thoughts of his own to keep him from an attitude of manfulness" (86). Similarly, when the fighting is over Henry is said to feel "gleeful and unregretting, for, in it, his public deeds were paraded in great and shining prominence. Those performances which had been witnessed by his fellows marched now in wide purple and gold, hiding various deflections" (133).

That Henry's prime motivation under fire is unconscious anger comes across most sharply in the account of the first combat of this day. The narrator says that "When, in a dream, it occurred to the youth that his rifle was an impotent stick, he lost sense of everything but his hate, his desire to smash into pulp the glittering smile of victory which he could feel upon the faces of his enemies . . . The youth was not conscious that he was erect upon his feet. He did not know the direction of the ground" (95). So all-consuming is this rage that Henry is not even aware that the enemy has retreated until someone from his own side forcibly points the fact out, at which time "there appeared upon the glazed vacancy of his eyes, a diamond-point of intelligence" (96). Even in a later moment when Henry might seem to perform a conscious act of unselfish heroism, recklessly exposing himself to enemy fire in an effort to rally his regiment when it has stalled during a charge, vanity and rage are the true engines, for his goal in this endeavor is to prove wrong the officer who earlier predicted just this outcome in saying that the regiment fights "'like a lot 'a mule-drivers'" (101). Specifically, Henry wishes to prove that *he* is no mule-driver, as the description of his thoughts at this moment reveals. We are told that "a scowl of mortification and rage was upon his face . . . His dreams had collapsed when the mule-drivers, dwindling rapidly, had wavered and hesitated on the little clearing and then had recoiled. And now the retreat of the mule-drivers was a march of shame to him" (111).

Despite the seemingly condemnatory nature of such passages, a number of critics have suggested that negative judgment of Henry on the bases of anger and vanity is contained in the minds of readers operating out of certain twentieth-century paradigms of courage rather than in the text itself. Philip Beidler argues that the reader must be aware of nineteenth-century concepts of heroism, both romantic and Darwinian, out of which Crane is writing. When Henry's thoughts and actions are viewed in the context of the contemporary "discourse of courage," Beidler says, it is possible, while not disregarding a great deal of complexity, to conclude that, for Crane,

Henry has proven commonly battleworthy by common definition, and specifically that he is as courageous as he or anyone else might expect to be ... Whether he is deluded or not *is* an issue and the focus throughout of a complex irony, but it is only so within this very specific context. He has simply been one of those left alive and accredited in the consensus of his fellows—and thus also in cultural memory—as having met the test.

(250)

And even within twentieth-century discourses of courage Henry's behavior may be regarded as normative rather than deficient. John Hersey concludes, on the basis of his observation of a marine unit's combat experience on Guadalcanal in 1942, that "except for the hard knot which is inside some men, courage is largely the desire to show other men that you have it" (qtd. in Monteiro, "Guadalcanal Report" 199-200). Tim O'Brien offers much the same assessment of men in Vietnam in *The Things They Carried*. Among those things, he says, is "the soldier's greatest fear, which was the fear of blushing. Men killed, and died, because they were embarrassed not to" (20-21).

One critical response to this less judgmental measure of Henry's courage has been to sever the connection Henry himself makes between heroism and manhood. Donald Pizer says that Henry's bravery on the second day does not differ in substance from his fear on the first "in their essential character as animal and instinctive responses to danger" (2), but he argues that Henry's experiences have run him through the whole gamut of human emotions and have thereby conferred some measure of growth upon him. "To have touched the great death as Henry has done," Pizer concludes, "and to have experienced as well the central emotions of life arising from this inescapable reality of the human condition, is indeed to have ... gained some degree of manhood" (6-7).

This is a sensitive and intelligent reading, one that takes into account the uncertain relationship between courage and maturity, but I would argue, as do a number of other critics, that it does not take into account Henry's lack of one emotion that for Crane is central to both manhood and heroism: compassion. In a letter dated January 12, 1896, just months after the publication of *The Red Badge,* Crane explained his view on this matter to Nellie Crouse, a young woman with whom he was enamored. "The final wall of the wise man's thought," he says, "is Human Kindness of course. If the road of disappointment, grief, pessimism, is followed far enough, it will arrive there ... Therefore do I strive to be as kind and as just as may be to those about me and in my meager success at it, I find the solitary pleasure of life" (*Correspondence* 180). It might be tempting to dismiss such a statement in such a context as youthful self-dramatization, but, as Crane says in the same letter, "[t]he cynical mind is an uneducated thing" (180), and *The Red Badge* bears out the philosophy of the letter, for Crane seems clearly to show that Henry is at fault for deriving his pleasure in life from other sources while consciously refusing to act out of human kindness.

The most glaring example of Henry's failure in this area spans both days of battle. Shortly after his flight on the first day, as he wanders behind the lines, Henry falls in with a column of wounded men, among whom he finds one of his best friends, Jim Conklin. Near death, Conklin asks Henry to keep him out of the road so he will not be run over by "'them damned artillery wagons'" (55). Henry responds, "hysterically," by the narrator's description, "'I'll take care of you! I swear to Gawd I will'" (55). Henry at this moment clearly does feel compassion, but the adverb *hysterically* suggests that this response may be, like his fear and courage, not entirely a matter of conscious will. When he is presented with a chance to show a more considered compassion a few moments later, he fails utterly. Following Conklin's death, another mortally wounded man who has befriended Henry shows solicitude for him, asking him where he has been wounded. Lacking a wound, Henry is afraid that this question will reveal that he is only behind the lines because he ran from the battle. As a result, he is "enraged against the tattered man and could have strangled him"; despite the man's entreaties that Henry stay with him, Henry walks away, leaving him "wandering about helplessly in the fields" (62).

At the end of the next day, as Henry is gleefully surveying his public deeds of courage, he recalls this man who displayed compassion and received none in return—"he who gored by bullets and faint for blood, had fretted concerning an imagined wound in another ... he who blind with weariness and pain had been deserted in the field" (134)—and the memory depresses him. This feeling does not proceed from any deep moral regret, however, but rather from "the thought that he might be detected in the thing" (134). In this new mood he fears that his comrades are "seeing his thoughts and scrutinizing each detail of the scene with the tattered soldier," but, as was the case with his flight on the first day, as soon as he realizes that this mistake too was performed in the dark his remorse vanishes. "[G]radually," the narrator says, "he mustered force to put the sin at a distance" and is able to conclude that "[h]e had been to touch the great death and found that, after all, it was but the great death. He was a man" (135).

However complicated Crane may make the relationship of courage to manhood, the irony in this juxtaposition of compassion and manhood seems clear: when Henry in fact confronted the great death in the form of the tattered soldier, he consciously *refused* to touch it, and so his assessment of himself is off by precisely 180 degrees. Pizer takes account of this flaw and acknowledges that it militates against Henry's having attained complete maturity, but further evidence suggests that compassion is a *sine qua non* of any sort of maturity for Crane and that he equally "conceives of humanity in heroism" (Zhu 6); for, as Zhu, Kevin J. Hayes, and Mary Neff Shaw have all noted, Henry's treatment of the tattered man is not an isolated episode but rather part of a pattern designed to show that Henry consistently behaves with "inhuman selfishness" (Zhu 6).[2] When Henry returns to his unit at the end of the first day with his story of separation and wounding, he is tended by his friend Wilson, who earlier had been boastful and quarrelsome but has been changed by his experiences under fire into the soul of compassion. He gives Henry his own canteen, dresses his wound, and puts him to bed in his own blankets. Henry is grateful, concluding that Wilson has "now climbed a peak of wisdom from which he could perceive himself as a very wee thing" (82), but he does not apply this analysis to himself and deal with Wilson in kind. Rather, when he fears that Wilson, like the tattered soldier, may unwittingly ask questions that will expose his cowardice, he recalls his knowledge of Wilson's own earlier fears, the tangible evidence of which is a packet of letters Wilson gave Henry, and "rejoice[s] in the possession of a small weapon with which he could prostrate his comrade at the first signs of a cross-examination. He was master. It would now be he who could laugh and shoot the shafts of derision" (85). Less developed but equally telling is Henry's behavior toward wounded men on the second day. Twice Henry encounters badly shot-up comrades, one "thrashing about in the grass, twisting his body into many strange postures [and] … screaming loudly" (99) and the other with his mouth pulped into "a pulsing mass of blood and teeth" (125-26), but in neither case does the vividness of his observation seem to evoke any sympathy for them; he merely notes their sufferings and moves along, intent on his own battle-fury.

It is this lack of compassion for the wounded that provides the link in terms of both plot and ideology to the short story "A Mystery of Heroism." Here Crane creates an equal number of significant parallels to and differences from the novel. Like Henry Fleming, Private Fred Collins, the protagonist of "Mystery," behaves bravely out of concern for the opinion of others, and like Henry he faces a challenge to act with compassion that entails personal risk in the face of the great death. Unlike Henry, however, Collins is capable of honest introspection and is therefore less sure of his own status as a man and a hero even though he passes the test of compassion as well as that of courage; and it would seem that his uncertainty provides a clear intertextual criticism of Henry.

The test of courage begins for Collins when, as his company is deployed at the edge of a meadow that is being shelled by Confederate artillery, he repeatedly complains of thirst and expresses a desire to drink from a well on the opposite side of the meadow. His comrades' reaction is to ask, "'Well, if yeh want a drink so bad, why don't yeh go git it?'" (50), which raises Collins's hackles. Before he fully realizes what he is doing, he takes the dare and asks his captain's and colonel's permission to make the hazardous run across the meadow. Although these officers deem his expedition foolhardy, they grant his request on condition that he take some other men's canteens with him, thus giving his action some semblance of purpose. At this point Collins's meditation on heroism begins. Unlike Henry prior to his first battle, he is not worried about fear; in fact, he feels none and wonders at this circumstance "because human expression had said loudly for centuries that men should feel afraid of certain things and that all men who did not feel this fear were phenomena, heroes" (53). Given this line of reasoning, Collins has no choice but to conclude that "[h]e was, then, a hero," but, again unlike Henry, he is not elated by this realization. Instead, we are told, "[h]e suffered that disappointment which we would all have"—all, apparently, but Henry—"if we discovered that we were ourselves capable of those deeds which we most admire in history and legend. This, then, was a hero. After all, heroes were not much" (53).

As downbeat as this induction is, Collins's meditation does not end here; rather, Crane has him descend from even this disheartening level. Collins finally decides that he is not a hero after all, for

> Heroes had no shame in their lives and, as for him, he remembered borrowing fifteen dollars from a friend and promising to pay it back the next day, and then avoiding that friend for ten months. When at home his mother had aroused him for the early labor of his life on the farm, it had often been his fashion to be irritable, childish, diabolical, and his mother had died since he had come to the war.
>
> (53)

Once more, the distance between Henry and Collins is sharp: whereas Henry leaves compassion out of his definition of his own heroism in putting "at a distance" his own "sin" of abandoning the tattered man, Collins feels that his significantly lesser failures to consider the needs of others render him "an intruder in the land of fine deeds" (53).

Collins's reflections end at this point, for once he begins his run across the meadow he has no time for introspection. Now, with shells exploding all around him, he does feel fear, but instead of wondering how this new access of emotion might affect his conception of himself, he is concerned only with getting out of jeopardy as fast as possible. Exasperated at how slowly the first canteen fills, he tosses aside all the canteens, instead fills a bucket he finds at the well, and begins the dash back to his own lines with that vessel. Then, out on the meadow, he encounters a mortally wounded Union officer pinned beneath his dead horse. In agony, the officer asks, "'Say, young man, give me a drink of water, can't you?'" (55). Collins, "mad from the threats of destruction," screams, "'I can't'" and continues running (55). An instant later, however, he turns, comes back, and, despite his continuing terror, attempts to succor the officer, who, with "the faintest shadow of a smile on his lips," gives "a sigh, a little primitive breath like that of a child" (56) even though all the trembling Collins can do for him is splash water on his face before dashing away again. In another moment, Collins reaches his regiment, his comrades cheer him—not, it would seem, for his small act of compassion but rather for the grand, foolhardy gesture of running the enemy's gauntlet—and the story ends by living up to its title: where at the end of *The Red Badge* we are treated to Henry's lengthy post-combat analysis of himself, here we know nothing about what conclusion Collins reaches regarding his experience; all we learn is that "two genial, sky-larking young lieutenants" wrestle playfully for the bucket until "[s]uddenly there was an oath, the thud of wood on the ground, and a swift murmur of astonishment from the ranks. The two lieutenants glared at each other. The bucket lay on the ground empty" (56).

Faced with this enigma, critics have wrestled as well, if less playfully than the lieutenants. Thomas Gullason sees this last image as Crane's final word on the mystery, asserting that "Collins's journey . . . invalidates the age-old notions regarding the meaning and value of heroism . . . The empty bucket sounds and resounds with aftereffects—of the praise lavished upon Collins by his fellow troopers, and the hollowness of his feat, with Collins graceless under pressure, where pride, panic, and group pressure have 'conspired' to make him an 'accidental' hero" (188). Similarly, George Monteiro says that "the irony [of the empty bucket] is unmistakable. Collins has risked his life for nothing. His heroics have gone for naught" (69). These are insightful and trenchant readings, but I would argue that in their focus on the end of the story they ignore the possible import of Collins's compassion for the wounded officer. My own view inclines more to those of Mary Neff Shaw and Patrick Dooley, who give attention to the final image of the bucket but also take heed of Collins's act of charity when the bucket still contains water. Shaw perceives a satiric opposition between the dash across the meadow and the moment of compassion, arguing that the former embodies "a superficial, self-centered attitude . . . that heroism is determined by social acclaim" and that the latter demonstrates that "[t]he primary constituent of Crane's personal concept of heroism is human kindness" (97). Dooley goes so far as to brand Collins's dash "immoral" because of the great disparity between its "serious cost and . . . trivial reward"; by contrast, Collins's giving water to the officer makes the point that "pain and suffering correctly appreciated by both the patient and the onlooker—and correctly responded to—[can transform] a foolish caper into a genuinely moral act of heroism" (125).

My affinity for these latter two readings is rooted in the fact that they take in more of the story than the first two, but even these two overlook still another mystery of heroism. Shaw and Dooley evidently assume that Collins's return to the officer is a conscious, willed act, but our lack of access to Collins's thoughts once he begins his race means that we cannot be sure this is the case. We are told only that he first runs past the officer and then comes back; we are not told what mental process, if any, has impelled this turnabout. Monteiro asserts that the return is in fact involuntary and that Crane thus "brushes aside the notion that heroism is an act of the will or intention" (69). I am not willing to go this far, but I concur with Monteiro's final assessment that this story "questions the notion that heroism can be defined essentially—which may be Crane's key to the mysteries of heroism" (70). Indeed, I would argue that when we read *The Red Badge of Courage* in the light of this story and vice versa Crane confronts us with not one but at least four mysteries of heroism: why men such as Henry Fleming and Fred Collins are willing to risk their lives for the sake of vanity, where the courage to perform a truly selfless act comes from, how Fleming can possibly regard himself as a hero, and how Collins can fail to do so.

Notes

1. For other discussions of this controversy, see Harold Beaver, "Stephen Crane: The Hero as Victim," *Yearbook of English Studies* 12 (1982): 186-93; Christine Brooke-Rose, "Ill Logics of Irony," *New Essays on The Red Badge of Courage,* ed. Lee Clark Mitchell (Cambridge: Cambridge UP, 1986), 129-46; John J. Conder, "*The Red Badge of Courage*: Form and Function," *Modern American Fiction: Form and Function,* Ed. Thomas Daniel Young (Baton Rouge: Louisiana State UP, 1989), 28-38; John Fraser, "Crime and Forgiveness: '*The Red Badge*' in Time

of War," *Criticism* 9 (1967): 243-56; Leland Krauth, "Heroes and Heroics: Stephen Crane's Moral Imperative," *South Dakota Review* 11 (1973): 86-93; Wayne Charles Miller, "A New Kind of War Demands a New Kind of Treatment: The Civil War and the Birth of American Realism," *An Armed America, Its Face in Fiction: A History of the American Military Novel* (New York: New York UP, 1970), 58-91; Donald Pizer, "Late Nineteenth-Century American Naturalism," *Realism and Naturalism in Nineteenth-Century American Literature* (Carbondale: Southern Illinois UP, 1966), 11-32; Kermit Vanderbilt and Daniel Weiss, "From Rifleman to Flagbearer: Henry Fleming's Separate Peace in *The Red Badge of Courage*," *Modern Fiction Studies* 11 (1966): 371-80; Daniel Weiss, "*The Red Badge of Courage*," *Psychoanalytic Review* 52 (1965): 176-96, 460-84.

2. See Hayes's "How Stephen Crane Shaped Henry Fleming," *Studies in the Novel* 22 (1990): 296-307; and Shaw's "Henry Fleming's Heroics in *The Red Badge of Courage*: A Satiric Search for a 'Kinder, Gentler' Heroism," *Studies in the Novel* 22 (1990): 418-28.

Works Cited

Beidler, Philip D. "Stephen Crane's *The Red Badge of Courage*: Henry Fleming's Courage in Its Contexts." *CLIO* 20 (1991): 235-51.

Clendenning, John. "Visions of War and Versions of Manhood." *Stephen Crane in War and Peace: A Special Edition of War, Literature & the Arts* (1999): 23-34.

Crane, Stephen. "A Mystery of Heroism." *Tales of War. Vol. VI, The Works of Stephen Crane.* Ed. Fredson Bowers. Charlottesville: U of Virginia P, 1970. 48-56.

———. *The Red Badge of Courage.* Vol. II, *The Works of Stephen Crane.* Ed. Fredson Bowers. Charlottesville, VA: U of Virginia P, 1975.

Dooley, Patrick. "'A Wound Gives Strange Dignity to Him Who Bears It': Stephen Crane's Metaphysics of Experience." *Stephen Crane in War and Peace: A Special Edition of War, Literature & the Arts* (1999): 116-27.

Gullason, Thomas. "Modern Pictures of War in Stephen Crane's Short Stories." *Stephen Crane in War and Peace: A Special Edition of War, Literature & the Arts* (1999): 183-96.

Horsford, Howard C. "He Was a Man." *New Essays on The Red Badge of Courage.* Ed. Lee Clark Mitchell. Cambridge: Cambridge UP, 1986. 109-27.

McDermott, John J. "Symbolism and Psychological Realism in *The Red Badge of Courage*." *Nineteenth-Century Fiction* 23 (1968): 324-31.

Monteiro, George. "After *The Red Badge*: Mysteries of Heroism, Death, and Burial in Stephen Crane's Fiction." *American Literary Realism* 28 (1995): 66-79.

———. "John Hersey's Guadalcanal Report: Drawing on Crane's War." *Stephen Crane in War and Peace: A Special Edition of War, Literature & the Arts* (1999): 197-208.

O'Brien, Tim. *The Things They Carried.* Boston: Houghton Mifflin, 1990.

Pizer, Donald. "Henry behind the Lines and the Concept of Manhood in *The Red Badge of Courage*." *Stephen Crane Studies* 10.1 (2001): 2-7.

Shaw, Mary Neff. "Apprehending the Mystery in Stephen Crane's 'A Mystery of Heroism.'" *CLA Journal* 39 (1995): 95-103.

Wertheim, Stanley, and Paul Sorrentino, eds. *The Correspondence of Stephen Crane.* 2 vols. New York: Columbia UP, 1988.

Zhu, Weihong Julia. "The Absurdity of Henry's Courage." *Stephen Crane Studies* 10.2 (2001): 2-11.

Charles Johanningsmeier (essay date 2008)

SOURCE: Johanningsmeier, Charles. "The 1894 Syndicated Newspaper Appearances of *The Red Badge of Courage*." *American Literary Realism*, vol. 40, no. 3, 2008, pp. 226-47.

[*In the following essay, Johanningsmeier provides a detailed history of the serial publication of* The Red Badge of Courage *(1895) and examines the differences between serial and book form of the novel that reveal how the publishing industry in this era shaped texts.*]

The general outline of how Stephen Crane's ***The Red Badge of Courage*** came to be serialized in numerous American newspapers in December 1894 is relatively well known among scholars. In January or February 1894, Crane submitted the manuscript of his novel to S. S. McClure for use either in his Associated Literary Press newspaper syndicate or in *McClure's Magazine* in hopes that its acceptance would help him achieve his first substantial success as a fiction author. Yet for a number of reasons neither McClure nor members of his staff made a quick decision about Crane's submission, resulting in months of anguished waiting for Crane. By fall Crane had finally lost his patience and asked for the manuscript back. Shortly thereafter he wrote to Hamlin Garland that "McClure was a Beast about the war-novel. . . . He kept it for six months until I was near mad." Disappointed, Crane submitted the manuscript to McClure's rival, newspaper syndicator Irving Bacheller. Bacheller later recalled that he took the manuscript home and with his wife Anna "spent more than half the night reading it aloud to each other." Bacheller, who was "thrilled by its power and vividness," promptly accepted the work for distribution by his syndicate.[1] Shortly thereafter, in early December, the novel began appearing serially in newspapers that subscribed to the Bacheller, Johnson, and Bacheller syndicate's fiction service.

Despite the significance of this episode to Crane's career—after all, previous to it he was a struggling writer who had experienced very limited success and recognition, and after it, he was a famous, sought-after author whose reputation among critics was destined to grow rapidly—it has received comparatively little scholarly attention and is not widely known outside the Crane scholarly community. Except for Joseph Katz's fairly detailed account in 1967, the history of *Red Badge*'s syndicated publication has typically merited only a few pages in most biographies, monographs, and articles about this classic American novel. Furthermore, the actual printed appearances of *Red Badge* in multiple American newspapers have, for the most part, been consigned to the shadows of Crane scholarship. Only a handful of scholars, mostly in the mid-1960s—Katz, Stanley Wertheim, and Thomas Gullason—have taken these publications seriously. In 1963 Stanley Wertheim reprinted one syndicated version as it appeared in the Philadelphia *Press* (Gullason did the same in 1967), and Katz in 1967 reprinted the New York *Press* version. A decade later, a number of its appearances were listed by Fredson Bowers in the University of Virginia edition of *Red Badge.* Since that time, however, no one has mentioned these texts except in passing. The lack of interest in them is best exemplified by their complete absence from the heated debate that took place between the late 1970s and the early 1990s about which textual version of *Red Badge* was most "authoritative" and thus worthy of study. Summing up this debate in 1994, Donald Pizer asserted, "There are three significant texts for *The Red Badge of Courage*: portions of a discarded draft; an almost complete manuscript; and the 1895 Appleton edition."[2] Most scholars, even if they do not agree with Pizer's preference for the 1895 Appleton edition, would concur that these are, indeed, the three most important versions of this text. Unfortunately, by implication—and omission—the syndicated versions are thus deemed "insignificant."[3]

It is not my intention here to reopen this debate and contend that the syndicated versions of *Red Badge* are most "authoritative" and thus deserve to be republished for use in the classroom and analysis by scholars instead of the other known versions. In fact, their publication history indicates that they do not reflect Crane's ultimate artistic intentions very well at all. Nonetheless, this episode in Crane's career, as well as the newspaper texts that emerged from it, are far from "insignificant," and they deserve to be better known and more closely scrutinized. Crane's experiences with McClure and Bacheller highlight the pivotal role that newspaper syndicates in the late-nineteenth century often played in launching unknown authors to fame. In addition, the serialized installments of *Red Badge* that appeared in newspapers across the country afford important insights into how the publishing industry at this time shaped literary texts; these were decidedly not the work of one individual, but were instead collaborative efforts, influenced and molded by many hands and forces. Most important, because these were the textual versions encountered by hundreds of thousands of readers in 1894, they allow us to understand better how Crane was perceived by the reading public at the beginning of his career and how these readers would have understood his work. In so doing, these serialized versions greatly aid the project of comprehending the kinds of "cultural work" the novel performed in the mid-1890s.

The important role that newspaper syndicates played in the American literary marketplace in the 1880s and 1890s is only slowly beginning to be understood and acknowledged by scholars. Crane, however, would have been well aware that syndicates could often prove critical to a beginning author's success. It is actually still unclear whether Crane intended to submit *Red Badge* to *McClure's Magazine* or to McClure's Associated Literary Press newspaper syndicate. Most likely he was unsure himself; after all, the majority of fictions that McClure published in the magazine from its first issue in June 1893 through 1894 were previously published via the syndicate—a form of "double-dipping" intended to get the most value out of his purchase of the serial rights to these works. Crane probably submitted his manuscript to McClure because it was well known that he was always on the lookout for new, talented writers, and that he had a reputation for paying authors handsomely for serial rights. Unfortunately, in early 1894 McClure was deeply involved in supervising the research and publication of the magazine's first major series, Ida Tarbell's history of Napoleon Bonaparte, whose first installment appeared in the November 1894 issue, and this might partially explain his inaction on Crane's manuscript. Crane scholars have repeatedly stated that McClure did not accept *Red Badge* because he was short of funds at the time. However, McClure during this period was expending large amounts of money on other fictions and non-fiction articles; and since common practice was not to have to pay an author until a work was published rather than when it was accepted, if McClure or a member of his staff had actually liked *Red Badge,* he would have accepted it for use in either the syndicate, the magazine, or both.

When Crane realized in late 1894 that McClure would not be publishing his work soon, he needed to find an alternate publishing outlet. Bacheller's firm was a natural second choice. Crane was directed to Bacheller not only by Edward Marshall of the New York *Press,* as has commonly been noted, but also most likely by Crane's mentor Hamlin Garland, who was also a friend of Bacheller's.[4] Garland was in a good position to know Bacheller's affairs at this time, and they just happened to coincide fortuitously with Crane's needs. Although Bacheller, like McClure, had begun his syndicate in 1884, his firm had published fiction only sporadically after 1891. However, Bacheller planned to re-enter the syndicated fiction market in late 1894 with a bang, and thus he needed a great number of manuscripts to fulfill his contracts with newspapers at at the same time Crane wanted to publish his novel. Not coincidentally, the first two short stories published in the syndicate's new service beginning in early November 1894 were by Bacheller and Crane's mutual friend Garland: "Old Mosinee Tom" on November 1 and "A Lynching in Mosinee" on November 2. Undoubtedly, Garland would not only have known about Bacheller's need for manuscripts but also would have been able to tell Crane that Bacheller was trustworthy and would pay on time if his work was accepted.

Newspaper syndicates such as McClure's and Bacheller's, while not well-known today, were very important to authors in the 1880s and 1890s because they constituted a large market for new fiction by known and unknown authors, generally paid quite well, and offered broad exposure. Bacheller's syndicate, like McClure's, would purchase a work from an author and then sell exclusive first serial rights to it to a single newspaper in each distribution area. Slightly before the projected publication date—which syndicators such as Bacheller ordered should be the same for all participating newspapers, so as to create the illusion for readers in each city that the story was "first" published there—the syndicator would send galley proof slips or stereotype plates of the fiction to the newspapers. By charging each of a great number of newspapers a relatively small fee for first publication rights, a syndicate manager such as Bacheller could collect enough money to pay authors quite well. Other authors Bacheller attracted with this scheme included Mary E. Wilkins, Sarah Orne Jewett, Rudyard Kipling, and Joel Chandler Harris.

In the end, Bacheller sent galley-proofs of *Red Badge* to newspaper editors in late November 1894 and the first installment appeared in numerous newspapers across the country on December 3. The novel generally ran for a total of six installments, usually ending on December 9 or 10, depending on whether the individual newspaper published on Sunday. Fredson Bowers in his 1975 edition of *Red Badge* reported six known syndicate printings: in the New York *Press* (complete in one issue on December 9), the Philadelphia *Press, Nebraska State Journal, Kansas City Star, Minneapolis Tribune,* and, in a clearly pirated version the following July, the *San Francisco Examiner.* In a 1980 addenda to Bowers, George Monteiro and Philip Eppard reported another appearance in the *Hartford Courant.* However, *Red Badge* was clearly published in many more outlets than this. John Berryman's assertion that it was published in at least two hundred small city dailies and 550-600 weekly papers across the country certainly cannot be dismissed. In the 1890s Bacheller typically sold individual fictions to approximately a hundred metropolitan daily newspapers, then allowed the A. N. Kellogg plate service and patent inside company to sell the works later to hundreds if not thousands of small country weeklies. As a result of Bacheller's circulation methods, many more printings of *Red Badge* are to be found by anyone with time and patience enough to scroll through microfilm or search digitized versions of old newspapers; in the past few years, for example, I have found three new appearances, in the *Rochester Herald,* the *Syracuse Daily Standard,* and the *Knoxville Journal.*[5] Given the subject of the novel and the many discussions about how it might have helped Northern and Southern readers look past sectional differences, the relative lack of Southern printings is significant and worthy of further investigation.

After a great deal of painful waiting, Crane in early December 1894 finally experienced a major breakthrough in his career: he was finally a widely-published author. What did this newspaper syndication mean to Crane? Clearly, like any beginning author, he was anxious about how the text would be received and what would result from it. Curtis Brown, an editor at the New York Sunday *Press,* recalled that he ran into Crane early on the Sunday morning of the *Press*'s publication of the novel and saw "Stephen on that bitter, wind-swept, acute corner of Park Row and Beekman Street. ... He was without an overcoat, but his face, thin and white, lit up when he saw me. He threw his arms around me and said: 'Oh, *do* you think it was good?'"⁶

Although critical acclaim for **Red Badge** would have to wait until after the book version was published in late September 1895, the success of the serialized newspaper version made Crane well-known among American readers and had important consequences for his future as a professional fiction author. As Katz succinctly puts it, the syndicated publication of **Red Badge** "was a major stage in Crane's rise to prominence." First, it significantly improved his finances. Willa Cather reported in 1900 that Crane told her he had received ninety dollars from Bacheller for the serial rights to **Red Badge,** and while the exact amount is unknown, Crane, in dire financial straits at the time, would have appreciated even the slightest remuneration.⁷

Second, the work's success established for Crane a solid connection with Bacheller's syndicate, which in the near future would provide him not only with much-needed backing for his travels but also an outlet for his work. In early 1895 Bacheller underwrote Crane's trip to the West and Mexico that would later inspire some of his best short stories; and in late 1896 Bacheller gave Crane his first opportunity to serve as a war correspondent, commissioning Crane to report on events in Cuba and providing him with $700 in gold for expenses. (Crane supposedly jettisoned this gold during the sinking of the *Commodore* on 2 January 1897.) From 1895 on, too, Bacheller's syndicate would circulate Crane's "The Pace of Youth," "A Mystery of Heroism," "One Dash—Horses," "A Grey Sleeve," "An Indiana Campaign," and many other sketches. The syndicated **Red Badge** also improved Crane's overall marketability, particularly with other syndicates. McClure joined the bandwagon and bought **The Third Violet** in 1896 for distribution by his own newspaper syndicate, and he later purchased even more works of fiction from Crane. By June 1896 an editorial writer in the *Echo* reported, "that apostle of Blood and Thunder and bad English, Stephen Crane, is besieged by orders from the syndicates and fixing his own prices."⁸

Third, acclaim for the syndicated **Red Badge** boosted Crane's morale and self-image as a writer at a time when he desperately needed it. Having previously toiled in relative obscurity, Crane suddenly was celebrated as an up-and-coming young author. Much of this adulation was the result of the perceived quality of **Red Badge** itself. An editorial in the Philadelphia *Press* of 7 December, for example, described **Red Badge** as "one of the best war stories going" and predicted that although "Stephen Crane is a new name now and unknown . . . everybody will be talking about him if he goes on as he has begun in this staving story." Years later Bacheller recalled that when he and Crane visited the Philadelphia *Press* newspaper office shortly after the newspaper publication of **Red Badge,** "Word flew from cellar to roof that the great Stephen Crane was in the office. Editors, reporters, compositors, proofreaders crowded around him shaking his hand." While the quality of the tale of course contributed to Crane's success, it should also be remembered that the Bacheller, Johnson, and Bacheller syndicate's pre-publication advertising for **Red Badge**—which to my knowledge has never been commented on by Crane scholars—also played a significant role in promoting Crane and his work. These ads, penned most likely by Irving Bacheller himself, were printed in a number of newspapers on December 2 or 3, 1894, immediately before the serial began appearing in most newspapers. Noting that "The 'Red Badge of Courage' [sic] is the best piece of fiction Mr. Crane has yet written"—establishing him as a veteran author for readers—the ad states, "It is a war story of remarkable power and contains descriptive passages that rise to the levels of Tolstoi and Zola." These comparisons to Tolstoi and Zola would have fostered in readers an idea that Crane was a "radical" writer and an expectation that his text would be similarly radical, which might have hurt Crane's reputation among certain readers. However, the ad balanced this perception by contributing to Crane's "success aura" with the statement, "W. D. Howells says of this young writer that he is the most promising now before the public. Hamlin Garland also ranks him very high in a bit of recent criticism." Such comparisons with and approval by these well-known, critically acclaimed authors undoubtedly would have raised not only Crane's self-esteem but also readers' regard for him.⁹

Fourth, the syndicated publication of **Red Badge** provided Crane with the publicity needed to launch his career as an author of national importance, some ten months before the first American book publication by D. Appleton in September 1895. As one contemporary put it, authors benefitted from syndication because the author's "name appears simultaneously in one hundred leading newspapers, thus presumably enhancing his reputation, and certainly giving his work a conspicuous opportunity to be read and admired." Another posited that syndicates could introduce authors "to a larger circle of readers than they could obtain through any magazine, or book."¹⁰ Certainly this was true in the case of **Red Badge,** for the newspapers in which it appeared were geographically widespread (except perhaps for the South) and had a combined readership of probably over a million. For the first time, Crane had broken out of being a chiefly New York author.

Thus it should be recognized that syndicated publication of *Red Badge* almost a year before the D. Appleton book edition was, in fact, the catalyst for Crane's first widespread fame. The popularity of the serialized version may even have predisposed book reviewers to take more notice of the novel than they otherwise would have. Further, the success of the serial could have prompted many readers to buy the book when it finally appeared. At this time it was commonly believed that newspaper and magazine serialization helped increase the sale of the work in volume form, and for this reason books were usually scheduled for publication slightly after the serial ended. Mark Twain certainly believed syndicated publication of his *The American Claimant* (1892) would boost sales of a cheap paperback version; he wrote to his publisher that in order to maximize sales, this edition "should issue a little before the last instalment ends in newspapers."[11] As a beginning author, Crane had no similar control over the publication schedule of *Red Badge,* but he might have nonetheless benefitted from the advance publicity that syndicated publication afforded.

In fact, perhaps the most important benefit of syndicated newspaper serialization for Crane was that it served as his entrée to editor Ripley Hitchcock at D. Appleton and Co. Instead of approaching Hitchcock as an unpublished, unknown author, Crane could show Hitchcock printed clippings of his abbreviated novel and published reports of his reception at the offices of the Philadelphia *Press.* Katz made the connection explicit, writing that the syndicate publication "led to the Appleton publication of the great American novel. The syndicate clippings had interested the publishing house, and the Philadelphia *Press* reception was useful as material with which to continue its wooing." These clippings and Crane's evident popularity were probably what convinced Hitchcock to ask to see a more complete version of *Red Badge* and subsequently to accept it for publication. Without the newspaper clippings, Appleton might have declined the manuscript, since publishing the work of an unknown author was a financially risky proposition; the syndicated publication and its reception, however, proved to Appleton that there was a market for such a book.[12]

Not all the effects of syndicated publication were positive, however. Most important, the various exigencies governing Bacheller's operations forced Crane, Bacheller, or both to extensively cut and edit the text of *Red Badge,* approximately 50,000 words long when submitted to McClure and Bacheller. As Hitchcock later put it, the 1895 book version "differed from the newspaper publication in containing much matter which had been cut out to meet journalistic requirements." It is primarily for this reason that scholars have privileged either a version of the manuscript that Crane had submitted to McClure and Bacheller or the 1895 D. Appleton book edition, which includes much more material than the syndicated versions. The reason why the text had to be cut for serialization is evident in the contract blank that Bacheller provided customers in late 1894, which promised editors that fictions would be divided into installments numbering between 2000 and 2500 words and that there would be no serials longer than six installments. These promises were not simply Bacheller's idiosyncratic whim; they were the result of his many years of experience with newspaper editors and what they believed their readers wanted. Editors who took Bacheller's service would never have accepted a work that ran for as many days (probably about twenty) as the uncut manuscript version would have required. Bacheller gave himself a heroic part when he later recalled that after reading the original manuscript, "I sent for Crane and made an arrangement with him to use about fifty thousand of his magic words as a serial. I had no place for a story of that length, but I decided to take the chance of putting it out in instalments far beyond the length of those permitted by my contracts. It was an experiment based on the hope that my judgment would swing my editors into line. They agreed with me."[13] In fact, though, Bacheller used only about 15,000 words of Crane's novel, and he sent the work out in six installments; neither the length of each installment nor their number exceeded the limits of his contract with editors. Indirectly, then, it was Bacheller's customers, the editors, who were most responsible for the extensive cuts.

The differences between the text that Bacheller sent to newspapers and what D. Appleton would publish in book form involved more than length, however. Due to the deletions, the number of chapters and their divisions are quite different: the syndicated text has only sixteen chapters, while the book version has twenty-four. The two texts also have very different tones, emphases, and endings. For example, as Katz has written, the newspaper version "is a fiction with fast pace, with less explicit introspection and with heavier use of narrative to push the plot along," making it "more the kind of blood-and-thunder story." Henry Fleming's observations of life behind the lines, his dialogues with fellow soldiers, the explicit questioning of military authority, and the gruesome descriptions of wounded soldiers and dead bodies are almost absent. The syndicated text also ends three chapters earlier than the book, with Henry Fleming and Wilson basking in the glow of the reported words of admiration from the colonel and the lieutenant, and the narrator commenting, "They were very happy." At the end of the book version, on the other hand, Henry has the chance to carry his brigade's colors into another battle and emerge feeling "a quiet manhood, non-assertive but of sturdy and strong blood." Furthermore, individual newspaper editors to whom Bacheller sent galley proof copy also made slight emendations to the text. Willa Cather recalled in 1900 that when she worked at the *Nebraska State Journal* she was partly responsible for making changes in the version of **Red Badge** that would appear in that paper, stating: "the grammatical construction of the story was so faulty that the managing editor had several times called on me to edit the copy."[14] Furthermore, typesetters at each newspaper inevitably made some mistakes when they retypeset this material from the galley proofs supplied by the syndicate. Thus, while Bacheller might have sent one "newspaper version" in galley proof form to editors, because each printing varied slightly, one is forced to use the plural "versions" whenever speaking of the newspaper publications.

When Crane sent the newspaper clippings of **Red Badge** to Ripley Hitchcock in December 1894 he wrote in his cover letter, "This is the war story in it's [sic] syndicated form—that is to say, much smaller and to my mind much worse than its original form." With the exception of Berryman, who contends that "most of the magnificent details are preserved in the cut version, the new jointing when necessary is done with skill, and the story holds astonishingly well," most scholars have concurred with Crane's assessment. Katz, while asserting that the syndicated version "was important . . . in part because it brought certain sections of the novel to further development," speaks for most scholars when he writes that "no man of taste would hesitate in choosing between the syndicated version and the complete achievement of the novel."[15] Given what these versions lack and that the book edition includes, the natural question is why should anyone bother to read the novel in its syndicated form.

For those scholars most interested in charting Crane's development as a writer and gauging his level of artistry, the answer to this question would probably seem rather obvious: one can safely ignore these newspaper versions. After all, they would respond, one should read and study the text that best represents Crane's artistic vision, and it is quite evident that Crane himself did not willingly choose to make the cuts required by the Bacheller syndicate; these were forced on him as a condition of publication. Those scholars who favor either a form of the manuscript of **Red Badge** or its 1895 D. Appleton first book version are also supported by quite traditional rationales of textual scholarship. The manuscript version of any given text can be regarded as best embodying the author's original intentions on those rare occasions when an author was coerced into cutting materials from his or her manuscript to win approval from a book publisher. In the majority of cases, however, textual editors have argued that the first book edition best embodies the author's artistry because for this edition authors typically have more time to revise their manuscripts for book publication, have the opportunity to consult with editors, and are allowed to review galley proofs before publication. Any serial publications that preceded volume publication, this line of reasoning asserts, can be lightly regarded because authors often were rushed during composition of serials and had to bow to editorial pressure and alter their ideal works in order to make them conform to certain length, pace, and subject matter requirements.

In recent years, though, some literary scholars have moved away from being so author-centered in their studies, concerned solely with the "authorized" texts that individual authors created. Instead, many have come to recognize the role of *readers* in creating the meaning of a text and have tried to understand their experiences. G. Thomas Tanselle, reflecting this new attitude, writes that "If . . . an unauthorized and carelessly produced edition of a work—one that had no connection with the author—was widely circulated, the historian cannot dismiss it, since many people would have encountered the author's ideas in this form."[16] Such a critical approach naturally opens the door to more serious consideration of serialized versions of literary texts, which often had more readers than the book versions had. In the case of **Red Badge,** a very large number of readers read this novel in its "corrupted" serialized forms—possibly as many as read it in book form before 1900—and so, if our goal is to better understand its readers rather than just Crane and his text, these serialized appearances deserve closer scrutiny.

One might first suggest that readers played a collaborative role in shaping the syndicated versions of **Red Badge.** Crane of course created the manuscript that he submitted to McClure and Bacheller. The reason it was shaped in the way that it was for syndication and why its multiple versions constitute such different experiences for readers, however, is that it needed to conform to certain conventions to please newspaper editors and readers. As noted earlier, for example, the drastic cuts in the manuscript's length are testimony to the power of editors' perceptions of what their readers wanted. In addition, as Wertheim notes, in a number of places in the early installments the language of Crane's soldiers is "standardized, probably in order to make it easier to read and less offensive to certain moral standards": "Words like 't'—morrah,' 'goin,' 'oncet,' and 'yeh' were given their proper spellings," and "Oaths such as 'hell's fire' and 'good Lord' were dropped." Little wonder that much of Henry Fleming's internal philosophizing was also excised. Editors commonly stated their belief to Bacheller and other syndicators that their readers wanted action, not introspection. This belief is manifested in one advertisement for the *Red Badge* that assured readers, "The story if [sic] full of action."[17] Explicit questioning of military authority and graphic presentation of soldiers' wounds and dead bodies also would not be something these editors—many of whom were using syndicated fiction to attract women and children as readers—would wish to include in their newspapers. Blood and gore were acceptable, even desirable elements on the news pages that were intended for male readers' eyes, but in the features pages these elements were usually either partially or completely missing.

Readers also indirectly influenced the ideological dimensions of the syndicated versions of *Red Badge*. Vital to the success of Bacheller's syndicate (as well as of other syndicates) was its ability to sell fiction to as many newspaper editors as possible. To do so, syndicate publishers generally believed the works they distributed needed to steer clear of politics and any hint of immorality. McClure, for example, sent a circular to authors in 1886 that stated, "no stories calculated to excite sectional feeling between the North and South, or to arouse any class prejudices, will be used," and undoubtedly Bacheller, who told authors he wanted stories full of "action & excitement," would have similarly preferred texts that avoided sectional or political controversy. In her landmark essay "The Spectacle of War in Crane's Revision of History," Amy Kaplan correctly notes that "In the outpour of nonfiction and fiction in the 1880s, writers consistently avoided referring to political conflicts over slavery or secession in favor of the theme of national reconciliation."[18] However, while she subtly implies that this was some kind of concerted hegemonic project to promote militarism, I would suggest that this avoidance of sectional conflict by many writers at the time might have had a more mundane explanation: magazine editors, book publishers, and syndicators discouraged writers from writing about controversial topics lest their inclusion hurt sales. One can frequently see evidence of this strategy in the way editors of all types purposely downplayed aspects of the fiction that might prove divisive. Significantly, for instance, only two newspapers used Crane's subtitle for *Red Badge*—**"An Episode of the American Civil War"**; in most versions, there was no subtitle included at all. The reason was probably less political than commercial.

One of the most important differences between the experiences of those who read *Red Badge* in its serialized form and those who read it in book form is that, except in the New York *Press,* newspaper readers read it in installments. In part this was because most newspaper editors believed their readers had short attention spans. The chief reason for publishing in installment form, though, was that editors wanted to encourage readers to buy the paper each day. This desire prompted editors to ask Bacheller that he edit works in such a way that at the end of each installment there was not necessarily a "cliffhanger" but at least what one might call an open-ended "leader" that inspired readers to be curious about what would happen next. Installment divisions in almost all the newspaper versions of *Red Badge* occurred at what in the book would be the middle of chapter three, the end of chapter six, the end of chapter nine, partly into chapter thirteen, and the end of chapter eighteen; the endings of these installments all anticipate what happens next. Typical is the end of the fifth installment, when Henry and the others, knowing they face overwhelming odds in the next battle, hear a "shaggy man" offer his ominous opinion, "We'll get swallered."[19] Such leaders, one can hypothesize, most likely prompted readers to focus on action and events rather than on Henry's internal moral development, which is what the book reading experience emphasized. Further, the publication of the novel in episodes might have prompted readers to understand better what many critics have suggested in the years since: that Crane was trying to show that a soldier's experience of war is not coherent and linear but an agglomeration of scenes which do not necessarily build on one another.

The less ambiguous ending of the newspaper version, too, was probably the result of Bacheller, Crane, or the newspaper editors believing that newspaper readers wanted and expected uncomplicated, happy endings. Deleting the final three chapters of the manuscript/book, for instance, leaves the reader with a greater sense of closure, of a goal achieved: Henry has faced his demons and emerges triumphant. He and Wilson "speedily forgot many things. The past held no pictures of error and disappointment." In sharp contrast, the final three chapters of the book indicate to the reader that flags such as the one Henry carries do advance, but also that they and the soldiers retreat on order, and that battles such as the one Henry experiences as all-important and life-changing are in fact rather insignificant; they come and go, with no end in sight. Most important, Henry is bothered in these final chapters of the book by nagging doubts about his earlier actions. Even though the book concludes that for Henry "The sultry nightmare was in the past," the reader has good reason for doubting such an assertion. After Henry recalls "with a thrill of joy the respectful comments of his fellows upon his conduct," "the ghost of his flight from the first engagement appeared to him" and there also "loomed the dogging memory of the tattered soldier" who had helped Jim Conklin and whom Henry had deserted.[20] Such doubt is absent from the syndicated version.

The experiences of contemporary readers of *Red Badge* in its newspaper form were different than those of book readers not only because its text was different but also because the contexts in which it appeared on the page were different. For example, while there were no illustrations included in the first book edition, readers of the syndicated *Red Badge* encountered in each installment two pen and ink illustrations, each a column wide, by G. Y. Kaufman of the Bacheller syndicate. Illustrations were supplied with the syndicated text because newspaper readers were generally less literate than book readers; the price differential between the two media alone (newspapers that included *Red Badge* installments cost two or three cents during the week and five cents on Sunday while the Appleton book cost a dollar) signals a class and educational difference. While newspapers that catered to more educated readers had more print and fewer illustrations, those catering to mass readers were full of illustrations. One contemporary commented, for example, that the New York *World*'s "pictorial and sensational features" made "it very popular with the masses." Less literate readers were likely to look to the illustrations for guidance, and as a result the illustrations influenced the ways in which they approached the text. The illustrations for the syndicated *Red Badge,* almost all of which involve action of some kind, prompted readers to view those specific scenes as the most important. The captions, which were provided by the Bacheller syndicate and included with most printings, also served to direct readers' attention to particular aspects of the text. In order of their appearance in most papers these are "He Sprang From His Bunk," "The Youth Forgot Many Things," "Directly He Was Working," "He Sped Towards the Rear," "He Stopped, Horror Stricken," "Gawd! Jim Conklin!," "He Could Hear the Tattered Man Bleating," "The Youth Climbed a Fence," "It Crushed Upon the Youth's Head," "Yeh've Been Grazed by a Ball," "Charge! Charge!," "Wrenched the Flag from the Dead Man's Hand," and "Several Men Came." Some editors, however, left the captions off, as in the *Rochester Herald* version, which included no captions after the first installment. In a few instances editors included most captions but left one or two out. The Philadelphia *Press,* for example, deleted "He Could Hear the Tattered Man Bleating" and the *Minneapolis Tribune* deleted "Wrenched the Flag from the Dead Man," possibly because both had unseemly implications. What were the likely effects of these illustrations on readers? The readers of versions without captions were in effect given more freedom to decide which scenes were most important, and certainly the word "bleating" would have negatively influenced attitudes towards this character. More generally, Kaplan has suggested that the text of "the newspaper version of the 'story,' which subordinates narrative context to theatrical events" emphasizes the idea of war as spectacle.[21] I would add, however, that the illustrations of the serialized *Red Badge,* even moreso than the text, prompted readers to view war as spectacle. After all, it is very difficult to create interesting illustrations of a person thinking.

In addition, unlike readers of *Red Badge* in book form, newspaper readers read a text very much enmeshed in a sea of short informational pieces and advertisements. Why care about the materials that surrounded the text and illustrations of *Red Badge* in the newspapers? After all, since Crane neither created them nor played a role in their placement, the other printed materials on the page would seem to be merely superfluous, ephemeral banter, unworthy of attention. Such has been the attitude of those Crane scholars who have previously examined the newspaper appearances. In their facsimile presentations of *Red Badge* newspaper versions, Wertheim, Gullason, and Katz reproduce only the text, and Bowers' bibliographical descriptions fail to take into consideration any materials unrelated to the text. Readers of *Red Badge,* though, did not make sense of the text solely by what Crane wrote or what the syndicates sent. The juxtapositions of the text of *Red Badge* with advertisements and other informational pieces in the pages of the paper are especially significant because these materials helped to shape readers' attitudes. That is, the texts of *Red Badge* as they appeared in newspapers form but single components of larger texts which we must read to understand better how readers interpreted the story.

One paratextual element that likely influenced readers' attitudes, for instance, was the head piece that was included at the beginning of all installments except the version in the New York *Press*. This woodcut is interesting for the way it portrays the disparity between the soldiers who fight wars and the "representers" of war, the authors who write about it.[22] The left side of this illustration shows a cleancut young man in a suit coat sitting at a desk writing; readers would have assumed that this represented Crane himself. Just to the right of this vignette, though, is an illustration of a bedraggled soldier holding a gun, sitting in front of a campfire. The effete writer would probably not have appeared very "masculine" to readers, and in some ways he might have seemed to be rather opportunistic in his writing about a war from the evident comfort of his study. No record exists of Crane's reaction to this illustration, but I suspect that it did not please him. This illustration, by positioning Crane as a young man in an orderly study, may even have contributed to the later controversy over how such a young author, who had never been to war, could write such a realistic novel about soldiering.

Because every newspaper editor who subscribed to Bacheller's service could position Crane's text on the page in any way he liked, the print contexts in which the syndicated *Red Badge* appeared varied widely. Still, there are some interesting patterns among the multiple printings. A number of critics have suggested that *Red Badge* symbolically works out a masculinity crisis in late nineteenth-century America; in this view, the tale does not glorify the virility of soldiers but instead interrogates the notion of individual agency in a complex, capitalistic, industrial world symbolized by the military "machine." Such a hypothesis is supported by the syndicated appearances of *Red Badge,* which appear as part and parcel of the masculinity crisis evident on the pages of the newspapers in which they were printed. This crisis is manifested most clearly by the fact that *The Red Badge of Courage* appeared most often not alongside advertisements for whisky, leather boots, guns, or other products coded as "masculine," but instead next to advertisements for "female" products such as "Mme. M. Yale's 3 Beauty Secrets" (tonics for gray hair, freckles, and wrinkles); Lydia E. Pinkham's Vegetable Compound; "Cuticura Soap"; "Kenyon's Closing-Out Sale of Fine Furs"; "Ladies' Desks" (which actually were vanities); and "Scott's Emulsion" (for "Babies and Children"). The proliferation of such ads is not surprising, since most newspaper editors bought syndicated fiction in hopes that its popularity would lead readers—especially female consumers—to pay more attention to advertisements placed next to it. Some installments, too, appeared directly next to articles about "Art and Society on Low-Cut Gowns" and "Hints to Housewives" (one of which addressed the "problem" of "Dancing-school frocks for girls of twelve to fifteen").

The besieged masculinity of American men is also often indicated in the few advertisements addressed to men that were placed in near proximity to installments of *Red Badge* as well as some articles that would likely have caught male readers' attention. In the *Rochester Herald,* for instance, Dr. Greene's Nerve Tablets were promoted with the headline, "Manhood Restored." These tablets, the ads proclaimed, could help those "who from *overwork, excesses, youthful indiscretion,* excessive use of stimulants, tobacco, or other causes suffer from Nervous Prostration, Weakened Memory, Loss of Power or Manhood." In Kansas City, too, readers of *Red Badge* would have seen the nearby ad that told how "Spanish Nerve Grains" could cure a host of maladies, including (again) "Lost Manhood." In the *Nebraska State Journal,* ads placed on the same page with installments of *Red Badge* included those for "Dr. E. C. West's Nerve and Brain Treatment," which promised to cure not only "Lost Manhood" but also "Lack of Confidence" and "Loss of Power of the Generative Organs in either sex," and another which exhorted, "WEAK MAN Cure Yourself in Two Weeks" of "NERVOUS WEAKNESS, LOST MANHOOD, and IMPOTENCY." On a similar theme, a group of would-be wolf hunters' misadventures were reported alongside *Red Badge* in the *Minneapolis Tribune.* The reason given for their ludicrously unsuccessful hunt—which killed only "a blackbird, a blue jay, and a large field mouse"—was that the male participants failed to take orders from their leader. "The result was the different divisions became separated and hopelessly were unable to unite and act in concert" and so the hunt "became a sort of go-as-you-please-affair, and every man hunted on his own responsibility." Such a scene is clearly reminiscent of what happens at various points to Henry Fleming's regiment. On the tamed Minnesota frontier and in battle thirty years earlier, it seems, excess individualism and the unwillingness to sacrifice for the good of the group and submit to authority could have dire consequences.[23]

True manhood thus clearly required self-discipline and sacrifice rather than thinking of one's selfish interests. This message was made quite explicit to readers of *Red Badge* in the Philadelphia *Press,* for in "Capt. George Dodd and His New Cossacks / American Cavalrymen Who Can Give the Czar's Reckless Riders Points" the reporter effuses not only about how horses and soldiers can be trained to act as one but also how a whole unit can be trained this way. He notes, "It is captivating to watch the advance of that solid column, to see it deploy and spread out in platoons, like the fan of some moving *machine*" (emphasis added). The reporter lauds this self-discipline by comparing the group to "the very sons of Ixion sweeping on as does the gale to vent their rage upon the luckless Lapidae."[24] Men who felt not so "masculine" at the time apparently had two routes they might take to regain their "lost manhood": either purchase the goods advertised for this purpose or act more like the U. S. cavalrymen who transformed themselves into Greek warriors by becoming machines at the command of higher authorities.

Finally, it is worth noting that those who could afford books and literary magazines were more likely to read at leisure in private, while newspapers were most often read hurriedly and in public. One contemporary opined that most papers were "'skimmed over' in the ten minutes which the average city dweller allows himself to read the paper." In fact, many city dwellers bought their newspapers at newsstands and read them in transit to and from work. As an 1895 report put it, "the modern business man never fails to read it [the newspaper] on the train, at least cursorily," and in Howells' *The Rise of Silas Lapham* (1885) Lapham skims two newspapers in the first twenty minutes or so of a ferry ride. As one contemporary commentator explained, "Continuous reading is impossible on a journey which is broken every five minutes by jerks and jolts." Readers who experienced the *Red Badge* in such conditions, one may surmise, were unlikely to pause long to consider the meaning of various symbols or the allusions in the Crane's text.[25] Instead, they read quickly, focusing chiefly on action scenes and perhaps gleaning some information useful to their lives, such as how to restore their "lost manhood."

Closer examination of the genesis and publication of the syndicated newspaper appearances of *The Red Badge of Courage* has broad implications for the study of literary realism at the end of the nineteenth century. For instance, it demonstrates even deeper ties between realist authors, their works, and newspapers than are commonly acknowledged. In addition, it reminds us that a large number of texts by realist authors now included in the canon, including ones not only by Crane but also by Howells, Garland, Jewett, James, London, and Norris, first appeared enmeshed in the thick of daily life in the newspaper, not separated from it in finely-printed books published by well-known and respected firms. Serial texts then as now were shaped not only by individual authors but by other members of the publishing community whose actions were often dictated by commercial considerations and unspoken assumptions about the target audience. This uneasy relationship between commercial and artistic interests in publishing is clearly evident on the newspaper pages where installments of *Red Badge* vied for the reader's attention with multiple advertisements.

The complete story of *Red Badge*'s first publication is perhaps most significant for what it tells us about readers. In the absence of actual readers' accounts of what they thought of works such as *Red Badge,* our best hope for recovering their experiences is a close examination of the elements comprising these experiences. The pages on which the installments of *Red Badge* were printed highlight how contemporary readers experienced serial fictions not in isolation but rather as part of larger, more heterogenous texts; this is a lesson that can be applied to all serial texts of the period. Until recently, consideration of readers' experiences were deemed secondary to the recovery of and critical inquiry into the author's "intended" text. The time has come, however, for more detailed investigation of these serial publications, no matter how different they are from an author's final intentions or whether critics view them as inferior to the book edition. In the case of *The Red Badge of Courage,* we need to find many more of its syndicated newspaper appearances and continue to analyze how patterns in the contexts in which they appeared might have influenced readers. We should, of course, continue to study the incomplete first draft of *Red Badge,* the more complete manuscript version, and the first book edition. But at the same time we should remember that a large number of readers first encountered this classic American novel in multiple American newspapers in early December 1894, and that these contexts in many ways determined their understanding of the text and its author as well as the cultural work they performed.

Notes

1. *The Correspondence of Stephen Crane,* ed. Stanley Wertheim and Paul Sorrentino (New York: Columbia Univ. Press, 1988) I, 79; Bacheller, *Coming Up the Road: Memories of a North Country Boyhood* (Indianapolis: Bobbs-Merrill, 1928), p. 278.

2. Joseph Katz, "Introduction" to *The Red Badge of Courage* (Gainesville: Scholars' Facsimiles and Reprints, 1967), pp. 9-44; Stanley Wertheim, "Stephen Crane's *The Red Badge of Courage*: A Study of Its Sources, Reputation, Imagery, and Structure," diss. New York Univ., 1963, pp. 215-27; Thomas Gullason, "The Newspaper Version of *The Red Badge of Courage*" in *The Complete Novels of Stephen Crane* (Garden City: Doubleday, 1967), pp. 155-95; Fredson Bowers, "The Text: History and Analysis," in *The Red Badge of Courage,* vol. 2 of the University of Virginia edition of Crane's works (Charlottesville: Univ. Press of Virginia, 1975), pp. 249-52; Donald Pizer, "A Note on the Text," *The Red Badge of Courage* (New York: Norton, 1994), p. ix.

3. This debate has focused chiefly on which form of *Red Badge* best reflects Crane's intentions and thus should be most widely read by students and analyzed by scholars: a version based on the 1895 first edition book published by D. Appleton or a form of Crane's 1894 manuscript. On one side of this debate are the traditionalists, well represented by Donald Pizer, James Colvert, and Michael Guemple, who argue that the 1895 D. Appleton first book edition best reflects Crane's final intentions for his work. On the other side Henry Binder, Hershel Parker, and Steven Mailloux contend that Crane greatly revised his original manuscript at the behest of editor Ripley Hitchcock and so the D. Appleton version is not a true indication of his artistic vision. This debate can be

followed chronologically in William Howarth, "*The Red Badge of Courage* Manuscript: New Evidence for a Critical Edition," *Studies in Bibliography,* 18 (1965), 229-46; Binder, "The *Red Badge of Courage* Nobody Knows," *Studies in the Novel,* 10 (1978), 9-47; Mailloux, "*The Red Badge of Courage* and Interpretive Conventions: Critical Response to a Maimed Text," *Studies in the Novel,* 10 (1978), 48-63; Pizer, "Self-Censorship and Textual Editing," *Textual Criticism and Literary Interpretation,* ed. Jerome J. McGann (Chicago: Univ. of Chicago Press, 1985), 144-61; Parker, "Getting Used to the 'Original Form' of *The Red Badge of Courage,*" in *New Essays on The Red Badge of Courage,* ed. Lee Clark Mitchell (Cambridge: Cambridge Univ. Press, 1986), pp. 25-47; Colvert, "Crane, Hitchcock, and the Binder Edition of *The Red Badge of Courage,*" in *Critical Essays on Stephen Crane's The Red Badge of Courage,* ed. Pizer (Boston: Hall, 1990), pp. 238-63; and Guemple, "A Case for the Appleton *Red Badge of Courage,*" *Resources for American Literary Study,* 21, i (1995), pp. 43-57.

4. Cather also asserted that Crane told her Howells had recommended Bacheller as an outlet for *Red Badge*; see "When I Knew Stephen Crane" (1900), rpt. in *Willa Cather. Stories, Poems, and Other Writings* (New York: Library of America, 1992), p. 933.

5. Bowers, pp. 249-52; George Monteiro and Philip B. Eppard, "Addenda to Bowers and Stallman: Unrecorded Contemporary Appearances of Stephen Crane's Work," *Publications of the Bibliographical Society of America,* 74 (1980), 74; John Berryman, *Stephen Crane* (n. p.: William Sloane Associates, 1950), p. 94n. See "The Red Badge of Courage," *Rochester Herald,* 3, 4, 5, 6, 7, and 8 December 1894, p. 5 each day; *Syracuse Daily Standard,* 4, 5, 6, 7, 8, and 10 December 1894, p. 3 each day; *Knoxville Journal,* 4, 5, 6, 7, 8, and 10 December 1894, p. 6 each day.

6. Curtis Brown, *Contacts* (New York and London: Harper and Bros., 1935), p. 261.

7. Joseph Katz, "Introduction" to *The Red Badge of Courage* (Columbus: Merrill, 1969), p. xii; Cather, p. 936.

8. [Percival Pollard], *Echo,* 1 June 1896, 60-61.

9. Philadelphia *Press* editorial reproduced in Katz (1967), p. 28; Bacheller, pp. 278-79; publicity advertisement, *Minneapolis Tribune,* 2 December 1894, p. 18; *Nebraska State Journal,* 3 December 1894, p. 6 (figure 1), and *Rochester Herald,* 2 December 1894, p. 5.

10. Bowers writes (244) that the novel was deposited for copyright on 27 September 1895 and that it was first advertised for sale in October. Leon Mead, "The Practical Side of Literature," *Gunton's,* 21 (1901), 443; Robert Donald, "Sunday Newspapers in the United States," *Universal Review,* (September-December 1890), 79.

11. *Mark Twain's Letters to His Publishers,* ed. Hamlin Hill (Berkeley: Univ. of California Press, 1967), p. 286.

12. Katz (1967), p. 38. On Crane's use of his clippings, see J. C. Levenson's introduction to *The Red Badge of Courage* (Charlottesville: Univ. Press of Virginia, 1975), p. lxxxix. On Hitchcock's early dealings with Crane, see his preface to *The Red Badge of Courage* (New York: D. Appleton, 1900), pp. v-vi.

13. Hitchcock, p. vi. See Katz (1967), pp. 22-23, for a copy of this contract blank. Levenson writes that it is uncertain who made the cuts in Crane's manuscript (lxxvii) while Katz argues that Crane prepared two typescripts—one for Bacheller and one for book publication (37). See also Bacheller, p. 278.

14. Katz (1967), p. 32; Katz (1969), p. xi; Cather, p. 933. No printings made from stereotype plates have yet been found. These would probably be more uniform than those typeset from galley proof copy, although editors could still have altered the texts by sawing off chunks of stereotyped text.

15. *The Correspondence of Stephen Crane,* I, 81; Berryman, pp. 93-94; Katz (1969), p. xii; Katz (1967), p. 31.

16. Tanselle, "The Bibliography and Textual Study of American Books," in *Needs and Opportunities in the History of the Book: America, 1639-1876,* ed. David D. Hall and John Hench (Worcester: American Antiquarian Society, 1987), p. 244.

17. Wertheim, p. 212; Publicity advertisement, *Nebraska State Journal,* 3 December 1894, p. 6.

18. Circular, October 1886, Scrapbook, S. S. McClure Papers, Lilly Library, Indiana Univ., Bloomington, Ind.; David Bonnell Green, "Sarah Orne Jewett's 'A Dark Night,'" *Papers of the Bibliographical Society of America,* 53 (1959), 331; Kaplan, "The Spectacle

of War in Crane's Revision of History," *New Essays on The Red Badge of Courage,* p. 79.

19. Gullason, p. 187.

20. Gullason, pp. 299, 195, 297.

21. "What Is Read in Syracuse," *Syracuse Daily Standard,* 7 June 1885, p. 7. For reproductions of the illustrations, see Katz (1967), pp. 34-36. For descriptions of illustration captions see Bowers, pp. 249-52; and Kaplan, p. 105.

22. Figure 3 is from the *Nebraska State Journal,* 5 December 1894, p. 5; this banner head can be seen in all the other newspaper versions of *Red Badge* mentioned previously, with the exception of the New York *Press.*

23. Advertisement for Dr. Greene's Nerve Tablets, *Rochester Herald,* 8 December 1894, p. 5; advertisement for "Spanish Nerve Grains," *Kansas City Star,* 6 December 1894, p. 3; advertisements, *Nebraska State Journal* 5 December 1894, p. 5, and 8 December 1894, p. 5; "Laugh In Their Sleeves," *Minneapolis Tribune,* 4 December 1894, p. 4.

24. "Capt. George Dodd," Philadelphia *Press,* 3 December 1894, p. 11.

25. "Newspaper Reading," *Boston Herald,* 15 November 1885, p. 12; G. T. C., "Reaching the Rich," *Printers' Ink,* 26 June 1895, p. 3; Howells, *The Rise of Silas Lapham* (1885; rpt. Bloomington: Indiana Univ. Press, 1971), pp. 78-79; "The Small Change of Literature," *Critic,* 12 (1889), p. 155.

Adam H. Wood (essay date 2009)

SOURCE: Wood, Adam H. "'Crimson Blotches on the Pages of the Past': Histories of Violence in Stephen Crane's *The Red Badge of Courage.*" *War, Literature, and the Arts,* vol. 21, nos. 1-2, 2009, pp. 38-57.

[*In the following essay, Wood discusses the critical contention that* The Red Badge of Courage *(1895) took place at the Battle of Chancellorsville, noting that the location is not as important to the novel as an understanding of whether or not "real" war can be fully conveyed in words.*]

> Future years will never know the seething hell and the black infernal background, the countless minor scenes and interiors of the secession war; and it is best they should not. The real war will never get in the books.
>
> Walt Whitman, *Specimen Days*

> We saw the lightning and that was the guns and then we heard the thunder and that was the big guns; and then we heard the rain falling and that was the blood falling; and when we came to get in the crops, it was dead men that we reaped.
>
> Harriet Tubman, from a postwar speech in Charleston

A great deal of critical attention has been put to identifying the historical actualities of Stephen Crane's ***The Red Badge of Courage: An Episode of the American Civil War.*** The seminal essay of this "historical" approach is surely Harold R. Hungerford's "'That Was at Chancellorsville': The Factual Framework of *The Red Badge of Courage,*" which argues that Crane's story of an aged Henry Fleming, "The Veteran," (published only a year after the novel) clearly establishes Chancellorsville as "a factual framework within to represent the perplexities of his young hero."[1] And surely Hungerford's conclusion is the correct one: indeed, as Hungerford notes, "If we turn to military history," much like Crane himself is said to have done in his perusal of *The Battles and Leaders* series, "we find that the evidence of place and time points directly to Chancellorsville."[2] Hungerford's research, too, is surely accurate in its discussion of the times, places, and movements of troops in the battle of Chancellorsville. And since the publication of Hungerford's essay, the factuality of his findings have little been questioned. Nor, I would suggest, should they be. If we put Crane's novel to the test of times and places, we will surely be led to agree that Hungerford is indeed correct. As Hungerford points out and even evidences in his article's title, it is a much older Henry himself who declares, in a moment of recollection to a youthful, post-Civil War audience, "that was at Chancellorsville."

The question that follows for us, though, is to what use is such historical material put? Or, perhaps, what purpose does isolating Crane's war novel into a single, specific event-frame serve? Or, again, what is at stake in attempting to prove that Crane's novel is *historical* and, certainly more importantly, what is the impetus of this particular style of historicism? That much of the time and place of ***The Red Badge of Courage*** may be—since I have no desire to argue against this position—based in the battle of Chancellorsville tells us what? Does it explain the function of the novel? Certainly the narrative itself—the singular perception of a young Henry Fleming in the midst of war—has little to do with a place called Chancellorsville. Were we to believe that Crane's extensive pouring over popular books and reports on the "factualities" of the Civil War influenced what Hungerford terms the "framework" of the novel and that this subject *requires* such extensive study as Hungerford's, we would have to ask why Crane offers up so little proof *within the novel* to lead to such specificities of time and place.

The desire to distill **Red Badge** to an essential set of "historical" facts can also be read as a desire to isolate the novel—to pigeonhole it—as a *specific* episode of *the Civil War* and not as indicative of the violence of war generally. That is, Crane's lack of acknowledgement of specific times and places—rather, his denial of them—seems of more crucial concern than what Crane knew but refused to admit into the narrative. This absence of history of time and place (of record, of "public" history) draws our attention to specifics because we seek to isolate it; we desire to put history *purely in the past*. In a sense, we might think of this as the reification of historical moments—the separation of events from any continued historical meaning and the subsequent categorization within an historical (c)age. What Hungerford's essay really urges us to do, then, is to ignore the *movement* of the narrative—its terror, violence, and trauma—in lieu of the moment of the "framework." Indeed, in many ways Hungerford's analysis does exactly what Crane's novel sought to undo. In Crane's own words, "the books won't tell me what I want to know." What is it, then, that Crane wants to know? Or, even more directly to our point here, to what extent does Crane have access to the "real" Civil War and, by extension, what role does **Red Badge** play in the construction of this history? Let's begin with another question: to what extent can "real" war be accessible? Surely, the annals of history are filled with war—any perusal of any given history book will certainly remind us of the import of wars in the course of human development. But perhaps that is not even sufficient enough to say; were we to invert the previous phrase, we might more likely arrive at the role of war in history. The course of human development is predicated on the role of war. (We might here borrow a phrase attributed to Mussolini: "blood alone moves the wheels of history.") Were we in a particularly dialectical mood, we might even go so far as to suggest that human development is virtually impossible without war. While this is most certainly not the position maintained here is largely not the point and, as well, this position refuses to offer us any insight. For the question is not to what extent war is part and parcel of human development, it is rather to what extent "real" war is accessible.

Histories of War, War Fictions, and the Space Between

There are, in effect, two distinct and disparate popular histories of the Civil War functioning, intermingling, and ultimately conflicting with each other in **Red Badge**. The first, as already hinted at, is the proliferation of Civil War "primary material." Embodied most thoroughly, and, we might add, most officially, by the *Battles and Leaders* series, this primary material is presented as the ultimate reference to the real war; this series, and others like it, attempt to present the Civil War both *subjectively* in interviews with soldiers and *objectively* in both the Generals' accounts and the new genre of photography. That is, a sense of coherence is imposed on the Civil War in that the selected subjective and objective accounts serve to justify, to "real"-ize, each other. But these "complete" accounts serve not so much to present the war as it was—the "real" war—but rather to present the war as a complete whole: an event beyond further discussion. This ideological impetus is even made clear in the introduction to the *Battles and Leaders* series:

> For the most part, each side has confined controversy to its own ranks, and both have emphasized the benefit as well as the glory of the issue. Coincident with the progress of the series during the past three years, may be noted a marked increase in the number of fraternal meetings between Union and Confederate veterans, enforcing the conviction that the nation is restored in spirit as in fact, and that each side is contributing its share to the new heritage of manhood and peace.[3]

Thus, as has been aptly pointed out by Amy Kaplan, these "histories" seek to present a sense of national post-war unity; indeed, as Kaplan argues, a great deal of these histories "excised political conflict from the collective memory of the war."[4] Or, to twist Kaplan's phrasing, we might suggest that the excision of political conflict functions to impose a collective memory of the war; that the war was, in fact, predicated on political conflict is erased in view of a post-war desire for national coherence and unity. This imposed unity serves two distinct purposes: 1) to establish the Civil War as a closed system, an event (ideologically) completed and, less our concern here (though it is largely Kaplan's concern), 2) to bolster nationalism in the face of an expanding American capitalistic imperialism and the resulting international wars.[5]

But Crane's novel endorses neither of these positions. Rather, what we might say Crane takes or borrows from histories such as *Great Battles and Leaders* is a matter of sheer location. That is, the uses to which Crane's primary textual research are put are essentially limited to descriptions of place. In point of fact, the conjecture that the central battle in **Red Badge** is considered to be modeled on the battle of Chancellorsville is based almost entirely on the placement of objects (rivers, roads, etc.) and the placement of troops. Thus, while we may rightly assume that the (literal) backdrop of the novel is the battle of Chancellorsville, this knowledge provides little insight into the actual subject matter of the novel. Even discussions of the Generals in **Red Badge** fail to reflect their representation in *Battles and Leaders*; what readers encounter of the Generals is almost entirely from the mouths of the nearly anonymous soldiers and, more importantly, presented in a less than positive tone. For example, Henry's understanding of the process of war attributes nothing to the Generals themselves: "'well, then, if we fight like the devil an' don't ever whip, it must be the general's fault [...] And I don't see any sense in fighting and fighting and fighting, yet always losing through some derned old lunkhead of a general'" (89).[6] Clearly, Crane is not interested in presenting the Civil War in the same manner as the *Battles and Leaders* series. Further, given the lack of attention put to the Generals in **Red Badge** in lieu of the attention put to the single soldier Henry (in direct contrast to the structure of *Battles and Leaders*), we must recognize that Crane's novel should not be seen as ideologically coherent with the dominant mode of reading the Civil War in the late 1890s.

The other "popular" representations of the Civil War that we may likely assume Crane had at least a familiarity with are the 19th century sentimental novels which, like Crane's novel, use the Civil War as a backdrop. These novels, though extremely popular and prolific, work in many ways to ideologically seal the Civil War in much the same fashion as many of the histories. Indeed, in an excellent review of much of this type of sentimental fiction, Kathleen Diffley, in her essay "The Roots of Tara: Making War Civil," argues that "Like the magazine fiction during and just after the war, these novels represent the postwar Union as a marriage between Northern hero and Southern heroine."[7] The purpose for representing the War in such romantic terms is quite clear for Diffley—a position quite agreed with here: "When it came time to shape the Civil War in popular culture, that ideal was in the ascendant."[8] That is, Diffley suggests that the sentimental fiction of the Civil War had, as its ultimate goal, to present the war in purely domestic terms, to present the war *as a necessity* to the ultimate union—read here as marriage—between the North and the South.

Crane's familiarity with such romantic, sentimentalized fiction is clear from the early pages of **Red Badge**. As the youth recalls leaving his small, hometown environment,

> there was [... a] darker [haired] girl whom he had gazed at steadfastly, and he thought she grew demure and sad at the sight of his blue and brass. As he had walked down the path between the row of oaks, he had turned his head and detected her at a window watching his departure. As he perceived her, she had immediately begun to stare up through the high tree branches at the sky. He had seen a good deal of flurry and haste in her movement as she changed her attitude.
>
> (6)

And while Crane tells us that "He often thought of her," this "darker girl" appears only once more and in a fantasy of *telling* a war story: "he imagined [...] the ejaculations of his mother and the young lady at the seminary as they drank his recitals" (86). Even Henry's belief in the "good deal of flurry" she displayed is augmented by the distorted line of vision Henry has: what he remembers seeing is merely what he desired to see.

There is a second—and perhaps more important—consideration of the romantic subplot a bit further into the novel when, more in line with Diffley's discussion, a young, southern woman appears. It is not, though, the sentimental affectation that Diffley identifies as the union of the northern hero and the southern heroine: "A rather fat soldier attempted to pilfer a horse from a dooryard [...] He was escaping with his prize when a young [southern] girl rushed from the house and grabbed the animal's mane. The young girl, with pink cheeks and shining eyes, stood like a dauntless statue" (15). And while Crane may, indeed, be playing on certain romantic notions by describing this young girl "with pink cheeks and shining eyes"—and image often associated with the flush of romance—her actions are anything but romantic. Thus, even though we are told that "The observant regiment, standing at rest in the roadway, whooped at once, and entered whole-souled upon the side of the maiden" (15), once again Crane sidesteps the romantic notion by adding that the regiment's support of the southern girl is less to her benefit than it is to belittle the fat soldier. Further, the novel debunks the romantic aspect by reminding the reader that this distraction is, in fact, just that: "The men became so engrossed in this affair that they entirely ceased to remember *their own large war*" (my emphasis 15). But, mere paragraphs later, the regiment returns to its military service. This brief section therefore inverts the tendencies of the popular, romantic Civil War novel: the romantic novel eschews the "large war"—that is, the actual war itself—in lieu of the romantic sub-plot while **Red Badge** introduces the northern/southern romantic subplot as a farce. Indeed, it is momentary distraction, and "real" romance is nowhere to be seen.[9]

That popular representations in the 1890s of the Civil War are either mired in a historicity of simple time and place or distracted by sentimentalized and romantic subplots may all be seen to function within an ideology of national (re)unification. Both types of accounts, then, are of interest not for what they tell us about the Civil War but rather for what they fail or refuse to tell us about it, what they "write out" of the history of the war: *the actual violence of war itself*. This phenomenon of omission has been effectively analyzed by Elaine Scarry in an excellent essay entitled "Injury and the Structure of War" where she argues that histories of war (both properly historical and literary) must exorcise violence (or, to use her term, injury) from representation in order to present war as "an outcome [that] cannot be (or should not, or must not be) contested."[10] In a lengthy paragraph that bears reproducing here, Scarry outlines the structure of war and the (necessitated) omission of violence:

> The main purpose of war is injuring. Though this fact is too self-evident and massive ever to be directly contested, it can be indirectly contested by many means and can disappear from view along many separated paths. It may disappear from view simply by being omitted: one can read many pages of an historic or strategic account of a particular military campaign [...] without encountering the acknowledgement that the purpose of the event described is to alter (to burn, to blast, to shell, to cut) human tissue, as well as to alter the surface, shape, and deep entirety of the objects that human beings recognize as extensions of themselves. In any given instance, omission may occur out of the sense that this activity is too self-evident to require articulation; it may instead originate in a failure of perception on the part of the describer; again [and this is largely Scarry's position] it may arise out of an active desire to misrepresent the central content of war's activity [...].[11]

Examining the multiple ways in which this misrepresentation by omission functions, Scarry argues that the predominant tendency of military histories is to alter or remove the language of the individuals in war and to substitute it with a meta-language *of* war:

> the intricacies and complications of the massive geographical interactions between two armies of opposing [sides] tend to be represented without frequent reference to the actual injuries occurring to the hundreds of thousands of soldiers involved: the movements and actions of the armies are emptied of human content and occur as a rarefied choreography of disembodied events.[12]

And this realization of omission is not lost on Crane. As Henry recalls the weeks before he enlisted, he remembers that "The newspapers, the gossip of the village, his own picturings, had aroused him to an uncheckable degree. They were *in truth* fighting finely down there. Almost every day the newspapers printed accounts of a decisive victory" (4, my emphasis). What Henry "hears" about the war—from the newspapers and local gossip, largely fueled, of course, by the local papers—is distinctly non-corporeal. As J. Cutler Andrews notes in his study *The North Reports the Civil War*, because of "the excited state of the public mind [...] both press and government [felt] that it was neither wise nor safe to reveal the exact truth of [a] disgraceful episode."[13] As a result, Cutler continues, "[m]ost Northerners so thoroughly believed that the South was playing a game of bluster and bluff that they fancied the war still might be won by a display of force and with a minimum of bloodshed" and, further, that the Northern press was quick to omit any Northern defeat and casualties "and to look forward to the future instead for victories yet to be one."[14] Not only is Henry's "side" (the North) well on its way to a "decisive victory," from these accounts there appears to be no wounded, virtually no deaths whatsoever.

Further, and still quite in line with Scarry's structuration of war, are what in the previous quote are identified as Henry's "own picturings." Just a page earlier in the novel, we are given view of what these picturings are—though we may rightly assert that they are not, in fact, merely his own individual picturings:

> He had, of course, dreamed of battles all his life—of vague and bloody conflicts that had thrilled him with their sweep and fire. In visions he had seen himself in many struggles. He had imagined peoples secure in the shadow of his eagle-eyed prowess. But awake he had regarded battles as crimson blotches on the pages of the past. He had put them as things of the bygone with his thought-images of heavy crowns and high castles. There was a portion of the world's history which he had regarded as the time of wars, but it, he thought, had been long gone over the horizon and had disappeared forever.
>
> (3)

The source(s) for these romanticized picturings are fairly obvious. Whether we want to locate the source in the Homeric myth-structure (as Warren D. Anderson has[15]) or Arthurian legends or any other romanticized representation of war, the effect is quite clear: while Henry does see blood in these struggles, it is always "vague" and absent. Actual violence and injury are surpassed by the "Greeklike struggle": "They might not be distinctly Homeric, but there seemed to be much glory in them" (3).

Thus, the first sign of actual death in *Red Badge* doesn't occur until the third chapter, and when it does, it is presented without blood and only after the fact of violence—that is, "the line encountered the body of a dead soldier" (22). What is unique, though, about this soldier's death is that Crane doesn't necessarily attribute the soldier's death to battle; there is no mention of blood, no mention of a wound of any kind. Instead, "it was as if fate had betrayed the soldier" (22). This betrayal, as Henry appears to read it, removes any chivalry or honor from the death. It is, Crane tells us, incapable of telling Henry (or the reader) anything about the nature of war: "He [Henry] vaguely desired walk around and around the body and stare; the impulse of the living to try to read in dead eyes the answer to the Question" (22). What, exactly, the "Question" is, though, Crane never tells us. Instead, he simply moves on to the next paragraph, leaving the image of the dead man behind.

The first real instance of battle *proper* doesn't occur until the sixth chapter in *Red Badge*, and in it is most certainly not chivalry or heroism. In the moment of battle, Henry's perceptions—up until this point largely mere conjecture as to how he might act in this moment—take what many critics have described as a distinctly impressionistic feel: Crane writes, "He began to exaggerate the endurance, the skill, and the valor of those who were coming. Himself reeling from exhaustion, he was astonished beyond measure at such persistency. They must be machines of steel" (39). As the tension increases, so does the impressionism: "To the youth it was an onslaught of redoubtable dragons [...] He waited in a sort of horrified, listening attitude. He seemed to shut his eyes and wait to be gobbled" (39). What Crane appears to be working towards here is clear; with the increase in tension, in fear, in the "unknown," metaphors become more impressionistic.[16] This increase in abstraction of meaning can be read as the increased difficulty Henry has in making any sort of sense for (and of) himself in the moment of battle. That is, Henry's resorting to the image of the dragon leads us back to the discussions of the Homeric or Arthurian sense of battle; clearly, though, the chivalry with which he once viewed such tales is ultimately inaccessible in this moment.

Paralleling Henry is another soldier, obviously in the same state of mortal peril, "whose face had borne an expression of exalted courage, the majesty of he who dares give his life, was, at an instant, smitten abject" (39). Once this other soldier "blanched like one who has come to the edge of a cliff at midnight and is suddenly made aware" (39), Crane largely abandons the surreal metaphors and opts for a more direct observation of action, not sensory perception: "There was a revelation. He, too, threw down his gun and fled. There was no shame in his face" (39). It should be noted that the "awareness" that this soldier appears to display is modified by the use of "like": Crane is not suggesting that this soldier, in fact, *did* become aware of something, but rather that his behavior, his *expression* is indescribable. There is no shame on his face to speak of because shame is an emotion that can occur retrospectively, in reading the moment (an issue I will address below). What this soldier experiences—as Crane writes—is the abject, the *inexpressible*: as Julia Kristeva posits in *Powers of Horror,*

> The abject has only one quality of the object—that of being opposed to *I*. If the object, however, through its opposition, settles me within the fragile texture of a desire for meaning, which, as a matter of fact, makes me ceaselessly and infinitely homologous to it, what is *abject,* on the contrary, the jettisoned object, is radically excluded and draws me toward the place where meaning collapses.[17]

Thus, the "trance" that Henry "shakes" as he, too, begins to run is that of an attempt to make meaning out of what amounts to, in the moment, a meaningless situation or, rather, a situation which is *contrary* to meaning. What was on his face, Crane tells us, "was the horror of those things which he imagined" (40). What he imagined, though, Crane won't—or, perhaps, can't—tell us. It is as if what runs through Henry's mind at this moment, like that which is reflected on his comrade's face, is also abject, also beyond representation.

Further, the second scene of death provides little more meaning than the first. In fact, against Henry's initial chivalric notions of war, we are told that "[t]here was a singular absence of heroic poses," and even the officers—those who should, ideally, be the exemplars of heroism—"neglected to stand in picturesque attitudes" (34). The captain of Henry's regiment, Crane writes, "had been killed in an early part of the action":

> His body lay stretched out in the position of a tired man resting, but upon his face there was an astonished and sorrowful look, as if he thought some friend had done him an ill turn. [...] Another grunted suddenly as if he had been struck by a club in the stomach. In his eyes was there was a mute, indefinite reproach.
>
> (35)

These two victims (though we don't really know if the second, in fact, died) work to reinforce the lesson of the dead man stumbled upon. Or, rather, they serve to reinforce that with death there is no lesson at all. The captain's face only provides an "astonished and sorrowful" look, and the second victim, similarly, displays only "a mute, indefinite reproach"—certainly not the grand meaning Henry hopes he should find in death. (It should be noted here that Crane reminds us of the *disunion* of the war in the phrase "as if [...] some friend had done him an ill turn": this is quite reminiscent of the cliché that the Civil War pitted brother against brother). A few paragraphs later, after the enemy "charge has been repulsed," the soldiers—Henry among them—are left "silent": "Apparently they were *trying* to contemplate themselves" (35, my emphasis). Again, Crane points out that the meaning of the event—of a series of deaths—is absent. That these representations occur so early in the novel is not peculiar; indeed, the entirety of the rest of the novel works predominantly to debunk such overly romantic notions of chivalry and glory.

It should be clear, then, that **Red Badge** acknowledges but ultimately refuses to merely reiterate dominant conceptions of the Civil War as presented in both popular histories and popular fictional accounts. Instead, what I will argue below, is that Crane's narrative works to reintroduce—to *reanimate*—the horror, the violence, and the injury of the Civil War that was largely omitted by stepping outside of any representation of the war that seeks to present it as a closed system, an historically isolated system, a system without the bodies and minds of the individuals—and the violence they enact and is enacted upon them—without which war itself would be an impossibility.

Reanimating Blood and Guts; or, a Different Kind of Specifics

"Nothing so delighted him," Alfred Kazin tells us, "as the conviction held by Civil War Veterans that Stephen Crane had been in the Civil War himself."[18] Thus, while many early critics of *Red Badge* charged Crane with antinationalism in his depictions of American soldiers as cowards (see the controversy within the pages of the *Dial* magazine, most notably the vicious response by Civil War veteran General Alexander C. McClurg[19]), obviously Crane's imagination had led him to something quintessential about the nature of the individual in the face of battle. Where Crane got his information, given that it has been established that this "information" is not from the histories, romance novels, or soldier's journals, we will likely never truly know. It is possible, perhaps, that Crane interviewed veterans, posing questions to them that had not been posed before; it is also possible, as Lars Ahnebrink suggests, that the "source" of the narrative derives largely from the influence of Tolstoy and Zola; or, as a third option, we might be led to agree with Larzer Ziff who suggests that "He would supply this from his imagination."[20] All of these are good possibilities but none of them account for his accuracy and, more importantly, specifics.

If, as I've argued above, Crane is little concerned with the specifics of time and place in terms of representing the Civil War, then we must look to a different kind of specifics. In an essay largely dedicated to the fiction of the Vietnam War, "War Stories: 'Truth' and Particulars," Sean M. Braswell asserts that authors of war stories, "somehow, through words, [...] might impress the impact of [...] experience on the very nerves of their listeners and make them understand what [the soldier in war] felt."[21] Further, Braswell poses a question we may likely assume Crane would have asked of a post-Civil War generation: "how can people truly understand something they have never themselves experienced?"[22] The answer, as Braswell sees it, is not in relating *verifiable* facts and events—times, places, names—but is instead in being able to convey exactly what times, places, and names can't get to: "the sheer unfamiliarity of it [...] the complete otherness of war."[23] In essence, Braswell suggests, in order to convey the "truth" of war (his term of use), the author must essentially defamiliarize and disrupt any preconceived notions about war in its entirety.[24]

In a little cited and discussed late essay, "Concerning the Accounts Given by the Residents of Hiroshima," Georges Bataille addresses what might be considered the central problem in *representing* "the truth" of war and the atrocities contained therein. And while Bataille's focus is obviously World War II and the hydrogen bomb that provided the closing "bracket" for that war, his essay suggests a more general phenomena: the disparity between accounts given in the moment (by those in the actuality and "action" of the war) and post-war accounts that attempt to render a certain (ideological) coherence or meaning to the moments of war. For those "in the action" of war (soldiers and civilians, victors and victims)—those actually existing between the concussions of bombs and discharges of firearms—the immediacy of war becomes (obviously, by means of necessity and the "death drive") the only available perspective. That is, according to Bataille, "it is in isolation and in complete ignorance of [the material violence of war that] was suddenly upon them, that the revelation—the meager, shattering unending revelation—began for each of them."[25] It is this "revelation" that Crane identifies within Henry. The revelation, though, is not a revelation of understanding—Henry here *does not* understand anything about the war or his place in it—but, rather, a revelation about the simple fact of death itself.

For the inhabitants of Hiroshima, Bataille continues, the largesse of the hydrogen bomb was lost in the attempts to make meaning in and only in that particular moment. It was not a moment of historic proportions for those who witnessed it—those who were *subject* to it—because "the individual in the streets [...] learned nothing from the colossal explosion. He submitted to it like an animal, not even knowing its gigantic scope. On the ground, for the isolated man, a bomb had exploded right near by; there was no momentous event, no leap into the future."[26] What the "individual on the ground" witnessed, then, was not a moment of history but rather a moment without history: a moment momentarily outside of history and, by extension, *outside of meaning*. It is of little surprise, then, that Henry's musings suggest that the nature of war—of history itself—seems to be beyond him. "For a time he had to labor to make himself believe," Crane writes, "He could not accept with assurance that he was about to mingle in one of those great affairs of the earth" (3). Henry cannot fathom himself as an agent of history because, at least in his own mind, as of yet, this moment has not been made historical.

The Red Badge of Courage is not a retelling of the events of the Civil War—as Hungerford and others have attempted to cast it—it is a "look at war, the red animal—war, the blood-swollen god" (23). The novel, then, must be read not as referencing some pre-existing written history, but (as Henry feels his place in war) the novel is "doomed alone to unwritten responsibilities" (23). And though I have no intention of suggesting that Henry is Crane or vice versa, we may apply this sense to what Crane felt his purpose was in writing the novel: to return to the history of war what had been up until then (and is still the case today in the 21st century) largely unwritten—violence, death, and chaos. While all of the historical accounts discussed above mention death, it is almost always presented in a highly abstracted form; indeed, even the most official of accounts—the *Battles and Leaders* texts—have, as the final entry, statistics on the death tolls and the causes (killed in action, died from wounds, etc.) but have *nothing* on the actual violence of combat. These numbers, therefore, can tell the reader nothing about battle.

We might be led, then, to assume that Crane's narrative fails to truly convey the horror and atrocity of war. This, however, is not the case. In order to understand the function of Crane's narrative, we may return to Braswell. For just as Braswell considers Vietnam war journalist Michael Herr's *Dispatches,* we can consider **Red Badge**: "He constructs no framework that a civilized reader can use to put the experience of war in perspective. Instead he allows the images and the soldiers to speak for themselves, bringing a surreal intensity to the events."[27] It is not the time and place of a battle that is of central import, then; it is what cannot be codified by history books and romantic revisions. Thus, what Crane's narrative attempts to convey—much like Herr's book—is what historical specificities cannot achieve: the perceptions of the soldiers in *the moment of violence*.

Attempting to return to his regiment after his flight from battle, Henry stumbles upon a procession of wounded soldiers, finding himself caught within a moment of violence: "The youth joined this crowd and marched along with it. The torn bodies expressed the awful machinery in which the men had been entangled" (50). This description of the "awful machinery" which functions *solely* by its "produc[tion of] corpses" is, in essence, what marks Crane's narrative as unique; war is not presented as an end result—a teleological system—but as a system of violent insatiability. War does not produce heroes; it produces mangled bodies. Of particular focus here is the soldier Crane identifies as "the tattered man," who is first presented as simply as bearing "an expression of awe and admiration" for a "bearded sergeant" (50). This initial image certainly seems to play off of the heroic nature of war until we realize that what initially appears to Henry as the "awe and admiration" for heroism is, most likely, a state of shock. As the tattered man attempts to talk with Henry, the violence this man has encountered becomes abundantly clear:

> After a time he began to sidle near to the youth, and in a different way try to make him a friend. Hs voice was gentle as a girl's voice and his eyes were pleading. The youth saw with surprise that the soldier had two wounds, one in the head, bound with a blood-soaked rag, and the other in the arm, making that member dangle like a broken bough.
>
> (50-51)

Again, the sheer corporeal violence enacted here works to de-romanticize the heroism of war. The tattered man's voice—not the heroic, masculinized ballast of wartime oaths and declarations—is presented as "gentle as a girl's." More importantly is Henry's realization of the actual violence sustained in battle of blood-soaked rags and dangling, near-amputated limbs, or, as Crane reemphasizes, "the bloody and grim figure" of the man (51).

Upon abandoning the tattered soldier (an equally unromantic move) and returning to his regiment—now with his own wound—Henry discovers that the violence of war he saw enacted on the tattered man is not exclusive to this single soldier. Indeed, Crane presents this image not as a peculiarity of war, but of the commonplace:

> About him were the rows and groups of men that he had dimly seen the previous night. They were getting a last draught of sleep before the awakening. The gaunt, care-worn features and dusty figures were made plain by this quaint light at the dawning, but it dressed the skin of the men in corpselike hues and made the tangled limbs appear pulseless and dead. [...] He believed for an instant that he was in the house of the dead, and he did not dare to move lest these corpses start up, squalling and squawking. [...] He saw that this somber picture was not a fact of the present, but a mere prophecy.
>
> (79)

The imagery here is strikingly similar to that of the tattered man—the corpselike appearance, the dangling, near-severed limbs. The similarity draws our attention not so much to the similarity *per se* but to the *reality* of the image, the insistence of the image. Thus, that Crane tells us that "this somber picture was not a fact of the present" takes nothing away from reading this as *the moment of violence,* but rather that this moment is one that seems to repeat itself *ad nauseum*. That it is "a mere prophecy" is not a future projection—for Henry, for anyone—as much as it is the irrepressible *truth* of war itself: it is "the pitiless monotony of conflicts" (118).

Meaning in Death; or, the Problem of Teleology

There are, of course, numerous images of the viscerality of violence scattered through the pages of **Red Badge** and, most, if not all, are also an examination of death itself. Two of the most moving, though, are quite similar in their depiction of death and the collapse of meaning. The first occurs after Henry's flight from battle. Attempting to find some sort of refuge (both physical and mental), Henry stumbles into what he perceives to be a sanctuary: "At length he reached place where the high, arching boughs made a chapel. [...] There was a religious half light" (46). This image of chapel implies a place of revelation, of, perhaps, the metaphysical understanding Henry so desperately seeks. Deliverance, though, is not to be found:

> Near the threshold he stopped, horror-stricken at the sight of a thing. He was being looked at by a dead man who was seated with his back against a columnlike tree. The corpse was dressed in a uniform that once had been blue, but was now faded to a melancholy shade of green. The eyes, staring at the youth, had changed to the dull hue to be seen on the side of a dead fish. The mouth was open. Its red had changed to an appalling yellow. Over the gray skin of the face ran little ants. One was trundling some sort of bundle along the upper lip.
>
> (46)

Far from providing Henry with the spiritual solace and understanding he seeks—it is Henry's own mind that transforms the forest into a chapel—the image of this dead soldier deconstructs any religious (and, we should note, nationalistic) symbolism. That is, Crane's descriptions certainly play off of religious, Christian imagery but ultimately fail to conjure any sense of piety. The dead man—seated as he is as God is often perceived between heavenly columns—is "faded," "melancholy," and "dull," not imbued with the glorious light of the heavens. Further, this dead man can offer no salvation. Holy words do not emanate from his open mouth; all that this dead man can express is death itself. Even the color of the mouth, once the red imagery of the saving blood of the Lord, is merely an "appalling yellow." To more fully understand the import of this image, we may return to Kristeva, "[a] wound with blood and pus, or the sickly, acrid smell of sweat, of decay, does not *signify* death. [...] The corpse, seen without God [...] is the utmost of abjection. It is death infecting life."[28] This dead body can provide no salvation for Henry; it can provide no meaning to the events he bears witness to.

The second image of a mouth incapable of expression occurs during the next battle. "The orderly sergeant of the youth's company was shot through the cheeks," Crane writes, "Its supports being injured, his jaw hung afar down, disclosing in the wide cavern of his mouth a pulsing mass of blood and teeth. And with it all he made attempts to cry out. In his endeavor there was a dreadful earnestness, as if he conceived that one great shriek would make him well" (121). Again, on the face of death there is only death; from the mouth of the sergeant—the authority, the "leader"—comes only corporeal material, blood, teeth. And despite his attempts to cry out—to express, to expurgate—he emits only silence. There is no ascension, no deliverance. The only movement, Crane describes, is "[t]he youth saw him presently go rearward" (121). This "rearward," is not a movement up to an understanding Heaven or even down to an equally understanding Hell, it is simply back, out of sight, out of meaning itself.

On this desire for death to have meaning, we may look to Bataille in his essay "Hegel, Death and Sacrifice" where he formulates the fundamental problem of seeking meaning in death: "In order for Man to reveal himself ultimately to himself, he would have to die, but he would have to do it while living—watching himself ceasing to be. In other words, death itself would have to become (self-)consciousness at the very moment that it annihilates the conscious being."[29] The possibility of this, obviously, is highly problematic. For death to have meaning it must be experienced by the individual who seeks this meaning but, if actually dead, no meaning for the individual can occur. The way around this, Bataille suggests, is through the subterfuge of the sacrifice: by imposing death on another animal body, "the sacrificer identifies himself with the animal that is struck down dead. And so he dies in seeing himself die [...] But it is a comedy! At least it would be a comedy if some other method existed which could reveal to the living the invasion of death [...]."[30] That is, the "knowledge," the "understanding" that is acquired in this subterfuge is not, in fact, the knowledge of death that is ultimately sought. For the individual soldier, the man on the ground in the moment of violence, there can be no genuine meaning whatsoever. Meaning in death—like any meaning constructed linguistically—can only occur by a negation of the individual (the erasure of difference) and an imposition of a totalizing meaning: *a meaning the same for all.*

Conclusion: Public Meaning, Private Memories

As I have attempted to establish, there is a conflict within **Red Badge** between what amounts to violence devoid of coherent meaning and the (later) imposition of meaning—of history—onto that violence. Tied to this, of course, is the central discrepancy of the perspective of the individual in the moment which is rooted in (and only in) the violence that is war and the imposed historical teleology that seeks, by omission, to negate the role of both violence and the individual. The omission of violence—of death itself—from the history of the Civil War is (as it is for any war) in many ways not terribly surprising. For the individual, the man on the ground, the omission of the visceral, corporeal, violence—in short, *the atrocity that is war*—is excised out of a need for survival. But it is now for a survival *beyond the moment*. That is, as Richard Holmes describes in *Acts of War: The Behavior of Men in Battle*, many soldiers upon exiting the realm of battle lock traumatic memories "away like an album of horrible photographs [...] viewed only with pain and reluctance: indeed, a few of the images may be so hideous that they are excised altogether."[31] But, of course, as Freud would outline more than fifty years after the Civil War, such trauma can never fully excised: There is, always, the return of the repressed. Most often, though, those who actually experienced the trauma of war are incapable of representing their trauma, their history. It is, as Cathy Carruth argues in her introduction to *Trauma: Explorations in Memory*, "the traumatized, we might say, carry an impossible history within them, or they become themselves the symptom of a history that they cannot entirely possess."[32]

That the subject of trauma becomes a "symptom" of history leads us to understand the omission of their perspectives from what becomes, only after the fact, history itself. That is, as with *The Battles and Leaders* series with which I began this analysis, what does not conform to a history that reduces war strictly to its political aftereffects—which, of course, seek to present the war as a closed system, a system already established in a meaning of (re)union—must be presented, if presented at all, as abhorrent. How, then, do we situate the war novel? Or, perhaps more accurately phrased, how do we read a novel with such specific historical connotations? The relationship between the war as event and the war as narrative—by "sheer volume" or intensity we might say—must be understood in terms specific to the unique place (as moment and discourse) that (the) war occupies. We must then pose a new set of questions to this unique historical and aesthetic relationship: To wht extent is the war, in fact, the subject? Or is the subject simply placed in the setting of war? To what extent is historical accuracy taken and, perhaps more importantly, which historical discourse(s) are prioritized (the victor or the victim, victor as moral victim, victim as moral victor)? How does the specific aesthetic form respond to and reanimate the event(s) to which it must ultimately claim as "source?" And, lastly, what function does the novel play in the (furthering) development of discourses of war and violence generally? *The Red Badge of Courage,* I have attempted to display, works to reanimate the abject, to return to war its essential aspects of violence—its injury, its death—in order to remind us, as readers, as secondary subjects of war: that the voices of those who cannot speak or are silenced may still be heard and, thus, may alter our awareness of a violent historical past and, more importantly, our ambivalence about our own violent present and potential future. *The Red Badge of Courage* functions, then, as Crane himself wrote, to reanimate those "crimson blotches on the pages of the past."

Notes

1. Harold R. Hungerford, "'That Was at Chancellorsville': The Factual Framework of *The Red Badge of Courage*," *American Literature* 64, no. 4 (1963): 520.

2. Ibid., 521.

3. Robert Johnson and Clarence Buel, eds. *Battles and Leaders of the Civil: The Opening Battles.* Vol.1. 1887 (New York: Century Co. 1887-88), X.

4. Amy Kaplan, *The Social Construction of American Realism* (Chicago: University of Chicago Press, 1992), 80.

5. For further discussion of the relationship between Crane's novel and capitalism, see Daniel Shanahan, "The Army Motif in *The Red Badge of Courage* as a Response to Industrial Capitalism," *Papers on Language and Literature* 32, no. 4 (1996): 399-410.

6. Stephen Crane, *The Red Badge of Courage: An Episode of the American Civil War* (New York: Bantam 1964), 89. All subsequent references are indicated parenthetically in the text of the essay.

7. Kathleen Diffley, "The Roots of Tara: Making War Civil," *American Quarterly* 63, no. 3 (1984): 369.

8. Ibid., 362.

9. See also Alice Fahs, "The Feminized Civil War: Gender, Northern Popular Literature, and the Memory of the War, 1861-1900," *The Journal of American History* 85, no. 4 (1989): 1461-94.

10. Elaine Scarry, "Injury and the Structure of War," *Representations* 10 (1985): 38.

11. Ibid., 1.

12. Ibid., 7.

13. J. Culter Andrews, *The North Reports the Civil War* (Pittsburgh: University of Pittsburgh Press, 1955), 77.

14. Ibid., 77, 100-101.

15. Warren D. Anderson, "Homer and Stephen Crane," *Nineteenth Century Fiction* 19, no. 1 (1964): 77-86.

16. See, for example, Joseph Conrad's discussions of Crane's fictive techniques in "Stephen Crane: A Note Without Dates" where he declares that Crane's greatest "gift" as a writer was his "impressionism of phrase." Further, Conrad notes that Crane

   > had indeed a wonderful power of vision, which he applied to the things of this earth and of our mortal humanity with a penetrating force that seemed to reach, within life's appearances and forms, the very spirit of life's truth. His ignorance of the world at large—he had seen very little of it—did not stand in the way of his imaginative grasp of facts, events, and picturesque men.

   Joseph Conrad, *Notes On Life and Letters,* ed. J. H. Stape (Cambridge: Cambridge University Press, 2004), 45.

17. Julia Kristeva, *Powers of Horror,* trans. Leon S. Roudiez (New York: Columbia University Press 1982), 1-2.

18. Alfred Kazin, introduction to *The Red Badge of Courage: An Episode of the American Civil War* (New York: Bantam, 1964), xiv.

19. The original source is from a letter written to the *Dial,* April 16 1896; reprinted in Richard Weatherford, *Stephen Crane* (New York: Routledge, 1997), 138-41.

20. Larzer Ziff, *The American 1890s: Life and Times of a Lost Generation* (New York: Viking, 1966), 195.

21. Sean Braswell, "War Stories: 'Truth' and Particulars," *War, Literature and the Arts* 11, no. 2 (1999), 148.

22. Ibid., 148.

23. Ibid., 149.

24. For a similar connective strategy, see James A. Stevenson, "Beyond Stephen Crane: *Full Metal Jacket*," *Literature/Film Quarterly* 16 (1988): 238-243.

25. Georges Bataille, "Concerning the Accounts Given by the Residents of Hiroshima," in *Trauma: Explorations in Memory,* ed. Cathy Carruth (Baltimore: Johns Hopkins University Press, 1995), 223.

26. Ibid., 224.

27. Braswell, "War Stories," 151.

28. Kristeva, *Powers of Horror,* 3-4.

29. Georges Bataille, "Hegel, Death, Sacrafice," *Yale French Studies* 78 (1990): 19.

30. Ibid., 19.

31. Richard Holmes, *Acts of War: The Behavior of Men in Battle* (New York: Free Press, 1986), 31.

32. Cathy Carruth, introduction to *Trauma: Explorations in Memory,* ed. Cathy Carruth (Baltimore: Johns Hopkins University Press, 1995), 5.

Joseph M. Meyer (essay date 2017)

SOURCE: Meyer, Joseph M. "Henry's Quest for Narrative in *The Red Badge of Courage.*" *Midwest Quarterly,* vol. 59, no. 1, 2017, pp. 23-38.

[*In the following essay, Meyer notes the critical debate over whether Henry Fleming has matured by the end of* The Red Badge of Courage *(1895) and suggests that his final thoughts are the beginning of his acceptance of a "personal narrative construction" to make sense of his trauma.*]

An ongoing debate surrounding Crane's ***The Red Badge of Courage*** concerns the validity of Henry Fleming's language at the end of the novel: should we or should we not believe that the young soldier has in some way matured, or does Crane's permeating irony—along with Fleming's romanticized views of war—automatically make us skeptical of any insights that he may have gained about what it means to be mature? John J. McDermott is one of the few critics who believes that the young soldier experiences a genuine movement "from sham heroics to genuine heroics for immature reasons, to a final pattern of courageous action performed primarily in response to his own matured demands on himself" (330). On the other side of the debate, Donald Pizer argues that Fleming's assertions at the end of the novel are an "exercise in sliding-door conscience" that "would appear to cast much doubt on the legitimacy" of his claims to maturity (2). One of the problems with this debate as it stands is that, as Charles Swann notes, "both readings are possible" (95). The ending of the novel certainly elicits strong reactions and invites us to carefully consider the evolution of Fleming's maturation. Rather than claiming my preference for one reading over the other, I would like to consider the impetus for the young soldier to say anything at all.

In light of the more recent research on PTSD and the use of narrative construction therapy, it is time for us to reconsider this debate. At the heart of the discussion is our judgment of Fleming's language and interpretation of the events he experiences—the story that makes up ***Red Badge***. However, perhaps it is not the story itself that we should be evaluating. Instead, I propose that we think about ***Red Badge*** as a type of narrative construction therapy.

This study focuses on the premise that what Fleming says at the conclusion of the novel is not as important as why he says it, or that he says it at all. The young soldier's sudden ability to make sense of the world around him may not sit well with many readers, but it does make sense in terms of his need to create a coherent narrative for his experiences, to give purpose to the chaos of his emotions. By viewing Crane's novel from the perspective of narrative construction and trauma, we begin to see that *The Red Badge of Courage* is not simply about the evolution of Fleming, the person—when we read it for this reason we are indeed left with the kind of ambiguity that critics have been writing about since the novel was published. Instead, if we read the novel through the scope of the trauma of personal narrative construction, we can see that Fleming's final thoughts are not an ending at all; they are a beginning. It is my contention that what we are reading in the *The Red Badge of Courage* is not the story of Henry Fleming; it is an attempt to process the thoughts that will eventually become the story of Henry Fleming.

Narrative Theory and Traumatic Emotional Responses

Before we engage the novel itself, it is important to establish the proper theoretical foundation for this discussion. Narrative theory "emphasizes how communities deal with the elusiveness of historical truths, and how history and narrative intersect when humans attempt to counteract historical uncertainty" (Nesler 3). Even when we discuss the private memories of an individual, they are often positioned against the collective memories of a community, adding an additional level of stress at the thought of how others interpret the same event. The question becomes: which memory will become the dominant one? In order for historical events to move from one generation to another, they must be conveyed in a coherent manner. Narrative often acts as the vehicle from which history is able to propagate into the future. Thus, there is always an urge to construct, or reconstruct, the past in a way that will most likely lead to its proliferation into the future. This impulse to construct narrative and create meaning, however, can be traumatic if events in history are blurry and inconsistent.

Cathy Caruth provides a good explanation of the disorienting effects of trauma on an individual's ability to build meaningful reference points throughout personal and collective history. She writes:

> it is here, in the equally widespread and bewildering encounter with trauma—both in its occurrence and in the attempt to understand it—that we can begin to recognize the possibility of a history that is no longer straightforwardly referential (that is, no longer based on simple models of experience and reference). Through the notion of trauma ... we can understand that a rethinking of reference is aimed not at eliminating history but at resituating it in our understanding, that is, at precisely permitting *history* to arise where *immediate understanding* may not.
>
> (11)

When we talk about "resituating our understanding" of our experiences, we are talking about narrative construction as much as we are talking about comprehension: the two are always, in some sense, connected. For Caruth, the aim of rethinking references poses no threat to history; it is merely a way of reestablishing reference points from which comprehension can occur. In Fleming's world, however, reestablishing reference points is a threat to history; it destroys the preconceived notions of narrative that he brings with him to the war. This is extremely traumatic for the young soldier because his future identity as hero is wrapped up in a present moment that does not yet exist. He is at all times simultaneously constructing narrative and identity. Therefore, any time that Fleming is faced with a situation that threatens the stability of his future narrative he acts defensively, subsuming the experience into his preconceived narrative as simply part of the original story. When we consider the role that Narrative Exposure Therapy (NET) plays in helping returning veterans who are suffering with PTSD, we begin to realize that what Fleming is doing is actually quite understandable.

Narrative Exposure Therapy allows individuals "to construct a narrative of their life up to and including the present. They are encouraged to elaborate on details surrounding traumatic experiences" (Gradus). One of the main goals of this therapy is to help establish a "consistent narrative ..., because memories and emotional processing are not always accurate, particularly when PTSD symptoms are involved" (Gradus). The key term here is consistency. It is understood that the memories attached to the traumatic event may not be accurate, but consistency in the narrative allows the individual to begin to process the emotional responses associated with traumatic memories (Gradus). Memories are still an important component to the NET, so in order to help stabilize memories and process them doctors and social workers are turning to Emotional Process Therapy (EMT).

In EMT, memories that are attached to particularly traumatic events are broken down into two categories: hot and cold memories. Hot memories are "thought to be stored as sensory-perceptual representational networks, containing memories of stimuli in different modalities, together with cognitive and emotional states experienced during the event" (Kangaslampi 3). These are the feelings that we attach to an event. Cold memories are "selective representations of the contextual and factual elements of the event, consciously and verbally accessible to the trauma survivor" (Kangaslampi 3). Thus, an individual might have a hot memory of the fear he or she was feeling in a specific moment and a cold memory of a particular color in the environment where the traumatic event had taken place. Individuals suffering with PTSD often face a problem in reconciling the two memory networks, especially when the individual experiences compounding traumatic events. The problem is that "the fear network grows, and the hot memories become increasingly disconnected from the contextual referents of the cold memories (such as time and place)" (Kangaslampi 3). This is why purely factual accounts of events are not as important in NET; it is more important that the individual create a clear, stable narrative from which memories can be processed. Scholars often point out the young soldier's propensity for equivocation. However, when we think about the compounding traumatic events that Fleming faces in **Red Badge,** his "self-deceiving rationalizations he constructs after the fact" become much more understandable (Horsford 110). They are a testament to his ongoing struggle to take dynamic events in real time and stabilize them into a coherent narrative. When we consider the fact that Fleming's understanding of war and heroism comes out of *The Iliad*, his choices and language begin to make more sense.

Homer and the Emotional Narrative

Upon reviewing the stories of *The Battles and Leaders of the Civil War,* published in *Century Magazine,* Crane famously told Corwin K. Linson, "I wonder that *some* of these fellows don't tell how they *felt* in those scraps! They spout eternally of what they *did,* but they are as emotionless as rocks!" (Linson 37). For Crane, what these soldiers actually did is not as important as the emotions that were produced out of these actions. Narrative theory bears out Crane's thoughts. As Bruner notes, "Narrative 'truth' is judged by its verisimilitude rather than its verifiability" (13). A narrative with emotion can appeal to a broader audience and can potentially create a universalizing appeal that goes beyond the particulars of any battle. When a soldier says he or she feels afraid for his or her life, many people can sympathize or empathize with such a fear. However, not nearly as many can understand the particulars of a fear that involves running toward an opposing company of armed troops during a war. Given Crane's preference for emotional response, it is no wonder that he decides to use Homer as the scaffold for Fleming's understanding of war. *The Iliad* is an epic poem of emotion, a story about the rage of Achilles, about the jealousy of kings, and about the hubris of great men and women. For Fleming, Homer's stories are real because they are emotionally charged with universal appeals to the human condition, not because they are historically factual.

The exchange between Fleming and his mother is the first genuinely Homeric moment in the story. Both Achilles and the young soldier are confronted by the difficult task of having to choose between competing narratives: on one hand, the epic hero, a narrative of excitement and immortality through story; on the other hand, there is the domestic narrative, a story of nobility and service to family, but one that lacks the immortality of greatness. Achilles openly acknowledges this dilemma to his mother. He says:

> A twofold fate conducts me to my death;—
> If I remain to fight beneath the walls
> Of Ilium, my return will be cut off,
> But deathless my renown; if I return
> To the dear land in which my fathers dwell,
> My glory will be nought, but long my life
> And late will come to me the stroke of death.
>
> (9.511-17)

Achilles is offered a long and prosperous life within the scope of a domestic narrative, but he refuses it, turning instead toward battle, glory, and death. Interestingly, like Achilles, it is the young soldier's mother who provides him with this choice of a domestic narrative in lieu of the more "glorious" one of war.

Fleming's mother attempts to offer him a path away from the war; however, this is not the direction that her son wants to take. The narrator tells us, "She could calmly . . . give him [Henry] many hundreds of reasons why he was of vastly more importance on the farm than on the field of battle" (4). What is interesting about this statement is that she phrases it in a heroic way: he is "of vastly more importance," as if there is glory in his staying. This interaction with his mother has a profound impact on Fleming, as there is a side to the young soldier that identifies "quite strongly with the maternal" (Sanner 3). In fact, it is in this scene with his mother that the young soldier begins to realize that narratives are not so easily created when others are involved.

Deep down, Fleming wants his mother to understand, as he does, that what he is doing by enlisting is glorious and world-changing, but his mother "had affected to look with some contempt upon the quality of his war ardor and patriotism" (5). There is some precedence for Fleming's concern here. In John Anthony Casey, Jr.'s essay on Crane, manhood, and Civil War veterans, he explores the anxiety within Fleming to participate in the war or be left behind as something that Crane could most likely relate to through the author's witnessing of the various interactions between

Civil War veterans and the general population. Young men in Crane's time were led to believe that "the last 'real' war had concluded decades ago" (Casey 5). Thus, a young man in the late nineteenth century had to find other means of achieving "manhood." Fleming's exchanges with his mother sound like a young man attempting to establish his identity as an adult. Given his naïve understanding of war, it is understandable that his mother tries to convince him that there are other paths to adulthood.

When Fleming initially attempts to tell his mother of his yearning to fight, she tells him, "don't you be a fool" (4). Instead of explaining to his mother why he feels the need to participate in the war, like an adult, Fleming waits until the next morning and enlists at a nearby farm, avoiding the conflict with his mother entirely. This interaction with his mother represents the first narrative breach, or deviation from the canonical script of a narrative (Bruner 11). Fleming's inability to face these breaches and come to terms with the fact that he is not in control of his perfect war narrative creates a pattern whereby the young soldier feels the need to constantly restructure how events should have happened in order to make them fit his preconceived notions of heroism. In doing so, Fleming places himself in a difficult position, one in which he must constantly struggle to fix his narrative on the spot in order to solidify it as authentically his. As the novel bears out, restructuring the narrative is a traumatic event in and of itself.

Henry Runs Away from His Narrative

Before we talk about Fleming's flight from battle, arguably the most traumatic event in the novel for the young soldier, we should recall that he initially experiences victory in his first test of combat. When he is confronted by the initial surge of Confederate troops, Fleming reveals that his mind is not concerned with survival; it is concerned with timing and order of events. The attack happens "Before he was ready to begin—before he had announced himself that he was about to fight" (32). Fleming came into the war with the belief that he would be given ample time to savor these moments and create lasting images in his mind for him to produce at a later date. However, he is cheated out of this moment.

Instead, Fleming is left in a space where he can only react. In doing so, he becomes "another thing" (24). The young soldier becomes mechanized himself, a part of the larger narrative happening around him. It is in this section of the novel that we witness some of the clearest thoughts from the young soldier. He "lost concern for himself..., welded into a common personality which was dominated by a single desire" (32). For this brief instance in the text, Fleming is actually living his narrative. Everything has gone to plan, so there is no need to restructure the events based upon his preconceived narrative of Fleming, the hero. However, this feeling does not last.

The Confederate forces manage to mount another attack, completely taking the young soldier by surprise. In Brian Croxall's recent discussion on the role of technology in *Red Badge,* he notes, Henry's "surprise ... is caused by how woefully inadequate his Homeric texts are for helping him frame the experience of a modern, mechanized war" (109). In the Homeric world, there is time for great speeches before, during, and after conflict—there is time to construct narrative. The speed of the current war, however, moves much too quickly for such things. As the second surge of Confederate troops make their way toward Fleming, he "stared. Surely, he thought, this impossible thing was not about to happen. He waited as if he expected the enemy to suddenly stop, apologize, and retire bowing. It was all a mistake" (38). Just prior to this second attack, Fleming had conferred upon himself the perfect ending to his story: he withstood a wave of enemy soldiers and achieved the type of victory he had desperately wanted—he earned his glory in battle. If there is no second wave of soldiers and Fleming's part in the war had ended there, he could go back home and tell everyone that he was victorious in battle, a true hero, but that is not what happens.

Fleming runs away from the second surge of Confederate troops, but he is not simply physically running away; he is also mentally and emotionally running away from having to face the failure of his narrative. He was not the only soldier to flee from the battle. It would be understandable for the young soldier to simply say that he was following others—that he was still a part of the machine. However, he is not there to follow others. In Ficociello's essay on *Red Badge* and subjectivity, he argues that "Fleming searches for his place in the war machine" (5). Certainly one of the young soldier's more positive moments is when he experiences collective victory with his fellow soldiers—solidifying his place as active participant in the machine. In fact, had Fleming simply accepted his place as part of the war machine—the same machine that both tasted victory and pushed through the difficult conflict of the second surge—the young soldier would not be faced with the daunting task of having to reconstruct the events to fit his personal narrative. The truth is that it is much more important to Fleming that he occupy a space outside of the machine. In true Homeric fashion, the war machine provides merely the backdrop from which the main narrative of individual heroism can emerge.

Fleming becomes so desperate to preserve his story of heroism that he does the only thing that makes sense to him at the time: he weaves his flight from the enemy into the original narrative without actually addressing what has happened. We are told, "[h]is actions had been sagacious things. They had been full of strategy. They were the work of a master's legs" (43). Again, the young soldier could have cited that there were others who fled from the onslaught. But, he does not. Such a decision would compromise the integrity of his story. Fleming does not in any way address his fear and confusion, nor does it address the fact that his actions were by and large reactionary, predicated more on the chaos of the moment than deliberation. Narratives are produced with carefully constructed language and memories. By constructing a rationale for his flight from the battle, he is able to instantaneously create hot and cold memories for himself, repairing the momentary breach in his narrative and establishing coherency once again. If the young soldier acknowledges his fears, he has to simultaneously acknowledge that the whole perception of heroism that lured him into the war is built upon a lie, and Fleming simply cannot bear such an admission.

Critics often acknowledge the trauma that Fleming experiences when he runs away from the second surge of Confederate troops. However, I would argue that the death of Jim Conklin and the degrading mental faculties of the tattered soldier are in many ways just as disturbing for Fleming. What he sees in both Jim Conklin and the tattered soldier is exactly what can happen when one no longer has creative control of his or her own story, and it frightens the young man. We need to unpack these two events separately to really see how the demise of these two characters creates additional sites of narrative trauma for Henry.

The death of Conklin is agonizing for Fleming to witness. However, he was never really supposed to see it. We are told, "At last, they saw [Conklin] stop and stand motionless. Hastening up, they perceived that his face wore an expression telling that he had at last found the place for which he had struggled" (54). The language here is important. Conklin shows agency in the decision for where he wishes to pass away. He is, at this point, controlling his own narrative, able to assert some say in how others view him for the last time. Repeatedly Conklin asks both Fleming and the tattered soldier to leave him alone. His final words are "don't tech me—leave me be" (55), a direct command for both Fleming and the tattered soldier to move on and forget about him, to let him pass away. The narrator tells us that "there was a curious and profound dignity in the firm lines of [Jim's] awful face" (55). These should be the final words that we hear of Jim Conklin: a mixture of the sad nature of death with the dignity of his acceptance. The problem is that Fleming and the tattered soldier do not listen to Conklin. They stay with him, and because of this decision, the last memories they have of Conklin are the expressions of "agony" and a "mouth . . . opened [with] teeth show[ing] in a laugh" (55). This is a grotesque final vision of Jim, and it is especially difficult on the young soldier because of the way in which Conklin loses all control of how others remember him. The death of Jim Conklin is not the only example of the ramifications of losing one's authorship of his or her narrative.

With the memory of Jim still fresh in Fleming's mind, the tattered soldier brings up the need to address the young soldier's wound. He says, "Yeh might have some queer kind 'a hurt yourself. Yeh can't never tell. Where is your'n located?" (58). This question reminds Fleming of the shame of his flight, but there is something else going on in this exchange that is not often discussed by critics. Fleming begins to focus his attention acutely on the demeanor of the tattered soldier. We are told that Fleming "could see that [the tattered soldier], too, like that other one, was beginning to act dumb and animal-like" (58). While these are harsh words, they do not change the fact that something appears to be wrong with the tattered soldier's mental faculties. The tattered soldier begins to ramble about his neighbor back home, Tom Jamison, going so far as to repeatedly refer to Fleming by this name. He yells, "Yeh wanta go trompin' off with a bad hurt. It ain't right—now—Tom Jamison—it ain't. Yeh wanta leave me take keer of yeh, Tom Jamison" (59). It is what Fleming does next that critics tend to label as unjustifiably cruel.

After the awkward exchange with the tattered soldier, we are told "The youth went on. Turning at distance he saw the tattered man wandering about helplessly in the field" (59). Fleming does nothing to help the tattered soldier. John E. Curran, Jr. believes, as other critics do, that Fleming is "so engrossed in egotism that he fails to evaluate in any meaningful way the events around him" (2). Fleming does in fact desert the tattered soldier, but it is not because of a lack of compassion or an inability to evaluate what is happening—if anything the young soldier is too sensitive to what is going on around him. The tattered soldier and Jim Conklin play an important role in our understanding of just how traumatizing narrative construction in war can be. These soldiers are not "devoid of human substance, devoid of comradery, devoid of heart," as Syed Afroz argues (202). Henry does bond with these men, and it is through their deaths that the young soldier is reminded again that at any moment extenuating circumstances can take control of one's personal narrative. The terrible truth that Fleming realizes is that one can become a Jim Conklin or a tattered soldier at any point; it could even happen to him.

The Ending in Light of Narrative Construction

One of the reasons why critics tend to find the ending of the novel so problematic is because there is a shift in the tone of the language. The narrator tells us, "[Henry] turned now with a lover's thirst to images of tranquil skies, fresh meadows, cool brooks—an existence of soft and eternal peace" (129). Admittedly, these words do create a disturbing sense of sudden resolution. How does Fleming come so quickly to a point of peace and clarity so quickly? Briefly returning to Caruth, she notes questions surrounding traumatic events "can never be asked in a straightforward way, but must, indeed, also be spoken in a language that is always somehow literary: a language that defies, even as it claims, our understanding" (5). The language that Henry uses at the end here is very literary. In fact, it is poetical, void of any hard memories or facts. Henry is not interested in creating history; he wants to create story. Aristotle's discussion about the difference between history and poetry can help further establish the point. The Greek philosopher states, "[history] relates things that have happened, [poetry] things that may happen. For this reason poetry is a more philosophical and more serious thing than history. Poetry tends to speak of universals, history of particulars" (97-8). Poetry, and all art for that matter, serves an important purpose: it captures not only a moment in time but adds the memorable element of emotional response to the text.

Jerome Bruner reminds us that "narratives do not exist ... in some real world, waiting there patiently and eternally to be veridically mirrored in a text" (8). There is far more that is involved in creating narrative. "The events themselves need to be *constituted* in the light of the overall narrative ..., to be made 'functions' of the story" (Bruner 8). The sudden shift in tone at the end of the novel indicates a beginning, not an ending. Fleming is just now beginning to put the events together into a narrative. He is just beginning to constitute the events in light of the overall story. The ending reads disingenuous to us because we have borne witness to the truth of the events. Just as Fleming and the tattered soldier had done in the scene with Jim Conklin, we have overstayed our welcome, have witnessed too much to enjoy the story that Fleming will tell others back home.

Does the young soldier experience a type of maturation here? The answer is most likely yes and no, but that never really appears to be the purpose in his going to war. As Fleming thinks about his flight from battle and treatment of the tattered soldier, he admits that his "plan for the utilization of a sin did not give him complete joy but it was the best sentiment he could formulate under the circumstances, and when it was combined with his success, or public deeds, he knew that he was quite contented" (128). Fleming's final words are not the words of an individual who wishes to reflect upon his experiences in order to become a more mature person. This is the language of narrative organization and composition. The impression we receive at the end of the novel is that Fleming's story—the one at least that he will tell people back home—has yet to be written, but when it is, it will contain some truth, some fiction, and a lot of emotion.

Works Cited

Aristotle. *Poetics. The Norton Anthology of Literary Criticism,* edited by Vincent B. Leitch, W.W. Norton & Company, 2001, pp. 86-117.

Bruner, Jerome. "The Narrative Construction of Reality." *Critical Inquiry,* vol. 18, no. 1, 1991, pp. 1-21. *JSTOR,* http://www.jstor.org/stable/1343711.

Caruth, Cathy. *Unclaimed Experiences.* Johns Hopkins UP, 1996.

Casey, John Anthony, Jr. "Searching for a War of One's Own: Stephen Crane, *The Red Badge of Courage,* and the Glorious Burden of the Civil War Veteran." *American Literary Realism,* vol. 44. no. 1, 2011, pp. 1-22. Literature Resource Center, http://go.galegroup.com.libproxy.albany.edu/ps/retrieve.do?tabID=T001&resultListType=RESULT_LIST&searchResultsType=MultiTab&searchType=AdvancedSearchForm&currentPosition=1&docId=GALE%7CA269029091&docType=Critical+essay&sort=RELEVANCE&contentSegment=&prodId=LitRC&contentSet=GALE%7CA269029091&searchId=R1&userGroupName=albanyu&inPS=true W.

Crane, Stephen. *The Red Badge of Courage: An Episode of the American Civil War. The Red Badge of Courage and Four Stories,* edited by R. W. Stallman, New American Library, 1997.

Croxall, Brian. "'Becoming Another Thing': Traumatic and Technological Transformation in *The Red Badge of Courage.*" *American Imago,* vol. 72, no. 1, 2015, pp. 101-27.

Curran, Jr., John E. "'Nobody seems to know where we go': Uncertainty, History, and Irony in *The Red Badge of Courage.*" *American Literary Studies,* vol. 26, no. 1, 1993, pp. 1-12.

Ficociello, Robert. "Crane's Episode Among Episodes in American War Discourse." *War, Literature, and the Arts: An International Journal of the Humanities,* vol. 25, 2013, *Ebscohost,* http://eds.a.ebscohost.com.libproxy.albany.edu/

eds/pdfviewer/pdfviewer?vid=14&sid=d7917589-0835-4b55-9428-70951c65be55%40sessionmgr4009&hid=4108.

Gradus, Jaimie L. "Epidemiology of PTSD." *U.S. Department of Veterans Affairs,* 8 Aug. 2016, http://www.ptsd.va.gov/professional/PTSD-overview/epidemiological-facts-ptsd.asp.

Homer. *The Iliad,* translated by William Cullen Bryant, vol. 1, Fields, Osgood & Co, 1870.

Horsford, Howard C. "'He Was a Man.'" *New Essays on The Red Badge of Courage,* edited by Lee Clark Mitchell, Cambridge University Press, 1986, pp. 109-27.

Kangaslampi, Samuli, et al. "Narrative Exposure Therapy for Immigrant Children Traumatized by War: Study Protocol for a Randomized Controlled Trial of Effectiveness and Mechanisms of Change." *BMC Psychiatry,* vol. 15, no. 1, 2015, pp. 1-14, *Ebscohost,* http://eds.a.ebscohost.com.libproxy.albany.edu/eds/detail/detail?vid=16&sid=d7917589-0835-4b55-9428-70951c65be55%40sessionmgr4009&hid=4108&bdata=JnNpdGU9ZWRzLWxpdmUmc2NvcGU9c2l0ZQ%3d%3d#AN=108306835&db=a2h.

Linson, Corwin K. *My Stephen Crane,* edited by Edwin H. Cady, Syracuse UP, 1958.

McDermott, John J. "Symbolism and Psychological Realism in *The Red Badge of Courage.*" *Nineteenth-Century Fiction,* vol. 23, no. 3, 1968, pp. 324-31.

Nesler, Miranda G. "'What Once I Was, and What Am Now': Narrative and Identity Constructions in *Samson Agonistes.*" *JNT: Journal of Narrative Theory,* vol. 37, no. 1, 2007, pp. 1-26, *Ebscohost,* http://eds.a.ebscohost.com.libproxy.albany.edu/eds/detail/detail?vid=18&sid=d7917589-0835-4b55-9428-70951c65be55%40sessionmgr4009&hid=4108&bdata=JnNpdGU9ZWRzLWxpdmUmc2NvcGU9c2l0ZQ%3d%3d#AN=edsgcl.1688737-74&db=edsglr.

Pizer, Donald. "Henry Behind the Lines and the Concept of Manhood in *The Red Badge of Courage.*" *Stephen Crane Studies,* vol. 10, no. 1, 2001, pp. 2-7.

Sanner, Kristin N. "Searching for Identity in *The Red Badge of Courage*: Henry Fleming's Battle with Gender." *Stephen Crane Studies,* vol. 18, no. 1, 2009, pp. 2-16.

Swann, Charles. "Stephen Crane and a Problem of Interpretation." *Literature and History,* vol. 7, no. 1, 1981, pp. 91-123.

Syed Afroz, Ashrafi. "Human Connections in *Red Badge of Courage.*" *International Journal of Applied Linguistics & English Literature,* vol. 5, no. 3, 2016, pp. 199-202.

FURTHER READING

Bibliographies

Dooley, Patrick K. *Stephen Crane: An Annotated Bibliography of Secondary Scholarship.* G. K. Hall, 1992.

    Includes nearly 1,900 annotated entries of writings in English about Crane from his death in 1900 to 1992. This list is updated periodically by the journal *Stephen Crane Studies.*

Schaefer, Michael W. *A Reader's Guide to the Short Stories of Stephen Crane.* G. K. Hall, 1996.

    Offers commentary on forty-nine of Crane's short stories, plus the novella *The Monster* (1899). In each entry Schaefer provides: "Publication History," "Circumstances of Composition," "Sources and Influences," and "Relationship with Other Works and Critical Studies."

Biographies

Colvert, James B. *Stephen Crane.* Harcourt Brace Jovanovich, 1984.

    Provides an informative biography of Crane, an even-handed assessment of the literary merits of his works, and a helpful interpretation of his literary creed. Colvert's study is an ideal introduction for beginning readers.

Kepnes, Caroline. *Stephen Crane.* Mitchell Lane Publishers, 2005.

    A generally reliable biography offering young readers five excellently cropped and colorized images of Crane from the Syracuse University Special Collections. Kepnes's volume is part of Mitchell Lane's academic children's book series.

Criticism

Fraser, John. "Crime and Forgiveness: *The Red Badge of Courage* in Time of War." *Criticism,* vol. 9, no. 3, 1967, pp. 243-56.

    Explicates differences between ethical norms in force for everyday life and those held in abeyance during combat to help readers appreciate how much Fleming grows, achieving moral equilibrium by the end of the second day of battle.

Frederic, Harold. "Stephen Crane's Triumph." *The New York Times,* 26 Jan. 1896, p. 22.

    Hails *The Red Badge of Courage* (1895) as among the finest American novels of Frederic's generation. [Included in *CLR,* Vol. 132.]

Foote, Shelby. Introduction. *The Red Badge of Courage and "The Veteran,"* by Stephen Crane, Modern Library, 2000, pp. vi-lii.

    Presents an elegant and poignant examination of the impact of *The Red Badge of Courage*. Foote concludes, "any true work having to do with war is bound, by definition, to turn out antiwar in its effect, and so, of course does this one."

Lawson, Andrew. "The Red Badge of Class: Stephen Crane and the Industrial Army." *Literature and History,* vol. 14, no. 2, 2005, pp. 53-68.

    Examines class concerns in *The Red Badge of Courage* by paying attention to the tensions between lower-class recruits and their upper-class officers.

Link, Eric Carl, editor. *Critical Insights:* The Red Badge of Courage *by Stephen Crane*. Salem Press, 2011.

    Includes seven new and fourteen reprinted essays, grouped under the headings "The Book and Author," "Critical Contexts," and "Critical Readings and Resources." These essays are among the best scholarly examinations on Crane and his most famous work.

Richardson, Mark. "Stephen Crane's *The Red Badge of Courage*." *American Writers Classics,* edited by Jay Parini, vol. 1, Scribner, 2003, pp. 237-55.

    Argues that Crane's startling, breakthrough style in *The Red Badge of Courage* enabled him to narrate "at once from inside and outside his hero's sensibilities."

Sorrentino, Paul M. *Student Companion to Stephen Crane.* Greenwood Press, 2006.

    Provides a valuable resource for studying Crane and his works. Sorrentino is arguably the finest Crane scholar of recent decades.

Stallman, Robert Wooster. Introduction. *The Red Badge of Courage,* by Stephen Crane, Modern Library, 1951, pp. v-xxxiii.

    Proposes that Christian symbols are the key to understanding *The Red Badge of Courage*. Focusing on Jim Conklin as a Christ figure, Stallman argues that the novel's central theme is redemption.

Additional information on Crane's life and works is contained in the following sources published by Gale: *American Writers; American Writers: The Classics,* **Vol. 1;** *Authors and Artists for Young Adults,* **Vol. 21;** *Beacham's Encyclopedia of Popular Fiction: Biography and Resources,* **Vol. 1;** *Beacham's Guide to Literature for Young Adults,* **Vol. 3;** *Children's Literature Review,* **Vol. 132;** *Concise Dictionary of American Literary Biography: 1865-1917; Contemporary Authors,* **Vols. 109, 140;** *Contemporary Authors New Revision Series,* **Vol. 84;** *Dictionary of Literary Biography,* **Vols. 12, 54, 78, 357, 378;** *DISCovering Authors; DISCovering Authors: British Edition; DISCovering Authors: Canadian Edition; DISCovering Authors Modules: Most-Studied Authors, Novelists,* **and** *Poets; DISCovering Authors 3.0; Exploring Novels; Exploring Short Stories; Gale Contextual Encyclopedia of American Literature,* **Vol. 1;** *Gale Literature Resource Center; Literary Movements for Students,* **Vol. 2;** *Literature and Its Times,* **Vol. 2;** *Modern American Literature,* **Ed. 5;** *Novels for Students,* **Vols. 4, 20;** *Poetry Criticism,* **Vol. 80;** *Poetry for Students,* **Vol. 9;** *Reference Guide to American Literature,* **Ed. 4;** *Reference Guide to Short Fiction,* **Ed. 2;** *Short Stories for Students,* **Vols. 4, 28, 34, 38;** *Short Story Criticism,* **Vols. 7, 56, 70, 129, 194, 223, 276, 291;** *Twayne's United States Authors; Twentieth-Century Literary Criticism,* **Vols. 11, 17, 32, 216;** *World Literature Criticism,* **Vol. 2;** *Writers for Young Adults;* **and** *Yesterday's Authors of Books for Children,* **Vol. 2.**

Charlotte's Web
E. B. White

(Full name Elwyn Brooks White) American children's fiction writer, essayist, nonfiction writer, and poet.

The following entry provides criticism of White's novel *Charlotte's Web* (1952). For additional information about White, see *CLR,* Volumes 1, 21, 107, and 238.

INTRODUCTION

Known for his pellucid style and impeccable handling of literary form, E. B. White (1899-1985) is remembered as the author of *Charlotte's Web,* a work often ranked among the best and most enduring children's novels of the twentieth century. In 1970 *Charlotte's Web* and White's first children's novel, *Stuart Little* (1945), shared the prestigious Laura Ingalls Wilder Medal for children's literature. Eloquent, engaging, and philosophical, the narrative of *Charlotte's Web* interweaves the story of Charlotte, a barnyard spider, and the pig Wilbur with that of Fern Arable's passage from childhood to preadolescence. A master stylist who revised William Strunk's famous 1918 writing guide *Elements of Style* (1959), White celebrates friendship, the pleasures of rural life, and the eternal cycles of nature, expressing these complex themes seemingly effortlessly through simple, graceful diction and syntax. Literary critics have long considered the story a standard against which to measure children's fiction. Scholars have also discussed the novel in relation to multiple philosophical and sociological perspectives, including early childhood development, feminism, and environmentalism.

In 1938, after a sixteen-year journalism career in Seattle and New York City, White and his wife, Katharine Angell White, moved to a farm in Brooklin, Maine. From there, he continued to contribute to *The New Yorker* and *Harper's* and eventually began writing children's books. Whereas *Stuart Little* is set in an urban environment and traces the adventures of its titular mouse protagonist in New York City, *Charlotte's Web* seems to have developed directly and exclusively out of White's enjoyment of his life in the countryside. He particularly enjoyed observing spiders closely and read extensively about them, compiling voluminous notes before writing the book. Archives preserved by Cornell University show that in draft after discarded draft White initially opened the novel by dwelling on the cozy, comfortable ambience of a barn. His essay "Death of a Pig" (1948)—a heartfelt account, written in "penitence and in grief," about his experience caring for a sick animal that explores the relationship between humans and farm animals—anticipates the revised opening scene of the almost-slaughtered pig, Wilbur, in *Charlotte's Web.*

PLOT AND MAJOR CHARACTERS

Charlotte's Web moves smoothly between two levels of related plot and theme. Eight-year-old Fern Arable convinces her father to allow her to keep the runt of a pig litter, normally destined for slaughter. Naming him Wilbur and treating him as a "baby" alongside her dolls, she bottle-feeds him until he is weaned. Bigger and stronger one month later, Wilbur is sold to Fern's uncle, Homer Zuckerman, and taken to his farm. The early pages of *Charlotte's Web* are a distanced, realistic, third-person account of Fern saving Wilbur and existence in the daily life of the barnyard. Once Wilbur speaks, he is personified and expresses human emotions, fears, pains, and even boredom. Like Wilbur, the other animals in the barnyard speak, too.

Once he is settled in the barn, Wilbur is lonely and yearns for companionship, but he is ignored by the other animals. However, he is befriended by Charlotte, a spider whose web is pitched over a door near Wilbur's enclosure and who begins to chat with him about many things, including her past and her arachnid nature. Eavesdropping on the other animals' conversations, Charlotte overhears the sheep and the geese foolishly and impoliticly discussing Wilbur's imminent demise; when she learns that Wilbur is going to be slaughtered for food, she devises an ingenious plan to save his life. Theorizing that farmer Zuckerman might be willing to spare Wilbur if he were a *famous* pig, Charlotte begins to weave words praising him into her web. The first phrase to appear, "SOME PIG," catches the attention of the barn hand, who reports to Zuckerman that a miracle has occurred. Indeed, Wilbur and the barn soon become famous, with tourists arriving to see the writing in the web for themselves. Charlotte subsequently weaves in the words "TERRIFIC," and then "RADIANT," attracting even more attention.

Not only do the barnyard animals speak, but Fern understands them, and she reports their conversation to her mother. Worried about the mental state of her unusual daughter, Mrs. Arable takes her to their family physician, Dr. Dorian, who reassures her that Fern's fascination with the barnyard is neither unusual nor unhealthy. He projects that Fern's fascination with the animals will naturally lessen as she grows older and develops other interests. Furthermore, Dr. Dorian suggests that we all might hear more if only we had the ears to listen.

As the summer goes on, farmer Zuckerman enters Wilbur into the county fair. The pig is accompanied on the journey there by Charlotte and a barn rat named Templeton. Although Wilbur does not win the highest prize, the jury awards him a special prize. Charlotte understands that this additional honor will help to prevent Zuckerman from slaughtering Wilbur and adds one more, final, word to her web—"HUMBLE." Satisfied that her friend's life is now safe, she begins to undergo the natural last phase of her own short life. In the meantime, Fern has matured from little girl to preadolescent and has developed an interest in boys. No longer preoccupied with Wilbur, she pays no attention to the events at the fair and enjoys riding the Ferris wheel in the company of her classmate Henry Fussy.

As the fair ends, Charlotte decides not to return to Zuckerman's farm with Wilbur and Templeton, instead remaining at the fairgrounds to await her death. Before Wilbur leaves, however, she entrusts her egg sac to him, placing it in his travel crate. Back at the farm, Wilbur enjoys the pampered life of a "celebrity." When spring arrives, Charlotte's numerous progeny hatch, although their mother died months before. Delighted at their birth, Wilbur is saddened when most of them leave the Zuckerman barn. Even though only three young spiders remain to keep him company, Wilbur is comforted by the knowledge that there will be multiple future generations of Charlotte's descendants to whom he can offer his friendship.

MAJOR THEMES

Friendship is the major theme of *Charlotte's Web*. Wilbur's life is saved through two instances of friendliness—first when Fern rescues him, and second when Charlotte's plan succeeds. Wilbur, in turn, pledges to the dying Charlotte that he will give her offspring "friendship, forever and ever." The book ends with the sentiment "it is not often that someone comes along who is a true friend and a good writer. Charlotte was both."

White expresses admiration for rural life through the novel's celebration of the barn. Of the nine surviving drafts of *Charlotte's Web,* several begin with loving, detailed descriptions of the barn and of the "dressing" in Wilbur's pen. White eventually discarded these and substituted the more dramatic opening line by Fern, "Where's Papa going with that ax?," but he retained the evocation of the barn and its comforting atmosphere, moving it to the opening of the third chapter of the book. Throughout *Charlotte's Web*, White intersperses similar celebrations of various aspects of the farm, depicting its seasonal activities tied to the cycles of life, death, and renewal.

Although some readers have found White's praise of country life in *Charlotte's Web* overly romantic, nostalgic, or even escapist, others have noted that it is situated in the mainstream of a Western literary tradition, traceable for millennia, carried through Vergil's *Eclogues* (42 BCE) and then on through such later works as James Thomson's *The Seasons* (1730). Just as in Thomson's poem and in Franz Joseph Haydn's 1801 oratorio based on it, lyrical intermezzos punctuate *Charlotte's Web*. For example, in chapter six White writes, "Early summer days are a jubilee time for birds. In the fields, around the house, in the barn, in the woods, in the swamp—everywhere love and songs and nests and eggs. On an apple bough, the phoebe teeters and wags its tail and says 'Phoebe, phoe-bee!' The song sparrow, who knows how brief and lovely life is, says, 'Sweet, sweet, sweet interlude.'" That interlude does not merely paint an affectionate portrait of the country; it sounds the classical note of *et in arcadia ego* (I [death], too, in paradise), announcing that even in the midst of life, there must come death. Charlotte dies when her natural lifespan has come to an end and when she has delivered her egg sac, ensuring that her progeny will start the cycle of life all over again.

CRITICAL RECEPTION

Charlotte's Web was published to immediate critical and popular acclaim. Reviewing the novel in *The New York Times Book Review,* the Pulitzer Prize-winning author Eudora Welty (1952) wrote, "As a piece of work it is just about perfect, and just about magical in the way it is done." Later commentators have echoed Welty's praise, especially in lauding how the novel depicts the themes of the nature of friendship, the life cycle, and patterns of maturation. Early criticism focused on White's book to define what constitutes a high-quality children's novel. Because many of these reviewers were also involved in establishing the legitimacy of children's literature as a field of study, they wrote about the novel's literary qualities, including complex themes; well-developed characterization, including appropriate character growth; sophisticated narrative structure; and a lack of overt didacticism, that is, direct moralizing aimed at child readers.

Rather than evaluating the novel with the aim of establishing the legitimacy of the scholarly study of children's literature, the next wave of critics interpreted *Charlotte's Web* on its own merits, examining it as they would any work of literature. Commentators have performed close readings that demonstrate how White uses the novel to explore Martin Heidegger's philosophy about coming to terms with the existential loneliness of human life through friendship and love. Others have employed Jean Piaget's developmental theory, Walter J. Ong's theories of the oral tradition, and Louise Rosenblatt's reader-response theory to analyze the parallel plot structures between the two realistic opening chapters of the novel and the fantasy that follows, pointing out that in both, a highly verbal female of another species saves Wilbur from attack by an aggressive male and, ultimately, from death. Still other critics have observed how the novel portrays transformations in individual behavior within communal and social structures, in particular during transitions from childhood to adulthood.

Early feminist readings of *Charlotte's Web* centered on how Nancy Chodorow's theories about the ways society teaches young girls to replicate their mothers' nurturing actions are enacted by Fern, then by Charlotte, and eventually by Wilbur himself as he nurtures Charlotte's egg sac after her death. Later feminist readings have used Jacques Lacan's concepts from *Écrits* (1966) to interpret Fern's and Charlotte's attitudes toward maternity, Wilbur's growth into language, and his inevitable separation from his mother-figures. Moreover, cultural studies scholars and historians have recognized that Wilbur emblematizes various eras of childhood, tracing historical changes to the role of the American child itself or arguing that Wilbur can be read as caught in the middle of a cultural paradigm shift first identified by US culture historian Warren Susman regarding the messaging children receive from novels about their character and advertisers about their personality.

Scholars have also explored the various influences on White's novel, including the American Transcendentalist movement of the 1840s, particularly its concern with the relationship between nature and design, Henry David Thoreau's *Walden* (1854), and historical juvenilia. They have frequently linked the accessible style of *Charlotte's Web* with White's writing handbook, *The Elements of Style*, where he admonishes writers to be clear, direct, and brief. Ecocritical interpretations have pointed out that Charlotte's web itself is the true miracle in the novel, since it serves as a vehicle for procuring food, transportation, and communication, as well as being a metaphor for the passage from life to death. In addition, ecocritics have admonished readers against viewing Wilbur simply as a stand-in for a child character, referencing the philosophy of Donna J. Haraway in discussing the ethics behind shifting the subjectivity of an animal companion into an object meant to be eaten.

Adapted by Jelena Krstovic from
Peter F. Neumeyer's entry
on White in *DLB*, Vol. 22

Academic Advisor: Roberta Seelinger Trites

Roberta Seelinger Trites is Distinguished Professor of English Emerita, Illinois State University, and the author of such works of literary criticism as *Waking Sleeping Beauty: Feminist Voices in Children's Literature* (1997); *Disturbing the Universe: Power and Repression in Adolescent Literature* (2000); and *Twain, Alcott, and the Birth of the Adolescent Reform Novel* (2007).

PRINCIPAL WORKS

Juvenile Books

Stuart Little. Harper, 1945. Print. (Novel)

Charlotte's Web. Harper, 1952. Print. (Novel)

The Trumpet of the Swan. Harper, 1970. Print. (Novel)

Other Major Works

Less than Nothing; or, The Life and Times of Sterling Finny. The New Yorker, 1927. Print. (Satire)

Is Sex Necessary? or, Why You Feel the Way You Do. With James Thurber. Harper, 1929. Print. (Essays)

The Lady Is Cold. Harper, 1929. Print. (Poetry)

Ho Hum: Newsbreaks from The New Yorker. Edited by E. B. White. Farrar and Rinehart, 1931. Print. (Miscellanea)

Another Ho Hum: More Newsbreaks from The New Yorker. Edited by White. Farrar and Rinehart, 1932. Print. (Miscellanea)

Every Day Is Saturday. Harper, 1934. Print. (Essays)

Farewell to Model T. As Lee Strout White. Putnam's, 1936. Print. (Essay)

The Fox of Peapack and Other Poems. Harper, 1938. Print. (Poetry)

Quo Vadimus? or, The Case for the Bicycle. Harper, 1938. Print. (Essays)

A Subtreasury of American Humor. Edited by White and Katharine S. White. Coward-McCann, 1941. Print. (Essays)

One Man's Meat. Harper, 1942. Rev. and enlarged ed. Harper, 1944. Print. (Essays)

The Wild Flag: Editorials from The New Yorker *on Federal World Government and Other Matters.* Houghton Mifflin, 1946. Print. (Essays)

Here Is New York. Harper, 1949. Print. (Essay)

**The Second Tree from the Corner.* Harper, 1954. Print. (Essays, poetry, and short stories)

The Elements of Style. By William Strunk, Jr. Rev. and expanded ed. Edited by White. Macmillan, 1959. Rev. ed. 1979. Print. (Handbook)

The Points of My Compass. Harper, 1962. Print. (Essays)

An E. B. White Reader. Edited by William W. Watt and Robert W. Bradford. Harper and Row, 1966. Print. (Essays)

Letters of E. B. White. Edited by Dorothy Lobrano Guth. Harper, 1976. Print. (Letters)

Essays of E. B. White. Harper, 1977. Print (Essays)

Poems and Sketches of E. B. White. Harper, 1981. Print. (Poems and sketches)

Writings from The New Yorker*: 1927-1976.* Edited by Rebecca M. Dale. Harper, 1990. Print. (Essays, reviews, and short stories)

In the Words of E. B. White: Quotations from America's Most Companionable of Writers. Cornell UP, 2011. Print. (Quotations)

*Includes the essay "Death of a Pig," first published in *Atlantic Monthly* in January 1948.

CRITICISM

PRIMARY SOURCE: *Charlotte's Web* (novel date 1952)

SOURCE: White, E. B. "Escape." *Charlotte's Web,* Harper and Row, 1952, pp. 13-14.

[*In the following excerpt, White establishes the primary setting for the novel—Mr. Zuckerman's barn—through an accretion of simple, specific, realistic imagery that conjures up its physical attributes as well as its overall atmosphere.*]

The barn was very large. It was very old. It smelled of hay and it smelled of manure. It smelled of the perspiration of tired horses and the wonderful sweet breath of patient cows. It often had a sort of peaceful smell—as though nothing bad could happen ever again in the world. It smelled of grain and of harness dressing and of axle grease and of rubber boots and of new rope. And whenever the cat was given a fish-head to eat, the barn would smell of fish. But mostly it smelled of hay, for there was always hay in the great loft up overhead. And there was always hay being pitched down to the cows and the horses and the sheep.

The barn was pleasantly warm in winter when the animals spent most of their time indoors, and it was pleasantly cool in summer when the big doors stood wide open to the breeze. The barn had stalls on the main floor for the work horses, tie-ups on the main floor for the cows, a sheepfold down below for the sheep, a pigpen down below for Wilbur, and it was full of all sorts of things that you find in barns: ladders, grindstones, pitch forks, monkey wrenches, scythes, lawn mowers, snow shovels, ax handles, milk pails, water buckets, empty grain sacks, and rusty rat traps. It was the kind of barn that swallows like to build their nests in. It was the kind of barn that children like to play in. And the whole thing was owned by Fern's uncle, Mr. Homer L. Zuckerman.

Dorothy G. Singer (essay date 1975)

SOURCE: Singer, Dorothy G. "*Charlotte's Web* and Erikson's Life Cycle." *School Library Journal,* vol. 22, no. 3, 1975, pp. 17-19.

[*In the following essay, Singer identifies how the characters in* Charlotte's Web *(1952) depict the eight developmental stages psychologist Erik Erikson identified in 1968, each of which involves an emotional crisis people must resolve as they grow.*]

A pig, a spider, a girl and boy illustrate in E. B. White's haunting tale, ***Charlotte's Web,*** the eight developmental stages of man that have been proposed by Erik Erikson (*Identity, Youth and Crisis,* Norton, 1968). White offers us the story of Wilbur, the runty pig, who is saved from slaughter at birth because of the love and concern of Fern, the farmer's eight-year-old daughter. As we follow the adventures of Wilbur, he meets Charlotte, a spider, who later is to help save his life by her weaving of words in her web that glorify Wilbur. Wilbur eventually interacts with all the barnyard characters and the life cycle from birth to death is unfolded.

Erikson believes in the "epigenetic principle which is derived from the growth of organisms in utero." According to him, "anything that grows has a ground plan and that out of this ground plan the parts arise, each part having its time of special ascendancy, until all parts have arisen to form a functioning whole."

When the baby is born he leaves the womb and must enter into society "where his gradually increasing capacities meet the opportunities and limitations of his culture." In *Charlotte's Web* the growth and development of Wilbur, the pig, Charlotte, the spider, and Fern, the preadolescent girl are presented and are analogous to Erikson's epigenetic theory of personality development as described in *Childhood and Society* and in *Identity, Youth and Crisis*. Perhaps this is why both adults and children find *Charlotte's Web* so appealing. We are able to identify with the characters and recognize our own strengths, weaknesses, conflicts and crises.

Erikson's stages are a richer extension of the five bio-sexual stages in Freudian theory. Erikson attempts to include the child's social growth, his cultural milieu and societal forces that contribute to the total personality. He believes that the individual meets a crisis in each stage, and must resolve this before moving on to the next stage. Crises for Erikson means a "turning point, a crucial point of increased vulnerability and heightened potential." In this way the crisis itself leads to either strength or maladjustment. All stages of man exist in some form at birth, but at each crucial period of development, one particular phase of personality is dominant. For example, a baby may show signs of independence at birth, but according to Erikson, the assertion of autonomy and struggle for independence does not become critical until the second year of life.

I feel certain that E. B. White wrote his story without any conscious awareness of Erikson's eight stages, and yet they are (from Stage I, *Basic Trust vs Mistrust*, to Stage VIII, *Integrity vs Despair*) exemplified with a remarkable lucidity in this imaginative tale. When the book opens, we discover that Wilbur is a weak pig and must be killed. Fern prevents his slaughter by entreaties and pleas to her father's sense of justice. Fern's job now is to care for the pig and raise it. Thus, the first stage evolves—*Basic Trust vs Mistrust*.

Wilbur learns about the world through his mouth. As Erikson states, "he (the baby) lives through and lives with his mouth, and the mother lives through and lives with her breasts or whatever parts of countenance and body convey eagerness to provide what he needs." Indeed, Fern assumes the role of mother who now holds her baby pig and feeds him his bottle: "Fern loved Wilbur more than anything. She loved to stroke him, to feed him, to put him to bed. Every morning as soon as she got up, she warmed his milk, tied his bib on and held his bottle for him."

Fern "mothers" Wilbur and Wilbur grows to trust and love Fern. He walks out to the road every morning as Fern goes off to school, and he "would stand and watch the bus until it vanished around a turn." The reciprocal love serves to reinforce Fern's mother role, and Wilbur's sense of trust. Once the infant learns to trust his mother and recognize a sameness and continuity in his world, he begins to trust his ability to cope with the environment. This developing sense of trust is based on the quality of the maternal relationship. Fern affords Wilbur this sense of trust through her concern for his feeding and sleeping habits. Fern is relieved when she realizes that her "baby would sleep covered up, and would stay warm." Erikson believes that mothers create this sense of trust in their offspring by their sensitive care of the baby and by a "firm sense of personal trustworthiness within the trusted framework of their community's life style."

As Wilbur grows, Fern's father insists that he must go. Wilbur is given to Uncle Homer Zuckerman who lives down the road and "sometimes raises pigs." This is convenient for Fern who can now visit Wilbur in his new home in a "manure pile" in the cellar of the Zuckerman's barn. This barn becomes the setting for Stage II, *Autonomy vs Shame and Doubt*. This stage, analogous to Freud's *Anal Stage*, is concerned with the child's "battle for autonomy." Through his muscle control of both bladder and bowels, the infant learns when to "hold on" and when "to let go." From this biological function of the eliminative organs, the child learns to expand his sense of autonomy and willfulness to other aspects of his environment. This stage of development is concerned with "good will and hateful self-insistence, between cooperation and willfulness, between self-expression and compulsive self-restraint or meek compliance." The child learns a sense of self-control without the loss of self-esteem. Here is the beginning of free will.

Wilbur is moving into this stage, not only physically by wallowing in the mud along the brook where "it was warm and moist and delightfully sticky and cozy," but emotionally by attempting to "escape" from the farm yard. Wilbur squeezes through the fence and finds himself free. When his friend the goose, asks him how he likes it, Wilbur replys, "I like it, that is, I *guess* I like it."

Wilbur feels strange and a bit frightened to be out on his own, and like any child aged two to four years who starts to run away, he is rather ashamed that he started the escapade in the first place, and doubtful about his ability to maintain independence for long. The barnyard animals urge Wilbur on by their chants:

> "Run downhill," suggested the cows
>
> "Run towards me," yelled the gander
>
> "Run uphill," cried the sheep
>
> "Look out for Zuckerman," yelled the gander
>
> "Watch out for the dog," cried the sheep

But poor Wilbur is crying and confused and frightened. After all, he "was a very young pig, not much more than a baby, really. He wished Fern were there to take him in her arms and comfort him." Finally, Wilbur, lured by a pail of warm slops, is tricked into returning through the fence into the yard. He is glad to be home and ready for bed. "I'm really too young to go out into the world alone, he thought as he lay down."

Poor Wilbur, who had been "dazed and frightened" by the noise and urgings of his barnyard friends, is experiencing the feeling of "shame" that Erikson describes as the bipolar emotion in Stage II. Wilbur "didn't like being the center of all this fuss." The young child who is developing a sense of autonomy may expose himself prematurely by attempting to do things he is not quite ready to master. The parent serves as a protector for the child's "untrained discrimination." Gradually, the child learns about what he can and cannot do, so that he may develop "into an independent individual who can choose and guide his own future."

Stage III, *Initiative vs Guilt,* is exemplified by the bungling attempts of Wilbur to imitate his new found friend Charlotte, the spider. Charlotte introduces herself to Wilbur one day when Wilbur is feeling particularly lonely. All the barnyard animals had rejected Wilbur's offers to play. Wilbur is depressed, dejected, and firendless. Charlotte offers Wilbur friendship and love. At first, Wilbur is taken aback by Charlotte's "bloodthirsty" way of trapping food. As Wilbur gets to know Charlotte, he admires her cleverness and compassionate nature. Charlotte is the one who saves Wilbur from the farmer's plan to kill him. Her plan is to spin a web and weave "Some Pig" in the center of it. Charlotte continues the "miracle" with words such as "Terrific" and "Radiant" spun on different occasions. This of course convinces Mr. Zuckerman that he should spare Wilbur from his fate and enter him in the local fair's pig contest.

These acts of Charlotte endear her to Wilbur completely, so that gradually he transfers his love from Fern to this clever spider who becomes mother, father, and friend to him. Wilbur is attempting to seek some sense of identity now. His future seems secure. He wants to become like Charlotte so much that he even attempts to spin a web! Wilbur asks Templeton, the barnyard rat to tie a string to his tail. Wilbur climbs to the top of a manure pile with his string trailing behind him. He throws himself into the air, and unfortunately falls "with a thud, crushed and hurt." Charlotte comforts him as usual.

When Charlotte tells Wilbur that she is a "sedentary spider" Wilbur claims that he is "sort of sedentary" too. Wilbur wants to be like Charlotte and needs her protection and love. Charlotte constantly chides the other animals for poking fun at Wilbur and in her "mother" role admonishes Wilbur to "eat" and "sleep" and to "never worry, never hurry."

Thus, Wilbur in Stage III begins to enter into the "politics" of the barnyard. He is in the intrusive mode characterized by "intrusion into space by vigorous locomotion (Wilbur's spinning, running away), intrusion into the unknown by consuming curiosity (continuous questioning by Wilbur of Charlotte's spinning mechanisms), intrusions into people's ears and minds by aggressive voice" (Wilbur's incessant chatting at night until finally Charlotte tells him "good night—no more talking, close your eyes and go to sleep"). Finally, Erikson says the most frightening intrusion for the young child is "the thought of the phallus intruding the female body." Wilbur's love for Charlotte never quite reaches the sexual form in this children's story, but certainly the desire to be totally like Charlotte, and to be close to her is expressed.

Industry vs Inferiority designates Erikson's Stage IV and this period roughly covers the early school years. Children begin to move outside of the family and turn to other models such as teachers and parents of other children. We begin to see such a movement on the part of Fern. She is now interested in someone other than Wilbur, namely a boy named Henry Fussy. Fern's budding heterosexual drive begins and Dr. Dorian, whom Mrs. Arable consults, feels convinced that Henry will become as interesting to Fern as pigs and spiders.

Fern's brother Avery epitomizes the Stage IV child. As Mrs. Arable puts it: "Avery is always fine. Of course, he gets into poison ivy and gets stung by wasps and bees and brings frogs and snakes home and breaks everything he lays his hands on. He's fine."

Avery generally walks around with his rifle in one hand, his wooden dagger in the other. Avery also enjoys the adventure and danger of his Uncle Zuckerman's swing. In one tense moment Avery is about to capture Charlotte, the spider, but fortunately for poor Wilbur, Avery loses his balance as he climbs over a fence, breaks an old goose egg that the rat Templeton had been hoarding and the stink is so bad that Avery is forced to retreat. We see Avery as the venturesome, fearless child attempting to master his environment. He is perpetually curious and works with his hands to make things. Erikson warns us that in this stage there may be the danger of an overly conforming child who accepts work as the only criterion of his worth. There is always the danger too that the child might lose some of his earlier imaginativeness and playfulness and submit to "what Marx called 'craft-idiocy,' i.e., become a slave of his technology and of its dominant role typology."

As childhood comes to an end, we enter Stage V or adolescence. Erikson calls this stage *Identity vs Identity Confusion*. White's discussion of Wilbur's need to imitate Charlotte in Stage III may be similarly used to illustrate Stage V. Wilbur has to accept the fact that he cannot be a spider. His attempts to spin a web were funny and acceptable for a baby pig trying to be like his adopted mother, but now as Wilbur matures he must accept himself as a "pig" just as each individual must attempt to carve out his own identity. In this period the adolescent readies himself for his future occupation. He clearly establishes his sexual identification. He seeks approval from peers and needs to belong to a group at the same time that he asserts his independence.

Charlotte's consistent praise of Wilbur through her weaving of words "radiant," "terrific," "some pig" help Wilbur gain some confidence in himself and eventually Wilbur becomes the center of attraction in the barnyard. Wilbur remains modest and usually felt "happy and confident." Sometimes he worries about the future and has fears of being slaughtered. But Charlotte's plan works so well, that Mr. Zuckerman enters Wilbur's name in the local fair. All the family hopes Wilbur would win a prize. Eventually Wilbur feels good about being a "pig," and becomes a pig "any man would be proud of." White describes Wilbur's attempts to live up to his reputation.

> When Charlotte's web said *Some Pig,* Wilbur had tried to look like some pig. When Charlotte's web said *Terrific,* Wilbur had tried to look terrific. And now that the web said *Radiant,* he did everything possible to make himself glow.

The young adolescent experiences many of the same highs and lows of Wilbur in this stage. Of course one of the prime concerns in this identity period is that of choices about future work and career. The sexual concerns are pressing in this period as well—and here is one area that White does not treat since this is a book for children. As mentioned we do get a small vignette dealing with Fern's attraction to Henry Fussy—but this is a minor part of the story.

Erikson discusses some further areas of concern for the adolescent—his clannishness and need to belong to a group; his willingness to accept idealogies and the inherent dangers in such acceptance of totalitarian doctrines. In ***Charlotte's Web,*** we see the democracy of the barnyard at work and the need for animals to help each other. Certainly, Templeton the miserly, overeating rat even learns to contribute to the welfare of the barnyard society through his help in finding words for Charlotte to copy, and later he helps to release Charlotte's egg sac from the ceiling. White demonstrates how each animal finds his place and purpose, just as Erikson describes in his discussions on identity.

The last three stages that Erikson deals with are those of the adult: *Intimacy vs Isolation, Generativity vs Stagnation,* and finally, *Integrity vs Despair.* Erikson sees these stages as those "beyond identity," and he suggests that some forms of identity crises may even occur in the later stages of the life cycle. The first of these stages beyond identity deals with intimacy. Erikson does not refer only to sexual intimacy, but to warm, close relationships between people. We see the warmth expressed in both the Arable and Zuckerman families that White writes about. Fern's parents give their children a secure and loving home, because their relationship as man and wife is presented as warm and loving. The Zuckermans are similarly portrayed. We witness the mutual cooperation and effort that the parents put forth in scrubbing Wilbur and readying him for the fair. We share in the joy of the Arables and Zuckermans as they hug and kiss each other when Wilbur wins a medal. As White puts it, "A great feeling of happiness swept over the Zuckermans and Arables. This was the greatest moment in Mr. Zuckerman's life. It is deeply satisfying to win a prize in front of a lot of people."

The pride is conveyed to Avery who does a wild dance, and of course all the others feel proud as well. We also see the intimacy that develops between Wilbur the pig and Charlotte the spider. Charlotte loves Wilbur but is also keenly aware of her function on earth, to spin webs, capture her food, and eventually form her egg sac. Her capacity to give love blends well with the following Erikson statement concerning love. "It is the guardian of that elusive and yet all-pervasive power of cultural and personal style which binds into a 'way of life' the affiliations of competition, and cooperation, production and procreation."

As ***Charlotte's Web*** draws to a close, White deals with Charlotte's procreation. Charlotte's love is so strong for Wilbur that she goes along to the fair with him in his crate despite her own weakened condition. She has reached the period in her life cycle when she must prepare an egg sac for her young. Nevertheless, she does spin her last tribute to Wilbur at the fair—the word *Humble.* Then Charlotte begins her final project—her "magnum opus" or her "great work—the finest thing I have ever made." Inside her sac are five hundred and fourteen eggs—all carefully counted by Charlotte. Charlotte informs Wilbur that her babies will be born in the following spring. Erikson states that generativity is "primarily the concern for establishing and guiding the next generation." Erikson makes an important point that the "mere fact of having or even wanting children does not achieve generativity." One must be a warm and tender caretaker. Erikson is also aware of those adults whose generativity drive takes the form of "altruistic concern" such as the performance of good works and concern for the community at large. In *Charlotte's Web* the theme of generativity is seen in the birth of Wilbur, the birth of the seven goslings, and finally the birth of Charlotte's babies.

The last adult stage, *Integrity* is sensitively treated by White through his description of Charlotte's death. The mature adult in this last phase of life fully accepts and does not fear his death. The aging person learns that only he, himself, is responsible for his own life, and that, "an individual life is the accidental coincidence of but one life cycle with but one segment of history, and that for him all human integrity stands and falls with the one style of integrity of which he partakes."

As Charlotte is about to die, her thoughts are for the future. She reminds Wilbur of the changing seasons, the sounds and smells in "this lovely world" and of the friendships he will continue to have. Just as Erikson delineates this eighth and final stage of life and expresses his thoughts about man's concern for those who live after him, Charlotte can only think of Wilbur and her unborn babies as she languishes. Charlotte's last speech to Wilbur is one of touching beauty. Wilbur is distraught to find that Charlotte is dying and shamefacedly he reminds her of how once he thought she was "cruel and bloodthirsty." Charlotte replies,

> "You have been my friend . . . I wove my webs for you because I liked you. After all, what's life, anyway? We're born, we live a little while, we die. A spider's life can't help being something of a mess, with all this trapping and eating of flies. By helping you, perhaps I was trying to lift up my life a trifle. Heavens knows anyone's life can stand a little of that."

Wilbur remains on the farm and in the spring, Charlotte's babies emerge from the egg sac. Each spring two or three spiders "set up housekeeping" in the doorway of Zuckerman's barn, and become friends of Wilbur. Wilbur has learned the meaning of love, compassion, and friendship from his spider friend, and indeed Charlotte's message to Wilbur blends so well with Erikson's statement,

> "I am what survives of me."

Virginia L. Wolf (essay date 1986)

SOURCE: Wolf, Virginia L. "The Cycle of the Seasons: Without and Within Time." *Children's Literature Association Quarterly,* vol. 10, no. 4, 1986, pp. 192-96.

[*In the following essay, Wolf relies on Northrop Frye's* The Anatomy of Criticism *(1957) to demonstrate how* Charlotte's Web *(1952), among other children's novels, relies on the passage of the seasons not only to create the narrative structure of time passing, but also to provide a communal vision of an idealized world that celebrates the life cycle of humans and animals.*]

Seeds grow to plants, yield their harvest, and die, the earth lying dormant and barren until the cycle begins anew. Within a year an animal may also progress from birth to full maturity, producing its own offspring. Similarly dependent upon the natural cycle, people find in the seasons multi-leveled and universal symbols. We see spring as childhood, summer as adolescence, fall as maturity, and winter as old age. On the religious or mythic level, the cycle of the seasons becomes the birth, death, and return of a divine being. In literature, according to Northrop Frye, there are *mythoi,* or generic plots, associated with the seasons—comedy with spring, romance with summer, tragedy with autumn, and irony with winter (162). The full cycle may suggest permanence, promising transcendence as spring follows winter or threatening endless repetition as summer leads to fall. Or, it may capture continuous change as each season offers new and unique experiences.

In a children's novel whose primary setting is home, formal requirements often necessitate the use of the cycle of the seasons. Novels using this setting differ enormously, depending on their individual content, especially the age of their protagonists, but besides their use of the seasons, they share other characteristics. Typically, they concentrate on a very small setting, introduce very little conflict, and celebrate a way of life. They may seem a collection of episodes with no clear-cut order. But, as I intend to demonstrate, the cycle of the seasons gives them form and, in the process, meaning.

Four such novels are E. B. White's *Charlotte's Web,* Laura Ingalls Wilder's *Little House in the Big Woods,* Eleanor Estes's *The Moffats,* and Louisa May Alcott's *Little Women, Part I.* All four are relatively stationary in space, focusing on their respective protagonists' homes, and all four have a strong female emphasis. None of them, furthermore, introduces serious conflict. On the other hand, there are many differences among them. *Charlotte's Web* runs from spring to spring, *The Moffats* from summer to summer, *Little House in the Big Woods* from autumn to autumn, and *Little Women* from winter to winter. Also differing are the seasons emphasized, ***Charlotte's Web*** and *The Moffats* stressing summer and *Little House in the Big Woods* and *Little Women* stressing winter. The most significant differences, however, are those created by the age range of the protagonists. Wilbur is one at the end of ***Charlotte's Web****,* Laura six at the end of *Little House,* Janey nine at the end of *The Moffats,* and Jo sixteen at the end of *Little Women.* The age of the protagonist is, of course, an essential factor in determining the age of the child reader of a novel and the form this novel can take. In their similarities and differences, in other words, these novels should provide the critic with the opportunity for increased understanding of the ways children's novels vary for the sake of audience.

At the same time, they also reveal the potential of the cycle of the seasons for structuring children's novels set in homes. In Northrop Frye's terms, ***Charlotte's Web*** and *Little House in the Big Woods* are romance, both very nearly becoming myth, and *The Moffats* and *Little Women* are comedy. Frye uses the term myth to refer to a communal vision controlling a work of literature. "Undisplaced myth, generally concerned with gods or demons" (139) he sees as the center of all literature, which often displaces, or adapts, myth to varying degrees for the sake of plausibility. To the extent that the techniques of mimesis—verisimilitude, fullness and accuracy of description, for example—characterize a literary work, in other words, myth is displaced (51, 139-140, 365-367). Romance Frye defines as "the mythos of literature concerned primarily with an idealized world" (367), and as the one which least displaces myth. Both similar and different, comedy is the mythos of literature in which myth is greatly displaced, resulting in romantic comedy to the extent that the ending represents an ideal, and ironic comedy to the extent that it does not (163-186). The tragic mythos, which begins in romance and ends in irony, its attention to mimesis qualified only by its heroic protagonist, and the ironic mythos, which parodies myth, its attention to mimesis offering demonic visions, are irrelevant here. These four novels show how the natural cycle can work against irony and, especially, tragedy. They use the cycle to elevate reality toward the ideal and to embody optimism, and in two of them story becomes a song of celebration.

Certainly ***Charlotte's Web*** is such a song, and White's careful evocation of the seasons are its chords. Quite deliberately, he invokes the various levels of meaning associated with each season. Spring as a time for birth begins and ends the novel. Wilbur the pig is born in spring, matures in summer and fall when, after Wilbur's triumph at the fair as a result of Charlotte's writing words in her web, she, his good friend and surrogate mother, dies. Through winter Wilbur guards Charlotte's egg sac, from which, the following spring, Charlotte's daughters are born. In the background of this story are White's tributes to the changes in vegetation and animals and Fern's turning from pigs to boys. On all but the explicitly religious level, in other words, the cycle informs ***Charlotte's Web,*** celebrating the cycle of life. In Wilbur's taking Charlotte's place as parent and in the novel's ending, as it began, with birth and spring, however, White offers us myth, suggesting that the reassurance of continuity is consolation for loss and change. Thus the novel stands at the top of Frye's wheel of *mythoi,* as a romance near the realm of myth.

This analysis of the novel's mythic structure, though, does not describe with sufficient specificity White's unique use of the seasons. Only two and a half chapters occur in spring, only one half chapter in winter, with seven in fall and twelve in summer. ***Charlotte's Web*** is mostly a novel of summer, celebrating growth—Wilbur's to maturity, Charlotte's in heroism, and Wilbur's and Charlotte's as friends The two occasions on which White literally breaks into song—that of the birds and that of the crickets—are, respectively, early and late summer. The first ends, "The song sparrow who knows how brief and lovely life is, says 'Sweet, sweet, sweet interlude; sweet, sweet, sweet interlude'" (43). The second begins, "The crickets sang in the grasses. They sang the song of summer's ending, a sad, monotonous song. 'Summer is over and gone,' they sang. 'Over and gone, over and gone. Summer is dying, dying.' ... Even on the most beautiful days in the whole year—the days when summer is changing into fall—the crickets spread the rumor of sadness and change" (113).

These passages capture the bittersweet quality of White's narrative. His great love for life balances his acute awareness of its rapid passing. Telling the story of a pig and a spider, his narrative also accentuates life's brevity—a pig reaching maturity in only one year, a spider living only from spring to autumn. What's more, as many have noticed, lovingly portraying even these lowly creatures, White shows us the beauty—the miracle—of all life. Summer is White's season precisely for this reason: "Everywhere you look is life; even the little ball of spit on the weed stalk, if you poke it apart, has a green worm in it. And on the under side of the leaf of the potato vine are the bright orange eggs of the potato bug" (43-44).

At the heart of ***Charlotte's Web*** lie summer and love—Wilbur's love for his manure pile, Charlotte's and Wilbur's love for one another, White's love for them, and the reader's growing awareness that love may somehow make change and loss—maybe even death—bearable. For the source of continuity is love: Charlotte guaranteeing Wilbur's survival,

Wilbur returning the favor with her daughters, and White singing his song of the life cycle to all his readers—those children who will grow up to take his place. Summer is the season of *Charlotte's Web,* the cycle of the seasons functioning to assure us of summer's return.

Winter, on the other hand, is the season of *Little House in the Big Woods.* In many ways nearly the opposite of *Charlotte's Web,* Wilder's novel nevertheless is also romance and at the top of Frye's wheel, near the realm of myth. Beginning and ending in autumn, devoting only one chapter each to spring and summer, but seven of its thirteen to winter, this novel celebrates not continuity but security and finally permanence. Similarly preoccupied with the small details of ordinary life among loved ones at home, *Little House in the Big Woods* does not, like *Charlotte's Web,* speak of loss or change or growth. It rather celebrates the constant, eternal vision at the heart of all the Little House books. Rather than the immediate reality alive in White's descriptions of nature, Wilder gives us a dream of the past, the myth of the pioneer in harmony with nature. Rather than sing of growth and change, this novel works against the cycle's tendency to suggest movement. By means of balanced images and the memory of a child's winter, it seems static, concluding in Laura's words, "'This is now.' She was glad that the cozy house, and Pa and Ma and the firelight and the music, were now. They could not be forgotten, she thought, because now is now. It can never be a long time ago" (176).

As I have pointed out elsewhere, balanced antitheses structure *Little House in the Big Woods*: home and wilderness, little and big, warm and cold, cozy and dangerous, Ma and Pa, play and work, story and reality, and so forth. This structure exists at the level of word, image, chapter, and book, achieving an equilibrium of opposites—a stasis. The winter setting augments this effect. For in the severe cold, the Ingallses, especially Laura, must stay inside the little house and limit their movement. Indeed, in the Big Woods, a child must always stay close to home. Finally, the reader's awareness that this winter's tale is that of a woman who "once upon a time, sixty years ago, . . . lived in the Big Woods" (1) creates an illusion of permanence, the novel offering the finished perfection of memory or art, the core of the person Laura Ingalls Wilder was.

Winter, the season of old age, pervades this tale of childhood as another sigh that the novel is memory. But winter also, as I've already noted, functions to focus our attention inside the house on Laura's Ma and Pa—her security. Ultimately, what this novel emphasizes is like one part of *Charlotte's Web*: Wilbur's dependence on Charlotte and Charlotte's nurture of Wilbur. Again there is a celebration of love, a source not of continuity but, rather, of security or permanence in an otherwise impermanent, constantly changing world. In the other Little House books Laura will grow up and take her place as a parent, as Wilbur does in the course of White's novel; in the human world growing up usually takes more time than in the vegetable or animal worlds. Thus *Little House in the Big Woods* portrays a little girl safe in her parents' love for her, internalizing the values that will one day enable her as a parent and writer to offer children the security of love. In every way, *Little House* is a vision, a winter dream, the cycle of the seasons functioning to balance opposites and to suggest permanence.

Estes' *The Moffats* returns us to summer and autumn, these seasons occupying four each of the twelve chapters with winter and spring occupying two each. Because no one season dominates, the cycle is more obvious than in the first two books discussed, especially so since the four chapters set in summer occur in two sets of two chapters each that begin and end the novel. The effect is to emphasize movement and passing time, and that is in keeping with a romantic comedy that is more removed from the mythic realm than either *Charlotte's Web* or *Little House in the Big Woods.*

Set within the human world, *The Moffats* offers a small town environment. Like the first two, this novel celebrates home, detailing the perfection of the yellow house exactly in the middle of New Dollar Street in Cranbury. But unlike the youngsters in either *Little House* or *Charlotte's Web,* the four Moffat children venture out into the community, meeting Mrs. Squire, Mr. Baxter, Dr. Witty, Chief Mulligan, Superintendent of Schools Pennypepper, and many others. Community is, of course, more characteristic of comedy than of romance, whose tendency is to focus on the isolated and special individual or group. To be sure, the community of Cranbury is a very good one—safe and loving. But the loss of the yellow house at the end of the novel, fear of its loss structuring the entire novel, distances *The Moffats* from the ideal vision central to the first two novels. The Moffats' poverty and Rufus's scarlet fever, which control the novel's winter chapters, also displace myth.

At first the myth structuring *Little House in the Big Woods* may seem to be present in *The Moffats*. Because we most often share Janey's point of view, we experience the yellow house as home—with all the warmth, security, and love associated with home. But we also experience her fear of its loss and her resistance to change. Indeed, these feelings provide the novel with its opening, middle, and last chapters, titled, respectively, "The Yellow House on New Dollar Street," "Another Sign on the Yellow House," and "The Last Chapter in the Yellow House," and they emerge as a motif throughout the novel. Janey attempts to cover the for-sale sign with mud, to ignore it, and in many other ways to make it go away. In the last chapter her thoughts still reveal her persistance. She fears losing all the joys of childhood. "But Jane has a feeling that just as surely as that they, the Moffats, were moving away from the yellow house that day, time would take these other keen delights from her too" (277). Another perspective balances Janey's lament. In the cycle of the seasons, Estes depicts the exciting variety of people and activities outside the yellow house. She elebrates change. And when Janey meets Nancy Stokes, who is her nextdoor neighbor at the Moffats' new home and becomes her first best friend, we hear Estes' distant invocation of the myth central to *Charlotte's Web*. Change brings loss but also new delights.

The reassurance of neither continuity nor permanence is given; myth is displaced. Janey is consoled by Nancy Stokes's existence and her offer of friendship, but only the reader sees what Estes implies—that leaving her childhood home, Janey moves toward adolescence and peer relationships. Because the book limits us to human life and to what might actually happen, we again have only a small part of the life cycle. Janey matures only slightly. Thus, rather than offer us the mythic accommodated to human existence as does romance, *The Moffats* is comedy, and the mythic dimension is relegated to the cyclical structure that counterpoints the novel's lament of loss.

Myth is even more displaced in *Little Women* than in *The Moffats,* irony more centrally informing. Like *Little House* it emphasizes winter, but like *The Moffats,* it uses the cycle somewhat more obviously than *Charlotte's Web* or *Little House,* dividing winter into two sets of chapters, the eight beginning and the six concluding ones. However, no other season gets as much attention as winter, fall occupying five chapters and spring and summer only two each. This emphasis on winter does not always, though, result in the cozy security of *Little House in the Big Woods.* The March girls, like the Moffats, do not stay home but rather venture out into a community—one less safe and less ideal than Cranbury. In addition, this community enters the March home, in the form of war to take Mr. and—eventually—Mrs. March away, in the form of scarlet fever nearly to kill Beth, and in the form of vanity and other sins to trouble Meg, Jo, and Amy. There is more difficulty—more of what Frye calls the demonic—in *Little Women* than in the other three novels. But this difficulty is internal rather than external. Psychology, rather than setting or adventure, is the focus of *Little Women*. It portrays the individual in conflict with society and is comic insofar as the individual's conformity and society's triumph seem justified and ironic insofar as they don't. But to the extent that Alcott idealizes character and setting, the novel is romantic comedy.

The ideal of home and female values forms the heart of *Little Women.* Self-sacrifice and living for others are what Marmee tries to teach and what Meg, Jo, Beth, and Amy try to learn. Beginning and ending near Christmas, the novel portrays the girls' efforts to internalize the Christian ethic. David Smith points out Alcott's use of Bunyan's *Pilgrim's Progress* to structure this effort. But we might notice other structures.

The obstacles of the first nine chapters are their father's absence, work, a lack of pretty possessions, certain moral failings—such as a quick temper, shyness, and vanity—and also wintry weather. After success in handling these problems, the girls relax somewhat from their pilgrims' progress for a holiday at home in the spring, summer, and early fall chapters. Then in the last nine chapters winter once again returns, and they confront their father's illness, their mother's absence, and Beth's near death. The first period of winter clearly prepares them for the greater difficulty of the second period, winter functioning here with all of its typical symbolism to suggest the demonic or ironic world. Home is the family refuge from winter as it is in *Little House,* not because it is physically safe but because it symbolizes spiritual safety—the possibility of eternal life.

The spiritual ideal is not realized in this novel, as Smith laments in his study of how it uses *Pilgrim's Progress.* Rather, the ideal of home functions as a goal toward which the girls work. They improve, but they also backslide. Alcott's concern with mimesis precludes their achieving the ideal; it requires their struggle, occasional failure, and partial success. Indeed, it requires that their success be psychological; that is, essentially they achieve increased self-awareness. Jo is typical. This passionate, energetic person is too impulsive—too quick to anger and to generosity. She feels so intensely that she can be blind to others' feelings and needs. Thus she fails to warn Amy about the thin ice, and Amy nearly drowns. Jo learns about the dangers of her temper; she learns some self-control. But even near the end of the novel she sells her hair to help her father and blurts out her opposition to Meg's engagement. Strong feelings still control her behavior, somewhat tempered by increased self-awareness and self-control.

On the other hand, Jo represents those values opposing home. An assertive, fully alive, non-traditional, creative young woman, she forces the reader to question Mr. and Mrs. March's efforts to get her to conform to the traditional female role. Jo's restless spirit functions like the winter wilderness in *Little House.* She is beautiful and admirable despite the dangers of her impulsiveness. As a character, she introduces irony for any reader recognizing that self-sacrifice for the sake of being good is self-destructive, and that giving of one's self constitutes maturity only when the giving is what one genuinely cares to do. There is significant tension in the novel between sympathy for Jo, whom Mr. March calls his "wild girl" (200), and the ideal of home, which Mrs. March promotes. Like many protagonists of romance, Jo opposes in her very being the loss of freedom—the loss of life—involved in conformity for the sake of security. Indeed, Jo's grief over her eventual loss of Meg somewhat qualifies the novel's happy ending with the family's reunion and Meg's engagement. Jo's resistance to growing up questions the value and degree of her conformity. Within the novel, in any case, she balances the "little women" as the winter wilderness balances the snug little house in Wilder's novel. Both she and her sisters are necessary to the novel because the ambiguity—the thematic richness—of *Little Women* resides in their opposition.

Clearly character, much more than setting, conveys meaning in *Little Women*, this emphasis on character displacing the kind of explicit reliance upon the seasonal symbolism that we find in ***Charlotte's Web*** and to a lesser extent in *Little House in the Big Woods* and *The Moffats*. Myth gives way gradually to mimesis and ambiguity as we move away from the natural cycle toward human life, away from the ideal toward the actual, away from dream toward nightmare, away from summer toward winter, and away from romance toward comedy. Arranged as I have discussed them, these four children's novels reveal such movement, each appealing to an audience increasingly mature. Altogether they represent only two of Frye's four *mythoi*. Because the seasonal cycle promises repetition and the settings—the four homes—are much more idyllic than demonic, none of these four novels is very ironic or at all tragic. They are nevertheless, I think, fairly typical of the children's novel as a genre. From ***Charlotte's Web*** to *Little Women*, we move from the use of the cycle of the seasons as mythic and clearly without the boundaries of time toward increased attention to the details of character and setting within time so that the mythic significance of the seasonal cycle is displaced. Indeed, in these four novels the promise of spring in ***Charlotte's Web***—of rebirth and eternal life—is replaced by the promise of Christmas in *Little Women*—the promise of a promise. In this fashion does literature for increasingly mature readers translate with increasing complexity the apparent simplicity of myths such as those associated with the cycle of the seasons.

References

Alcott, Louisa M. *Little Women*. Boston: Little Brown & Co., 1968; Boston: Roberts Brothers, 1868.

Estes, Eleanor. *The Moffats*. New York: Harcourt, Brace, & World, 1941.

Frye, Northrop. *The Anatomy of Criticism*. Princeton, NJ: Princeton University Press, 1957.

Smith, David E. *John Bunyan's America*. Bloomington, IN: Indiana University Press, 1966.

White, E. B. *Charlotte's Web*. New York: Harper & Row, 1952.

Wilder, Laura Ingalls. *Little House in the Big Woods*. New York: Harper & Brothers, 1932.

Wolf, Virginia. "The Symbolic Center: *Little House in the Big Woods*." *Children's Literature in Education* 13 (Autumn 1982): 107-114.

Ashraf H. A. Rushdy (essay date 1991)

SOURCE: Rushdy, Ashraf H. A. "'The Miracle of the Web': Community, Desire, and Narrativity in *Charlotte's Web*." *The Lion and the Unicorn*, vol. 15, no. 2, 1991, pp. 35-60.

[*In the following essay, Rushdy contrasts the intellectual history around concepts of art, psychology, and ideology as they both reflect culture and shape, weave, or change culture. He contends that the web in* Charlotte's Web *(1952) becomes a potent symbol for how words, such as "some pig" or "humble," can change the meaning of a childhood ideology.*]

In the opening scene of ***Charlotte's Web***, Mr. Arable sets out to slaughter the recently-born runt because, as he tells his daughter, a "weakling makes trouble" within the "litter" (3). At the end of the novel, we are told that "Mr. Zuckerman took fine care of Wilbur all the rest of his days" (183). What happens between Wilbur's perilous beginning and his auspicious maturity has much to do with a sense of community. Regarded as a nuisance within and to his original community, the litter into which he was born, Wilbur is saved from the fate of most pigs—"smoked bacon and ham" as the insensitive old sheep puts it (49)—because at the end he is made to belong to another community made up of his human "friends and admirers." Wilbur's integration into this human community, of course, is the result of Charlotte's work. Those who "often visited" Wilbur do so *because* they never forgot "the year of his triumph and the miracle of the web" (183). Also, as most readers realize, Wilbur's integration into the human community is just one example of the novel's concern with demonstrating other forms of integration, especially Fern's maturation and entry into the order of sexuality. In fact, these two forms of integration form parallel plots in this novel. At the very moment Wilbur receives a special award from the Fair committee, and thereby gains a license to live without the fear of gracing a dinner table, Fern runs off "ducking and dodging through the crowd, in search of Henry" (156). Several enlightening congruences exist between Wilbur's integration into the human community and Fern's into the realm of sexual desire (symbolized by her search for Henry Fussy), but the basic similarity involves the issue I would argue to be underlying the novel as a whole. **Charlotte's Web** may be said to be a representation of the integral function of narratives in the orientation and reorientation of individual and communal desires.

As such a representation, White's novel anticipates some recent theorizing about desire as a social construct. Arguing against a recrudescence of a facile romanticism which stipulates that desire is the expression of an innate recognition of absence (that it is a form of *natural* longing), Gilles Deleuze and Félix Guattari contend that desire "has nothing to do with a natural or spontaneous determination; there is no desire but assembling, assembled, desire" (399). In the same vein, René Girard states that desire is never original and never natural. Rather, an individual learns to desire an object because that individual sees a representation of another individual—fictional or real—desiring the same object or a simulacrum of the same object (*Deceit* 1-52). As he phrases it elsewhere, desire is always "a second-hand desire" ("Mimetic Desire" 2). It is second-hand because it is imitative (as Girard puts it), an "assemblage" (as Deleuze and Guattari put it), or a result of conforming to an already established pattern. Desire is, in other words, a construct of culture. In **Charlotte's Web,** White represents this theoretical debate on desire as either a natural effluence or a cultural form in the scene of Mrs. Arable's visit to Dr. Dorian.

Thinking that her daughter's interest in the animals at the Zuckermans' farm "didn't seem natural," Mrs. Arable decides to visit Dr. Dorian (107). The visit falls into two distinct parts. In the first part, Dr. Dorian opens his diagnosis with some preliminary remarks on the difference between culture and nature. Seemingly unimpressed by the fact that the spider had written a word in her web, Dr. Dorian notes that the very act of a spider's weaving a web is itself a "miracle" (109). In response to Mrs. Arable's contention that she herself can knit and crochet, Dr. Dorian notes that she was "taught" to do so while a spider "knows how to spin a web without any instructions from anybody." While Mrs. Arable is taught to perform her manual work and thereby belongs to the realm of culture, Charlotte, who is not taught but driven by instinct to spin a web, belongs to the realm of nature. According to the good doctor, such instinctual response is what constitutes a "miracle" (110). On the surface, Dr. Dorian appears to have romantic ideals about nature. Despite what appear to be facile romantic ideals, though, Dr. Dorian does not finally subscribe to a simple naturalism to explain the process of a child's maturation. Indeed, he makes the distinction between natural instinct and cultural education in order to return to Mrs. Arable's original concern—her daughter.

In the second part of their meeting, Dr. Dorian asks Mrs. Arable whether her daughter knows any boys. She responds brightly, by noting that Fern knows Henry Fussy—the same Henry after whom Fern will eventually go ducking and dodging. After initially noting the limited appeal of Henry—"I would say, offhand, that spiders and pigs were fully as interesting as Henry Fussy"—Dr. Dorian nonetheless assures Mrs. Arable that Fern will soon develop a deeper interest in boys. As he says, "I predict that the day will come when even Henry will drop some chance remark that catches Fern's attention" (111). This, then, appears to be Dr. Dorian's two-part diagnosis. The work of culture is done within communities—the elders teach those younger how to react to given environmental conditions, just as Mrs. Arable had been taught to knit and crochet by her mother. Communities are formed by two interactive agents—desire and narrative. Fern will one day attend to Henry as a potential suitor because her sense of what is desirable will change. At the same time, her sense of what is desirable will change because she will have been the auditor of a series of cultural stories about how desire should be directed. Indeed, but two chapters later Fern will wear her prettiest dress to the County Fair "because she knew she would see boys at the Fair" (119). Fern learns desire, we might say, by hearing stories about what is desirable. Moreover, because she has some idea of the form and content of those acculturating stories, she will respond, as Dr. Dorian predicted, to Henry's own narrative gifts with some attention. When Henry is able to drop the right "chance remark," it will be *right* because it has a place in Fern's expectations of what constitutes adolescent courtship. It is not likely that Henry will break new ground in the rhetoric of romance. He will succeed only because he happens to use the discourse which Fern has been prepared to understand. And, of course, Fern's expectations are developed and nurtured by the stories she grows up hearing and reading. So, according to Dr. Dorian's diagnosis of civilization and its contents, cultural transmission works essentially because the stories a community tells its initiates operate on and direct those initiates' desires.

In other words, individuals are solicited within communities by narratives which direct their desires toward certain objects because these stories predominantly tell of the rewards for following such directed desires (especially the reward of a sense of community) and the punishments meted out to those who do not follow those directions (especially a sense of ostracization). What is true of Fern's integration into communal relations with other human children, especially romantic relations with boys, is also true of Wilbur's integration into the human community. Communal sensibilities are formed, White seems to be telling us, by narratives which operate on desires. We can say of this novel that community is a process of the recognition of integration and diversity, of how individuals come to belong to a larger social reality and also learn to note the differences within and beyond that social reality. Moreover, community is especially directed by these two inter-related impulses or agencies—desire and narrative. With this insight, White has indeed anticipated many recent cultural and literary theories regarding the relationship among narrative, culture, and desire.

Some contemporary theorists of "narrativity"—which, in its most significant form, is that branch of general narrative theory concerned with defining the sociohistorical interplay of text and reader—have attempted to discern in what ways and to what degree narrative forms and narrative acts define the relationship between desire and community.[1] These theorists attempt to see the basic play among desire as the intuition of an organic absence in the life of the psyche, narrative as the formal organization of stories which supplement the sense of absence, and community as the social organism within which desire is mediated and stories related.

One such theorist is Jean-François Lyotard. According to Lyotard, "desire" is one name for a general "principle of interaction and integration." In other words, desire, even what appears to be individual desire, is always mediated by a community, always a way of dealing with others and becoming one with others. In fact, Lyotard goes on to define "community" itself as "the desire experienced by diversity." According to Lyotard, individual desires become incorporated into communities by way of the subject's accession to a certain form of knowing: "With the willing of the will, there is displayed a time, memory and project, heritage and program. A narrative" (221). For Lyotard, then, the encompassing form of knowledge which promotes interaction and integration is narrative. Lyotard's attempt to describe how desire works within a community is part of a larger project of theorizing the work of narratives, the ways that narratives direct and redirect desires, produce communal sentiments, and act as transmitters for cultural norms and precedents.

One of the key contributors to that larger project has been Teresa de Lauretis. She has given us a rich paradigm to explain how narratives work upon desires. De Lauretis notes in *Alice Doesn't* that "a story . . . is always a question of desire" (112). Desire also, it turns out, is a question of narrative. To identify oneself as what she calls "a subject in a process" requires one to be "actively involved" in the acculturating stories in which one becomes imbricated (141). In her most recent volume, *Technologies of Gender*, she has reworked the term "narrativity" to describe the "effective functioning of narrative on and with the reader," thereby producing the "subject of reading" (108). De Lauretis offers us a description of how texts involve the reader into their workings and thereby transform the original desires the reader had brought to the narrative. Although de Lauretis is by no means losing sight of how any written text operates in a cultural framework—that is, any text is inscribing a pattern of desires which has already been articulated in other forms of social control such as law and decorum—she is nonetheless more interested in theorizing how individuals become caught up in the narratives they are taught to inhabit. Her concern, then, is to define the redirection in a reader's desire when the reader becomes *involved* in a text. In a somewhat different vein, Lyotard describes how narratives transmute individual desires into communal patterns. His overall concern, though, is like de Lauretis's in that he wishes to discern the alteration in an individual's desires when that individual becomes "interpellated" into a community.[2] There are, however, two unasked questions behind both these schemes. How do communities come to tell the particular stories they tell? And, more importantly, how can those who do not belong to certain communities—those who are not invited to participate in this congenial act of "integration"—act on those communities they wish to enter in such a way as to solicit that invitation?

Charlotte's Web, it seems to me, is a story about those two unasked questions. I wish to offer a reading of ***Charlotte's Web*** as a novel concerned with describing how individual agents can manipulate a given community's narrative *forms* and thereby alter the ways that the community directs individual desires. Once what John Fiske calls these "socially interested agents" (173) are able to act on a community's narrative *forms* to the degree of altering them and the desires they orient, then the community will tell itself stories which are more inviting for those individuals who are not yet a part of the community. What we have to define, then, is a pattern which incorporates narrative, desire, and community. To do so, we need to clarify the grounds upon which we are treading. Because we are dealing with narrative, we must elaborate a poetics. Because we are interested in thinking and desire, we must construct a psychology (which is, in turn, underwritten by an epistemology). Because we are discussing a community, we have to define an ideology. In less abstract terms, we can say that in order to define a pattern which describes the interplay of narrative, desire, and community we have to ask three pertinent questions. First, in a given model what is the metaphor capable of describing the relationship between art and society? This question defines the model's poetics. Second, what is the metaphor which is capable of describing the relationship between the mind and the environment? This question configures the model's psychology. Finally, what is the relationship between these metaphors and the ways societies interpellate their subjects? This question helps us define a given model's ideology. There has always been one dominant metaphor and one dominant model to answer these three questions—the metaphor of the mirror and what we may call the "reflective model" of interpellation. In *Charlotte's Web,* though, White challenges this dominant metaphor and, in doing so, he represents what can be called the "narrative model" of cultural transmission. Before we consider the articulation of that challenge in the novel itself, we need to have before us the terms of the two models.[3]

Reflective and Narrative Models of Cultural Transmission

The reflective model holds that texts work upon our sentiments and solicit our interest by claiming to mirror reality for us and, therefore, inviting us to inhabit a world which is apparently reflective of our own. Hayden White, one of our leading theorists of the relationship between narrative forms and historical events, has recently suggested that we ought to study the ways texts call up a "specific subjectivity" in the reader "who is supposed to entertain this representation of the world as a realistic one in virtue of its congeniality to the imaginary relationship the subject bears to his own social and cultural situation" (193). That is, the reader becomes involved in a text because that text is held up as a mirror to psychological verities and supposedly reflects actual social relations. In other words, in an echo of Aristotle's revision of the basic Platonic metaphor of art, narratives act as mirrors held up to nature. In answer to our first question, then, the metaphor best able to describe the relationship between art and society is the mirror.

According to the theorists of the reflective model, the answer to our second question—regarding the metaphor describing the relationship between mind and environment—is the same as the answer to the first. The metaphor that best describes how the mind works on the environment is that of the mirror. As Richard Rorty has demonstrated, the dominant tradition in Western philosophy suggests that "knowledge [is] a set of immaterial representations" which the mind reflects (93). This tradition begins, Rorty states, as do so many others, with Aristotle who argued that "intellect ... is both mirror and eye in one" (45). Even a philosophical tradition apparently as different from Aristotle's as was Francis Bacon's still employed the same specular imagery. As Bacon has it, although the "mind of man is far from the nature of a clear and equal glass wherein the beams of things should reflect according to their true incidence," it nonetheless could aspire to that state (127). Rorty is right to note that this image of the "mind as a great mirror" holds "traditional philosophy captive" (12). Indeed, even contemporary philosophers who set out to challenge this tradition seem to falter when they come to close grips with it. Hilary Putnam, for instance, argues that while *language* does not reflect a given situation, "speakers" of language do "mirror the world" in the sense of their "constructing a symbolic representation" of their environment. This constitutes what Putnam calls "internal realism" (483). According to thinkers otherwise as different as Rorty and Robert Nozick, Putnam's "internal realism" fails because in Rorty's estimation it does not escape the traditional imagery of reflection (298-99) and in Nozick's estimation it cannot avoid the charges liable against any skeptical epistemology (168-69). The epistemology of the reflective model, then, is firmly based on the metaphor of the mirror.

When we take up the supplementary question of how desire operates in the psychology of the reflective model, we find again that the image of the mirror dominates discussion. The reflective model suggests that because desire operates in a narcissistic fashion it may be represented by a mirror. The major theorist here is Jacques Lacan. Although he does employ the metaphor of the mirror to explain the way that desire can be specular, Lacan (especially the Lacan of the 1964 seminars) avoids some of the problems of mirror-imagery because he posits a mirror that is substantially refractory—"As a specular mirage, love is essentially deception" (*Four Fundamental Concepts* 268). Even in the early essay of 1949, "The Mirror-Stage," Lacan had suggested that all investigation into desire should start "from the *function of méconnaissance* that characterizes the ego in all its structures" (*Écrits* 6).[4] Deception and misrecognition are not the usual modes of perception emphasized by theorists who use the metaphor of the mirror. We can even follow Lacan's advice, given in a paper of 1958, that "one should not be deceived by the metaphor of the mirror," but, in that case, we should also heed his question, asked in the same paper, "what is metaphor if not an effect of positive meaning[?]" (*Écrits* 229, 258). In any case, by 1964 Lacan had answered his own question with an affirmation that a metaphor is more than an "effect" of positive meaning; it is indeed a veritable agency of it. Lacan concludes his 1964 lectures by noting that transference, like all forms of love, can be mapped "only in the field of narcissism." Lacan, in the end, can represent only the model of desire as reflection. No statement more demonstrates this than his pronouncement that "To love is, essentially, to wish to be loved" (*Four Fundamental Concepts* 253). Or, as Girard puts it, "Desire is always reflection on desire" (*Things Hidden* 328). In the reflective model, desire is always a product of narcissism and it is always represented by a mirror-structure.

We have now before us a theory of how artifacts act as mirrors of society, how minds faithfully reflect the environment, and how desires are wrought of specular identification. To complete the theory of the reflective model, we need to define its formulation of how communities solicit individuals into their systems of thinking, believing, and representing. The foremost theorist here is Louis Althusser. According to Althusser, ideological interpellation is primarily reflective. The structure of ideology, he writes, is "*speculary,* i.e. a mirror-structure." This "mirror duplication is constitutive of ideology and ensures its functioning." The subject of the state is subjected to the State by believing that it (the subject) can "contemplate its own image (present and future)" in the mirror-structure of ideology and, therefore, be "guarantee[d] that everything really is so" (*Lenin and Philosophy* 180-81). Althusser elsewhere calls this structure "the vicious circle of the mirror relation of ideological recognition" (*Reading Capital* 53). The state's ideological apparatus interpellates its subjects by proposing that this speculary model is primary. Once the subjects of that state see themselves reflected in its workings, they accede to their place in the ongoing history of subjection.[5]

That, in sum, is the reflective model, a model solidly based on the metaphor of the mirror in its exploration of how texts work on society (by mimetic reflection), how the mind interacts with the environment (by mirroring it), how desires are provoked in individuals (by narcissistic reflection), and how individuals become members of a community (by speculary interpellation). It does not take much reflection to see that this model does not help us to understand how White answers the questions concerning the interplay of narrative, desire, and community. ***Charlotte's Web*** does not subscribe to either the metaphors or the presuppositions of the reflective model. It is in its title, I suggest, that we might find the answer to those three questions with which we began our analysis of the reflective model. Rather than suggesting that thinking and art are *reflections* of social relations, White suggests that thinking and art are *connected* to social relations. In other words, the mind and the novel are not mirrors of an external given but rather both are part of the construction of that external given. Mind and art are woven into the social relations they represent. The metaphor for the narrative model is thus a *web*—a tissue of connections in which mind, art, and society are wholly imbricated.[6]

We have already seen in our analysis of the reflective model how the metaphor which describes thinking and desire (its psychology) is also the metaphor which describes art (its poetics). It is no different for the narrative model. John Dewey, one of the foremost theorists of both the pragmatic process of mentation and the pragmatic purpose of art, elaborates a poetics for the narrative model. We can begin with examining the answer to the second question first—the question of what metaphor describes the relationship between mind and environment. Dewey's career, to a large extent, was an extended critique of specular theories of knowledge. Any "theory of knowing" which "is modeled after what was supposed to take place in the act of vision," he notes, produces as its "inevitable outcome" a "spectator theory of knowledge." It is Dewey's genius to have discerned the shift from speculation as a mental phenomenon to spectatorship as a human attitude toward the world. The problem with a spectator theory of knowledge, of course, is that it negates the productive nature of inquiry (*Quest for Certainty* 19). Knowledge, according to Dewey, does not work that way because it itself is a productive process: "consciousness of meanings, or having ideas, denotes an exigent re-making of meanings" (*Experience and Nature* 262). Arguing against the idea that the mind is a mirror reflecting the external world whence meanings lay and are derived, Dewey proposes a model of the mind as an agent constantly restructuring the ideas it re-makes. Dewey's interest is not in discerning how the ideas came to inhere in the mind, but rather in understanding what the mind can do with ideas once there—with the ideas, that is, once they start to play a role in the socialization of any individual within a community. In fact, following George Herbert Mead, Dewey defines "Mind" itself as a "function of social interactions" (*Experience* 6; Mead 50, 132-33). Earlier in his career he had defined "mind" as the "interaction of biological aptitudes with a social environment" (*Human Nature and Conduct* 3). In other words, "mind" is established in a process in which human "impulse" asserts itself deliberately against "an existing custom" (*Human Nature* 62). Reason in this model of mind is emphatically "not . . . a mere idle mirroring of pre-existent facts" (*Human Nature* 55). Reason, as Dewey remarks, depends on what "outlets and inhibitions" the social environment provides for any impulse to be "interwoven with other impulses" (*Human Nature* 69). In other words, the metaphor which describes how reason operates on the external environment is that of the web. Mind is not a mirror but an agent, not a place in which all external things are reflected in their supposed order but a recreating part of that external order.

According to Dewey, because thinking is an active process conducted within society, all human functions assume a significance in relation to other processes. Every human act is possessed of "infinite import" because the "little part of the scheme of affairs which is modifiable by our efforts is continuous with the rest of the world." With this psychology and this insight into the connectedness of diverse phenomena, Dewey is able to construct a poetics in which social relations are not mirrored but rather incorporated into the artwork. Art, according to Dewey, intimates the significance of human actions and evokes an appreciation of that significance by weaving a desire for reforming the world into the "texture of our lives" (*Human Nature* 180). Art is not simply a faithful reflection of what is out there; rather "all art is a process of making the world a different place in which to live" (*Experience* 272). Like thinking, art is an "active productive process" (*Experience* 281). Because art shares with rhetoric a desire for altering what it represents, and because (to borrow a phrase) our thinking makes it so, the world takes on a different permutation in Dewey's pragmatic conception: "The universe is no infinite self-representative series, if only because the addition within it of a representation makes it a different universe" (*Experience* 310). Dewey is one of the most thorough theorists of the narrative model because he insists that perception, identification, even the environment take on narrative form. Indeed, he goes so far as to cast "nature" into the mode of narrative: "when nature is viewed as consisting of events rather than substances, it is characterized by *histories*, that is, by continuity of change proceeding from beginnings to endings" (*Experience* 5-6). In Dewey's world, thinking is not a reflection of nature, nor is nature simply a static entity (substance), nor art merely thinking the reflection of nature into an aesthetic object. Rather, thinking is the representation of nature and art is therefore a representation of nature which changes nature by telling a different story of it (and, thereby, expanding nature by one more representation). The metaphor best able to describe the work of art in Dewey's world, then, is the "web." Rather than elaborating a reflective mimesis, Dewey gives us an entangling mimesis. What makes a work of art significant is not its fidelity to the surface features of our social reality, but rather its modification of the reality. A story is not simply a reflection of an event; it is itself an event woven into the world it represents.

According to the narrative model's answer to the first two questions, both art and thinking (both its poetics and its psychology) are based on the metaphor of the web. We come now to our third question. What is the relationship between the metaphor of the web and the process by which a community solicits its subjects? Society itself, writes the very first theorist of the narrative model, is web-like. In Plato's *Statesman*, the Stranger tells the young Socrates and Theodorus that the "web of state" (308e) is woven by the statesman who is best able to "make the fabric [of state] close and firm by working common convictions in the hearts of each type of citizen" (311a). Where Althusser had argued that the state conscripts its subjects by forcing them to reflect on how the life of the state is a mirror of the life of the individual, Plato argues that society involves its members by educating and indoctrinating them, by weaving into their hearts the sentiments necessary to promoting the society's interests. The narrative model, then, has its metaphor and its paradigm of social conscription. Using the web as the metaphor for describing the work of art and the process of thought, the narrative model also uses the web to suggest another way of representing the strategies of socialization.

One thing yet remains for us to do. It might be noted that I have not yet offered an elaboration of how desire *works* in the narrative model. In order to see the work of desire, we had first of all to have the rest of the model before us. The reflective model's expression of the workings of desire makes immediate sense because we have, on the whole, incorporated into our thinking the basic features of how mirrors reflect our social existence. So, when Lacan and Girard describe love or desire as reflection, they are situating the question of love or desire within a complete system of thought. Now that we have a better idea of the structures of the narrative model, we can better describe the operation of desire. Just as the reflective model finds its expression of narcissistic love in Lacan's statement that "To love is, essentially, to wish to be loved," so does the narrative model find its expression of implicating love in La Rochefoucauld's famous pronouncement that "Some people would never have fallen in love if they had never heard of love" (*Maxims* 54). Love, like all cultural phenomena, is not the product of reflection, but the effect of the stories we tell each other, the anecdotal relations that form our identities as persons, citizens, insiders, or outsiders, the histories that implicate us into cultures, in a word, the narratives that give us selfhood, subjectivity, and forms of expression like love.

The most important and most contemporary theorist of the consummate narrative model is Kenneth Burke. He, and perhaps he alone, theorizes the narrative model as a coherent and integral process. More importantly, though, Burke offers us the best description of the microstructural workings of the narrative model. Like Dewey, Burke is interested in understanding how education involves the individual into the social order. Like Plato, Burke assumes that the process works by making connections between what an individual believes within and what he or she hears from without.

According to Burke, the "formation" of an individual in a community depends on what "formal equipment" is used to bring that individual within the community. As Burke says, only "those voices from without are effective which can speak in the language of a voice within" (*Rhetoric* 563). Those voices make up what Burke calls "ideology," which it must be remembered operates as a piece of "formal equipment." Indeed, as Burke notes, for inner persuasion to be effective the subject must "resort to images or ideas that are *formative*" (*Rhetoric* 563, my italics). This multiple insistence on "form" is important because "form," as Burke had noted in his first book, has to do "with the creation and gratification of needs" (*Counter-Statement* 138).

Form operates at the level of social integration, according to Burke, because education directs the individual to strive to form herself or himself in accordance with the "communicative norms that match the cooperative ways" of the given society (*Rhetoric* 563). We must notice that when Burke talks about how representations make their way from without (society) to within (subject), and about how individuals become subjects by internalizing those representations, he is emphatically talking about "communicative norms." For Burke, communicative norms are what involve any individual into a social program. Here we begin to see Burke's tracing of the microstructural workings of desire within a symbolic order. First of all, Burke sets out the conditions of the symbolic order. He notes that all human attitudes have "an overall double provenience." The first is language. Once individuals learn a language they no longer experience a sensation solely as a sensation. Their "newfound ways with language" enable them "to *duplicate* the *sensory* experience in 'transcendent' terms of a *nonsensory* medium" (*Attitudes Toward History* 382). With language, experience takes on a new *form*. The basic unit of language—the word—then acts as a symbol; that is, it operates as the "verbal parallel to a pattern of experience" (*Counter-Statement* 152). The second provenience of human attitudes is narrative. Once sensations can be cast into language, these sensations get expressed in the *form* of stories which are told in different ways depending on whether the auditor has experienced the sensation or not (*Attitudes Toward History* 383). Once a society develops a repertoire of possible experiences, it forms a set of narratives to invite future members to participate in these experiences, or to warn them of the consequences of participation.

It is obvious that the relationship between words and stories (language and narrative) is integral. Consider what Burke asks in one of those beautiful rhetorical questions that make his career a delight to follow: "Can we ever clearly know what a tangle came into the world when our ancestors began learning language, and thereby Story was born" (*Attitudes Toward History* 411)? First of all, we note that Burke fully revels in the metaphor of the web. Narrative is a "tangle" not only because it is fully involved with language, but also because it is connected to the world in a way quite different than simply being reflective of any given external reality. Second, narrative is entangling because it is primarily the *form* of desire. Now we come to the microstructural workings of desire. Recall that Burke had maintained that form had to do with the "creation and gratification of needs." Therefore, according to Burke, "desire" is the middle ground between form and ideology. As he notes under the heading "Form and Ideology," the "artist's manipulations of the reader's desires involve his use of what the reader considers desirable" (*Counter-Statement* 146). For Burke, desire is never merely (or primarily) reflective. It is wrought in the interconnective space between the subject and ideology, between the two forms of production of desire (the reader's and the writer's). The subject's desire is reoriented by her or his internalizing the external forms and representations (in a word, narratives) which society uses to construct, to direct, and to orient that subject's subjectivity.

The narrative model of desiring, given this "tangle" of language and story, works in two ways. Desire is produced, first, by an ongoing revision of linguistic values and valencies (at the level of words), and, second, by a consistent subjective socialization (at the level of narrative). In fact, in the narrative model, we can go so far as to say that desire is the effect of verbal and narrative mediation. The precondition of story is the word. "Words," writes Burke, "are a mediatory realm, that join us with wordless nature while at the same time standing between us and wordless nature." Words, that is to say, operate essentially in the space that is the mode of desire. If desire, according to Burke, is a "sense of union with something with which one is identified but from which one is divided," then "words" which simultaneously join us to and disjoin us from "wordless nature" are our only mediators of desire (*Attitudes* 372-73). In the narrative model of desire, then, the subject does not "reflect" at all. Desire is wrought out of the absence that words create and intimate. Desire, in Burke's model, therefore, works by narrative "entanglement." As Burke has noted, once words become the mediators of sensory experience, narrative enters the scene.

Narrative, in the end, orients both individual and communal desires. For the individual, the process of indoctrination is one in which the subject of a society is imbricated into a given society by acquiring its language, and then learning how to experience sensations by acceding to that society's stories (its histories, its narratives of propriety) and, finally, learning how to narrativize his or her own history in accord with the *forms* of those stories. For the community, the process of change occurs when a new narrative works to effect a categorical alteration in the way the community defines its ends and its repertoire of experiences; it is when a community finds itself telling a differently symbolic story. The symbol, according to Burke, "might be called a word invented by the artist to specify a particular grouping or pattern or emphasizing of experiences—and the work of art in which the Symbol figures might be called a definition of this word" (*Counter-Statement* 153). In the end, though, all is interconnected. Everything operates in that "tangle" of language and narrative. In effect, then, the narrative model demonstrates how it works by employing the metaphor of the web to define its poetics, its psychology, and its ideology. It is a model and metaphor that seems more promising for an analysis of how individual and communal desires are oriented, disoriented, and reoriented in ***Charlotte's Web.***

THE NARRATIVE MODEL EXEMPLIFIED: A READING OF *CHARLOTTE'S WEB*

Few readers, at least few published readers besides Roger Sale (258-61), take at face value White's claim that he wrote **Charlotte's Web** as a "hymn to the barn" (quoted in Neumeyer 493). Some of the more lyrical passages in the novel, such as that arresting description of the "wonderful sweet breath of patient cows" (13), might indeed attest to White's declared desire to write a georgic. Most other features of the novel, however, seem less a hymn to the barn and more a testament to the advertising agency. The basis of the story, after all, is Charlotte's elaborate demonstration of her dictum that "people are very gullible" (67). After the goose suggests that Charlotte use "terrific" to describe Wilbur in her second web, Wilbur demurs: "But Charlotte, . . . I'm *not* terrific." "That doesn't make a particle of difference," replies Charlotte, "Not a particle. People believe almost anything they see in print" (89). Indeed, it will turn out that not only people but pigs too believe almost anything they see in print. After a day of standing under a web labelling him "terrific," Wilbur begins *feeling* terrific (96). During the next meeting of the animals, when "radiant" is proposed as a description of Wilbur, Charlotte is unsure of its applicability to its referent—"I'm not sure Wilbur's action is exactly radiant"—but Wilbur, by now, is eager to assume the qualities accruing to whatever signifier he is assigned: "'Actually,' said Wilbur, 'I *feel* radiant'" (101). We might say, then, that this is a hymn to the barn containing some pragmatic behaviorist animals. Charlotte seems to have read her George Herbert Mead.

She also seems familiar with her Kenneth Burke. What Charlotte does, when she takes the Zuckermans' desire to eat Wilbur for Christmas dinner and reorients this into a desire to keep Wilbur as a pet, is effect a categorical change of the sort Burke called "perspective by incongruity." According to Burke, every "word belongs by custom to a certain category." What someone who wishes to effect a "perspective by incongruity" does is take a given key word and "wrench it loose" from its consensual category by "metaphorically apply[ing] it to a different category" (*Attitudes* 308). Moreover, while effecting a perspective by incongruity is not done by a narrative act, it is the foundation, indeed the very precondition of narrativity. We know that Charlotte does not tell stories (at least not in the act of saving Wilbur by writing in her web). It is not that she is prohibited by her spiderly incapacities—as Mrs. Arable tells Fern, "You know spiders don't tell stories" (105)—but that, for one thing, her web has its limits. As John Griffith acutely notes, Charlotte's "entire published canon was only five words" (117). Even so, I will argue, it is not because of the logistics of the web that Charlotte does not tell formal stories. It is for her own strategic reasons that Charlotte chooses to create the preconditions for storytelling rather than telling stories. To appreciate what those preconditions are, we need to theorize how words become narratives. The model for that transformation we borrow from Burke's examination of how words mediate things.

Here, we might turn to one of Burke's most brilliant pieces, his essay of 1962—"What Are Signs of What? A Theory of Entitlement." Burke's thesis is that "in mediating between the social realm and the realm of nonverbal nature, words communicate to things the spirit that the society imposes upon the words which have come to be the 'names' for them. The things are in effect the visible tangible material embodiments of the spirit that infuses them through the medium of words. And in this sense, things become the the signs of the genius that resides in words" (*Language as Symbolic Action* 362). Nature "as so conceived and perceived," he writes, "would be infused with the spirit of words, and of the social orders that are implicit in any given complex verbal structure" (379). We have seen already how Burke argues that words mediate nature, and how nature, according to Dewey, is possessed of intrinsic narratives. Returning our attention to ***Charlotte's Web,*** we can now see how Charlotte achieves an end (effecting a perspective by incongruity) by using this method of abbreviating a narrative into key words.

Let us consider the scene of Charlotte's first assay. At the end of the third chapter, Lurvy, the Zuckermans' hired hand, looks at Wilbur and says, "He's quite a pig." Zuckerman replies, "Yes, he'll make a good pig" (23-24). What Zuckerman unequivocally means is that Wilbur will make good ham (he is employing what we might call the discourse of *jambon*). In chapter eleven, Charlotte writes her first advertisement of Wilbur: "Some Pig." The scene of Lurvy and Zuckerman's first encounter of the web is worth examining in full:

> Zuckerman stared at the writing on the web. Then he murmured the words, "Some Pig." Then he looked at Lurvy. Then they both began to tremble. Charlotte, sleepy after her night's exertions, smiled as she watched. Wilbur came and stood directly under the web.
>
> "Some pig!" muttered Lurvy in a low voice.
>
> "Some pig!" whispered Mr. Zuckerman. They stared and stared for a long time at Wilbur. Then they stared at Charlotte.
>
> (79)

After this, Zuckerman and Lurvy start to elaborate a new grammar—and that grammar is literally transformative. In a series of exclamations, they call Wilbur "a very unusual pig"; a "pig completely out of the ordinary"; "no ordinary pig"; and a "solid pig" (79-81). Lurvy concludes this litany by calling Wilbur "quite a pig" and "some pig" (82). That is, Lurvy uses exactly the same phrase he had used earlier when he was talking about Wilbur in the discourse of *jambon* to talk about Wilbur in what we should call the discourse of *cochon*: "quite a pig" (23, 82). The difference is the other phrase Lurvy utters, which is Charlotte's contribution toward establishing a "perspective by incongruity": "Some pig." Likewise, Zuckerman's penultimate reference to Wilbur is to call him an "extra good" pig. Again, Zuckerman is no longer talking about now Wilbur will "make a good pig" (as in make a good ham in the discourse of *jambon*), but about how Wilbur is a "good" pig (as in make a good pet in the discourse of *cochon*). Charlotte has done nothing less than effected a categorical change in the discursive habits of Lurvy and Zuckerman. By doing so, she establishes the preconditions for the narrative which will prevent Wilbur from being felled by the human desire for pork. She has changed Wilbur's status by positing the possibility for telling another story—the story of Wilbur as *cochon*. It is done in what is called the "miracle of the web" (183). And the "web" here is not just the medium in which Charlotte has physically woven the words that change how Zuckerman and Lurvy view Wilbur; that web is also the social system of beliefs about what forms a community, of values about what forms a social bond, of narratives about what direction desires should take towards any given object.

What Charlotte does, then, is use a phrase of entitlement to establish the preconditions for a narrative. The phrase "some pig" can hardly be called a narrative. What is significant about the phrase is, first of all, that it can bridge the two discursive realms of *jambon* and *cochon*. The phrase belongs to the description of pork in the same way that "quite a pig" and "good pig" do. And while, as Janice Alberghene notes, Charlotte chose the phrase "by herself" (37), she chose it with an understanding of the discursive realms she was negotiating. Because it bridges the realm of thinking of pigs as pork or as pets, the phrase sets up the possibility for reorienting thinking. And it does that by establishing the preconditions of narrative. First of all, people start telling stories about the role of Wilbur within their realm of experience. All the people who come to read the web go away saying "they had never seen such a pig before in their lives" (84). The phrase in the web acts as a text that imbricates Wilbur into people's lives. Wilbur is no longer an anonymous pig, but a pig who has now some relationship to an event significant for the life of this particular community. Indeed, the community even incorporates Wilbur into its religious life. Not only does the minister give Wilbur ecclesiastical sanction—"There can be no doubt that you have a most unusual pig" (82)—but he also involves Charlotte's phrase into the religious life of his parish: "He said the words on the spider's web proved that human beings must always be on the watch for the coming of wonders" (85). Even though "some pig" is not a narrative, the phrase itself and its referent (Wilbur) are woven into the community's narrative of its life—and that, as Charlotte knew, was the way to become part of the community (instead of part of its diet).

Second, once the grammar is in place for reorienting the desires of the community, the community can start to tell a coherent and integral story which will incorporate Wilbur into their society in his new role. By the end of the fifth word of Charlotte's publishing career, the community as a whole is telling a complete narrative of Wilbur's life. The "loud speaker" at the fair, a disembodied voice embodying the community's standards, tells the story of how Wilbur came to be what he is now. It is worth noting the form of the loud speaker's story. Wilbur is "some pig." That goes almost without saying. The loud speaker does not suggest that Wilbur is "some pig" because Charlotte's web signified as much. Rather, he cites the phrase from Charlotte's web as confirmation of what is already given. "In the words of the spider's web, ladies and gentlemen, this is some pig" (157). Almost oblivious as to where his information comes from, the loud speaker continues telling the story of Wilbur's emergence without even referring to Charlotte's web in the second instance. "This magnificent animal," continued the loud speaker, 'is truly terrific.'" In the third instance, the loud speaker goes as far as possible in reversing the order of signifier and signified (or, in Burke's homelier terms, word and thing). "Note the general radiance of this animal! Then remember the day when the word 'radiant' appeared clearly in the web" (158). According to the loud speaker's narrative, Wilbur's radiance is not the effect of Charlotte's writing but the autonomous signified of it. Charlotte, we should recall, had her reservations about Wilbur's radiance. In response to Wilbur's affirmation that he felt radiant, Charlotte responds, "you're a good little pig, and radiant you *shall be*" (101, my italics). To judge by the loud speaker's faith, Wilbur has indeed been made radiant. And, to judge by the loud speaker's discursive *form*, which does employ a temporal, dynamic narrative structure, Charlotte's strategy of positing the preconditions for narrative has succeeded. Words have become story.

Charlotte's strategy for saving Wilbur is successful because she manipulates the discourses the community uses to describe things as edible or as amiable. Once the community has a new way of thinking about old words, Wilbur himself is changed from being pork to becoming pig. And once the community thinks anew of Wilbur, it starts to tell stories that socialize him into that community's narrative. No longer in danger of becoming an anonymous meal, Wilbur becomes a pig who is part of the community *because* the community has changed its representation of the world. "Mr. Zuckerman took fine care of Wilbur all the rest of his days, and the pig was often visited by friends and admirers, for nobody ever forgot the year of his triumph and the miracle of the web" (183).

Now, let us return once more to the question of the relationship between Wilbur's fate and Fern's. As Perry Nodelman has noted, the first two chapters of **Charlotte's Web** tell a story that is "a shorter but nevertheless complete version of the story the rest of the book tells" (119). Just as the rest of the book tells the story of how Charlotte saves Wilbur's life, so too do the first two chapters tell the story of how Fern saved Wilbur's life. According to Nodelman, the major difference is that whereas Charlotte "saves Wilbur by using her knowledge," Fern "saves Wilbur because she has *no* knowledge of the world, and because her father wants to keep her that way" (120). We can dispute this reading on several grounds. First of all, Mr. Arable hardly hides the knowledge of the ways of the world from Fern. To her query about where he is going with the ax, he remarks that a "weakling makes trouble" (3). In other words, the ways of the world are so clear that they do not need explicit defining. On a farm, whatever makes trouble is exterminated. Second, Fern saves Wilbur by employing the same method Charlotte would use later—that is, establishing a perspective by incongruity. When Mr. Arable wishes to slaughter Wilbur because Wilbur is a runt, Fern asks whether he would have slaughtered her if she had turned out a runt. He tries to explain that the situations are incongruous:

"But this is different. A little girl is one thing, a little runty pig is another." Her reply is more sophisticated than Mr. Arable might ever realize: "I see no difference" (3). What Fern does, like Charlotte but in a different way, is problematize *difference*. As a runt, Wilbur's life is in danger because he is different from the other pigs; Fern saves his life by suggesting that there is no difference between girlhood and pighood, by suggesting that all living things deserve to live. We can hardly agree with Nodelman's argument that "Fern is rewarded for being weak, vulnerable, and in need of protection" (121). She is rewarded for being astute enough to interrogate the very question of "difference." And this interrogation immediately affects Mr. Arable's ordering of the world.

After Fern suggests to Mr. Arable that the difference between a "little runty pig" and a "little girl" is not so very great, he begins to view the pig in a new way. No longer simply a "little runty pig" or a "weakling," the "runt" becomes "like a baby" (3). *Pace* Nodelman, then, we note that Fern is rewarded for being able to effect a categorical change in her father's perspective. She offers Mr. Arable a new way of determining the bonds and boundaries of community. By making difference a key issue—by making community a situation more accepting of diversity—Fern promotes the possibility for the human community's extending an invitation to Wilbur. In a way, Charlotte too highlights the questions of difference and community. As a pig, Wilbur's life is in danger because he is no different from any other pig; Charlotte saves his life by suggesting that there is a difference between *jambon* and *cochon*. What both Fern and Charlotte do is organize the possibility for telling different stories about Wilbur. In both cases, the communal desire to kill Wilbur (as runt or as Christmas dinner) is reoriented into a desire to keep Wilbur as a pet—in the first case as a family pet, in the second as a community pet.

Finally, what I am calling Fern's interrogation of the question of difference is also significant for our examination of Fern's entry into adolescence—into an order some romanticize as spontaneous and natural love and some examine under Adrienne Rich's term "compulsory heterosexuality" (23-75). If we accept Nodelman's reading that Fern is rewarded for being weak, vulnerable and relatively ignorant of the world, we encounter a dilemma. When we consider the five illustrations in the first two chapters (these are Garth Williams's illustrations), we notice that there is an almost parodic representation of opposite gender roles. The second picture is of Avery, armed to the teeth with a rifle and a knife (5). Both hands are fully occupied with grasping his weapons: "an air rifle in one hand, a wooden dagger in the other" (4). The third picture is of Fern "seated on the floor in the corner of the kitchen with her infant between her knees, teaching it to suck from the bottle" (6-7). In the following illustration Fern will be sitting outside watching "her baby" play outside in his new house (9). In the final illustration of chapter two, Fern is hold the bottle in her right hand while standing beside her carriage containing both her doll and Wilbur—"her infants" (10-11). The contrast is fairly clear. Girls nurture, boys get ready to kill.

If we accept Nodelman's reading of Fern's disposition, we have no way of accounting for the first illustration. The book opens with a picture of Mr. Arable and Fern struggling over the handle of a large ax (2). It is important to recognize Fern's aggressive resistance to her father's order of the world because it is the one symbol of an otherwise relentless representation of reified gender roles in the first two chapters of **Charlotte's Web**. The illustration renders ineffectual Nodelman's argument that this is a little girl who succeeds in getting her way by acquiescing to a stereotype of ignorant vulnerability. If anything, Fern's early aggressive resistance to her father—both in the aptitude of her questions and in her physical determination—demonstrates for us her strength and her wisdom. In the end, Nodelman is quite correct to note that the first two chapters do represent "a shorter but nevertheless complete version of the story the rest of the book tells." These first two chapters foretell the story of how a strong female character saves Wilbur's life. Moreover, they also foretell the story of how that strong female character is subject to an order of acculturation. For Fern's early resistance to her father demonstrates that gender roles are not *natural* acquisitions. As much as her father would like her to believe that a "little girl is one thing," Fern resists his definition of girlhood just as she resists his desire to slaughter Wilbur (3). But **Charlotte's Web** also demonstrates that even though gender roles are cultural acquisitions, they are nonetheless difficult to resist because of the community's relentless narrative constructions. It does not take long for Mrs. Arable to decide that it wasn't "natural for a little girl to be so interested in animals" (107). Just like her husband, Mrs. Arable seems to have a determined sense of what constitutes "a little girl."

There is another especially worthwhile story which explores how a little girl attempts to resist the definition of girlhood by associating herself with animals and making herself immune to narratives of feminine propriety. In Alice Munro's "Boys and Girls," the unnamed narrator finds that as she turns eleven the combined forces of her mother and her grandmother come into play in defining for her a gender. Her mother insists on telling her stories of how things had been when the mother herself "was a little girl"—narratives of "what certain dresses of hers had looked like" and stories of "boys she had gone out with later on when she was grown up" (310). Her mother, that is, acculturates her by telling her narratives of historical female behavior. That same year the grandmother came to visit and the narrator "heard other things." These other things are narratives of propriety defining "girlhood." "'Girls don't slam doors like that.' 'Girls keep their knees together when they sit down.' And worse still, when I asked some questions, 'That's none of girls' business'" (312). The narrator comes to the realization that although the "word *girl* had formerly seemed . . . innocent and unburdened, like the word *child*," it had now become "a definition, always touched with emphasis, with reproach and disappointment." "A girl was not, as I had supposed, simply what I was; it was what I had to become" (312). She resists, as does Fern, by identifying herself with the animals on the farm. In her case, she does so by effecting the escape of a mare her father was going to slaughter. Eventually, the horse is caught and killed and the narrator apparently acquiesces to her father's judgment that she was "only a girl" (318). No small part of that transformation occurs because she also begins to tell herself stories like the stories her mother had told her. As she drifts off to sleep, she tells herself stories in which "something different was happening." "A story might start off in the old way, with a spectacular danger, a fire or wild animals, and for a while I might rescue people; then things would change around, and instead, somebody would be rescuing me. It might be a boy from our class at school . . . [and] at this point the story concerned itself at great length with what I looked like . . . and what kind of dress I had on" (317). The stories she now tells herself have incorporated both her grandmother's rules for what girls do or don't do and her mother's plots for what girls are concerned about—boys and dresses. Munro's story is also the story of Fern—of what happens when the word *girl* becomes a definition.

Both Munro's story and White's suggest how narratives work to acculturate an individual into a social role. Both show how little girls define themselves with certain animals in order to avoid having themselves defined according to cultural imperatives. There is a difference, though. Whereas Munro's story suggests the impossibility of resisting the roles a community establishes for its little girls, by having both the little girl acquiesce to a definition of her gender and the animal with whom she identified killed according to the order of farm life, White's narrative seems to offer a hope of resistance by representing for us two different scenarios. On the one hand, Fern will eventually become enmeshed in the narratives defining girlhood. At the Fair, she eventually does ride the Ferris wheel with Henry. As her mother looks up at her daughter and Henry, she smiles and says to herself, "My, my, . . . Henry Fussy. Think of that" (139). That night as Mrs. Arable tucks her daughter into bed, she promotes Fern's emergent adolescence by telling her that what happened at the fair was indeed "nice" (143). By the next day, Fern begins to think of the world in a new way and to create quite different scenarios in her imaginative life. "As they passed the Ferris wheel, Fern gazed up at it and wished she were in the topmost car with Henry Fussy at her side" (154). On the other hand, though, the pig lives. Charlotte, completing the work Fern began, alters the way the community determines Wilbur's role by writing a new set of words defining him and thereby producing the possibility for the community to tell a different narrative of his place in their culture. The new narrative in place, Wilbur's life is safe. Because White does suggest the link between Wilbur's and Fern's fates, **Charlotte's Web** is able to offer both a diagnosis of and a hope for the workings of acculturation. White demonstrates how cultures use words (like "little girl" and "pig") and narratives (like the life of a little girl or the life of a pig) to define both communal and individual desires. White also shows us, though, that words and narratives are pliable. Even though a community has an established pattern of determining what role anything should take in the community's system of production and reproduction, there exists the chance that there can be a different story.

To conclude, let me point out how White himself envisaged such a different story. As we know, White wrote one other famous narrative about a pig. Five years before the publication of **Charlotte's Web,** he wrote his charming essay **"Death of a Pig."** In this essay, White describes what happens when a pig assumes difference, that is when a pig is no longer healthy and perceived as *jambon* but when the pig becomes ill and is perceived as *cochon*. As he buries the deceased pig, he notes that his grief is directed by a different discourse: "The loss we felt was not the loss of ham but the loss of pig" (***Essays*** 18). Like Charlotte, White comes to realize that the signifier one assigns to an entity ("ham" or "pig") is already a way of determining one's desire towards that entity. Moreover, the way desire is oriented determines the story that gets told. As White notes in his essay, he "feels driven to account" for the days in September when he tended to his ailing pig because "the pig died at last, and I lived, and things might easily have gone the other way round." In other words, like Fern, White comes to realize what a different world can exist once one begins to interrogate what seem to be obvious "differences."

White's novel, like the inchoate form of it in the essay, is exemplary of the narrative model of desire and the processes of narrative identification. The writing in the web changes the value and valency of words. Once words signify hitherto unexplored differences and effect a perspective by incongruity, there exists a renewed possibility for integration, for telling stories that imbricate more and diverse individuals into communities. Words reorient desires by demonstrating that things are desirable because they are signified and, therefore, significant. Narratives reorient desires by demonstrating that things are desirable because they are socialized and, therefore, significant for others.

Notes

I would like to thank my friend and colleague Roderick McGillis, whose conversation and inspiration helped me a great deal in my thinking about the subject of this article. A slightly different version of this paper was read to the 10th Congress of the Societe Internationale de Recherche en Litterature d'Enfance et de Jeunesse in Paris in September 1991. I would like to thank Jean Perrot for his kind invitation to address the Congress and the participants in my session for their generous comments on the earlier paper.

1. According to Shlomith Rimmon-Kenan, the term "narrativity" was apparently first developed by Claude Bremond as a way of describing what Vladimir Propp meant by an "immanent story structure" (7). The form of narrativity I am talking about was most cogently developed by Teresa de Lauretis as being "the structuring and destructuring, even destructive, processes at work in the textual and semiotic relations of spectatorship" or reading (*Technologies* 118). I discuss the history of the term more fully elsewhere (*Empty Garden* 483n6).

2. The term "interpellation" is taken, obviously, from the work of Louis Althusser. In a general sense, he uses it to mean the way that a social order solicits or "calls" its subjects into its workings (*Lenin and Philosophy* 174). As such, then, it has been popularly used simply to describe the way that any political system confers subjectivity or subjection on its citizens or victims. Paul Smith gives a useful introduction to Althusserian interpellation (14-23). See also note 5.

3. Just a note on my practice here. By "model" I mean to suggest something like what Marx intuited to be superstructure. It is perhaps best to say that a model is concerned with limning the relationship between actions (or practice) and representations. In this way a model is that mediating realm which Kenneth Burke would call a "program" when he notes that "Action requires programs—programs require vocabulary (*Attitudes* 4). The idea of tracing the workings of a model by discerning the metaphors used to describe its operation might seem farfetched or commonsensical, depending on where you stand. From

where I stand, it is commonsensical. With Richard Rorty, I agree that "metaphors ... determine most of our philosophical convictions" (12); with Stuart Hall, I concur that "metaphors are serious things [which] ... affect one's practice" (282).

4. Lacan's paper was first delivered under the title "Le stade du miroir" in August 1936, and translated as "The Looking-glass Stage" in the 1937 issue of *The International Journal of Psychoanalysis*. The version in *Écrits* was first delivered in July 1949, and was published in the 1949 issue of the *Revue française de psychanalyse*. I will be citing exclusively from the translation of the 1949 version in *Écrits: A Selection*.

5. I have elsewhere offered a critique of the reactionary politics behind Althusser's structuralist theory of interpellation (*Empty Garden* 41-64).

6. Actually "imbricated" is not the world I should be using. Because it belongs to the discourse of architecture it does not quite fit the purpose. The ideal word I should be using is "texturation" (from the Latin for "web" [*textura*] referring both to the work of the weaver and the poet). I do not use the term in the body of my paper, however, because I am reluctant to introduce another neologism into a discipline rife with them, at least reluctant to do so except in the relative safety of a footnote.

Works Cited

Alberghene, Janice M. "Writing in *Charlotte's Web*." *Children's Literature in Education* 16 (1985): 32-44.

Althusser, Louis. *Lenin and Philosophy and Other Essays*. Trans. Ben Brewster. New York: Monthly Press, 1971.

Althusser, Louis, and Etienne Balibar. *Reading Capital*. Trans. Ben Brewster. London: Verso, 1979.

Bacon, Francis. *The Advancement of Learning and New Atlantis*. Ed. Arthur Johnston. Oxford: Clarendon, 1974.

Burke, Kenneth. *Attitudes Toward History*. 1937. 3d ed. Berkeley: U of California P, 1984.

———. *Counter-Statement*. 1931. Berkeley: U of California P, 1952.

———. *Language as Symbolic Action: Essays on Life, Literature, and Method*. Berkeley: U of California P, 1966.

———. *A Rhetoric of Motives*. 1950. *A Grammar of Motives and A Rhetoric of Motives*. Cleveland: World, 1962.

De Lauretis, Teresa. *Alice Doesn't: Feminism, Semiotics, Cinema*. Bloomington: Indiana UP, 1984.

———. *Technologies of Gender: Essays on Theory, Film, and Fiction*. Bloomington: Indiana UP, 1987.

Deleuze, Gilles, and Félix Guattari. *A Thousand Plateaus: Capitalism and Schizophrenia*. Trans. Brian Massumi. Minneapolis: U of Minnesota P, 1987.

Dewey, John. *Experience and Nature*. 1925. *John Dewey: The Later Works, 1925-1953*. Vol. 1. Ed. Jo Ann Boydston. Carbondale: Southern Illinois UP, 1981.

———. *Human Nature and Conduct*. 1922. *John Dewey: The Middle Works, 1899-1924*. Vol. 14. Ed. Jo Ann Boydston. Carbondale: Southern Illinois UP, 1983.

———. *The Quest for Certainty*. 1929. *John Dewey: The Later Works, 1925-1953,* Vol. 4. Ed. Jo Ann Boydston. Carbondale: Southern Illinois UP, 1984.

Fiske, John. "Cultural Studies and the Culture of Everyday Life." Grossberg et al. 154-73.

Girard, René. *Deceit, Desire, and the Novel: Self and Other in Literary Structure*. Trans. Yvonne Freccero. Baltimore: Johns Hopkins UP, 1965.

———. "The Mimetic Desire of Paolo and Francesca." Trans. Petra Morrison. *"To Double Business Bound": Essays on Literature, Mimesis, and Anthropology*. Baltimore: Johns Hopkins UP, 1978: 1-8.

———. *Things Hidden Since the Foundation of the World*. Trans. Stephen Bann and Michael Metteer. Stanford: Stanford UP, 1987.

Griffith, John. "*Charlotte's Web:* A Lonely Fantasy of Love." *Children's Literature* 8 (1980): 111-17.

Grossberg, Lawrence, Cary Nelson, and Paula Treichler, eds. *Cultural Studies*. New York: Routledge, 1992.

Hall, Stuart. "Cultural Studies and Its Theoretical Legacies." Grossberg et al. 277-86.

Lacan, Jacques. *Écrits: A Selection*. Trans. Alan Sheridan. London: Tavistock, 1977.

———. *The Four Fundamental Concepts of Psychoanalysis*. Trans. Alan Sheridan. New York: Norton, 1977.

La Rochefoucauld, François. *Maxims*. Trans. Leonard Tancock. Harmondsworth: Penguin, 1959.

Lyotard, Jean-François. "Sensus communis: The Subject in *statu nascendi*." Trans. Marian Hobson. *Who Comes After the Subject?* Eds. Eduardo Cadava, Peter Connor, and Jean-Luc Nancy. London: Routledge, 1991. 217-35.

Mead, George Herbert. *Mind, Self, and Society from the Standpoint of a Social Behaviorist.* Ed. Charles W. Morris. Chicago: U of Chicago P, 1962.

Munro, Alice. "Boys and Girls." *The Norton Introduction to Literature.* 4th ed. Ed. Carl E. Bain et al. New York: Norton, 1986. 307-18.

Neumeyer, Peter F. "The Creation of *Charlotte's Web*: From Drafts to Book, Part I." *The Horn Book* 58 (Oct. 1982): 489-97. "Part II." (Dec. 1982) 617-25.

Nodelman, Perry. "Text as Teacher: The Beginning of *Charlotte's Web*." *Children's Literature* 13 (1985): 109-27.

Nozick, Robert. *Philosophical Explanations.* Cambridge, Mass.: Harvard UP, 1981.

Plato. *Statesman.* Trans. J. B. Skemp. *Plato: The Collected Dialogues.* Eds. Edith Hamilton and Huntington Cairns. Princeton: Princeton UP, 1961. 1018-85.

Putnam, Hilary. "Realism and Reason." *Proceedings and Addresses of the American Philosophical Association* 50.6 (1977): 483-98.

Rich, Adrienne. "Compulsory Heterosexuality and Lesbian Existence." *Blood, Bread, and Poetry: Selected Prose 1979-1985.* New York: Norton, 1986. 23-75.

Rimmon-Kenan, Shlomith. *Narrative Fiction: Contemporary Poetics.* London: Methuen, 1983.

Rorty, Richard. *Philosophy and the Mirror of Nature.* Oxford: Basil Blackwell, 1980.

Rushdy, Ashraf H. A. *The Empty Garden: The Subject of Late Milton.* Pittsburgh: U of Pittsburgh P, 1992.

Sale, Roger. *Fairy Tales and After: From Snow White to E. B. White.* Cambridge, Mass.: Harvard UP, 1978.

Smith, Paul. *Discerning the Subject.* Minneapolis: U of Minnesota P, 1988.

White, E. B. *Charlotte's Web.* 1952. New York: Harper, 1980.

———. *Essays of E. B. White.* New York: Harper, 1977.

White, Hayden. *The Content of the Form: Narrative Discourse and Historical Representation.* Baltimore: Johns Hopkins UP, 1987.

Cathlena Martin (essay date 2009)

SOURCE: Martin, Cathlena. "Charlotte's Website: Media Transformation and the Intertextual Web of Children's Culture." *Adaptation in Contemporary Culture: Textual Infidelities,* edited by Rachel Carroll, London, Continuum International Publishing, 2009, pp. 85-95.

[*In the following essay, Martin employs transmedia studies to examine various film and game adaptations of* Charlotte's Web *(1952), focusing specifically on how the game relies more on familiar marketing strategies and commonplace video graphics than on White's original text.*]

Children's literature provides a rich heritage of stories from which to draw material for twenty-first-century media. Adapted texts saturate children's culture—lining toy stores, pervading bookshelves, filling television time slots, and permeating internet websites. Media theorists Marsha Kinder (1999) and Henry Jenkins (2006), among others, examine transmedia intertextuality and transmedia storytelling by focusing on a narrative arc that transitions across multiple media. Postmodern literary critic N. Katherine Hayles (2005) explores a similar strain of a print text transformed into an electronic text, but refers to the process as media translation. Media transformations are inundating current children's culture, and this chapter will examine the transitions and convergences between old and new media. In particular, I will provide connections between children's print media and digital media using multiple versions of **Charlotte's Web** as a way to approach questions of fidelity/infidelity within adaptation. Additionally, given the primary theme of death in E. B. White's **Charlotte's Web** (1952), the video game version presents a case study for textual infidelity because of its lack of violence or player death. The game thus contradicts the normative stereotype of video games as being equated with violence, and denies a major theme from the original print text in doing so.

Adaptation usually places texts in a hierarchy of source text as original and adaptation as derivative. This common strain of adaptation theory largely focuses on the fidelity of the adaptation to the original, with most media adaptation studies spotlighting literature and film. But film adaptation studies have increasingly approached film as a series of intertexts, thus opening up adaptation to the notion of intertextuality, following James Naremore's assertion that 'The study of adaptation needs to be joined with the study of recycling, remaking, and every other form of retelling in the age of mechanical reproduction and electronic communication' (2000: 15). Intertextuality broadens the scope of adaptation, placing the derivative text within its cultural moment and linking it to a web of other texts and influences.

Intertextuality can come from anywhere and everywhere, referencing, alluding to and transforming texts from any medium, but what mass culture is currently experiencing in its reanimation of classical and established texts is not merely intertextuality. Authors, producers and directors are not simply making reference to other cultural works, be they movies, video games or print texts, but through intertextuality, transmedia crossing and convergence, they are redefining those cultural works. This is particularly true among children's texts, a complex area of textual transformation across media.

Because of the expanded media used by children, children's texts have increased and become an area of boundary crossing and blurred divisions. In the introduction to their edited collection *Toys, Games and Media* (2004), Jeffrey Goldstein, David Buckingham and Gilles Brougere state:

> Children's culture is now highly intertextual: Every 'text' (including commodities such as toys) effectively draws upon and feeds into every other text. When children play with Pokemon cards or toys, for example, they draw on knowledge and expertise they have derived from watching the TV shows and movies, or from playing the computer games. Each play event is a broader flow of events that crosses from one medium or 'platform' to another. This is play that involves . . . flexibility across different media and modes of communication.
>
> (2004: 2-3)

This overlapping, intertextual nature of children's culture has happened in the past, but its mass prevalence is part of the larger scope of today's digital era. In *Remediation: Understanding New Media* (2000), Jay Bolter and Richard Grusin posit that all media forms draw on their predecessors for remediation design options, and that old media can be hypermediated through new media. More specifically, comparative media theorist Jenkins explores old and new media convergence in *Convergence Culture* (2006). He explains convergence as:

> A word that describes technological, industrial, cultural, and social changes in the ways media circulates within our culture. . . . Perhaps most broadly, media convergence refers to a situation in which multiple media systems coexist and where media content flows fluidly across them. Convergence is understood here as an ongoing process or series of intersections between different media systems, not a fixed relationship.
>
> (2006: 282)

Convergence is important for the study of children's literature and adaptation, because it exemplifies the current moment in popular children's culture and allows scholarship of children's literature to grow with the expanding digital era. With the increased accessibility of print and digital media, children's texts are transforming in terms of transmedia storytelling, participatory culture, and marketing. In tandem with adaptation and intertextuality, convergence provides another avenue into discussing children's texts that have been transformed across media.

The transmedia effect in children's texts can be seen in multiple dimensions. Yet children's texts are becoming a franchise: these texts refuse to be confined to one medium, and need to be examined across a range of media for their cultural significance. The child consumer is probably largely unaware of this media convergence as a new occurrence because computers, video games and the internet have always been an everyday part of his/her life. These are the children of the digital age, or the 'net generation' as Don Tapscott describes them in *Growing Up Digital* (1998). *Charlotte's Web* serves as an example of adaptation where a children's text is being transferred or converted from one medium to another. Specifically, the transformation of **Charlotte's Web** as a text/artifact in American culture, since its original publication in the 1950s, both reflects moments of past American media culture, and encapsulates the present digital age.

In 1952, more than a decade and a half before the internet started brewing in the labs of the Pentagon's Defense Advanced Research Projects Agency (DARPA), a little spider communicated through the simple lines of a web thread. E.B. White's *Charlotte's Web* (1952) was published in the second golden age of children's literature. The book won White a Newbery Honor in 1953.

For many years, the original 1952 novel by White comprised the entirety of the story of **Charlotte's Web.** Today, however, stories do not stay confined to one medium. The Hanna-Barbera animated film was released in 1973, with a sequel in 2003: *Charlotte's Web 2: Wilbur's Great Adventure.* Finally, in 2006 the live action film was released, along with a video game. These print and media versions converge to create a larger ur-text. In the mind of the consumer there may not be a clear division between original and adaptation, depending on which version the consumer was exposed to first. With the creation of film and video game versions of the story, modern audiences can now experience the narrative of 'Charlotte's Web' as a broader and more inclusive text than just the original printed novel. 'Charlotte's Web,' the story, now consists of an amalgam of print, film and digital sources, which combine to create what the reader interprets and assimilates as 'Charlotte's Web.' Each of the media versions of 'Charlotte's web' *is* **Charlotte's Web,** yet each of them is also distinct and unique. The novel's account of Charlotte and Wilbur's friendship is different from that of the animated film, through the basic change in form and narrative, yet they are both 'Charlotte's Web.' In this instance the print version came first chronologically, and therefore most other versions look back to it as the original. But these additional texts can also be studied independently. Instead of being simply an adaptation or a rewriting of an original, a new media version of a text expands the text's boundaries, generating an additional primary text within that story's scope. A new media version of the text creates a type of convergence—transmedia storytelling—that expands the text's scope, generating an additional primary text and expanding the boundaries of what we perceive as the narrative, while adding the assets of its own medium.

Peter Neumeyer, in annotating **Charlotte's Web,** notes:

> This great American children's novel has stood by itself without the aid of notes for over forty years. Certainly, it could continue to be read without. But if selected insights into the workshop of a thoroughly self-aware author enrich the reading for some ... then this edition justifies its existence.
>
> (1994: xviii)

This great work can also continue to be read without any awareness or recognition of the other media texts associated by name, but additional texts could also enrich the reading for some, and may be the only engagement with 'Charlotte's Web' that some children experience. This begins to fulfil André Bazin's prophetic statement that the 'critic of the year 2050 would find not a novel out of which a play and a film had been "made," but rather a single work reflected through three art forms, an artistic pyramid with three sides, all equal in the eyes of the critic' (2000: 26). We are at the forefront of that movement now, but Bazin omitted one art form—the video game. Adult readers may resist multimedia adaptation, relying on the supremacy of print text as 'high art' compared to 'lowbrow' video games, but consumer children experience transmedia stories on a regular basis; they no longer view the printed text as the only way to experience 'Charlotte's Web' because multimedia adaptations of texts have been the normal publishing practice in their lifetime.

Immediately after the book's publication in 1952, various people tried to secure the rights to handle the adaptation, including Disney Studios, but White was concerned about his work being adapted and 'was skeptical of and cautious about film versions of *Charlotte's Web*' (Apseloff 1983: 174). He wrote in his letters that he did not want an adaptation to violate 'the spirit and meaning of the story,' and he wanted 'the chance to edit the script' (quoted in Apseloff 1983: 172). According to Marilyn Apseloff, 'many of White's fears came to pass' (1983: 175) when the animated film was released 21 years after the book had been first published. She describes how the animated version of *Charlotte's Web* 'captures the spirit in part, but too often the cartoon intrudes' (Apseloff 1983: 180), and she ultimately concludes that:

> the film *Charlotte's Web* can stand on its own as an entertaining, rather skillfully animated musical for children and adults, well voiced, with distinctive characters and some memorable songs and visual effects. It is when the adaptation is compared with the book and the book's *intent* that its divergence from White's work is realized.
>
> (1983: 181)

Her sentiments embody much of what is insufficient about the fidelity approach to adaptation, with the secondary text paling in comparison to the original.

But this type of fidelity analysis in adaptation is quickly losing ground with critics such as Linda Hutcheon, who believes that 'an adaptation is a derivation that is not derivative—a work that is second without being secondary' (2006: 9). Reference books on children's media such as *From Page to Screen* (1992), edited by Joyce Moss and George Wilson, show the changing thoughts on fidelity by providing both an adaptation rating to 'indicate how closely the film adaptation reflects its literary source,' and a cinematic rating to 'indicate the film's strength independent of the book' (1992: xiv). Adaptations can be looked at in addition to the original to comprehend the entirety of what **Charlotte's Web** has become as it is constructed across media, and not solely to judge how faithful the adaptations are to the original text.

Also, the notion of interpretation and the degree of adaptation become questionable. 'White wrote to one entrepreneur hoping to film the barnyard saga, "I saw a spider spin the egg sac described in the story, and I wouldn't trade the sight for all the animated chimpmunks in filmland"' (quoted in Neumeyer 1994: xxix). Here, White is describing a first-hand visual account that he experienced and subsequently penned into the story through a textual rendering in descriptive narrative form, thus providing one level of transformation. White's text then proceeds to incorporate another level of transformation by illustrating the text with pictures by Garth Williams. Williams's illustrations do more than just add pictures: they enhance the meaning of the story and work cooperatively with the written text to create an interplay of image and text that becomes the novel. For example, after the line 'When she was finished ripping things out, her web looked something like this': there is a line drawing of a web (White, 1952: 92). This displays a visual interpretation of the intended meaning of White's words in a similar way to how a film version would, but with one image instead of 24 frames per second.

Similarly, Neumeyer annotates another picture of Charlotte's web, now complete with the word 'Terrific' in the centre and Wilbur positioned underneath: 'since White doesn't describe the expression on Wilbur's face, this illustration is testimonial to Williams's own creative bent' (1994: 95). White approves the illustrations, yet he is opposed to revisualizing his retelling of the event on film. His opposition may have been due to White's need for control over his story, but in the end adaptations were made.

The film and media transformations of *Charlotte's Web* exemplify the larger movements in American culture through the various technological shifts in available film techniques, from animated cells to computer-generated imagery (CGI). The animated feature film by Hanna-Barbera added a musical twist which was also popular with the other cartoon powerhouse, Disney. The 1970s were a unique time because a legacy had died with Walt Disney in 1966, but other cartoon production companies became more active. Film historian Leonard Maltin speculated that the 70s witnessed a 'cartoon renaissance' that 'saw a remarkable proliferation of feature cartoons, from here and abroad, for every possible type of audience' (1980: 342). The closest Disney release to Hanna-Barbera's *Charlotte's Web* (1973) was also a children's book adaptation, *Winnie the Pooh and Tigger Too* (1974), though this was an animated short.

The animated feature contributes to the overall story of *Charlotte's Web*, just as the live action film (made with the aid of live animals and computer animation) brought *Charlotte's Web* to life and also reintroduced the story to a new generation. In 2006, with CGI graphics becoming more and more realistic and feasible, the cultural moment called for a live action remake. The year before, Hutch Parker, president of production at 20th Century Fox Film, claimed: 'Even five years ago, we shot one or two movies a year with a significant number of effects. Today, 50 per cent have significant effects. They're a character in the movie' (quoted in Thompson, 2005: np). *Charlotte's Web* had behind it the legacy of another live action hit, with a talking pig—*Babe* (directed by Chris Noonan, 1995). Winning the 1996 Oscar for Best Effects, Visual Effects, *Babe* paved the way for a live action, barnyard family movie.

A video game, marketed as based on the 2006 film version of *Charlotte's Web,* was released in November 2006 on several platforms including PC, GameBoyAdvance, Play Station2, and Nintendo DS, illustrating the typical progression of children's classic texts from print to film to video game. Since the original children's book was written well before today's millennial generation was born, the release of a lone video game of *Charlotte's Web* may not have had its name recognized by the child purchaser. Since the text's original audience was not the video game's target audience, the game needed first to be presented through a movie in order to introduce children to the characters their parents were already familiar with. Each new text links to the previous one, but also remains its own text. In *Intertextuality* (2000), Graham Allen posits: 'The idea of the text, and thus of intertextuality, depends, as Barthes argues, on the figure of the web, the weave, the garment (text) woven from the threads of the "already written and the already read"' (2000: 6). *Charlotte's Web* is no different. Each text builds on the central radial hub but adds additional threads, part and parcel of creating the larger web, or ur-text.

Most video games that accompany the release of a live action film are largely dependent on that film because of shared graphics and a similar marketing plan; however, the *Charlotte's Web* video game is not simply a playable version of the film or the novel. The game reverted back to animated visuals; it was distinct from both the film and the book's narrative, but freely drew source material from both. The DS game returns to a first draft of Charlotte's Web where, according to White, 'the story did not contain Fern' since he added her character at the last minute before sending the manuscript to the publisher (***Letters of E. B. White,*** 1976: 648). The game does not use Fern as the primary playable character. Using her may have exacerbated the gender divide, whereas playing as Wilbur is gender-neutral and opens the game up to a wider audience. Fern as the avatar might promote the game's classification as a girl's game, thus limiting its selling range. Instead Fern is displayed occasionally, primarily in the role of healer to pet Wilbur to preserve his health, thus increasing the longevity of his game life.

In place of Fern, Wilbur is the main playable character. Again, the game has reverted to a pre-publication version of *Charlotte's Web.* Neumeyer writes that White intended 'that chapter in praise of the barn [Chapter Three] to open the book' (1994: xxix). The adventure portion of the video game begins in 'Level 1: Zuckerman's Barn.' Stills from the live action movie accompany the game's narration: 'I was born in a barn . . . just a plain old barn. But every barn needs a pig!' After this short-cut scene the game begins by waking Wilbur up in the barn, where the player then controls Wilbur and learns his actions through a short tutorial. The player guides Wilbur, and occasionally Templeton, through 16 levels from the barn to the state fair, collecting letters along the way. Just as the beginning of the game skips a section of the novel, it also ends before the novel concludes. 'Level 16: Say Uncle' concludes the game at the state fair after Wilbur and Templeton find Charlotte's egg sac.

The game consists of three modes: adventure, mini-games and storybook. The storybook mode displays stills from the live action movie with an abbreviated and adapted version of the novel. The story in the storybook mode begins:

> Wilbur was born the runt of the litter. Since Wilbur is not able to fend for himself, Mr Arable decides to give him to his daughter, Fern. Fern loves Wilbur, and tends to his every need, including long walks. When Wilbur grows too old to stay in the Arable house, Fern give him to her Uncle Zuckerman to take care of, on a great, big farm.
>
> (2006)

The story continues with a still picture from the movie in the upper screen and a short text in the bottom screen, presenting the entire story, or rather the video game version of the story, in 16 sentences.

Even though the game presents its own interpretation of the story in the various modes, being able to play *Charlotte's Web* adds a new level of interaction with the story. The adventure mode is the most obvious form, but the mini-games creatively adapt the story into short, active games, pushing the boundaries of the story. The mini-games sometimes take themes or instances from the story and rework them into short games that can be played in one sitting. Pulling from the gathering of words for Charlotte's web, one mini-game gives the player a jumble of letters and s/he has to create words of three letters or more. In another game the player helps Templeton catch food droppings to eat at the fair. Some games are based on those that Fern, Henry and Avery may have played at the fair, such as bumper cars and ring toss. Some are thematically linked to a barn—as in 'Bale Out,' where the player manoeuvres Wilbur through a hay-bale maze. The PC version of the game added a special game not found on the DS, 'Petting Pen,' where players can care for Wilbur. In this instance there is no need for a visual avatar of Fern because the player literally becomes the Fern character by taking care of Wilbur.

While the current strain of adaptation theory is pushing against the established debate about fidelity to the original text, instances of infidelity still prove noteworthy. Critics are largely concerned with how faithful a film or video game is to the original work, but breaches of fidelity prove interesting—particularly with the video game *Charlotte's Web*, which chooses to delete a central theme in the novel: death.

Charlotte's Web is, according to children's literature pioneer Francelia Butler, 'One of the most notable treatments of death in children's literature' (1984: 85). Neumeyer claims the work as 'one of the first children's books to deal seriously, without sentimentality or condescension, with death' (1994: xix). Animal death was part of White's everyday life on his Maine farm from 1938 to 1944. He loved being in the barn and around animals, and death on a farm is inevitable. But this sort of raw reality is foreign to mainstream American children today. For them, images of death are usually mediated through television, movies and video games. The *Charlotte's Web* video game chose to preserve the innocence of a childhood unmarred by thoughts or images of death: death, as well as violence, are completely removed from both the narrative and the game play, reflecting a backlash of political and parental activism against media violence. Instead of remaining faithful to a key theme of the novel, the video game distances itself from both the novel and any potential controversy, presenting a sanitized version of ***Charlotte's Web***. This may be an attempt by SEGA, the game's publisher, to address current concerns about video game violence.

Because children are largely removed from natural death, educators and others connected with children are concerned by the type of death and violence that children are now experiencing vicariously, particularly through various media. But the novel ***Charlotte's Web*** is a story whose themes include life, death, salvation and rebirth. In particular, the opening includes a strong presentation of killing and death.

'Where's Papa going with that ax?' opens the text (White, 1952: 1). Fern, because she 'was only eight' (White, 1952: 1), does not link her father or the axe with danger, violence or death, and thus asks her question in a very casual way—that of someone who sees her father with an axe regularly. It is not until her mother gently breaks the news to Fern that her father is going to 'do away' with a runt pig that Fern becomes agitated. Because she has grown up on a farm, Fern understands the euphemism and translates it into the harsh reality that her father is going to '*kill*' the runt [emphasis in original]. As Mr Arable's intentions are disclosed, White uses the tension created by death and killing as a plot device to both hook the reader and drive the action forward.

Potential violence is again implied with the introduction of Fern's ten-year-old brother Avery: 'He was heavily armed—an air rifle in one hand, a wooden dagger in the other' (White, 1952: 4). But then tension subsides as the possible death is averted. Of course the tension associated with impending death recurs throughout the entire novel, propelling the action and keeping Wilbur and readers wondering if he is going to be slaughtered. Only when Wilbur is finally safe does Charlotte die. Hers is a peaceful, yet heartbreaking, death not associated with any violence, but presented as the natural conclusion to life. Yet this conclusion is not the end. There is renewal in the spring as Charlotte's children are born and three decide to stay with Wilbur, providing a happy ending to the cyclical tale of life, death and rebirth.

Not only does the text of the novel present a violent tension, but the first two illustrations also visually increase the tone of violence. The escalation of emotions during the conversation between Fern and her mother is heightened by Garth Williams' drawing of Fern struggling with the axe in her father's hands (White 1952: 2). In the next illustration, the reader is visually introduced to a boy holding a rifle and clutching a knife (White 1952: 5). In the third illustration peace resumes, illustrated by a maternal scene of Fern cradling Wilbur in her arms and feeding him from a bottle. He has become 'her infant' and through her motherly love peace is restored, and violence and death diverted (White 1952: 6). No other illustration in the text contains man-made weapons. The most violent scene portrayed after the first chapter's pictures is Avery trying to capture Charlotte by knocking her into a box with a stick, but that image carries a comedic tone by showing Avery landing on his head with his feet in the air (White 1952: 73). The violence is also neutralized by the stench of a rotten goose egg that Avery breaks open when he falls.

Compared to the opening chapter in the novel, the video game version of *Charlotte's Web* (2006) contains no killing, violence, or death. Something so central to the novel—death—is completely removed from the video game. In the adventure mode, Wilbur is never in fear of dying at the hands of either Fern's father or Mr Zuckerman. Wilbur does have to evade Lurvy in one chapter of the game but, as in the book chapter 'Escape,' there is no immediate threat. Even if a player tries to kill Wilbur by letting him drown in a water obstacle, he cannot really die. He squirms comically, his health bar drops to zero, and the game restarts at the most recent checkpoint to give the player yet another chance. No matter how many times Wilbur runs out of health, the game always restarts with new lives for Wilbur. Violence in video games is a politically charged topic, but the video game *Charlotte's Web* deflates the notion in its adventure mode, which purposefully avoids death and violence, thus remaining unfaithful to a key theme presented in the novel.

The storybook mode does not delete every instance of potential death in the novel, but glosses over Wilbur's potential fate by euphemistically stating: 'Learning that Wilbur is destined to become a holiday ham, Charlotte tries to save his life by letting everyone know, he's "Some Pig."' But Wilbur's fate is never mentioned again. Also, his first brush with death is removed so that the humane Mr Arable 'decides to give him to his daughter, Fern' instead of Fern having to plead for Wilbur's life.

As well as avoiding death, the video game also leaves out the cycle of life and rebirth. The adventure mode ends at the fair, and does not continue back to the barn. The storybook mode goes one episode further: 'When Wilbur comes home, he watches Charlotte's babies hatch and fly away.' Both modes, in sanitizing the story by removing the cycle of life, death and rebirth, provide a cultural commentary on the sanctioned avoidance of such topics for today's children, regardless of their inclusion in the original text.

As is the case with *Charlotte's Web,* where a book has become a revered 'classic' most readers will evaluate its film, and especially video game, adaptations on the basis of fidelity. Throughout the history of adaptation studies, questions of fidelity to the source have dominated theoretical discussion by questioning whether (for example) the movie faithfully represents the text, leading to a strong critique on points of departure from the original. With the current trend for releasing movies and games based on popular children's books, the fidelity question is at its nadir. However, sometimes points of infidelity prove the most interesting, especially in the convergent web of intertexts.

Bibliography

Allen, Graham (2000), *Intertextuality.* London: Routledge.

Apseloff, Marilyn (1983), '*Charlotte's Web*: flaws in the weaving,' in Douglas Street (ed.), *Children's Novels and the Movies.* New York: Frederick Ungar Publishing pp. 171-81.

Babe (1995). USA, dir. Chris Noonan.

Bazin, Andre (2000), 'Adaptation, or the cinema as digest,' in James Naremore (ed.), *Film Adaptation.* New Brunswick, NJ: Rutgers University Press pp. 19-27.

Bolter, Jay David and Richard Grusin (2000), *Remediation: Understanding New Media.* Cambridge, MA: MIT.

Butler, Francelia (1984), 'Death in children's literature,' in Francelia Butler and Richard Rotert (eds), *Reflections on Literature for Children.* Connecticut, USA: Library Professional Publications pp. 72-90.

Cartmell, Deborah and Imelda Whelehan (2005), 'Harry Potter and the fidelity debate,' in Mireia Aragay (ed.), *Books in Motion: Adaptation, Intertextuality, Authorship.* New York: Rodopi pp. 37-49.

Charlotte's Web (1973). USA, dir. Charles A. Nichols and Iwao Takamoto.

Charlotte's Web (2006). USA, dir. Gary Winick.

Charlotte's Web (2006) (electronic video game). USA, Sega.

Cook, David A. (2000), *Lost Illusions: American Cinema in the Shadow of Watergate and Vietnam, 1970-1979*. History of the American Cinema vol. 9. New York: Charles Scribner's Sons.

Goldstein, Jeffrey, David Buckingham and Gilles Brougere (eds) (2004), *Toys, Games, and Media*. Mahwah, NJ: Lawrence Erlbaum Associates.

Hayles, N. Katherine (2005), *My Mother Was a Computer: Digital Subjects and Literary Texts*. Chicago: Chicago University Press.

Hutcheon, Linda (2006), *A Theory of Adaptation*. New York: Routledge.

Jenkins, Henry (2006), *Convergence Culture: Where Old and New Media Collide*. New York: New York University Press.

Kinder, Marsha (1999), *Kid's Media Culture*. Durham, NC: Duke University Press.

Maltin, Leonard. (1980), *Of Mice and Magic: A History of American Animated Cartoons*. New York: McGraw-Hill.

Moss, Joyce and George Wilson (eds) (1992), *From Page to Screen: Children's and Young Adult Books on Film and Video*. Detroit, MI: Gale Research.

Naremore, James (ed.) (2000), *Film Adaptation*. New Brunswick, NJ: Rutgers University Press.

Neumeyer, Peter F. (1994), *The Annotated Charlotte's Web*. New York: HarperCollins.

Sutherland, Zena (1997), *Children and Books*. 9th edn. New York: Longman.

Tapscott, Don (1998), *Growing Up Digital*. New York: McGraw-Hill.

Thompson, Anne (2005), 'F/X gods: the 10 visual effects wizards who rule Hollywood'. *Wired*, 13 February. <http://www.wired.com/wired/archive/13.02/fxgods.html?pg=1&topic=fxgods&topic_set=>.

White, E. B. (1952), *Charlotte's Web*. New York: HarperCollins.

———. (1976), *Letters of E. B. White*, ed. Dorothy Lobrano Guth. New York: Harper & Row.

Thomas Crisp (essay date 2011)

SOURCE: Crisp, Thomas. "'Some Dead Spider!': Three Variations on the Death of Charlotte in Print and Film." *Crossing Textual Boundaries in International Children's Literature,* edited by Lance Weldy, Newcastle upon Tyne, Cambridge Scholars Publishing, 2011, pp. 94-108.

[*In the following essay, Crisp provides a history of* Charlotte's Web *(1952) on film, then discusses the treatment of the death of Charlotte in two filmed versions and the unfilmed script of a third, "exploring how the variations in interpretation are intended to operate on their implied viewers."*]

As one of the most canonical pieces of American children's literature, E. B. White's 1952 novel **Charlotte's Web** is often, as Perry Nodelman notes, the first extended narrative read to children.[1] In the nearly sixty years since its publication, the book has continued to captivate readers, critics, and scholars of children's literature—volumes have been written interpreting (and re-interpreting) what Eudora Welty called a "just about perfect" children's book.[2] **Charlotte's Web** has been explored through such varied theoretical lenses as reader response[3] and Lacanian subjectivity.[4] Who and what the novel is ultimately "about" is the subject of much conversation among readers:[5] the book seems to be as much about Charlotte or Templeton as it is about Wilbur or Fern; it is as much about environmental ethics[6] and farm life[7] as it is about mothering,[8] the cycle of life,[9] or the power of writing.[10] White himself believed that **Charlotte's Web** is not a moral tale, nor did he see in it any symbolism or political meaning: it is "a straight report from the barn cellar"; a "hymn to the barn."[11]

In children's literature textbooks and classrooms, the novel operates as an exemplar of children's fiction: many textbooks extensively use White's novel as an example of various literary elements, techniques, and structures; the assumption seeming to be that most—or all—readers will already be familiar with the book or that most—or all—will read it in class or be inspired to pick it up and read it independently. At the same time, for some, the novel's loss of the 1953 Newbery Medal to Ann Nolan Clark's *Secret of the Andes* serves as a ready example of the subjective nature of children's book awards and as testament that the ways in which a text is read and understood is socially constructed and can change across time.

Despite the loss of the Newbery gold, Web's novel received a number of awards, including the Newbery Honor, Horn Book Fanfare, the Lewis Carroll Shelf Award, the Laura Ingalls Wilder Medal, and it was named an ALA Notable Children's Book. The positive reviews of readers across a range of ages, its numerable awards, and the range of scholarly conversations that continue to revolve around and intertwine with this book provide evidence of its enduring power and canonical status.

OFF TO THE CINEMA: TRANSFORMING *CHARLOTTE'S WEB* FROM NOVEL TO FILM

With the popular tendency to compare a film interpretation of a book with its original literary counterpart, the decision to make a cinematic adaptation of such a canonical piece of fiction may seem like a recipe for disaster—it would be nearly impossible to "get it right" and avoid purist complaints about the shade of Fern's hair, the tenor of Wilbur's voice, or the filmmaker's fidelity to the original text. At the same time, however, it is difficult to imagine a filmmaker, studio, or production company *not* wanting to make a film interpretation of the novel—its status as iconic cultural artifact would almost necessarily mean financial success for any cinematic undertaking. In fact, it was not long after the publication of the novel that a number of film makers (including animators John and Faith Hubley) and production companies (like Disney) began courting White for the film rights to his novel, but it would be more than two decades before the first film interpretation would be produced and completed.

One roadblock to the successful creation of a film adaptation of the novel was what E. B. White himself acknowledged were extensive demands for creative control. White required a "right of approval clause" that would protect him from any motion picture version of *Charlotte's Web* that "violates the spirit and meaning of the story." He wanted access to the screenplay, sketches of principal characters, the right to hear and approve principal voices, and "the chance to edit the script wherever anything turns up that is a gross departure or a gross violation. I also would like to be protected against the insertion of wholly new material—songs, jokes, capers, episodes."[12] Upon the initial suggestion of an animated film adaptation, White's correspondences reveal particular trepidation. In a letter dated June 28, 1961, he writes, "While animation is a perfect device for satire, *Charlotte's Web* is not really a satire [...] because of this, it has occurred to me that the book, if handled with imagination, might make a motion picture in live action—real girl, real barn, real creatures."[13]

In 1971, a decade after that letter was written, White appears to have been persuaded that an animated version of the novel may indeed work and he enters into an agreement in which he would collaborate with animator Gene Deitch to create a film adaptation of *CHarlotte's Web.* Correspondences between the two make clear that Deitch was willing to work closely with White: reading pieces of a script White had started previously as well as entertaining White's advice on themes, music, and characterization. In a January 12, 1971 letter, White tells Deitch, "You are stuck with my scheme and will probably come out better if you go along with it."[14] What seems like a promising relationship between animator and author falls apart when later in 1971, Deitch is removed from the project and replaced by Joseph Barbera and the Hanna-Barbera and Sagittarius production companies. Sagittarius and Hanna-Barbera sent White a script written by Earl Hamner, Jr. upon which their animated film was to be based. Although White subsequently spent ten days writing copious notes and annotations on the content of Hamner's script, Hamner and Hanna-Barbera paid little attention to these suggestions.[15] It will not be surprising, then, to find that White was strongly disappointed by Hanna-Barbera's film. On March 26, 1973, he wrote, "The movie of Charlotte is about what I expected it to be. The story is interrupted every few minutes so that somebody can sing a jolly song. I don't care much for jolly songs. The Blue Hill Fair, which I tried to report faithfully in the book, has become a Disney world, with 76 trombones. But that's what you get for getting embroiled with Hollywood."[16]

In her 1983 essay, "*Charlotte's Web*: Flaws in the Weaving," Marilyn Apseloff details some of the history behind the creation of White's novel before moving into a discussion (really, a comparison) of the 1973 animated film and the original novel. Although Apseloff nods to scholarship suggesting films can stand on their own as interpretations, she ultimately rejects that approach, concluding that, "it is when the adaptation is compared with the book and the book's *intent* that its divergence from White's work is realized."[17] She explores what she views as the misinterpretation of White's novel by examining the order, content, and addition/removal of scenes and characters, and how these alterations impact the authorial intent of the novel. It is tempting (and often pleasing) to compare an artistic interpretation of a novel to the "original," but as George Bluestone writes in the preface to *Novels into Film,* literature and film are "marked by such essentially different traits that they belong to separate artistic genera. [...] [T]he novel is a linguistic medium, the film essentially visual."[18] Bluestone argues that film and literature are as different as ballet and architecture and he asserts that a filmmaker is not the translator for the author of the literary text, but is instead "a new author in his own right."[19]

In the first major collection of critical essays focusing on children's novels and their film interpretations, editor Douglas Street finds more of a relationship between film and fiction, noting that the two mediums freely borrow from one another. But even he concludes that "the transformation of the writer's visual language into the filmmakers language of vision requires essential alterations of the original."[20] Ultimately, changes in film adaptations of texts are inevitable. Andrew Horton and Joan Magretta write that "adaptation can be a lively and creative art, and that attention to this art will enhance our understanding of film. [. . .] The study of adaptation is clearly a form of source study and thus should trace the *genesis* (not the destruction) of works deemed worthy of close examination in and of themselves"[21]

Ian Wojcik-Andrews writes, "to know something about a film is to know something about how society sees them and how they might in turn see society."[22] Film history, social history, and the depiction of social issues in motion pictures constantly interact. Examining children's films and the ways in which viewers are positioned in the textual event contributes to an understanding of what these films reveal about the context in which they were created, released, and consumed. In the rest of this essay, I want to take up the project that Apseloff rejects by examining one particular scene in **Charlotte's Web** and critically exploring various ways in which it has been interpreted for two major feature film releases (the animated film released by Hanna-Barbera Productions in 1973 referenced earlier, and the recent 2006 Paramount Pictures live-action/computer generated graphics release) as well as in a pedagogically-oriented reader's theater script written in 1993/2006 by Patsy Carey and Susan Kilpatrick.

THE DEATH OF CHARLOTTE

For many readers, the death of Charlotte in the penultimate chapter of White's novel stands as one of the most poignant and powerful moments in the text, and each of these three interpretations presents it differently. While my inner literary purist may find it difficult, in this paper, I work to separate my tendency toward aesthetic readings of film that privilege the literary text to instead situate this work within a sociological/historical approach to children's film adaptation by exploring how the variations in interpretation are intended to operate on their implied viewers. Just as **Charlotte's Web** classification as "children's literature" is about genre and not an indication of readership, the marketing of **Charlotte's Web** as a "family film" eliminates any real or imagined differences between child and adult readers. Robin Wood writes that the uniquely American "family film"[23] reconstructs adult viewers as child viewers because they are "intellectually undemanding" and employ special effects that prevent audiences from thinking too critically about what they are viewing. These films serve to reassure viewers and encourage them to "evade responsibility and thought." Often, family films reproduce patriarchal myths of the nuclear family and social stability,[24] and this remains true in both of the *Web* films, with transformations that include heightened focus on the relationship between Fern and Henry Fussy as well the construction of Mr. Arable as quintessential patriarch of the family.

The 1960s and 1970s were a time of social and political unrest in the United States, with the Civil Rights and feminist movements and the ongoing Vietnam War all contributing to feelings of lost confidence experienced by many American citizens. Terrorism—including airplane hijackings, bombings, kidnapping, and mass murder—was increasingly visible around the world and violence and gang activity in American cities were on the rise. Aspects of life that had previously been taken for granted were being questioned and often displaced: even the media depiction of the American family was changing, with sitcoms like "Maude," The Mary Tyler Moore Show," and "All in the Family" replacing "The Donna Reed Show" and "Leave it to Beaver."

On March 1, 1973, in the same year that saw the release of films like *The Exorcist, American Graffiti, The Way We Were,* and Disney's *Robin Hood,* Hanna-Barbera and Sagittarius productions released the animated film *Charlotte's Web*. The film was initially marketed in the United States as *E. B. White's Charlotte's Web,* drawing a direct link from White's book to this film transformation. This film interpretation of **Charlotte's Web** attempts to build on the late 1960s success of a "trio of high budget, musical adaptations" that attempted to "outdo the popularity of television,"[25] including *Mary Poppins, Doctor Dolittle,* and *Chitty Chitty Bang Bang*. It is just one of several 1970s films that testify to a renewed interest in the animated feature and a turn toward children's literature for storylines and profits in films like *The Hobbit* and *The Lion, the Witch, and the Wardrobe*.

Upon its release, *Charlotte's Web* met with modest critical review and commercial success thanks, in part, to a cast which included the vocal talents of Debbie Reynolds as Charlotte, Henry Gibson as Wilbur, Agnes Moorehead as the Goose, and Paul Lynde as Templeton. The film was released internationally, from West Germany (March 30) and Sweden (August 11) to Japan (August 25). Although many reviewers comment that the movie is a faithful adaptation of the book, others criticize the music and the "Saturday morning cartoon quality" of the animation.[26] Still others refer to it as being "downright bad,"[27] but even many of these critics find some aspects of the film worthy of praise. For example, Dan Jardine writes that the film "retains just enough of White's elegant prose in the dialogue and narration to keep the film from being simply a painfully well-intended experiment,"[28] and Christopher Null asserts that ultimately, White's novel "needs little to make it come to life."[29] Writing specifically of the depiction of the death of Charlotte, Craig Butler writes that in the film, "no attempt has been made to soften the existential sadness at the story's core."[30]

Lucy Rollin writes that White's novel, focused on the domestic sphere (which has traditionally and stereotypically constructed as a "female" sphere), is filled with nurturing females. It initially positions Fern as a mother to Wilbur, and later, when Wilbur is moved to the barnyard, Charlotte fulfills this role as well. Rollin notes Charlotte's "indulgent fondness"[31] for Wilbur: she is affectionate, even when she scolds Wilbur, she sets goals and makes plans for his future, and builds his ego and self-confidence.[32] This theme is picked up in the 1973 animated film, focusing on the mothering of characters like Mrs. Arable, Fern, and Charlotte.

In the 1973 film, "The Last Day" sequence opens with Charlotte commenting on the medal Wilbur has just received at the fair. Although nothing in her animated physical appearance or in Debbie Reynolds vocal performance of Charlotte appears any different than it was throughout the film, Wilbur senses something is wrong and asks Charlotte if she is alright, remarking that she does not sound like herself. Climbing her gossamer to the top of the pen, Charlotte simply replies she is tired. At this point, the angle of the shot shifts to Wilbur's perspective, aimed upward toward Charlotte as she remarks, "What's a life anyway? We're born, we live a little while, and we die." Charlotte continues to speak, but the film only frames Wilbur, in a medium shot, what John Golden has argued is a neutral shot—the viewer may listen to Charlotte's words, but attention is entirely focused on Wilbur. Viewers may be positioned to view the scene from Wilbur's point of view, but at no point during this sequence are viewers situated to identify with Charlotte. On one level, this makes sense: the story is ultimately Wilbur's tale; however, the decision to minimize any identification with Charlotte provides further evidence of the "family film's" reduction of all viewers to child viewers. Even in the climactic moment in which Charlotte reveals she will not be returning to the barn, the camera continues to be positioned to focus on Wilbur and his response.

Further, when Charlotte reveals she is dying, Wilbur is seen from a wide angle or long shot, positioning the viewer to hear, but not see, Charlotte. The use of "neutral shots" or wide angles within this sequence all work to distance the viewer from the immediacy of the action and emotion. Viewers are generally positioned outside and expected to empathize with and feel sympathy for Wilbur as the camera remains focused on him.

It is only when Charlotte says that she hasn't the strength to climb down into the crate that the camera has moved back to frame her from a low angle, just above eye-level. Viewers are placed slightly below her body, viewing Charlotte as she gazes downward toward Wilbur, the character who has until now played the role of her child. Immediately after Charlotte's revelation, the camera returns to a medium ("neutral") shot of Wilbur moaning and sobbing while Charlotte's voice is again heard comforting him from off-screen. The angle of the camera moves to a close up of Wilbur's lined and pained face, bright blue tears pouring from his eyes.

Then suddenly, Charlotte (filling the role of mother) appears in the shot, having climbed down to comfort the pig. One has to wonder why the filmmakers would break the sequence of shots focusing on Wilbur, cut to Charlotte just long enough for her to declare that she hasn't the strength to climb down, and then contradict that statement only moments later by showing her descend to comfort the grieving Wilbur. If **Charlotte's Web** is ostensibly about mothering, with characters like Charlotte and Fern alternating in the role of mother to "the child," Wilbur, this cinematic transformation reflects and builds upon that theme by using cinematic techniques to manipulate viewers into identifying with Wilbur at the expense of other characters. Although White's novel is primarily Wilbur's story, space is provided in the text through which readers can resist dominant readings and instead identify with a character like Fern or Charlotte. A film interpretation could provide similar spaces through which viewers could identify with any range of characters, but the filmmakers work to eliminate these alternative perspectives in an effort to position all readers as "Wilbur," the child whose world will never be the same after the death of his "mother," Charlotte.

Emerging in the post-Civil Rights and women's liberation era, and in the midst of the Vietnam War, the film's focus on the "female"-socialized image of woman as mother, as well as the patriarchal constructions of family, operate as a throw-back to "safer" times. The filmmaker's decision to have Charlotte lower herself to comfort Wilbur after stating she hasn't the strength (or gossamer in her spinnerets) to climb down suggests that the thematic role of Charlotte as caregiver and mother-figure for Wilbur drives the film so powerfully that it comes at the expense even of logic and consistency within the film.

After Templeton has retrieved Charlotte's egg sack, Wilbur promises her that her children are safe, but Charlotte does not respond. Fearing she has died, Wilbur panics until Charlotte tells him that she is simply sitting quietly, thinking of his life. Instead of reflecting on her own life—having it flash before her many eyes—or thinking about the potential lives of her *actual* children; Charlotte remains focused on the life of Wilbur. She begins to sing of autumn days, and the film fades into a flashback sequence. "Contemporary Wilbur" is still visible, gazing up presumably at Charlotte as she sings, but this image is in soft focus with the predominant sequence consisting of images of Wilbur's life superimposed around him. The film moves back and forth: sometimes with Contemporary Wilbur dissolving away entirely so that the moments of his past come into sharp relief, and at other times, the reverse is true as Wilbur—almost smiling—looks up toward Charlotte, while the replaying of past experiences fades into the background.

The sequence shows a caregiver who has succeeded in raising her young, and, now that her duty is fulfilled, she can die (and does so while reflecting not on her own life, but the life of the child). As the song continues toward its end, Charlotte's voice becomes a mere whisper. Wilbur realizes Charlotte has died, slumping and sobbing while the melody of the song Charlotte just sang plays in the background. Wilbur crawls into his crate, and the scene dissolves as an image of Zuckerman's barn fades in and brings the action back home to the farm, where Wilbur assumes the role of mother to Charlotte's young spiders. Although White's novel clearly indicates that "No one was with her when she died,"[33] in this depiction of the death of Charlotte, the filmmakers have decided that Charlotte should not be left alone when her life ends—Charlotte dies while Wilbur and Templeton are still with her. She dies surrounded by friends, and Wilbur (with whom the viewer has been positioned to identify) has closure in that he is allowed to be beside Charlotte as she passes and is able to watch over the spider who watched over him almost from birth.

The 1973 animated interpretation of **Charlotte's Web** may have had mediocre critical review and commercial success upon its release, but its enduring popularity in VHS—and later DVD—format inspired Paramount Pictures to release an animated sequel on March 18, 2003, entitled, *Charlotte's Web 2: Wilbur's Great Adventure* (internally distributed by Universal Pictures). The film, produced by Paramount, Universal and Universal Cartoon Studios, and Nickelodeon met with some of the same criticism of its predecessor, mainly, the "Saturday morning cartoon" nature and mediocre animation and plot. However, it is rumored that this straight-to-video release was successful enough to inspire Paramount, Walden Media and Kerner Entertainment Companies, and Nickelodeon Movies to mount a live-action/computer-animated feature film, with a screenplay by Susannah Grant and Karey Kirkpatrick and direction by Gary Winick.

Released on December 15, 2006, this iteration of *Charlotte's Web* was created without any connection to E. B. White's estate[34] and features the vocal talents of Dakota Fanning as Fern, Kevin Anderson as Mr. Arable, Beau Bridges as Dr. Dorian, Julia Roberts as Charlotte, Steve Buscemi as Templeton, as well as John Cleese, Oprah Winfrey, Cedric the Entertainer, Kathy Bates, Reba McEntire, Robert Redford, and more. This time, reviews were more positive, with Michael Medved awarding the film 3.5 out of four stars, calling the film "irresistible" and "glowing with goodness."[35] In *Entertainment Weekly*, Owen Geiberman writes that although the film is "a bit noisy," the director deserves applause for putting "the book, in all its glorious tall-tall reverence, right up on the screen."[36] In one particularly colorful review, Colm Andrew of the *Manx Independent* gives the film 6/10, citing "the ultra-cute characterization of Wilbur [which resulted] in half the audience rooting for his demise." In the end, even Andrew writes this film interpretation is "a competent retelling of a classic story that won't offend."[37] The release of the 2006 film provides testimony to the commodification and commercialism of children's literature as argued by scholars like Jack Zipes: coupled with the release of the film were a range of products—from plush and plastic toys and dolls, board games, and a computer game to clothing and party supplies like hats, plates, napkins. The politics of children's publishing, as described by Joel Taxel, are evident in the simultaneous release of picture books based on White's novel, picture books based on the film, and picture books extending White's text.

In this version of the "Last Day" sequence, Charlotte and Wilbur converse about Charlotte's egg sack and the 514 spiders inside. It is when Wilbur suggests that it will be "really radiant" back on the farm that Charlotte explains that she will not be returning home. The camera pans from a pacing Wilbur upward toward Charlotte and then back again in an uninterrupted single long shot until the moment in which Charlotte explains that she hasn't the strength to climb down to the crate to return to the barnyard. At this point, the shot ends and a new one begins, notably from Charlotte's perspective: a close-up of Wilbur as he begs her to climb down so he can carry her home. Throughout the subsequent exchange between these two characters, the camera angles alternate from Charlotte's perspective gazing down at Wilbur to Wilbur's perspective looking up at Charlotte. Unlike the 1973 film, which works to situate viewers squarely with Wilbur, the cinematic techniques employed by the current filmmakers provide a range of options for viewers: as examples, they can identify with either or both characters, they can participate in a little of each perspective and get a sense of how each is reacting within the scene, or they can remain unattached and distance themselves from the film.

Wilbur admits that "I didn't do anything, Charlotte. You did it all," but Charlotte dismisses this by stating, "My webs were no miracle. I was only describing what I saw. The miracle ... is you." There is a beat and then Charlotte and Wilbur see the Zuckermans' truck approaching. After Templeton drops Charlotte's egg sac down to Wilbur, the pig puts it in his mouth just before being situated in the crate and loaded on the truck. As the vehicle begins to depart, the shot returns to Charlotte framed in a close up as she speaks her final words in the film: "Goodbye, my sweet, sweet, Wilbur." The next shot shows Wilbur pushing his face through the slats of the crate and placing his left hoof on one of the planks as if straining to see his friend for as long as possible. Wilbur has apparently deposited the egg sack somewhere in the crate, because he looks up at Charlotte and says, "Goodbye, Charlotte. I love you." His snout quivers as the sounds of Wilbur's crying mix with sentimental orchestral music and the truck departs, fading away as Charlotte is shown closing her eyes: the web in which the word "Humble" had been spun waves in the wind, disheveled and torn. Unlike the novel (which, again, explicitly states that no one is with Charlotte when she dies) or the 1973 animated film in which Wilbur is with Charlotte when she dies, this interpretation goes a step further: Wilbur has the chance to say goodbye to Charlotte and tell her that he loves her. The ending may be sad, but it is satisfying because it fits a pattern of the cycle of life that is comforting and pleasing: not only does Wilbur get to say goodbye, but he also gets to say "I love you" one last time.

Like the 1973 version of the film, the 2006 iteration of *Charlotte's Web* was released during a time of political and social unrest. But while both film interpretations highlight the importance of good mothering, the 2006 film is also about safe goodbyes. For many Americans, the terrorist attacks on the pentagon and World Trade Center in 2001, perceived crises in education and industry, ongoing military action in Afghanistan and Iraq, and a growing LGBTQ rights movement contributed to feelings of uncertainty and insecurity, prompting many to call for a return to more "traditional" value systems and structures. Walden Media and Kerner Entertainment, two of the companies behind this production of *Charlotte's Web* have been cited as having evangelical Christian beliefs and a "Christian mission" and using these beliefs to rewrite the stories they are producing as films. Giving Wilbur (and viewers) the opportunity to say "goodbye" and "I love you" to Charlotte may operate here as a fantasy of closure; an acceptable version of the cycle of life and death.

Some (Dead?) Spider: *Charlotte's Web* as Theatrical Script

Although quite different in its purposes from the cinematic interpretations of *Charlotte's Web*, one final depiction of the death of Charlotte is worthy of a brief exploration: a reader's theatre script found in the Teacher Created Resources' *Guide for Using Charlotte's Web in the Classroom*. Teacher Created Resources is a national educational publishing company that produces products that are "created *by* teachers *for* teachers and parents."[38] Their guides for children's literature are among the top-selling in the nation. The contents of this guide include a range of materials: lesson plans, background information about the book and author, and activities for language arts and "related" curriculum (i.e., math and science). Finally, the guide includes "culminating activities" including a reader's theater script intended to be performed for caregivers, but which could also be performed in other classrooms or elsewhere in the community. This interpretation is a departure from the two film transformations, as reader's theatre is a pedagogical tool intended to increase fluency, prosody, and sometimes the comprehension of young readers. Like most reader's theater scripts, Patsy Carey and Susan Kilpatrick's interpretation of *Charlotte's Web* is brief (a mere four pages); everything is minimal. In the *Guide for Using Charlotte's Web in the Classroom*, Charlotte's death is alluded to even on the cover of the guide, which positions Charlotte, Wilbur, and Templeton in front of a web in which the word "humble" has been woven (the word Charlotte weaves in her final web at the fair).

In this interpretation, an announcer and three narrators guide much of the action, but performers also take on the roles of characters like Wilbur and Charlotte. The final sequence in the script unfolds as follows:

NARRATOR 3:

> Mr. Zuckerman decided to take his famous pig to the county fair. While they were at the fair, Charlotte wrote one more word in her web. The word was "Humble."

NARRATOR 1:

> Wilbur was awarded a special prize and fainted from all the excitement.

NARRATOR 3:

> Wilbur was very grateful to Charlotte.

WILBUR:

    When I first met you, Charlotte, I thought you were bloodthirsty, but now you have saved my life. I don't deserve a friend like you.

CHARLOTTE:

    You have been a good and loyal friend, Wilbur. That, in itself, is a tremendous thing.

WILBUR:

    You have saved me, Charlotte, and I would gladly give my life for you.

CHARLOTTE:

    I'm sure you would. Thank you, Wilbur.

NARRATOR 1:

    Charlotte and Wilbur were true friends to the very end.

NARRATOR 2:

    Wilbur had a chance to repay Charlotte when he carried her egg sac back to the farm.

NARRATOR 3:

    Wilbur never forgot what a wonderful friend Charlotte had been to him. Wilbur and Charlotte are not going to read a poem to each other. Listen for some of the descriptive words they use. [*Teacher: Two new children can be designated to read the poems on page 20. You may wish to involve small groups or assign half the class to read one poem, and the other half to read the second poem. Adapt the Announcer's preceding lines to fit the situation.*][39]

ANNOUNCER:

    We will now sing a song entitled "Some Pig!" *(When the song is finished the announcer or another student thanks the audience for coming and invites everyone to enjoy the food and classroom displays.)*[40]

Fitting with other interpretations of White's novel, Charlotte's final words ("Thank you, Wilbur") are for and about Wilbur, and in this version of the story, the narrators immediately step into the scene to tell viewers (or readers of the script) that Charlotte and Wilbur "were true friends *to the very end.*"[41] The death of Charlotte is implicit here, further underscored by the comment that "Wilbur never forgot what a wonderful friend Charlotte *had been* to him."[42] Immediately after these two lines, however, the potential impact Charlotte's death may have is erased when Charlotte and Wilbur return to the stage to read a poem to one another. Viewers see both characters interacting with one another as they read a poem (which is actually a song all about Wilbur, including such lyrics as "If you believe you're radiant, / Then let your bright line shine. / So don't feel down, / No need to frown. / Remember you're no swine!")[43]

There could be a number of reasons that the death of Charlotte has been minimized in this interpretation. It could be that the script, as reader's theatre, relies upon the assumption that those enacting or viewing the performance have read the novel and will recognize the death of Charlotte in its subtle representation (the authorial suggestion that this be performed for an outside audience may undermine this interpretation) or maybe it is simply a matter of length and time, or perhaps the authors wanted to spare the audience from watching the melodramatic "death" of a young child as Charlotte. Regardless of intent, the removal of Charlotte's death has profound implications in that it minimizes one of the most powerful lessons about the cycle of life, one that has been integral in all other interpretations of the story. Beyond the elimination of Charlotte's death, there are several other transformations of interest, for example, the reconstruction of the character of Wilbur. Narrator 3, speaking directly to the audience, declares that "Wilbur never forgot what a wonderful friend Charlotte had been to him," but, more interestingly, Narrator 2 announces that "Wilbur had a chance to repay Charlotte when he carried her egg sac back to the farm." This is not open to interpretation, disagreement, or discussion among participants and audience members. The authors of the script have decided that this one act for Charlotte repays her for all that she had done for Wilbur across his life, and alternative reader responses are eliminated through the explicit text of the script.

CONCLUSION

This analysis begins to explore a few of the ways in which each of these films and the reader's theater script establishes a particular way of understanding the relationship between Wilbur and Charlotte and Charlotte's death (or death followed by immediate resurrection). Each filmmaker, director, writer, and producer has worked to decide which meanings and themes should be gleaned by viewing the various interpretations explored in this paper. One focuses on the reproduction of mothering, with Charlotte comforting Wilbur and reflecting on his life while her own slips away (in this case, she dies surrounded by friends), where another presents the death of Charlotte in a safe and satisfying way (giving Wilbur the chance to say goodbye). A third interpretation seeks to protect viewers by almost entirely eliminating Charlotte's death. While it is possible to resist what these various players choose to highlight, and while viewers can revise these scenes in multiple ways (or rewrite them entirely), the techniques of filming direct attention and situate viewers within a particular perspective.

When the individual components (angle, shot, music, and so forth) are brought together, it serves to privilege one particular "reading" over others. Ultimately, films aren't copies of the literary original, but unique interpretations shaped through careful and purposeful decisions. These conscious efforts advance particular themes, manipulate audiences, and promote ideologies that reflect the forces behind the film and are intended to reflect and shape the perceived cultural views of members of the society in which these interpretations are released.

Notes

1. Perry Nodelman, "Text as Teacher: The Beginning of *Charlotte's Web*," *Children's Literature* 15 (1985): 159.

2. Eudora Welty, "Review of *Charlotte's Web*," *New York Times Book Review* (October 19, 1952): 49.

3. Peggy J. Miller, "Peter Rabbit and Mr. McGregor Reconciled, Charlotte Lives: Preschoolers Recreate the Classics," *The Horn Book Magazine* 73, no.3 (May/June 1997): 282-288.

4. Karen Coats, "Lacan with Runt Pigs," *Children's Literature* 27 (1999): 105-128.

5. Norton V. Kinghorn, "The Real Miracle of *Charlotte's Web*," *Children's Literature Association Quarterly* 11, no.1 (Spring 1986): 4-9.

6. Mark Sagoff, "Zuckerman's Dilemma: A Plea for Environmental Ethics," *The Hastings Center Report* 21, no.5 (September 1991): 32-40.

7. Roger Sale, *Fairy Tales and After: From Snow White to E. B. White*. (Cambridge, MA: Harvard University Press, 1978).

8. Lucy Rollin, "The Reproduction of Mothering in *Charlotte's Web*," in *Psychoanalytic Responses to Children's Literature*, ed. Lucy Rollin and Mark I. West (Jefferson, NC: McFarland & Co., 1999), 53-64.

9. Eudora Welty, "Review of *Charlotte's Web*," *New York Times Book Review* (19 October 1952): 49.

10. Janice M. Alberghene, "Writing in *Charlotte's Web*," *Children's Literature in Education* 16, no.1 (March 1985): 32-44.

11. Dorothy Lobrano Guth and Martha White, *Letters of E. B. White: Revised Edition* (New York: HarperCollins, 2006), 562-3.

12. Ibid., 500.

13. Ibid., 439.

14. Ibid., 563.

15. Ibid., 577.

16. Ibid., 595.

17. Marilyn Apseloff, "*Charlotte's Web*: Flaws in the Weaving," in *Children's Novels and the Movies*, ed. Douglas Street (New York: Frederick Ungar Publishing Co., 1983), 171-181.

18. George Bluestone, *Novels into Film*, (Los Angeles: University of California Press), viii.

19. Ibid., 62.

20. Douglas Street, "Introduction," in *Children's Novels and the Movies*, ed. Douglas Street (New York: Frederick Ungar Publishing Co., 1983), xvii.

21. Andrew Horton and Joan Magretta, *Modern European Film Makers and the Art of Adaptation* (New York: Frederick Ungar Publishing Co., 1981), 1.

22. Ian Wojcik-Andrews, *Children's Films: History, Ideology, Pedagogy, Theory* (New York: Garland Publishing, 2000), 2.

23. "Children's films" (not family films) outside of the United States take a decidedly different stance toward what children's movies are and should be.

24. Robin Wood, *Hollywood from Vietnam to Reagan* (New York: Columbia University Press, 1986), 165-172.

25. Ian Wojcik-Andrews, *Children's Films: History, Ideology, Pedagogy, Theory* (New York: Garland Publishing, 2000), 88.

26. Dan Jardine, review of *Charlotte's Web, Apollo Guide,* <http://apolloguide.com/mov_fullrev.asp?CID=3484> (19 September 2009).

27. Christopher Null, review of *Charlotte's Web, filmcritic.com,* 9 June 2001, <http://www.filmcritic.com/reviews/1973/charlottes-web> (19 September 2009).

28. Jardine.

29. Null.

30. Craig Butler, review of *Charlotte's Web, All-Movie Guide,* <http://www.allmovie.com/work/9012/review> (19 September 2009).

31. Lucy Rollin, "The Reproduction of Mothering in *Charlotte's Web*," *Children's Literature* 18 (1990): 45.

32. Rollin demonstrates how Wilbur's acquisition of Charlotte's egg sac places him in the position of mothering, suggesting that (like the death of Charlotte), all the actions within the novel are essentially focused on Wilbur.

33. Peter Neumeyer, *The Annotated Charlotte's Web* (New York: Harper Trophy, 1994): 171.

34. Henry Garfield, "E. B. White's Web," *Bangor Metro*, 10 May 2007, <http://www.bangormetro.com/media/Bangor-Metro/May-2007/E-B-Whites-Web> (27 March 2010).

35. Michael Medved, review of *Charlotte's Web, Michael Medved's Eye on Entertainment,* 15 December 2006, <http://www.michaelmedved.com/pg/jsp/eot/review.jsp?pid=3649> (27 March 2010).

36. Owen Gleiberman, review of *Charlotte's Web, Entertainment Weekly,* 15 December 2006, <http://www.ew.com/ew/article/0,,1569403,00.html> (27 March 2010).

37. Colm Andrew, "FilmReview: A Sugar-Coated Web," *Manx Independent,* 15 February 2007, <http://www.iomtoday.co.im/what-where-when/FILMREVIEW-A-SUGARCOATED-WEB.2052021.jp> (27 March 2010).

38. Teacher Created Resources, *Company Info,* <http://www.teachercreated.com/company> (27 March 2010) (emphasis mine)

39. Patsy Carey and Susan Kilpatrick, *Guide for Using Charlotte's Web in the Classroom* (Westminster, CA: Teacher Created Resources, 1993/2006), 47.

40. Ibid.

41. Ibid. (emphasis mine).

42. Ibid. (emphasis mine).

43. Ibid., 42.

Amy Ratelle (essay date 2014)

SOURCE: Ratelle, Amy. "Ethics and Edibility in *Charlotte's Web.*" *The Lion and the Unicorn,* vol. 38, no. 3, 2014, pp. 327-41.

[*In the following essay, Ratelle asserts that Wilbur should not be interpreted simply as a stand-in for a child character. Ratelle employs ecocritical philosophy, including the work of such ecocritics as Donna J. Haraway, to explore the ethics behind shifting the subjectivity of an animal companion, such as a pig, into an object meant to be eaten.*]

Dying in season evokes no terrors.

(115) John Griffith, *"Charlotte's Web: A Lonely Fantasy of Love"*

E. B. White's ***Charlotte's Web*** (1952) has long been considered by scholars and educators to be a classic of children's literature. Most analyses of the text retain the practice of seeing the animal body as a stand-in for human values, emotions, and experiences. Early scholarship on ***Charlotte's Web*** focuses on its structural elements, including White's proficiency with poetic language. Peter Neumeyer, for example, attends to the "mythopoetic dimension" (66) of the novel, clearly positioning it within the pastoral tradition. Perry Nodelman similarly examines the narrativity of the novel in the larger framework of folklore studies. Karen Coats, meanwhile, has recently approached the novel through a psychoanalytic lens, contending that "reading ***Charlotte's Web*** through Lacan's theory of subjectivity . . . enables us to come to an understanding of just how complicated the Other (as other people, as our own unconscious, as language itself) is in the formation of our identities" (105). Coats is correct in envisioning the Other as a means by which identity is formed, but her analysis remains focused on the creation of human identity, unproblematically using Wilbur as a stand-in for the human child. Ashraf Rushdy similarly prioritizes the human experience, positioning ***Charlotte's Web*** as "a representation of individual and communal desires" (36), by which he is referring to *human* desires. Rushdy further characterizes Wilbur as becoming, by the end of the novel, "integrated into the human community" (37), despite the fact that, while occasionally visited by "friends and admirers" (White 183), the pig remains in the barn with Charlotte's descendants for company. Although granted a reprieve from the fate of most livestock, Wilbur's integration into human society is only partially complete, as he does not develop close relationships with any other human characters after Fern, and never returns to a fully domestic space.

Examining the politics of animal subjectivity in ***Charlotte's Web*** as part of the larger context of White's other writings on animals, however, reveals a deeper ambivalence on the author's part regarding the West's culture of animal consumption. Through an animality studies reading of ***Charlotte's Web,*** I aim to push the boundaries of what "subjectivity" and "community" mean in both the novel and in the larger framework of Western culture. An analysis that accounts for Wilbur as an actual nonhuman animal instead of as a representative of the concept of the human child calls into question the naturalization of what Jacques Derrida refers to as the "noncriminal putting to death" of the animal for human consumption (112).

In my analysis of White's writing, I highlight the importance of animal subjectivity in a companion-species relationship. My examination of *Charlotte's Web* accounts for the wider implications of granting subjectivity to a singular animal and not to all animals. More specifically, I investigate the crucially important relationship of ethics to edibility. Expanding on Donna Haraway's conception of companion species, I explore White's rhetorically sympathetic fusion of children and animals, as well as the possibility of interspecies friendship. *Charlotte's Web* promotes a vision of subjectivity for the individual animal at odds with the West's "carnophallogocentric" (Derrida 113) paradigm of meat consumption.

A Brief History of Hogs

Sanders Spencer, founder of the British Pig Association, characterized the pig as "a machine for the conversion of farm produce into meat" (132), a straightforward and utilitarian view of the animal consistent with René Descartes's conception of the animal as an unfeeling beast-machine for the human to put to use as seen fit. As journalist William Hedgepeth posits, however, the development of human civilization advanced "hand-in-hoof ... in a symbiotic sort of equilibrium" (43) with the domestication of the wild pig. Naturalist Roger Caras believes that, historically, this symbiosis facilitated the shift toward stable agriculturally based societies across Europe and Asia (118). The human domestication of animals in general had, between eight and ten thousand years ago, already encompassed other livestock, as well as dogs, but the stubborn swine's refusal to be herded made it difficult to assimilate the species into a nomadic lifestyle. The animals' destructive foraging habits made confinement an attractive idea because this ensured no direct competition between swine and humans for the same resources. Possessed of a lively natural curiosity, the pig's inclination to roam was circumscribed by farmyard fences (Malcolmson and Mastoris 19).

Reliance on confinement had significant repercussions for the pig, changing its previous behaviors. As a wild beast, the pig would seek shade from the heat of the sun or root for food in the ground; after domestication it was restricted to wallowing in mud to keep cool, and became dependent on its keeper for its meals. Human perceptions of the pig changed accordingly, and the pig became aligned with filth and indolence. In this vein, Robert Malcolmson and Stephane Mastoris observe that, historically, the pig has "fared poorly" in comparison to the human treatment of other livestock such as cattle and horses (33). Where horses in particular became an "embodiment of untamed natural force" (Dingley 245) and a figure around which the early animal rights movement coalesced, the pig became representative of all that was "disagreeable or uncouth, or even revolting or beyond the pale" (Malcolmson and Mastoris 2). Author and lexicographer Samuel Johnson, for example, defined the swine in his 1755 dictionary as a creature "remarkable for stupidity and nastiness" (906). Prevailing opinions historically held pigs to be stupid, filthy creatures lacking in intelligence and sociability.

Despite the important role the domesticated swine played in establishing human civilization, this development did not lead to the same kind of affection and mutual respect that has characterized human relationships with, for example, dogs.[1] And yet, according to philosopher Jeffrey Mousaieff Masson, pigs have more in common with humans than canines:

> Like us, pigs dream and can see colors. Also like us, and like dogs and wolves, pigs are sociable. ... The females form stable families led by a matriarch with her children and female relatives. Piglets are particularly fond of play, just as human children are, and chase one another, play-fight, play-love, tumble down hills, and generally engage in a wide variety of enjoyable activities.
>
> (19-20)

Despite humans having more in common with porcines than canines, the absence of the kind of companion relationship experienced by dogs stems primarily from the pig's primary status as "a critically important, highly productive, low-cost maintenance meat animal" (Caras 111).[2] For Masson, the crucial difference between companion and edible animals stems from the way they are treated (18). Dogs sleep on our beds and are often fed from our tables as companions. Hogs are comestibles, confined to barns and farmyards.

In her recent study, *When Species Meet,* Donna Haraway foregrounds the intersections between food and friendship, but differentiates between "companion animal" and "companion species" (16). What Haraway envisions is a table at which humans and animals sit together in mutual subjectivity, not a table at which the animal body is eaten by the human as the meal. What Haraway calls "becoming with" is rooted in this mutual subjectivity, making it impossible to become with the meat animal because its transformation into dinner is predicated on the disavowal of animal subjectivity.

Vegan activist Carol Adams similarly argues that meat constitutes an "absent referent" (51); that is, animals in name and body are made absent *as animals* for meat to exist. Animals' lives precede and enable the existence of meat. If animals are alive, they cannot be meat. Thus a dead body replaces the live animal. Without animals, there would be no meat-eating, yet they are absent from the act of eating meat because they have been transformed into food.

(51)

In accord with Masson, Adams posits that the denial of the animal's subjectivity prior to its death is manifested in part by the conditions in which it is kept and how it is treated. More specifically, humans generally segregate meat animals by keeping them out of the domestic space and confining them to farmyards, a move that ensures they are treated not as integral members of the community but as a distinct entity with which there is no need to interact in any extensive or meaningful way.

As an animal advocate working to reform the meat industry, Temple Grandin regrets that the human diet includes meat. She prefers that "humans would have evolved to be plant eaters, so we wouldn't have to kill animals for food. But we didn't, and I don't see the human race converting to vegetarianism anytime soon" (179). Grandin's objective, like Jeremy Bentham's, is to minimize suffering.[3] Because the animal has no foreknowledge of its death, it cannot experience any tormented anticipation. All the human owes to the animal is a swift, painless death, ensuring that the animal does not suffer overmuch in the act of killing. In accord with Bentham, Grandin contends that the animal "should feel as little pain as possible, and he should die as quick as possible" (180). While Grandin aligns herself with animal subjectivity, she is unwilling to challenge the paradigms of mass meat consumption in the Western world.

Masson takes exception, however, to visions like Grandin's of a "kind death" for animals (41). He views the concept as remaining complicit in a systemic disavowal of subjectivity to all animals on the grounds that we are "supposed" to eat them. Masson observes that "it is in our own self-interest *not* to know them; it is easier to disconnect from whom we are eating if we know nothing at all about them" (283). There is thus a critical ethical conflict between acknowledging individual animals as unique subjects while not allowing for an overarching notion of subjectivity for all animals. This crisis is echoed by White throughout his writing career.

E. B. White, Self-professed Animal Murderer

Michael Sims contends that White situated **Charlotte's Web** in the animal world because "throughout his long life animals were White's favorite acquaintances" (3). Lynn Overholt Wake likewise characterizes White as a nature-writer, positing that his witty, urbane columns for *The New Yorker* and *Harper's Magazine* and his "animal fables" for children "should not be divided into two separate provinces; his accomplishment was more holistic than it was fragmented" (103). Both Sims and Wake propose a nuanced vision of White and his literary works, which encompass the city and the countryside, as well as the creatures—both human and nonhuman—found there. White often makes no clear distinctions between nature and culture, finding each in the other. In "Art of the Essay," for example, he contends that the city is

part of the country. When I had an apartment on the East Forty-eighth Street, my backyard during the migratory season yielded more birds than I ever saw in Maine. I could step out on my porch, spring or fall, and there was the hermit thrush, picking around in McEvoy's yard. Or the white-throated sparrow, the brown thrasher, the jay, the kinglet. John Kieran has recorded the immense variety of flora and fauna within the limits of Greater New York. But it is not just a question of birds and animals. The urban scene is a spectacle that fascinates me. People are animals, and the city is full of people in strange plumage, defending their territorial rights, digging for their supper.

(Plimpton and Crowther)

White's writing career is characterized by the unexpected entwining, or even subversion, of the accepted opposition of nature and culture, stemming from his childhood association with animals and the outdoors.

Born in Mount Vernon, New York, White experienced a childhood that was a mixture of time spent in the city as well as on holiday in the Maine countryside. He spent many hours developing a kinship with the horses and assorted stray dogs sheltered in the family's stable. White "found the dark and pungent stable intoxicatingly rich in romantic associations of life and death and adventure" (Sims 11). Similarly, as a young reader, White was a fan of wild animal adventure stories, such as those of Canadian author Ernest Thompson Seton. He appreciated the blending of scientific observation with fantastic tales of animal daring (43). Seton in particular emphasized kinship with animals, prefacing *Wild Animals I Have Known* (1898) by boldly stating, "we and the beasts are kin. Man has nothing that the animals have not at least a vestige of, the animals have nothing that man does not in some degree share." This sentiment resonated with White, who even as a child sought to develop the kind of companion-species relationship Haraway describes as situated in mutual subjectivity.

Never a robust child, White was often confined to bed with complications from his allergies. During one such confinement, he made friends with a particularly friendly and curious mouse. With little else to do during his enforced rest, he devoted his efforts to gaining the mouse's trust. White spent long hours observing the mouse going about its business (Agosta 6), observations he would later put to good use in *Stuart Little* (1945). White's earliest published piece is in fact a poem dedicated to that mouse, and it won him a prize from *The Woman's Home Companion* in 1909 (Elledge 30). White was only nine years old, but this preliminary publication helped set the tone of his adult career.

White's affinity for nature is carried over into his novels for children. The author delighted in keeping animals as pets and, when he bought his farm in 1933, he immediately stocked it with sheep, cattle, geese, and of course pigs (Griffith, *Salvation* 55). White re-creates his daily farm routines and the structures of rural life in *Charlotte's Web,* and this attention to detail and distinct tethering to the real world make it impossible to dismiss the novel as mere fantasy.[4] White's inspiration for *Charlotte's Web* stems from an incident in his second career as a gentleman farmer, and his ambivalence toward his own role as butcher. In his famous essay **"Death of a Pig"** (1948), he recounts how he fought to save the life of his pig, stricken ill with erysipelas. White notes with his characteristic gentle irony that he felt baffled by a situation in which he would feel so badly for the premature death of an animal he would have killed anyway. In the course of raising his pig, the author merged his own state of well-being with that of the animal, an identity conflation that Haraway explains as a form of "natureculture" (*Companion Species Manifesto* 8). Haraway positions "natureculture" as a site of intersection and overlap between the established binary of nature and culture. She posits that engaging with the nonhuman animal itself presents a new means by which to explore human/animal relations in a way that no longer privileges the human. White similarly observes that, from "the lustiness of a healthy pig a man derives a feeling of personal lustiness ... and when this suddenly comes to an end and food lies stale and untouched, souring in the sun, the pig's imbalance becomes the man's, vicariously, and life seems insecure, displaced, transitory" (**"Death of a Pig"**). Foregrounding his affinity with animals, White's alignment of human and animal health and well-being in this essay forms a counter argument against the enforced segregation of human and animal, and as such, becomes an implicit endorsement of animal rights.[5]

White directly addresses the hypocrisy inherent to raising an animal for its meat in the essay "Pigs and Spiders" (1953). The author writes that a farm is "a peculiar problem" for anybody who actually likes animals: "the fate of most livestock is that they are murdered by their benefactors. The creatures may live serenely but they end violently, and the odor of doom hangs about them always" (49). Noting his keen efforts in raising his pigs over the years, White confesses: "The relationship bothered me. Day by day I became better acquainted with my pig, and he with me, and the fact that the whole adventure pointed toward an eventual piece of double-dealing on my part lent an eerie quality to the thing" (49). White's thorough account of his conflation with the animal in **"Death of a Pig"** and his desire in "Pigs and Spiders" to redress the wrong he feels he is doing to a trusting fellow creature provides a direct impetus for creating Wilbur. Here he has given himself a pig that he gets to save by granting him a unique subjectivity, thus removing Wilbur from what Derrida calls the "carnophallogocentric" paradigm of Western meat consumption (113). Like Haraway, White foregrounds issues of edibility, seeking to invite the animal to the table as a guest, if not the dinner.

The Western Carnophallogocentric Paradigm in *Charlotte's Web*

Through an animality studies reading of *Charlotte's Web*, I wish to push the boundaries of the dominant Western conception of animal subjectivity. By following White's lead in accounting for Wilbur as an actual animal and not a metaphor for a human child, I am able to articulate White's own espousal of a model of animal subjectivity that contradicts the anthropocentric scholarly interpretations that have dominated White studies to date. Expanding on Haraway's vision of companion species, I aim to address the innovations and limitations of White's rhetorically sympathetic fusion of children and animals, as well as interspecies friendship. *Charlotte's Web* promotes a notion of animal subjectivity at odds with the carnophallogocentric paradigm of meat consumption.

Derrida describes the "ideal" subject as a human, male, meat-eating individual, actively "possessing" nature and accepting the sacrifice inherent to eating flesh (114). Rooted in the Judeo-Christian myth of God's granting dominion to man over animals, this authority becomes inherent to the act of consuming flesh by the adult male subject. According to Derrida, carnophallogocentric cultures construct their social structures and morality around this schema, the noncriminal putting to death of the animal in order to evade the ethical consequences of what White himself characterizes as "murder" in both **"Death of a Pig"** (14) and *Charlotte's Web* (49). According to John Desmond, Derrida deconstructs the

> prevailing assumption inherent in logocentrism, which presumed speech to be more pure than writing. He later appended the phallus, or signifier of male power, to logocentrism, in questioning the presumed superiority of the

male. In his final articulation of "carno" to phallogocentrism, he calls into question the bases of the assumption that humans have the legal right to kill animals.

(240)

For Derrida, then, the authority of the phallogocentric subject is granted to "the man (*homo* and *vir*) rather than to the woman, and to the woman rather than to the animal. And of course to the adult male rather than to the child. The virile strength of the adult male, the father, the husband, or brother... belongs to the schema that dominates the concept of the subject" (114). White's desire to "save" a pig is far more than a wish to help or rescue it, rooted instead in the wish to develop an undeniable subjectivity for the fictional Wilbur in a context that sees human dominion over animals as divinely granted.[6] White's framing of killing his pig at harvest time as "double dealing" and "betrayal" (49) reveals what Derrida calls the "*sacrificial* structure" of the Western paradigm of meat consumption and the discourses surrounding edibility (112). What both Derrida and White wish to problematize is the tradition of not extending the biblical prohibition "Thou shalt not kill" to animals as well as humans. Through an adaptation of Derrida's position, I wish to demonstrate White's own ambivalence toward the Western culture of meat-eating, which encourages the young to question the ethics of animal consumption, but only insofar as nonhuman animals ultimately remain a potential resource.

Charlotte's Web is the story of the young pig Wilbur and his friendship with Charlotte, a spider. Charlotte develops an ingenious plan to prevent Wilbur from being killed as part of the fall harvest, aiming to make the human community complicit in the recognition of Wilbur as an individual. As the spider knows, if the humans recognize the pig's subjectivity, he will not be killed at harvest time. As Charlotte calls attention to Wilbur's subjectivity, so too does the reader become implicated in Wilbur's removal from the carnophallogocentric framework.

The act of putting to death is central to White's novel. The text in fact opens with murderous intent. Young Fern Arable, hearing that her father John is about to kill the runt of a litter of pigs, is deeply distressed and intervenes. Karen Coats asserts that Fern does not necessarily care about this particular pig, but instead wishes to challenge her father's authority in general, grabbing his axe in order to threaten the symbolic male power structure (108). Such a reading, however, ignores the ostensibly natural sympathy children have toward animals. Fern's tactic, like White's, is to align herself rhetorically with the animal in order to force her father to acknowledge the artificial separation between animal and human. "The pig couldn't help being born small, could it?" she argues: "If *I* had been very small at birth, would you have killed *me*?" (3). John maintains the boundary between human and animal, replying that "this is different. A little girl is one thing, a runty pig another" (3). Fern reiterates that there is no appreciable difference and her father, who clearly does not relish the task anyway, gives in to Fern and brings the runt into the home. According to Ashraf Rushdy, what Fern offers her father is "a new way of determining the bonds and boundaries of community" (53), one that can encompass the meat animal. This exchange between father and daughter lays out White's objective for the novel, which continually undermines the established structures that alienates and disempowers the meat animal.

Though John is ostensibly merciful, White's immediate description of the kitchen smelling of, among other things, bacon, implies that the little pig has only been granted a temporary reprieve (3). The evocation of food terminology, however, further underscores the nature of our relationships with food animals. White's inclusion of bacon in an opening scene in which a live animal has been brought symbolically into the home deftly implies that there is a culturally marked difference between the living animal and its function as food. As Adams observes, moreover, the act of transforming a live pig into breakfast is not only enacted by the death and dismemberment of the animal, but by the renaming of the inert parts. Live animals are, she argues, "the absent referents in the concept of meat. ... When we eat animals, we change the way we talk about them, for instance, we no longer talk about baby animals, but veal or lamb" (51-53). In accord with Adams's insight, White's reference to the scent of bacon permeating the novel's opening scene establishes an ethical conundrum between meat and animal subjectivity that the remainder of the novel attempts to unravel.

Fern's treatment of Wilbur as a human baby does not effectively challenge her father's view of the pig's destiny. As Wilbur thrives in Fern's care and grows large enough to sustain himself, John becomes adamant that the pig must be sold, as it is costing too much in food and upkeep. His wife negotiates a compromise, suggesting that "Uncle Homer" Zuckerman might take Wilbur and allow Fern to visit him in the barn (12). Once sold and relegated to the barn, however, Wilbur no longer benefits from his status as a beloved pet. White compensates for this by moving the narrative from Fern's point of view to Wilbur's. Though Agosta positions the Zuckerman barn as idyllic and life-affirming (81, 85), in reality, the mundane loneliness of Wilbur's existence underscores the differences in the human treatment of companion-species animals and food animals. Masson notes that "pigs were rarely seen as companions," even on small, family-owned farms (32). In the novel, Fern can visit Wilbur under his new identity as livestock, but she is no longer allowed to relate to it as a friend or a human baby. This forced separation is the cultural means of ensuring her acceptance of Wilbur's status as a meat animal. In the original edition of the novel, Garth Williams's illustration of Fern watching Wilbur in the barn reinforces the segregation of the meat animal from not only the human, but also other livestock (White 14-15). Peering over a fence at her old friend, Fern is flanked by a sheep on her right and a goose on her left, suggesting a cross-species community. Indeed, as per Williams's design, the girl is separated from Wilbur not only by a wooden division, but also by the very gutter of the page. Williams would have been well aware that his illustration had to work around the intrusion of the gutter. What he does is effectively isolate the pig on one page, while allowing all the other living beings to stand as a community on the other, contributing to the subjectivist politics of White's own narrative.

Fern resists her indoctrination as a meat eater, frequently visiting the barn to observe the animals, gaining their trust and becoming privy to their conversations and subjectivity. One discussion that Fern does not overhear is Wilbur's introduction to Charlotte the spider. At the end of what Wilbur considers the worst day of his life thus far, a small voice from "out of the darkness" (31) offers the kind of friendship and comfort he previously experienced as Fern's pet. White undermines the false idealism of this happy interlude, however, by setting Wilbur up as already entangled in the web of ideological structures pertaining to the eating of animals. Wilbur is aghast that Charlotte kills and eats flies, but fails to realize, as the goose contemptuously thinks to herself, that "Mr. Zuckerman and Lurvy are plotting to kill him" around Christmastime, so that Wilbur's dead body will provide meat over the winter (40). As Emmanuel Levinas points out, eating is not necessarily reducible to "the chemistry of alimentation" (128); but rather, "the act of eating involves above all ... the way the I, the absolute commencement, is suspended on the non-I" (128-29). In other words, the consumption of flesh positions the eater as a subject, and the consumed as a "thing." Because Charlotte kills and eats her own flies, she is a consuming subject and, as such, has the ontological authority to stand in for White in order to save Wilbur, (unlike, for example, Templeton the rat, whom it is implied has a similarly murderous nature). Templeton's capacity for killing is revealed in an episode in which he bargains for a "dud" egg that did not survive to be hatched (45). While the goose allows him to take the egg, he is sternly warned away from the living goslings by the gander under threat of violence. Like White himself, Haraway similarly acknowledges the deep ambivalence toward edible animals, noting that because "eating and killing cannot be hygienically separated does *not* mean that just any way of eating and killing is fine, merely a matter of taste and culture" (295). More simply, some ways of killing and eating are more ethically palatable than others. Templeton, for example, is vermin—as a scavenger, he can find food in many places, but instead has been known to kill and eat the small goslings, a selfish and unnecessary act, not unlike the humans' act of killing and eating pigs. Charlotte, on the other hand, can be considered a killer, but catching and eating flies is positioned both as her sole source of sustenance and a public service, lest flies "multiply and become so numerous that they'd destroy the earth, wipe out everything" (40). In this framework, Charlotte stands out as altruistic in her killing of flies and other insects for food, and can claim the moral authority to intervene on Wilbur's behalf.

Charlotte's authority is reinforced in the episode in which the old sheep lets Wilbur know of his impending murder. The pig and the spider have been friends long enough for Wilbur no longer to be bothered by the deaths of unsuspecting flies; in fact, he finds Charlotte's insect pain management admirable (48). By normalizing the killing and eating of insects, and moreover, presenting that act as public service (40), White increases Wilbur's shock at finding out that he himself is to be killed and eaten. The old sheep tells Wilbur that his destiny is to be "smoked bacon and ham. ... Almost all the young pigs get murdered by the farmer as soon as the real cold weather sets in" (49). Fern, in the barn visiting, is attuned to Wilbur's anguish and becomes tense and upset because, as Griffith notes, "creatures who speak the same language as the author and his readers have souls; that is to say, their deaths are just as significant as the death of a human being" (45). For Fern, Wilbur's impending doom is especially upsetting, as she had naïvely assumed that, by rescuing Wilbur from her father's axe, he would be safe forever. Williams's illustration for this conversation between the pig and the sheep depicts Wilbur's distressed reaction, with the informant looking on in a disapproving fashion at the pig's display of emotion. Williams captures the sheep's sense of superiority and self-righteous distancing from the meat animal, while maintaining the visual distinction between Wilbur and the rest of the animal community by depicting the sheep on the opposite side of the fence (White 50).

In Charlotte's view (as in White's own), the secrecy around the animal's scheduled death is a form of unethical betrayal. Charlotte's challenge, then, is to make Wilbur's subjectivity manifest to the Zuckermans and the larger human community through the appropriation of human language. As Adams notes, the carnophallogocentric power structure is maintained by the double distancination of the living animal through language. Just as the dead animal becomes meat; the living animal is further denied subjectivity through objectifying pronouns such as "it." In Adams's formulation, "the generic 'it' erases the living, breathing nature of the animals and reifies their object status" (75).[7] Both living and dead animals in this worldview are continually denied subjectivity in order to enact the noncriminal aspect of the death of the animal for human consumption. Similarly arguing for the transformative power of language, Agosta posits that words "operate as true miracles in our world. They call things into being that did not exist before. They transform and create. Language is the creator of reality and is responsible for the formation of a self" (99). Just as words can deny subjectivity to the meat animal, Wilbur's subjectivity can be made legible to the novel's human characters by Charlotte through the power of language. Griffith argues, however, that, if Charlotte's efforts on his behalf revealed

> that Wilbur is a person (which would presumably lead to the greater revelation that all animals are people), and therefore that to kill him would be murder, presumably her web-words would be very different: something like "Wilbur has a soul!" or "Meat is murder!" But she proposes to leave people in their misconception that animals are mere things, and to save Wilbur by convincing them that he is a wonderful thing, a thing worth saving.
>
> (*Salvation* 48)

What Griffith overlooks is that White himself has already characterized the act of killing an animal as murder, in both the text itself and the essays surrounding its conception. Becoming a writer in her own right, Charlotte functions as a voice for White himself, using language to highlight the plight of a single animal by startling the humans out of their complacent thoughts about animals.

Despite the subtlety of his exploration into carnophallogocentrism, White ultimately gets trapped in the web of discourse politics. Toward the end of the novel, the author reinforces entrenched human attitudes toward animals when he contrasts a "radiant" (114) Wilbur with the common vulgarity of "Uncle," the pig against whom Wilbur is to compete for the blue ribbon at the fair. Though of the same age and anthropomorphized in the same fashion as Wilbur, Uncle is depicted as much larger and more grotesque, even more adult. Uncle is covered in coarse, shaggy hair and the downward slope of his eyes makes him appear dull and stupid (White 135). Although his name implies that Uncle is the member of a human family or community, it distances him as well since, unlike "Wilbur," it is not an actual name, but instead a descriptive signifier, signaling a degree of separation from the nuclear family. At the same time, the name adds a further element of adultness that counters any potential sympathy that the young reader—meant to identify with the perpetually childlike Wilbur—might develop for the second pig. Charlotte's conversation with Uncle similarly renders him an unsympathetic character. According to the spider, he is "too familiar, too noisy, and he cracks weak jokes. Also, he's not anywhere near as clean as you are, nor as pleasant. I took quite a dislike to him in our brief interview" (135). By contrast, Wilbur is an exceptional individual, worthy of Charlotte's (and the reader's) efforts on his behalf. White thus undermines his arguments for an inclusive notion of animal subjectivity by presenting a second individual pig that reinforces negative porcine stereotypes of filth, stupidity and indolence. In short, White sacrifices all the others of the porcine species in order to foreground the subjectivity and ensure the safety of his deserving hero.

* * *

In *Charlotte's Web*, White can be seen as ultimately reinforcing the carnophallogocentrism of which he was so critical both in this novel and his other writings. He rhetorically encourages his readers to animal husbandry and stewardship, but only insofar as the nonhuman animal remains a potential resource. Despite his acknowledgment that meat entails murder, the author is not actually out to unravel the false logic of the dominant paradigm so much as to express regret that Western rhetoric around the death of the food animal works so hard to disguise itself. Charlotte's web, in this sense, is the web in which White finds himself entangled—that of a discourse already engrained in his humanist sense of self and thus already structured to counteract any individual's attempt to speak outside of its essentialist façade of human privilege.

Notes

1. Peter Singer similarly contends that of all the meat animals, the pig is undoubtedly the most intelligent, making them a logical choice for George Orwell to cast as the leaders of the animal revolution in *Animal Farm* (*Animal Liberation* 119).

2. Caras notes further that its meat value supercedes all of the pig's other skills and attributes, including cart pulling and truffle hunting. Contrasted to other livestock like sheep, goats, cattle, and horses, the pig alone is solely valued for its edibility (111).

3. Bentham, however, advocated the eating of animals, stating that humans should eat animals, because "we are the better for it, and they are never the worse" (311).

4. John Griffith rightly points out that the most fantastical elements in *Charlotte's Web* stem from White's socioeconomic bracket, which insulated him from the realities of subsistence farming or fighting to retain land and make money in an increasingly corporatized industry.

5. In *Animal Farm*, Orwell similarly conflates human and animal at the end of his novel, albeit to call attention to the corrupting nature of political power and the plight of the working poor. According to Orwell, "men exploit animals in much the same way as the rich exploit the proletariat" ("Author's Preface" 405).

6. Matthew Scully addresses this topic further in *Dominion*, in which he challenges the Judeo-Christian mythos that human rule over animals is not only granted by God, but includes the right of humans to inflict untold suffering upon them.

7. Microsoft Word insists that it is incorrect to use "who" instead when referring to animals. Both grammar and technology are thus programmed to discourage the conflation of human and animal subjectivity.

Works Cited

Adams, Carol J. *The Sexual Politics of Meat: A Feminist-Vegetarian Critical Theory*. 1990. New York: Continuum, 2000.

Agosta, Lucien L. *E. B. White: The Children's Books*. New York: Twayne P, 1995.

Bentham, Jeremy. *An Introduction to the Principles of Morals and Legislation*. 1780. Oxford: Clarendon, 1879.

Caras, Roger. *A Perfect Harmony: The Intertwining Lives of Animals and Humans Throughout History*. West Lafayette, IN: NotaBell Books, 1996.

Coats, Karen. "Lacan with Runt Pigs." *Children's Literature* 27 (1999): 105-28.

Coppin, Dawn. "Hog Futures: The Birth of Mega-Hog Farms." *Sociological Quarterly* 44.4 (Autumn 2003): 597-616.

Derrida, Jacques. "'Eating Well,' or the Calculation of the Subject: An Interview with Jacques Derrida." Trans. Peter Connor and Avital Ronell. Eds. Eduardo Cadava, Peter Connor, and Jean-Luc Nancy. *Who Comes After the Subject?* New York: Routledge, 1991.

Desmond, John. "A Summons to the Consuming Animal." *Business Ethics: A European Review*. 19.3 (July 2010): 238-52.

Dingley, Robert. "A Horse of a Different Color: 'Black Beauty' and the Pressures of Indebtedness." *Victorian Literature and Culture*. 25.2 (1997): 241-51.

Elledge, Scott. *E. B. White: A Biography*. New York: W. W. Norton, 1984.

Grandin, Temple. *Animals in Translation: Using the Mysteries of Autism to Decode Animal Behaviour*. New York: Scribner, 2005.

Griffith, John. "*Charlotte's Web*: A Lonely Fantasy of Love." *Children's Literature* 8 (1980): 111-17.

———. *Charlotte's Web: A Pig's Salvation*. New York: Twayne P, 1993.

Haraway, Donna. *The Companion Species Manifesto: Dogs, People, and Significant Otherness*. Chicago: Prickly Paradigm P, 2003.

———. *When Species Meet*. Minneapolis: U of Minnesota P, 2008.

Hedgepeth, William. *The Hog Book*. Athens, GA: U of Georgia P, 1998.

Johnson, Samuel. *English Dictionary*. 1755. Boston: Nathan Hale, 1835.

Levinas, Emmanuel. *Totality and Infinity An Essay on Exteriority*. Trans. Alphonso Lingis. Pittsburgh: Duquesne UP, 1969.

Malcolmson, Robert and Stephanos Mastoris. *The English Pig: A History*. London: The Hambledon P, 1998.

Masson, Jeffrey Moussaieff. *The Pig Who Sang to the Moon: The Emotional Lives of Farm Animals*. New York: Ballantine Books, 2003.

Neumeyer, Peter. "What Makes a Good Children's Book? The Texture of *Charlotte's Web*." *South Atlantic Bulletin* 44.2 (May 1979): 66-75.

Nodelman, Perry. "Text as Teacher: The Beginning of *Charlotte's Web*." *Children's Literature* (1985): 109-27.

Orwell, George. *Animal Farm*. 1945. Toronto: Penguin Books, 1989.

———. "Author's Preface to the Ukranian Edition of *Animal Farm*." *Collected Essays, Journalism and Letters of George Orwell, Volume 3*. Eds. Sonia Orwell and Ian Angus. New York: Harcourt, Brace and World, 1968.

Plimpton, George A., and Frank H. Crowther. Interview with E. B. White. "The Art of the Essay, I: E. B. White." *Paris Review* 48 (Fall 1969): 65-88. 1 June 2011 <http://

www.theparisreview.org/interviews/4155/the-art-of-the-essay-no-1-e-b-white>.

Rushdy, Ashraf H. A. " 'The Miracle of the Web': Community, Desire and Narrativity in *Charlotte's Web*." *The Lion and the Unicorn* 15 (1991): 35-60.

Scully, Matthew. *Dominion: The Power of Man, the Suffering of Animals, and the Call to Mercy*. New York: St. Martin's P, 2002.

Seton, Ernest Thompson. *Wild Animals I Have Known*. Project Gutenberg, October 2009. Web. 4 Dec. 2010. <http://www.gutenberg.org/files/3031/3031-h/3031-h.htm>.

Sims, Michael. *The Story of* Charlotte's Web: *E. B. White's Eccentric Life and the Birth of an American Classic*. New York: Walker, 2011.

Singer, Peter. *Animal Liberation*. 1975. New York: HarperCollins, 2009.

Spencer, Sanders. *The Pig: Breeding, Rearing and Marketing*. 1919. Cookhill, UK: Read Country Books, 2008.

Wake, Lynn Overholt. "E. B. White's Paean to Life: The Environmental Imagination of *Charlotte's Web*." Eds. Sidney I. Dobrin and Kenneth B. Kidd. *Wild Things: Children's Culture and Ecocritisism*. Detroit: Wayne State UP, 2004.

White, E. B. *Charlotte's Web*. 1952. New York: HarperCollins, 1980.

———. "Death of a Pig." *Atlantic Monthly* 181.1 (Jan. 1948): 28-33. <http://www.theatlantic.com/ideastour/animals/white-full.html>. Accessed 1 June 2011.

———. "Pigs and Spiders." *McClurg's Book News* (Jan. 1953): 49.

Juliet McMaster (essay date 2019)

SOURCE: McMaster, Juliet. "White's Wilbur and Whiteley's Peter Paul Rubens." *Journal of Juvenilia Studies*, vol. 2, no. 1, 2019, pp. 46-54.

[*In the following essay, McMaster discusses one possible literary influence on* Charlotte's Web *(1952): the childhood diary of Opal Whiteley, which was published serially in the* Atlantic Monthly *in 1920. Most notably, Opal's favorite pig—Peter Paul Rubens—shares many characteristics with Wilbur, including following the girl to school, making "such a sweet picture" as he stood in the classroom doorway, and eventually succumbing to the death that Wilbur fears when he learns that he is slated to become food for the Avery family.*]

Michael Sims's book called *The Story of Charlotte's Web* makes no mention of Opal Whiteley or her famous diary, published in 1920. Nevertheless, I want to convince you that Opal Whiteley's diary is a notable part of the story of **Charlotte's Web**. If I succeed, then Opal Whiteley's diary becomes a striking instance of juvenile writing as a shaping influence on a major work of American literature.

E. B. White, as we all know, cared a great deal about pigs. And before he ever came to write **Charlotte's Web,** the story of the rescue of a pig from going the way of all porcine flesh, he had come to feel poignantly about the predestined fate of spring pigs. As he wrote in his essay **"Death of a Pig,"**

> The science of buying a spring pig in in blossomtime, feeding it through summer and fall, and butchering it when the cold weather arrives, is a familiar scheme to me and follows an antique pattern. It is a tragedy enacted on most farms with perfect fidelity to the original script. The murder, being premeditated, is in the first degree but quick and skillful, and the smoked bacon and ham provide a ceremonial ending whose fitness is seldom questioned.
>
> (*Essays* 17)

Questioned seldom, but not never. And White's essay, by describing the premature death of a pig from natural causes, shows how its author came to question that familiar script, and to imagine a new script in which the tragic trajectory is bent and redirected by the intervention of a talented and devoted friend: Charlotte, the author-spider.

"Death of a Pig" shows White's familiar artistry—his appealing simple directness that still combines with wry irony. The writer, a no-nonsense unsentimental farmer, can accept and justify the "murder," and make it happen, for his own gain. But when nature intervenes and strikes the pig with a different threat, he is thrust into the new role of nurse. As he works for the pig's life, it becomes a fellow creature rather than bacon-in-the-making. And when the pig dies he grieves genuinely. "The loss we felt was not the loss of ham but the loss of pig" (**"Death"** 18).

Such an experience, it is easy to see, was a catalyst for the creation of **Charlotte's Web** some four years later. White wrote about the autobiographical origins of the story. "The idea of the writing of **Charlotte's Web** came to me one day when I was on my way down through the orchard carrying a pail of slops to my pig. I had made up my mind to write a children's book about animals, and I needed a way to save a pig's life, and I had been watching a large spider in the backhouse, and what with one thing and another, the idea came to me" (*Letters* 375). Asked by a man named Wilbur why he had called the pig in the story Wilbur, he responded, "The Wilbur of the book was named not after you but after a pig I used to have named Wilbur. It's that simple" (*Letters* 375). One can guess that the historical Wilbur was the pig who had died of natural causes, the one who convinced him he "needed a way to save a pig's life."[1]

That connection is well known. But I suggest that another intertext for *Charlotte's Web,* and a work that prepared White to receive the message delivered by his sick pig, was a diary by a seven-year-old girl who loved and lost a pig called Peter Paul Rubens.

Born in 1897, some two years ahead of White, Opal Whiteley was a child of the logging camps of Oregon, abused by her mother, and she wrote her diary secretly, with coloured crayons, in a childish script of all capitals, on any scraps of paper she could lay her hands on. At some point the diary was discovered and partially destroyed by her younger sister. As a teenager this gifted child distinguished herself by her nature talks and work with children. In her early twenties, she approached Ellery Sedgwick, editor of the *Atlantic Monthly.* Sedgwick became interested in the young author and her life, and he asked her if she had ever kept a diary (Sedgwick 255). The diary was sent for, and the multitudinous scraps of script were painstakingly reconstructed, in a process that he witnessed and oversaw.

The Story of Opal: The Journal of an Understanding Heart was published serially in the *Atlantic Monthly* in 1920, to enormous acclaim. At the time E. B. White was a student and an aspiring journalist at Cornell, working on the Cornell paper the *Daily Sun,* and it is a sure bet that he was reading the *Atlantic,* like other literary people of the day. The chronicle of a young girl's response to nature and her relation with animals brought a greatly increased circulation to the *Atlantic,* and celebrity for the young author. Famous overnight, she and her family were hounded by the media. But then came a backlash, as has happened to other young authors such as Daisy Ashford with the *Young Visiters.*[2] The work is too sophisticated, too knowledgeable, too *good,* so the argument goes, to be the work of a child.

It did not help that Opal had purveyed what we suppose is fantasy as fact: She claimed that she was merely adopted by the Whiteleys, and that her real parents were "Angel Father" and "Angel Mother," who were of the French royal family. Detected in one falsehood, she lost all credibility. Much the same thing happened to Thomas Chatterton, when it was discovered he had invented the mediaeval monk Thomas Rowley. Chatterton took poison and died at seventeen.[3] Opal survived into her nineties, but her last four decades were spent in a mental hospital. The documentary evidence for the time of writing, however, remained incontrovertible; and Ellery Sedgwick, a man of culture and integrity who had seen the whole process leading to publication, continued to believe in Opal and the genuineness of her remarkable production.[4]

Little Opal Whiteley, as we learn from her diary, was a fanatic observer of anniversaries. She seems to have had access to an almanac that provided copious information on the "borning days" and "going-away days" of notable historical figures, from Charlemagne to Tennyson. (In our Juvenilia Press edition of a selection from Opal's diary we were able to date the many events of the narrative.) Her animals, therefore, gathered distinguished names. She calls the calf "with poetry in her tracks" Elizabeth Barrett Browning; the draught horse is William Shakespeare; her pet rat is Thomas Chatterton Jupiter Zeus; and her pig is Peter Paul Rubens, because she first saw him on Rubens's birthday, 29 June. It is he who is the tragic hero of the present essay.

Opal introduces Peter Paul Rubens as "a very plump young pig with a little red-ribbon squeal, and a wanting to go everywhere I did go" (Whiteley 108). The first incident of the diary that involves him is the day he follows Opal to school, and she does not have the heart to take him back to the pig-pen.

> So we just went along to school together.
>
> When we got there, school was already took up. I went in first. The new teacher came back to tell me I was tardy again. She did look out the door. She saw my dear Peter Paul Rubens. She did ask me where that pig came from. I just started in to tell her all about him, from the day I first met him.
>
> She did look long looks at me. She did look those looks for a long time . . . I did ask her what she was looking those long looks at me for. She said, "I'm screwtineyesing you." I never did hear that word before—it is a new word. It does have an interest sound. I think I will have uses for it. Now when I am looking long looks at a thing, I will print I did *screwtineyes* it.
>
> (Whiteley 109)[5]

It is easy to see parallels with *Charlotte's Web* here. Wilbur follows Fern around the place (*CW* 10), and Fern like Opal is inattentive at school because she is thinking about her pig (*CW* 7). More specific to White's concerns is Opal's sensitivity to words, her tendency to pounce on a new one like "scrutinize" and store it away for future use. Words are treasures for Opal, as they are for White and for Charlotte.

To return to Peter Paul Rubens in the classroom: "It wasn't long until he walked right in. I felt such an amount of satisfaction, having him at school. Teacher felt not so" (109). In fact, teacher is so far from feeling so that she goes after Peter Paul Rubens with a stick; and when Opal defends him she sends them both home. Opal ponders the wide difference between her own response to the pig and teacher's:

> Now I have wonders about things. I wonder why was it teacher didn't want Peter Paul Rubens coming to school. Why, he did make such a sweet picture as he did stand in the doorway, looking looks about. And the grunts he gave, they were such nice ones. He stood there saying, "*I have come to your school—what class are you going to put me in?*" He said in plain grunts the very same words I did say the first day *I* came to school. . . . But I guess our teacher didn't have understanding of pig talk.
>
> (109-110)

Peter Paul Rubens's "plain grunts" are as articulate to Opal as Wilbur's and Charlotte's talk is to Fern, and her teacher's failure to understand "pig talk" is cognate with the adult's usual lack understanding.

It seems that Opal's wisdom filtered through White to Dr. Dorian of *Charlotte's Web.* When asked if he believes animals talk he responds,

> "It is quite possible that an animal has spoken civilly to me and that I didn't catch the remark because I wasn't paying attention. Children pay better attention than grownups. If Fern says the animals in Zukerman's barn talk I'm quite ready to believe her."
>
> (*CW* 110)

Opal certainly pays attention. It is not often that she actually attributes dialogue to animals. But she communicates in one way or another not only with Peter Paul Rubens but also with the shepherd dog and the draught horse and the calf and the crow and the wood-rat and the field-mouse; with sheep and chickens, with wasps and moths, with trees and flowers, and even with lowly potatoes in their "brown dresses" (120). Opal has in abundance what Keats called negative capability: she can suspend her own identity and inhabit that of some other creature. For instance, after a trip in the woods, she discovers a chrysalis in her hair: "I put it to my ear, and I did listen. It had a little voice. It was not a tone voice; it was a heart voice. While I did listen, I did feel its feels. It had lovely ones" (143). That is a child who knows how to pay attention.

In both narratives the composition process is to the fore. Charlotte replaces the old "script" for a pig's existence with a new and saving script, consisting of words laboriously inscribed in a spider's web. Opal's editor Ellery Sedgwick paid attention to the diary's status as a document. He wrote of the "myriad fragments" of the manuscript, the weeks spent "piecing it together, sheet by sheet; each page a kind of picture-puzzle, lettered on both sides in colored chalks, the characters, printed with a child's unskilfulness of hand, nearly an inch high" (Sedgwick, *Atlantic,* March 290). The volume version included two pages of striking facsimile. Opal herself also brings the "printing" of her record into her account. She prints in the woods, in school, and under the bed where "the mamma" orders her to go in disgrace until she can find time to spank her. Opal's coloured pencils, so essential for figuring out the order of the scraps of paper, are contributed by "the man that wears grey neckties and is kind to mice," as she always calls him. And she is explicit about her ambition to be a writer. "When I grow up," she says, "I am going to write for children—and for grownups that haven't grown up too much" (121).

In the same way White's Charlotte is remarkable for being "both a true friend and a good writer," as the last words of *Charlotte's Web* emphasise (184). And her most vigorous action consists of her acrobatic feats in creating the letters in her web, "all capitals and no punctuation—much like the inscriptions dug up by archaeologists," as Sedgwick said of Opal's script (*Atlantic* 249).

"Now, let's see, the first letter is T," Charlotte soliloquises as she prepares to write "TERRIFIC" in her web. And for a full page we follow her progress in constructing one letter after another, each one larger than herself (*CW* 93a-4). Janice Alberghene, in discussing Charlotte's writing in the same passage, points out that "the physical practice of writing, routine that it is for adults, is enormously complicated for children. For them, forming letters is analogous to Charlotte's writing" (84). She might have been writing about Opal Whiteley.

Many readers have wondered why Charlotte, who has an excellent vocabulary, should need words for her web supplied by the rat. But Templeton's ferreting around in the dump to find her words on scraps of paper draws attention to the materiality of the composition process, the need for light, paper, pencils, or spinnerets that has to be part of the writer's multiple concerns, as it is both Opal's and Charlotte's.[6]

Opal the child writer, I believe, passes on part of herself both to Fern the child and Charlotte the writer. She has Fern's innocence and lack of power to control the world around her, as well as Charlotte's wisdom and delight in language.

Fern is peripheral to the plot of *Charlotte's Web,* as many readers have noticed; and White's biographer, Scott Elledge, has shown that the opening that includes her came relatively late in White's composition process (Elledge 295). After her one brave stand against injustice when she saves the runt pig from slaughter, Fern settles for being merely a witness of Wilbur's drama. Since the main work of saving Wilbur from the predestined fate of spring pigs is taken on by Charlotte, one might wonder why White needed Fern at all. White himself explained that the book was virtually finished without her, when he "decided something was wrong, or lacking" (*Letters* 649). White's step-son Roger Angell similarly recorded that the first version of ***Charlotte's Web*** was virtually complete when White set it aside for several months, before rewriting it and enlarging the role of Fern. Late in the day, it seems, White discovered that he needed a way to save a pig's life not just for himself, but for a little girl—eight-year-old Fern, named after a beautiful plant, stands in for seven-year-old Opal, named after a beautiful stone.

"This is the most terrible case of injustice I ever heard of," Fern famously cries as her father takes the axe to slaughter the runt of the litter. "A queer look came over John Arable's face," White wrote memorably. "He seemed almost ready to cry himself" (*CW* 3). It is that moment of awakening consciousness, a sudden awareness that pigs *matter,* that White himself had felt: a moment triggered by a child.

Fern and Opal both baby their pigs. Fern feeds Wilbur with a human baby's bottle and puts a bib on him. Opal likewise adorns her pet pigs with red ribbons and christening robes. Both initially show an ominous lack of anxiety about the destiny of the pig: the Arables are having bacon for breakfast on the morning that Fern protests against the injustice of killing the runt pig; in the diary Opal takes on the massive job of carving the ham intended for "the breakfasts and dinners and suppers of the papa and the mamma" (Whiteley 131)—apparently unaware that the ham is the *corpus dilecti* of Peter Paul Rubens's predecessor. White the adult *is* aware that "smoked bacon and ham provide a ceremonial ending to the pig's tragedy," but the little girls who care about pigs are unconscious of the grim irony that connects their breakfasts with the animals they treat as human.

Opal learns the hard way. And readers of the diary, who have followed her activities with Peter Paul Rubens and learned to understand how important he is to this child who is constantly rated and beaten by her mother, likewise receive a jolt we are is not likely to forget. I must quote the passage at some length.

> I am feeling all queer inside. Yesterday was butchering day. Among the hogs they butchered was Peter Paul Rubens.
>
> The mamma let me go off to the woods all day, after my morning's work was done. Brave Horatius and Lars Porsena of Clusium [the shepherd dog and the crow] went with me. . . .
>
> We had not gone far, when we heard an awful squeal—so different from the way pigs squeal when they want their supper. I felt cold all over. Then I did have knowings why the mamma had let me start away to the woods without scolding. And I ran a quick run to save my dear Peter Paul Rubens—but already he was dying. And he died with his head in my lap. I sat there feeling dead, too, until my knees were all wet with blood from the throat of my dear Peter Paul Rubens.
>
> (Whiteley 155-56)

The shock and the violence are almost unbearable. And the pain is made worse by the fact that Opal had actually been delighted at the unwonted indulgence of being allowed for once to set out on one of her expeditions without being scolded. One is appalled by the bad faith of a mother who tricks her child into believing she has a treat, in order to get her out of the way, and then fails to comfort or protect her from being drenched in her beloved animal's blood. The dose of reality in a hard world is too much. Like White, after reading this passage we are *all* likely to want to find a way to save a pig's life for a little girl.

There are other notable parallels between the works. Fern's brother Avery, with his casual brutality and stock of weapons, is a milder form of the "chore boy" of the diary, who mocks Opal for her concern for the animals, and deliberately shoots her pet crow in front of her (152, 295). When Avery threatens to "knock that ol' spider into this box," Charlotte is saved by the fortunate accident of the breaking of an egg, which fills the air with "terrible gasses and smells" before which both Avery and Fern retreat (72). There is a rotten egg incident in the diary too, when an egg Opal is carrying breaks dramatically, and delivers a "a queer odor that one does have longings to run away from" (316). And I have sometimes wondered whether Templeton's rather aristocratic name may be a distant echo of the grand name Opal gives her wood-rat, Thomas Chatterton Jupiter Zeus.

When Wilbur gets a buttermilk bath before the fair, he comes out "the cleanest, prettiest pig you ever saw" (*CW* 121). Likewise when Opal bathes her piglet, he comes out "the pinkest white pig you ever saw" (Whiteley 216). Charlotte and Wilbur devote great care to Charlotte's *magnum opus,* the egg sac. Opal too is careful and attentive when she finds spider egg-sacs:

> Under that old grey board were five little silk bags. They were white, and they did feel lumps. I know baby spiders will come out of them when comes spring days, because last year I found bags like these, and this year in the spring,

> baby spiders walked out. They were very figdgety youngsters.
>
> (141)

Wilbur too learns about fidgety spider youngsters.

Such incidents, it might be argued, are common occurrences in the rural setting that both authors present. But it is not every narrative of country life that includes a rotten-egg incident and a spider's egg-sac incident, as well as an adopted piglet episode.

The closest affinity between White's fiction and Opal's diary is also the hardest to demonstrate, because it pertains not to words and incidents but to a whole world view. One might claim for both of them the status of nature poets. They are the prose Wordsworths of rural America, recording their epiphanies in the face of a natural world of great beauty and moral force.

The narratives of character and incident include lyric passages that celebrate the earth and the seasons. Characteristically, Whiteley and White do not talk *to* Nature or its manifestations: no apostrophes to skylarks or wild west winds or nightingales; rather they *listen* as nature talks to *them*. Hear each of them on that most evocative of seasons, the fall. This is Opal:

> Now are come the days of brown leaves. They fall from the trees; they flutter to the ground. When the brown leaves flutter, they are saying little things. They talk with the wind. I hear them tell of their borning days, when they did come into the world as leaves. ... They talked on and on, and I did listen to what they were telling the wind and the earth in their whisperings.
>
> (138)

And now White:

> The crickets sang in the grasses. They sang the song of summer's ending, a sad, monotonous song. "Summer is over and gone," they sang. "Over and gone, over and gone. Summer is dying, dying."
>
> The crickets felt it was their duty to warn everybody that summertime cannot last forever. Even on the most beautiful days in the whole year,—the days when summer is changing into fall—the crickets spread the rumor of sadness and change.
>
> (*CW* 113)

Such lyric interludes in prose narratives provide a particular rhythm and harmony for both works. Both authors present a knowledge all too intimate with death and pain and loss. Both can incorporate the sadness into a world vision that celebrates life and love, friendship and natural beauty. "Now I think I shall go out the bedroom window and talk to the stars," writes Opal. "They always smile so friendly. This is a very wonderful world to live in" (107). "All I hope to say in books," says White, "all that I ever hope to say, is that I love the world" (DiCamillo [v]).

Convinced as I am that E. B. White read and responded to Opal Whiteley's diary, and that his mission to write a story about saving a pig's life arises from his compassion for Peter Paul Rubens as well as from his experience with his own sick pig, I find it sad that he seems never to have acknowledged any admiration for *The Story of Opal*. It is one more note of sadness in the painful story of an exceptionally gifted child who snatched a temporary fame out of an abused childhood, then suffered another kind of abuse in being accused of falsehood, and sank into insanity and obscurity. After the cooked-up "exposure" of the diary, it was hardly respectable to refer to her. The personal portrait of White that Angell provided suggests that White was diffident about his writing, and perhaps shy of acknowledging a source that had lost credibility ("Andy").

But I do find what I consider to be an *implicit* acknowledgement, if not an explicit one. For all his success with the *New Yorker,* White had early been rejected by the high temple of Boston culture, the *Atlantic*. When his reputation had grown sufficiently, however, the *Atlantic* came courting him, and invited him to contribute an essay to the issue celebrating its ninetieth anniversary. It was in the journal that brought Peter Paul Rubens to the public that White chose to publish his own story on **"The Death of a Pig,"** which led to the story of the saving of another pig.

Notes

1. For the obvious connection between "Death of a Pig" and *Charlotte's Web,* see, for instance, Beverley Gherman's biography of White for children, *E. B. White: Some Writer!*

2. Daisy Ashford's *The Young Visiters,* written at nine and published in 1919 as edited by James Barrie, sold 230,000 copies in the first two years. But suspicions arose that Barrie of *Peter Pan* fame must have had a hand in its composition. Having worked on the manuscript, now in the Berg Collection in New York, I have no doubt of its being the true unassisted work of a nine-year-old. The only interventions in the manuscript are the addition of more spelling errors. Although the editor did not invent new errors, he made existing ones, such as "idear" for "idea," consistent. See Jeffrey Mather's introduction to the Juvenilia Press edition of *The Young Visiters*.

3. So goes the usual argument, inherited from the Romantics and further purveyed by Henry Wallis's

famous 1856 painting of the death of Chatterton, "Cut is the branch that might have grown full straight." Nick Grooms has suggested, however, that Chatterton's death from arsenic might have been an accidental overdose of a purported cure for venereal disease ("Literary Sleuthing").

4. "Of the rightness and honesty of the manuscript as the *Atlantic* printed it, I am utterly convinced; more certain am I than of the authorship of many another famous diary, for I have watched the original copy reborn and subjected to the closest scrutiny" (Sedgwick 263).

5. I quote from Benjamin Hoff's edition, *The Singing Creek where the Willows Grow*, since it is readily available. His edition is based on the volume, *The Story of Opal: The Journal of an Understanding Heart* (1920), which includes passages that were omitted from the serial run in the *Atlantic*. Hoff preserves the sequence of words, but provides his own chapter divisions, paragraphs, and punctuation.

6. Another contributory text for *Charlotte's Web*, I believe, is Don Marquis's *vers libre* serial for the *Sun*, *archy and mehitabel*. Archy the poet cockroach, who writes his copy by diving headfirst onto the keys of a typewriter, and therefore all in lower case, is surely a forerunner of Charlotte the author spider. And White wrote the introduction to the 1950 Doubleday edition of *archy and mehitabel*, not long before swinging into the composition of *Charlotte's Web* (published in 1952). White found the process of writing laborious, and he sympathised with Archy and his author Don Marquis. "Archy's physical limitations (his inability to operate the shift key) relieved Marquis of the troublesome business of capital letters, apostrophes, and quotation marks, those small irritations that slow up all men who are hoping their spirit will soar in time to catch the edition." Indeed Archy becomes for White "blood brother to writing men": "he cast himself with all his force upon a key, head downward. So do we all" (*Essays* 251). White, Archy, Charlotte and Opal share the heavy duty of creating with words, and manipulating difficult implements to form articulate inscriptions on paper hard to find or in webs fragile and transitory, and subject to the depredations of cats, flies, and little sisters.

Works Cited

Alberghene, Janice M. "Writing in *Charlotte's Web*. *Critical Essays on E. B. White*, edited by Robert L. Root, Jr., G. K. Hall, 1994, pp. 78-87.

Ashford, Daisy. *The Young Visiters or Mr Salteena's Plan*. Edited by Juliet McMaster and others. Juvenilia Press, 1997. Limited edition.

DiCamillo, Kate. Foreword. *Charlotte's Web*, by E. B. White, HarperCollins, 2012, pp. [v-vii].

Elledge, Scott. *E. B. White: A Biography*. W. W. Norton, 1984.

Gherman, Beverly. *E. B. White: Some Writer!* New York: Beech Tree Paperback, 1994.

Mather, Jeffrey. Introduction. *The Young Visiters or Mr. Salteena's Plan*, by Daisy Ashford, edited by Juliet McMaster and others, Juvenilia Press, 1997, pp. ix-xiv.

Sedgwick, Ellery. "An Opalescent Chapter." *The Happy Profession*, Little, Brown, 1946, pp. 252-266.

Sims, Michael. *The Story of Charlotte's Web*. Walker and Company, 2011.

White, E. B. *Charlotte's Web*. 1952. HarperCollins, 2012.

———. "Death of a Pig." *Atlantic Monthly*, vol. 181, no. 1, Jan. 1948, pp. 30-3. 90th Anniversary Issue.

———. "Death of a Pig." *Essays of E. B. White*. Harper and Rowe, 1977, pp. 17-24.

———. *Letters of E. B. White*. Edited by Dorothy Lobrano Guth, Harper and Rowe, 1977, pp. 17-24.

Whiteley, Opal. *Peter Paul Rubens and Other Friendly Folk*. Edited by Laura Cappello, Juliet McMaster, Lesley Peterson, and Chris Wangler, Juvenilia Press, 2001.

———. *The Singing Creek Where the Willows Grow: The Mystical Nature Diary of Opal Whiteley*, Biography and Afterword by Benjamin Hoff, Penguin Books, 1994.

———. *The Story of Opal: The Journal of an Understanding Heart*. Atlantic Monthly Press, 1920.

FURTHER READING

Biographies

Elledge, Scott. *E. B. White: A Biography*. W. W. Norton, 1984.

The authoritative biography of White. [An excerpt from this book is included in *CLR*, Vol. 21.]

Sims, Michael. *The Story of* Charlotte's Web: *E. B. White's Eccentric Life in Nature and the Birth of an American Classic*. Walker, 2011.

A biography that focuses on White's relationship with the natural world, including animals. Sims describes how this painfully shy child, still reticent as an adult, transformed his love of nature into a genre of fantasy that is grounded in realism. Sims also discusses the long creative process that went into the writing of *Charlotte's Web* (1952), as well as White's relationship with his wife, *New Yorker* editor Katharine Angell White, and the renowned Harper and Brothers children's book editor Ursula Nordstrom.

Criticism

Agosta, Lucien L. *E. B. White: The Children's Books*. Twayne Publishers, 1995.

Introduces White's books for children and provides useful information about the literary reception of *Charlotte's Web* over time.

Ceraldi, Gabrielle. "Advertising the Self: The Culture of Personality in E. B White's *Charlotte's Web*." *Jeunesse*, vol. 6, no. 1, 2014, pp. 77-94.

Proposes that Wilbur can be read as caught in the middle of a cultural paradigm shift: he is at once developing his character, as children were taught to do in nineteenth-century novels, and his personality, as advertising agencies taught youth to do in the twentieth century. [Included in *CLR*, Vol. 238.]

Coats, Karen. "Lacan with Runt Pigs." *Children's Literature*, vol. 27, 1999, pp. 105-28.

Employs *Charlotte's Web* to instruct scholars of children's literature on the ways Lacanian theory can be employed in the analysis of children's literature. Specifically, Coats uses Jacques Lacan's concepts to interpret Fern's and Charlotte's maternity, Wilbur's growth into language, and his separation from his mother-figures.

Gagnon, Laurence. "Webs of Concern: *The Little Prince* and *Charlotte's Web*." *Children's Literature*, vol. 2, 1973, pp. 61-66.

Provides a Heideggerian reading of what it means to live authentically, including what it means to be true to one's self and to understand that one is being-unto-death, which is the concept that every living thing has within it the seeds of its own death. [Included in *CLR*, Vol. 21 and in the Antoine De Saint-Exupéry entry in *CLR*, Vol. 10.]

Griffith, John. "*Charlotte's Web*: A Lonely Fantasy of Love." *Children's Literature*, vol. 8, 1980, pp. 111-17.

Asserts that "White creates a consoling fantasy in which a small Everyman survives and triumphs over the pathos of being alone"; Wilbur overcomes his fear of change and death by learning to be himself, to accept help from others, and to understand the importance of language. [Included in *CLR*, Vol. 21.]

Kinghorn, Norton D. "The Real Miracle of *Charlotte's Web*." *Children's Literature Association Quarterly*, vol. 11, no. 1, 1986, pp. 4-9.

Argues that the real miracle of *Charlotte's Web* is the web itself, which serves the spider on a literal level as a source of food, a form of transportation, and a way to communicate with others. On a more metaphorical level, the web represents the passage from life to death and a way for the child Fern (or the child reader) to navigate between daily living and the otherworldly nature of life in the barn. [Included in *CLR*, Vol. 21 and in the Religion in Children's Literature entry in *CLR*, Vol. 121.]

Lukens, Rebecca. "The Child, the Critic, and a Good Book." *Language Arts*, vol. 55, no. 4, 1978, pp. 452+.

Defends the study of children's literature as a legitimate field of literary criticism. As one example, Lukens praises *Charlotte's Web* for its literary style: "E. B. White uses every stylistic device open to children both to please them and to help them understand the nature of friendship, of maternal love, and of death's inevitability. Connotative meanings, metaphors, similes, onomatopoeia, hyperbole and understatement as well as sound devices and rhythm are all parts of *Charlotte's Web*." She also examines White's use of folktales and parody in *Charlotte's Web* as a further example of his sophisticated literary style.

Mason, Bobbie Ann. "PROFILE: The Elements of E. B. White's Style." *Language Arts*, vol. 56, no. 6, 1979, pp. 692-96.

Attributes White's elegant stylistic phrasing to his being mentored by William Strunk, whose book *Elements of Style* White edited for its second edition in 1959. [Included in *CLR*, Vol. 21.]

Misheff, Sue. "Beneath the Web and Over the Stream: The Search for Safe Places in *Charlotte's Web* and *Bridge to Terabithia*." *Children's Literature in Education*, vol. 29, no. 3, 1998, pp. 131-41.

Examines how Romantic idealism is enacted in *Charlotte's Web*, comparing it to Katherine Paterson's *Bridge to Terabithia* (1977). In both, a female savior figure imagines into being a safe space for the male character, who is able to grow imaginatively because of this space and the female savior's sacrificial death.

Neumeyer, Peter. "What Makes a Good Children's Book? The Texture of *Charlotte's Web*." *South Atlantic Bulletin*, vol. 44, no. 2, 1979, pp. 66-75.

Praises *Charlotte's Web* as a well-textured work of art. Neumeyer calls attention to the novel's diction, character and dialogue, syntax, plot, rhetoric, and the way it flows within the patterns of "the Western literary tradition."

———. *The Annotated Charlotte's Web.* HarperCollins Publishers, 1994.

Draws from a broad array of sources, including Scott Elledge's biography (see above) and White's letters, to provide readers with the definitive edition of *Charlotte's Web,* complete with photographs of manuscript pages, information about what White read that influenced the novel and the writing process that went into it, and interesting facts related to the novel's composition and reception.

Nodelman, Perry. "Text as Teacher: The Beginning of *Charlotte's Web.*" *Children's Literature,* vol. 13, 1985, pp. 109-27.

Demonstrates how the first two chapters of *Charlotte's Web*—both of which are entirely realistic—teach children how to read the fantasy story of a pig saved from death at the hands of an aggressive male by a female of another species via the significance of her compassion and her word usage. [Included in *CLR,* Vol. 107.]

Rollin, Lucy. "The Reproduction of Mothering in *Charlotte's Web.*" *Children's Literature,* vol. 18, 1990, pp. 42-52.

Perceives that Nancy Chodorow's description of how mothering roles are replicated over generations, articulated in *The Reproduction of Mothering* (1978), works itself out in *Charlotte's Web,* first in terms of Fern's babying of Wilbur, then in Charlotte's treatment of him as a child growing into adulthood, only for him to become himself a surrogate parent to Charlotte's children in a less-gendered depiction of motherhood being reproduced cross-generationally. [Included in *CLR,* Vol. 107.]

Sampson, Edward C. "Stories for Children." *E. B. White,* Twayne, 1974, pp. 94-105.

Offers an early critique of *Charlotte's Web,* arguing that it and White's other works for young readers are written "in the classical tradition of children's stories."

Thomas, Trudelle H. "The Arc of the Rope Swing: Humour, Poetry, and Spirituality in *Charlotte's Web* by E. B. White." *International Journal of Children's Spirituality,* vol. 21, nos. 3-4, 2016, pp. 201-15.

Explains how White's humor and poetic writing style convey spirituality inspired by the child's relationship with nature. Thomas references Transcendentalist writing, including Ralph Waldo Emerson's "The Oversoul" (1841) and Henry David Thoreau's *Walden* (1854), as potential influences on White.

Wake, Lynn Overholt. "E. B. White's Paean to Life: The Environmental Imagination of *Charlotte's Web.*" *Wild Things: Children's Culture and Ecocriticism,* edited by Sidney I. Dobrin and Kenneth B. Kidd, Wayne State UP, 2004, pp. 101-14.

Examines the celebration of life and its interrelationship with the natural world, acknowledging the central influence of Thoreau's *Walden* on White and *Charlotte's Web.* Wake also examines the relationship between *Charlotte's Web* and William Strunk and White's *Elements of Style* in terms of simplicity and design.

Welty, Eudora. "Life in the Barn Was Very Good." *The New York Times,* 19 Oct. 1952, p. BR49.

Praises the variety of characters in *Charlotte's Web* and the positive traits of Wilbur specifically. [Included in *CLR,* Vol. 21.]

Additional information on White's life and works is contained in the following sources published by Gale: *American Writers Supplement,* **Vol. 1;** *Authors and Artists for Young Adults,* **Vol. 62;** *Authors in the News,* **Vol. 2;** *Children's Literature Review,* **Vols. 1, 21, 107, 238;** *Concise Dictionary of American Literary Biography Supplement;* *Contemporary Authors,* **Vols. 13-16R, 116;** *Contemporary Authors New Revision Series,* **Vols. 16, 37;** *Contemporary Literary Criticism,* **Vols. 10, 34, 39;** *Contemporary Popular Writers;* *Dictionary of Literary Biography,* **Vols. 11, 22;** *DISCovering Authors Modules: Popular Fiction and Genre Authors;* *DISCovering Authors 3.0;* *Encyclopedia of World Literature in the 20th Century,* **Ed. 3;** *Gale Contextual Encyclopedia of American Literature,* **Vol. 4;** *Gale Literature Resource Center;* *Major Authors and Illustrators for Children and Young Adults,* **Eds. 1, 2;** *Major 20th-Century Writers,* **Eds. 1, 2;** *Major 21st-Century Writers;* *Modern American Literature,* **Ed. 5;** *Nonfiction Classics for Students,* **Vol. 5;** *Reference Guide to American Literature,* **Ed. 4;** *St. James Guide to Fantasy Writers;* *Science Fiction, Fantasy, and Horror Writers;* **and** *Something about the Author,* **Vols. 2, 29, 44, 100.**

How to Use This Index

The main references

> **Calvino, Italo**
> 1923-1985 .... CLC 5, 8, 11, 22, 33, 39,
> 73; SSC 3, 48

list all author entries in the following Gale Literary Criticism series:

AAL = Asian American Literature
BG = The Beat Generation: A Gale Critical Companion
BLC = Black Literature Criticism
BLCS = Black Literature Criticism Supplement
CLC = Contemporary Literary Criticism
CLR = Children's Literature Review
CMLC = Classical and Medieval Literature Criticism
DC = Drama Criticism
FL = Feminism in Literature: A Gale Critical Companion
GL = Gothic Literature: A Gale Critical Companion
HLC = Hispanic Literature Criticism
HLCS = Hispanic Literature Criticism Supplement
HR = Harlem Renaissance: A Gale Critical Companion
LC = Literature Criticism from 1400 to 1800
NCLC = Nineteenth-Century Literature Criticism
NNAL = Native North American Literature
PC = Poetry Criticism
SSC = Short Story Criticism
TCLC = Twentieth-Century Literary Criticism
WLC = World Literature Criticism, 1500 to the Present
WLCS = World Literature Criticism Supplement

The cross-references

> See also CA 85-88, 116; CANR 23, 61;
> DAM NOV; DLB 196; EW 13; MTCW 1, 2;
> RGSF 2; RGWL 2; SFW 4; SSFS 12

list all author entries in the following Gale biographical and literary sources:

AAYA = Authors & Artists for Young Adults
AFAW = African American Writers
AFW = African Writers
AITN = Authors in the News
AMW = American Writers
AMWR = American Writers Retrospective Supplement
AMWS = American Writers Supplement
ANW = American Nature Writers
AW = Ancient Writers
BEST = Bestsellers
BPFB = Beacham's Encyclopedia of Popular Fiction: Biography and Resources
BRW = British Writers
BRWS = British Writers Supplement
BW = Black Writers
BYA = Beacham's Guide to Literature for Young Adults
CA = Contemporary Authors
CAAS = Contemporary Authors Autobiography Series
CABS = Contemporary Authors Bibliographical Series
CAD = Contemporary American Dramatists
CANR = Contemporary Authors New Revision Series
CAP = Contemporary Authors Permanent Series
CBD = Contemporary British Dramatists
CCA = Contemporary Canadian Authors

CD = Contemporary Dramatists
CDALB = Concise Dictionary of American Literary Biography
CDALBS = Concise Dictionary of American Literary Biography Supplement
CDBLB = Concise Dictionary of British Literary Biography
CMW = St. James Guide to Crime & Mystery Writers
CN = Contemporary Novelists
CP = Contemporary Poets
CPW = Contemporary Popular Writers
CSW = Contemporary Southern Writers
CWD = Contemporary Women Dramatists
CWP = Contemporary Women Poets
CWRI = St. James Guide to Children's Writers
CWW = Contemporary World Writers
DA = DISCovering Authors
DA3 = DISCovering Authors 3.0
DAB = DISCovering Authors: British Edition
DAC = DISCovering Authors: Canadian Edition
DAM = DISCovering Authors: Modules
   DRAM: Dramatists Module; **MST:** Most-studied Authors Module;
   MULT: Multicultural Authors Module; **NOV:** Novelists Module;
   POET: Poets Module; **POP:** Popular Fiction and Genre Authors Module
DFS = Drama for Students
DLB = Dictionary of Literary Biography
DLBD = Dictionary of Literary Biography Documentary Series
DLBY = Dictionary of Literary Biography Yearbook
DNFS = Literature of Developing Nations for Students
EFS = Epics for Students
EW = European Writers
EWL = Encyclopedia of World Literature in the 20th Century
EXPN = Exploring Novels
EXPP = Exploring Poetry
EXPS = Exploring Short Stories
FANT = St. James Guide to Fantasy Writers
FW = Feminist Writers
GFL = Guide to French Literature, Beginnings to 1789; 1789 to the Present
GLL = Gay and Lesbian Literature
HGG = St. James Guide to Horror, Ghost & Gothic Writers
HW = Hispanic Writers
IDFW = International Dictionary of Films and Filmmakers: Writers and Production Artists
IDTP = International Dictionary of Theatre: Playwrights
LAIT = Literature and Its Times
LAW = Latin American Writers
JRDA = Junior DISCovering Authors
MAICYA = Major Authors and Illustrators for Children and Young Adults
MAICYAS = Major Authors and Illustrators for Children and Young Adults Supplement
MAWW = Modern American Women Writers
MJW = Modern Japanese Writers
MTCW = Major 20th-Century Writers
NCFS = Nonfiction Classics for Students
NFS = Novels for Students
PAB = Poets: American and British
PFS = Poetry for Students
RGAL = Reference Guide to American Literature
RGEL = Reference Guide to English Literature
RGSF = Reference Guide to Short Fiction
RGWL = Reference Guide to World Literature
RHW = Twentieth-Century Romance and Historical Writers
SAAS = Something about the Author Autobiography Series
SATA = Something about the Author
SFW = St. James Guide to Science Fiction Writers
SSFS = Short Stories for Students
TCWW = Twentieth-Century Western Writers
WLIT = World Literature and Its Times
WP = World Poets
YABC = Yesterday's Authors of Books for Children
YAW = St. James Guide to Young Adult Writers

CLR Cumulative Author Index

Aardema, Verna 1911-2000 .... **17**
See also CA 5-8R; 189; CANR 3, 18, 39; CWRI 5; MAICYA 1, 2; SAAS 8; SATA 4, 68, 107; SATA-Obit 119

Aaseng, Nate
See Aaseng, Nathan

Aaseng, Nathan 1953- **54**
See also AAYA 27; CA 106, 317; CAAE 317; CANR 36, 103; JRDA; MAICYA 1, 2; SAAS 12; SATA 51, 88, 172, 236; SATA-Brief 38; SATA-Essay 236

Abbott, Jacob 1803-1879 .... **208**
See also DLB 1, 42, 243; SATA 22

Abbott, Manager Henry
See Stratemeyer, Edward L.

Abbott, Sarah
See Zolotow, Charlotte

Abingdon, Alexander
See Dr. Seuss

Achebe, Albert Chinualumogu
See Achebe, Chinua

Achebe, Chinua 1930- **20, 156**
See also AAYA 15; AFW; BLC 1:1, 2:1; BPFB 1; BRWC 2; BW 2, 3; CA 1-4R; CANR 6, 26, 47, 124, 220; CDWLB 3; CLC 1, 3, 5, 7, 11, 26, 51, 75, 127, 152, 272, 278, 325; CN 1, 2, 3, 4, 5, 6, 7; CP 2, 3, 4, 5, 6, 7; CWRI 5; DA; DA3; DAB; DAC; DAM MST, MULT, NOV; DLB 117; DNFS 1; EWL 3; EXPN; EXPS; LAIT 2; LATS 1:2; MAICYA 1, 2; MTCW 1, 2; MTFW 2005; NFS 2, 33; RGEL 2; RGSF 2; SATA 38, 40; SATA-Brief 38; SSC 105; SSFS 3, 13, 30; TWA; WLC 1; WLIT 2; WWE 1

Ada, Alma Flor 1938- **62**
See also CA 123; CANR 87, 122, 166; MAICYA 2; SATA 43, 84, 143, 181, 222; SATA-Essay 222

Adams, Adrienne 1906- **73**
See also CA 49-52; CANR 1, 35, 104; MAICYA 2; MAICYAS 1; SATA 8, 90

Adams, Harrison
See Stratemeyer, Edward L.
See also CA 19-20; CANR 26; CAP 2

Adams, Richard 1920- **20, 121**
See also AAYA 16; AITN 1, 2; BPFB 1; BYA 5; CA 49-52; CANR 3, 35, 128; CLC 4, 5, 18; CN 4, 5, 6, 7; DAM NOV; DLB 261; FANT; JRDA; LAIT 5; MAICYA 1, 2; MTCW 1, 2; NFS 11; SATA 7, 69; YAW

Adams, Richard George
See Adams, Richard

Adelberg, Doris
See Orgel, Doris

Adkins, Jan 1944- **7, 77**
See also CA 33-36R, 293; CAAE 293; CANR 103, 126; MAICYA 1, 2; SAAS 19; SATA 8, 69, 144, 210; SATA-Essay 210

Adler, C. S. 1932- **78**
See also AAYA 4, 41; CA 89-92; CANR 19, 40, 101; CLC 35; JRDA; MAICYA 1, 2; SAAS 15; SATA 26, 63, 102, 126; YAW

Adler, Carole Schwerdtfeger
See Adler, C. S.

Adler, David A. 1947- **108**
See also CA 57-60; CANR 7, 23, 88, 163, 202; MAICYA 1, 2; SATA 14, 70, 106, 151, 178, 231

Adler, Irving 1913- **27**
See also CA 5-8R; CANR 2, 47, 114; MAICYA 1, 2; SAAS 15; SATA 1, 29; SATA-Essay 164

Adoff, Arnold 1935- **7**
See also AAYA 3, 50; AITN 1; CA 41-44R; CANR 20, 37, 67, 126; CWRI 5; DLBY 2001; JRDA; MAICYA 1, 2; SAAS 15; SATA 5, 57, 96

Aesop 620(?)BCE-560(?)BCE **14**
See also CMTW 24; MAICYA 1, 2; SATA 64; SSC 164

Aesop, Abraham
See Newbery, John

Affabee, Eric
See Stine, R.L.

Agapida, Fray Antonio
See Irving, Washington

Aghill, Gordon
See Silverberg, Robert

Ahlberg, Allan 1938- **18, 233**
See also CA 111, 114; CANR 38, 70, 98, 151; CWRI 5; MAICYA 1, 2; SATA 68, 120, 165, 214; SATA-Brief 35

Ahlberg, Janet 1944-1994 .... **18**
See also CA 111; 114; 147; CANR 79, 104; CWRI 5; MAICYA 1, 2; MAICYAS 1; SATA 68, 120; SATA-Brief 32; SATA-Obit 83

Aiken, Joan (Delano) 1924-2004 ... **1, 19, 90**
See also AAYA 1, 25; CA 9-12R, 182; 223; CAAE 182; CANR 4, 23, 34, 64, 121; CLC 35; DLB 161; FANT; HGG; JRDA; MAICYA 1, 2; MTCW 1; RHW; SAAS 1; SATA 2, 30, 73; SATA-Essay 109; SATA-Obit 152; SSFS 33; SUFW 2; WYA; YAW

Akers, Floyd
See Baum, L. Frank

Albrecht, Karl
See Salten, Felix

Alcock, Vivien (Dolores) 1924-2003 .... **26**
See also AAYA 8, 57; BYA 5, 6; CA 110; 222; CANR 41, 105; JRDA; MAICYA 1, 2; SATA 45, 76; SATA-Brief 38; SATA-Obit 148; YAW

Alcott, Louisa May
1832-1888 ...... **1, 38, 109, 195, 196, 222**
See also AAYA 20; AMWS 1; BPFB 1; BYA 2; CDALB 1865-1917; DA; DA3; DAB; DAC; DAM MST, NOV; DLB 1, 42, 79, 223, 239, 242; DLBD 14; FL 1:2; FW; JRDA; LAIT 2; MAICYA 1, 2; NCLC 6, 58, 83, 218; NFS 12; RGAL 4; SATA 100; SSC 27, 98, 164; TUS; WCH; WLC 1; WYA; YABC 1; YAW

Alda, Arlene 1933- **93**
See also CA 114; CANR 142; SATA 44, 106, 158, 205; SATA-Brief 36

Aldiss, Brian W. 1925- **197**
See also AAYA 42; BRWS 19; CA 5-8R; 190; CAAS 2; CANR 5, 28, 64, 121, 168; CLC 5, 14, 40, 290; CMTFW; CN 1, 2, 3, 4, 5, 6, 7; DAM NOV; DLB 14, 261, 271; MBL 2; MTCW 1, 2; MTFW 2; SATA 34; SCFW 1, 2; SFW 4; SSC 36

Aldon, Adair
See Meigs, Cornelia Lynde

Aldrich, Ann
See Meaker, Marijane

Aldrich, Bess Streeter 1881-1954 .... **70**
See also TCLC 125; TCWW 2

Alexander, Lloyd 1924-2007 .... **1, 5, 48, 227**
See also AAYA 1, 27; BPFB 1; BYA 5, 6, 7, 9, 10, 11; CA 1-4R; 260; CANR 1, 24, 38, 55, 113; CLC 35; CWRI 5; DLB 52; FANT; JRDA; MAICYA 1, 2; MAICYAS 1; MTCW 1; SAAS 19; SATA 3, 49, 81, 129, 135; SATA-Obit 182; SSFHW; SUFW; TUS; WYA; YAW

Alexander, Lloyd Chudley
See Alexander, Lloyd

Alexie, Sherman 1966- **179**
See also AAYA 28, 85; BYA 15; CA 138; CANR 65, 95, 133, 174; CLC 96, 154, 312; CN 7; DA3; DAM MULT; DLB 175, 206, 278; LATS 1:2; MTCW 2; MTFW 2005; NNAL; NFS 17, 31, 38; PC 53; PFS 39; SSC 107; SSFS 18, 36

Alger, Horatio, Jr.
See Stratemeyer, Edward L.

Alger, Horatio, Jr. 1832-1899 ... **87, 170, 221**
See also DLB 42; LAIT 2; NCLC 8, 83, 260; RGAL 4; SATA 16; TUS

Aliki
See Brandenberg, Aliki

Allan, Mabel Esther 1915-1998 .... **43**
See also CA 5-8R; 167; CANR 2, 18, 47, 104; CWRI 5; MAICYA 1, 2; SAAS 11; SATA 5, 32, 75

Allard, Harry, Jr. 1928- **85**
See also CA 113; CANR 38; INT CA-113; MAICYA 1, 2; SATA 42, 102, 216

Allard, Harry G.
See Allard, Harry, Jr.

Allen, Adam
See Epstein, Beryl; Epstein, Samuel

Allen, Alex B.
See Heide, Florence Parry

Allen, Pamela (Kay) 1934- **44**
See also CA 126; CANR 53, 118; CWRI 5; MAICYA 2; SATA 50, 81, 123

Allende, Isabel 1942- **99, 171**
See also AAYA 18, 70; CA 125; 130; CANR 51, 74, 129, 165, 208; CDWLB 3; CLC 39,

57, 97, 170, 264; CWW 2; DA3; DAM MULT, NOV; DLB 145; DNFS 1; EWL 3; FL 1:5; FW; HLC 1; HW 1, 2; INT CA-130; LAIT 5; LAWS 1; LMFS 2; MTCW 1, 2; MTFW 2005; NCFS 1; NFS 6, 18, 29; RGSF 2; RGWL 3; SATA 163; SSC 65; SSFS 11, 16; WLCS; WLIT 1

Alleyn, Ellen
See Rossetti, Christina

Almond, David 1951- **85, 168, 258**
See also AAYA 38, 87; BYA 16; CA 186; CANR 142, 200, 252, 302; MAICYA 2; SATA 114, 158, 233, 307, 342, 377

Altman, Suzanne
See Orgel, Doris

Alyer, Philip A.
See Stratemeyer, Edward L.

Anaya, Rudolfo 1937- **129**
See also AAYA 20; BYA 13; CA 45-48; CAAS 4; CANR 1, 32, 51, 124, 169; CLC 23, 148, 255; CN 4, 5, 6, 7; DAM MULT, NOV; DLB 82, 206, 278; HLC 1; HW 1; LAIT 4; LLW; MAL 5; MTCW 1, 2; MTFW 2005; NFS 12; RGAL 4; RGSF 2; TCWW 2; WLIT 1

Anaya, Rudolfo A.
See Anaya, Rudolfo

Anaya, Rudolpho Alfonso
See Anaya, Rudolfo

Andersen, Hans Christian
1805-1875 .... **6, 113**
See also AAYA 57; DA; DA3; DAB; DAC; DAM MST, POP; EW 6; MAICYA 1, 2; NCLC 7, 79, 214; RGSF 2; RGWL 2, 3; SATA 100; SSC 6, 56; TWA; WCH; WLC 1; YABC 1

Anderson, Laurie Halse 1961- **138, 213**
See also AAYA 39, 84; BYA 16; CA 160; CANR 103, 135, 171, 206; MTFW 2005; NFS 31, 35; SATA 95, 132, 186

Anderson, Poul 1926-2001 .... **58**
See also AAYA 5, 34; BPFB 1; BYA 6, 8, 9; CA 1-4R, 181; 199; CAAE 181; CAAS 2; CANR 2, 15, 34, 64, 110; CLC 15; DLB 8; FANT; INT CANR-15; MTCW 1, 2; MTFW 2005; SATA 90; SATA-Brief 39; SATA-Essay 106; SCFW 1, 2; SFW 4; SUFW 1, 2

Andrews, Julie 1935- **85**
See also CA 37-40R; CANR 139, 201; SATA 7, 153

Angeli, Marguerite (Lofft) de
See de Angeli, Marguerite (Lofft)

Angell, Judie
See Angell, Judie

Angell, Judie 1937- **33**
See also AAYA 11, 71; BYA 6; CA 77-80; CANR 49; CLC 30; JRDA; SATA 22, 78; WYA; YAW

Angelou, Maya 1928-2014 .... **53, 184, 266**
See also AAYA 7, 20; AMWS 4; BLC 1:1; BPFB 1; BW 2, 3; BYA 2; CA 65-68; CANR 19, 42, 65, 111, 133, 204, 265; CDALBS; CLC 12, 35, 64, 77, 155, 389; CP 4, 5, 6, 7; CPW; CSW; CWP; DA; DA3; DAB; DAC; DAM MST, MULT, POET, POP; DLB 38; EWL 3; EXPN; EXPP; FL 1:5; LAIT 4; MAICYA 2; MAICYAS 1; MAL 5; MBL; MTCW 1, 2; MTFW 2005; NCFS 2; NFS 2; PC 32; PFS 2, 3, 33, 38, 42, 47, 53; RGAL 4; SATA 49, 136, 281; TCLE 1:1; WLCS; WYA; YAW

Anglund, Joan Walsh 1926- **1, 94**
See also CA 5-8R; CANR 15; MAICYA 2; SATA 2

Anno, Mitsumasa 1926- **2, 14, 122**
See also CA 49-52; CANR 4, 44, 141; MAICYA 1, 2; SATA 5, 38, 77, 157

Anthony, John
See Ciardi, John (Anthony)

Anthony, Piers 1934- **118**
See also AAYA 11, 48; BYA 7; CA 200; CAAE 200; CANR 28, 56, 73, 102, 133, 202; CLC 35; CPW; DAM POP; DLB 8; FANT; MAICYA 2; MAICYAS 1; MTCW 1, 2; MTFW 2005; SAAS 22; SATA 84, 129; SATA-Essay 129; SFW 4; SUFW 1, 2; YAW

Applegate, K.A.
See Applegate, Katherine

Applegate, Katherine 1956- **90**
See also AAYA 37; BYA 14, 16; CA 171; CANR 138, 187; SATA 109, 162, 196; WYAS 1

Applegate, Katherine Alice
See Applegate, Katherine

Appleton, Victor
See Stratemeyer, Edward L.

Ardizzone, Edward (Jeffrey Irving)
1900-1979 .... **3**
See also CA 5-8R; 89-92; CANR 8, 78; CWRI 5; DLB 160; MAICYA 1, 2; SATA 1, 28; SATA-Obit 21; WCH

Armstrong, Jennifer 1961- **66**
See also AAYA 28; CA 145; CANR 67, 134; SAAS 24; SATA 77, 111, 165; SATA-Essay 120; YAW

Armstrong, William H(oward)
1914-1999 .... **1, 117**
See also AAYA 18; AITN 1; BYA 3; CA 17-20R; 177; CANR 9, 69, 104; JRDA; MAICYA 1, 2; SAAS 7; SATA 4; SATA-Obit 111; YAW

Arnette, Robert
See Silverberg, Robert

Arnold, Caroline 1944- **61**
See also CA 107; CANR 24, 137; SAAS 23; SATA 36, 85, 131, 174, 228; SATA-Brief 34

Arnold, Emily 1939- **46**
See also CA 109, 180; CANR 103; CWRI 5; MAICYA 1, 2; MAICYAS 1; SAAS 7; SATA 5, 50, 76, 110, 134, 210; SATA-Essay 134

Arnold, Gillian Clare
See Cross, Gillian

Arnosky, James Edward 1946- **93**
See also CA 69-72; CANR 12, 32, 126; MAICYA 1, 2; SATA 70, 118, 189

Arnosky, Jim
See Arnosky, James Edward

Arrick, Fran
See Angell, Judie

Aruego, Jose 1932- **5**
See also CA 37-40R; CANR 42, 105; MAICYA 1, 2; SATA 6, 68, 125, 178

Aruego, Jose Espiritu
See Aruego, Jose

Arundel, Honor (Morfydd) 1919-1973 .... **35**
See also CA 21-22; 41-44R; CAP 2; CLC 17; CWRI 5; SATA 4; SATA-Obit 24

Asbjornsen, Peter Christen 1812-1885 .. **104**
See also DLB 354; MAICYA 1, 2; SATA 15; WCH

Ashabranner, Brent 1921- **28**
See also AAYA 6, 46; BYA 1; CA 5-8R; CANR 10, 27, 57, 110; JRDA; MAICYA 1, 2; SAAS 14; SATA 1, 67, 130, 166; YAW

Ashabranner, Brent Kenneth
See Ashabranner, Brent

Asheron, Sara
See Moore, Lilian

Ashey, Bella
See Breinburg, Petronella

Ashley, Bernard (John) 1935- **4, 189**
See also CA 93-96; CANR 25, 44, 140; MAICYA 1, 2; SATA 47, 79, 155; SATA-Brief 39; YAW

Asimov, Isaac 1920-1992 .... **12, 79**
See also AAYA 13; BEST 90:2; BPFB 1; BYA 4, 6, 7, 9; CA 1-4R; 137; CANR 2, 19, 36, 60, 125; CLC 1, 3, 9, 19, 26, 76, 92; CMW 4; CN 1, 2, 3, 4, 5; CPW; DA3; DAM POP; DLB 8; DLBY 1992; INT CANR-19; JRDA; LAIT 5; LMFS 2; MAICYA 1, 2; MAL 5; MTCW 1, 2; MTFW 2005; NFS 29; RGAL 4; SATA 1, 26, 74; SCFW 1, 2; SFW 4; SSC 148; SSFS 17, 33; TUS; YAW

Aston, James
See White, T(erence) H(anbury)

Atwater, Florence 1896-1979 .... **19**
See also CA 135; MAICYA 1, 2; SATA 16, 66

Atwater, Florence Hasseltine Carroll
See Atwater, Florence

Atwater, Richard 1892-1948 .... **19**
See also CA 111; 135; CWRI 5; MAICYA 1, 2; SATA 54, 66; SATA-Brief 27

Atwater, Richard Tupper
See Atwater, Richard

Aunt Weedy
See Alcott, Louisa May

Avi 1937- **24, 68, 188**
See also AAYA 10, 37; BYA 1, 10; CA 69-72; CANR 12, 42, 120, 178; JRDA; MAICYA 1, 2; MAICYAS 1; NFS 34; SATA 14, 71, 108, 156, 190, 226; WYA; YAW

Awdry, Wilbert Vere 1911-1997 .... **23**
See also CA 103; 157; CWRI 5; DLB 160; MAICYA 2; MAICYAS 1; SATA 94

Aylesworth, Jim 1943- **89**
See also CA 106; CANR 22, 45; CWRI 5; SATA 38, 89, 139, 213

Aylesworth, Thomas G(ibbons)
1927-1995 .... **6**
See also CA 25-28R; 149; CANR 10, 26; SAAS 17; SATA 4, 88

Ayme, Marcel (Andre) 1902-1967 .... **25**
See also CA 89-92; CANR 67, 137; CLC 11; DLB 72; EW 12; EWL 3; GFL 1789 to the Present; RGSF 2; RGWL 2, 3; SATA 91; SSC 41

Babbitt, Natalie 1932- **2, 53, 141**
See also AAYA 51; BYA 5; CA 49-52; CANR 2, 19, 38, 126, 185; CWRI 5; DLB 52; JRDA; MAICYA 1, 2; SAAS 5; SATA 6, 68, 106, 194

Babbitt, Natalie Zane Moore
See Babbitt, Natalie

Bachman, Richard
See King, Stephen

Bacon, Martha Sherman 1917-1981 .... **3**
See also CA 85-88; 104; CWRI 5; SATA 18; SATA-Obit 27

Bahlke, Valerie Worth -1994
See Worth, Valerie

Baillie, Allan 1943- **49**
See also AAYA 25; CA 118; CANR 42, 135, 159; SAAS 21; SATA 87, 151; YAW

Baillie, Allan Stuart
See Baillie, Allan

Baker, Jeannie 1950- **28**
See also CA 97-100; CANR 69, 102; CWRI 5; MAICYA 2; MAICYAS 1; SATA 23, 88, 156

Baldwin, James 1924-1987 .... **191, 255**
See also AAYA 4, 34; AMWS 2:1; AFAW 1, 2; AMWR 2; AMWS 1; BLC 1:1, 2:1; BPFB 1; BW 1; CA 1-4R, 124; CABS 1; CAD; CANR 3, 24; CDALB 1941-1968; CN 1, 2, 3, 4; CLC 1, 2, 3, 4, 5, 8, 13, 15, 17, 42, 50, 67, 90, 127; CPW; DA; DA3; DAB; DAC; DAM MST, MULT, NOV, POP; DC 1; DFS 11, 15; DLB 2, 7, 33, 249, 278; DLBY 1987; EWL 3; EXPS; LAIT 5; MAL 5; MTCW 1, 2; MTFW 2005; NCFS 4; NFS 4; RGAL 4; RGSF 2; SATA 9;

SATA-Obit 54; SSC 10, 33, 98, 134, 199, 286, 295; SSFS 2, 18, 44; TCLC 229, 376, 377, 422; TUS; WLC 1
Ballantyne, R(obert) M(ichael) 1825-1894 .... **137, 228**
See also DLB 163; JRDA; NCLC 301; RGEL 2; SATA 24
Ballard, Robert D(uane) 1942- **60**
See also CA 112; CANR 96; SATA 85
Banat, D. R.
See Bradbury, Ray
Bancroft, Laura
See Baum, L. Frank
Bang, Garrett
See Bang, Molly
Bang, Molly 1943- **8**
See also CA 102; CANR 126; CWRI 5; MAICYA 1, 2; SATA 24, 69, 111, 158, 215
Banks, Lynne Reid
See Reid Banks, Lynne
Banner, Angela
See Maddison, Angela Mary
Bannerman, Helen (Brodie Cowan Watson) 1862(?)-1946 .... **21, 144**
See also CA 136, 111; CWRI 5; DLB 141; MAICYA 1, 2; SATA 19
Barbauld, Anna Laetitia 1743-1825 ...... **160**
See also DLB 107, 109, 142, 158, 336; NCLC 50, 185; RGEL 2
Barclay, Bill
See Moorcock, Michael
Barclay, William Ewert
See Moorcock, Michael
Barker, Cicely Mary 1895-1973 .... **88**
See also CA 121; 117; CWRI 5; SATA 49; SATA-Brief 39
Barklem, Jill 1951- **31**
See also CA 161; CANR 137; SATA 96
Barnum, P. T., Jr.
See Stratemeyer, Edward L.
Barnum, Theodore
See Stratemeyer, Edward L.
Barrett, Judi
See Barrett, Judith
Barrett, Judith 1941- **98**
See also CA 103; MAICYA 2; SATA 26, 204
Barrie, Baronet
See Barrie, J. M.
Barrie, J. M. 1860-1937 .... **16, 124, 244**
See also BRWS 3; BYA 4, 5; CA 104, 136; CANR 77; CDBLB 1890-1914; CWRI 5; DA3; DAB; DAM DRAM; DFS 7; DLB 10, 141, 156, 352; EWL 3; FANT; MAICYA 1, 2; MBL 2; MTCW 2; MTFW 2005; SATA 100; SUFW; TCLC 2, 164; WCH; WLIT 4; YABC 1
Barrie, James Matthew
See Barrie, J. M.
Barrington, Michael
See Moorcock, Michael
Barron, T.A. 1952- **86**
See also AAYA 30; BYA 12, 13, 14; CA 150; CANR 105, 122, 182; SATA 83, 126, 192; YAW
Barron, Thomas Archibald
See Barron, T.A.
Barron, Tom
See Barron, T.A.
Base, Graeme 1958- **22**
See also CA 134; CANR 69, 128; CWRI 5; MAICYA 1, 2; SATA 67, 101, 162
Base, Graeme Rowland
See Base, Graeme
Bashevis, Isaac
See Singer, Isaac Bashevis
Bashevis, Yitskhok
See Singer, Isaac Bashevis
Baum, L. Frank 1856-1919 .... **15, 107, 175, 216**

See also AAYA 46; BYA 16; CA 108; 133; CWRI 5; DLB 22; FANT; JRDA; MAICYA 1, 2; MTCW 1, 2; NFS 13; RGAL 4; SATA 18, 100; TCLC 7, 132; WCH
Baum, Louis F.
See Baum, L. Frank
Baum, Lyman Frank
See Baum, L. Frank
Baumann, Hans 1914- **35**
See also CA 5-8R; CANR 3; SATA 2
Bawden, Nina 1925- **2, 51**
See also CA 17-20R; CANR 8, 29, 54, 180; CN 1, 2, 3, 4, 5, 6, 7; DAB; DLB 14, 161, 207; JRDA; MAICYA 1, 2; SAAS 16; SATA 4, 72, 132; YAW
Bawden, Nina Mary Mabey
See Bawden, Nina
Baxter, Virginia
See Hilton, Margaret Lynette
Baylor, Byrd 1924- **3**
See also CA 81-84; CANR 115; MAICYA 1, 2; SATA 16, 69, 136
Beagle, Peter S. 1939- **220**
See also AAYA 47; BPFB 1; BYA 9, 10, 16; CA 9-12R; CANR 4, 51, 73, 110, 213; CLC 7, 104; CMTFW 1; DA3; DLB 1980; FANT; MTCW 2; MTFW; SATA 60, 130; SUFW 1, 2; YAW;
Bean, Normal
See Burroughs, Edgar Rice
Bear, Greg 1951- **175**
See also AAYA 24; BPFB 1; BYA 9, 10; CA 113; CANR 35, 81, 145, 199; CN 7; SATA 65, 105; SCFW 2; SFW 4
Bear, Gregory Dale
See Bear, Greg
Becker, Karin
See Salten, Felix
Beckman, Gunnel 1910- **25**
See also CA 33-36R; CANR 15, 114; CLC 26; MAICYA 1, 2; SAAS 9; SATA 6
Bedard, Michael 1949- **35**
See also AAYA 22; CA 159; CANR 118; CWRI 5; MAICYA 2; MAICYAS 1; SATA 93, 154
Beeler, Janet
See Shaw, Janet
Belaney, Archibald Stansfeld
See Grey Owl
Bell, Emerson
See Stratemeyer, Edward L.
Bell, William 1945- **91**
See also AAYA 75; CA 155; CANR 123; MAICYA 2; SATA 90; YAW
Bellairs, John (Anthony) 1938-1991 .... **37**
See also BYA 4, 5; CA 21-24R; 133; CANR 8, 24; FANT; JRDA; MAICYA 1, 2; SATA 2, 68, 160; SATA-Obit 66
Beller, Susan Provost 1949- **106**
See also CA 151; CANR 109; SATA 84, 128
Belloc, Hilaire 1870-1953 .... **102, 224**
See also CA 106, 152; CWRI 5; DAM POET; DLB 19, 100, 141, 174; EWL 3; MTCW 2; MTFW 2005; PC 24; SATA 112; TCLC 7, 18; WCH; YABC 1
Belloc, Joseph Hilaire Pierre Sebastien Rene Swanton
See Belloc, Hilaire
Belloc, Joseph Peter Rene Hilaire
See Belloc, Hilaire
Belloc, Joseph Pierre Hilaire
See Belloc, Hilaire
Bemelmans, Ludwig 1898-1962 .... **6, 93**
See also CA 73-76; CANR 81; CWRI 5; DLB 22; MAICYA 1, 2; RGAL 4; SATA 15, 100; WCH
Benary, Margot
See Benary-Isbert, Margot

Benary-Isbert, Margot 1889-1979 .... **12**
See also CA 5-8R; 89-92; CANR 4, 72; CLC 12; MAICYA 1, 2; SATA 2; SATA-Obit 21
Bendick, Jeanne 1919- **5**
See also CA 5-8R; CANR 2, 48, 113; MAICYA 1, 2; SAAS 4; SATA 2, 68, 135, 238; SATA-Essay 238
Berenstain, Jan 1923- **19, 150**
See also CA 25-28R; CANR 14, 36, 77, 108; CWRI 5; MAICYA 1, 2; SAAS 20; SATA 12, 64, 129, 135
Berenstain, Janice
See Berenstain, Jan
Berenstain, Stan 1923-2005 .... **19, 150**
See also CA 25-28R; 245; CANR 14, 36, 108; CWRI 5; MAICYA 1, 2; SAAS 20; SATA 12, 64, 129, 135; SATA-Obit 169
Berenstain, Stanley
See Berenstain, Stan
Berger, Melvin H. 1927- **32**
See also CA 5-8R; CANR 4, 142; CLC 12; SAAS 2; SATA 5, 88, 158; SATA-Essay 124
Berna, Paul 1910-1994 .... **19**
See also CA 73-76; 143; CANR 78; SATA 15; SATA-Obit 78
Berry, James 1924- **22, 143**
See also AAYA 30; BYA 9; CA 135; CANR 102; CP 5, 7; CWRI 5; DLB 347; JRDA; MAICYA 2; MAICYAS 1; SATA 67, 110
Beskow, Elsa (Maartman) 1874-1953 ...... **17**
See also CA 135; MAICYA 1, 2; SATA 20
Bess, Clayton
See Locke, Robert
Bethancourt, T. Ernesto
See Paisley, Tom
Bethlen, T.D.
See Silverberg, Robert
Betts, James
See Haynes, Betsy
Beynon, John
See Wyndham, John
Bianco, Margery
See Bianco, Margery Williams
Bianco, Margery Williams 1881-1944 .... **19, 146**
See also CA 109; 155; CWRI 5; DLB 160; MAICYA 1, 2; SATA 15; WCH
Bickerstaff, Isaac
See Swift, Jonathan
Biegel, Paul 1925- **27**
See also CA 77-80; CANR 14, 32, 73; SAAS 18; SATA 16, 79
Billout, Guy (Rene) 1941- **33**
See also CA 85-88; CANR 26, 124; SATA 10, 144
Biro, B.
See Biro, B. S.
Biro, B. S. 1921- **28**
See also CA 25-28R; CANR 11, 39, 77; CWRI 5; MAICYA 1, 2; SAAS 13; SATA 1
Biro, Balint Stephen
See Biro, B. S.
Biro, Val
See Biro, B. S.
Bishop, Claire Huchet 1899(?)-1993 .... **80**
See also CA 73-76; 140; CANR 36; CWRI 5; MAICYA 1, 2; SATA 14; SATA-Obit 74
Bjoerk, Christina 1938- **22**
See also CA 135; SATA 67, 99
Bjork, Christina
See Bjoerk, Christina
Blacklin, Malcolm
See Chambers, Aidan
Blade, Alexander
See Silverberg, Robert

Blades, Ann (Sager) 1947- **15**
See also CA 77-80; CANR 13, 48; CWRI 5; JRDA; MAICYA 1, 2; SATA 16, 69

Blair, Eric
See Orwell, George

Blair, Eric Arthur
See Orwell, George

Blair, Pauline Hunter
See Clarke, Pauline

Blake, Quentin 1932- **31**
See also CA 25-28R; CANR 11, 37, 67, 105; CWRI 5; MAICYA 1, 2; SATA 9, 52, 96, 125, 211

Blake, William 1757-1827 .... **52**
See also AAYA 47; BRW 3; BRWR 1; CDBLB 1789-1832; DA; DA3; DAB; DAC; DAM MST, POET; DLB 93, 154, 163; EXPP; LATS 1:1; LMFS 1; MAICYA 1, 2; NCLC 13, 37, 57, 127, 173, 190, 201; PAB; PC 12, 63; PFS 2, 12, 24, 34, 40; SATA 30; TEA; WCH; WLC 1; WLIT 3; WP

Bland, E.
See Nesbit, E.

Bland, Edith Nesbit
See Nesbit, E.

Bland, Fabian
See Nesbit, E.

Bliss, Frederick
See Card, Orson Scott

Bliss, Gillian
See Paton Walsh, Jill

Bliss, Reginald
See Wells, H. G.

Block, Francesca Lia 1962- **33, 116, 185**
See also AAYA 13, 34; BYA 8, 10; CA 131; CANR 56, 77, 94, 135, 183; MAICYA 2; MAICYAS 1; MTFW 2005; SAAS 21; SATA 80, 116, 158, 213; WYA; YAW

Blos, Joan W. 1928- **18**
See also BYA 1; CA 101; CANR 21, 128, 184; CWRI 5; JRDA; MAICYA 1, 2; SAAS 11; SATA 33, 69, 109, 153; SATA-Brief 27; SATA-Essay 153; YAW

Blos, Joan Winsor
See Blos, Joan W.

Blue, Zachary
See Stine, R.L.

Bluggage, Oranthy
See Alcott, Louisa May

Blumberg, Rhoda 1917- **21**
See also CA 65-68; CANR 9, 26, 101; MAICYA 1, 2; SATA 35, 70, 123

Blume, Judy 1938- **2, 15, 69, 176**
See also AAYA 3, 26; BYA 1, 8, 12; CA 29-32R; CANR 13, 37, 66, 124, 186; CLC 12, 30, 325; CPW; DA3; DAM NOV, POP; DLB 52; JRDA; MAICYA 1, 2; MAICYAS 1; MTCW 1, 2; MTFW 2005; NFS 24; SATA 2, 31, 79, 142, 195; WYA; YAW

Blume, Judy Sussman
See Blume, Judy

Blutig, Eduard
See Gorey, Edward (St. John)

Blyton, Enid 1897-1968 .... **31, 204**
See also CA 77-80; 25-28R; CANR 33; CWRI 5; DLB 160; MAICYA 1, 2; SATA 25

Blyton, Enid Mary
See Blyton, Enid

Bodker, Cecil
See Bodker, Cecil

Bodker, Cecil 1927- **23**
See also CA 73-76; CANR 13, 44, 111; CLC 21; MAICYA 1, 2; SATA 14, 133

Bogart, Jo Ellen 1945- **59**
See also CA 156; CANR 110; SATA 92, 222

Bolton, Elizabeth
See St. John, Nicole

Bolton, Evelyn
See Bunting, Eve

Bond, (Thomas) Michael 1926- **1, 95**
See also CA 5-8R; CANR 4, 24, 49, 101; CWRI 5; DLB 161; INT CANR-24; MAICYA 1, 2; SAAS 3; SATA 6, 58, 157

Bond, Nancy 1945- **11**
See also CA 65-68; CAAE 250; CANR 9, 36; JRDA; MAICYA 1, 2; SAAS 13; SATA 22, 82, 159; SATA-Essay 159; YAW

Bond, Nancy Barbara
See Bond, Nancy

Bond, Ruskin 1934- **171**
See also CA 29-32R; CANR 14, 31, 52; CWRI 5; RGSF 2; SATA 14, 87

Bonehill, Captain Ralph
See Stratemeyer, Edward L.

Bontemps, Arna 1902-1973 .... **6**
See also BLC 1:1; BW 1; CA 1-4R; 41-44R; CANR 4, 35; CLC 1, 18; CP 1; CWRI 5; DA3; DAM MULT, NOV, POET; DLB 48, 51; HR 1:2; JRDA; MAICYA 1, 2; MAL 5; MTCW 1, 2; PFS 32; SATA 2, 44; SATA-Obit 24; WCH; WP

Bontemps, Arnaud Wendell
See Bontemps, Arna

Bookman, Charlotte
See Zolotow, Charlotte

Boston, L(ucy) M(aria Wood) 1892-1990 .... **3**
See also CA 73-76; 131; CANR 58; CWRI 5; DLB 161; FANT; JRDA; MAICYA 1, 2; SATA 19; SATA-Obit 64; YAW

Boutet de Monvel, (Louis) M(aurice) 1850(?)-1913 .... **32**
See also CA 177; MAICYA 2; MAICYAS 1; SATA 30

Bova, Ben 1932- **3, 96**
See also AAYA 16; CA 5-8R; CAAS 18; CANR 11, 56, 94, 111, 157, 219; CLC 45; DLBY 1981; INT CANR-11; MAICYA 1, 2; MTCW 1; SATA 6, 68, 133; SFW 4

Bova, Benjamin William
See Bova, Ben

Bowie, Jim
See Stratemeyer, Edward L.

Bowler, Jan Brett
See Brett, Jan

Boyd, Candy Dawson 1946- **50**
See also BW 2, 3; CA 138; CANR 81; JRDA; MAICYA 2; SATA 72

Boynton, Sandra (Keith) 1953- **105**
See also CA 126; CANR 53, 136; MAICYA 2; SATA 57, 107, 152; SATA-Brief 38

Boz
See Dickens, Charles

Bradbury, Edward P.
See Moorcock, Michael

Bradbury, Ray 1920- **174**
See also AAYA 15, 84; AITN 1, 2; AMWS 4; BPFB 1; BYA 4, 5, 11; CA 1-4R; CANR 2, 30, 75, 125, 186; CDALB 1968-1988; CLC 1, 3, 10, 15, 42, 98, 235; CN 1, 2, 3, 4, 5, 6, 7; CPW; DA; DA3; DAB; DAC; DAM MST, NOV, POP; DLB 2, 8; EXPN; EXPS; HGG; LAIT 3, 5; LATS 1:2; LMFS 2; MAL 5; MTCW 1, 2; MTFW 2005; NFS 1, 22, 29; RGAL 4; RGSF 2; SATA 11, 64, 123; SCFW 1, 2; SFW 4; SSC 29, 53, 157; SSFS 1, 20, 28; SUFW 1, 2; TUS; WLC 1; YAW

Bradbury, Ray Douglas
See Bradbury, Ray

Bradley, Marion Zimmer 1930-1999 ..... **158**
See also AAYA 40; BPFB 1; CA 57-60; 185; CAAS 10; CANR 7, 31, 51, 75, 107; CLC 30; CPW; DA3; DAM POP; DLB 8; FANT; FW; GLL 1; MTCW 1, 2; MTFW 2005; NFS 40; SATA 90, 139; SATA-Obit 116; SFW 4; SUFW 2; YAW

Brancato, Robin F. 1936- **32**
See also AAYA 9, 68; BYA 6; CA 69-72; CANR 11, 45; CLC 35; JRDA; MAICYA 2; MAICYAS 1; SAAS 9; SATA 97; WYA; YAW

Brancato, Robin Fidler
See Brancato, Robin F.

Brandenberg, Aliki 1929- **9, 71**
See also CA 1-4R; CANR 4, 12, 30, 102; CWRI 5; MAICYA 1, 2; SATA 2, 35, 75, 113, 157

Brandenberg, Aliki Liacouras
See Brandenberg, Aliki

Branley, Franklyn M(ansfield) 1915-2002 .... **13**
See also CA 33-36R; 207; CANR 14, 39; CLC 21; MAICYA 1, 2; SAAS 16; SATA 4, 68, 136

Brashares, Ann 1967- **113**
See also AAYA 52; CA 218; CANR 152, 203; SATA 145, 188

Brazil, Angela 1869(?)-1947 .... **157**
See also CA 112; CWRI 5

Breinburg, Petronella 1927- **31**
See also CA 53-56; CANR 4; SATA 11

Breskin, Jane
See Zalben, Jane Breskin

Brett, Jan 1949- **27**
See also CA 116; CANR 41, 110; CWRI 5; MAICYA 1, 2; SATA 42, 71, 130, 171, 234

Brett, Jan Churchill
See Brett, Jan

Brett Bowler, Jan
See Brett, Jan

Bridgers, Sue Ellen 1942- **18, 199**
See also AAYA 8, 49; BYA 7, 8; CA 65-68; CANR 11, 36; CLC 26; DLB 52; JRDA; MAICYA 1, 2; SAAS 1; SATA 22, 90; SATA-Essay 109; SSFS 39; WYA; YAW

Bridwell, Norman (Ray) 1928- **96**
See also CA 13-16R; CANR 5, 20, 46, 117; CWRI 5; MAICYA 1, 2; SATA 4, 68, 138

Briggs, Raymond 1934- **10, 168**
See also CA 73-76; CANR 70, 148, 169; CWRI 5; MAICYA 1, 2; SATA 23, 66, 131, 184

Briggs, Raymond Redvers
See Briggs, Raymond

Brindle, Max
See Fleischman, Sid

Brink, Carol Ryrie 1895-1981 .... **30, 149**
See also BYA 1; CA 1-4R; 104; CANR 3, 65; CWRI 5; JRDA; MAICYA 1, 2; SATA 1, 31, 100; SATA-Obit 27; TCWW 2; WCH

Brinsmead, H. F.
See Brinsmead, H(esba) F(ay)

Brinsmead, H. F(ay)
See Brinsmead, H(esba) F(ay)

Brinsmead, H(esba) F(ay) 1922- **47**
See also CA 21-24R; CANR 10; CLC 21; CWRI 5; MAICYA 1, 2; SAAS 5; SATA 18, 78

Brooke, L(eonard) Leslie 1862-1940 .... **20**
See also CWRI 5; DLB 141; MAICYA 1, 2; SATA 17

Brooks, Bruce 1950- **25**
See also AAYA 8, 36; BYA 7, 9; CA 137; CANR 140; JRDA; MAICYA 1, 2; SATA 72, 112; SATA-Brief 53; WYA; YAW

Brooks, George
See Baum, L. Frank

Brooks, Gwendolyn 1917-2000 .... **27**
See also AAYA 20; AFAW 1, 2; AITN 1; AMWS 3; BLC 1:1, 2:1; BW 2, 3; CA 1-4R; 190; CANR 1, 27, 52, 75, 132; CDALB 1941-1968; CLC 1, 2, 4, 5, 15, 49, 125; CP 1, 2, 3, 4, 5, 6, 7; CWP; DA; DA3; DAC; DAM MST, MULT, POET; DLB 5, 76, 165;

EWL 3; EXPP; FL 1:5; MAL 5; MBL; MTCW 1, 2; MTFW 2005; PC 7; PFS 1, 2, 4, 6, 32, 40; RGAL 4; SATA 6; SATA-Obit 123; SSFS 35; TUS; WLC 1; WP

Brooks, Gwendolyn Elizabeth
See Brooks, Gwendolyn

Brooks, Kevin 1959- **201**
See also CA 225; CANR 176; SATA 150, 197, 254

Brothers Grimm
See Grimm, Jacob Ludwig Karl; Grimm, Wilhelm Karl

Brown, Marc (Tolon) 1946- **29**
See also CA 69-72; CANR 36, 79, 130; CWRI 5; MAICYA 1, 2; SATA 10, 53, 80, 145

Brown, Marcia (Joan) 1918- **12**
See also CA 41-44R; CANR 46; CWRI 5; DLB 61; MAICYA 1, 2; MAICYAS 1; SATA 7, 47

Brown, Margaret Wise 1910-1952 ... **10, 107**
See also CA 108; 136; CANR 78; CWRI 5; DLB 22; MAICYA 1, 2; SATA 100; YABC 2

Brown, Roderick (Langmere) Haig-
See Haig-Brown, Roderick (Langmere)

Browne, Anthony 1946- **19, 156, 254**
See also CA 97-100; CANR 36, 78, 82, 176; CWRI 5; MAICYA 1, 2; MAICYAS 1; SATA 45, 61, 105, 163, 280, 343, 370; SATA-Brief 44

Browne, Anthony Edward Tudor
See Browne, Anthony

Browning, Robert 1812-1889 .... **97**
See also BRW 4; BRWC 2; BRWR 3; CDBLB 1832-1890; DA; DA3; DAB; DAC; DAM MST, POET; DLB 32, 163; EXPP; LATS 1:1; NCLC 19, 79; PAB; PC 2, 61, 97; PFS 1, 15, 41; RGEL 2; TEA; WLCS; WLIT 4; WP; YABC 1

Bruchac, Joseph III
See Bruchac, Joseph

Bruchac, Joseph 1942- **46**
See also AAYA 19; CA 33-36R, 256; CAAE 256; CANR 13, 47, 75, 94, 137, 161, 204; CWRI 5; DAM MULT; DLB 342; JRDA; MAICYA 2; MAICYAS 1; MTCW 2; MTFW 2005; NNAL; PFS 36; SATA 42, 89, 131, 176, 228; SATA-Essay 176

Bruna, Dick 1927- **7**
See also CA 112; CANR 36; MAICYA 1, 2; SATA 43, 76; SATA-Brief 30

Brunhoff, Jean de 1899-1937 .... **4, 116**
See also CA 118; 137; MAICYA 1, 2; SATA 24; TWA; WCH

Brunhoff, Laurent de 1925- **4, 116**
See also CA 73-76; CANR 45, 129; MAICYA 1, 2; SATA 24, 71, 150

Bryan, Ashley 1923- **18, 66**
See also AAYA 68; BW 2; CA 107; CANR 26, 43, 156; CWRI 5; MAICYA 1, 2; MAICYAS 1; SATA 31, 72, 132, 178

Bryan, Ashley F.
See Bryan, Ashley

Buck, Pearl S. 1892-1973 .... **238**
See also AAYA 42; AITN 1; AMWS 2; BPFB 1; CA 1-4R, 41-44R; CANR 1, 34; CDALBS; CLC 7, 11, 18, 127; CN 1; DA; DA3; DAB; DAC; DAM MST, NOV; DLB 9, 102, 329; EWL 3; LAIT 3; MAL 5; MTCW 1, 2; MTFW 2005; NFS 25; RGAL 4; RHW; SATA 1, 25; SSFS 33, 39; TUS

Buffie, Margaret 1945- **39**
See also AAYA 23; CA 160; CANR 146; CWRI 5; JRDA; MAICYA 2; MAICYAS 1; SATA 71, 107, 161

Bunting, A.E.
See Bunting, Eve

Bunting, Anne Evelyn
See Bunting, Eve

Bunting, Eve 1928- **28, 56, 82, 189**
See also AAYA 5, 61; BYA 8; CA 53-56; CANR 5, 19, 59, 142, 187; JRDA; MAICYA 1, 2; MAICYAS 1; SATA 18, 64, 110, 158, 196, 235; WYA; YAW

Bunyan, John 1628-1688 .... **124**
See also BRW 2; BYA 5; CDBLB 1660-1789; DA; DAB; DAC; DAM MST; DLB 39; LC 4, 69, 180; NFS 32; RGEL 2; TEA; WCH; WLC 1; WLIT 3

Burbank, L.
See Dr. Seuss

Burch, Robert J(oseph) 1925- **63**
See also BYA 3; CA 5-8R; CANR 2, 17, 71; DLB 52; JRDA; MAICYA 1, 2; SATA 1, 74; YAW

Burgess, Starling
See Tudor, Tasha

Burke, Ralph
See Silverberg, Robert

Burnett, Frances Eliza Hodgson
See Burnett, Frances Hodgson

Burnett, Frances Hodgson 1849-1924 .... **24, 122, 182, 215, 231**
See also BYA 3; CA 108, 136; CWRI 5; DLB 42, 141; DLBD 13, 14; JRDA; MAICYA 1, 2; MTFW 2005; RGAL 4; RGEL 2; SATA 100; TEA; WCH; YABC 2

Burnford, S. D.
See Burnford, Sheila (Philip Cochrane Every)

Burnford, Sheila (Philip Cochrane Every) 1918-1984 .... **2**
See also CA 1-4R; 112; CANR 1, 49; CWRI 5; JRDA; MAICYA 1, 2; SATA 3; SATA-Obit 38

Burningham, John 1936- **9**
See also CA 73-76; CANR 36, 78; CWRI 5; MAICYA 1, 2; SATA 16, 59, 111, 160, 225

Burningham, John Mackintosh
See Burningham, John

Burroughs, Edgar Rice 1875-1950 .... **157**
See also AAYA 11; BPFB 1; BYA 4, 9; CA 104; 132; CANR 131; DA3; DAM NOV; DLB 8, 364; FANT; MTCW 1, 2; MTFW 2005; RGAL 4; SATA 41; SCFW 1, 2; SFW 4; TCLC 2, 32; TCWW 1, 2; TUS; YAW

Burton, Hester (Wood-Hill) 1913-2000 ...... **1**
See also CA 9-12R; CANR 10; DLB 161; MAICYA 1, 2; SAAS 8; SATA 7, 74; YAW

Burton, Virginia Lee 1909-1968 .... **11**
See also CA 13-14; 25-28R; CANR 86; CAP 1; CWRI 5; DLB 22; MAICYA 1, 2; SATA 2, 100; WCH

Buss, Helen M.
See Clarke, Margaret

Butler, Octavia 1947-2006 .... **65, 186**
See also AAYA 18, 48; AFAW 2; AMWS 13; BLC 2:1; BLCS; BPFB 1; BW 2, 3; CA 73-76; 248; CANR 12, 24, 38, 73, 145, 240; CLC 38, 121, 230, 240; CN 7; CPW; DA3; DAM MULT, POP; DLB 33; LATS 1:2; MTCW 1, 2; MTFW 2005; NFS 8, 21, 34; SATA 84; SCFW 2; SFW 4; SSFS 6; TCLE 1:1; YAW

Butler, Octavia E.
See Butler, Octavia

Butler, Octavia Estelle
See Butler, Octavia

Buxton, Ralph
See Silverstein, Alvin; Silverstein, Virginia B.

Byars, Betsy 1928- **1, 16, 72**
See also AAYA 19; BYA 3; CA 33-36R, 183; CAAE 183; CANR 18, 36, 57, 102, 148; CLC 35; DLB 52; INT CANR-18; JRDA; MAICYA 1, 2; MAICYAS 1; MTCW 1; SAAS 1; SATA 4, 46, 80, 163, 223; SATA-Essay 108; WYA; YAW

Byars, Betsy Cromer
See Byars, Betsy

C. 3. 3.
See Wilde, Oscar

Cabot, Meg 1967- **85**
See also AAYA 50; BYA 16; CA 197; CANR 163, 195; SATA 127, 175, 217

Cabot, Meggin
See Cabot, Meg

Cabot, Meggin Patricia
See Cabot, Meg

Cabot, Patricia
See Cabot, Meg

Cadnum, Michael 1949- **78**
See also AAYA 23; BYA 9, 11, 13; CA 151; CANR 90, 147, 176; HGG; SATA 87, 121, 165, 225; WYAS 1; YAW

Caines, Jeannette (Franklin) 1938- **24**
See also BW 2; CA 152; SATA 78; SATA-Brief 43

Caldecott, Randolph (J.) 1846-1886 ... **14, 110**
See also AAYA 64; DLB 163; MAICYA 1, 2; SATA 17, 100

Calhoun, Mary
See Wilkins, Mary Huiskamp

Calkins, Franklin
See Stratemeyer, Edward L.

Calvert, John
See Leaf, (Wilbur) Munro

Cameron, Eleanor (Frances) 1912-1996 .... **1, 72**
See also BYA 3, 5; CA 1-4R; 154; CANR 2, 22; DLB 52; JRDA; MAICYA 1, 2; MAICYAS 1; MTCW 1; SAAS 10; SATA 1, 25; SATA-Obit 93; YAW

Camp, Madeleine L'Engle
See L'Engle, Madeleine

Campbell, Bruce
See Epstein, Samuel

Canfield, Dorothea F.
See Fisher, Dorothy (Frances) Canfield

Canfield, Dorothea Frances
See Fisher, Dorothy (Frances) Canfield

Canfield, Dorothy
See Fisher, Dorothy (Frances) Canfield

Cannon, Janell 1957- **120**
See also MAICYA 2; SATA 78, 128

Cantab, Carl
See Alger, Horatio, Jr.

Card, Orson Scott 1951- **116**
See also AAYA 11, 42; BPFB 1; BYA 5, 8; CA 102; CANR 27, 47, 73, 102, 106, 133, 184; CLC 44, 47, 50, 279; CPW; DA3; DAM POP; FANT; INT CANR-27; MTCW 1, 2; MTFW 2005; NFS 5; SATA 83, 127; SCFW 2; SFW 4; SUFW 2; YAW

Carigiet, Alois 1902-1985 .... **38**
See also CA 73-76; 119; SATA 24; SATA-Obit 47

Carle, Eric 1929- **10, 72**
See also CA 25-28R; CANR 10, 25, 98; CWRI 5; MAICYA 1, 2; SAAS 6; SATA 4, 65, 120, 163

Carroll, Jenny
See Cabot, Meg

Carroll, Lewis 1832-1898 ..... **2, 18, 108, 230**
See also AAYA 39; BRW 5; BYA 5, 13; CDBLB 1832-1890; DA; DA3; DAB; DAC; DAM MST, NOV, POET; DLB 18, 163, 178, 375, 376; DLBY 1998; EXPN; EXPP; FANT; JRDA; LAIT 1, 2; MAICYA 1, 2; NCLC 2, 53, 139, 258, 308; NFS 7; PC 18, 74; PFS 11, 30; RGEL 2; SATA 100; SSFHW 27; SUFW 1; TEA; WCH; WLC 1; YABC 2

Carter, Alden R 1947- 22
See also AAYA 17, 54; CA 135; CANR 58, 114, 154; SAAS 18; SATA 67, 137; WYA; YAW

Carter, Alden Richardson
See Carter, Alden R

Carter, Nick
See Stratemeyer, Edward L.

Carwell, L'Ann
See McKissack, Patricia C.

Cassedy, Sylvia 1930-1989 26
See also CA 105; CANR 22; CWRI 5; JRDA; MAICYA 2; MAICYAS 1; SATA 27, 77; SATA-Obit 61; YAW

Catalanotto, Peter 1959- 68
See also CA 138; CANR 68; MAICYA 2; MAICYAS 1; SAAS 25; SATA 70, 114, 159, 195; SATA-Essay 113

Cather, Willa 1873-1947 98
See also AAYA 24; AMW; AMWC 1; AMWR 1; BPFB 1; CA 104; 128; CDALB 1865-1917; DA; DA3; DAB; DAC; DAM MST, NOV; DLB 9, 54, 78, 256; DLBD 1; EWL 3; EXPN; EXPS; FL 1:5; LAIT 3; LATS 1:1; MAL 5; MBL; MTCW 1, 2; MTFW 2005; NFS 2, 19, 33; RGAL 4; RGSF 2; RHW; SATA 30; SSC 2, 50, 114; SSFS 2, 7, 16, 27; TCLC 1, 11, 31, 99, 132, 152, 264; TCWW 1, 2; TUS; WLC 1

Cather, Willa Sibert
See Cather, Willa

Causley, Charles (Stanley) 1917-2003 30
See also CA 9-12R; 223; CANR 5, 35, 94; CLC 7; CP 1, 2, 3, 4, 5; CWRI 5; DLB 27; MTCW 1; SATA 3, 66; SATA-Obit 149

Chambers, Aidan 1934- 151
See also AAYA 27, 86; CA 25-28R; CANR 12, 31, 58, 116; CLC 35; JRDA; MAICYA 1, 2; SAAS 12; SATA 1, 69, 108, 171; WYA; YAW

Chambers, Catherine E.
See St. John, Nicole

Chambers, Kate
See St. John, Nicole

Chance, Stephen
See Turner, Philip (William)

Chapman, Jean 65
See also CA 97-100; SATA 34, 104

Chapman, Lee
See Bradley, Marion Zimmer

Chapman, Walker
See Silverberg, Robert

Charles, Louis
See Stratemeyer, Edward L.

Charles, Nicholas
See Kuskin, Karla

Charles, Nicholas J.
See Kuskin, Karla

Charlip, Remy 1929- 8
See also CA 33-36R; CANR 44, 97; MAICYA 1, 2; SATA 4, 68, 119

Chase, Alice
See McHargue, Georgess

Chauncy, Nan(cen Beryl Masterman) 1900-1970 6
See also CA 1-4R; CANR 4; CWRI 5; MAICYA 1, 2; SATA 6

Childress, Alice 1920-1994 14
See also AAYA 8; BLC 1:1; BW 2, 3; BYA 2; CA 45-48; 146; CAD; CANR 3, 27, 50, 74; CLC 12, 15, 86, 96; CWD; DA3; DAM DRAM, MULT, NOV; DC 4; DFS 2, 8, 14, 26; DLB 7, 38, 249; JRDA; LAIT 5; MAICYA 1, 2; MAICYAS 1; MAL 5; MTCW 1, 2; MTFW 2005; RGAL 4; SATA 7, 48, 81; TCLC 116; TUS; WYA; YAW

Chimaera
See Farjeon, Eleanor

Choi, Sook Nyul 1937- 53
See also AAYA 38; CA 197; CAAE 197; MAICYA 2; MAICYAS 1; NFS 29; SATA 73; SATA-Essay 126

Christie, Ann Philippa
See Pearce, Philippa

Christie, Philippa
See Pearce, Philippa

Christopher, John
See Youd, Samuel

Christopher, Matt(hew Frederick) 1917-1997 .... 33, 119
See also BYA 8; CA 1-4R; 161; CANR 5, 36, 104; JRDA; MAICYA 1, 2; SAAS 9; SATA 2, 47, 80; SATA-Obit 99

Chukovsky, Kornei Ivanovich 1882-1969 239
See also CA 5-8R, 25-28R; CANR 4, 42; MAICYA 1, 2; SATA 5, 34

Ciardi, John (Anthony) 1916-1986 19
See also CA 5-8R; 118; CAAS 2; CANR 5, 33; CLC 10, 40, 44, 129; CP 1, 2, 3, 4; CWRI 5; DAM POET; DLB 5; DLBY 1986; INT CANR-5; MAICYA 1, 2; MAL 5; MTCW 1, 2; MTFW 2005; PC 69; RGAL 4; SAAS 26; SATA 1, 65; SATA-Obit 46

Cisneros, Sandra 1954- 123
See also AAYA 9, 53; AMWS 7; CA 131; CANR 64, 118; CLC 69, 118, 193, 305; CN 7; CWP; DA3; DAM MULT; DLB 122, 152; EWL 3; EXPN; EXPS; FL 1:5; FW; HLC 1; HW 1, 2; LAIT 5; LATS 1:2; LLW; MAICYA 2; MAL 5; MTCW 2; MTFW 2005; NFS 2; PC 52; PFS 19; RGAL 4; RGSF 2; SSC 32, 72, 143; SSFS 3, 13, 27, 32; WLIT 1; YAW

Clare, Helen
See Clarke, Pauline

Clark, Ann Nolan 1896-1995 16
See also BYA 4; CA 5-8R; 150; CANR 2, 48; CWRI 5; DLB 52; MAICYA 1, 2; MAICYAS 1; SAAS 16; SATA 4, 82; SATA-Obit 87

Clark, M. R.
See Clark, Mavis Thorpe

Clark, Mavis Thorpe 1909-1999 30
See also CA 57-60; CANR 8, 37, 107; CLC 12; CWRI 5; MAICYA 1, 2; SAAS 5; SATA 8, 74

Clarke, Arthur
See Clarke, Arthur C.

Clarke, Arthur C. 1917-2008 119
See also AAYA 4, 33; BPFB 1; BYA 13; CA 1-4R; 270; CANR 2, 28, 55, 74, 130, 196; CLC 1, 4, 13, 18, 35, 136; CN 1, 2, 3, 4, 5, 6, 7; CPW; DA3; DAM POP; DLB 261; JRDA; LAIT 5; MAICYA 1, 2; MTCW 1, 2; MTFW 2005; SATA 13, 70, 115; SATA-Obit 191; SCFW 1, 2; SFW 4; SSC 3; SSFS 4, 18, 29; TCLE 1:1; YAW

Clarke, Arthur Charles
See Clarke, Arthur C.

Clarke, J.
See Clarke, Judith

Clarke, Judith 1943- 61
See also AAYA 34; CA 142; CANR 123, 184; SATA 75, 110, 164

Clarke, Margaret 1941- 99
See also CA 130

Clarke, Pauline 1921- 28
See also CANR 45; CWRI 5; DLB 161; MAICYA 1, 2; SATA 3, 131

Cleary, Beverly 1916- 2, 8, 72, 229
See also AAYA 6, 62; BYA 1; CA 1-4R; CANR 2, 19, 36, 66, 85, 129; CMTFW; CWRI 5; DA3; DLB 52; INT CANR-19; JRDA; MAICYA 1, 2; MTCW 1, 2; MTFW 2005; SAAS 20; SATA 2, 43, 79, 121; TUS

Cleary, Beverly Atlee Bunn
See Cleary, Beverly

Cleaver, Bill
See Cleaver, William J.

Cleaver, Elizabeth (Ann Mrazik) 1939-1985 13
See also CA 97-100; 117; MAICYA 2; MAICYAS 1; SATA 23; SATA-Obit 43

Cleaver, Vera 1919-1993 6
See also AAYA 12; BYA 3; CA 73-76; 161; CANR 38; DLB 52; JRDA; MAICYA 1, 2; SATA 22, 76; WYA; YAW 1

Cleaver, Vera Allen
See Cleaver, Vera

Cleaver, William J. 1920-1981 6
See also BYA 3; CA 175; 104; CANR 38; DLB 52; JRDA; MAICYA 1, 2; SATA 22; SATA-Obit 27; WYA; YAW

Cleaver, William Joseph
See Cleaver, William J.

Cleishbotham, Jebediah
See Scott, Sir Walter

Clemens, Samuel
See Twain, Mark

Clemens, Samuel Langhorne
See Twain, Mark

Clement, Hal 1922-2003 197
See also CA 13-16R; 224; CAAS 16; CANR 7, 26; DLB 8; SCFW 1, 2; SFW 4

Clerk, N. W.
See Lewis, C. S.

Clifton, Lucille 1936-2010 .... 5, 251
See also AFAW 2; BLC 1:1, 2:1; BW 2, 3; CA 49-52; CANR 2, 24, 42, 76, 97, 138; CLC 19, 66, 162, 283; CMTFW; CP 2, 3, 4, 5, 6, 7; CSW; CWP; CWRI 5; DA3; DAM MULT, POET; DLB 5, 41; EXPP; MAICYA 1, 2; MTCW 1, 2; MTFW 2005; PC 17, 148; PFS 1, 14, 29, 41; SATA 20, 69, 128, 284; SSFS 34; WP

Clifton, Thelma Lucille
See Clifton, Lucille

Climo, Shirley 1928- 69
See also CA 107; CANR 24, 49, 91, 152; CWRI 5; SATA 39, 77, 166; SATA-Brief 35; SATA-Essay 110

Clinton, Dirk
See Silverberg, Robert

Clowes, Daniel 1961- 198
See also AAYA 42; CA 191; CANR 186, 226; CMTFW; MTFW

Coatsworth, Elizabeth (Jane) 1893-1986 2
See also BYA 5; CA 5-8R; 120; CANR 4, 78; CWRI 5; DLB 22; MAICYA 1, 2; SATA 2, 56, 100; SATA-Obit 49; YAW

Cobalt, Martin
See Mayne, William

Cobb, Vicki 1938- 2
See also CA 33-36R; CANR 14; JRDA; MAICYA 1, 2; SAAS 6; SATA 8, 69, 131, 136; SATA-Essay 136

Coburton, John
See Tarkington, Booth

Coe, Douglas
See Epstein, Beryl; Epstein, Samuel

Cohen, Daniel (E.) 1936- 3, 43
See also AAYA 7; CA 45-48; CANR 1, 20, 44; JRDA; MAICYA 1, 2; SAAS 4; SATA 8, 70

Cole, Brock 1938- 18
See also AAYA 15, 45; BYA 10; CA 136; CANR 115, 191; JRDA; MAICYA 1, 2; SATA 72, 136, 200; WYA; YAW

Cole, Joanna 1944- 5, 40
See also CA 115; CANR 36, 55, 70, 98; MAICYA 1, 2; SATA 49, 81, 120, 168, 231; SATA-Brief 37

Colfer, Eoin 1965- **112**
See also AAYA 48; BYA 16; CA 205; CANR 131, 181; SATA 148, 197

Colin, Ann
See Ure, Jean

Collier, Christopher 1930- **126**
See also AAYA 13; BYA 2; CA 33-36R; CANR 13, 33, 102; CLC 30; JRDA; MAICYA 1, 2; NFS 38; SATA 16, 70; WYA; YAW 1

Collier, James Lincoln 1928- **3, 126**
See also AAYA 13; BYA 2; CA 9-12R; CANR 4, 33, 60, 102, 208; CLC 30; DAM POP; JRDA; MAICYA 1, 2; NFS 38; SAAS 21; SATA 8, 70, 166; WYA; YAW 1

Collins, Suzanne 1962- **203**
See also AAYA 86; CA 258; CANR 207, 268; CLC 355; SATA 180, 224, 280

Collodi, Carlo 1826-1890 .... **5, 120**
See also MAICYA 1,2; NCLC 54; SATA 29, 100; WCH; WLIT 7

Colt, Martin
See Epstein, Beryl; Epstein, Samuel

Colum, Padraic 1881-1972 .... **36**
See also AAYA by 4; CA 73-76; 33-36R; CANR 35; CLC 28; CP 1; CWRI 5; DLB 19; MAICYA 1, 2; MTCW 1; RGEL 2; SATA 15; WCH

Colvin, James
See Moorcock, Michael

Comenius, John Amos 1592-1670 .... **191**

Comus
See Ballantyne, R(obert) M(ichael)

Conan Doyle, Arthur
See Doyle, Sir Arthur Conan

Conford, Ellen 1942- **10, 71**
See also AAYA 10, 70; CA 33-36R; CANR 13, 29, 54, 111; JRDA; MAICYA 1, 2; SATA 6, 68, 110, 162; YAW

Conly, Robert Leslie
See O'Brien, Robert C.

Conrad, Pam 1947-1996 .... **18**
See also AAYA 18; BYA 7, 8; CA 121; 151; CANR 36, 78, 111; JRDA; MAICYA 1, 2; MAICYAS 1; SAAS 19; SATA 52, 80, 133; SATA-Brief 49; SATA-Obit 90; YAW

Cook, Roy
See Silverberg, Robert

Cooke, Ann
See Cole, Joanna

Cooke, John Estes
See Baum, L. Frank

Susan Coolidge 1835-1905 .... **206**
See also CA 115; DLB 42

Cooney, Barbara 1917-2000 .... **23**
See also CA 5-8R; 190; CANR 3, 37, 67; CWRI 5; MAICYA 1, 2; SATA 6, 59, 96; SATA-Obit 123

Cooper, Floyd **60**
See also CA 161; CANR 124, 173; MAICYA 2; MAICYAS 1; SATA 96, 144, 187, 227

Cooper, James Fenimore 1789-1851 ... **105, 188**
See also AAYA 22; AMW; BPFB 1; CDALB 1640-1865; DA3; DLB 3, 183, 250, 254; LAIT 1; NCLC 1, 27, 54, 203; NFS 25; RGAL 4; SATA 19; TUS; WCH

Cooper, Susan 1935- **4, 67, 161, 253**
See also AAYA 13, 41; BYA 5; CA 29-32R, 369; CANR 15, 37, 63, 103, 137; DLB 161, 261; FANT; JRDA; MAICYA 1, 2; MTCW 2; MTFW 2005; SAAS 6; SATA 4, 64, 104, 151, 256, 332, 361; SSFHW; SUFW 2; YAW

Corbett, Scott 1913- **1**
See also CA 1-4R; CANR 1, 23; CWRI 5; JRDA; MAICYA 1, 2; SAAS 2; SATA 2, 42

Corbett, W(illiam) J(esse) 1938- **19**
See also CA 137; CWRI 5; FANT; MAICYA 1, 2; SATA 50, 102; SATA-Brief 44

Corcoran, Barbara (Asenath) 1911-2003 **50**
See also AAYA 14; CA 21-24R, 191; CAAE 191; CAAS 2; CANR 11, 28, 48; CLC 17; DLB 52; JRDA; MAICYA 2; MAICYAS 1; RHW; SAAS 20; SATA 3, 77; SATA-Essay 125

Cormier, Robert 1925-2000 .... **12, 55, 167, 243**
See also AAYA 3, 19; BYA 1, 2, 6, 8, 9; CA 1-4R; CANR 5, 23, 76, 93; CDALB 1968-1988; CLC 12, 30; DA; DAB; DAC; DAM MST, NOV; DLB 52; EXPN; INT CANR-23; JRDA; LAIT 5; MAICYA 1, 2; MTCW 1, 2; MTFW 2005; NFS 2, 18; SATA 10, 45, 83; SATA-Obit 122; WYA; YAW

Cormier, Robert Edmund
See Cormier, Robert

Cowles, Kathleen
See Krull, Kathleen

Cowley, Cassia Joy
See Cowley, Joy

Cowley, Joy 1936- **55**
See also CA 25-28R; CANR 11, 57, 124, 203; CWRI 5; MAICYA 2; SAAS 26; SATA 4, 90, 164; SATA-Essay 118

Cox, Palmer 1840-1924 .... **24**
See also CA 111; 185; DLB 42; SATA 24

Cracken, Jael
See Aldiss, Brian W.

Craig, A. A.
See Anderson, Poul

Crane, Stephen 1871-1900 .... **132, 272**
See also AAYA 21; AMW; AMWC 1; BPFB 1; BYA 3; CA 109, 140; CANR 84; CDALB 1865-1917; DA; DA3; DAB; DAC; DAM MST, NOV, POET; DLB 12, 54, 78, 357, 378; EXPN; EXPS; LAIT 2; LMFS 2; MAL 5; NFS 4, 20; PC 80; PFS 9; RGAL 4; RGSF 2; SSC 7, 56, 70, 129, 194, 223, 276, 291; SSFS 4, 28, 34, 38; TCLC 11, 17, 32, 216; TUS; WLC 2; WYA; YABC 2

Crane, Stephen Townley
See Crane, Stephen

Crane, Walter 1845-1915 .... **56**
See also CA 168; DLB 163; MAICYA 1, 2; SATA 18, 100

Cranshaw, Stanley
See Fisher, Dorothy (Frances) Canfield

Crayon, Geoffrey
See Irving, Washington

Creech, Sharon 1945- **42, 89, 164**
See also AAYA 21, 52; BYA 9, 11, 12; CA 159; CANR 113, 188; MAICYA 2; MAICYAS 1; SATA 94, 139, 172, 226; WYAS 1; YAW

Cresswell, Helen 1934-2005 .... **18**
See also AAYA 25; CA 17-20R; 243; CANR 8, 37; CWRI 5; DLB 161; JRDA; MAICYA 1, 2; SAAS 20; SATA 1, 48, 79; SATA-Obit 168

Crew, Gary 1947- **42**
See also AAYA 17; CA 142; CANR 83, 148; HGG; MAICYA 2; SATA 75, 110, 163; YAW

Crews, Donald 1938- **7**
See also CA 108; CANR 83, 104; CWRI 5; MAICYA 1, 2; SATA 32, 76; SATA-Brief 30

Cronin, Doreen 1966(?)- **105, 136**
See also SATA 178

Cronin, Doreen A.
See Cronin, Doreen

Crosby, Margaret
See Rathmann, Peggy

Cross, Gillian 1945- **28**
See also AAYA 24; BYA 9; CA 111; CANR 38, 81, 151, 193; DLB 161; JRDA; MAICYA 1, 2; MAICYAS 1; SATA 38, 71, 110, 165, 178; SATA-Essay 178; YAW

Cross, Gillian Clare
See Cross, Gillian

Crossley-Holland, Kevin 1941- **47, 84**
See also AAYA 57; CA 41-44R; CANR 47, 84, 102; CP 1, 2, 3, 4, 5, 6, 7; DLB 40, 161; MAICYA 1, 2; SAAS 20; SATA 5, 74, 120, 165; YAW

Crowfield, Christopher
See Stowe, Harriet Beecher

Cruikshank, George 1792-1878 .... **63**
See also SATA 22

Crutcher, Chris 1946- **28, 159**
See also AAYA 9, 39; BYA 8, 14, 15; CA 113; CANR 36, 84, 134, 187; JRDA; MAICYA 1, 2; MAICYAS 1; MTFW 2005; NFS 11, 32; SATA 52, 99, 153, 196; WYA; YAW

Crutcher, Christopher C.
See Crutcher, Chris

Culper, Felix
See McCaughrean, Geraldine

Cummings, Pat 1950- **48**
See also BW 2; CA 122; CANR 44, 88; CWRI 5; MAICYA 1, 2; MAICYAS 1; SAAS 13; SATA 42, 71, 107, 203

Curry, Jane L(ouise) 1932- **31**
See also CA 17-20R; CANR 7, 24, 44; CWRI 5; MAICYA 1, 2; SAAS 6; SATA 1, 52, 90, 138; SATA-Essay 138

Curtis, Christopher Paul
1953- **68, 172**
See also AAYA 37; BW 3; BYA 11, 13; CA 159; CANR 80, 119, 173; MAICYA 2; SATA 93, 140, 187; YAW

Curtis, Jamie Lee 1958- **88**
See also CA 160; CANR 124; SATA 95, 144

Cushman, Karen 1941- **55**
See also AAYA 22, 60; BYA 9, 13; CA 155; CANR 130; MAICYA 2; MAICYAS 1; SATA 89, 147; WYAS 1; YAW

Dahl, Roald 1916-1990 .... **1, 7, 41, 111, 224**
See also AAYA 15; BPFB 1; BRWS 4; BYA 5; CA 1-4R, 133; CANR 6, 32, 37, 62; CLC 1, 6, 18, 79; CN 1, 2, 3, 4; CPW; DA3; DAB; DAC; DAM MST, NOV, POP; DLB 139, 255; HGG; JRDA; MAICYA 1, 2; MTCW 1, 2; MTFW 2005; RGSF 2; SATA 1, 26, 73; SATA-Obit 65; SSC 252; SSFS 4, 30; TCLC 173, 312; TEA; YAW

Dale, George E.
See Asimov, Isaac

Dalgliesh, Alice 1893-1979 .... **62**
See also CA 73-76; 89-92; CWRI 5; MAICYA 1, 2; SATA 17; SATA-Obit 21

Daly, Jim
See Stratemeyer, Edward L.

Daly, Maureen 1921-2006 .... **96, 262**
See also AAYA 5, 58; BYA 6; CA 253; CANR 37, 83, 108; CLC 17; DLB 389; JRDA; MAICYA 1, 2; SAAS 1; SATA 2, 129; SATA-Obit 176; WYA; YAW

Daly, Nicholas
See Daly, Niki

Daly, Niki 1946- **41**
See also CA 111; CANR 36, 123, 212; CWRI 5; MAICYA 1, 2; SAAS 21; SATA 37, 76, 114, 164, 198

Dangerfield, Balfour
See McCloskey, (John) Robert

Danziger, Paula 1944-2004 .... **20**
See also AAYA 4, 36; BYA 6, 7, 14; CA 112; 115; 229; CANR 37, 132; CLC 21; JRDA; MAICYA 1, 2; MTFW 2005; SATA 36, 63, 102, 149; SATA-Brief 30; SATA-Obit 155; WYA; YAW

Dare, Geena
See McNicoll, Sylvia (Marilyn)

Darling, Sandra Louise Woodward
See Day, Alexandra

Daugherty, James (Henry) 1889-1974 ..... **78**
See also BYA 1, 3; CA 73-76; 49-52; CANR 81; CWRI 5; MAICYA 1, 2; SATA 13; WCH

d'Aulaire, Edgar Parin 1898-1986 .... **21**
See also CA 49-52; 119; CANR 29; CWRI 5; DLB 22; MAICYA 1, 2; SATA 5, 66; SATA-Obit 47

d'Aulaire, Ingri 1904-1980 .... **21**
See also CA 49-52; 102; CANR 29; CWRI 5; DLB 22; MAICYA 1, 2; SATA 5, 66; SATA-Obit 24

d'Aulaire, Ingri Mortenson Parin
See d'Aulaire, Ingri

Davis, Ossie 1917-2005 .... **56**
See also AAYA 17; BW 2, 3; CA 112; 236; CAD; CANR 26, 53, 76; CD 5, 6; CSW; DA3; DAM DRAM, MULT; DLB 7, 38, 249; MTCW 2; SATA 81

Day, Alexandra 1941- **22**
See also CA 136; MAICYA 2; MAICYAS 1; SAAS 19; SATA 67, 97, 169, 197; SATA-Essay 197

de Angeli, Marguerite (Lofft) 1889-1987 .. **1**
See also AITN 2; BYA 1; CA 5-8R; 122; CANR 3; CWRI 5; DLB 22; MAICYA 1, 2; SATA 1, 27, 100; SATA-Obit 51

de Brissac, Malcolm
See Dickinson, Peter

de Brunhoff, Jean
See Brunhoff, Jean de

De Brunhoff, Laurent
See Brunhoff, Laurent de

DeClements, Barthe 1920- **23**
See also CA 105; CANR 22, 45, 103; JRDA; MAICYA 2; MAICYAS 1; SATA 35, 71, 131

DeClements, Barthe Faith
See DeClements, Barthe

de Conte, Sieur Louis
See Twain, Mark

Defoe, Daniel 1660(?)-1731 .... **61, 164**
See also AAYA 27; BRW 3; BRWR 1; BYA 4; CDBLB 1660-1789; DA; DA3; DAB; DAC; DAM MST, NOV; DLB 39, 95, 101, 336; JRDA; LAIT 1; LC 1, 42, 105, 180; LMFS 1; MAICYA 1, 2; NFS 9, 13, 30; RGEL 2; SATA 22; TEA; WCH; WLC 2; WLIT 3

DeJong, Meindert 1906-1991 .... **1, 73**
See also BYA 2, 3; CA 13-16R; 134; CANR 36, 105; CWRI 5; DLB 52; MAICYA 1, 2; SATA 2; SATA-Obit 68

de la Mare, Walter (John)
1873-1956 .... **23, 148**
See also AAYA 81; CA 163; CDBLB 1914-1945; CWRI 5; DA3; DAB; DAC; DAM MST, POET; DLB 19, 153, 162, 255, 284; EWL 3; EXPP; HGG; MAICYA 1, 2; MTCW 2; MTFW 2005; PC 77; PFS 39; RGEL 2; RGSF 2; SATA 16; SSC 14; SUFW 1; TCLC 4, 53; TEA; WCH; WLC 2

Delessert, Etienne 1941- **81**
See also CA 21-24R; CANR 13, 37, 102, 165; MAICYA 1, 2; SATA 46, 130, 179; SATA-Brief 27

Delving, Michael
See Williams, Jay

Demi 1942- **58**
See also CA 61-64; CANR 8, 35; MAICYA 1, 2; SATA 11, 66, 102, 152, 210

Demijohn, Thom
See Disch, Thomas M.

Denim, Sue
See Pilkey, Dav

Denslow, W(illiam) W(allace) 1856-1915 ... **15**
See also CA 211; DLB 188; SATA 16

Denton, Kady MacDonald **71**
See also CA 134; MAICYA 2; SATA 66, 110, 181

dePaola, Thomas Anthony 1934- **4, 24, 81**
See also CA 49-52; CANR 2, 37, 130; CWRI 5; DLB 61; MAICYA 1, 2; MTFW 2005; SAAS 15; SATA 11, 59, 108, 155, 200

dePaola, Tomie
See dePaola, Thomas Anthony

de Roo, Anne Louise 1931-1997 .... **63**
See also CA 103; CANR 51; CWRI 5; SATA 25, 84

Derry Down Derry
See Lear, Edward

Desai, Anita 1937- **249**
See also AAYA 85; BRWS 5; CA 81-84; CANR 33, 53, 95, 133; CLC 19, 37, 97, 175, 271; CMTFW; CN 1, 2, 3, 4, 5, 6, 7; CWRI 5; DA3; DAB; DAM NOV; DLB 271, 323; DNFS 2; EWL 3; FW; MTCW 1, 2; MTFW 2005; NFS 44; SATA 63, 126; SSC 168; SSFS 28, 31

Dessen Sarah 1970- **192**
See also AAYA 39, 86; BYA 12, 16; CA 196; CANR 155, 203; SATA 120, 172, 252

Dexter, John
See Bradley, Marion Zimmer

de Zubizarreta, Alma
See Ada, Alma Flor

Dhondy, Farrukh 1944- **41, 234**
See also AAYA 24; CA 132; CANR 81, 138; MAICYA 1, 2; SATA 65, 152; YAW

Diaz, David 1959(?)- **65**
See also MAICYA 2; MAICYAS 1; SATA 96, 150, 189, 229

di Bassetto, Corno
See Shaw, George Bernard

DiCamillo, Kate 1964- **117, 216**
See also AAYA 47; BYA 15; CA 192; CANR 148, 183; SATA 121, 163, 202

Dickens, Charles 1812-1870 ..... **95, 162, 271**
See also AAYA 23; BRW 5; BRWC 1, 2; BYA 1, 2, 3, 13, 14; CDBLB 1832-1890; CMW 4; DA; DA3; DAB; DAC; DAM MST, NOV; DLB 21, 55, 70, 159, 166; EXPN; GL 2; HGG; JRDA; LAIT 1, 2; LATS 1:1; LMFS 1; MAICYA 1, 2; NCLC 3, 8, 18, 26, 37, 50, 86, 105, 113, 161, 187, 203, 206, 211, 217, 219, 230, 231, 239, 285, 307, 318, 341, 410, 420; NFS 4, 5, 10, 14, 20, 25, 30, 33, 41; RGEL 2; RGSF 2; SATA 15; SSC 17, 49, 88, 215, 298, 310, 324; SUFW 1; TEA; WCH; WLC 2; WLIT 4; WYA

Dickens, Charles John Huffam
See Dickens, Charles

Dickinson, Mary-Anne
See Rodda, Emily

Dickinson, Peter 1927- **29, 125**
See also AAYA 9, 49; BYA 5; CA 41-44R; CANR 31, 58, 88, 134, 195; CLC 12, 35; CMW 4; DLB 87, 161, 276; JRDA; MAICYA 1, 2; SATA 5, 62, 95, 150, 229; SFW 4; WYA; YAW

Dickinson, Peter Malcolm de Brissac
See Dickinson, Peter

Dillon, Diane 1933- **44**
See also MAICYA 1, 2; SATA 15, 51, 106, 194

Dillon, Diane Claire
See Dillon, Diane

Dillon, Eilis 1920-1994 .... **26**
See also CA 9-12R; 147; CAAE 182; CAAS 3; CANR 4, 38, 78; CLC 17; MAICYA 1, 2; MAICYAS 1; SATA 2, 74; SATA-Essay 105; SATA-Obit 83; YAW

Dillon, Leo 1933- **44**
See also MAICYA 1, 2; SATA 15, 51, 106, 194

Disch, Thomas M. 1940-2008 .... **18**
See also AAYA 17; BPFB 1; CA 21-24R; 274; CAAS 4; CANR 17, 36, 54, 89; CLC 7, 36, 325; CP 5, 6, 7; DA3; DLB 8, 282; HGG; MAICYA 1, 2; MTCW 1, 2; MTFW 2005; SAAS 15; SATA 92; SATA-Obit 195; SCFW 1, 2; SFW 4; SUFW 2

Disch, Thomas Michael
See Disch, Thomas M.

Disch, Tom
See Disch, Thomas M.

Disney, Walt 1901-1966 .... **223**
See also AAYA 22; CA 107, 159; DLB 22; IDFW 3, 4; SATA 27, 28

Dixon, Franklin W.
See McFarlane, Leslie; Stratemeyer, Edward L.

Dixon, Paige
See Corcoran, Barbara (Asenath)

Doctor X
See Nourse, Alan E(dward)

Doctorow, Cory 1971- **194**
See also AAYA 84; CA 221; CANR 203, 252; CLC 273; SATA 254

Dodd, Lynley (Stuart) 1941- **62**
See also CA 107; CANR 25, 51; CWRI 5; SATA 35, 86, 132

Dodge, Mary (Elizabeth) Mapes
1831(?)-1905 .... **62**
See also BYA 2; CA 109; 137; DLB 42, 79; DLBD 13; MAICYA 1, 2; SATA 21, 100; WCH

Dodgson, Charles Lutwidge
See Carroll, Lewis

Dogyear, Drew
See Gorey, Edward (St. John)

Doherty, Berlie 1943- **21**
See also AAYA 18, 75; CA 131; CANR 126; JRDA; MAICYA 1, 2; SAAS 16; SATA 72, 111; YAW

Domanska, Janina 1913(?)-1995 .... **40**
See also AITN 1; CA 17-20R; 147; CANR 11, 45; MAICYA 1, 2; MAICYAS 1; SAAS 18; SATA 6, 68; SATA-Obit 84

Donnelly, Elfie 1950- **104**

Donovan, John 1928-1992 .... **3, 183**
See also AAYA 20; CA 97-100; 137; CLC 35; MAICYA 1, 2; SATA 72; SATA-Brief 29; YAW

Dorris, Michael 1945-1997 .... **58**
See also AAYA 20; BEST 90:1; BYA 12; CA 102; 157; CANR 19, 46, 75; CLC 109; DA3; DAM MULT, NOV; DLB 175; LAIT 5; MTCW 2; MTFW 2005; NFS 3; NNAL; RGAL 4; SATA 75; SATA-Obit 94; TCWW 2; YAW

Dorris, Michael A.
See Dorris, Michael

Dorris, Michael Anthony
See Dorris, Michael

Dorritt, Susan
See Schlein, Miriam

Dorros, Arthur 1950- **42**
See also CA 146; CANR 93, 157; MAICYA 2; MAICYAS 1; SAAS 20; SATA 78, 122, 168

Dorros, Arthur M.
See Dorros, Arthur

Douglas, Leonard
See Bradbury, Ray

Dowdy, Mrs. Regera
See Gorey, Edward (St. John)

Doyle, A. Conan
See Doyle, Sir Arthur Conan

Doyle, Sir Arthur Conan 1859-1930 ..... **106**
See also AAYA 14; BPFB 1; BRWS 2; BYA 4, 5, 11; CA 104; 122; CANR 131; CDBLB 1890-1914; CMW 4; DA; DA3; DAB; DAC; DAM MST, NOV; DLB 18, 70, 156, 178; EXPS; HGG; LAIT 2; MSW; MTCW 1, 2; MTFW 2005; NFS 28; RGEL 2; RGSF 2; RHW; SATA 24; SCFW 1, 2; SFW 4; SSC 12, 83, 95; SSFS 2; TCLC 7; TEA; WCH; WLC 2; WLIT 4; WYA; YAW

Doyle, Brian 1935- **22**
See also AAYA 16; CA 135; CANR 55, 140, 194; CCA 1; JRDA; MAICYA 1, 2; SAAS 16; SATA 67, 104, 156; YAW

Doyle, Conan
See Doyle, Sir Arthur Conan

Doyle, Malachy 1954- **83**
See also CA 191; CANR 156; SATA 120, 165
Doyle, Sir A. Conan
See Doyle, Sir Arthur Conan
Dr. A
See Asimov, Isaac; Silverstein, Alvin; Silverstein, Virginia B.
Dr. Seuss 1904-1991 .... **1, 9, 53, 100, 211**
See also AAYA 48; AMWS 16; CA 13-16R; 135; CANR 13, 32, 132; DA3; DLB 61; DLBY 1991; MAICYA 1, 2; MTCW 1, 2; MTFW 2005; SATA 1, 28, 75, 100; SATA-Obit 67; TUS
Draper, Sharon
See Draper, Sharon M.
Draper, Sharon M. 1948- **57**
See also AAYA 28; CANR 124, 169, 186; MAICYA 2; SATA 98, 146, 195; SATA-Essay 146; YAW
Draper, Sharon Mills
See Draper, Sharon M.
Drapier, M. B.
See Swift, Jonathan
Drescher, Henrik 1955- **20**
See also CA 135; MAICYA 1, 2; SATA 67, 105, 172
Driving Hawk, Virginia
See Sneve, Virginia Driving Hawk
Drummond, Walter
See Silverberg, Robert
Druse, Eleanor
See King, Stephen
Dryden, Pamela
See St. John, Nicole
D.T., Hughes
See Hughes, Dean
du Bois, William Pene
See Pene du Bois, William (Sherman)
Duder, Tessa 1940- **43**
See also CA 147; CANR 96; MAICYA 2; MAICYAS 1; SAAS 23; SATA 80, 117; YAW
Duke, Kate 1956- **51**
See also CA 188; MAICYA 2; SATA 90, 148, 192
Dumas, Alexandre (père)
1802-1870 .... **134, 205, 257, 271**
See also AAYA 22; BYA 3; DA; DA3; DAB; DAC; DAM MST, NOV; DLB 119, 192; EW 6; GFL 1789 to the Present; LAIT 1, 2; NCLC 11, 71, 271, 399; NFS 14, 19, 41; RGWL 2, 3; SATA 18; TWA; WCH; WLC 2
Duncan, Lois 1934- **29, 129**
See also AAYA 4, 34; BYA 6, 8; CA 1-4R; CANR 2, 23, 36, 111; CLC 26; JRDA; MAICYA 1, 2; MAICYAS 1; MTFW 2005; SAAS 2; SATA 1, 36, 75, 133, 141, 219; SATA-Essay 141; WYA; YAW
Dunne, Marie
See Clark, Ann Nolan
Duvoisin, Roger (Antoine) 1904-1980 ...... **23**
See also CA 13-16R; 101; CANR 11; CWRI 5; DLB 61; MAICYA 1, 2; SATA 2, 30; SATA-Obit 23
Eager, Edward (McMaken) 1911-1964 .... **43**
See also CA 73-76; CANR 87; CWRI 5; DLB 22; FANT; MAICYA 1, 2; SATA 17
Eastman, Charles Alexander 1858-1939 .. **214**
See also CA 179; CANR 91; DLB 175; DAM MULT; NNAL; TCLC 55; YABC
Eckenpfeifer, Jeremias
See Salten, Felix
Eckert, Horst 1931- **26**
See also CA 37-40R; CANR 38; MAICYA 1, 2; SATA 8, 72
Edgeworth, Maria 1768-1849 .... **153**
See also BRWS 3; DLB 116, 159, 163; FL 1:3; FW; NCLC 1, 51, 158; RGEL 2; SATA 21; SSC 86; TEA; WLIT 3

Edgy, Wardore
See Gorey, Edward (St. John)
Edison, Theodore
See Stratemeyer, Edward L.
Edmund, Sean
See Pringle, Laurence
Edwards, Al
See Nourse, Alan E(dward)
Edwards, Julia
See Stratemeyer, Edward L.
Edwards, Julie
See Andrews, Julie
Edwards, Julie Andrews
See Andrews, Julie
Ehlert, Lois 1934- **28**
See also CA 137; CANR 107, 174; CWRI 5; MAICYA 1, 2; SATA 35, 69, 128, 172, 237
Ehlert, Lois Jane
See Ehlert, Lois
Eliot, Dan
See Silverberg, Robert
Ellen, Jaye
See Nixon, Joan Lowery
Elliott, Don
See Silverberg, Robert
Elliott, William
See Bradbury, Ray
Ellis, Sarah 1952- **42**
See also AAYA 57; CA 123; CANR 50, 84, 165; JRDA; MAICYA 2; MAICYAS 1; SATA 68, 131, 179; YAW
Ellison, Ralph 1914-1994 .... **197**
See also AAYA 19; AFAW 1, 2; AMWC 2; AMWR 2; AMWS 2; BPFB 1; BW 1, 3; BYA 2; CA 9-12R; 145; CANR 24, 53; CDALB 1941-1968; CN 1, 2, 3, 4, 5; CSW; DA; DA3; DAB; DAC; DAM MST, MULT, NOV; DLB 2, 76, 227; DLBY 1994; EWL 3; EXPN; EXPS; LAIT 4; MAL 5; MTCW 1, 2; MTFW 2005; NCFS 3; NFS 2, 21; RGAL 4; RGSF 2; SSFS 1, 11; YAW
Emberley, Barbara A. 1932- **5**
See also CA 5-8R; CANR 5, 129; MAICYA 1, 2; SATA 8, 70, 146
Emberley, Barbara Anne
See Emberley, Barbara A.
Emberley, Ed 1931- **5, 81**
See also CA 5-8R; CANR 5, 36, 82, 129, 193; MAICYA 1, 2; SATA 8, 70, 146
Emberley, Edward Randolph
See Emberley, Ed
Emecheta, Buchi 1944- **158**
See also AAYA 67; AFW; BLC 1:2; BW 2, 3; CA 81-84; CANR 27, 81, 126; CDWLB 3; CLC 14, 48, 128, 214; CN 4, 5, 6, 7; CWRI 5; DA3; DAM MULT; DLB 117; EWL 3; FL 1:5; FW; MTCW 1, 2; MTFW 2005; NFS 12, 14; SATA 66; WLIT 2
Emecheta, Florence Onye Buchi
See Emecheta, Buchi
Ende, Michael (Andreas Helmuth)
1929-1995 .... **14, 138**
See also BYA 5; CA 118; 124; 149; CANR 36, 110; CLC 31; DLB 75; MAICYA 1, 2; MAICYAS 1; SATA 61, 130; SATA-Brief 42; SATA-Obit 86
Engdahl, Sylvia Louise 1933- **2**
See also AAYA 36; BYA 4; CA 29-32R, 195; CAAE 195; CANR 14, 85, 95; JRDA; MAICYA 1, 2; SAAS 5; SATA 4; SATA-Essay 122; SFW 4; YAW
Enright, Elizabeth (Wright) 1909-1968 ..... **4**
See also BYA 3; CA 61-64; 25-28R; CANR 83; CWRI 5; DLB 22, 335; MAICYA 1, 2; SATA 9; WCH
Epstein, Beryl 1910- **26**
See also CA 5-8R; CANR 2, 18, 39; SAAS 17; SATA 1, 31

Epstein, Beryl M. Williams
See Epstein, Beryl
Epstein, Samuel 1909-2000 .... **26**
See also CA 9-12R; CANR 4, 18, 39; SAAS 17; SATA 1, 31
Estes, Eleanor (Ruth) 1906-1988 .... **2, 70**
See also BYA 1; CA 1-4R; 126; CANR 5, 20, 84; CWRI 5; DLB 22; JRDA; MAICYA 1, 2; SATA 7, 91; SATA-Obit 56
Estoril, Jean
See Allan, Mabel Esther
Ets, Marie Hall 1893-1984 .... **33**
See also CA 1-4R; CANR 4, 83; CWRI 5; DLB 22; MAICYA 1, 2; SATA 2
Ewing, Juliana (Horatia Gatty)
1841-1885 .... **78**
See also DLB 21, 163; SATA 16; WCH
Fairfield, Flora
See Alcott, Louisa May
Falconer, Ian 1959- **90, 146**
See also CA 197; SATA 125, 179
Farjeon, Eleanor 1881-1965 .... **34**
See also CA 11-12; CAP 1; CWRI 5; DLB 160; MAICYA 1, 2; SATA 2; WCH
Farmer, Penelope (Jane) 1939- **8**
See also CA 13-16R; CANR 9, 37, 84; DLB 161; FANT; JRDA; MAICYA 1, 2; SAAS 22; SATA 40, 105; SATA-Brief 39; YAW
Farmer, Philip José 1918-2009 .... **201**
See also AAYA 28; BPFB 1; CA 1-4R, 283; CANR 4, 35, 111, 220; CLC 1, 19, 299; CMTFW; DLB 8; MTCW 1; SATA 93, 201; SCFW 1, 2; SFW 4;
Farquharson, Martha
See Finley, Martha
Feelings, Muriel 1938- **5**
See also BW 1; CA 93-96; MAICYA 1, 2; SAAS 8; SATA 16
Feelings, Muriel Lavita Grey
See Feelings, Muriel
Feelings, Thomas 1933-2003 .... **5, 58**
See also AAYA 25; BW 1; CA 49-52; 222; CANR 25; MAICYA 1, 2; MAICYAS 1; SAAS 19; SATA 8, 69; SATA-Obit 148; YAW
Feelings, Tom
See Feelings, Thomas
Ferris, James Cody
See McFarlane, Leslie
Ferry, Charles 1927- **34**
See also AAYA 29; CA 97-100; CANR 16, 57; SAAS 20; SATA 43, 92
Field, Rachel (Lyman) 1894-1942 .... **21**
See also BYA 5; CA 109; 137; CANR 79; CWRI 5; DLB 9, 22; MAICYA 1, 2; RHW; SATA 15; WCH
Fielding, Sarah 1710-1768 .... **253**
See also DLB 39; LC 1, 44, 223; RGEL 2; TEA
Finder, Martin
See Salten, Felix
Fine, Anne 1947- **25, 180**
See also AAYA 20; CA 105; CANR 38, 83, 105, 159, 188; CWRI 5; JRDA; MAICYA 1, 2; MAICYAS 1; SAAS 15; SATA 29, 72, 111, 160, 197
Finley, Martha 1828-1909 .... **148**
See also CA 118; DLB 42; SATA 43
Fisher, Aileen (Lucia) 1906-2002 .... **49**
See also CA 5-8R; 216; CANR 2, 17, 37, 84; CWRI 5; MAICYA 1, 2; SATA 1, 25, 73; SATA-Obit 143
Fisher, Dorothy (Frances) Canfield
1879-1958 .... **71**
See also CA 114; 136; CANR 80; CWRI 5; DLB 9, 102, 284; MAICYA 1, 2; MAL 5; TCLC 87; YABC 1

Fisher, Leonard Everett 1924- **18**
See also CA 1-4R; CANR 2, 37, 77, 98; CWRI 5; DLB 61; MAICYA 1, 2; SAAS 1; SATA 4, 34, 73, 120, 176; SATA-Essay 122

Fisher, Suzanne
See Staples, Suzanne Fisher

Fitch, John IV
See Cormier, Robert

Fitzgerald, Captain Hugh
See Baum, L. Frank

Fitzgerald, F. Scott 1896-1940 .... **176, 269**
See also AAYA 24; AITN 1; AMW; AMWC 2; AMWR 1; BPFB 1; BYA 2; CA 110, 123; CDALB 1917-1929; DA; DA3; DAB; DAC; DAM MST, NOV; DLB 4, 9, 86, 219, 273; DLBD 1, 15, 16; DLBY 1981, 1996; EWL 3; EXPN; EXPS; LAIT 3; MAL 5; MTCW 1, 2; MTFW 2005; NFS 2, 19, 20, 49; RGAL 4; RGSF 2; SSC 6, 31, 75, 143, 233, 285, 313; SSFS 4, 15, 21, 25, 36; TCLC 1, 6, 14, 28, 55, 157, 280, 311, 441, 451; TUS; WLC 2

Fitzgerald, John D(ennis) 1907(?)-1988 ..... **1**
See also CA 93-96; 126; CANR 84; CWRI 5; MAICYA 1, 2; SATA 20; SATA-Obit 56

Fitzgerald, William
See Leinster, Murray

Fitzhardinge, Joan Margaret 1912- **5**
See also AAYA 14; CA 13-16R; CANR 6, 23, 36; MAICYA 1, 2; SAAS 3; SATA 2, 73; YAW

Fitzhugh, Louise (Perkins)
1928-1974 .... **1, 72, 187**
See also AAYA 18; CA 29-32; 53-56; CANR 34, 84; CAP 2; CWRI 5; DLB 52; JRDA; MAICYA 1, 2; SATA 1, 45; SATA-Obit 24

Flack, Marjorie 1897-1958 .... **28**
See also CA 112; 136; CANR 84; CWRI 5; MAICYA 1, 2; SATA 100; YABC 2

Fleischman, Albert Sidney
See Fleischman, Sid

Fleischman, Paul 1952- **20, 66**
See also AAYA 11, 35; BYA 5, 6, 8, 11, 12, 16; CA 113; CANR 37, 84, 105, 207; JRDA; MAICYA 1, 2; MAICYAS 1; SAAS 20; SATA 39, 72, 110, 156; SATA-Brief 32; WYAS 1; YAW

Fleischman, Sid 1920-2010 .... **1, 15**
See also BYA 4, 11; CA 1-4R; CANR 5, 37, 67, 131, 156; CWRI 5; JRDA; MAICYA 1, 2; SATA 8, 59, 96, 148, 185

Fletcher, Ralph 1953- **104**
See also CA 173; CANR 132, 186; SATA 105, 149, 195

Fletcher, Ralph J.
See Fletcher, Ralph

Forbes, Esther 1891-1967 .... **27, 147**
See also AAYA 17; BYA 2; CA 13-14; 25-28R; CAP 1; CLC 12; DLB 22; JRDA; MAICYA 1, 2; RHW; SATA 2, 100; YAW

Ford, Albert Lee
See Stratemeyer, Edward L.

Ford, Hilary
See Youd, Samuel

Foreman, Michael 1938- **32**
See also CA 21-24R; CANR 10, 38, 68, 108, 169; CWRI 5; MAICYA 1, 2; MAICYAS 1; SAAS 21; SATA 2, 73, 129, 135, 184, 216

Foster, Genevieve (Stump) 1893-1979 .... **7**
See also CA 5-8R; 89-92; CANR 4; DLB 61; MAICYA 1, 2; SATA 2; SATA-Obit 23

Fox, J. N.
See Janeczko, Paul B(ryan)

Fox, Mem 1946- **23, 80**
See also CA 127; CANR 84; CWRI 5; MAICYA 1, 2; SATA 51, 103, 155, 211

Fox, Merrion Frances
See Fox, Mem

Fox, Norma Diane
See Mazer, Norma Fox

Fox, Paula 1923- **1, 44, 96**
See also AAYA 3, 37; BYA 3, 8; CA 73-76; CANR 20, 36, 62, 105, 200; CLC 2, 8, 121; DLB 52; JRDA; MAICYA 1, 2; MTCW 1; NFS 12; SATA 17, 60, 120, 167; WYA; YAW

Frank, Anne 1929-1945 .... **101, 189**
See also AAYA 12; BYA 1; CA 113; 133; CANR 68; DA; DA3; DAB; DAC; DAM MST; LAIT 4; MAICYA 2; MAICYAS 1; MTCW 1, 2; MTFW 2005; NCFS 2; RGHL; SATA 87; SATA-Brief 42; TCLC 17; WLC 2; WYA; YAW

Frank, Annelies Marie
See Frank, Anne

Frank, Pat 1907-1964 .... **193**
See also CA 5-8R; CANR 80; NFS 29; SFW 4

Franklin, Madeleine
See L'Engle, Madeleine

Franklin, Madeleine L'Engle
See L'Engle, Madeleine

Franklin, Madeleine L'Engle Camp
See L'Engle, Madeleine

Freedman, Russell 1929- **20, 71**
See also AAYA 4, 24; BYA 2, 11, 14; CA 17-20R; CANR 7, 23, 46, 81, 101, 160, 208; JRDA; MAICYA 1, 2; MAICYAS 1; SATA 16, 71, 123, 175, 235; WYA; YAW

Freedman, Russell Bruce
See Freedman, Russell

Freeman, Don 1908-1978 .... **30, 90**
See also CA 77-80; CANR 44; CWRI 5; MAICYA 1, 2; SATA 17

French, Fiona 1944- **37**
See also CA 29-32R; CANR 40; CWRI 5; MAICYA 1, 2; SAAS 21; SATA 6, 75, 132

French, Paul
See Asimov, Isaac

Fritz, Jean (Guttery) 1915- **2, 14, 96**
See also BYA 2, 3, 14, 16; CA 1-4R; CANR 5, 16, 37, 97; DLB 52; INT CANR-16; JRDA; MAICYA 1, 2; SAAS 2; SATA 1, 29, 72, 119, 163; SATA-Essay 122

Frost, Robert 1874-1963 .... **67**
See also AAYA 21; AMW; AMWR 1; CA 89-92; CANR 33; CDALB 1917-1929; CLC 1, 3, 4, 9, 10, 13, 15, 26, 34, 44; DA; DA3; DAB; DAC; DAM MST, POET; DLB 54, 284, 342; DLBD 7; EWL 3; EXPP; MAL 5; MTCW 1, 2; MTFW 2005; PAB; PC 1, 39, 71; PFS 1, 2, 3, 4, 5, 6, 7, 10, 13, 32, 35, 41; RGAL 4; SATA 14; TCLC 236; TUS; WLC 2; WP; WYA

Frost, Robert Lee
See Frost, Robert

Fujikawa, Gyo 1908-1998 .... **25**
See also CA 113; 172; CANR 46; CWRI 5; MAICYA 1, 2; SAAS 16; SATA 39, 76; SATA-Brief 30; SATA-Obit 110

Fuller, Maud
See Petersham, Maud

Funke, Cornelia 1958- **145**
See also AAYA 68; CA 221; CANR 157, 205; SATA 154, 174, 209

Funke, Cornelia Caroline
See Funke, Cornelia

Furlonger, Patricia
See Wrightson, Patricia

Gaberman, Judie Angell
See Angell, Judie

Gag, Wanda (Hazel) 1893-1946 .... **4, 150**
See also CA 113; 137; CWRI 5; DLB 22; MAICYA 1, 2; SATA 100; WCH; YABC 1

Gaiman, Neil 1960- **109, 177, 205, 207**
See also AAYA 19, 42, 82; CA 133; CANR 81, 129, 188; CLC 319; DLB 261; HGG; MTFW 2005; SATA 85, 146, 197, 228; SFW 4; SUFW 2

Gaiman, Neil Richard
See Gaiman, Neil

Gaines, Ernest J. 1933- **62**
See also AAYA 18; AFAW 1, 2; AITN 1; BLC 1:2; BPFB 2; BW 2, 3; BYA 6; CA 9-12R; CANR 6, 24, 42, 75, 126; CDALB 1968-1988; CLC 3, 11, 18, 86, 181, 300; CN 1, 2, 3, 4, 5, 6, 7; CSW; DA3; DAM MULT; DLB 2, 33, 152; DLBY 1980; EWL 3; EXPN; LAIT 5; LATS 1:2; MAL 5; MTCW 1, 2; MTFW 2005; NFS 5, 7, 16; RGAL 4; RGSF 2; RHW; SATA 86; SSC 68, 137; SSFS 5; YAW

Gaines, Ernest James
See Gaines, Ernest J.

Gal, Laszlo 1933- **61**
See also CA 161; CWRI 5; MAICYA 2; MAICYAS 1; SATA 52, 96; SATA-Brief 32

Galdone, Paul 1907(?)-1986 .... **16**
See also CA 73-76; 121; CANR 13, 76; MAICYA 1, 2; SATA 17, 66; SATA-Obit 49

Gallant, Roy A(rthur) 1924- **30**
See also CA 5-8R; CANR 4, 29, 54, 117; CLC 17; MAICYA 1, 2; SATA 4, 68, 110

Gallaz, Christophe 1948- **126**
See also CA 238; SATA 162

Gammell, Stephen 1943- **83**
See also CA 135; CANR 55, 107; MAICYA 1, 2; SATA 53, 81, 128, 226

Gantos, Jack 1951- **18, 85**
See also AAYA 40; CA 65-68; CANR 15, 56, 97, 181; SATA 20, 81, 119, 169

Gantos, John Bryan, Jr.
See Gantos, Jack

Gard, Janice
See Latham, Jean Lee

Gardam, Jane 1928- **12**
See also CA 49-52; CANR 2, 18, 33, 54, 106, 167, 206; CLC 43; DLB 14, 161, 231; MAICYA 1, 2; MTCW 1; SAAS 9; SATA 39, 76, 130; SATA-Brief 28; YAW

Gardam, Jane Mary
See Gardam, Jane

Garden, Nancy 1938-2014 .... **51, 199**
See also AAYA 18, 55; BYA 7; CA 33-36R; CANR 13, 30, 84, 171; JRDA; MAICYA 2; MAICYAS 1; SAAS 8; SATA 12, 77, 114; SATA-Essay 147; WYAS 1; YAW

Gardner, Miriam
See Bradley, Marion Zimmer

Garfield, Leon 1921-1996 .... **21, 166**
See also AAYA 8, 69; BYA 1, 3; CA 17-20R; 152; CANR 38, 41, 78; CLC 12; DLB 161; JRDA; MAICYA 1, 2; MAICYAS 1; SATA 1, 32, 76; SATA-Obit 90; TEA; WYA; YAW

Garner, Alan 1934- **20, 130**
See also AAYA 18; BYA 3, 5; CA 73-76, 178; CAAE 178; CANR 15, 64, 134; CLC 17; CPW; DAB; DAM POP; DLB 161, 261; FANT; MAICYA 1, 2; MTCW 1, 2; MTFW 2005; SATA 18, 69; SATA-Essay 108; SUFW 1, 2; YAW

Garnet, A. H.
See Slote, Alfred

Gatty, Juliana Horatia
See Ewing, Juliana (Horatia Gatty)

Gauch, Patricia Lee 1934- **56**
See also CA 57-60; CANR 9; CWRI 5; MAICYA 2; MAICYAS 1; SAAS 21; SATA 26, 80, 228

Gay, Marie-Louise 1952- **27**
See also CA 135; CANR 105; CWRI 5; MAICYA 2; MAICYAS 1; SAAS 21; SATA 68, 126, 179

Gaze, Gillian
See Barklem, Jill

Gee, Maurice 1931- **56**
See also AAYA 42; CA 97-100; CANR 67, 123, 204; CLC 29; CN 2, 3, 4, 5, 6, 7; CWRI 5; EWL 3; MAICYA 2; RGSF 2; SATA 46, 101, 227

Gee, Maurice Gough
See Gee, Maurice

Geisel, Theodor Seuss
See Dr. Seuss

Geisert, Arthur 1941- **87**
See also CA 120; CANR 44, 57, 111; MAICYA 2; MAICYAS 1; SAAS 23; SATA 56, 92, 133, 171, 237; SATA-Brief 52

Geisert, Arthur Frederick
See Geisert, Arthur

George, Jean
See George, Jean Craighead

George, Jean C.
See George, Jean Craighead

George, Jean Craighead 1919- **1, 80, 136**
See also AAYA 8, 69; BYA 2, 4; CA 5-8R; CANR 25, 198; CLC 35; DLB 52; JRDA; MAICYA 1, 2; SATA 2, 68, 124, 170, 226; WYA; YAW

Gerrard, Roy 1935-1997 .... **23**
See also CA 110; 160; CANR 57; MAICYA 2; MAICYAS 1; SATA 47, 90; SATA-Brief 45; SATA-Obit 99

Gerstein, Mordicai 1935- **102**
See also AAYA 69; CA 117; 127; CANR 36, 56, 82, 121, 163; MAICYA 1, 2; SATA 47, 81, 142, 178, 222; SATA-Brief 36

Gewe, Raddory
See Gorey, Edward (St. John)

Gibbons, Gail 1944- **8**
See also CA 69-72; CANR 12, 129; CWRI 5; MAICYA 1, 2; SAAS 12; SATA 23, 72, 104, 160, 201

Gibbons, Gail Gretchen
See Gibbons, Gail

Giblin, James Cross 1933- **29**
See also AAYA 39; BYA 9, 10; CA 106; CANR 24, 100, 161, 188; MAICYA 1, 2; SAAS 12; SATA 33, 75, 122, 197

Ginsburg, Mirra 1909-2000 .... **45**
See also CA 17-20R; 193; CANR 11, 28, 54; MAICYA 1; MAICYAS 1; SATA 6, 92

Giovanni, Nikki 1943- **6, 73**
See also AAYA 22, 85; AITN 1; BLC 1:2; BW 2, 3; CA 29-32R; CAAS 6; CANR 18, 41, 60, 91, 130, 175; CDALBS; CLC 2, 4, 19, 64, 117; CP 2, 3, 4, 5, 6, 7; CSW; CWP; CWRI 5; DA; DA3; DAB; DAC; DAM MST, MULT, POET; DLB 5, 41; EWL 3; EXPP; INT CANR-18; MAICYA 1, 2; MAL 5; MTCW 1, 2; MTFW 2005; PC 19; PFS 17, 28, 35; RGAL 4; SATA 24, 107, 208; TUS; WLCS; YAW

Giovanni, Yolanda Cornelia
See Giovanni, Nikki

Giovanni, Yolande Cornelia
See Giovanni, Nikki

Giovanni, Yolande Cornelia, Jr.
See Giovanni, Nikki

Glasscock, Amnesia
See Steinbeck, John

Gleitzman, Morris 1953- **88**
See also CA 131; CANR 140; CWRI 5; SATA 88, 156, 234

Glenn, Mel 1943- **51**
See also AAYA 25; CA 123; CANR 49, 68, 127; MAICYA 2; MAICYAS 1; SATA 51, 93; SATA-Brief 45; WYAS 1; YAW

Glockenhammer, Walker
See Wells, H. G.

Glubok, Shirley (Astor) **1**
See also CA 5-8R; CANR 4, 43; MAICYA 1, 2; SAAS 7; SATA 6, 68, 146; SATA-Essay 146

Gobbletree, Richard
See Quackenbush, Robert M(ead)

Goble, Paul 1933- **21**
See also CA 93-96; CANR 16; CWRI 5; MAICYA 1, 2; SATA 25, 69, 131

Godden, (Margaret) Rumer 1907-1998 ... **20**
See also AAYA 6; BPFB 2; BYA 2, 5; CA 5-8R; 172; CANR 4, 27, 36, 55, 80; CLC 53; CN 1, 2, 3, 4, 5, 6; CWRI 5; DLB 161; MAICYA 1, 2; RHW; SAAS 12; SATA 3, 36; SATA-Obit 109; TEA

Godfrey, Martyn
See Godfrey, Martyn N.; Godfrey, Martyn N.

Godfrey, Martyn N. 1949-2000 .... **57**
See also CA 126; CANR 68; SATA 95

Godfrey, William
See Youd, Samuel

Goffstein, Brooke
See Goffstein, Marilyn Brooke

Goffstein, M. B.
See Goffstein, Marilyn Brooke

Goffstein, Marilyn Brooke 1940- **3**
See also CA 21-24R; CANR 9, 28; DLB 61; MAICYA 1, 2; SATA 8, 70

Golding, William 1911-1993 .... **94, 130**
See also AAYA 5, 44; BPFB 2; BRWR 1; BRWS 1; BYA 2; CA 5-8R; 141; CANR 13, 33, 54; CD 5; CDBLB 1945-1960; CLC 1, 2, 3, 8, 10, 17, 27, 58, 81; CN 1, 2, 3, 4; DA; DA3; DAB; DAC; DAM MST, NOV; DLB 15, 100, 255, 326, 330; EWL 3; EXPN; HGG; LAIT 4; MTCW 1, 2; MTFW 2005; NFS 2, 36; RGEL 2; RHW; SFW 4; TEA; WLC 3; WLIT 4; YAW

Golding, William Gerald
See Golding, William

Goldsmith, Oliver 1730?-1774 .... **208**
See also BRW 3; CDBLB 1660-1789; DA; DAB; DAC; DAM DRAM, MST, NOV, POET; DC 8; DFS 1; DLB 39, 89, 104, 109, 142, 336; IDTP; LC 2, 48, 122; PC 77; RGEL 2; SATA 26; TEA; WLC 3; WLIT 3

Goldszmit, Henryk 1878-1942 .... **152**
See also CA 133; RGHL; SATA 65

Gomi, Taro 1945- **57**
See also CA 162; MAICYA 2; SATA 64, 103

Goodall, John S(trickland) 1908-1996 ..... **25**
See also CA 33-36R; 152; MAICYA 1, 2; MAICYAS 1; SATA 4, 66; SATA-Obit 91

Goodrich, Samuel Griswold 1793-1860 .. **212**
See also DLB 1, 42, 73, 243; SATA 23

Gordon, Gaelyn 1939-1997 .... **75**
See also CWRI 5

Gordon, Sheila 1927- **27**
See also CA 132; NFS 40; SATA 88

Gorey, Edward (St. John)
1925-2000 .... **36, 246**
See also AAYA 40; CA 5-8R; 187; CANR 9, 30, 78; CWRI 5; DLB 61; INT CANR-30; MAICYA 1, 2; SATA 29, 70; SATA-Brief 27; SATA-Obit 118

Goscinny, René 1926-1977 .... **37, 198**
See also CA 113; 117; SATA 47; SATA-Brief 39

Goudge, Elizabeth (de Beauchamp)
1900-1984 .... **94**
See also CA 5-8R; 112; CANR 5; CWRI 5; DLB 191; MAICYA 1, 2; RHW; SATA 2; SATA-Obit 38

Graaf, Peter
See Youd, Samuel

Graham, Bob 1942- **31**
See also CA 165; CANR 123, 173; CWRI 5; MAICYA 2; SATA 63, 101, 151, 187

Graham, Lorenz (Bell) 1902-1989 .... **10**
See also BW 1; CA 9-12R; 129; CANR 25; DLB 76; MAICYA 1, 2; SAAS 5; SATA 2, 74; SATA-Obit 63; YAW

Grahame, Kenneth
1859-1932 .... **5, 135, 211, 226**
See also BYA 5; CA 108, 136; CANR 80; CWRI 5; DA3; DAB; DLB 34, 141, 178; FANT; MAICYA 1, 2; MBL 2; MTCW 2; NFS 20; RGEL 2; SATA 100; TCLC 64, 136; TEA; WCH; YABC 1

Gramatky, Hardie 1907-1979 .... **22**
See also AITN 1; CA 1-4R; 85-88; CANR 3; CWRI 5; DLB 22; MAICYA 1, 2; SATA 1, 30; SATA-Obit 23

Graves, Valerie
See Bradley, Marion Zimmer

Green, Brian
See Card, Orson Scott

Green, John 1977- **204**
See also AAYA 82; CA 243; CANR 183, 263; NFS 48; SATA 170, 235

Greenaway, Kate 1846-1901 .... **6, 111**
See also AAYA 56; CA 137; DLB 141; MAICYA 1, 2; SATA 100; YABC 2

Greene, Bette 1934- **2, 140**
See also AAYA 7, 69; BYA 3; CA 53-56; CANR 4, 146; CLC 30; CWRI 5; JRDA; LAIT 4; MAICYA 1, 2; NFS 10; SAAS 16; SATA 8, 102, 161; WYA; YAW

Greene, Constance C(larke) 1924- **62**
See also AAYA 7; CA 61-64; CANR 8, 38; CWRI 5; JRDA; MAICYA 1, 2; SAAS 11; SATA 11, 72

Greenfield, Eloise 1929- **4, 38**
See also BW 2; CA 49-52; CANR 1, 19, 43, 127; CWRI 5; INT CANR-19; JRDA; MAICYA 1, 2; SAAS 16; SATA 19, 61, 105, 155

Greer, Richard
See Silverberg, Robert

Gregory, Jean
See Ure, Jean

Grewdead, Roy
See Gorey, Edward (St. John)

Grey Owl 1888-1938 .... **32, 227**
See also CA 114; DLB 92; DLBD 17; SATA 24

Grifalconi, Ann 1929- **35**
See also CA 5-8R; CANR 9, 35, 111, 206; MAICYA 1, 2; SAAS 16; SATA 2, 66, 133, 210

Griffin, John Howard 1920-1980 .... **211**
See also AITN 1; CA 1-4R, 101; CANR 2; CLC 68

Griffiths, Helen 1939- **75**
See also CA 17-20R; CANR 7, 25, 51; CWRI 5; SAAS 5; SATA 5, 86

Grimes, Nikki 1950- **42**
See also AAYA 53; CA 77-80; CANR 60, 115, 157; CWRI 5; MAICYA 2; MAICYAS 1; SATA 93, 136, 174, 218

Grimm, Jacob Ludwig Karl
1785-1863 .... **112**
See also DLB 90; MAICYA 1, 2; NCLC 3, 77; RGSF 2; RGWL 2, 3; SATA 22; SSC 36, 88; WCH

Grimm, Wilhelm Karl 1786-1859 .... **112**
See also CDWLB 2; DLB 90; MAICYA 1, 2; NCLC 3, 77; RGSF 2; RGWL 2, 3; SATA 22; SSC 36; WCH

Grimm and Grim
See Grimm, Jacob Ludwig Karl; Grimm, Wilhelm Karl

Grimm Brothers
See Grimm, Jacob Ludwig Karl; Grimm, Wilhelm Karl

Gripe, Maria 1923- **5**
See also CA 29-32R; CANR 17, 39, 147; DLB 257; MAICYA 1, 2; SATA 2, 74

Gripe, Maria Kristina
See Gripe, Maria

Grode, Redway
See Gorey, Edward (St. John)

Gruelle, John 1880-1938 .... **34**
See also CA 115; 175; CWRI 5; DLB 22; MAICYA 2; MAICYAS 1; SATA 35; SATA-Brief 32

Gruelle, John Barton
See Gruelle, John

Gruelle, Johnny
See Gruelle, John

Guillot, Rene 1900-1969 .... **22**
See also CA 49-52; CANR 39; SATA 7

Gump, P. Q.
See Card, Orson Scott

Guy, Rosa 1925- **13, 137**
See also AAYA 4, 37; BW 2; CA 17-20R; CANR 14, 34, 83; CLC 26; DLB 33; DNFS 1; JRDA; MAICYA 1, 2; SATA 14, 62, 122; YAW

Guy, Rosa Cuthbert
See Guy, Rosa

Haar, Jaap ter
See ter Haar, Jaap

Haddon, Mark 1962- **188**
See also CA 222; CANR 173, 256; CMTFW 1; SATA 155, 223

Hadley, Lee 1934-1995 .... **40**
See also AAYA 13; BYA 8; CA 101; 149; CANR 19, 36, 83; MAICYA 1, 2; MAICYAS 1; SAAS 14; SATA 47, 89; SATA-Brief 38; SATA-Obit 86; WYA; YAW

Haenel, Wolfram 1956- **64**
See also CA 155; SATA 89

Hagon, Priscilla
See Allan, Mabel Esther

Haig-Brown, Roderick (Langmere) 1908-1976 .... **31**
See also CA 5-8R; 69-72; CANR 4, 38, 83; CLC 21; CWRI 5; DLB 88; MAICYA 1, 2; SATA 12; TCWW 2

Haij, Vera
See Jansson, Tove (Marika)

Hakadah
See Eastman, Charles Alexander

Hale, Lucretia P.
See Hale, Lucretia Peabody

Hale, Lucretia Peabody 1820-1900 .... **105**
See also CA 122; 136; DLB 42; MAICYA 1, 2; SATA 26; WCH

Haley, Alex 1921-1992 .... **192, 256**
See also AAYA 26; BLC 2; BPFB 2; BW 2, 3; CA 77-80; 136; CANR 61; CDALBS; CLC 8, 12, 76; CPW; CSW; DA; DA3; DAB; DAC; DAM MST, MULT, POP; DLB 38; LAIT 5; MTCW 1, 2; NFS 9; TCLC 147

Haley, Gail E(inhart) 1939- **21**
See also CA 21-24R; CANR 14, 35, 82, 115; MAICYA 1, 2; SAAS 13; SATA 43, 78, 136, 161; SATA-Brief 28; SATA-Essay 161

Halse, Laurie Beth
See Anderson, Laurie Halse

Hamilton, Clive
See Lewis, C. S.

Hamilton, Franklin
See Silverberg, Robert

Hamilton, Gail
See Corcoran, Barbara (Asenath)

Hamilton, Ralph
See Stratemeyer, Edward L.

Hamilton, Virginia 1936-2002 .... **1, 11, 40, 127**
See also AAYA 2, 21; BW 2, 3; BYA 1, 2, 8; CA 25-28R; 206; CANR 20, 37, 73, 126; CLC 26; DAM MULT; DLB 33, 52; DLBY 2001; INT CANR-20; JRDA; LAIT 5; MAICYA 1, 2; MAICYAS 1; MTCW 1, 2; MTFW 2005; SATA 4, 56, 79, 123; SATA-Obit 132; WYA; YAW

Hamilton, Virginia Esther
See Hamilton, Virginia

Hamley, D. C.
See Hamley, Dennis

Hamley, Dennis 1935- **47**
See also CA 57-60; CANR 11, 26, 193; SAAS 22; SATA 39, 69

Hamley, Dennis C.
See Hamley, Dennis

Hampton, Harry
See Alger, Horatio, Jr.

Handford, Martin (John) 1956- **22**
See also CA 137; MAICYA 1, 2; SATA 64

Handler, Daniel
See Snicket, Lemony

Hanel, Wolfram
See Haenel, Wolfram

Hansberry, Lorraine 1930-1965 .... **265**
See also AAYA 25; AFAW 1, 2; AMWS 4; BLC 1:2, 2:2; BW 1, 3; CA 25-28R, 109; CABS 3; CAD; CANR 58; CDALB 1941-1968; CLC 17, 62; CWD; DA; DA3; DAB; DAC; DAM DRAM, MST, MULT; DC 2, 57; DFS 2, 29; DLB 7, 38; EWL 3; FL 1:6; FW; LAIT 4; MAL 5; MTCW 1, 2; MTFW 2005; RGAL 4; TCLC 192, 402; TUS

Hansen, Joyce 1942- **21**
See also AAYA 41; BW 2; CA 105; CANR 43, 87, 143; CWRI 5; JRDA; MAICYA 1, 2; SAAS 15; SATA 46, 101, 172; SATA-Brief 39; SATA-Essay 172

Hansen, Joyce Viola
See Hansen, Joyce

Hargrave, Leonie
See Disch, Thomas M.

Harkaway, Hal
See Stratemeyer, Edward L.

Harlan, Judith 1949- **81**
See also CA 204; SATA 74, 135

Harris, Christie
See Harris, Christie (Lucy) Irwin

Harris, Christie (Lucy) Irwin 1907-2002 ... **47**
See also CA 5-8R; CANR 6, 83; CLC 12; DLB 88; JRDA; MAICYA 1, 2; SAAS 10; SATA 6, 74; SATA-Essay 116

Harris, Joel Chandler 1845-1908 .... **49, 128, 237**
See also CA 104; 137; CANR 80; DLB 11, 23, 42, 78, 91; LAIT 2; MAICYA 1, 2; RGSF 2; SATA 100; SSC 19, 103; TCLC 2; WCH; YABC 1

Harris, J. W. B.
See Wyndham, John

Harris, John Beynon
See Wyndham, John

Harris, John Wyndham Parkes Lucas Beynon
See Wyndham, John

Harris, Johnson
See Wyndham, John

Harris, Lavinia
See St. John, Nicole

Harris, Rosemary (Jeanne) **30**
See also CA 33-36R; CANR 13, 30, 84; CWRI 5; SAAS 7; SATA 4, 82

Hartling, Peter
See Hartling, Peter

Hartling, Peter 1933- **29**
See also CA 101; CANR 22, 48; DLB 75; MAICYA 1, 2; SATA 66

Haskins, James
See Haskins, James S.

Haskins, James S. 1941-2005 .... **3, 39**
See also AAYA 14; BW 2, 3; CA 33-36R; 241; CANR 25, 48, 79; JRDA; MAICYA 1, 2; MAICYAS 1; SAAS 4; SATA 9, 69, 105, 132; SATA-Essay 132; WYAS 1; YAW

Haskins, Jim
See Haskins, James S.

Hastings, Victor
See Disch, Thomas M.

Hauff, Wilhelm 1802-1827 .... **155**
See also DLB 90; NCLC 185; SUFW 1

Haugaard, Erik Christian 1923- **11, 173**
See also AAYA 36; BYA 1; CA 5-8R; CANR 3, 38; CWRI 5; JRDA; MAICYA 1, 2; SAAS 12; SATA 4, 68

Hausman, Gerald 1945- **89**
See also CA 45-48; CANR 2, 17, 38, 108, 164; SATA 13, 90, 132, 180

Hausman, Gerry
See Hausman, Gerald

Hautman, Pete 1952– **176**
See also AAYA 49; CA 144; CANR 72, 107, 155, 178; SATA 82, 128, 173

Hautzig, Esther Rudomin 1930-2009 .... **22**
See also BYA 1; CA 1-4R; CANR 5, 20, 46, 85, 132; JRDA; LAIT 4; MAICYA 1, 2; SAAS 15; SATA 4, 68, 148; YAW

Hawthorne, Nathaniel 1804-1864 .... **103, 163, 267**
See also AAYA 18; AMW; AMWC 1; AMWR 1; BPFB 2; BYA 3; CDALB 1640-1865; DA; DA3; DAB; DAC; DAM MST, NOV; DLB 1, 74, 183, 223, 269; EXPN; EXPS; GL 2; HGG; LAIT 1; NCLC 2, 10, 17, 23, 39, 79, 95, 158, 171, 191, 226, 426; NFS 1, 20; RGAL 4; RGSF 2; SSC 3, 29, 39, 89, 130, 166, 176, 185, 190, 195, 214, 227, 232, 257, 269, 294; SSFS 1, 7, 11, 15, 30, 35, 42; SUFW 1; TUS; WCH; WLC 3; YABC 2

Hay, Timothy
See Brown, Margaret Wise

Haynes, Betsy 1937- **90**
See also CA 57-60; CANR 8, 67; SATA 48, 94; SATA-Brief 37

Hays, Wilma Pitchford 1909- **59**
See also CA 1-4R; CANR 5, 45; MAICYA 1, 2; SAAS 3; SATA 1, 28

Haywood, Carolyn 1898-1990 .... **22**
See also CA 5-8R; 130; CANR 5, 20, 83; CWRI 5; MAICYA 1, 2; SATA 1, 29, 75; SATA-Obit 64

Hearn, Lian
See Rubinstein, Gillian

Heide, Florence Parry 1919-2011 .... **60**
See also CA 93-96; CANR 19, 84, 96, 163, 182; CWRI 5; JRDA; MAICYA 1, 2; SAAS 6; SATA 32, 69, 118, 192

Heine, Helme 1941- **18**
See also CA 135; MAICYA 1, 2; SATA 67, 135

Heinlein, Robert A. 1907-1988 .... **75**
See also AAYA 17; BPFB 2; BYA 4, 13; CA 1-4R; 125; CANR 1, 20, 53; CLC 1, 3, 8, 14, 26, 55; CN 1, 2, 3, 4; CPW; DA3; DAM POP; DLB 8; EXPS; JRDA; LAIT 5; LMFS 2; MAICYA 1, 2; MTCW 1, 2; MTFW 2005; NFS 40; RGAL 4; SATA 9, 69; SATA-Obit 56; SCFW 1, 2; SFW 4; SSC 55; SSFS 7; YAW

Heinrich, Karl
See Salten, Felix

Hemingway, Ernest 1899-1961 .... **168, 201**
See also AAYA 19; AMW; AMWC 1; AMWR 1; BPFB 2; BYA 2, 3, 13, 15; CA 77-80; CANR 34; CDALB 1917-1929; CLC 1, 3, 6, 8, 10, 13, 19, 30, 34, 39, 41, 44, 50, 61, 80; DA; DA3; DAB; DAC; DAM MST, NOV; DLB 4, 9, 102, 210, 308, 316, 330; DLBD 1, 15, 16; DLBY 1981, 1987, 1996, 1998; EWL 3; EXPN; EXPS; LAIT 3, 4; LATS 1:1; MAL 5; MTCW 1, 2; MTFW 2005; NFS 1, 5, 6, 14; RGAL 4; RGSF 2; SSC 1, 25, 36, 40, 63, 117, 137, 168; SSFS 17; TCLC 115, 203; TUS; WLC 3; WYA

Hemingway, Ernest Miller
See Hemingway, Ernest

Hemmer, Marie
See Salten, Felix

Henkes, Kevin 1960- **23, 108**
See also AAYA 59; CA 114; CANR 38, 139; MAICYA 1, 2; SATA 43, 76, 108, 154, 207

Henry, Marguerite 1902-1997 .... **4**
See also BYA 2; CA 17-20R; 162; CANR 9; CWRI 5; DLB 22; JRDA; MAICYA 1, 2; SAAS 7; SATA 100; SATA-Obit 99

Hentoff, Nat(han Irving) 1925- **1, 52**
See also AAYA 4, 42; BYA 6; CA 1-4R; CAAS 6; CANR 5, 25, 77, 114; CLC 26; DLB 345; INT CANR-25; JRDA; MAICYA 1, 2; SATA 42, 69, 133; SATA-Brief 27; WYA; YAW

Henty, G(eorge) A(lfred) 1832-1902 ... **76, 249**
See also CA 112, 177; DLB 18, 141; RGEL 2; SATA 64

Herald, Kathleen
See Peyton, Kathleen Wendy

Hergé 1907-1983 .... **6, 114, 241**
See also AAYA 55; CA 69-72, 109; CANR 31; SATA 13; SATA-Obit 32; UGN

Herriot, James 1916-1995 .... **80**
See also AAYA 1, 54; BPFB 2; CA 77-80; 148; CANR 40; CLC 12; CPW; DAM POP; LAIT 3; MAICYA 2; MAICYAS 1; MTCW 2; SATA 86, 135; SATA-Brief 44; TEA; YAW

Hesse, Karen 1952- **54, 141**
See also AAYA 27, 52; BYA 9; CA 168; CANR 118; MAICYA 2; SAAS 25; SATA 74, 103, 158, 215; SATA-Essay 113; WYAS 1; YAW

Hicks, Harvey
See Stratemeyer, Edward L.

Highwater, Jamake (Mamake) 1942(?)-2001 .... **17**
See also AAYA 7, 69; BPFB 2; BYA 4; CA 65-68; 199; CAAS 7; CANR 10, 34, 84; CLC 12; CWRI 5; DLB 52; DLBY 1985; JRDA; MAICYA 1, 2; SATA 32, 69; SATA-Brief 30

Hill, Eric 1927- **13**
See also CA 134; CANR 111; MAICYA 1, 2; SATA 66, 133; SATA-Brief 53

Hilton, Margaret Lynette 1946- **25**
See also CA 136; CANR 105; SAAS 21; SATA 68, 105

Hilton, Nette
See Hilton, Margaret Lynette

Hilton-Bruce, Anne
See Hilton, Margaret Lynette

Hinton, S. E. 1950- **3, 23**
See also AAYA 2, 33; BPFB 2; BYA 2, 3; CA 81-84; CANR 32, 62, 92, 133; CDALBS; CLC 30, 111; CPW; DA; DA3; DAB; DAC; DAM MST, NOV; JRDA; LAIT 5; MAICYA 1, 2; MTCW 1, 2; MTFW 2005; NFS 5, 9, 15, 16, 35; SATA 19, 58, 115, 160; WYA; YAW

Hinton, Susan Eloise
See Hinton, S. E.

Hitz, Demi
See Demi

Ho, Minfong 1951- **28**
See also AAYA 29; CA 77-80; CANR 67, 150; MAICYA 2; MAICYAS 1; SATA 15, 94, 151; YAW

Hoban, Lillian 1925-1998 .... **67**
See also CA 69-72; 169; CANR 23; MAICYA 1, 2; SATA 22, 69; SATA-Obit 104

Hoban, Russell 1925-2011 .... **3, 69, 139, 242**
See also BPFB 2; CA 5-8R; CANR 23, 37, 66, 114, 138, 218; CLC 7, 25; CMTFW; CN 4, 5, 6, 7; CWRI 5; DAM NOV; DLB 52; FANT; MAICYA 1, 2; MTCW 1, 2; MTFW 2005; SATA 1, 40, 78, 136, 254; SFW 4; SUFW 2; TCLE 1:1

Hoban, Russell Conwell
See Hoban, Russell

Hoban, Tana 1917(?)-2006 .... **13, 76**
See also CA 93-96; 247; CANR 23, 141; MAICYA 1, 2; SAAS 12; SATA 22, 70, 104; SATA-Obit 173

Hobbie, Holly 1942- **88**
See also SATA 178, 225

Hobbs, Valerie 1941- **148**
See also AAYA 28, 78; CA 159; CANR 127, 184; SATA 93, 145, 193; SATA-Essay 145

Hobbs, Will 1947- **59**
See also AAYA 14, 39; BYA 6; CA 180; CANR 124, 162; MAICYA 2; MAICYAS 1; SATA 72, 110, 177; SATA-Essay 127; WYA; YAW

Hobbs, William Carl
See Hobbs, Will

Hoberman, Mary Ann 1930- **22**
See also CA 41-44R; CANR 124, 194; CWRI 5; MAICYA 1, 2; SAAS 18; SATA 5, 72, 111, 158, 228

Hoff, Syd(ney) 1912-2004 .... **83**
See also CA 5-8R; 227; CANR 4, 38, 117; CWRI 5; MAICYA 1, 2; SAAS 4; SATA 9, 72, 138; SATA-Obit 154

Hoffmann, E(rnst) T(heodor) A(madeus) 1776-1822 .... **133**
See also CDWLB 2; DLB 90; EW 5; GL 2; NCLC 2, 183; RGSF 2; RGWL 2, 3; SATA 27; SSC 13, 92; SUFW 1; WCH

Hoffmann, Heinrich 1809-1894 .... **70, 122**
See also WCH

Hogrogian, Nonny 1932- **2, 95**
See also CA 45-48; CANR 2, 49; MAICYA 1, 2; SAAS 1; SATA 7, 74; SATA-Essay 127

Holland, Isabelle (Christian) 1920-2002 .... **57**
See also AAYA 11, 64; CA 21-24R; 205; CAAE 181; CANR 10, 25, 47; CLC 21; CWRI 5; JRDA; LAIT 4; MAICYA 1, 2; SATA 8, 70; SATA-Essay 103; SATA-Obit 132; WYA

Hollander, Paul
See Silverberg, Robert

Holling, Holling C(lancy) 1900-1973 .... **50**
See also CA 106; CWRI 5; MAICYA 1, 2; SATA 15; SATA-Obit 26

Holm, (Else) Anne (Lise) 1922-1998 .... **75**
See also CA 17-20R; MAICYA 1, 2; SAAS 7; SATA 1; YAW

Holton, Leonard
See Wibberley, Leonard

Hopkins, Lee Bennett 1938- **44**
See also AAYA 18; CA 25-28R; CANR 29, 55, 104; JRDA; MAICYA 1, 2; MAICYAS 1; SAAS 4; SATA 3, 68, 125, 168, 215

Hopkinson, Deborah 1952- **118**
See also CA 143, 260; CAAE 260; CANR 72; SATA 76, 108, 159, 180, 216; SATA-Essay 180

Horvath, Polly 1957- **90**
See also CA 132; CANR 185; SATA 85, 140, 194

Houston, James A(rchibald) 1921-2005 .... **3**
See also AAYA 18; CA 65-68; 238; CANR 38, 60, 108; DAC; DAM MST; JRDA; MAICYA 1, 2; SAAS 17; SATA 13, 74; SATA-Obit 163; YAW

Howe, James 1946- **9**
See also CA 105; CANR 22, 46, 71, 146; CWRI 5; JRDA; MAICYA 1, 2; SATA 29, 71, 111, 161, 224

Howker, Janni 1957- **14**
See also AAYA 9, 68; CA 137; JRDA; MAICYA 1, 2; SAAS 13; SATA 72; SATA-Brief 46; YAW

Hudson, Jan 1954-1990 .... **40**
See also AAYA 22; BYA 15; CA 136; CWRI 5; JRDA; MAICYA 2; MAICYAS 1; NFS 28; SATA 77

Hughes, D. T.
See Hughes, Dean

Hughes, Dean 1943- **76**
See also AAYA 53; CA 106; CANR 22, 162; SATA 33, 77, 139, 235; YAW

Hughes, D.T.
See Hughes, Dean

Hughes, Edward James
See Hughes, Ted

Hughes, James Langston
See Hughes, Langston

Hughes, Langston 1902-1967 .... **17**
See also AAYA 12; AFAW 1, 2; AMWR 1; AMWS 1; BLC 1:2; BW 1, 3; CA 1-4R; 25-28R; CANR 1, 34, 82; CDALB 1929-1941; CLC 1, 5, 10, 15, 35, 44, 108; DA; DA3; DAB; DAC; DAM DRAM, MST, MULT, POET; DC 3; DFS 6, 18; DLB 4, 7, 48, 51, 86, 228, 315; EWL 3; EXPP; EXPS; HR 1:2; JRDA; LAIT 3; LMFS 2; MAICYA 1, 2; MAL 5; MTCW 1, 2; MTFW 2005; NFS 21; PAB; PC 1, 53; PFS 1, 3, 6, 10, 15, 30, 38; RGAL 4; RGSF 2; SATA 4, 33; SSC 6, 90; SSFS 4, 7, 29; TUS; WCH; WLC 3; WP; YAW

Hughes, Monica 1925-2003 .... **9, 60**
See also AAYA 19; BYA 6, 14, 15; CA 77-80; CANR 23, 46, 110; JRDA; MAICYA 1, 2; SAAS 11; SATA 15, 70, 119, 162; WYA; YAW

Hughes, Monica Ince
See Hughes, Monica

Hughes, Shirley 1927- **15**
See also CA 85-88; CANR 24, 47, 144; CWRI 5; MAICYA 1, 2; SATA 16, 70, 110, 159

Hughes, Ted 1930-1998 .... **3, 131**
See also BRWC 2; BRWR 2; BRWS 1; CA 1-4R; 171; CANR 1, 33, 66, 108; CLC 2, 4, 9, 14, 37, 119; CP 1, 2, 3, 4, 5, 6; DA3; DAB; DAC; DAM MST, POET; DLB 40, 161; EWL 3; EXPP; MAICYA 1, 2; MTCW 1, 2; MTFW 2005; PAB; PC 7, 89; PFS 4, 19, 32; RGEL 2; SATA 49; SATA-Brief 27; SATA-Obit 107; TEA; YAW

Hughes, Thomas 1822-1896 .... **160**
See also BYA 3; DLB 18, 163; LAIT 2; NCLC 207; RGEL 2; SATA 31

Hungerford, Hesba Fay
See Brinsmead, H(esba) F(ay)

Hungerford, Pixie
See Brinsmead, H(esba) F(ay)

Hunt, Charlotte Dumaresq
See Demi

Hunt, Francesca
See Holland, Isabelle (Christian)

Hunt, Irene 1907-2001 .... **1**
See also AAYA 18; BYA 1, 3; CA 17-20R; CANR 8, 57; DLB 52; JRDA; LAIT 2; MAICYA 1, 2; SATA 2, 91; YAW

Hunter, Kristin
See Lattany, Kristin Hunter

Hunter, Mollie 1922- **25**
See also AAYA 13, 71; BYA 6; CANR 37, 78; CLC 21; DLB 161; JRDA; MAICYA 1, 2; SAAS 7; SATA 2, 54, 106, 139; SATA-Essay 139; WYA; YAW

Hunter Blair, Pauline
See Clarke, Pauline

Hurd, Clement (G.) 1908-1988 .... **49**
See also CA 29-32R; 124; CANR 9, 24; MAICYA 1, 2; SATA 2, 64; SATA-Obit 54

Hurd, Edith Thacher 1910-1997 .... **49**
See also CA 13-16R; 156; CANR 9, 24; MAICYA 1, 2; MAICYAS 1; SAAS 13; SATA 2, 64; SATA-Obit 95

Hurmence, Belinda 1921- **25**
See also AAYA 17; CA 145; JRDA; MAICYA 2; MAICYAS 1; SAAS 20; SATA 77

Hurston, Zora Neale 1891-1960 .... **177**
See also AAYA 15, 71; AFAW 1, 2; AMWS 6; BLC 1:2; BW 1, 3; BYA 12; CA 85-88; CANR 61; CDALBS; CLC 7, 30, 61; DA; DA3; DAC; DAM MST, MULT, NOV; DC 12; DFS 6, 30; DLB 51, 86; EWL 3; EXPN; EXPS; FL 1:6; FW; HR 1:2; LAIT 3; LATS 1:1; LMFS 2; MAL 5; MBL;

MTCW 1, 2; MTFW 2005; NFS 3; RGAL 4; RGSF 2; SSC 4, 80; SSFS 1, 6, 11, 19, 21; TCLC 121, 131, 285; TUS; WLCS; YAW

Hutchins, Pat 1942- **20**
See also CA 81-84; CANR 15, 32, 64, 125; CWRI 5; MAICYA 1, 2; SAAS 16; SATA 15, 70, 111, 178

Huxley, Aldous 1894-1963 .... **151**
See also AAYA 11; BPFB 2; BRW 7; CA 85-88; CANR 44, 99; CDBLB 1914-1945; CLC 1, 3, 4, 5, 8, 11, 18, 35, 79; DA; DA3; DAB; DAC; DAM MST, NOV; DLB 36, 100, 162, 195, 255; EWL 3; EXPN; LAIT 5; LMFS 2; MTCW 1, 2; MTFW 2005; NFS 6; RGEL 2; SATA 63; SCFW 1, 2; SFW 4; SSC 39; TEA; WLC 3; YAW

Huxley, Aldous Leonard
See Huxley, Aldous

Hyde, Margaret O. 1917- **23**
See also CA 1-4R; CANR 1, 36, 137, 181; CLC 21; JRDA; MAICYA 1, 2; SAAS 8; SATA 1, 42, 76, 139

Hyde, Margaret Oldroyd
See Hyde, Margaret O.

Hyman, Trina Schart 1939-2004 .... **50**
See also CA 49-52; 233; CANR 24, 70; CWRI 5; DLB 61; MAICYA 1, 2; MAICYAS 1; SATA 7, 46, 95; SATA-Obit 158

Ichikawa, Satomi 1949- **62**
See also CA 116; 126; CANR 129; MAICYA 2; MAICYAS 1; SATA 47, 78, 146, 208; SATA-Brief 36

Innocenti, Roberto 1940- **56, 126**
See also MAICYA 2; MAICYAS 1; SATA 96, 159

Innocenti and Gallaz
See Gallaz, Christophe; Innocenti, Roberto

Irving, Robert
See Adler, Irving

Irving, Washington 1783-1859 .... **97**
See also AAYA 56; AMW; CDALB 1640-1865; DA; DA3; DAB; DAC; DAM MST; DLB 3, 11, 30, 59, 73, 74, 183, 186, 250, 254; EXPS; GL 2; LAIT 1; NCLC 2, 19, 95, 242; RGAL 4; RGSF 2; SSC 2, 37, 104; SSFS 1, 8, 16; SUFW 1; TUS; WCH; WLC 3; YABC 2

Irwin, Ann(abelle Bowen) 1915-1998 ...... **40**
See also AAYA 13; BYA 8; CA 101; 170; CANR 19, 36; MAICYA 1, 2; SAAS 14; SATA 44, 89; SATA-Brief 38; SATA-Obit 106; WYA; YAW

Irwin, Hadley
See Hadley, Lee; Irwin, Ann(abelle Bowen)

Isadora, Rachel 1953(?)- **7**
See also CA 111; 137; CANR 99, 151; CWRI 5; MAICYA 1, 2; SATA 54, 79, 121, 165, 204; SATA-Brief 32

Ives, Morgan
See Bradley, Marion Zimmer

Iwamatsu, Jun Atsushi 1908-1994 .... **4**
See also CA 73-76; 146; CANR 45; CWRI 5; MAICYA 1, 2; MAICYAS 1; SATA 14, 81

Iwasaki (Matsumoto), Chihiro 1918-1974 .... **18**
See also CA 233

Jackson, Jesse 1908-1983 .... **28**
See also BW 1; CA 25-28R; 109; CANR 27; CLC 12; CWRI 5; MAICYA 1, 2; SATA 2, 29; SATA-Obit 48

Jacques, Brian 1939-2011 .... **21**
See also AAYA 20; BYA 16; CA 127; CANR 68, 117, 161; FANT; JRDA; MAICYA 2; MAICYAS 1; SATA 62, 95, 138, 176; YAW

James, Captain Lew
See Stratemeyer, Edward L.

James, Dynely
See Mayne, William

James, Henry 1843-1916 .... **189, 255**
See also AAYA 84; AMW; AMWC 1; AMWR 1; BPFB 2; BRW 6; CA 104;132; CDALB 1865-1917; DA; DA3; DAB; DAC; DAM MST, NOV; DC 41; DLB 12, 71, 74, 189, 381; DLBD 13; EWL 3; EXPS; GCEAL; GL 2; HGG; LAIT 2; MAL 5; MBL 2; MTCW 1, 2; MTFW 2005; NFS 12, 16, 19, 32, 37, 44; RGAL 4; RGEL 2; RGSF 2; SSC 8, 32, 47, 108, 150, 196, 201, 205, 237, 239, 248, 285, 303; SSFS 9; SUFW 1; TCLC 2, 11, 24, 40, 47, 64, 171; TUS; WLC 3

James, Mary
See Meaker, Marijane

James, Philip
See Moorcock, Michael

Janeczko, Paul B(ryan) 1945- **47**
See also AAYA 9, 28; CA 104; CANR 22, 49, 105, 155; MAICYA 2; MAICYAS 1; SAAS 18; SATA 53, 98, 155; YAW

Janosch
See Eckert, Horst

Janson, Hank
See Moorcock, Michael

Jansson, Tove (Marika) 1914-2001 .... **2, 125**
See also CA 17-20R; 196; CANR 38, 118; CWW 2; DLB 257; EWL 3; MAICYA 1, 2; RGSF 2; SATA 3, 41; SSC 96

Jarrell, Randall 1914-1965 .... **6, 111**
See also AMW; BYA 5; CA 5-8R; 25-28R; CABS 2; CANR 6, 34; CDALB 1941-1968; CLC 1, 2, 6, 9, 13, 49; CWRI 5; DAM POET; DLB 48, 52; EWL 3; EXPP; MAICYA 1, 2; MAL 5; MTCW 1, 2; PAB; PC 41; PFS 2, 31; RGAL 4; SATA 7; TCLC 177

Jarvis, E.K.
See Silverberg, Robert

Jefferies, Richard 1848-1887 .... **217**
See also BRWS 15; DLB 98, 141; NCLC 47; RGEL 2; SFW 4; SATA 16

Jeffers, Susan 1942- **30**
See also CA 97-100; CANR 44; MAICYA 1, 2; SATA 17, 70, 129, 137, 202

Jenkins, Will F.
See Leinster, Murray

Jennings, Paul 1943- **40**
See also AAYA 28; CA 170; CANR 93, 151; DLB 352; MAICYA 2; MAICYAS 1; SATA 88, 165

Jennison, C. S.
See Starbird, Kaye

Johnson, Angela 1961- **33**
See also AAYA 32, 86; CA 138; CANR 92, 134, 174; CWRI 5; MAICYA 2; MAICYAS 1; SATA 69, 102, 150, 188

Johnson, Crockett
See Leisk, David (Johnson)

Johnson, James Weldon 1871-1938 ... **32, 247**
See also AAYA 73; AFAW 1, 2; BLC 1:2; BW 1, 3; CA 104; 125; CANR 82; CDALB 1917-1929; DA3; DAM MULT, POET; DLB 51; EWL 3; EXPP; HR 1:3; LMFS 2; MAL 5; MTCW 1, 2; MTFW 2005; NFS 22; PC 24; PFS 1; RGAL 4; SATA 31; TCLC 3, 19, 175; TUS

Johnson, Marguerite Annie
See Angelou, Maya

Johnson, Stacie
See Myers, Walter Dean

Johnston, Julie 1941- **41**
See also AAYA 27; CA 146; CANR 69, 122; MAICYA 2; MAICYAS 1; SAAS 24; SATA 78, 110; SATA-Essay 128; YAW

Johnston, Norma
See St. John, Nicole

Jonas, Ann 1932- **12, 74**
See also CA 118; 136; CWRI 5; MAICYA 1, 2; SATA 50, 135; SATA-Brief 42

Jones, Diana Wynne 1934-2011 .... **23, 120**
See also AAYA 12; BYA 6, 7, 9, 11, 13, 16; CA 49-52; CANR 4, 26, 56, 120, 167; CLC 26; DLB 161; FANT; JRDA; MAICYA 1, 2; MTFW 2005; SAAS 7; SATA 9, 70, 108, 160, 234; SFW 4; SUFW 2; YAW

Jones, Geraldine
See McCaughrean, Geraldine

Jones, Tim Wynne
See Wynne-Jones, Tim

Jordan, June 1936-2002 .... **10**
See also AAYA 2, 66; AFAW 1, 2; BLCS; BW 2, 3; CA 33-36R; 206; CANR 25, 70, 114, 154; CLC 5, 11, 23, 114, 230; CP 3, 4, 5, 6, 7; CWP; DAM MULT, POET; DLB 38; GLL 2; LAIT 5; MAICYA 1, 2; MTCW 1; PC 38; SATA 4, 136; YAW

Jordan, June Meyer
See Jordan, June

Jorgenson, Ivar
See Silverberg, Robert

Josh
See Twain, Mark

Joyce, Bill
See Joyce, William

Joyce, William 1957- **26**
See also AAYA 38; CA 124; CANR 96, 172; CWRI 5; MAICYA 2; MAICYAS 1; SATA 72, 118; SATA-Brief 46

Juster, Norton 1929- **112**
See also BYA 5; CA 13-16R; CANR 13, 44, 83, 148; FANT; JRDA; MAICYA 1, 2; SATA 3, 132, 220; YAW

Kadohata, Cynthia 1956(?)- **121**
See also AAYA 71; CA 140; CANR 124, 205; CLC 59, 122; LNFS 1; SATA 155, 180, 228

Kadohata, Cynthia L.
See Kadohata, Cynthia

Kaestner, Erich 1899-1974 .... **4, 153**
See also CA 73-76; 49-52; CANR 40; DLB 56; EWL 3; IDFW 4; MAICYA 1, 2; SATA 14; WCH

Kafka, Franz 1883-1924 .... **193**
See also AAYA 31; BPFB 2; CA 105; 126; CDWLB 2; DA; DA3; DAB; DAC; DAM MST, NOV; DLB 81; EW 9; EWL 3; EXPS; LATS 1:1; LMFS 2; MTCW 1, 2; MTFW 2005; NFS 7, 34; RGSF 2; RGWL 2, 3; SFW 4; SSFS 3, 7, 12, 33; TWA

Kalman, Maira 1949- **32**
See also CA 161; CANR 116; MAICYA 2; MAICYAS 1; SATA 96, 137

Karageorge, Michael
See Anderson, Poul

Kark, Nina Mary
See Bawden, Nina

Kastel, Warren
See Silverberg, Robert

Kastner, Erich
See Kaestner, Erich

Katz, Welwyn Wilton 1948- **45**
See also AAYA 19; CA 154; CANR 127; JRDA; MAICYA 2; MAICYAS 1; SATA 62, 96; SATA-Essay 118; YAW

Kaur Khalsa, Dayal
See Khalsa, Dayal Kaur

Keats, Ezra Jack 1916-1983 .... **1, 35**
See also AITN 1; CA 77-80; 109; CANR 85; CWRI 5; DLB 61; MAICYA 1, 2; SATA 14, 57; SATA-Obit 34

Keene, Carolyn
See McFarlane, Leslie; Stratemeyer, Edward L.

Keeping, Charles (William James) 1924-1988 .... **34**
See also AAYA 26; CA 21-24R; 125; CANR 11, 43; CWRI 5; MAICYA 1, 2; SATA 9, 69; SATA-Obit 56

Kelleher, Victor (Michael Kitchener) 1939- **36**

See also AAYA 31; CA 126; CANR 56, 109; CN 5, 6, 7; HGG; SATA 75, 129; SATA-Brief 52; YAW

Keller, Holly 1942- **45**
See also CA 118; 235; MAICYA 2; SATA 76, 108, 157, 216; SATA-Brief 42

Kellogg, Steven 1941- **6**
See also CA 49-52; CANR 1, 110, 162; CWRI 5; DLB 61; MAICYA 1, 2; SATA 8, 57, 130, 177

Kellogg, Steven Castle
See Kellogg, Steven

Kemp, Gene 1926- **29**
See also CA 69-72; CANR 12, 85; CWRI 5; MAICYA 1, 2; SATA 25, 75

Kendall, Katherine
See Applegate, Katherine

Kennedy, Joseph Charles
See Kennedy, X. J.

Kennedy, X. J. 1929- **27**
See also AMWS 15; CA 1-4R, 201; CAAE 201; CAAS 1; CANR 4, 30, 40, 214; CLC 8, 42; CP 1, 2, 3, 4, 5, 6, 7; CWRI 5; DLB 5; MAICYA 2; MAICYAS 1; PC 93; SAAS 22; SATA 14, 86, 130; SATA-Essay 130

Kenny, Kathryn
See Krull, Kathleen

Kenny, Kevin
See Krull, Kathleen

Kerr, M. E.
See Meaker, Marijane

Kerry, Lois
See Duncan, Lois

Kesey, Ken 1935-2001 .... **170**
See also AAYA 25; BG 1:3; BPFB 2; CA 1-4R; 204; CANR 22, 38, 66, 124; CDALB 1968-1988; CLC 1, 3, 6, 11, 46, 64, 184; CN 1, 2, 3, 4, 5, 6, 7; CPW; DA; DA3; DAB; DAC; DAM MST, NOV, POP; DLB 2, 16, 206; EWL 3; EXPN; LAIT 4; MAL 5; MTCW 1, 2; MTFW 2005; NFS 2; RGAL 4; SATA 66; SATA-Obit 131; TUS; WLC 3; YAW

Khalsa, Dayal Kaur 1943-1989 .... **30**
See also CA 137; 129; CANR 85; CWRI 5; MAICYA 1, 2; SATA 62

Kherdian, David 1931- **24**
See also AAYA 42; CA 21-24R, 192; CAAE 192; CAAS 2; CANR 39, 78; CLC 6, 9; JRDA; LAIT 3; MAICYA 1, 2; SATA 16, 74; SATA-Essay 125

Kilgalen, Milton
See Tarkington, Booth

Kincaid, Jamaica 1949- **63**
See also AAYA 13, 56; AFAW; AMWS 7; BLC 1:2, 2:2; BRWS 7; BW 2, 3; CA 125; CANR 47, 59, 95, 133; CDALBS; CDWLB 3; CLC 43, 68, 137, 234; CN 4, 5, 6, 7; DA3; DAM MULT, NOV; DLB 157, 227; DNFS 1; EWL 3; EXPS; FW; LATS 1:2; LMFS 2; MAL 5; MTCW 2; MTFW 2005; NCFS 1; NFS 3; SSC 72; SSFS 5, 7; TUS; WWE 1; YAW

Kindl, Patrice 1951- **132**
See also AAYA 55; CA 149; CANR 115; SATA 82, 128

King, Martin Luther, Jr. 1929-1968 .... **206**
See also BLC 2; BW 2, 3; CA 25-28; CANR 27, 44; CAP 2; CLC 83; DA; DAB; DAC; DAM MST, DAM MULT; DA3; LAIT 5; LAITS 1; MTCW 1, 2; MTFW; SATA 14; WLCS 1

King, Stephen 1947- **124, 194**
See also AAYA 1, 17, 82; AMWS 5; BEST 90:1; BPFB 2; CA 61-64; CANR 1, 30, 52, 76, 119, 134, 168, 227; CLC 12, 26, 37, 61, 113, 228, 244; CN 7; CPW; DA3; DAM NOV, POP; DLB 143, 350; DLBY 1980; HGG; JRDA; LAIT 5; LNFS 1; MTCW 1, 2; MTFW 2005; RGAL 4; SATA 9, 55, 161; SSC 17, 55; SSFS 30; SUFW 1, 2; WYAS 1; YAW

King, Stephen Edwin
See King, Stephen

King, Steve
See King, Stephen

Kingsley, Charles 1819-1875 .... **77, 167, 234**
See also BRWS 16; DLB 21, 32, 163, 178, 190; FANT; MAICYA 2; MAICYAS 1; NCLC 35; RGEL 2; WCH; YABC 2

King-Smith, Dick 1922-2011 .... **40**
See also CA 105; CANR 85; CWRI 5; MAICYA 1, 2; SATA 47, 80, 135, 192; SATA-Brief 38

Kipling, Joseph Rudyard
See Kipling, Rudyard

Kipling, Rudyard 1865-1936 .... **39, 65, 83, 199, 212, 257, 259**
See also AAYA 32; BRW 6; BRWC 1, 2; BRWR 3; BYA 4; CA 105, 120; CANR 33; CDBLB 1890-1914; CLC 17; DA; DA3; DAB; DAC; DAM MST, POET; DLB 19, 34, 141, 156, 330; EWL 3; EXPS; FANT; LAIT 3; LMFS 1; MAICYA 1, 2; MBL 2; MTCW 1, 2; MTFW 2005; NFS 21; PC 3, 91; PFS 22; RGEL 2; RGSF 2; SATA 100; SFW 4; SSC 5, 54, 110, 207, 217, 222; SSFHW; SSFS 8, 21, 22, 32; SUFW 1; TCLC 8, 17, 167; TEA; WCH; WLC 3; WLIT 4; YABC 2

Kirkham, Dinah
See Card, Orson Scott

Kitamura, Satoshi 1956- **60**
See also CA 165; CANR 122; SATA 62, 98, 143, 201

Kjelgaard, James Arthur 1910-1959 .... **81**
See also CA 109; 137; CANR 84; CWRI 5; JRDA; MAICYA 1, 2; SATA 17

Kjelgaard, Jim
See Kjelgaard, James Arthur

Klause, Annette Curtis 1953- **104**
See also AAYA 27; BPFA 14; BYA 12; CA 147; CANR 83, 162; SATA 79, 175; WYAS 1; YAW

Klein, Norma 1938-1989 .... **2, 19, 162**
See also AAYA 2, 35; BPFB 2; BYA 6, 7, 8; CA 41-44R; 128; CANR 15, 37; CLC 30; INT CANR-15; JRDA; MAICYA 1, 2; SAAS 1; SATA 7, 57; WYA; YAW

Klein, Robin 1936- **21**
See also AAYA 21; CA 116; CANR 40, 150; JRDA; MAICYA 1, 2; SATA 55, 80, 164; SATA-Brief 45; YAW

Kleven, Elisa 1958- **85**
See also CA 143; SATA 76, 173, 217

Knickerbocker, Diedrich
See Irving, Washington

Knight, David C(arpenter) 1925-1984 ..... **38**
See also CA 73-76; SATA 14

Knight, Kathryn Lasky
See Lasky, Kathryn

Knowles, John 1926-2001 .... **98**
See also AAYA 10, 72; AMWS 12; BPFB 2; BYA 3; CA 17-20R; 203; CANR 40, 74, 76, 132; CDALB 1968-1988; CLC 1, 4, 10, 26; CN 1, 2, 3, 4, 5, 6, 7; DA; DAC; DAM MST, NOV; DLB 6; EXPN; MTCW 1, 2; MTFW 2005; NFS 2; RGAL 4; SATA 8, 89; SATA-Obit 134; YAW

Knox, Calvin M.
See Silverberg, Robert

Knye, Cassandra
See Disch, Thomas M.

Koller, Jackie French 1948- **68**
See also AAYA 28; CA 170; CANR 141; SATA 72, 109, 157

Konigsburg, E.L. 1930- **1, 47, 81**
See also AAYA 3, 41; BYA 1, 2, 3, 9; CA 21-24R; CANR 17, 39, 59, 106, 155, 185; CWRI 5; DLB 52; INT CANR-17; JRDA; MAICYA 1, 2; MAICYAS 1; MTCW 1; SATA 4, 48, 94, 126, 194; TUS; YAW

Konigsburg, Elaine Lobl
See Konigsburg, E.L.

Korczak, Janusz
See Goldsmit, Henryk

Korinets, Iurii Iosifovich
See Korinetz, Yuri (Iosifovich)

Korinetz, Yuri (Iosifovich) 1923- **4**
See also CA 61-64; CANR 11; SATA 9

Korman, Gordon 1963- **25**
See also AAYA 10, 44; CA 112; CANR 34, 56, 90, 154, 197; CCA 1; CWRI 5; JRDA; MAICYA 1, 2; SATA 49, 81, 119, 167, 226; SATA-Brief 41; WYA

Korman, Gordon Richard
See Korman, Gordon

Kotzwinkle, William 1938- **6**
See also BPFB 2; CA 45-48; CANR 3, 44, 84, 129; CLC 5, 14, 35; CN 7; DLB 173; FANT; MAICYA 1, 2; SATA 24, 70, 146; SFW 4; SUFW 2; YAW

Kovalski, Maryann 1951- **34**
See also CA 163; CANR 149; SAAS 21; SATA 58, 97, 175

Krahn, Fernando 1935- **3**
See also CA 65-68; CANR 11; SATA 49; SATA-Brief 31

Krasilovsky, Phyllis 1926- **83**
See also CA 29-32R; CANR 11, 45, 85; CWRI 5; MAICYA 1, 2; SAAS 5; SATA 1, 38

Krauss, Ruth 1911-1993 .... **42**
See also CA 1-4R; 141; CAD; CANR 1, 13, 47, 83; CWD; CWRI 5; DLB 52; MAICYA 1, 2; SATA 1, 30; SATA-Obit 75

Krauss, Ruth Ida
See Krauss, Ruth

Krementz, Jill 1940- **5**
See also AITN 1, 2; CA 41-44R; CANR 23, 46, 112; INT CANR-23; MAICYA 1, 2; SAAS 8; SATA 17, 71, 134

Kropp, Paul 1948- **96**
See also CA 112; CANR 96, 187; SATA 38; SATA-Brief 34; YAW

Kropp, Paul Stephan
See Kropp, Paul

Kruess, James
See Kruss, James

Krull, Kathleen 1952- **44**
See also CA 106; CANR 132, 169; MAICYA 2; MAICYAS 1; SATA 52, 80, 149, 184, 229; SATA-Brief 39; SATA-Essay 106

Kruss, James 1926-1997 .... **9**
See also CA 53-56; CANR 5; MAICYA 1, 2; SATA 8

Kuklin, Susan 1941- **51**
See also AAYA 27; CA 130; CANR 67, 149, 207; MAICYA 2; SATA 63, 95, 163

Kuratomi, Chizuko 1939- **32**
See also CA 21-24R; CANR 10; SATA 12

Kurelek, William 1927-1977 .... **2, 210**
See also CA 49-52; CANR 3, 85; CCA 1; CWRI 5; JRDA; MAICYA 1, 2; SATA 8; SATA-Obit 27

Kurtz, Jane 1952- **123**
See also CA 155; SATA 91, 139

Kurtzman, Harvey 1924-1993 .... **209**
See also CA 216

Kushner, Donn (J.) 1927- **55**
See also CA 113; CANR 35; CWRI 5; SATA 52

Kuskin, Karla 1932-2009 .... **4**
See also CA 1-4R; 289; CANR 4, 22, 41, 136; CWRI 5; MAICYA 1, 2; SAAS 3; SATA 2, 68, 111, 164; SATA-Obit 206

Kuskin, Karla Seidman
See Kuskin, Karla

Lackey, Mercedes 1950- 193
See also AAYA 13; BPFB 2; CA 126; CANR 51, 97, 146, 211, 242; FANT; SATA 81, 127; SUFW; YAW

Lagerloef, Selma
See Lagerlof, Selma

Lagerloef, Selma Ottiliana Lovisa
See Lagerlof, Selma

Lagerlof, Selma 1858-1940 7
See also CA 108; 188; DLB 259, 331; MTCW 2; RGWL 2, 3; SATA 15; SSFS 18, 35; TCLC 4, 36

Lagerlof, Selma Ottiliana Lovisa
See Lagerlof, Selma

Laird, Elizabeth 1943- 65
See also AAYA 63; CA 128; CANR 65, 127; SATA 77, 114, 159, 228

Laird, Elizabeth Mary Risk
See Laird, Elizabeth

Lang, Andrew 1844-1912 .... 101, 174, 227
See also CA 114, 137; CANR 85; DLB 98, 141, 184; FANT; MAICYA 1, 2; MBL 2; RGEL 2; SATA 16; TCLC 16; WCH

Lang, T.T.
See Taylor, Theodore

Langstaff, John 1920-2005 3
See also CA 1-4R; 246; CANR 4, 49; MAICYA 1, 2; SATA 6, 68; SATA-Obit 172

Langstaff, John Meredith
See Langstaff, John

Langstaff, Launcelot
See Irving, Washington

Langton, Jane 1922- 33
See also BYA 5; CA 1-4R; CANR 1, 18, 40, 83, 109, 191; CMW 4; MAICYA 1, 2; SAAS 5; SATA 3, 68, 129, 140, 200; SATA-Essay 140; YAW

Lanzelot, Sacha
See Salten, Felix

Larkin, Maia
See Wojciechowska, Maia (Teresa)

Lasky, Kathryn 1944- 11, 140
See also AAYA 19; BYA 6; CA 69-72; CANR 11, 84, 141, 206; JRDA; MAICYA 1, 2; SATA 13, 69, 112, 157, 210, 236; WYA; YAW

Lasky Knight, Kathryn
See Lasky, Kathryn

Latham, Jean Lee 1902-1995 50
See also AITN 1; BYA 1; CA 5-8R; CANR 7, 84; CLC 12; MAICYA 1, 2; SATA 2, 68; YAW

Latham, Mavis
See Clark, Mavis Thorpe

Lattany, Kristin
See Lattany, Kristin Hunter

Lattany, Kristin Elaine Eggleston Hunter
See Lattany, Kristin Hunter

Lattany, Kristin Hunter 1931-2008 3
See also AITN 1; BW 1; BYA 3; CA 13-16R; CANR 13, 108; CLC 35; CN 1, 2, 3, 4, 5, 6; DLB 33; INT CANR-13; MAICYA 1, 2; SAAS 10; SATA 12, 132; YAW

Lauber, Patricia (Grace) 1924- 16
See also CA 9-12R; CANR 6, 24, 38, 117; JRDA; MAICYA 1, 2; SATA 1, 33, 75, 138

Lavine, Sigmund Arnold 1908-1986 35
See also CA 1-4R; CANR 4, 19, 41; SATA 3, 82

Lawson, Julie 1947- 89
See also CA 196; CANR 170; SATA 79, 126

Lawson, Robert 1892-1957 .... 2, 73
See also BYA 5; CA 118; 137; CWRI 5; DLB 22; MAICYA 1, 2; SATA 100; WCH; YABC 2

Lea, Joan
See Neufeld, John (Arthur)

Leaf, (Wilbur) Munro 1905-1976 25
See also CA 73-76; 69-72; CANR 29, 85; CWRI 5; MAICYA 1, 2; SATA 20

Lear, Edward 1812-1888 .... 1, 75, 169
See also CA 48; BRW 5; DLB 32, 163, 166; MAICYA 1, 2; NCLC 3; PC 65; RGEL 2; SATA 18, 100; WCH; WP

Lee, Dennis (Beynon) 1939- 3
See also CA 25-28R; CANR 11, 31, 57, 61, 119; CP 1, 2, 3, 4, 5, 6, 7; CWRI 5; DAC; DLB 53; MAICYA 1, 2; SATA 14, 102

Lee, Harper 1926- 169
See also AAYA 13; AMWS 8; BPFB 2; BYA 3; CA 13-16R; CANR 51, 128; CDALB 1941-1968; CLC 12, 60, 194; CSW; DA; DA3; DAB; DAC; DAM MST, NOV; DLB 6; EXPN; LAIT 3; MAL 5; MTCW 1, 2; MTFW 2005; NFS 2, 32; SATA 11; WLC 4; WYA; YAW

Lee, Julian
See Latham, Jean Lee

Lee, Louisa Carter
See Leinster, Murray

Lee, Nelle Harper
See Lee, Harper

Lee, Stan 1922- 207
See also AAYA 5, 49; CMTFW; CA 108, 111; CANR 129; CLC 17; MTFW

Le Guin, Ursula K. 1929- 3, 28, 91, 173
See also AAYA 9, 27, 84; AITN 1; BPFB 2; BYA 5, 8, 11, 14; CA 21-24R; CANR 9, 32, 52, 74, 132, 192; CDALB 1968-1988; CLC 8, 13, 22, 45, 71, 136, 310; CN 2, 3, 4, 5, 6, 7; CPW; DA3; DAB; DAC; DAM MST, POP; DLB 8, 52, 256, 275; EXPS; FANT; FW; INT CANR-32; JRDA; LAIT 5; MAICYA 1, 2; MAL 5; MTCW 1, 2; MTFW 2005; NFS 6, 9; SATA 4, 52, 99, 149, 194; SCFW 1, 2; SFW 4; SSC 12, 69; SSFS 2; SUFW 1, 2; WYA; YAW

Le Guin, Ursula Kroeber
See Le Guin, Ursula K.

Leisk, David (Johnson) 1906-1975 98
See also CA 9-12R; 57-60; CWRI 5; MAICYA 1, 2; SATA 1, 30; SATA-Obit 26

Leinster, Murray 1896-1975 192
See also CA 9-12R; 57-60; CANR 4, 63; DLB 8; SCFW 1, 2; SFW 4; TCWW 1, 2

L'Engle, Madeleine 1918-2007 ...... 1, 14, 57, 172, 261
See also AAYA 1, 28; AITN 2; BPFB 2; BYA 2, 4, 5, 7; CA 1-4R, 264; CANR 3, 21, 39, 66, 107, 207; CLC 12; CMTFW; CPW; CWRI 5; DA3; DAM POP; DLB 52, 389; JRDA; MAICYA 1, 2; MTCW 1, 2; MTFW 2005; NFS 32; SAAS 15; SATA 1, 27, 75, 128; SATA-Obit 186; SFW 4; SSFHW; WYA; YAW

L'Engle, Madeleine Camp Franklin
See L'Engle, Madeleine

Lenski, Lois 1893-1974 26
See also BYA 3; CA 13-14; 53-56; CANR 41, 80; CAP 1; CWRI 5; DLB 22; MAICYA 1, 2; SATA 1, 26, 100

Lerner, Carol 1927- 34
See also CA 102; CANR 70; MAICYA 2; MAICYAS 1; SAAS 12; SATA 33, 86

LeShan, Eda J(oan) 1922-2002 6
See also CA 13-16R; 205; CANR 21; SATA 21

LeSieg, Theo.
See Dr. Seuss

Lester, Julius 1939- 2, 41, 143
See also AAYA 12, 51; BLC 2:2; BW 2; BYA 3, 9, 11, 12; CA 17-20R; CANR 8, 23, 43, 129, 174; JRDA; MAICYA 1, 2; MAICYAS 1; MTFW 2005; SATA 12, 74, 112, 157; YAW

Lester, Julius Bernard
See Lester, Julius

Levine, Gail Carson 1947- 85
See also AAYA 37; BYA 11; CA 166; CANR 118, 165, 186; MAICYA 2; SATA 98, 161, 195, 239

Levithan, David 1972- 181
See also AAYA 85; CA 242; CANR 188; SATA 166, 235

Levitin, Sonia 1934- 53
See also AAYA 13, 48; CA 29-32R; CANR 14, 32, 79, 182; CLC 17; JRDA; MAICYA 1, 2; SAAS 2; SATA 4, 68, 119, 131, 192; SATA-Essay 131; YAW

Levon, O. U.
See Kesey, Ken

Lewin, Hugh 1939- 9
See also CA 113; CANR 38; MAICYA 1, 2; SATA 72; SATA-Brief 40

Lewis, C. S. 1898-1963 .... 3, 27, 109, 173, 242
See also AAYA 3, 39; BPFB 2; BRWS 3; BYA 15, 16; CA 81-84; CANR 33, 71, 132; CDBLB 1945-1960; CLC 1, 3, 6, 14, 27, 124; CWRI 5; DA; DA3; DAB; DAC; DAM MST, NOV, POP; DLB 15, 100, 160, 255; EWL 3; FANT; JRDA; LMFS 2; MAICYA 1, 2; MTCW 1, 2; MTFW 2005; NFS 24; RGEL 2; SATA 13, 100; SCFW 1, 2; SFW 4; SUFW 1; TCLC 380, 382, 393; TEA; WCH; WLC 4; WYA; YAW

Lewis, Clive Staples
See Lewis, C. S.

Lindgren, Astrid (Anna Emilia Ericsson) 1907-2002 .... 1, 39, 119, 260
See also BYA 5; CA 13-16R, 204; CANR 39, 80, 117; CLC 361; CWW 2; DLB 257; MAICYA 1, 2; SATA 2, 38, 291; SATA-Obit 128; TWA

Lindgren, Barbro 1937- 20, 86
See also CA 149; CANR 119; SATA 63, 120, 207; SATA-Brief 46

Lindsay, Norman Alfred William 1879-1969 8
See also CA 102; CANR 79; CWRI 5; DLB 260; SATA 67

Lingard, Joan (Amelia) 1932- 89
See also AAYA 38; BYA 12; CA 41-44R; CANR 18, 40, 79; JRDA; MAICYA 1, 2; SAAS 5; SATA 8, 74, 114, 130; SATA-Essay 130; YAW

Lionni, Leo(nard) 1910-1999 .... 7, 71
See also CA 53-56; 187; CANR 38; CWRI 5; DLB 61; MAICYA 1, 2; SATA 8, 72; SATA-Obit 118

Lipsyte, Robert 1938- 23, 76
See also AAYA 7, 45; CA 17-20R; CANR 8, 57, 146, 189; CLC 21; DA; DAC; DAM MST, NOV; JRDA; LAIT 5; MAICYA 1, 2; NFS 35; SATA 5, 68, 113, 161, 198; WYA; YAW

Lipsyte, Robert Michael
See Lipsyte, Robert

Little, (Flora) Jean 1932- 4
See also AAYA 43; CA 21-24R; CANR 42, 66, 121; CWRI 5; DAC; DAM MST; JRDA; MAICYA 1, 2; SAAS 17; SATA 2, 68, 106, 149; YAW

Lively, Penelope 1933- 7, 159
See also BPFB 2; CA 41-44R; CANR 29, 67, 79, 131, 172, 222; CLC 32, 50, 306; CN 5, 6, 7; CWRI 5; DAM NOV; DLB 14, 161, 207, 326; FANT; JRDA; MAICYA 1, 2; MTCW 1, 2; MTFW 2005; SATA 7, 60, 101, 164; TEA

Lively, Penelope Margaret
See Lively, Penelope

Livingston, Myra Cohn 1926-1996 7
See also CA 1-4R; 153; CANR 1, 33, 58; CWRI 5; DLB 61; INT CANR-33; MAICYA 1, 2; MAICYAS 1; SAAS 1; SATA 5, 68; SATA-Obit 92

Lobel, Arnold (Stark) 1933-1987 .... **5**
See also AITN 1; CA 1-4R; 124; CANR 2, 33, 79; CWRI 5; DLB 61; MAICYA 1, 2; SATA 6, 55; SATA-Obit 54

Locke, Robert 1944- **39**
See also CA 129; SATA 63

Locker, Thomas 1937- **14**
See also CA 128; CANR 66, 91; MAICYA 1, 2; SATA 59, 109

Lofting, Hugh (John) 1886-1947 ...... **19, 143**
See also BYA 5; CA 109; 137; CANR 73; CWRI 5; DLB 160; FANT; MAICYA 1, 2; SATA 15, 100; TEA; WCH

London, Jack 1876-1916 .... **108**
See also AAYA 13, 75; AITN 2; AMW; BPFB 2; BYA 4, 13; CA 110; 119; CANR 73; CDALB 1865-1917; DA; DA3; DAB; DAC; DAM MST, NOV; DLB 8, 12, 78, 212; EWL 3; EXPS; JRDA; LAIT 3; MAICYA 1, 2,; MAL 5; MTCW 1, 2; MTFW 2005; NFS 8, 19, 35; RGAL 4; RGSF 2; SATA 18; SFW 4; SSC 4, 49, 133; SSFS 7, 35; TCLC 9, 15, 39; TCWW 1, 2; TUS; WLC 4; WYA; YAW

London, John Griffith
See London, Jack

Longfellow, Henry Wadsworth 1807-1882 .... **99**
See also AMW; AMWR 2; CDALB 1640-1865; DA; DA3; DAB; DAC; DAM MST, POET; DLB 1, 59, 235; EXPP; NCLC 2, 45, 101, 103, 235; PAB; PC 30; PFS 2, 7, 17, 31, 39; RGAL 4; SATA 19; TUS; WLCS; WP

Longway, A. Hugh
See Lang, Andrew

Lord, Bette Bao 1938- **151**
See also AAL; BEST 90:3; BPFB 2; CA 107; CANR 41, 79; CLC 23; INT CA-107; SATA 58

Louisburgh, Sheila Burnford
See Burnford, Sheila (Philip Cochrane Every)

Lovelace, Maud Hart 1892-1980 .... **231**
See also CA 5-8 R, 104; CANR 39, 79; CWRI 5; FW; MAICYA 1, 2; SATA 2, 23

Low, Penelope Margaret
See Lively, Penelope

Lowry, Lois 1937- **6, 46, 72, 199, 261**
See also AAYA 5, 32; BYA 4, 6, 14; CA 69-72, 200; CAAE 200; CANR 13, 43, 70, 131, 162, 202; CMTFW; DLB 52; INT CANR-13; JRDA; MAICYA 1, 2; MAICYAS 1; MTCW 2; MTFW 2005; NFS 3, 39; SAAS 3; SATA 23, 70, 111, 127, 177, 230, 312, 366; SATA-Essay 127; WYA; YAW

Lowry, Lois Hammersberg
See Lowry, Lois

Lumley, Robert
See Moorcock, Michael

Lunn, Janet (Louise Swoboda) 1928- **18**
See also AAYA 38; CA 33-36R; CANR 22, 80; CWRI 5; JRDA; MAICYA 1, 2; SAAS 12; SATA 4, 68, 110

Lynch, Chris 1962- **58**
See also AAYA 19, 44; BYA 10, 12, 15; CA 154; CANR 163, 205; MAICYA 2; MAICYAS 1; SATA 95, 131, 171, 209; WYA; YAW

Lynch, Patricia (Nora) 1898-1972 .... **167**
See also CA 11-12; CANR 70; CAP 1; CWRI 5; DLB 160; SATA 9

Macaulay, David (Alexander) 1946- **3, 14**
See also AAYA 21; BEST 89:2; BYA 1; CA 53-56; CANR 5, 34; CWRI 5; DLB 61; INT CANR-34; MAICYA 2; SATA 46, 72, 137; SATA-Brief 27

MacDonald, Anson
See Heinlein, Robert A.

Macdonald, Caroline 1948- **60**
See also CA 152; 171; CANR 90; CWRI 5; SATA 86; SATA-Obit 111

MacDonald, George 1824-1905 .... **67, 233**
See also AAYA 57; BYA 5; CA 106, 137; CANR 80; DLB 18, 163, 178; FANT; MAICYA 1, 2; RGEL 2; SATA 33, 100; SFW 4; SSFHW; SUFW; TCLC 9, 113, 207; WCH

MacDonald, Golden
See Brown, Margaret Wise

Mackay, Claire 1930- **43**
See also CA 105; CANR 22, 50, 92; CWRI 5; SATA 40, 97; SATA-Essay 124

MacLachlan, Patricia 1938- **14**
See also AAYA 18; BYA 3; CA 118; 136; CANR 130, 201; CWRI 5; JRDA; MAICYA 1, 2; SATA 62, 107, 168, 229; SATA-Brief 42

Maddison, Angela Mary 1923- **24**
See also CA 53-56; CANR 89; CWRI 5; SATA 10

Maestro, Betsy (Crippen) 1944- **45**
See also CA 61-64; CANR 8, 23, 37; MAICYA 1, 2; SATA 59, 106; SATA-Brief 30

Maestro, Giulio 1942- **45**
See also CA 57-60; CANR 8, 23, 37; MAICYA 1, 2; SATA 8, 59, 106

Mahony, Elizabeth Winthrop
See Winthrop, Elizabeth

Mahy, Margaret 1936-2012 ... **7, 78, 155, 240**
See also AAYA 8, 46; BYA 6, 7, 8; CA 69-72; CANR 13, 30, 38, 77, 157; CWRI 5; FANT; JRDA; MAICYA 1, 2; MAICYAS 1; SATA 14, 69, 119, 171, 251; SSFHW; WYA; YAW

Mahy, Margaret May
See Mahy, Margaret

Major, Kevin (Gerald) 1949- **11**
See also AAYA 16; CA 97-100; CANR 21, 38, 112; CLC 26; DAC; DLB 60; INT CANR-21; JRDA; MAICYA 1, 2; MAICYAS 1; SATA 32, 82, 134; WYA; YAW

Malcolm, Dan
See Silverberg, Robert

Manley, Seon 1921- **3**
See also CA 85-88; SAAS 2; SATA 15

March, Carl
See Fleischman, Sid

Marciano, John Bemelmans 1970- **93**
See also SATA 118, 167

Mark, Jan 1943-2006 .... **11**
See also CA 93-96; 247; CANR 17, 42, 77, 150; MAICYA 1, 2; SATA 22, 69, 114, 164; SATA-Obit 173; YAW

Mark, Janet Marjorie
See Mark, Jan

Markoosie
See Patsauq, Markoosie

Marks, J.
See Highwater, Jamake (Mamake)

Marks-Highwater, J.
See Highwater, Jamake (Mamake)

Marrin, Albert 1936- **53**
See also AAYA 35; CA 49-52; CANR 30, 58, 106, 184; MAICYA 2; MAICYAS 1; SATA 53, 90, 126, 193; SATA-Brief 43

Marsden, John 1950- **34**
See also AAYA 20; CA 135; CANR 129, 191; MAICYA 2; MAICYAS 1; SAAS 22; SATA 66, 97, 146; YAW

Marshall, Edward
See Marshall, James

Marshall, James 1942-1992 .... **21**
See also CA 41-44R; 139; CANR 38, 77; CWRI 5; DLB 61; MAICYA 1, 2; MAICYAS 1; SATA 6, 51, 75

Marshall, James Edward
See Marshall, James

Martin, Ann M. 1955- **32**
See also AAYA 6, 42; BYA 8, 14; CA 111; CANR 32, 106, 182; INT CANR-32; JRDA; MAICYA 1, 2; SATA 44, 70, 126, 192, 234; SATA-Brief 41

Martin, Bill, Jr. 1916-2004 .... **97**
See also CA 117; 130; 229; CANR 192; MAICYA 1, 2; SATA 40, 67, 145; SATA-Brief 40

Martin, Fredric
See Christopher, Matt(hew Frederick)

Martin, Webber
See Silverberg, Robert

Martin, William Ivan, Jr.
See Martin, Bill, Jr.

Maruki, Toshi 1912-2000 .... **19**
See also SATA 112

Masefield, John (Edward) 1878-1967 .... **164**
See also CA 19-20; 25-28R; CANR 33; CAP 2; CDBLB 1890-1914; CLC 11, 47; DAM POET; DLB 10, 19, 153, 160; EWL 3; EXPP; FANT; MTCW 1, 2; PC 78; PFS 5; RGEL 2; SATA 19

Matas, Carol 1949- **52**
See also AAYA 22; BYA 15; CA 158; CANR 144, 185; MAICYA 2; MAICYAS 1; SATA 93, 194; SATA-Essay 112; YAW

Mathers, Petra 1945- **76**
See also CA 194; CWRI 5; SATA 119, 176

Mathis, Sharon Bell 1937- **3, 147**
See also AAYA 12; BW 2; CA 41-44R; DLB 33; JRDA; MAICYA 1, 2; SAAS 3; SATA 7, 58; YAW

Matthew, James
See Barrie, J. M.

Mattingley, Christobel (Rosemary) 1931- **24**
See also CA 97-100; CANR 20, 47; CWRI 5; MAICYA 1, 2; SAAS 18; SATA 37, 85

Mayer, Mercer 1943- **11**
See also CA 85-88; CANR 38, 77, 109; CWRI 5; DLB 61; MAICYA 1, 2; SATA 16, 32, 73, 129, 137

Mayne, William 1928-2010 .... **25, 123**
See also AAYA 20; CA 9-12R; CANR 37, 80, 100; CLC 12; FANT; JRDA; MAICYA 1, 2; MAICYAS 1; SAAS 11; SATA 6, 68, 122; SUFW 2; YAW

Mayne, William James Carter
See Mayne, William

Mazer, Harry 1925- **16**
See also AAYA 5, 36; BYA 6; CA 97-100; CANR 32, 129; INT CA-97-100; JRDA; MAICYA 1, 2; SAAS 11; SATA 31, 67, 105, 167; WYA; YAW

Mazer, Norma Fox 1931-2009 .... **23**
See also AAYA 5, 36; BYA 1, 8; CA 69-72; 292; CANR 12, 32, 66, 129, 189; CLC 26; JRDA; MAICYA 1, 2; SAAS 1; SATA 24, 67, 105, 168, 198; WYA; YAW

McBratney, Sam 1943- **44**
See also CA 155; CANR 115, 195; CWRI 5; MAICYA 2; MAICYAS 1; SATA 89, 164, 203

McCaffrey, Anne 1926-2011 .... **49, 130**
See also AAYA 6, 34; AITN 2; BEST 89:2; BPFB 2; BYA 5; CA 25-28R, 227; CAAE 227; CANR 15, 35, 55, 96, 169, 234; CLC 17; CPW; DA3; DAM NOV, POP; DLB 8; JRDA; MAICYA 1, 2; MTCW 1, 2; MTFW 2005; SAAS 11; SATA 8, 70, 116, 152; SATA-Essay 152; SFW 4; SUFW 2; WYA; YAW

McCaffrey, Anne Inez
See McCaffrey, Anne

McCaughrean, Geraldine 1951- **38**
See also AAYA 83; CA 117; CANR 52, 111, 156; MAICYA 2; MAICYAS 1; SATA 87, 139, 173; YAW

McCloskey, (John) Robert 1914-2003 ...... **7**
See also CA 9-12R; 217; CANR 47; CWRI 5; DLB 22; MAICYA 1, 2; SATA 2, 39, 100; SATA-Obit 146

McClung, Robert M(arshall) 1916- **11**
See also AITN 2; CA 13-16R; CANR 6, 21, 46, 77, 113; MAICYA 1, 2; SAAS 15; SATA 2, 68, 135

McCord, David (Thompson Watson)
1897-1997 .... **9**
See also CA 73-76; 157; CANR 38; CWRI 5; DLB 61; MAICYA 1, 2; MAICYAS 1; SATA 18; SATA-Obit 96

McCulloch, John Tyler
See Burroughs, Edgar Rice

McCulloch, Sarah
See Ure, Jean

McCully, Emily Arnold
See Arnold, Emily

McDermott, Gerald (Edward) 1941- **9**
See also AITN 2; CA 85-88; CWRI 5; MAICYA 1, 2; SATA 16, 74, 163

McDonald, Jamie
See Heide, Florence Parry

McDonald, Megan 1958- **94**
See also CA 135; CANR 131, 193; SATA 67, 99, 148, 151, 202; SATA-Essay 151

McFadden, Kevin Christopher
See Pike, Christopher

McFarlane, Leslie 1902-1977 .... **61, 118**
See also BYA 4; CA 112, 17-20R, 19-20; CANR 37, 27, 56; CAP 2; CCA 1; DLB 88; JRDA; MAICYA 1, 2; SATA 31, 1, 65, 67, 100

McFarlane, Leslie Charles
See McFarlane, Leslie

McGivern, Maureen Daly
See Daly, Maureen

McGivern, Maureen Patricia Daly
See Daly, Maureen

McGovern, Ann 1930- **50**
See also CA 49-52; CANR 2, 44; MAICYA 1, 2; SAAS 17; SATA 8, 69, 70, 132

McHargue, Georgess 1941-2011 .... **2**
See also CA 25-28R; CANR 24; JRDA; SAAS 5; SATA 4, 77

McIlwraith, Maureen Mollie Hunter
See Hunter, Mollie

McKean, Dave 1963- **186**
See also CA 217; SATA 197

McKee, David (John) 1935- **38**
See also CA 137; CANR 143; CWRI 5; MAICYA 1, 2; SATA 70, 107, 158

McKillip, Patricia A. 1948- **213**
See also AAYA 14, 82; BPFB

McKinley, Robin 1952- **10, 81, 127**
See also AAYA 4, 33, 87; BYA 4, 5, 6, 12, 16; CA 107; CANR 31, 64, 110, 186; DLB 52; FANT; JRDA; LAIT 1; MAICYA 1, 2; MTFW 2005; NFS 33; SATA 50, 89, 130, 195, 229; SATA-Brief 32; YAW

McKissack, Fredrick L. 1939- **55**
See also BYA 15; CA 120; CANR 49, 96, 147; CWRI 5; SATA 73, 117, 162; SATA-Brief 53

McKissack, Fredrick Lemuel
See McKissack, Fredrick L.

McKissack, Patricia C. 1944- **23, 55, 129**
See also AAYA 38; BW 2; BYA 15; CA 118; CANR 38, 96, 147, 186; CWRI 5; JRDA; MAICYA 1, 2; MAICYAS 1; SATA 51, 73, 117, 162, 195

McKissack, Patricia L'Ann Carwell
See McKissack, Patricia C.

McKissack and McKissack
See McKissack, Fredrick L.; McKissack, Patricia C.

McMillan, Bruce 1947- **47**
See also CA 73-76; CANR 13, 35, 89, 110, 182; MAICYA 1, 2; SATA 22, 70, 129, 192

McMillan, Naomi
See Grimes, Nikki

McNaughton, Colin 1951- **54**
See also CA 112; CANR 47, 112; SATA 39, 92, 134, 211

McNicoll, Sylvia (Marilyn) 1954- **99**
See also CA 163; CANR 139; SATA 113

Meade, Elizabeth Thomasina
1844-1914 .... **163, 236**
See also CA 112; DLB 141

Meade, L. T.
See Meade, Elizabeth Thomasina

Meaker, M. J.
See Meaker, Marijane

Meaker, Marijane 1927- **29**
See also AAYA 2, 23, 82; BYA 1, 7, 8; CA 107; CANR 37, 63, 145, 180; CLC 12, 35; GLL 2; INT CA-107; JRDA; MAICYA 1, 2; MAICYAS 1; MTCW 1; SAAS 1; SATA 20, 61, 99, 160; SATA-Essay 111; WYA; YAW

Meaker, Marijane Agnes
See Meaker, Marijane

Means, Florence Crannell 1891-1980 .... **56**
See also CA 1-4R; 103; CANR 37; MAICYA 1, 2; SATA 1; SATA-Obit 25; YAW

Meigs, Cornelia Lynde 1884-1973 .... **55**
See also BYA 2; CA 9-12R; 45-48; JRDA; MAICYA 1, 2; SATA 6; WCH; YAW

Melmoth, Sebastian
See Wilde, Oscar

Meltzer, Milton 1915-2009 .... **13**
See also AAYA 8, 45; BYA 2, 6; CA 13-16R; 290; CANR 38, 92, 107, 192; CLC 26; DLB 61; JRDA; MAICYA 1, 2; SAAS 1; SATA 1, 50, 80, 128, 201; SATA-Essay 124; WYA; YAW

Mendicant, Arch
See Aldiss, Brian W.

Merker, Sebastian
See Salten, Felix

Merriam, Eve 1916-1992 .... **14**
See also CA 5-8R; 137; CANR 29, 80; DLB 61; EXPP; MAICYA 1, 2; PFS 6, 37; SATA 3, 40, 73; YAW

Merrill, Jean (Fairbanks) 1923- **52**
See also BYA 5; CA 1-4R; CANR 4, 38; CWRI 5; MAICYA 1, 2; SATA 1, 82

Merriman, Alex
See Silverberg, Robert

Merry, Robert
See Goodrich, Samuel Griswold

Metcalf, Suzanne
See Baum, L. Frank

Meyer, June
See Jordan, June

Meyer, Stephenie 1973- **142, 180**
See also AAYA 77; CA 253; CANR 192; CLC 280; SATA 193

Michaëlis, Karin 1872-1950 .... **237**
See also DLB 214

Militant
See Sandburg, Carl

Miller, Arthur 1915-2005 .... **195, 269**
See also AAYA 15; AITN 1; AMW; AMWC 1; CA 1-4R, 236; CABS 3; CANR 2, 30, 54, 76, 132; CAD; CD 5, 6; CDALB 1941-1968; CLC 1, 2, 6, 10, 15, 26, 47, 78, 179, 428; CMTFW 1; DA; DA3; DAB; DAC; DAM DRAM, MST; DC 1, 31; DFS 1, 3, 8, 27, 32; DLB 7, 266; EWL 3; LAIT 1, 4; LATS 1:2; MAL 5; MTCW 1, 2; MTFW 2005; RGAL 4; RGHL; TUS; WLC 4; WYAS 1

Milligan, Spike
See Milligan, Terence Alan

Milligan, Terence Alan 1918-2002 .... **92**
See also CA 9-12R; 207; CANR 4, 33, 64; DLB 352; MTCW 1; SATA 29; SATA-Obit 134

Milne, A. A. 1882-1956 ... **1, 26, 108, 226, 270**
See also BRWS 5; CA 104, 133; CMW 4; CWRI 5; DA3; DAB; DAC; DAM MST; DLB 10, 77, 100, 160, 352; FANT; MAICYA 1, 2; MBL 2; MTCW 1, 2; MTFW 2005; RGEL 2; SATA 100; TCLC 6, 88; WCH; YABC 1

Milne, Alan Alexander
See Milne, A. A.

Milne, Lorus J. **22**
See also CA 33-36R; CANR 14; SAAS 18; SATA 5

Milne, Margery **22**
See also CA 33-36R; CANR 14; SAAS 18; SATA 5

Minarik, Else Holmelund 1920- **33**
See also CA 73-76; CANR 48, 91; CWRI 5; MAICYA 1, 2; SATA 15, 127

Mitchell, Clyde
See Silverberg, Robert

Mitchell, Margaret 1900-1949 .... **190**
See also AAYA 23; BPFB 2; BYA 1; CA 109, 125; CANR 55, 94; CDALBS; CEAL; DA3; DAM NOV, POP; DLB 9; LAIT 2; MAL 5; MTCW 1, 2; MTFW 2005; NFS 9, 38; RGAL 4; RHW; TCLC 11, 170; TUS; WYAS 1; YAW

Moe, Jorgen (Ingebretsen) 1813-1882 ... **104**
See also DLB 354; WCH

Mohr, Nicholasa 1938- **22, 209**
See also AAYA 8, 46; CA 49-52; CANR 1, 32, 64; CLC 12; DAM MULT; DLB 145; HLC 2; HW 1, 2; JRDA; LAIT 5; LLW; MAICYA 2; MAICYAS 1; RGAL 4; SAAS 8; SATA 8, 97; SATA-Essay 113; WYA; YAW

Mole, John 1941- **61**
See also CA 101; CANR 18, 41, 83; CP 2, 3, 4, 5, 6, 7; SATA 36, 103

Molesworth, Mary Louisa 1839-1921 .... **166**
See also CA 165; DLB 135; HGG; SATA 98; WCH

Molin, Charles
See Mayne, William

Monjo, F(erdinand) N(icholas III)
1924-1978 .... **2**
See also CA 81-84; CANR 37, 83; CWRI 5; MAICYA 1, 2; SATA 16

Monroe, Lyle
See Heinlein, Robert A.

Montgomery, L. M.
1874-1942 .... **8, 91, 145, 270**
See also AAYA 12; BYA 1; CA 108, 137; DA3; DAC; DAM MST; DLB 92, 362; DLBD 14; JRDA; MAICYA 1, 2; MTCW 2; MTFW 2005; RGEL 2; SATA 100; TCLC 51, 140; TWA; WCH; WYA; YABC 1

Montgomery, Lucy Maud
See Montgomery, L. M.

Moody, Minerva
See Alcott, Louisa May

Moorcock, Michael 1939- **203**
See also AAYA 26; CMTFW; CA 45-48; CAAS 5; CANR 2, 17, 38, 64, 122, 203; CLC 5, 27, 58, 236; CN 5, 6, 7; DLB 14, 231, 261, 319; FANT; MTCW 1, 2; MTFW; SFW; SFFHW; SATA 93, 166; SUFW 1, 2

Moore, Alan 1953- **209**
See also AAYA 51; CMTFW; CA 204; CANR 138, 184; CLC 230; DLB 261; MTFW; SFW

Moore, Lilian 1909-2004 .... **15**
See also CA 103; 229; CANR 38, 116; MAICYA 1, 2; SATA 52, 137; SATA-Obit 155

Mora, Pat 1942- **58**
See also AMWS 13; CA 129; CANR 57, 81, 112, 171; DAM MULT; DLB 209; HLC 2; HW 1, 2; LLW; MAICYA 2; MTFW 2005; PFS 33, 35, 40; SATA 92, 134, 186, 232

Mora, Patricia
See Mora, Pat

Moreton, Andrew Esq.
See Defoe, Daniel

Morgan, Jane
See Cooper, James Fenimore

Mori, Kyoko 1957- **64**
See also AAYA 25; BYA 13; CA 153; CANR 102; DLB 312; LATS 1:2; MAICYA 2; MAICYAS 1; MTFW 2005; NFS 15; SAAS 26; SATA 122; SATA-Essay 126; WYAS 1; YAW

Morpurgo, Michael 1943- **51**
See also AAYA 37; BYA 15; CA 158; CANR 122, 169; MAICYA 2; MAICYAS 1; SATA 93, 143, 184, 225; YAW

Morrison, Chloe Anthony Wofford
See Morrison, Toni

Morrison, Toni 1931-2019 .... **99, 190, 258**
See also AAYA 1, 22, 61; AFAW 1, 2; AMWC 1; AMWS 3; BLC 1:3, 2:3; BPFB 2; BW 2, 3; CA 29-32R; CANR 27, 42, 67, 113, 124, 204, 254, 298; CDALB 1968-1988; CLC 4, 10, 22, 55, 81, 87, 173, 194, 344, 363, 366, 474, 480; CN 3, 4, 5, 6, 7; CPW; DA; DA3; DAB; DAC; DAM MST, MULT, NOV, POP; DLB 6, 33, 143, 331; DLBY 1981; EWL 3; EXPN; FL 1:6; FW; GL 3; LAIT 2, 4; LATS 1:2; LMFS 2; MAL 5; MAWW; MBL; MTCW 1, 2; MTFW 2005; NFS 1, 6, 8, 14, 37, 40, 46; RGAL 4; RHW; SATA 57, 144, 235, 350; SSC 26; SSFS 5; TCLE 1:2; TUS; WLC 4; YAW

Moser, Barry 1940- **49**
See also CA 196; CANR 170; MAICYA 1, 2; SAAS 15; SATA 56, 79, 138, 185

Moss, Marissa 1959- **134**
See also CA 171; CANR 130; SATA 71, 104, 163, 216

Mowat, Farley 1921-2014 .... **20, 248**
See also AAYA 1, 50; BYA 2; CA 1-4R; CANR 4, 24, 42, 68, 108; CLC 26; CMTFW; CPW; DAC; DAM MST; DLB 68; INT CANR-24; JRDA; MAICYA 1, 2; MTCW 1, 2; MTFW 2005; SATA 3, 55; YAW

Mowat, Farley McGill
See Mowat, Farley

Mowry, Jess 1960- **65**
See also AAYA 29; BYA 10; CA 133; MAICYA 2; SATA 109, 131; SATA-Essay 131; YAW

Mude, O.
See Gorey, Edward (St. John)

Mueller, Jorg 1942- **43**
See also CA 136; MAICYA 2; SATA 67

Mukerji, Dhan Gopal 1890-1936 .... **10**
See also BYA 5; CA 119; 136; CANR 90; CWRI 5; MAICYA 1, 2; SATA 40

Muller, Jorg
See Mueller, Jorg

Mun
See Leaf, (Wilbur) Munro

Munari, Bruno 1907-1998 .... **9**
See also CA 73-76; CANR 38; MAICYA 1, 2; SATA 15

Muñoz, Elías Miguel 1954- **218**
See also LLW

Munsch, Bob
See Munsch, Robert (Norman)

Munsch, Robert (Norman) 1945- **19**
See also CA 121; CANR 37, 87; CWRI 5; MAICYA 1, 2; SATA 50, 83, 120; SATA-Brief 48

Murphy, Jill 1949- **39**
See also CA 105; CANR 44, 50, 84, 121; CWRI 5; MAICYA 1, 2; SATA 37, 70, 142, 214

Murphy, Jill Frances
See Murphy, Jill

Murphy, Jim 1947- **53**
See also AAYA 20; BYA 10, 11, 16; CA 111; CANR 170; CWRI 5; MAICYA 2; MAICYAS 1; SATA 37, 77, 124, 185, 224; SATA-Brief 32

Murphy, Tim
See Murphy, Jim

Myers, Christopher 1975- **97**
See also SATA 183

Myers, Walter Dean 1937-2014 .... **4, 16, 35, 110, 185, 206, 267**
See also AAYA 4, 23, 88; BLC 1:3, 2:3; BW 2; BYA 6, 8, 11; CA 33-36R; CANR 20, 42, 67, 108, 184, 312; CLC 35; CMTFW; DAM MULT, NOV; DLB 33, 391; INT CANR-20; JRDA; LAIT 5; LNFS 1; MAICYA 1, 2; MAICYAS 1; MTCW 1; MTFW 2005; NFS 30, 33, 40, 45; SAAS 2; SATA 41, 71, 109, 157, 193, 229, 280, 325; SATA-Brief 27; SSFS 31; WYA; YAW

Myers, Walter M.
See Myers, Walter Dean

Naidoo, Beverley 1943- **29**
See also AAYA 23; CA 160; CANR 113; MAICYA 2; MAICYAS 1; SATA 63, 135, 180; YAW

Nakatani, Chiyoko 1930-1981 .... **30**
See also CA 77-80; SATA 55; SATA-Brief 40

Namioka, Lensey 1929- **48**
See also AAYA 27; CA 69-72; CANR 11, 27, 52, 84, 141; MAICYA 2; SAAS 24; SATA 27, 89, 157; SATA-Essay 116; YAW

Napoli, Donna Jo 1948- **51**
See also AAYA 25; BYA 10, 11; CA 156; CANR 96, 169; MAICYA 2; SAAS 23; SATA 92, 137, 190, 230; SATA-Essay 230; WYAS 1; YAW

Naylor, Gloria 1950- **202**
See also AAYA 6, 39; AFAW 1, 2; AMWS 8; BLC 1:3; BW 2, 3; CA 107; CANR 27, 51, 74, 130; CLC 28, 52, 156, 261, 375, 383; CN 4, 5, 6, 7; CPW; DA; DA3; DAM MST, MULT, NOV, POP; DLB 173; EWL 3; FW; MAL 5; MTCW 1, 2; MTFW 2005; NFS 4, 7; RGAL 4; TCLE 1:2; TUS; WLCS

Naylor, Phyllis 1933-
See Naylor, Phyllis Reynolds

Naylor, Phyllis Reynolds 1933- **17, 135**
See also AAYA 4, 29; BYA 7, 8; CA 21-24R; CANR 8, 24, 59, 121, 177, 205; CWRI 5; JRDA; MAICYA 1, 2; MAICYAS 1; SAAS 10; SATA 209; SATA-Essay 152; WYA; YAW

Needle, Jan 1943- **43**
See also AAYA 23; CA 106; CANR 28, 84; SAAS 23; SATA 30, 98; YAW

Nesbit, E. 1858-1924 .... **3, 70, 252**
See also BYA 5; CA 118; 137; CWRI 5; DLB 141, 153, 178; FANT; HGG; MAICYA 1, 2; MTCW 2; RGEL 2; SATA 100; WCH; YABC 1

Nesbit, Edith
See Nesbit, E.

Ness, Evaline (Michelow) 1911-1986 .... **6**
See also CA 5-8R; 120; CANR 5, 37; CWRI 5; DLB 61; MAICYA 1, 2; SAAS 1; SATA 1, 26; SATA-Obit 49

Neufeld, John (Arthur) 1938- **52**
See also AAYA 11; CA 25-28R; CANR 11, 37, 56; CLC 17; MAICYA 1, 2; SAAS 3; SATA 6, 81, 131; SATA-Essay 131; YAW

Newbery, John 1713-1767 .... **147**
See also DLB 154; MAICYA 1, 2; SATA 20

Nichols, Peter
See Youd, Samuel

Nichols, (Joanna) Ruth 1948- **149**
See also CA 25-28R; CANR 16, 37, 84; CWRI 5; DLB 60; FANT; JRDA; SATA 15

Nicholson, William 1872-1949 .... **76**
See also CWRI 5; DLB 141

Nielsen, Kay (Rasmus) 1886-1957 .... **16**
See also CA 177; MAICYA 1, 2; SATA 16

Nimmo, Jenny 1944- **44**
See also CA 108; CANR 52, 83, 124; CWRI 5; FANT; MAICYA 2; SATA 87, 144

Nix, Garth 1963- **68, 187**
See also AAYA 27; BYA 14, 16; CA 164; CANR 122, 206; SATA 97, 143, 210; YAW

Nixon, Joan Lowery 1927-2003 .... **24**
See also AAYA 12, 54; BYA 16; CA 9-12R; 217; CANR 7, 24, 38, 135; JRDA; MAICYA 1, 2; MAICYAS 1; SAAS 9; SATA 8, 44, 78, 115; SATA-Obit 146; WYA; YAW

Noestlinger, Christine
See Nostlinger, Christine

North, Andrew
See Norton, Andre

North, Captain George
See Stevenson, Robert Louis

Norton, Alice Mary
See Norton, Andre

Norton, Andre 1912-2005 .... **50, 184**
See also AAYA 83; BPFB 2; BYA 4, 10, 12; CA 1-4R; 237; CANR 2, 31, 68, 108, 149; CLC 12; DLB 8, 52; JRDA; MAICYA 1, 2; MTCW 1; SATA 1, 43, 91; SUFW 1, 2; YAW

Norton, Mary 1903-1992 .... **6, 140**
See also CA 97-100, 139; CWRI 5; DLB 160; FANT; MAICYA 1, 2; MAICYAS 1; SATA 18, 60; SATA-Obit 72; TEA

Nostlinger, Christine 1936- **12**
See also CA 115; 123; CANR 38, 147; MAICYA 1, 2; SATA 64, 162; SATA-Brief 37; YAW

Nourse, Alan E(dward) 1928-1992 .... **33**
See also CA 1-4R; 145; CANR 3, 21, 45, 84; DLB 8; SATA 48; SFW 4

Numeroff, Laura 1953- **85**
See also CA 106; CANR 58, 118; MAICYA 2; SATA 28, 90, 142, 206

Numeroff Joffe, Laura
See Numeroff, Laura

Nwapa, Flora (Nwanzuruaha) 1931-1993 .... **162**
See also BLCS; BW 2; CA 143; CANR 83; CDWLB 3; CLC 133; CWRI 5; DLB 125; EWL 3; WLIT 2

Nye, Naomi Shihab 1952- **59, 193**
See also AAYA 27; AMWS 13; CA 146; CANR 70, 126, 190; CP 6, 7; CSW; CWP; DLB 120; MAICYA 2; MTFW 2005; PFS 24, 33; SATA 86, 147, 198

Oakley, Graham 1929- **7**
See also CA 106; CANR 38, 54, 85; CWRI 5; MAICYA 1, 2; SATA 30, 84

Oberman, Sheldon 1949-2004 .... **54**
See also CA 152; 226; CANR 120; SAAS 26; SATA 85; SATA-Essay 114; SATA-Obit 153

O'Brian, E.G.
See Clarke, Arthur C.

O'Brien, E.G.
See Clarke, Arthur C.

O'Brien, Robert C. 1918-1973 .... **2**
See also AAYA 6; CA 73-76; 41-44R; MAICYA 1, 2; SATA 23; YAW

O'Connor, Patrick
See Wibberley, Leonard

O'Dell, Scott 1898-1989 .... **1, 16, 126**
See also AAYA 3, 44; BPFB 3; BYA 1, 2, 3, 5; CA 61-64; 129; CANR 12, 30, 112; CLC 30; DLB 52; JRDA; MAICYA 1, 2; SATA 12, 60, 134; WYA; YAW

Ofek, Uriel 1926- **28**
See also CA 101; CANR 18; SATA 36

Ogilvy, Gavin
See Barrie, J. M.

Ohi yesa
See Eastman, Charles Alexander

o huigin, sean 1942- **75**
See also CA 208; SATA 138

Old Boy
See Hughes, Thomas

Oldstyle, Jonathan
See Irving, Washington

Om
See Gorey, Edward (St. John)

O Mude
See Gorey, Edward (St. John)

Oneal, Elizabeth 1934- **13, 169**
See also AAYA 5, 41; BYA 13; CA 106; CANR 28, 84; CLC 30; JRDA; MAICYA 1, 2; SATA 30, 82; WYA; YAW

Oneal, Zibby
See Oneal, Elizabeth

Optic, Oliver
See Stratemeyer, Edward L.

Orgel, Doris 1929- **48**
See also AITN 1; CA 45-48; CANR 2, 131; SAAS 19; SATA 7, 85, 148; YAW

Orlev, Uri 1931- **30, 191**
See also AAYA 20; CA 101; CANR 34, 84, 113; MAICYA 2; MAICYAS 1; RGHL; SAAS 19; SATA 58, 135; YAW

Ormerod, Jan 1946- **20**
See also CA 113; CANR 35; MAICYA 1, 2; SATA 55, 70, 132, 210; SATA-Brief 44

Ormerod, Janette Louise
See Ormerod, Jan

Orwell, George 1903-1950 .... **68, 171, 196**
See also BPFB 3; BRW 7; BYA 5; CA 104; 132; CDBLB 1945-1960; DA; DA3; DAB; DAC; DAM MST, NOV; DLB 15, 98, 195, 255; EWL 3; EXPN; LAIT 4, 5; LATS 1:1; MTCW 1, 2; MTFW 2005; NFS 3, 7; RGEL 2; SATA 29; SCFW 1, 2; SFW 4; SSC 68; SSFS 4; TCLC 2, 6, 15, 31, 51, 123, 128, 129; TEA; WLC 4; WLIT 4; YAW X

Osborne, David
See Silverberg, Robert

Osborne, George
See Silverberg, Robert

Osborne, Mary Pope 1949- **88**
See also CA 111; CANR 29, 62, 124; SATA 41, 55, 98, 144

Osborne, Thos. Mott, '27
See Dr. Seuss

O'Shea, Catherine Patricia Shiels
See O'Shea, Pat

O'Shea, Pat 1931-2007 .... **18**
See also CA 145; CANR 84, 157; CWRI 5; FANT; SATA 87

Ottley, Reginald Leslie 1909-1985 .... **16**
See also CA 93-96; CANR 34; MAICYA 1, 2; SATA 26

Ouida 1839-1908 .... **208**
See also CA 204; DLB 18, 156; RGEL 2; SATA 20; TCLC 43

Owen, (John) Gareth 1936-2002 .... **31**
See also CA 150; CANR 101; CWRI 5; SAAS 14; SATA 83, 162

Oxenbury, Helen 1938- **22, 70**
See also CA 25-28R; CANR 35, 79, 133; CWRI 5; MAICYA 1, 2; SATA 3, 68, 149

Packer, Vin
See Meaker, Marijane

Pad, Peter
See Stratemeyer, Edward L.

Paisley, Tom 1932- **3**
See also AAYA 20; CA 61-64; CANR 15; SATA 11; WYA; YAW

Paolini, Christopher 1983- **102**
See also AAYA 71; CA 219; CANR 204; LNFS 3; SATA 157

Parish, Margaret 1927-1988 .... **22**
See also CA 73-76; 127; CANR 18, 38, 81; CWRI 5; MAICYA 1, 2; SATA 17, 73; SATA-Obit 59

Parish, Margaret Cecile
See Parish, Margaret

Parish, Peggy
See Parish, Margaret

Park, Barbara 1947- **34**
See also CA 113; CANR 101; MAICYA 2; SATA 40, 78, 123; SATA-Brief 35

Park, Linda Sue 1960- **84**
See also AAYA 49; CA 197; CANR 191; MAICYA 2; SATA 127, 173, 200

Park, Rosina Ruth Lucia
See Park, Ruth

Park, Ruth 1917(?)-2010 .... **51**
See also CA 105; CANR 65; DLB 260; MAICYA 2; SATA 25, 93

Parkes, Lucas
See Wyndham, John

Parley, Peter
See Goodrich, Samuel Griswold

Parson Lot
See Kingsley, Charles

Pascal, Francine 1938- **25**
See also AAYA 1, 40; CA 115; 123; CANR 39, 50, 97; JRDA; MAICYA 1, 2; SATA 51, 80, 143; SATA-Brief 37; YAW

Passailaigue, Thomas E.
See Paisley, Tom

Patent, Dorothy Hinshaw 1940- **19**
See also CA 61-64; CANR 9, 24, 98, 161; MAICYA 1, 2; SAAS 13; SATA 22, 69, 120, 162; SATA-Essay 162

Paterson, Katherine 1932- **7, 50, 127, 218**
See also AAYA 1, 31; BYA 1, 2, 7; CA 21-24R; CANR 28, 59, 111, 173, 196; CLC 12, 30; CWRI 5; DLB 52; JRDA; LAIT 4; MAICYA 1, 2; MAICYAS 1; MTCW 1; SATA 13, 53, 92, 133, 204; WYA; YAW

Paterson, Katherine Womeldorf
See Paterson, Katherine

Paton Walsh, Gillian
See Paton Walsh, Jill

Paton Walsh, Jill 1937- **2, 6, 128**
See also AAYA 11, 47; BYA 1, 8; CA 262; CAAE 262; CANR 38, 83, 158, 229; CLC 35; DLB 161; JRDA; MAICYA 1, 2; SAAS 3; SATA 4, 72, 109, 190; SATA-Essay 190; WYA; YAW

Patsauq, Markoosie 1942- **23**
See also CA 101; CWRI 5; DAM MULT; NNAL

Paul, Hamish Vigne Christie 1951- **87**
See also SATA 151

Paul, Korky
See Paul, Hamish Vigne Christie

Paulsen, Gary 1939- **19, 54, 82**
See also AAYA 2, 17; BYA 6, 7, 8, 10, 11; CA 73-76; CANR 30, 54, 83, 126, 177; JRDA; MAICYA 1, 2; MAICYAS 1; SATA 22, 50, 54, 79, 111, 158, 189, 231; TCWW 2; WYA; YAW

Pearce, Ann Philippa
See Pearce, Philippa

Pearce, Philippa 1920-2006 .... **9**
See also BYA 5; CA 5-8R; 255; CANR 4, 109; CLC 21; CWRI 5; DLB 161; FANT; MAICYA 1; SATA 1, 67, 129; SATA-Obit 179

Pearson, Jean Mary
See Gardam, Jane

Pearson, Kit 1947- **26**
See also AAYA 19; CA 145; CANR 71; CCA 1; JRDA; MAICYA 2; MAICYAS 1; SATA 77; SATA-Essay 117; YAW

Peck, Richard 1934- **15, 142**
See also AAYA 1, 24; BYA 1, 6, 8, 11; CA 85-88; CANR 19, 38, 129, 178; CLC 21; INT CANR-19; JRDA; MAICYA 1, 2; SAAS 2; SATA 18, 55, 97, 110, 158, 190, 228; SATA-Essay 110; WYA; YAW

Peck, Richard Wayne
See Peck, Richard

Peck, Robert Newton 1928- **45, 163**
See also AAYA 3, 43; BYA 1, 6; CA 81-84; 182; CAAE 182; CANR 31, 63, 127; CLC 17; DA; DAC; DAM MST; DLB; LAIT 3; MAICYA 1, 2; NFS 29; SAAS 1; SATA 21, 62, 111, 156; SATA-Essay 108; WYA; YAW

Peet, Bill
See Peet, William Bartlett

Peet, William Bartlett 1915-2002 .... **12**
See also CA 17-20R; 207; CANR 38, 84; CWRI 5; MAICYA 1, 2; SATA 2, 41, 78; SATA-Obit 137

Pene du Bois, William (Sherman) 1916-1993 .... **1**
See also CA 5-8R; 140; CANR 17, 41; CWRI 5; DLB 61; MAICYA 1, 2; SATA 4, 68; SATA-Obit 74

Perrault, Charles 1628-1703 .... **79, 134, 203**
See also BYA 4; DLB 268; GFL Beginnings to 1789; LC 2, 56; MAICYA 1, 2; RGWL 2, 3; SATA 25; SSC 144; WCH

Peter
See Stratemeyer, Edward L.

Petersham, Maud 1890-1971 .... **24**
See also CA 73-76; 33-36R; CANR 29, 84; CWRI 5; DLB 22; MAICYA 1, 2; SATA 17

Petersham, Maud Sylvia Fuller
See Petersham, Maud

Petersham, Miska 1888-1960 .... **24**
See also CA 73-76; CANR 29, 83; CWRI 5; DLB 22; MAICYA 1, 2; SATA 17

Petri, Arnold
See Petry, Ann

Petry, Ann 1908-1997 .... **12, 214**
See also AFAW 1, 2; BPFB 3; BW 1, 3; BYA 2; CA 5-8R; 157; CAAS 6; CANR 4, 46; CLC 1, 7, 18; CN 1, 2, 3, 4, 5, 6; DLB 76; EWL 3; JRDA; LAIT 1; MAICYA 1, 2; MAICYAS 1; MTCW 1; NFS 33; RGAL 4; SATA 5; SATA-Obit 94; SSC 161; TCLC 112; TUS

Petry, Ann Lane
See Petry, Ann

Peyton, K. M.
See Peyton, Kathleen Wendy

Peyton, Kathleen Wendy 1929- **3**
See also AAYA 20; CA 69-72; CANR 32, 69, 142; DLB 161; JRDA; MAICYA 1, 2; SAAS 17; SATA 15, 62, 157; WYA; YAW

Peyton, Kathleen Wendy Herald
See Peyton, Kathleen Wendy

Pfeffer, Susan Beth 1948- **11**
See also AAYA 12, 55; BYA 8; CA 29-32R; CANR 31, 58, 164; JRDA; MAICYA 2; MAICYAS 1; SAAS 17; SATA 4, 83, 180; WYA

Pfister, Marcus **42**
   See also CA 185; MAICYA 2; SATA 83, 150, 207
Phillips, Jack
   See Sandburg, Carl
Phipson, Joan
   See Fitzhardinge, Joan Margaret
Pica, Peter
   See Aldiss, Brian W.
Pienkowski, Jan (Michal) 1936- **6**
   See also CA 65-68; CANR 11, 38; MAICYA 1, 2; SATA 6, 58, 131
Pierce, Meredith Ann 1958- **20**
   See also AAYA 13, 60; BYA 5; CA 108; CANR 26, 48, 87, 106; FANT; JRDA; MAICYA 1, 2; SATA 67, 127; SATA-Brief 48; YAW
Piers, Robert
   See Anthony, Piers
Pig, Edward
   See Gorey, Edward (St. John)
Pike, Christopher 1954(?)- **29**
   See also AAYA 13; CA 136; CANR 66, 141, 185; HGG; JRDA; MAICYA 2; MAICYAS 1; SATA 68, 156, 239; WYAS 1; YAW
Pilgrim, Anne
   See Allan, Mabel Esther
Pilkey, Dav 1966- **48, 160**
   See also CA 136; CANR 122; MAICYA 2; SATA 68, 115, 166
Pilkey, David Murray, Jr.
   See Pilkey, Dav
Pinkney, Brian 1961- **54**
   See also CWRI 5; MAICYA 2; MAICYAS 1; SATA 74, 148, 206
Pinkney, J. Brian
   See Pinkney, Brian
Pinkney, Jerry 1939- **43**
   See also MAICYA 1, 2; MAICYAS 1; SAAS 12; SATA 41, 71, 107, 151, 198; SATA-Brief 32; SATA-Essay 198
Pinkwater, D. Manus
   See Pinkwater, Daniel
Pinkwater, Daniel 1941- **4, 175**
   See also AAYA 1, 46; BYA 9; CA 29-32R; CANR 12, 38, 89, 143; CLC 35; CSW; FANT; JRDA; MAICYA 1, 2; SAAS 3; SATA 8, 46, 76, 114, 158, 210; SFW 4; YAW
Pinkwater, Daniel M.
   See Pinkwater, Daniel
Pinkwater, Daniel Manus
   See Pinkwater, Daniel
Pinkwater, Manus
   See Pinkwater, Daniel
Polacco, Patricia 1944- **40**
   See also CA 185; CANR 101; CWRI 5; MAICYA 2; MAICYAS 1; SATA 74, 123, 180, 212
Polacco, Patricia Ann
   See Polacco, Patricia
Polder, Markus
   See Kruss, James
Politi, Leo 1908-1996 .... **29**
   See also CA 17-20R; 151; CANR 13, 47; MAICYA 1, 2; MAICYAS 1; SATA 1, 47; SATA-Obit 88
Pollock, Mary
   See Blyton, Enid
Porter, Eleanor H(odgman) 1868-1920 .... **110, 217**
   See also BYA 3; CA 108; DLB 9; RHW
Porter, Gene Stratton
   See Stratton-Porter, Gene
Porter, Geneva Grace
   See Stratton-Porter, Gene
Potok, Chaim 1929-2002 .... **92**
   See also AAYA 15, 50; AITN 1, 2; BPFB 3; BYA 1; CA 17-20R; 208; CANR 19, 35, 64, 98; CLC 2, 7, 14, 26, 112, 325; CN 4, 5, 6; DA3; DAM NOV; DLB 28, 152; EXPN; INT CANR-19; LAIT 4; MTCW 1, 2; MTFW 2005; NFS 4, 34, 38; RGHL; SATA 33, 106; SATA-Obit 134; TUS; YAW
Potok, Herbert Harold
   See Potok, Chaim
Potok, Herman Harold
   See Potok, Chaim
Potter, Beatrix 1866-1943 .... **1, 19, 73, 165, 213**
   See also BRWS 3; CA 108; 137; CANR 107; CWRI 5; DLB 141; MAICYA 1, 2; MTCW 2; MTFW 2005; SATA 100, 132; TEA; WCH; YABC 1
Potter, Helen Beatrix
   See Potter, Beatrix
Poulin, Stephane 1961- **28**
   See also CA 165; MAICYA 2; SATA 98
Pratchett, Terence David John
   See Pratchett, Terry
Pratchett, Terry 1948-2015 .... **64, 225**
   See also AAYA 19, 54; BPFB 3; CA 143; CANR 87, 126, 170, 248, 281; CLC 197; CN 6, 7; CPW; CWRI 5; FANT; MTFW 2005; SATA 82, 139, 185, 253, 291; SFW 4; SUFW 2
Prelutsky, Jack 1940- **13, 115**
   See also CA 93-96; CANR 38, 118, 198; CWRI 5; DLB 61; MAICYA 1, 2; SATA 22, 66, 118, 171
Preston, Caroline F.
   See Alger, Horatio, Jr.
Preston, Charles F.
   See Alger, Horatio, Jr.
Pringle, Laurence 1935- **4, 57**
   See also CA 29-32R; 273; CAAE 273; CANR 14, 60, 139, 178; CWRI 5; MAICYA 1, 2; SAAS 6; SATA 4, 68, 104, 154, 201; SATA-Essay 201
Pringle, Laurence Patrick
   See Pringle, Laurence
Proeysen, Alf 1914-1970 .... **24**
   See also CA 136; SATA 67
Provensen, Alice 1918- **11**
   See also CA 53-56; CANR 5, 44, 128; MAICYA 1, 2; SATA 9, 70, 147
Provensen, Martin 1916-1987 .... **11**
   See also CA 53-56; 122; CANR 5, 44; MAICYA 1, 2; SATA 9, 70; SATA-Obit 51
Provensen, Martin Elias
   See Provensen, Martin
Proysen, Alf
   See Proeysen, Alf
Pullman, Philip 1946- **20, 62, 84, 202**
   See also AAYA 15, 41; BRWS 3; BYA 8, 13; CA 127; CANR 50, 77, 105, 134, 190; CLC 245; JRDA; MAICYA 1, 2; MAICYAS 1; MTFW 2005; SAAS 17; SATA 65, 103, 150, 198; SUFW 2; WYAS 1; YAW
Putnam, Arthur Lee
   See Alger, Horatio, Jr.
Pyle, Howard 1853-1911 .... **22, 117**
   See also AAYA 57; BYA 2, 4; CA 109; 137; DLB 42, 188; DLBD 13; LAIT 1; MAICYA 1, 2; SATA 16, 100; TCLC 81; WCH; YAW
Quackenbush, Robert M(ead) 1929- **122**
   See also CA 45-48; CANR 2, 17, 38, 78, 112; MAICYA 1, 2; SAAS 7; SATA 7, 70, 133; SATA-Essay 133
Rackham, Arthur 1867-1939 .... **57**
   See also AAYA 31; CA 179; DLB 141; MAICYA 1, 2; SATA 15, 100
Rael, Elsa Okon 1927- **84**
Ramal, Walter
   See de la Mare, Walter (John)
Randall, Robert
   See Silverberg, Robert
Ransome, Arthur (Michell) 1884-1967 .... **8, 215**
   See also CA 73-76; CANR 81; CWRI 5; DLB 160; MAICYA 1, 2; SATA 22; TEA; WCH
Ransome, James E. 1961- **86**
   See also SATA 76, 123, 178, 227
Raskin, Ellen 1928-1984 .... **1, 12**
   See also BYA 4; CA 21-24R; 113; CANR 37; DLB 52; MAICYA 1, 2; SATA 2, 38, 139; YAW
Rathmann, Peggy 1953- **77**
   See also CA 159; CANR 142; CWRI 5; MAICYA 2; MAICYAS 1; SATA 94, 157
Rau, Margaret 1913- **8**
   See also CA 61-64; CANR 8; SATA 9, 168
Rawlings, Marjorie Kinnan 1896-1953 ... **63**
   See also AAYA 20; AMWS 10; ANW; BPFB 3; BYA 5; CA 104; 137; CANR 74; DLB 9, 22, 102; DLBD 17; JRDA; MAICYA 1, 2; MAL 5; MTCW 2; MTFW 2005; RGAL 4; SATA 100; TCLC 4, 248; WCH; YABC 1; YAW
Rawls, (Woodrow) Wilson 1913-1984 .... **81**
   See also AAYA 21; AITN 1; BYA 12; CA 1-4R; CANR 5, 131; JRDA; MAICYA 2; SATA 22
Rayner, Mary 1933- **41**
   See also CA 69-72; CANR 12, 29, 52, 80; CWRI 5; MAICYA 2; MAICYAS 1; SATA 22, 87
Reed, Talbot Baines 1852-1893 .... **76**
   See also DLB 141
Reeder, Carolyn 1937- **69**
   See also AAYA 32; CA 135; CANR 153; MAICYA 2; MAICYAS 1; SATA 66, 97
Reid, Barbara (Jane) 1957- **64**
   See also MAICYA 2; MAICYAS 1; SATA 93
Reid, Desmond
   See Moorcock, Michael
Reid Banks, Lynne 1929- **24, 86**
   See also AAYA 6; BYA 7; CA 1-4R; CANR 6, 22, 38, 87; CLC 23; CN 4, 5, 6; JRDA; MAICYA 1, 2; SATA 22, 75, 111, 165; YAW
Reiss, Johanna 1929(?)- **19**
   See also CA 85-88; CANR 207; JRDA; SATA 18; YAW
Reiss, Johanna de Leeuw
   See Reiss, Johanna
Remark, Erich Paul
   See Remarque, Erich Maria
Remarque, Erich Maria 1898-1970 .... **159**
   See also AAYA 27; BPFB 3; CA 77-80; 29-32R; CDWLB 2; CLC 21; DA; DA3; DAB; DAC; DAM MST, NOV; DLB 56; EWL 3; EXPN; LAIT 3; MTCW 1, 2; MTFW 2005; NFS 4, 36; RGHL; RGWL 2, 3
Remi, Georges Prosper
   See Hergé
Remy, Georges
   See Hergé
Rey, H. A. 1898-1977 .... **5, 93**
   See also CA 5-8R; 73-76; CANR 6, 90; CWRI 5; DLB 22; MAICYA 1, 2; SATA 1, 26, 69, 100
Rey, Hans Augusto
   See Rey, H. A.
Rey, Margret 1906-1996 .... **5, 93**
   See also CA 105; 155; CANR 38; CWRI 5; MAICYA 1, 2; MAICYAS 1; SATA 26, 86; SATA-Obit 93
Rey, Margret Elisabeth
   See Rey, Margret
Rhine, Richard
   See Silverstein, Alvin; Silverstein, Virginia B.

Rhue, Morton
See Strasser, Todd

Richards, Laura E(lizabeth Howe)
1850-1943 54
See also CA 120; 137; CWRI 5; DLB 42; MAICYA 1, 2; WCH; YABC 1

Richler, Mordecai 1931-2001 17
See also AITN 1; CA 65-68; 201; CANR 31, 62, 111; CCA 1; CLC 3, 5, 9, 13, 18, 46, 70, 185, 271; CN 1, 2, 3, 4, 5, 7; CWRI 5; DAC; DAM MST, NOV; DLB 53; EWL 3; MAICYA 1, 2; MTCW 1, 2; MTFW 2005; RGEL 2; RGHL; SATA 44, 98; SATA-Brief 27; TWA

Richter, Hans Peter
1925-1993 21
See also BYA 1; CA 45-48; CANR 2; MAICYA 1, 2; SAAS 11; SATA 6; YAW

Rigg, Sharon
See Creech, Sharon

Rinaldi, Ann 1934- 46
See also AAYA 15; BYA 6, 7, 8; CA 111; CANR 95, 147, 193; JRDA; MAICYA 2; MAICYAS 1; SATA 51, 78, 117, 161, 202; SATA-Brief 50; WYA; YAW

Ringgold, Faith 1930- 30, 174
See also AAYA 19; CA 154; CANR 88, 161; CWRI 5; MAICYA 2; MAICYAS 1; SATA 71, 114, 187

Riordan, Rick 1964- 190
See also AAYA 80; CA 201; CANR 152, 179, 250; SATA 174, 208, 238

Riq
See Atwater, Richard

Ritter, Felix
See Kruss, James

Rivers, Elfrida
See Bradley, Marion Zimmer

Riverside, John
See Heinlein, Robert A.

R. J.
See Jefferies, Richard

Robert, Adrian
See St. John, Nicole

Roberts, Charles G(eorge) D(ouglas)
1860-1943 33
See also CA 105; 188; CWRI 5; DLB 92; RGEL 2; RGSF 2; SATA 88; SATA-Brief 29; SSC 91; TCLC 8

Roberts, Elizabeth Madox 1886-1941 100
See also CA 111; 166; CWRI 5; DLB 9, 54, 102; RGAL 4; RHW; SATA 33; SATA-Brief 27; TCLC 68; TCWW 2; WCH

Roberts, Willo Davis 1928-2004 95
See also AAYA 13; CA 49-52; 235; CANR 3, 19, 47, 112; JRDA; MAICYA 1, 2; MAICYAS 1; RHW; SAAS 8; SATA 21, 70, 133, 150; SATA-Essay 150; SATA-Obit 160; YAW

Robertson, Ellis
See Silverberg, Robert

Robinet, Harriette Gillem 1931- 64
See also AAYA 50; BW 2; BYA 13, 14, 15; CA 69-72; CANR 42, 153; MAICYA 2; SATA 27, 104

Robinson, Lloyd
See Silverberg, Robert

Rockwell, Thomas 1933- 6
See also CA 29-32R; CANR 44; MAICYA 1, 2; SATA 7, 70, 231

Rockwood, Roy
See McFarlane, Leslie; Stratemeyer, Edward L.

Rodari, Gianni 1920-1980 24
See also CA 219

Rodda, Emily 1948- 32
See also CA 164; CANR 127, 198; SATA 97, 146, 230

Rodgers, Mary 1931- 20
See also BYA 5; CA 49-52; CANR 8, 55, 90; CLC 12; CWRI 5; DFS 28; INT CANR-8; JRDA; MAICYA 1, 2; SATA 8, 130

Rodman, Eric
See Silverberg, Robert

Rodman, Maia
See Wojciechowska, Maia (Teresa)

Rohmann, Eric 1957- 100
See also SATA 171, 239

Rosen, Michael 1946- 45
See also CA 25-28R; CANR 15, 32, 52, 92, 166; CWRI 5; MAICYA 2; SATA 48, 84, 137, 181, 229; SATA-Brief 40

Rosen, Michael Wayne
See Rosen, Michael

Rossetti, Christina 1830-1894 115
See also AAYA 51; BRW 5; BRWR 3; BYA 4; DA; DA3; DAB; DAC; DAM MST, POET; DLB 35, 163, 240; EXPP; FL 1:3; LATS 1:1; MAICYA 1, 2; NCLC 2, 50, 66, 186; PC 7, 119; PFS 10, 14, 27, 34; RGEL 2; SATA 20; TEA; WCH; WLC 5

Rossetti, Christina Georgina
See Rossetti, Christina

Rossetti, D. G., '25
See Dr. Seuss

Roughsey, Dick 1921(?)-1985 41
See also CA 109; CANR 80; CWRI 5; SATA 35

Roughsey, Goobalathaldin
See Roughsey, Dick

Rowe, Jennifer
See Rodda, Emily

Rowling, J.K. 1965- 66, 80, 112, 183, 235
See also AAYA 34, 82; BRWS 16; BYA 11, 13, 14; CA 173; CANR 128, 157, 263, 310; CLC 137, 217; CMTFW; DLB 377; LNFS 1, 2, 3; MAICYA 2; MTFW 2005; SATA 109, 174, 291; SUFW 2

Rowling, Joanne Kathleen
See Rowling, J.K.

Rubinstein, Gillian 1942- 35
See also AAYA 22; CA 136; CANR 86, 143, 177; SAAS 25; SATA 68, 105, 158; SATA-Essay 116; YAW

Rubinstein, Gillian Margaret
See Rubinstein, Gillian

Rudomin, Esther
See Hautzig, Esther Rudomin

Runciman, John
See Aldiss, Brian W.

Rushdie, Ahmed Salman
See Rushdie, Salman

Rushdie, Salman 1947- 125
See also AAYA 65; BEST 89:3; BPFB 3; BRWS 4; CA 108; 111; CANR 33, 56, 108, 133, 192; CLC 23, 31, 55, 100, 191, 272; CN 4, 5, 6, 7; CPW 1; DA3; DAB; DAC; DAM MST, NOV, POP; DLB 194, 323, 326; EWL 3; FANT; INT CA-111; LATS 1:2; LMFS 2; MTCW 1, 2; MTFW 2005; NFS 22, 23; RGEL 2; RGSF 2; SSC 83; TEA; WLCS; WLIT 4

Ryder, Joanne 1946- 37
See also CA 112; 133; CANR 90; CWRI 5; MAICYA 1, 2; SATA 65, 122, 163, 226; SATA-Brief 34

Rye, Anthony
See Youd, Samuel

Rylant, Cynthia 1954- 15, 86, 187
See also AAYA 10, 45; BYA 6, 7; CA 136; CANR 79, 140; CWRI 5; JRDA; MAICYA 1, 2; MAICYAS 1; SAAS 13; SATA 50, 76, 112, 160, 195; SATA-Brief 44; WYAS 1; YAW

S. L. C.
See Twain, Mark

Sachar, Louis 1954- 28, 79, 161, 200
See also AAYA 35; CA 81-84; CANR 15, 33, 131, 176; CWRI 5; JRDA; MAICYA 2; MAICYAS 1; NFS 37; SATA 63, 104, 154, 238; SATA-Brief 50; WYAS 1

Sachs, Marilyn 1927- 2
See also AAYA 2; BYA 6; CA 17-20R; CANR 13, 47, 150; CLC 35; JRDA; MAICYA 1, 2; SAAS 2; SATA 3, 68, 164; SATA-Essay 110; WYA; YAW

Sachs, Marilyn Stickle
See Sachs, Marilyn

Sage, Juniper
See Brown, Margaret Wise; Hurd, Edith Thacher

Saint-Exupéry, Antoine de
1900-1944 .... 10, 142, 229
See also AAYA 63; BPFB 3; BYA 3; CA 108; 132; DA3; DAM NOV; DLB 72; EW 12; EWL 3; GFL 1789 to the Present; LAIT 3; MAICYA 1, 2; MTCW 1, 2; MTFW 2005; NFS 30; RGWL 2, 3; SATA 20; TCLC 2, 56, 169; TWA; WLC

Saint-Exupery, Antoine Jean Baptiste Marie Roger de
See Saint-Exupery, Antoine de

St. George, Judith 1931- 57
See also AAYA 7, 72; CA 69-72; CANR 14, 148, 196; JRDA; SAAS 12; SATA 13, 99, 161

St. George, Judith Alexander
See St. George, Judith

St. John, Nicole 46
See also AAYA 12, 57; CANR 32; JRDA; SAAS 7; SATA 29, 89, 143; SATA-Essay 143; WYA

St. Meyer, Ned
See Stratemeyer, Edward L.

St. Myer, Ned
See Stratemeyer, Edward L.

Salinger, J.D. 1919-2010 .... 18, 181
See also AAYA 2, 36; AMW; AMWC 1; BPFB 3; CA 5-8R; CANR 39, 129; CDALB 1941-1968; CLC 1, 3, 8, 12, 55, 56, 138, 243, 318; CN 1, 2, 3, 4, 5, 6, 7; CPW 1; DA; DA3; DAB; DAC; DAM MST, NOV, POP; DLB 2, 102, 173; EWL 3; EXPN; LAIT 4; MAICYA 1, 2; MAL 5; MTCW 1, 2; MTFW 2005; NFS 1; PFS 38; RGAL 4; RGSF 2; SATA 67; SSC 2, 28, 65, 146; SSFS 17; TUS; WLC 5; WYA; YAW

Salinger, Jerome David
See Salinger, J.D.

Salten, Felix 1869-1945 215
See also CA 108; 137; MAICYA 1, 2; SATA 25; WCH

Sanchez, Alex 1957- 181
See also AAYA 51; CA 226; CANR 80; SATA 151

Sanchez, Sonia 1934- 18
See also BLC 1:3, 2:3; BW 2, 3; CA 33-36R; CANR 24, 49, 74, 115; CLC 5, 116, 215; CP 2, 3, 4, 5, 6, 7; CSW; CWP; DA3; DAM MULT; DLB 41; DLBD 8; EWL 3; MAICYA 1, 2; MAL 5; MTCW 1, 2; MTFW 2005; PC 9; PFS 26; SATA 22, 136; WP

Sanchez-Silva, Jose Maria 1911- 12
See also CA 73-76; MAICYA 1, 2; SATA 16, 132

Sandburg, Carl 1878-1967 67
See also AAYA 24; AMW; BYA 1, 3; CA 5-8R; 25-28R; CANR 35; CDALB 1865-1917; CLC 1, 4, 10, 15, 35; DA; DA3; DAB; DAC; DAM MST, POET; DLB 17, 54, 284; EWL 3; EXPP; LAIT 2; MAICYA 1, 2; MAL 5; MTCW 1, 2; MTFW 2005; PAB; PC 2, 41; PFS 3, 6, 12, 33, 36; RGAL 4; SATA 8; TUS; WCH; WLC 5; WP; WYA

Sandburg, Carl August
See Sandburg, Carl
Sandburg, Charles
See Sandburg, Carl
Sandburg, Charles A.
See Sandburg, Carl
Sanders, Winston P.
See Anderson, Poul
Sanford, Rose
See Simmonds, Posy
San Souci, Robert D. 1946- 43
See also CA 108; CANR 46, 79, 143; MAICYA 2; MAICYAS 1; SATA 40, 81, 117, 158, 220
Santos, Helen
See Griffiths, Helen
Sasek, Miroslav 1916-1980 4
See also CA 73-76; 101; SATA 16; SATA-Obit 23
Satrapi, Marjane 1969- 185
See also AAYA 55; CA 246; CLC 332
Sattler, Helen Roney 1921-1992 24
See also CA 33-36R; CANR 14, 31; SATA 4, 74
Saunders, Caleb
See Heinlein, Robert A.
Sawyer, Ruth 1880-1970 36
See also BYA 3; CA 73-76; CANR 37, 83; CWRI 5; DLB 22; MAICYA 1, 2; SATA 17; WCH
Say, Allen 1937- 22, 135
See also CA 29-32R; CANR 30, 146; CWRI 5; JRDA; MAICYA 1, 2; MAICYAS 1; SATA 28, 69, 110, 161
Scamander, Newt
See Rowling, J.K.
Scarlett, Susan
See Streatfeild, Noel
Scarry, Richard (McClure) 1919-1994 ... 3, 41
See also CA 17-20R; 145; CANR 18, 39, 83; CWRI 5; DLB 61; MAICYA 1, 2; MAICYAS 1; SATA 2, 35, 75; SATA-Obit 90
Schlein, Miriam 1926-2004 41
See also CA 1-4R; 233; CANR 2, 52, 87; CWRI 5; MAICYA 2; SATA 2, 87, 130; SATA-Obit 159
Schmidt, Annie M. G. 1911-1995 22
See also CA 135; 152; SATA 67; SATA-Obit 91
Schneider, Elisa
See Kleven, Elisa
Schulz, Charles M. 1922-2000 188
See also AAYA 39; CA 9-12R, 187; CANR 6, 132; CLC 12; CMTFW 1; MTFW 2005; SATA 10, 118
Schwartz, Alvin 1927-1992 .... 3, 89
See also CA 13-16R; 137; CANR 7, 24, 49, 86; MAICYA 1, 2; SATA 4, 56; SATA-Obit 71
Schwartz, Amy 1954- 25
See also CA 110; CANR 29, 57, 130; INT CANR-29; MAICYA 2; MAICYAS 1; SAAS 18; SATA 47, 83, 131, 189; SATA-Brief 41
Schweitzer, Byrd Baylor
See Baylor, Byrd
Scieszka, Jon 1954- 27, 107
See also AAYA 21; CA 135; CANR 84, 145, 190; CWRI 5; MAICYA 2; MAICYAS 1; SATA 68, 105, 160, 199, 238
Scott, Jack Denton 1915-1995 20
See also CA 108; CANR 48, 86; MAICYA 1, 2; MAICYAS 1; SAAS 14; SATA 31, 83
Scott, Sir Walter 1771-1832 154
See also AAYA 22; BRW 4; BYA 2; CDBLB 1789-1832; DA; DAB; DAC; DAM MST, NOV, POET; DLB 93, 107, 116, 144, 159, 366; GL 3; HGG; LAIT 1; NCLC 15, 69, 110, 209, 241; NFS 31; PC 13; RGEL 2;
RGSF 2; SSC 32; SSFS 10; SUFW 1; TEA; WLC 5; WLIT 3; YABC 2
Sebastian, Lee
See Silverberg, Robert
Sebestyen, Igen
See Sebestyen, Ouida
Sebestyen, Ouida 1924- 17
See also AAYA 8; BYA 7; CA 107; CANR 40, 114; CLC 30; JRDA; MAICYA 1, 2; SAAS 10; SATA 39, 140; WYA; YAW
Seed, Cecile Eugenie 1930- 76
See also CA 21-24R; CANR 26, 51, 83; CWRI 5; SATA 8, 86
Seed, Jenny
See Seed, Cecile Eugenie
Sefton, Catherine
See Waddell, Martin
Seidman, Karla
See Kuskin, Karla
Selden, George
See Thompson, George Selden
Selsam, Millicent E(llis) 1912-1996 1
See also CA 9-12R; 154; CANR 5, 38; MAICYA 1, 2; MAICYAS 1; SATA 1, 29; SATA-Obit 92
Sendak, Maurice 1928- .. 1, 17, 74, 131, 196
See also CA 5-8R; CANR 11, 39, 112; CWRI 5; DLB 61; INT CANR-11; MAICYA 1, 2; MAICYAS 1; MTCW 1, 2; MTFW 2005; SATA 1, 27, 113, 165; TUS
Seredy, Kate 1899-1975 10
See also BYA 1, 4; CA 5-8R; 57-60; CANR 83; CWRI 5; DLB 22; MAICYA 1, 2; SATA 1; SATA-Obit 24; WCH
Serraillier, Ian (Lucien) 1912-1994 2
See also BYA 3, 4; CA 1-4R; 147; CANR 1, 83; DLB 161; MAICYA 1, 2; MAICYAS 1; SAAS 3; SATA 1, 73; SATA-Obit 83; YAW
Seton, Ernest (Evan) Thompson 1860-1946 59
See also ANW; BYA 3; CA 109; 204; DLB 92; DLBD 13; JRDA; SATA 18; TCLC 31
Seton-Thompson, Ernest
See Seton, Ernest (Evan) Thompson
Seuss, Dr.
See Dr. Seuss
Seuss, T.
See Dr. Seuss
Seuss, Theophrastus
See Dr. Seuss
Sewell, Anna 1820-1878 .... 17, 219
See also BYA 1; DLB 163; JRDA; MAICYA 1, 2; NFS 22; SATA 24, 100; WCH
Shackleton, C. C.
See Aldiss, Brian W.
Shannon, David 1959- 87
See also SATA 107, 152, 228
Sharp, Margery 1905-1991 27
See also CA 21-24R; 134; CANR 18, 85; CN 1, 2, 3, 4; CWRI 5; DLB 161; MAICYA 1, 2; SATA 1, 29; SATA-Obit 67
Shaw, Bernard
See Shaw, George Bernard
Shaw, G. Bernard
See Shaw, George Bernard
Shaw, George Bernard 1856-1950 252
See also AAYA 61; BRW 6; BRWC 1; BRWR 2; CA 104, 128; CDBLB 1914-1945; DA; DA3; DAB; DAC; DAM DRAM, MST; DC 23; DFS 1, 3, 6, 11, 19, 22, 30; DLB 10, 57, 190, 332; EWL 3; LAIT 3; LATS 1:1; MBL 2; MTCW 1, 2; MTFW 2005; RGEL 2; TCLC 3, 9, 21, 45, 205, 293, 415; TEA; WLC 5; WLIT 4
Shaw, Janet 1937- 96
See also CA 127; CANR 127; SATA 61, 146
Shaw, Janet Beeler
See Shaw, Janet
Shearer, John 1947- 34
See also CA 125; SATA 43; SATA-Brief 27
Shelley, Mary
See Shelley, Mary Wollstonecraft
Shelley, Mary Wollstonecraft 1797-1851 133
See also AAYA 20; BPFB 3; BRW 3; BRWC 2; BRWR 3; BRWS 3; BYA 5; CDBLB 1789-1832; DA; DA3; DAB; DAC; DAM MST, NOV; DLB 110, 116, 159, 178; EXPN; FL 1:3; GL 3; HGG; LAIT 1; LMFS 1, 2; NCLC 14, 59, 103, 170; NFS 1, 37; RGEL 2; SATA 29; SCFW 1, 2; SFW 4; SSC 92; TEA; WLC 5; WLIT 3
Shepard, Ernest Howard 1879-1976 27
See also CA 9-12R; 65-68; CANR 23, 86; DLB 160; MAICYA 1, 2; SATA 3, 33, 100; SATA-Obit 24
Shippen, Katherine B(inney) 1892-1980 36
See also CA 5-8R; 93-96; CANR 86; SATA 1; SATA-Obit 23
Showers, Paul C. 1910-1999 6
See also CA 1-4R; 183; CANR 4, 38, 59; MAICYA 1, 2; SAAS 7; SATA 21, 92; SATA-Obit 114
Shulevitz, Uri 1935- 5, 61
See also CA 9-12R; CANR 3; CWRI 5; DLB 61; MAICYA 1, 2; SATA 3, 50, 106, 165
Silverberg, Robert 1935- 59
See also AAYA 24; BPFB 3; BYA 7, 9; CA 1-4R, 186; CAAE 186; CAAS 3; CANR 1, 20, 36, 85, 140, 175; CLC 7, 140; CN 6, 7; CPW; DAM POP; DLB 8; INT CANR-20; MAICYA 1, 2; MTCW 1, 2; MTFW 2005; SATA 13, 91; SATA-Essay 104; SCFW 1, 2; SFW 4; SUFW 2
Silverstein, Alvin 1933- 25
See also CA 49-52; CANR 2; CLC 17; JRDA; MAICYA 1, 2; SATA 8, 69, 124
Silverstein, Shel 1930-1999 .... 5, 96, 232
See also AAYA 40; BW 3; CA 107, 179; CANR 47, 74, 81, 244; CMTFW; CWRI 5; JRDA; MAICYA 1, 2; MTCW 2; MTFW 2005; PC 49; SATA 33, 92, 255; SATA-Brief 27; SATA-Obit 116
Silverstein, Sheldon Allan
See Silverstein, Shel
Silverstein, Virginia B. 1937- 25
See also CA 49-52; CANR 2; CLC 17; JRDA; MAICYA 1, 2; SATA 8, 69, 124
Silverstein, Virginia Barbara Opshelor
See Silverstein, Virginia B.
Simmonds, Posy 1945- 23
See also CA 199; CANR 197; SATA 130
Simmonds, Rosemary Elizabeth
See Simmonds, Posy
Simon, Hilda Rita 1921- 39
See also CA 77-80; SATA 28
Simon, Seymour 1931- 9, 63
See also CA 25-28R; CANR 11, 29, 117; MAICYA 1, 2; SATA 4, 73, 138, 202
Sinclair, Catherine 1800-1864 183
See also DLB 163
Singer, Isaac
See Singer, Isaac Bashevis
Singer, Isaac Bashevis 1904-1991 1
See also AAYA 32; AITN 1, 2; AMW; AMWR 2; BPFB 3; BYA 1, 4; CA 1-4R; 134; CANR 1, 39, 106; CDALB 1941-1968; CLC 1, 3, 6, 9, 11, 15, 23, 38, 69, 111; CN 1, 2, 3, 4; CWRI 5; DA; DA3; DAB; DAC; DAM MST, NOV; DLB 6, 28, 52, 278, 332, 333; DLBY 1991; EWL 3; EXPS; HGG; JRDA; LAIT 3; MAICYA 1, 2; MAL 5; MTCW 1, 2; MTFW 2005; RGAL 4; RGHL; RGSF 2; SATA 3, 27;

SATA-Obit 68; SSC 3, 53, 80, 154; SSFS 2, 12, 16, 27, 30; TUS; TWA; WLC 5

Singer, Marilyn 1948- **48**
See also CA 65-68, 248; CAAE 248; CANR 9, 39, 85, 105, 192; JRDA; MAICYA 1, 2; SAAS 13; SATA 48, 80, 125, 158, 201, 234; SATA-Brief 38; SATA-Essay 158; YAW

Sis, Peter 1949- **45, 110**
See also CANR 98, 132; SATA 149, 192

Sleator, William 1945-2011 .... **29, 128**
See also AAYA 5, 39; BYA 4, 6, 7, 8, 9, 10, 11, 16; CA 29-32R; CANR 46, 83, 97, 174, 203; JRDA; LAIT 5; MAICYA 1, 2; SATA 3, 68, 118, 161, 208; WYA; YAW

Sleator, William Warner III
See Sleator, William

Slote, Alfred 1926- **4**
See also CA 203; CWRI 5; JRDA; MAICYA 1, 2; SAAS 21; SATA 8, 72

Small, David 1945- **53**
See also CLC 299; MAICYA 2; SATA 50, 95, 126, 183, 216; SATA-Brief 46

Smalls, Irene
See Smalls-Hector, Irene

Smalls-Hector, Irene 1950- **103**
See also CA 220; SATA 73, 146

Smith, Betty 1896-1972 .... **202**
See also AAYA 72; AMWS 23; BPFB 3; BYA 3; CA 5-8R; 33-36R; CLC 19; DLBY 1982; LAIT 3; NFS 31; RGAL 4; SATA 6

Smith, Dick King
See King-Smith, Dick

Smith, Jessie Willcox 1863-1935 .... **59**
See also CA 190; DLB 188; MAICYA 1, 2; SATA 21

Smith, Johnston
See Crane, Stephen

Smith, Lane 1959- **47**
See also AAYA 21; CA 143; MAICYA 2; MAICYAS 1; SATA 76, 131, 179, 224

Smith, Sosthenes
See Wells, H. G.

Smucker, Barbara 1915-2003 .... **10**
See also CA 106; CANR 23; CWRI 5; JRDA; MAICYA 1, 2; SAAS 11; SATA 29, 76, 130

Smucker, Barbara Claassen
See Smucker, Barbara

Sneve, Virginia Driving Hawk 1933- **2**
See also CA 49-52; CANR 3, 68; SATA 8, 95; SSFS 28

Snicket, Lemony 1970- **79, 182**
See also AAYA 46; BYA 15; CA 195; CANR 173, 211; MTFW 2005; SATA 126, 187, 215

Snodgrass, Quentin Curtius
See Twain, Mark

Snodgrass, Thomas Jefferson
See Twain, Mark

Snyder, Zilpha Keatley 1927- **31, 121**
See also AAYA 15; BYA 1; CA 9-12R, 252; CAAE 252; CANR 38, 202; CLC 17; JRDA; MAICYA 1, 2; SAAS 2; SATA 1, 28, 75, 110, 163, 226; SATA-Essay 112, 163; YAW

Sobol, Donald J. 1924- **4**
See also CA 1-4R; CANR 1, 18, 38, 201; CWRI 5; JRDA; MAICYA 1, 2; SATA 1, 31, 73, 132

Sonnenblick, Jordan 1969- **144**
See also AAYA 78; CA 264; SATA 185, 223

Soto, Gary 1952- **38**
See also AAYA 10, 37; BYA 11; CA 119; 125; CANR 50, 74, 107, 157, 219; CLC 32, 80; CP 4, 5, 6, 7; DAM MULT; DFS 26; DLB 82; EWL 3; EXPP; HLC 2; HW 1, 2; INT CA-125; JRDA; LLW; MAICYA 2; MAICYAS 1; MAL 5; MTCW 2; MTFW 2005; PC 28; PFS 7, 30; RGAL 4; SATA 80, 120, 174; SSFS 33; WYA; YAW

Souci, Robert D. San
See San Souci, Robert D.

Southall, Ivan 1921-2008 .... **2, 165**
See also AAYA 22; BYA 2; CA 9-12R; CANR 7, 47; JRDA; MAICYA 1, 2; SAAS 3; SATA 3, 68, 134; SATA-Essay 134; YAW

Southall, Ivan Francis
See Southall, Ivan

Sparks, Beatrice (Mathews) 1918- **139**
See also BYA 14; CA 97-100; CANR 143; SATA 44; SATA-Brief 28

Spaulding, Douglas
See Bradbury, Ray

Spaulding, Leonard
See Bradbury, Ray

Speare, Elizabeth George 1908-1994 .... **8**
See also AAYA 76; BYA 1, 3; CA 1-4R; 147; JRDA; MAICYA 1, 2; MAICYAS 1; SATA 5, 62; SATA-Obit 83; YAW

Spence, Eleanor (Rachel) 1928- **26**
See also CA 49-52; CANR 3; SATA 21; YAW

Spencer, Leonard G.
See Silverberg, Robert

Spier, Peter (Edward) 1927- **5**
See also CA 5-8R; CANR 41; CWRI 5; DLB 61; MAICYA 1, 2; SATA 4, 54

Spinelli, Jerry 1941- **26, 82, 200**
See also AAYA 11, 41; BYA 7, 9, 10; CA 111; CANR 30, 45, 119, 186; JRDA; MAICYA 1, 2; SATA 39, 71, 110, 158, 195; WYA; YAW

Spirin, Gennadii
See Spirin, Gennady

Spirin, Gennadij
See Spirin, Gennady

Spirin, Gennady 1948- **88**
See also CWRI 5; MAICYA 2; MAICYAS 1; SATA 95, 134, 204

Spykman, E(lizabeth) C(hoate) 1896-1965 .. **35**
See also CA 101; CWRI 5; SATA 10

Spyri, Johanna (Heusser) 1827-1901 .. **13, 115**
See also BYA 2; CA 137; MAICYA 1, 2; SATA 19, 100; WCH

Stanley, Diane 1943- **46**
See also CA 112; CANR 32, 64, 132; CWRI 5; MAICYA 2; MAICYAS 1; SAAS 15; SATA 37, 80, 115, 164, 213; SATA-Brief 32

Stanton, Schuyler
See Baum, L. Frank

Staples, Suzanne Fisher 1945- **60, 137**
See also AAYA 26; BYA 15; CA 132; CANR 82, 201; MAICYA 2; MAICYAS 1; NFS 35; SATA 70, 105, 151, 207; WYAS 1; YAW

Starbird, Kaye 1916- **60**
See also CA 17-20R; CANR 38; MAICYA 1, 2; SATA 6

Starr, Julian
See Alger, Horatio, Jr.

Staunton, Schuyler
See Baum, L. Frank

Steig, William 1907-2003 .... **2, 15, 103**
See also AITN 1; CA 77-80; 224; CANR 21, 44, 119; CWRI 5; DLB 61; INT CANR-21; MAICYA 1, 2; MTFW 2005; SATA 18, 70, 111; SATA-Obit 149

Steig, William H.
See Steig, William

Steinbeck, John 1902-1968 .... **172, 194, 195, 251**
See also AAYA 12; AMW; BPFB 3; BYA 2, 3, 13; CA 1-4R, 25-28R; CANR 1, 35; CDALB 1929-1941; CLC 1, 5, 9, 13, 21, 34, 45, 75, 124; DA; DA3; DAB; DAC; DAM DRAM, MST, NOV; DC 46; DLB 7, 9, 212, 275, 309, 332, 364; DLBD 2; EWL 3; EXPS; LAIT 3; MAL 5; MTCW 1, 2; MTFW 2005; NFS 1, 5, 7, 17, 19, 28, 34, 37, 39, 46, 53; RGAL 4; RGSF 2; RHW; SATA 9; SSC 11, 37, 77, 135, 265; SSFS 3, 6, 22; TCLC 135, 369, 408; TCWW 1, 2; TUS; WLC 5; WYA; YAW

Steinbeck, John Ernst
See Steinbeck, John

Steptoe, John (Lewis) 1950-1989 .... **2, 12**
See also BW 1; CA 49-52; 129; CANR 3, 26, 81; CWRI 5; MAICYA 1, 2; SATA 8, 63

Sterling, Brett
See Bradbury, Ray

Sterling, Dorothy 1913-2008 .... **1**
See also CA 9-12R, 201; 280; CAAE 201; CANR 5, 28; JRDA; MAICYA 1, 2; SAAS 2; SATA 1, 83; SATA-Essay 127; SATA-Obit 200

Stevens, Margaret Dean
See Aldrich, Bess Streeter

Stevenson, James 1929- **17**
See also CA 115; CANR 47, 101, 186; CWRI 5; MAICYA 1, 2; SATA 42, 71, 113, 161, 195; SATA-Brief 34

Stevenson, Robert Louis 1850-1894 ... **10, 11, 107, 180, 204, 210, 221**
See also AAYA 24; BPFB 3; BRW 5; BRWC 1; BRWR 1; BYA 1, 2, 4, 13; CDBLB 1890-1914; DA; DA3; DAB; DAC; DAM MST, NOV; DLB 18, 57, 141, 156, 174; DLBD 13; GL 3; HGG; JRDA; LAIT 1, 3; MAICYA 1, 2; NCLC 5, 14, 63, 193, 274, 289, 292, 308; NFS 11, 20, 33; PC 84; RGEL 2; RGSF 2; SATA 100; SSC 11, 51, 126, 228, 235; SUFW; TEA; WCH; WLC 5; WLIT 4; WYA; YABC 2; YAW

Stevenson, Robert Louis Balfour
See Stevenson, Robert Louis

Stewart, Eleanor
See Porter, Eleanor H(odgman)

Stine, Jovial Bob
See Stine, R.L.

Stine, R.L. 1943- **37, 111**
See also AAYA 13; CA 105; CANR 22, 53, 109, 185; CPW; HGG; JRDA; MAICYA 2; MAICYAS 1; MTCW 2; MTFW 2005; SATA 31, 76, 129, 194; WYAS 1; YAW

Stine, Robert Lawrence
See Stine, R.L.

Stoker, Bram 1847-1912 .... **178**
See also AAYA 23; BPFB 3; BRWS 3; BYA 5; CA 105; 150; CDBLB 1890-1914; DA; DA3; DAB; DAC; DAM MST, NOV; DLB 304; GL 3; HGG; LATS 1:1; MTFW 2005; NFS 18; RGEL 2; SATA 29; SSC 62; SUFW; TCLC 8, 144; TEA; WLC 6; WLIT 4

Stollberg, Ferdinand
See Salten, Felix

Stone, Rosetta
See Dr. Seuss

Stowe, Harriet Beecher 1811-1896 .... **131**
See also AAYA 53; AMWS 1; CDALB 1865-1917; DA; DA3; DAB; DAC; DAM MST, NOV; DLB 1, 12, 42, 74, 189, 239, 243; EXPN; FL 1:3; JRDA; LAIT 2; MAICYA 1, 2; NCLC 3, 50, 133, 195; NFS 6; RGAL 4; SSC 159; TUS; WLC 6; YABC 1

Stowe, Harriet Elizabeth Beecher
See Stowe, Harriet Beecher

Strasser, Todd 1950- **11**
See also AAYA 2, 35; BYA 6, 8, 9, 12; CA 117; 123; CANR 47, 130, 176; JRDA; MAICYA 1, 2; SATA 41, 45, 71, 107, 153, 215; WYA; YAW

Stratemeyer, Edward L. 1862-1930 .... **166**
See also Adams, Harrison
See also CA 19-20; CANR 27; CAP 2; CCA 1; DLB 42; MAICYA 1, 2; SATA 1, 67, 100; WYA

Stratton-Porter, Gene 1863-1924 ...... **87, 220**
See also AMWS 20; ANW; BPFB 3; CA 112; 137; CWRI 5; DLB 221; DLBD 14; MAICYA 1, 2; RHW; SATA 15; TCLC 21

Stratton-Porter, Geneva Grace
See Stratton-Porter, Gene

Strayer, E. Ward
See Stratemeyer, Edward L.

Streatfeild, Mary Noel
See Streatfeild, Noel

Streatfeild, Noel 1897(?)-1986 .... **17, 83**
See also CA 81-84; 120; CANR 31; CLC 21; CWRI 5; DLB 160; MAICYA 1, 2; SATA 20; SATA-Obit 48

Stren, Patti 1949- **5**
See also CA 117; 124; SATA 88; SATA-Brief 41

Strong, Charles
See Epstein, Beryl; Epstein, Samuel

Stroud, Jonathan 1970- **134**
See also CA 169; CANR 144, 204; SATA 102, 159, 213

Stuart, Eleanor
See Porter, Eleanor H(odgman)

Suhl, Yuri (Menachem) 1908-1986 .... **2**
See also CA 45-48; 121; CANR 2, 38; MAICYA 1, 2; SAAS 1; SATA 8; SATA-Obit 50

Summers, Cassia Joy
See Cowley, Joy

Sutcliff, Rosemary 1920-1992 ...... **1, 37, 138**
See also AAYA 10; BRWS 16; BYA 1, 4; CA 5-8R; 139; CANR 37; CLC 26; CPW; DAB; DAC; DAM MST, POP; JRDA; LATS 1:1; MAICYA 1, 2; MAICYAS 1; RHW; SATA 6, 44, 78; SATA-Obit 73; WYA; YAW

Swann, E.L.
See Lasky, Kathryn

Swift, Jonathan 1667-1745 .... **53, 161**
See also AAYA 41; BRW 3; BRWC 1; BRWR 1; BYA 5, 14; CDBLB 1660-1789; DA; DA3; DAB; DAC; DAM MST, NOV, POET; DLB 39, 95, 101; EXPN; LAIT 1; LC 1, 42, 101, 201; NFS 6; PC 9; PFS 27, 37; RGEL 2; SATA 19; TEA; WCH; WLC 6; WLIT 3

Swithen, John
See King, Stephen

Taback, Simms 1932- **100**
See also CA 115; 171; CANR 145; MAICYA 2; SATA 40, 104, 170; SATA-Brief 36

Tafuri, Nancy 1946- **74**
See also CA 118, 269; CAAE 269; CANR 44; CWRI 5; MAICYA 1, 2; SAAS 14; SATA 39, 75, 130, 192; SATA-Essay 192

Tan, Shaun 1974- **184**
See also AAYA 85; CA 303; NFS 42; SATA 198, 251

Tarkington, Booth 1869-1946 .... **241**
See also BPFB 3; BYA 3; CA 110, 143; CWRI 5; DLB 9, 102; MAL 5; MTCW 2; NFS 34; RGAL 4; SATA 17; TCLC 9

Tarry, Ellen 1906-2008 .... **26**
See also BW 1, 3; CA 73-76; CANR 69; SAAS 16; SATA 16

Tate, Eleanora E. 1948- **37**
See also AAYA 25; BW 2, 3; CA 105; CANR 25, 43, 81, 183; CWRI 5; JRDA; MAICYA 2; MAICYAS 1; SATA 38, 94, 191

Tate, Eleanora Elaine
See Tate, Eleanora E.

Taylor, Cora (Lorraine) 1936- **63**
See also CA 124; CANR 125; CWRI 5; SATA 64, 103

Taylor, Mildred D. 1943- ... **9, 59, 90, 144, 241**
See also AAYA 10, 47; BW 1; BYA 3, 8; CA 85-88; CANR 25, 115, 136; CLC 21; CMTFW; CSW; DLB 52; JRDA; LAIT 3; MAICYA 1, 2; MTFW 2005; SAAS 5; SATA 15, 70, 135; WYA; YAW

Taylor, Sydney 1904-1978 .... **178**
See also CA 5-8R; CA 77-80; CANR 4; MAICYA 1, 2; CWRI 5; SATA 1, 28; SATA-Obit 26

Taylor, Theodore 1921-2006 .... **30**
See also AAYA 2, 19, 76; BYA 1; CA 21-24R; 254; CANR 9, 25, 38, 50, 108, 150; JRDA; MAICYA 1, 2; MAICYAS 1; SAAS 4; SATA 5, 54, 83, 128; SATA-Obit 177; WYA; YAW

Taylor, William 1938- **63**
See also CA 146; CANR 94, 150; CWRI 5; SATA 78, 113, 164

Tedesco, P.R.
See Naylor, Phyllis Reynolds

Tejima
See Tejima, Keizaburo

Tejima, Keizaburo 1931- **20**
See also SATA 139

Telescope, Tom
See Newbery, John

Tenneshaw, S.M.
See Silverberg, Robert

Tenniel, John 1820-1914 .... **18, 146, 243**
See also CA 111; MAICYA 1, 2; SATA 74; SATA-Brief 27

ter Haar, Jaap 1922- **15**
See also CA 37-40R; SATA 6

Thiele, Colin 1920-2006 .... **27**
See also CA 29-32R; CANR 12, 28, 53, 105; CLC 17; CP 1, 2; DLB 289; MAICYA 1, 2; SAAS 2; SATA 14, 72, 125; YAW

Thomas, Angie 1988- **259**
See also CA 411; CLC 506; SATA 356

Thomas, Ianthe 1951- **8**
See also SATA 139; SATA-Brief 42

Thomas, Joyce Carol 1938- **19**
See also AAYA 12, 54; BW 2, 3; CA 113; 116; CANR 48, 114, 135, 206; CLC 35; DLB 33; INT CA-116; JRDA; MAICYA 1, 2; MTCW 1, 2; MTFW 2005; SAAS 7; SATA 40, 78, 123, 137, 210; SATA-Essay 137; WYA; YAW

Thompson, George Selden 1929-1989 .... **8**
See also CA 5-8R; 130; CANR 21, 37; CWRI 5; DLB 52; FANT; INT CANR-21; MAICYA 1, 2; SATA 4, 73; SATA-Obit 63

Thompson, Julian F(rancis) 1927- **24**
See also AAYA 9, 70; CA 111; CANR 30, 56, 102; JRDA; MAICYA 1, 2; SAAS 13; SATA 55, 99, 155; SATA-Brief 40; WYA

Thompson, Kay 1912(?)-1998 .... **22**
See also CA 85-88; 169; MAICYA 1, 2; SATA 16

Thornton, Hall
See Silverberg, Robert

Tobias, Tobi 1938- **4**
See also CA 29-32R; CANR 16, 135; SATA 5, 82

Tolkien, J. R. R.
1892-1973 .... **56, 152, 236, 240**
See also AAYA 10; AITN 1; BPFB 3; BRWC 2; BRWS 2; CA 17-18, 45-48; CANR 36, 134; CAP 2; CDBLB 1914-1945; CLC 1, 2, 3, 8, 12, 38; CN 1; CPW 1; CWRI 5; DA; DA3; DAB; DAC; DAM MST, NOV, POP; DLB 15, 160, 255; EFS 1:2, 2:1; EWL 3; FANT; JRDA; LAIT 1; LATS 1:2; LMFS 2; MAICYA 1, 2; MBL; MTCW 1, 2; MTFW 2005; NFS 8, 26; RGEL 2; SATA 2, 32, 100; SATA-Obit 24; SFW 4; SSC 156; SSFHW; SUFW; TCLC 137, 299; TEA; WCH; WLC 6; WYA; YAW

Tolkien, John Ronald Reuel
See Tolkien, J. R. R.

Tomfool
See Farjeon, Eleanor

Tomlinson, Theresa 1946- **60**
See also BYA 11; CA 170; CANR 133, 196; MAICYA 2; SATA 103, 165

Totham, Mary
See Breinburg, Petronella

Townsend, John Rowe 1922- **2**
See also AAYA 11; BYA 1; CA 37-40R; CANR 41; JRDA; MAICYA 1, 2; SAAS 2; SATA 4, 68, 132; SATA-Essay 132; YAW

Travers, P(amela) L(yndon)
1899-1996 .... **2, 93, 262**
See also CA 33-36R; 152; CANR 30; CWRI 5; DLB 160; MAICYA 1, 2; MAICYAS 1; SAAS 2; SATA 4, 54, 100; SATA-Obit 90; TEA

Trease, (Robert) Geoffrey 1909-1998 .... **42**
See also CA 5-8R; 165; CANR 7, 22, 38; MAICYA 1, 2; SAAS 6; SATA 2, 60; SATA-Obit 101; YAW

Treece, Henry 1912-1966 .... **2**
See also BYA 4; CA 1-4R; 25-28R; CANR 6, 60; DLB 160; MAICYA 1, 2; RHW; SATA 2

Tresselt, Alvin 1916-2000 .... **30**
See also CA 49-52; 189; CANR 1; CWRI 5; MAICYA 1, 2; SATA 7

Trezise, Percy 1923- **41**
See also CA 132; CWRI 5

Trezise, Percy James
See Trezise, Percy

Trout, Kilgore
See Farmer, Philip José

Tudor, Edward
See Browne, Anthony

Tudor, Tasha 1915-2008 .... **13**
See also CA 81-84; 276; CANR 145; MAICYA 1, 2; SATA 20, 69, 160; SATA-Obit 205

Tunis, Edwin (Burdett) 1897-1973 .... **2**
See also CA 5-8R; 45-48; CANR 7; MAICYA 1, 2; SATA 1, 28; SATA-Obit 24

Turner, Philip (William) 1925- **89**
See also CA 25-28R; CANR 11, 27; CWRI 5; SAAS 6; SATA 11, 83

Twain, Mark 1835-1910 ...... **58, 60, 66, 156, 187, 245, 254, 266**
See also AAYA 20; AMW; AMWC 1; BPFB 3; BYA 2, 3, 11, 14; CA 104, 135; CDALB 1865-1917; DA; DA3; DAB; DAC; DAM MST, NOV; DLB 11, 12, 23, 64, 74, 186, 189, 343; EXPN; EXPS; FANT; JRDA; LAIT 2; LMFS 1; MAICYA 1, 2; MAL 5; NCFS 4; NFS 1, 6; RGAL 4; RGSF 2; SATA 100; SFW 4; SSC 6, 26, 34, 87, 119, 210, 234, 258, 286; SSFS 1, 7, 16, 21, 27, 33, 42; SUFW; TCLC 6, 12, 19, 36, 48, 59, 161, 185, 260; TUS; WCH; WLC 6; WYA; YABC 2; YAW

Twohill, Maggie
See Angell, Judie

Uchida, Yoshiko 1921-1992 .... **6, 56**
See also AAL; AAYA 16; BYA 2, 3; CA 13-16R; 139; CANR 6, 22, 47, 61; CDALBS 7; CWRI 5; DLB 312; JRDA; MAICYA 1, 2; MTCW 1, 2; MTFW 2005; NFS 26; SAAS 1; SATA 1, 53; SATA-Obit 72; SSFS 31

Uderzo, Albert 1927- **37**
See also CA 230

Uncle Gus
See Rey, H. A.

Uncle Shelby
See Silverstein, Shel

Ungerer, (Jean) Thomas 1931- **3, 77**
See also CA 41-44R; CWRI 5; MAICYA 1, 2; SATA 5, 33, 106

Ungerer, Tomi 1931-
See Ungerer, (Jean) Thomas

Unnerstad, Edith (Totterman)
1900-1982 .... **36**
See also CA 5-8R; CANR 6, 72; SATA 3

Ure, Jean 1943- **34**
See also AAYA 33; BYA 6; CA 125, 261; CANR 48, 92, 109, 182; JRDA; MAICYA 1, 2; SAAS 14; SATA 48, 78, 129, 192; SATA-Essay 192; YAW

Usher, Margo Scegge
See McHargue, Georgess

Van Allsburg, Chris 1949- **5, 13, 113**
See also AAYA 69; CA 113; 117; CANR 38, 120; CWRI 5; DLB 61; MAICYA 1, 2; SATA 37, 53, 105, 156

Vance, Gerald
See Silverberg, Robert

Vande Velde, Vivian 1951- **145**
See also AAYA 32; BYA 6; CA 160; CANR 120; MAICYA 2; SATA 62, 95, 141, 211

Van Dyne, Edith
See Baum, L. Frank

Vega, Diego
See Adkins, Jan

Ventura, Piero (Luigi) 1937- **16**
See also CA 103; CANR 39; MAICYA 1, 2; SATA 61; SATA-Brief 43

Verne, Jules 1828-1905 .... **88, 212, 232**
See also AAYA 16; BYA 4; CA 110, 131; DA3; DLB 123; GFL 1789 to the Present; JRDA; LAIT 2; LMFS 2; MAICYA 1, 2; MTFW 2005; NFS 30, 34; RGWL 2, 3; SATA 21; SCFW 1, 2; SFW 4; SSFHW; TCLC 6, 52, 245, 375; TWA; WCH

Verne, Jules Gabriel
See Verne, Jules

Vestly, Anne-Cath(arina) 1920-2008 .... **99**
See also CA 85-88; CANR 18, 41; SATA 14

Viator, Vacuus
See Hughes, Thomas

Vincent, Gabrielle 1928-2000 .... **13**
See also CA 126; CANR 99; MAICYA 1, 2; SATA 61, 121

Viorst, Judith 1931- **3, 90**
See also BEST 90:1; CA 49-52; CANR 2, 26, 59, 101, 155, 185; CPW; CWRI 5; DAM POP; DLB 52; INT CANR-26; MAICYA 1, 2; SATA 7, 70, 123, 172

Viramontes, Helena Maria 1954- **285**
See also CA 159; CANR 182; DLB 122, 350; HLCS 2; HW 2; LLW; SSC 149

Vogel, Ilse-Margret 1914-2001 .... **170**
See also CA 13-16R; CANR 7; SATA 14

Voigt, Cynthia 1942- **13, 48, 141**
See also AAYA 3, 30; BYA 1, 3, 6, 7, 8; CA 106; CANR 18, 37, 40, 94, 145; CLC 30; INT CANR-18; JRDA; LAIT 5; MAICYA 1, 2; MAICYAS 1; MTFW 2005; SATA 48, 79, 116, 160; SATA-Brief 33; WYA; YAW

von Ziegesar, Cecily 1970- **239**
See also AAYA 56; CA 241; CANR 225, 332; SATA 161, 281

Vonnegut, Kurt 1922-2007 .... **265**
See also AAYA 6, 44; AITN 1; AMWS 2; BEST 90:4; BPFB 3; BYA 3, 14; CA 1-4R; 259; CANR 1, 25, 49, 75, 92, 207; CDALB 1968-1988; CLC 1, 2, 3, 4, 5, 8, 12, 22, 40, 60, 111, 212, 254, 387; CN 1, 2, 3, 4, 5, 6, 7; CPW 1; DA; DA3; DAB; DAC; DAM MST, NOV, POP; DLB 2, 8, 152; DLBD 3; DLBY 1980; EWL 3; EXPN; EXPS; LAIT 4; LMFS 2; MAL 5; MTCW 1, 2; MTFW 2005; NFS 3, 28; RGAL; SSC 8, 155; WLC 6

Vos, Ida 1931-2006 .... **85**
See also CA 137; CANR 99; SATA 69, 121; YAW

Vugteveen, Verna Aardema
See Aardema, Verna

Waber, Bernard 1924- **55**
See also CA 1-4R; CANR 2, 38, 68, 140; CWRI 5; MAICYA 1, 2; SATA 47, 95, 155; SATA-Brief 40

Waddell, Martin 1941- **31**
See also AAYA 23; CA 113; CANR 34, 56, 107; CWRI 5; MAICYA 2; MAICYAS 1; SAAS 15; SATA 43, 81, 127, 129, 232; SATA-Essay 129

Walker, Alice 1944- **198, 256**
See also AAYA 3, 33; AFAW 1, 2; AMWS 3; BEST 89:4; BLC 1:3, 2:3; BPFB 3; BW 2, 3; CA 37-40R; CANR 9, 27, 49, 66, 82, 131, 191, 238; CDALB 1968-1988; CLC 5, 6, 9, 19, 27, 46, 58, 103, 167, 319; CMTFW; CN 4, 5, 6, 7; CPW; CSW; DA; DA3; DAB; DAC; DAM MST, MULT, NOV, POET, POP; DLB 6, 33, 143; EWL 3; EXPN; EXPS; FL 1:6; FW; LAIT 3; MAL 5; MAWW; MBL; MTCW 1, 2; MTFW 2005; NFS 5, 44; PC 30; PFS 30, 34; RGAL 4; RGSF 2; SATA 31; SSC 5, 272; SSFS 2, 11; TUS; WLCS; YAW 1, 2

Wallace, Barbara Brooks 1922- **150**
See also CA 29-32R; CANR 11, 28, 115; MAICYA 2; SAAS 17; SATA 4, 78, 136

Wallace, Ian 1950- **37**
See also CA 107; CANR 25, 38, 50, 120; CWRI 5; MAICYA 1, 2; SATA 53, 56, 141, 219

Walley, Byron
See Card, Orson Scott

Walsh, Gillian Paton
See Paton Walsh, Jill

Walsh, Jill Paton
See Paton Walsh, Jill

Walter, Mildred Pitts 1922- **15, 61**
See also BW 2; CA 138; CWRI 5; JRDA; MAICYA 1, 2; MAICYAS 1; SAAS 12; SATA 69, 133; SATA-Brief 45; YAW

Walter, Villiam Christian
See Andersen, Hans Christian

Ward, E. D.
See Gorey, Edward (St. John)

Ward, Ed
See Stratemeyer, Edward L.

Ward, Jesmyn **222**

Ward, Tom
See Stratemeyer, Edward L.

Ware, Chris 1967- **191**
See also AAYA 47; CA 175; CANR 119; CMTFW; MTFW; SATA 140

Warner, Susan 1819-1885 .... **179, 219**
See also AMWS 18; DLB 3, 42, 239, 250, 254; NCLC 31, 146

Warshofsky, Isaac
See Singer, Isaac Bashevis

Wa-Sha-Quon-Asin
See Belaney, Archibald Stansfeld

Wa-sha-quon-asin
See Belaney, Archibald Stansfeld

Watanabe, Shigeo 1928- **8**
See also CA 112; CANR 45; MAICYA 1, 2; SATA 39, 131; SATA-Brief 32

Watkins, Yoko Kawashima 1933- **182**
See also BYA 14; CA 158; LAIT 4; NFS 28; SATA 93

Watson, Clyde 1947- **3**
See also CA 49-52; CANR 4, 39; MAICYA 1, 2; SATA 5, 68

Watson, John H.
See Farmer, Philip José

Watson, John H., M.D.
See Moorcock, Michael

Watson, Richard F.
See Silverberg, Robert

Waystaff, Simon
See Swift, Jonathan

Weary, Ogdred
See Gorey, Edward (St. John)

Webb, Christopher
See Wibberley, Leonard

Weiss, Harvey 1922- **4**
See also CA 5-8R; CANR 6, 38; MAICYA 1, 2; SAAS 19; SATA 1, 27, 76

Weiss, Miriam
See Schlein, Miriam

Wells, H. G. 1866-1946 ...... **64, 133, 200, 250**
See also AAYA 18; BPFB 3; BRW 6; CA 110, 121; CDBLB 1914-1945; DA; DA3; DAB; DAC; DAM MST, NOV; DLB 34, 70, 156, 178; EWL 3; EXPS; HGG; LAIT 3; LMFS 2; MBL; MTCW 1, 2; MTFW 2005; NFS 17, 20, 36; RGEL 2; RGSF 2; SATA 20; SCFW 1, 2; SFW 4; SSC 6, 70, 151, 264; SSFHW; SSFS 3, 34; SUFW; TCLC 6, 12, 19, 133, 317; TEA; WCH; WLC 6; WLIT 4; YAW

Wells, Herbert George
See Wells, H. G.

Wells, Rosemary 1943- **16, 69**
See also AAYA 13; BYA 7, 8; CA 85-88; CANR 48, 120, 179; CLC 12; CWRI 5; MAICYA 1, 2; SAAS 1; SATA 18, 69, 114, 156, 207, 237; YAW

Wersba, Barbara 1932- **3, 78**
See also AAYA 2, 30; BYA 6, 12, 13; CA 29-32R, 182; CAAE 182; CANR 16, 38; CLC 30; DLB 52; JRDA; MAICYA 1, 2; SAAS 2; SATA 1, 58; SATA-Essay 103; WYA; YAW

Westall, Robert (Atkinson) 1929-1993 .... **13, 177**
See also AAYA 12; BYA 2, 6, 7, 8, 9, 15; CA 69-72; 141; CANR 18, 68; CLC 17; FANT; JRDA; MAICYA 1, 2; MAICYAS 1; SAAS 2; SATA 23, 69; SATA-Obit 75; WYA; YAW

Westerfeld, Scott 1963- **225**
See also AAYA 80; CA 218; CANR 168, 289; SATA 161, 230, 300

Weston, Allen
See Norton, Andre

Wetherell, Elizabeth
See Warner, Susan

Wharton, Edith 1862-1937 .... **136**
See also AAYA 25; AMW; AMWC 2; AMWR 1; BPFB 3; CA 104; 132; CDALB 1865-1917; DA; DA3; DAB; DAC; DAM MST, NOV; DLB 4, 9, 12, 78, 189; DLBD 13; EWL 3; EXPS; FL 1:6; GL 3; HGG; LAIT 2, 3; LATS 1:1; MAL 5; MBL; MTCW 1, 2; MTFW 2005; NFS 5, 11, 15, 20, 37; RGAL 4; RGSF 2; RHW; SSC 6, 84, 120; SSFS 6, 7; SUFW; TCLC 3, 9, 27, 53, 129, 149; TUS; WLC 6

Wharton, Edith Newbold Jones
See Wharton, Edith

Whelan, Gloria 1923- **90**
See also AAYA 42; BYA 15; CA 101; CANR 108, 151, 204; MAICYA 2; SATA 85, 128, 178, 224

Whelan, Gloria Ann
See Whelan, Gloria

Whisp, Kennilworthy
See Rowling, J.K.

White, E. B. 1899-1985 ... **1, 21, 107, 238, 272**
See also AAYA 62; AITN 2; AMWS 1; CA 13-16R, 116; CANR 16, 37; CDALBS; CLC 10, 34, 39; CPW; DA3; DAM POP; DLB 11, 22; EWL 3; FANT; MAICYA 1, 2; MAL 5; MTCW 1, 2; MTFW 2005; NCFS 5; RGAL 4; SATA 2, 29, 100; SATA-Obit 44; SSFHW; TUS

White, Elwyn Brooks
See White, E. B.

White, Lee Strout
See White, E. B.

White, Robb 1909-1990 .... **3**
See also AAYA 29; CA 1-4R; CANR 1; SAAS 1; SATA 1, 83; YAW

White, T(erence) H(anbury) 1906-1964 ... 139
See also AAYA 22; BPFB 3; BYA 4, 5; CA 73-76; CANR 37; CLC 30; DLB 160; FANT; JRDA; LAIT 1; MAICYA 1, 2; NFS 30; RGEL 2; SATA 12; SUFW 1; YAW

Whitney, Phyllis A. 1903-2008 ... 59
See also AAYA 36; AITN 2; BEST 90:3; CA 1-4R; 269; CANR 3, 25, 38, 60; CLC 42; CMW 4; CPW; DA3; DAM POP; JRDA; MAICYA 1, 2; MTCW 2; RHW; SATA 1, 30; SATA-Obit 189; YAW

Whitney, Phyllis Ayame
See Whitney, Phyllis A.

Wibberley, Leonard 1915-1983 ... 3
See also CA 5-8R; 111; CANR 3; MSW; SATA 2, 45; SATA-Obit 36

Wibberley, Leonard Patrick O'Connor
See Wibberley, Leonard

Wiese, Kurt 1887-1974 ... 86
See also CA 9-12R; 49-52; CANR 77; MAICYA 1, 2; SATA 3, 36; SATA-Obit 24

Wiesel, Elie 1928- ... 192
See also AAYA 7, 54; AITN 1; CA 5-8R; CAAS 4; CANR 8, 40, 65, 125, 207; CDALBS; CWW 2; DA; DA3; DAB; DAC; DAM MST, NOV; DLB 83, 299; DLBY 1987; EWL 3; INT CANR-8; LAIT 4; MTCW 1, 2; MTFW 2005; NCFS 4; NFS 4; RGHL; RGWL 3; SATA 56; YAW

Wiesner, David 1956- ... 43, 84
See also CA 209; CWRI 5; MAICYA 2; MAICYAS 1; SATA 72, 117, 139, 181

Wiggin, Kate Douglas (Smith) 1856-1923 ... 52, 179
See also BYA 3; CA 111; 160; CWRI 5; DLB 42; MAICYA 1, 2; WCH; YABC 1

Wight, James Alfred
See Herriot, James

Wilde, Oscar 1854-1900 ... 114, 264
See also AAYA 49; BRW 5; BRWC 1, 2; BRWR 2; BYA 15; CA 104, 119; CANR 112; CDBLB 1890-1914; DA; DA3; DAB; DAC; DAM DRAM, MST, NOV; DC 17, 57; DFS 4, 8, 9, 21; DLB 10, 19, 34, 57, 141, 156, 190, 344; EXPS; FANT; GL 3; LATS 1:1; NFS 20; PC 111; RGEL 2; RGSF 2; SATA 24; SSC 11, 77, 208, 293; SSFS 7, 41; SUFW; TCLC 1, 8, 23, 41, 175, 272, 349; TEA; WCH; WLC 6; WLIT 4

Wilde, Oscar Fingal O'Flahertie Willis
See Wilde, Oscar

Wilder, Laura Elizabeth Ingalls
See Wilder, Laura Ingalls

Wilder, Laura Ingalls 1867-1957 ... 2, 111, 229
See also AAYA 26; BYA 2; CA 111; 137; CWRI 5; DA3; DLB 22, 256; JRDA; MAICYA 1, 2; MTCW 2; MTFW 2005; SATA 15, 29, 100; TCLC 344; TCWW 2; TUS; WCH; WYA

Wildsmith, Brian 1930- ... 2, 52
See also CA 35-88; CANR 35; MAICYA 1, 2; SAAS 5; SATA 16, 69, 124

Wilhelm, Hans 1945- ... 46
See also CA 119, 274; CAAE 274; CANR 48, 113; SAAS 21; SATA 58, 135, 196; SATA-Essay 196

Wilkins, Mary Huiskamp 1926- ... 42
See also CA 5-8R; CANR 2, 18, 118; MAICYA 1; MAICYAS 1; SATA 2

Wilkins, Mary Huiskamp Calhoun
See Wilkins, Mary Huiskamp

Wilkinson, Brenda 1946- ... 20
See also BW 2; CA 69-72; CANR 26, 51; JRDA; MAICYA 2; MAICYAS 1; SATA 14, 91; WYA; YAW

Willard, Barbara (Mary) 1909-1994 ... 2
See also CA 81-84; 144; CANR 15; DLB 161; MAICYA 1, 2; MAICYAS 1; SAAS 5; SATA 17, 74; YAW

Willard, Nancy 1936- ... 5
See also BYA 5; CA 89-92; CANR 10, 39, 68, 107, 152, 186; CLC 7, 37; CP 2, 3, 4, 5; CWP; CWRI 5; DLB 5, 52; FANT; MAICYA 1, 2; MTCW 1; SATA 37, 71, 127, 191; SATA-Brief 30; SUFW 2; TCLE 1:2

Willems, Mo ... 114
See also AAYA 71; SATA 154, 180, 228

William, Kate
See Armstrong, Jennifer

Williams, Barbara 1925- ... 48
See also CA 49-52; CANR 1, 17; MAICYA 2; SAAS 16; SATA 11, 107

Williams, Beryl
See Epstein, Beryl

Williams, Charles
See Collier, James Lincoln

Williams, Garth (Montgomery) 1912-1996 ... 57
See also CA 134; 152; DLB 22; MAICYA 1, 2; MAICYAS 1; SAAS 7; SATA 18, 66; SATA-Obit 90

Williams, Jay 1914-1978 ... 8
See also CA 1-4R; 81-84; CANR 2, 39; MAICYA 1, 2; SATA 3, 41; SATA-Obit 24

Williams, Kit 1946(?)- ... 4
See also CA 107; SATA 44

Williams, Margery
See Bianco, Margery Williams

Williams, Vera B(aker) 1927- ... 9
See also CA 123; CANR 38, 123; CWRI 5; MAICYA 1, 2; MAICYAS 1; SATA 53, 102; SATA-Brief 33

Williams-Garcia, Rita 1957- ... 36
See also AAYA 22, 87; CA 159; CANR 87, 145, 209; SATA 98, 160; WYAS 1

Willis, Charles
See Clarke, Arthur C.

Willis, Connie 1945- ... 66
See also AAYA 30, 74; CA 114, 203; CAAE 203; CANR 35, 91, 151; CN 6, 7; FANT; MAICYA 2; SATA 110; SCFW 2; SFW 4

Winchester, Stanley
See Youd, Samuel

Winfield, Arthur M.
See Stratemeyer, Edward L.

Winfield, Edna
See Stratemeyer, Edward L.

Winfield, Julia
See Armstrong, Jennifer

Winthrop, Elizabeth 1948- ... 89
See also CA 41-44R; CANR 110; MAICYA 2; MAICYAS 1; SATA 8, 76, 164; SATA-Essay 116

Wisniewski, David 1953-2002 ... 51
See also CA 160; 209; CWRI 5; MAICYA 2; MAICYAS 1; SATA 95; SATA-Obit 139

Wodge, Dreary
See Gorey, Edward (St. John)

Wojciechowska, Maia (Teresa) 1927-2002 ... 1
See also AAYA 8, 46; BYA 3; CA 9-12R, 183; 209; CAAE 183; CANR 4, 41; CLC 26; JRDA; MAICYA 1, 2; SAAS 1; SATA 1, 28, 83; SATA-Essay 104; SATA-Obit 134; YAW

Wolff, Sonia
See Levitin, Sonia

Wolff, Virginia Euwer 1937- ... 62
See also AAYA 26; CA 107; CANR 111, 209; MAICYA 2; MAICYAS 1; NFS 35; SATA 78, 137; WYA; YAW

Wolny, P.
See Janeczko, Paul B(ryan)

Wong, Janet S. 1962- ... 94
See also CA 166; CANR 132, 206; SATA 98, 148, 210

Wood, Audrey ... 26
See also CA 137; CANR 118; MAICYA 1, 2; SATA 50, 81, 139, 198; SATA-Brief 44

Wood, Don 1945- ... 26
See also CA 136; MAICYA 1, 2; SATA 50; SATA-Brief 44

Wood, June Rae 1946- ... 82
See also AAYA 39; CA 191; CANR 173; SATA 79, 120

Woodford, Cecil
See Tarkington, Booth

Woods, Nat
See Stratemeyer, Edward L.

Woodson, Jacqueline 1963- ... 49, 260
See also AAYA 54, 84; CA 159; CANR 87, 129, 177, 253, 292, 324; CMTFW; DLB 389; GLL 2; MAICYA 2; MAICYAS 1; MTFW 2005; NFS 46, 52; SATA 94, 139, 189, 246, 318; WYAS 1; YAW

Woolsey, Sarah Chauncey
See Coolidge, Susan

Worth, Valerie 1933-1994 ... 21
See also CA 41-44R; 146; CANR 15, 44, 192; CWRI 5; MAICYA 1, 2; SATA 8, 70, 81

Wortis, Avi
See Avi

Wortis, Edward Irving
See Avi

Wrightson, Alice Patricia
See Wrightson, Patricia

Wrightson, Patricia 1921-2010 ... 4, 14, 154
See also AAYA 5, 58; BYA 5, 6; CA 45-48; CANR 3, 19, 36; DLB 289; FANT; JRDA; MAICYA 1, 2; SAAS 4; SATA 8, 66, 112; SATA-Obit 215; YAW

Wryde, Dogear
See Gorey, Edward (St. John)

Wyeth, N(ewell) C(onvers) 1882-1945 ... 106
See also DLB 188; DLBD 16; MAICYA 1, 2; SATA 17

Wyndham, John 1903-1969 ... 190
See also BRWS 13; CA 89-92, 102; CANR 84; CLC 19; DLB 255; SATA 118; SCFW 1, 2; SFW 4

Wynne-Jones, Tim 1948- ... 21, 58
See also AAYA 31; CA 105; CANR 39, 145; CWRI 5; MAICYA 2; MAICYAS 1; SATA 67, 96, 136, 186; SATA-Essay 136

Wynne-Jones, Timothy
See Wynne-Jones, Tim

Wyss, Johann David Von 1743-1818 ... 92
See also JRDA; MAICYA 1, 2; NCLC 10; SATA 29; SATA-Brief 27

Yaffe, Alan
See Yorinks, Arthur

Yang, Gene Luen 1973- ... 178, 246
See also AAYA 82; CA 267, 383; CAAE 383; CANR 253; NFS 39; SATA 248, 285

Yarbrough, Camille 1938- ... 29
See also BW 2; CA 105; 125; SATA 79

Yashima, Taro
See Iwamatsu, Jun Atsushi

Yee, Paul 1956- ... 44
See also AAYA 24; CA 135; CANR 81, 122; CWRI 5; JRDA; MAICYA 2; MAICYAS 1; SATA 67, 96, 143, 211

Yeoman, John 1934- ... 46
See also CA 106; SATA 28, 80

Yep, Laurence 1948- ... 3, 17, 54, 132
See also AAYA 5, 31; BYA 7; CA 49-52; CANR 1, 46, 92, 161; CLC 35; DLB 52, 312; FANT; JRDA; MAICYA 1, 2; MAICYAS 1; SATA 7, 69, 123, 176, 213; WYA; YAW

Yep, Laurence Michael
See Yep, Laurence

Yolen, Jane 1939- **4, 44, 149, 248**
See also AAYA 4, 22, 85; BPFB 3; BYA 9, 10, 11, 14, 16; CA 13-16R; CANR 11, 29, 56, 91, 126, 185, 245, 344; CLC 256; CMTFW; CWRI 5; DLB 52; FANT; INT CANR-29; JRDA; MAICYA 1, 2; MTFW 2005; NFS 30; SAAS 1; SATA 4, 40, 75, 112, 158, 194, 230, 300, 327; SATA-Essay 111; SFW 4; SSFHW; SSFS 29; SUFW 2; WYA; YAW

Yolen, Jane Hyatt
See Yolen, Jane

Yonge, Charlotte Mary 1823-1901 .... **210**
See also BRWS 17; CA 109, 163; DLB 18, 163; RGEL 2; SATA 17; TCLC 48, 245; WCH

Yorinks, Arthur 1953- **20**
See also CA 106; CANR 38, 125, 192; CWRI 5; MAICYA 1, 2; SATA 33, 49, 85, 144, 200

York, Simon
See Heinlein, Robert A.

Youd, C. S.
See Youd, Samuel

Youd, Christopher Samuel
See Youd, Samuel

Youd, Samuel 1922- **2**
See also AAYA 22; BYA 4, 8; CA 77-80; CANR 37, 114; DLB 255; JRDA; MAICYA 1, 2; SAAS 6; SATA 47, 135; SATA-Brief 30; SFW 4; YAW

Young, Clarence
See Stratemeyer, Edward L.

Young, Ed 1931- **27**
See also CA 116; 130; CANR 100; CWRI 5; MAICYA 1, 2; MAICYAS 1; SATA 10, 74, 122, 173, 211

Young, Ed Tse-chun
See Young, Ed

Zalben, Jane Breskin 1950- **84**
See also CA 49-52; CANR 4, 98, 173; SATA 7, 79, 120, 170; YAW

Zei, Alki 1925- **6**
See also BYA 13; CA 77-80; SATA 24

Zelinsky, Paul O. 1953- **55**
See also CA 121; CANR 38; CWRI 5; MAICYA 1, 2; SATA 49, 102, 154; SATA-Brief 33

Zephaniah, Benjamin 1958- **220**
BLC 3; CA 147; CANR 103, 156, 177; CP 5, 6, 7; DLB 347; SATA 86, 140, 189

Zim, Herbert S(pencer) 1909-1994 .... **2**
See also CA 13-16R; 147; CANR 17; JRDA; MAICYA 1, 2; MAICYAS 1; SAAS 2; SATA 1, 30; SATA-Obit 85

Zimmy
See Stratemeyer, Edward L.

Zimnik, Reiner 1930- **3**
See also CA 77-80; SATA 36

Zindel, Paul 1936-2003 .... **3, 45, 85, 186**
See also AAYA 2, 37; BYA 2, 3, 8, 11, 14; CA 73-76; 213; CAD; CANR 31, 65, 108; CD 5, 6; CDALBS; CLC 6, 26; DA; DA3; DAB; DAC; DAM DRAM, MST, NOV; DC 5; DFS 12; DLB 7, 52; JRDA; LAIT 5; MAICYA 1, 2; MTCW 1, 2; MTFW 2005; NFS 14; SATA 16, 58, 102; SATA-Obit 142; WYA; YAW

Zinger, Yitskhok
See Singer, Isaac Bashevis

Zolotow, Charlotte 1915- **2, 77**
See also CA 5-8R; CANR 3, 18, 38, 117, 172; CWRI 5; DLB 52; MAICYA 1, 2; SATA 1, 35, 78, 138

Zolotow, Charlotte Gertrude Shapiro
See Zolotow, Charlotte

Zuromskis, Diane
See Stanley, Diane

Zuromskis, Diane Stanley
See Stanley, Diane

Zusak, Markus 1975- **250**
See also AAYA 79; CA 223; CANR 163, 248; LNFS 3; NFS 44; SATA 149, 251, 342

Zwerger, Lisbeth 1954- **46**
See also MAICYA 1, 2; SAAS 13; SATA 66, 130, 194

Literary Criticism Series Cumulative Topic Index

This index lists all topic entries in Gale's *Children's Literature Review* (CLR), *Classical and Medieval Literature Criticism* (CMLC), *Contemporary Literary Criticism* (CLC), *Drama Criticism* (DC), *Literature Criticism from 1400 to 1800* (LC), *Nineteenth-Century Literature Criticism* (NCLC), *Poetry Criticism* (PC), *Short Story Criticism* (SSC), and *Twentieth-Century Literary Criticism* (TCLC). The index also lists topic entries in the Gale Critical Companion Collection, which includes the following publications: *The Beat Generation* (BG), *Feminism in Literature* (FL), *Gothic Literature* (GL), and *Harlem Renaissance* (HR).

Abbey Theatre TCLC 258: 1-123
 overview and history, 2-71
 major figures, 71-109
 plays and productions, 109-123

Abbey Theatre in the Irish Literary Renaissance TCLC 154: 1-114
 origins and development, 2-14
 major figures, 14-30
 plays and controversies, 30-59
 artistic vision and significance, 59-114

Abolitionist Literature of Cuba and Brazil, Nineteenth-Century NCLC 132: 1-94
 overviews, 2-11
 origins and development, 11-23
 sociopolitical concerns, 23-39
 poetry, 39-47
 prose, 47-93

The Aborigine in Nineteenth-Century Australian Literature NCLC 120: 1-88
 overviews, 2-27
 representations of the Aborigine in Australian literature, 27-58
 Aboriginal myth, literature, and oral tradition, 58-88

Acting on the Restoration and Eighteenth-Century English Stage LC 148: 1-116
 overviews 2-23
 acting styles 23-43
 influential actors 43-70
 introduction of actresses 70-86
 influence of the actress 86-115

Activist Children's Literature CLR 263: 1-178
 primary sources, 6-8
 environmentalism in children's literature, 8-32
 marginalization in children's literature, 32-151
 general commentary on activism in children's literature, 151-76

Addiction in Children's Literature CLR 262: 1-49

Adultery in 19th-Century Literature NCLC 220:1-102
 background: transgression and moral rhetoric, 2-6
 adultery and censure, 6-38
 major authors and significant works, 38-101

Adventure Literature TCLC 202: 1-89
 overviews and general studies 2-32
 juvenile adventure narratives 32-8
 adventure literature and imperialism 38-57
 war and adventure 57-88

The Aesopic Fable LC 51: 1-100
 the British Aesopic Fable, 1-54
 the Aesopic tradition in non-English-speaking cultures, 55-66
 political uses of the Aesopic fable, 67-88
 the evolution of the Aesopic fable, 89-99

Aesop's Fables CLR 115: 1-55
 overviews and general studies, 4-29
 morality in Aesop's fables, 29-39
 historical editions of Aesop's fables, 39-53
 reviews of contemporary editions of Aesop's fables, 53-55

African-American Folklore and Literature TCLC 126: 1-67
 African-American folk tradition, 1-16
 representative writers, 16-34
 hallmark works, 35-48
 the study of African-American literature and folklore, 48-64

Age of al-Andalus CMLC 81: 1-174
 overviews, 1-48
 history, society, and culture, 48-127
 Andalusī poetry, 127-73

Age of Eleanor of Aquitaine CMLC 125: 1-72
 overview, 4-21
 courtly love, 21-53
 medieval verse romances, 53-71

Age of Johnson LC 15: 1-87
 Johnson's London, 3-15
 aesthetics of neoclassicism, 15-36
 "age of prose and reason," 36-45
 clubmen and bluestockings, 45-56
 printing technology, 56-62
 periodicals: "a map of busy life," 62-74
 transition, 74-86

The Age of King Alfred the Great CMLC 79: 1-141
 overviews and historical background, 4-17
 the Alfredian translations, 17-43
 King Alfred's prefaces, 43-84
 Alfred and Boethius, 84-140

Age of Spenser LC 39: 1-70
 overviews and general studies, 2-21
 literary style, 22-34
 poets and the crown, 34-70

AIDS in Literature CLC 81: 365-416

Alchemy in Seventeenth-Century England LC 148: 117-241
 overviews 118-47
 the last alchemists 147-69
 Ben Jonson and *The Alchemist* 169-88
 alchemy and poetry 188-239

Alcohol and Literature TCLC 70: 1-58
 overview, 2-8
 fiction, 8-48
 poetry and drama, 48-58

Alexander the Great in Literature CMLC 112: 1-255
 overviews and major works, 2-57
 Alexander according to Greek and Roman historians, 57-178
 the Medieval Alexander, 178-255

The Algonquin Round Table TCLC 242: 1-46
 overviews, 2-15
 political and social pressures, 15-45

American Abolitionism NCLC 44: 1-73
 overviews and general studies, 2-26
 abolitionist ideals, 26-46
 the literature of abolitionism, 46-72

American Autobiography TCLC 86: 1-115
 overviews and general studies, 3-36
 American authors and autobiography, 36-82
 African-American autobiography, 82-114

American Black Humor Fiction TCLC 54: 1-85
 characteristics of black humor, 2-13
 origins and development, 13-38
 black humor distinguished from related literary trends, 38-60
 black humor and society, 60-75
 black humor reconsidered, 75-83

American Civil War Era Memoirs and Autobiographies NCLC 272: 1-133
 memoirs by generals and officers, 3-21
 memoirs by common soldiers, 21-110
 memoirs by civilians, 110-130

American Civil War in Literature NCLC 32: 1-109
- overviews and general studies, 2-20
- regional perspectives, 20-54
- fiction popular during the war, 54-79
- the historical novel, 79-108
- NCLC 212: 1-148
- overviews, 4-32
- gender roles, 32-70
- race and slavery, 70-104
- physicality and mortality, 104-47

The American Dream in Literature TCLC 210: 1-105
- overviews, 2-11
- the American Dream and popular culture, 11-27
- the immigrant experience and the American Dream, 27-40
- American authors and the American Dream, 40-105

American Frontier in Literature NCLC 28: 1-103
- definitions, 2-12
- development, 12-17
- nonfiction writing about the frontier, 17-30
- frontier fiction, 30-45
- frontier protagonists, 45-66
- portrayals of Native Americans, 66-86
- feminist readings, 86-98
- twentieth-century reaction against frontier literature, 98-100

American Frontier Literature TCLC 194: 1-125
- overviews and general studies, 2-26
- the frontier thesis and frontier literature, 26-51
- major authors and frontier literature, 51-125

American Humor Writing NCLC 52: 1-59
- overviews and general studies, 2-12
- the Old Southwest, 12-42
- broader impacts, 42-5
- women humorists, 45-58
- NCLC 232: 1-95
- race, 2-49
- Southwestern writers, 49-62
- women writers, 62-95

American Immigrant Literature TCLC 206: 1-131
- overviews and general studies, 2-33
- cultural displacement, 33-78
- stereotypes, identity, representation, 78-104
- literary technique and use of language, 104-31

American Literary Naturalism TCLC 182: 1-95
- overviews, 2-20
- major authors, 20-77
- themes and literary techniques, 77-94

The American Literary Renaissance NCLC 184: 1-107
- overviews, 3-22
- race and revolution, 22-40
- gender, 41-106

American Mercury, **The** TCLC 74: 1-80

American Naturalism in Short Fiction SSC 77: 1-103
- overviews and general studies, 2-30
- major authors of American literary Naturalism, 30-102
  - Ambrose Bierce, 30
  - Stephen Crane, 30-53
  - Theodore Dreiser, 53-65
  - Jack London, 65-80
  - Frank Norris, 80-9
  - Edith Wharton, 89-102

American Novel of Manners TCLC 130: 1-42
- history of the Novel of Manners in America, 4-10
- representative writers, 10-18
- relevancy of the Novel of Manners, 18-24
- hallmark works in the Novel of Manners, 24-36
- Novel of Manners and other media, 36-40

American Poetry of the Vietnam War PC 143: 1-87
- overviews and general studies, 5-44
- civilian poetry, 44-61
- veteran poetry, 61-78
- writing from the margins, 78-85

American Political Drama TCLC 242: 47-168
- political drama and the Communist Movement, 49-83
- political drama in the Cold War years, 83-140
- political drama and the Civil Rights Movement: the late 1950s and '60s, 140-61
- political drama and Women's Movement: the late 1960s through the '80s, 161-67

American Popular Song, Golden Age of TCLC 42: 1-49
- background and major figures, 2-34
- the lyrics of popular songs, 34-47

American Proletarian Literature TCLC 54: 86-175
- overviews and general studies, 87-95
- American proletarian literature and the American Communist Party, 95-111
- ideology and literary merit, 111-17
- novels, 117-36
- Gastonia, 136-48
- drama, 148-54
- journalism, 154-9
- proletarian literature in the United States, 159-74

American Realism NCLC 120: 89-246
- overviews, 91-112
- background and sources, 112-72
- social issues, 172-223
- women and realism, 223-45

American Reform Writers TCLC 266: 1-124
- urban reform, 2-10
- social reformers, 10-50
- women reformers, 50-124

American Renaissance SSC 64: 46-193
- overviews and general studies, 47-103
- major authors of short fiction, 103-92

American Romanticism NCLC 44: 74-138
- overviews and general studies, 74-84
- sociopolitical influences, 84-104
- romanticism and the American frontier, 104-15
- thematic concerns, 115-37

American Romanticism NCLC 440: 1-292

American Short Fiction since World War II TCLC 282: 1-110
- overview, 2-18
- major authors, 18-46
- women authors, 46-72
- multiculturalism in the short story, 72-90
- regionalism and "place," 90-110

American Transcendentalism NCLC 224: 1-116
- overviews, 3-26
- religion and spirituality, 27-57
- women authors, 57-115

American Western Literature TCLC 46: 1-100
- definition and development of American Western literature, 2-7
- characteristics of the Western novel, 8-23
- Westerns as history and fiction, 23-34
- critical reception of American Western literature, 34-41
- the Western hero, 41-73
- women in Western fiction, 73-91
- later Western fiction, 91-9

American Westerns, Contemporary See **Westerns, Contemporary American**

American Writers in Paris TCLC 98: 1-156
- overviews and general studies, 2-155

The Amis and Amiloun Tradition CMLC 177: 1-65
- overviews and general studies, 3-14
- chivalry and Christianity in the Middle-English *Amis and Amiloun,* 14-44
- gender in the Amis and Amiloun tradition, 44-56
- the influence of the Amis and Amiloun tradition, 57-63

Anarchism NCLC 84: 1-97
- overviews and general studies, 2-23
- the French anarchist tradition, 23-56
- Anglo-American anarchism, 56-68
- anarchism: incidents and issues, 68-97

Angry Young Men TCLC 166: 1-80
- overviews, 2-18
- major figures, 18-58
- themes and style, 58-79

Animal Stories CLR 132: 1-37
- overviews and general studies, 5-7
- animal fantasies in children's literature, 7-25
- realistic children's animal stories, 25-36

Animals in Literature TCLC 106: 1-120
- overviews and general studies, 2-8
- animals in American literature, 8-45
- animals in Canadian literature, 45-57
- animals in European literature, 57-100
- animals in Latin American literature, 100-06
- animals in women's literature, 106-20

Antebellum South, Literature of the NCLC 112:1-188
- overviews, 4-55
- culture of the Old South, 55-68
- antebellum fiction: pastoral and heroic romance, 68-120
- role of women: a subdued rebellion, 120-59
- slavery and the slave narrative, 159-85

Anti-Americanism TCLC 158: 1-98
- overviews and general studies, 3-18
- literary and intellectual perspectives, 18-36
- social and political reactions, 36-98

Anti-Apartheid TCLC 162: 1-121
- overviews, 3-45
- major authors, 45-74
- anti-apartheid literature and the liberal tradition, 74-101
- writing under apartheid: historical views, 101-20

Antitheatrical Writing of the Renaissance LC 164: 1-140
- overviews, 2-37
- Stephen Gosson and Philip Stubbes, 37-65
- antitheatrical drama, 65-104
- antitheatrical rhetoric and religion, 104-39

The Apocalypse Theme in Twentieth-Century Literature TCLC 218: 1-113
- overviews and general studies, 2-36
- the theme of apocalypse in fiction, 36-77
- the theme of apocalypse in poetry, 77-112

The Apocalyptic Movement TCLC 106: 121-69

Apollo Myth in Classical and Medieval Literature CMLC 113: 1-106
   Apollo and the Greeks, 3-55
   Apollo and the Romans, 55-65
   The Myth of Apollo in the Middle Ages, 65-106

Argentine Literature TCLC 210: 106-209
   overviews, 108-31
   dictatorship and its aftermath, 131-48
   Borges and Cortázar, 148-81
   women and minorities in Argentine literature, 181-209

The Aristotelian Arts Masters Controversy CMLC 136: 1-142
   overview, 4-11
   major figures, 11-52
   the condemnation of 1277, 52-78
   philosophical legacy of the condemnation, 78-140

Aristotle CMLC 31: 1-397
   philosophy, 3-100
   poetics, 101-219
   rhetoric, 220-301
   science, 302-397

Ars moriendi LC 172
   overviews, 3-49
   ars moriendi and the reformation, 49-86
   ars moriendi and literature, 86-126
   ars moriendi and women, 126-35

Art and Literature TCLC 54: 176-248
   overviews and general studies, 176-93
   definitions, 193-219
   influence of visual arts on literature, 219-31
   spatial form in literature, 231-47

Arthurian Legends for Children CLR 155: 1-75
   overviews and general studies, 6-31
   Howard Pyle and the Arthurian legend, 32-44
   Sir Gawain stories for children, 44-60
   contemporary Arthur stories for children, 50-75

Arthurian Literature CMLC 10: 1-127
   historical context and literary beginnings, 2-27
   development of the legend through Malory, 27-64
   development of the legend from Malory to the Victorian Age, 65-81
   themes and motifs, 81-95
   principal characters, 95-125

Arthurian Revival NCLC 36: 1-77
   overviews and general studies, 2-12
   Tennyson and his influence, 12-43
   other leading figures, 43-73
   the Arthurian legend in the visual arts, 73-6

Asian American Literature CLC 340: 1-163
   theorizing Asian American literature, 4-59
   themes of transnationalism, 59-109
   themes of sexuality and sexual identity, 109-38
   the role of food in identity formation, 138-52
   Asian American spirituality, 152-62

Astronomy in Nineteenth-Century Literature NCLC 228: 1-59
   Herman Melville, 2-19
   poetry, 19-47
   women writers, 47-59

The Audience and Nineteenth-Century Literature NCLC 160: 1-158
   overviews, 3-35
   race, class, gender, 35-89
   America, 89-102
   Britain and Europe, 102-30
   genre and audience, 130-57

Australian Children's Literature CLR 148: 1-58
   overviews and general studies, 4-24
   nineteenth-century Australian children's literature, 24-36
   multiculturalism in Australian children's literature, 36-58

Australian Cultural Identity in Nineteenth-Century Literature NCLC 124: 1-164
   overviews and general studies, 4-22
   poetry, 22-67
   fiction, 67-135
   role of women writers, 135-64

Australian Literature TCLC 50: 1-94
   origins and development, 2-21
   characteristics of Australian literature, 21-33
   historical and critical perspectives, 33-41
   poetry, 41-58
   fiction, 58-76
   drama, 76-82
   Aboriginal literature, 82-91

Australian Literature TCLC 278: 1-152
   background: white settler nationalism, 4-32
   national identity and themes of place, 33-65
   the Aboriginal response, 65-92
   postcolonial perspectives, 92-118
   major authors, 118-50

Autobiographical Writing TCLC 214: 1-134
   overviews and general studies, 3-34
   significant autobiographical works, 34-66
   African American autobiographical writing, 66-87
   immigrant autobiographies, 87-134

Aztec Myths and Literature LC 122: 1-182
   overviews and general studies, 3-68
   cosmology, 68-136
   language and literature, 136-81

Baseball in Contemporary Literature CLC 333: 1-83
   introduction to baseball in contemporary literature, 1-6
   major themes, 6-32
   a gendered fiction, 32-67
   the many genres of baseball literature, 67-83

The Beat Generation BG 1:1-562
   the Beat Generation: an overview, 1-137
      primary sources, 3-32
      overviews and general studies, 32-47
      Beat Generation as a social phenomenon, 47-65
      drugs, inspiration, and the Beat Generation, 65-92
      religion and the Beat Generation, 92-124
      women of the Beat Generation, 124-36
   Beat "scene": East and West, 139-259
      primary sources, 141-77
      Beat scene in the East, 177-218
      Beat scene in the West, 218-59
   Beat Generation publishing: periodicals, small presses, and censorship, 261-349
      primary sources, 263-74
      overview, 274-88
      Beat periodicals: "little magazines," 288-311
      Beat publishing: small presses, 311-24
      Beat battles with censorship, 324-49
   performing arts and the Beat Generation, 351-417
      primary sources, 353-58
      Beats and film, 358-81
      Beats and music, 381-415
   visual arts and the Beat Generation, 419-91
      primary sources, 421-24
      critical commentary, 424-90

The Beat Generation TCLC 222: 1-129
   overviews, 2-59
   major authors of the Beat Generation, 60-110
   Beat poetry, 110-28

Beat Generation, Literature of the TCLC 42: 50-102
   overviews and general studies, 51-9
   the Beat generation as a social phenomenon, 59-62
   development, 62-5
   Beat literature, 66-96
   influence, 97-100

The Bell Curve Controversy CLC 91: 281-330

Bereavement in Nineteenth-Century Literature NCLC 216: 1-103
   overview, 3-13
   psychological interpretations, 13-60
   elegies, 60-102
   major authors, 62-115
   technique and narrative, 115-127

Betrayal in Short Fiction SSC 194: 1-116
   betrayal in short stories about love, 4-7
   betrayal in short stories about good and evil, 7-35
   betrayal, order, and disorder, 35-58
   the betrayal of ideals, 58-64
   betrayal and cultural difference, 64-115

The Bible and Children's Literature CLR 145: 1-72
   overviews and general studies, 3-24
   biblical influence on children's literature, 24-67
   responses to the Bible in children's literature, 67-72

Bildungsroman **in Nineteenth-Century Literature** NCLC 20: 92-168
   surveys, 93-113
   in Germany, 113-40
   in England, 140-56
   female *Bildungsromane*, 156-67
   NCLC 152: 1-129
   overview, 3-16
   definition and issues, 16-52
   female *Bildungsromane*, 52-83
   ideology and nationhood, 83-128
   NCLC 240: 1-110
   overviews, 1-39
   female *Bildungsromane*, 39-80
   national and cultural identity, 80-109

Black, Asian, and Minority Ethnic (BAME) British Authors CLR 228: 81-187
   the publishing industry and education system, 85-100
   colonialism, immigration, and place, 100-45
   race, gender, and identity, 145-85

Black Humor, Contemporary CLC 196: 1-128
   overviews and general studies, 2-18
   black humor in American fiction, 18-28
   development and history, 29-62
   major authors, 62-115
   technique and narrative, 115-127

Black Humor in Children's Literature CLR 104: 76-145
   overviews and general studies, 79-96
   examples of black humor in Victorian children's literature, 96-110
   examples of black humor in twentieth-century children's literature, 110-28
   black humor in the works of Roald Dahl, 128-44

Black Mountain Poets TCLC 230: 1-86
  overviews, 2-23
  Olson and Creeley, 23-68
  other figures, 68-86

The Bloomsbury Group TCLC 34: 1-73
  history and major figures, 2-13
  definitions, 13-7
  influences, 17-27
  thought, 27-40
  prose, 40-52
  and literary criticism, 52-4
  political ideals, 54-61
  response to, 61-71
  TCLC 138: 1-59
  representative members of the Bloomsbury Group, 9-24
  literary relevance of the Bloomsbury Group, 24-36
  Bloomsbury's hallmark works, 36-48
  other modernists studied with the Bloomsbury Group, 48-54
  TCLC 266: 126-216
  major figures, 126-73
  legacy and themes, 173-216

The Blues in Literature TCLC 82: 1-71

The Bluestockings LC 189: 1-153
  overviews, 3-22
  the learned ladies, 22-74
  Bluestocking ideas and ideals, 74-153

Bly, Robert, *Iron John: A Book about Men and Men's Work* CLC 70: 414-62

Book Clubs, Contemporary and Historic CLC 235: 1-94
  the book club phenomenon, 1-72
  Oprah Winfrey's book club, 72-90
  reviews of books about book clubs, 90-94

The Book of Common Prayer LC 118: 1-76
  overviews, 2-43
  translation and diffusion, 44-63
  influence of the Prayer Book, 63-76

The Book of J CLC 65: 289-311

Brazilian Literature TCLC 134: 1-126
  overviews and general studies, 3-33
  Brazilian poetry, 33-48
  contemporary Brazilian writing, 48-76
  culture, politics, and race in Brazilian writing, 76-100
  modernism and postmodernism in Brazil, 100-25

Brazilian Literature, Contemporary CLC 311: 94-190
  race relations and national identity in Brazil, 96-113
  background trends in poetry, 113-23
  surveys: fiction and poetry, 123-68
  major authors, 168-89

British Abolitionist Literature NCLC 450: 1-293

British Ephemeral Literature LC 59: 1-70
  overviews and general studies, 1-9
  broadside ballads, 10-40
  chapbooks, jestbooks, pamphlets, and newspapers, 40-69

British Laboring-Class Women's Poetry of the Eighteenth Century PC 145: 1-132
  general and thematic studies, 3-24
  Mary Collier, 25-43
  Mary Barber, 43-65
  Mary Leapor, 65-81
  Ann Yearsley, 81-93
  Janet Little, 93-8
  Mary Scott, 98-108
  Anne Wilson, 108-19
  Elizabeth Hands, 119-30

British Women Poets of World War I PC 162: 165-254
  overviews and general studies, 167-80
  recovering women's voices, 180-94
  comparative studies, 194-225
  poetry and women's experiences of war, 225-53

British Working-Class Literature NCLC 246: 1-162
  literary depictions by the working class, 4-54
  Chartist literature, 54-95
  literary depictions of the working class, 95-135
  relationship between class and gender, 135-60

Buddhism and Literature TCLC 70: 59-164
  eastern literature, 60-113
  western literature, 113-63

Buddhism in the Nineteenth-Century Western World NCLC 164: 1-88
  overviews, 3-47
  Buddhism and Western Philosophers, 47-74
  Buddhism in Western Literature, 74-88

The *Bulletin* and the Rise of Australian Literary Nationalism NCLC 116: 1-121
  overviews, 3-32
  legend of the nineties, 32-55
  Bulletin style, 55-71
  Australian literary nationalism, 71-98
  myth of the bush, 98-120

Businessman in American Literature TCLC 26: 1-48
  portrayal of the businessman, 1-32
  themes and techniques in business fiction, 32-47

The Calendar LC 55: 1-92
  overviews and general studies, 2-19
  measuring time, 19-28
  calendars and culture, 28-60
  calendar reform, 60-92

Calvinism in Nineteenth-Century Literature NCLC 192: 1-90
  challenges to Calvinism, 2-13
  literary expressions of Calvinist doctrine, 13-89

Canadian Literature TCLC 206: 132-233
  overviews, 133-60
  personal identity and national identity, 160-74
  Native Canadian authors, 174-93
  other major authors, 193-232

Canadian Poetry in English, Contemporary CLC 298: 1-105
  overviews, 4-20
  major Canadian poets, 20-51
  diasporic voices, 51-67
  experimental voices, 67-105

Canadian Short Fiction, Contemporary CLC 314: 175-265
  two solitudes: Canadian short fiction in English and French, 178-193
  women's and gender issues in Canadian short fiction, 193-228
  identity and cultural crossings in Canadian short fiction, 228-250
  history and memory: the past versus the present in Canadian short fiction, 250-264

Canadian Short Fiction SSC 157: 70-237
  overviews, 71-95
  major authors, 95-158
  race, nationality, ethnicity, and identity in Canadian short fiction, 159-205
  female authors and gender issues, 205-236

Canadian Women Writers TCLC 238: 1-141
  overviews, 3-34
  major authors, 34-80
  feminism and gender, 80-114
  ethnicity and race, 114-41

Captivity Narratives LC 82: 71-172
  overviews, 72-107
  captivity narratives and Puritanism, 108-34
  captivity narratives and Native Americans, 134-49
  influence on American literature, 149-72

Captivity Narratives, Nineteenth-Century NCLC 80:131-218
  overview, 132-37
  the political significance of captivity narratives, 137-67
  images of gender, 167-96
  moral instruction, 197-217

Caribbean Literature TCLC 138: 60-135
  overviews and general studies, 61-9
  ethnic and national identity, 69-107
  expatriate Caribbean literature, 107-23
  literary histoiography, 123-35

The Carolingian Renaissance CMLC 127: 1-114
  overviews and major themes, 3-53
  Charlemagne and the Church, 53-93
  major figures, 93-113

Catholicism in Nineteenth-Century American Literature NCLC 64: 1-58
  overviews, 3-14
  polemical literature, 14-46
  Catholicism in literature, 47-57

Cavalier Poetry and Drama LC 107: 1-71
  overviews, 2-36
  Cavalier drama, 36-48
  major figures, 48-70

Celtic Mythology CMLC 26: 1-111
  overviews and general studies, 2-22
  Celtic myth as literature and history, 22-48
  Celtic religion: Druids and divinities, 48-80
  Fionn MacCuhaill and the Fenian cycle, 80-111

Celtic Twilight See **Irish Literary Renaissance**

Censorship and Contemporary World Literature CLC 194: 1-80
  overviews and general studies, 2-19
  notorious cases, 19-59
  censorship in the global context, 59-79

Censorship in Children's Literature CLR 118: 29-87
  overviews and general studies, 33-49
  regional examples of children's literature censorship, 49-67
  censorship in the juvenile fantasy and pulp novel genres, 67-78
  author responses to the censorship of children's literature, 78-87

Censorship of the Press in the Nineteenth Century NCLC 156: 1-133
  overviews, 3-29
  censorship in Austria, Germany, and Russia, 29-87
  censorship in France and Spain, 87-120
  censorship in England and America, 120-33

Censorship in Twentieth-Century Literature TCLC 154: 115-238
  overviews and general studies, 117-25
  censorship and obscenity trials, 125-61
  censorship and sexual politics, 161-81
  censorship and war, 181-207
  political censorship and the state, 207-28
  censorship and the writer, 228-38

The Chartist Movement and Literature
NCLC 60: 1-84
  overview: nineteenth-century working-class fiction, 2-19
  Chartist fiction and poetry, 19-73
  the Chartist press, 73-84

The Chicago Renaissance TCLC 154: 239-341
  overviews and general studies, 240-60
  definitions and growth, 260-82
  the language debate, 282-318
  major authors, 318-40

Chicano/a Literature, Contemporary
CLC 205: 82-181
  overviews, 84-124
  Chicana studies, 124-40
  some representative works, 140-80

Chicano/a Short Fiction SSC 162: 1-102
  overviews, 3-14
  the search for identity, 14-67
  crossing borders and boundaries, 67-84
  reading and marketing strategies, 84-102

Chick-Lit and Lad-Lit CLC 210: 115-64
  overviews, 117-25
  the debate over Chick Lit, 125-46
  representative authors, 146-64

Chick Lit and the Emergence of Postfeminism CLC 508: 1-80
  primary sources, 5-6
  overviews and general studies, 6-75

Child Labor in Nineteenth-Century Literature NCLC 108: 1-133
  overviews, 3-10
  climbing boys and chimney sweeps, 10-16
  the international traffic in children, 16-45
  critics and reformers, 45-82
  fictional representations of child laborers, 83-132

Childhood in Nineteenth-Century Literature
NCLC 172: 1-140
  overviews, 2-20
  romanticism and childhood, 20-46
  childhood in the works of William Wordsworth, 46-72
  childhood in the works of Charles Dickens, 72-106
  childhood in the works of Leo Tolstoy, 106-29
  childhood in the works of Emily Dickinson, 129-39

Children's Biography CLR 129: 69-132
  overviews and general studies, 69-93
  critical approaches to children's biographies, 93-106
  children's biographies on ethnic and minority figures, 106-32

Children's Diaries CLR 141: 18-94
  overviews of Holocaust diaries, 20-41
  critical evaluations of Anne Frank's "The Diary of a Young Girl," 41-57
  critical evaluations of other Holocaust diaries, 57-62
  critical evaluations of Victorian children's diaries, 62-76
  critical evaluations of contemporary children's diaries, 76-94

Children's Fantasy CLR 150: 21-117
  some representative works, 23-4
  nineteenth century children's fantasy 24-55
  children's fantasy, 1960-1989, 55-95
  children's fantasy, 1990-2009, 95-117

Children's Literature Awards CLR 139: 1-52
  overviews and general studies, 4-13
  multicultural children's literature awards, 13-23

themes and trends in children's literature award winners, 23-52

Children's Literature Illustration CLR 144: 44-112
  overviews and general studies, 47-84
  history of children's book illustration, 84-88
  communicative relationship between text and illustration in children's texts, 88-102
  analyses of illustrative arts used in books: topographic, nonfiction, and nursery rhymes, 102-11

Children's Literature, Nineteenth-Century
NCLC 52: 60-135
  overviews and general studies, 61-72
  moral tales, 72-89
  fairy tales and fantasy, 90-119
  making men/making women, 119-34

Children's Periodicals CLR 138: 25-125
  overviews and general studies, 27-65
  early children's periodicals, 65-70
  St. Nicholas Magazine, 70-104
  children's periodicals and war, 104-24

Children's Poetry CLR 120: 15-100
  overviews and general studies, 19-48
  defining children's poetry, 48-68
  teaching children's poetry, 68-71
  poetry for children in the nineteenth, twentieth, and twenty-first centuries, 71-99

Chilean Literature TCLC 206: 234-366
  overviews, 235-53
  major chilean authors, 253-313
  chilean literature and politics, 313-65

Chilean Short-Fiction Writers SSC 215: 69-131
  overview and general study, 73-75
  early-twentieth-century fiction of oppression, 75-95
  themes of identity and exile in boom and post-boom fiction, 95-111
  depictions of women's lives, 112-129

Christian Saints and Mystics of the Early Modern Era LC 153: 1-128
  overviews, 3-18
  the great mystic saints, 18-44
  lesser-known mystics, 44-89
  mystic poets, 89-127

Christianity in Nineteenth-Century Literature NCLC 180: 1-111
  overviews, 4-32
  women writers, 32-66
  social and political discourse, 66-77
  Russian literature, 77-110

Christianity in Twentieth-Century Literature
TCLC 110: 1-79
  overviews and general studies, 2-31
  Christianity in twentieth-century fiction, 31-78

Chronicle Plays LC 89: 1-106
  development of the genre, 2-33
  historiography and literature, 33-56
  genre and performance, 56-88
  politics and ideology, 88-106

Cinderella in Children's Literature CLR 149: 40-131
  overviews and general studies, 43-68
  origins of the Cinderella story, 68-76
  studies of international variants of the Cinderella story, 76-120
  contemporized versions of the Cinderella story, 120-131

The City and Literature TCLC 90: 1-124
  overviews and general studies, 2-9
  the city in American literature, 9-86
  the city in European literature, 86-124

The City in Short Fiction SSC 153: 80-214
  the city in short fiction—U.S., Canada, and South America, 81-133
  short fiction and the European city, 133-65
  short fiction—the African and Asian city, 165-213

City Comedy LC 118: 77-211
  origins and development, 79-113
  economic issues, 113-32
  women and city comedy, 132-82
  the plays of Thomas Middleton, 182-211

Civic Critics, Russian NCLC 20: 402-46
  principal figures and background, 402-9
  and Russian Nihilism, 410-6
  aesthetic and critical views, 416-45

Civic Pageants LC 154: 1-123
  overview and history, 2-16
  pageants in text and performance, 16-69
  pageantry and politics, 69-111
  Restoration pageantry, 111-22

Civil Rights Literature TCLC 210: 210-354
  major authors and voices, 212-96
  memoirs and autobiographies, 296-320
  rhetoric and strategy, 320-53

Closet Drama DC 60: 1-254
  the closet versus the stage, 4-61
  sociopolitical interpretations, 62-181
  women and closet drama, 181-253

The Cockney School NCLC 68: 1-64
  overview, 2-7
  Blackwood's Magazine and the contemporary critical response, 7-24
  the political and social import of the Cockneys and their critics, 24-63

Cold War Literature TCLC 186: 1-136
  overviews 2-52
  novels and the cold war 52-102
  social, political, and cultural response 102-36

Colonial America: The Intellectual Background LC 25: 1-98
  overviews and general studies, 2-17
  philosophy and politics, 17-31
  early religious influences in Colonial America, 31-60
  consequences of the Revolution, 60-78
  religious influences in post-revolutionary America, 78-87
  colonial literary genres, 87-97

Colonialism in Victorian English Literature
NCLC 56: 1-77
  overviews and general studies, 2-34
  colonialism and gender, 34-51
  monsters and the occult, 51-76

Colombian Literature TCLC 254: 1-99
  colonialism and national identity, 2-16
  film and theater, 16-33
  major authors, 33-72
  major themes, 73-99

Columbus, Christopher, Books on the Quincentennial of His Arrival in the New World CLC 70: 329-60

Comic Books TCLC 66: 1-139
  historical and critical perspectives, 2-48
  superheroes, 48-67
  underground comix, 67-88
  comic books and society, 88-122
  adult comics and graphic novels, 122-36

Comedy of Manners LC 92: 1-75
  overviews, 2-21
  comedy of manners and society, 21-47
  comedy of manners and women, 47-74

Coming-of-Age Story SSC 130: 29-146
  aspects of the initiation narrative, 32-61
  themes of sexual awakening, 61-77
  gender-specific rites of passage, 77-103
  culturally-driven rites of passage, 103-131
  variations on the Bildungsroman archetype, 131-45

Commedia dell'Arte LC 83: 1-147
  overviews, 2-7
  origins and development, 7-23
  characters and actors, 23-45
  performance, 45-62
  texts and authors, 62-100
  influence in Europe, 100-46

Commonwealth Literature TCLC 198: 1-137
  overviews and general studies, 2-14
  perceptions and definitions, 14-23
  merging cultures, 23-73
  commonwealth literature and post-colonial theory, 73-113
  language and power113-36

Conduct Books in Nineteenth-Century Literature NCLC 152: 130-229
  women's education, 131-68
  feminist revisions, 168-82
  American behavioral literature: cultivating national identity, 182-209
  English behavioral literature: defining a middle class, 209-27

Confessional School of Poetry, The TCLC 258: 124-204
  overviews and background, 126-54
  major authors, 154-203

Connecticut Wits NCLC 48: 1-95
  overviews and general studies, 2-40
  major works, 40-76
  intellectual context, 76-95

Contemporary African American Short Fiction SSC 344: 1-292

Contemporary Brazilian Literature See Brazilian Literature, Contemporary

Contemporary Lebanese Writers CLC 401: 1-62
  comparative analyses, 7-35
  gender issues, 35-53
  responses to violence, 53-61

Contemporary Scottish Novelists CLC 388: 1-274
  political and social issues, 5-58
  literary elements and context, 58-176
  genre novelists, 176-233
  gender and sexuality, 233-71

Contemporary Syrian Authors CLC 408: 71-113
  the position of the contemporary Syrian author, 74-84
  Syrian fiction about wartime and exile, 84-6
  Syrian poetry: love and politics, 86-91
  women's issues in contemporary Syrian literature, 91-112

Counter-Reformation Literature See Literature of the Counter-Reformation

Country House Literature TCLC 190: 1-117
  overviews 2-20
  major works 20-58
  gender and country house literature 58-77
  the big house motif in Irish literature 77-117

Courtesans in Nineteenth-Century French Literature NCLC 247: 77-106
  background studies, 80-110
  major authors and significant works, 111-33
  La Dame aux Camélias, 133-51
  Nana, 151-69
  the courtesan as novelist and memoirist, 169-205

Creation Myths CMLC 110: 203-380
  overviews 204-18
  Themes and Motifs 218-81
  Creation Myths in the Americas 281-332
  Genesis 332-380

Crime, Criminals, and Nineteenth-Century Literature NCLC 243: 1-140
  overviews, 6-28
  the aesthetics of crime writing, 28-61
  sociology and psychology, 61-92
  true crime and fiction, 92-111
  fictionalizations of true crimes, 111-38

Crime Fiction, Contemporary CLC 209: 34-192
  overviews, 37-61
  ethnicity and race in crime fiction, 61-105
  literary traditions and crime fiction, 105-43
  themes, 143-81
  representative authors, 181-92

Crime in Literature TCLC 54: 249-307
  evolution of the criminal figure in literature, 250-61
  crime and society, 261-77
  literary perspectives on crime and punishment, 277-88
  writings by criminals, 288-306

Crime-Mystery-Detective Stories SSC 59:89-226
  overviews and general studies, 90-140
  origins and early masters of the crime-mystery-detective story, 140-73
  hard-boiled crime-mystery-detective fiction, 173-209
  diversity in the crime-mystery-detective story, 210-25

Critical Pluralism TCLC 298: 253-340
  overviews and surveys of Critical Pluralism, 254-271
  specific applications of Critical Pluralism, 271-320
  endorsements of Critical Pluralism, 320-338

The Crusades CMLC 38: 1-144
  history of the Crusades, 3-60
  literature of the Crusades, 60-116
  the Crusades and the people: attitudes and influences, 116-44

Cuban Exile Literature, Contemporary CLC 207: 1-100
  overviews, 2-20
  Cubana writers and exile, 20-48
  some representative works, 48-100

Cubism in Literature TCLC 274:1-305
  contemporaries of Cubism, 2-52
  Cubism: intersections between image and word, 52-63
  Cubism and later twentieth-century writers, 63-85

Cyberpunk TCLC 106: 170-366
  overviews and general studies, 171-88
  feminism and cyberpunk, 188-230
  history and cyberpunk, 230-70
  sexuality and cyberpunk, 270-98
  social issues and cyberpunk, 299-366

Cyberpunk Fiction CLC 497: 1-270
  primary sources, 4-8
  androids, cyborgs, and the post-human body, 8-71
  gender issues: feminism, masculinity, and queerness, 71-131
  social influences, 131-80
  depicting dystopia and post-utopia, 180-207
  genre influences and connections, 207-70

Cyberpunk Short Fiction SSC 60: 44-108
  overviews and general studies, 46-78
  major writers of cyberpunk fiction, 78-81
  sexuality and cyberpunk fiction, 81-97
  additional pieces, 97-108

Czechoslovakian Literature of the Twentieth Century TCLC 42:103-96
  through World War II, 104-35
  de-Stalinization, the Prague Spring, and contemporary literature, 135-72
  Slovak literature, 172-85
  Czech science fiction, 185-93

Dadaism TCLC 46: 101-71
  background and major figures, 102-16
  definitions, 116-26
  manifestos and commentary by Dadaists, 126-40
  theater and film, 140-58
  nature and characteristics of Dadaist writing, 158-70

Dance in Nineteenth-Century Literature NCLC 204: 1-96
  French literature, 2-40
  Jane Austen, 40-61
  danse macabre, 61-95

Dandyism in Nineteenth-Century Literature NCLC 240: 111-208
  overviews, 113-45
  identity and cultural commentary, 145-81
  Charles Baudelaire and Barbey d'Aurevilly, 181-99
  Oscar Wilde, 199-208

Danish Literature See Twentieth-Century Danish Literature

Darwinism NCLC 224: 117-215
  gender and race, 118-74
  literary representations of Darwinism, 174-214

Darwinism and Literature NCLC 32: 110-206
  background, 110-31
  direct responses to Darwin, 131-71
  collateral effects of Darwinism, 171-205

The Dead Sea Scrolls CMLC 113: 107-269
  Literary, Religious, and Historical Themes, 108-136
  The Scrolls and the Old Testament, 136-155
  The Scrolls and the New Testament, 155-210
  Jesus and the Dead Sea Scrolls, 210-267

Death in American Literature NCLC 92: 1-170
  overviews and general studies, 2-32
  death in the works of Emily Dickinson, 32-72
  death in the works of Herman Melville, 72-101
  death in the works of Edgar Allan Poe, 101-43
  death in the works of Walt Whitman, 143-70

Death in Literature TCLC 78: 1-183
  fiction, 2-115
  poetry, 115-46
  drama, 146-81

Death in Nineteenth-Century British Literature NCLC 68: 65-142
  overviews and general studies, 66-92
  responses to death, 92-102
  feminist perspectives, 103-17
  striving for immortality, 117-41

Death in the Short Story SSC 141: 1-152
  the death motif in American fiction, 4-61
  the death motif in British and European short fiction, 61-118
  death in Latino short stories, 118-51

Decadence in Nineteenth-Century Literature NCLC 164: 90-191
  overviews, 90-132

Decadent literary subjects, 132-44
Decadence in British literature, 144-57
Decadence in French literature, 158-79
women writers and Decadence, 179-90

Deconstruction TCLC 138: 136-256
overviews and general studies, 137-83
deconstruction and literature, 183-221
deconstruction in philosophy and history, 221-56

Defense of Women Pamphlets in Early Modern England LC 191: 102-222
overviews, 103-38
the women pamphleteers, 138-222

Deism LC 157: 81-156
overviews, 83-110
European deism, 111-39
American deism, 139-54

de Man, Paul, Wartime Journalism of CLC 55: 382-424

Democracy in Nineteenth-Century Literature NCLC 180: 112-245
overviews, 113-27
anti-democratic sentiment, 127-68
Walt Whitman, 168-84
romanticism, 184-211
Henry James and American women, 211-44

Depictions of Islam in Modern Literature TCLC 166: 81-198
overviews, 82-115
literature in the Muslim world, 115-56
Western interpretations, 156-82
women, Islam, and literature, 182-97

Detective Fiction NCLC 148: 1-161
overviews, 3-26
origins and influences, 26-63
major authors, 63-134
Freud and detective fiction, 134-61

Detective Fiction, Nineteenth-Century NCLC 36: 78-148
origins of the genre, 79-100
history of nineteenth-century detective fiction, 101-33
significance of nineteenth-century detective fiction, 133-46
NCLC 148: 1-161
overviews, 3-26
origins and influences, 26-63
major authors, 63-134
Freud and detective fiction, 134-59

Detective Fiction, Twentieth-Century TCLC 38: 1-96
genesis and history of the detective story, 3-22
defining detective fiction, 22-32
evolution and varieties, 32-77
the appeal of detective fiction, 77-90

Detective Story See Crime-Mystery-Detective Stories

Dime Novels NCLC 84: 98-168
overviews and general studies, 99-123
popular characters, 123-39
major figures and influences, 139-52
socio-political concerns, 152-167

Disabilities in Children's Literature CLR 126: 34-106
overviews and general studies, 37-60
presentation of mental disabilities in children's literature, 60-72
presentation of physical disabilities in children's literature, 72-84
presentation of cognitive and emotional disabilities in children's literature, 84-106

Disability in the Literature of Antiquity CMLC 235: 1-290

The Disability Memoir Boom CLC 484: 177-304
primary sources, 182-85
overviews and general studies, 185-301

Disease and Literature TCLC 66: 140-283
overviews and general studies, 141-65
disease in nineteenth-century literature, 165-81
tuberculosis and literature, 181-94
women and disease in literature, 194-221
plague literature, 221-53
AIDS in literature, 253-82

Diversities in Children's and Young Adult Literature CLR 268: 1-188

Domestic Violence in Literature TCLC 428: 132-304

Domesticity in Nineteenth-Century Literature NCLC 240: 209-310
overview, 211-25
female identity and individualism, 225-61
race and nationalism, 261-309

El Dorado, The Legend of See The Legend of El Dorado

The Double in Nineteenth-Century Literature NCLC 40: 1-95
genesis and development of the theme, 2-15
the double and romanticism, 16-27
sociological views, 27-52
psychological interpretations, 52-87
philosophical considerations, 87-95
NCLC 192: 91-217
overviews and general studies, 93-151
psychology and the double, 151-93
race, gender, and the double, 193-216

The Double in Short Fiction SSC 149: 68-159
the symbolic significance of the double, 69-127
major short fiction works featuring the motif of the double, 127-58

Dramatic Realism NCLC 44: 139-202
overviews and general studies, 140-50
origins and definitions, 150-66
impact and influence, 166-93
realist drama and tragedy, 193-201

Drugs and Literature TCLC 78: 184-282
overviews and general studies, 185-201
pre-twentieth-century literature, 201-42
twentieth-century literature, 242-82

Dystopias in Contemporary Literature CLC 168: 1-91
overviews and general studies, 2-52
dystopian views in Margaret Atwood's *The Handmaid's Tale* (1985), 52-71
feminist readings of dystopias, 71-90

Early Modern Education: An Introduction LC 318: 1-165

Early Modern English Science Fiction LC 205: 1-136
overviews, 2-49
authors and their works, 49-136

Early Modern Folk Literature LC 171: 123-288
overviews, 125-45
popular themes and figures, 145-69
folk literature in Britain, 169-240
folk literature in Europe, 240-88

Early Twentieth-Century Children's Literature TCLC 246: 1-110
overviews and general studies, 2-40
early twentieth-century children's fantasists, 40-70
early twentieth-century girls' books, 70-99
early twentieth-century nursery books, 99-109

Early Twentieth-Century Drama TCLC 246: 111-97

American realism, 114-47
realism and the Moscow Art Theatre, 147-82
the Irish literary renaissance and the Abbey Theatre, 182-96

Early Welsh Saga Poetry CMLC 191: 1-134
overviews and general studies, 3-23
the historical context of early Welsh saga poetry, 23-93
influences on the development of early Welsh saga poetry, 93-132

East Asian Literature TCLC 254: 100-77
overviews and major themes, 102-12
China and Taiwan, 112-36
Japan and Korea, 136-76

Eastern Mythology CMLC 26: 112-92
heroes and kings, 113-51
cross-cultural perspective, 151-69
relations to history and society, 169-92

Ecocriticism and Nineteenth-Century Literature NCLC 140: 1-168
overviews, 3-20
American literature: Romantics and Realists, 20-76
American explorers and naturalists, 76-123
English literature: Romantics and Victorians, 123-67

Ecofeminism and Nineteenth-Century Literature NCLC 136: 1-110
overviews, 2-24
the local landscape, 24-72
travel writing, 72-109

Ecofeminism in Literature TCLC 278: 153-218
overviews and history, 154-79
representative studies, 179-216

The Ecological Short Story SSC 163: 59-195
overviews, 60-70
Faulkner and Ecological Short Fiction, 70-94
Short Ecofiction: Topics, Themes, Styles, 94-161
Latin American Ecological Short Fiction, 162-77
Ecofeminist Short Fiction, 177-94

Edwardian Literature TCLC 186: 137-282
overviews 138-74
culture and society in the edwardian age 174-203
nation and empire 203-34
images of money 234-52
Edwardians and Modernists 252-71
Edwardian novels 271-81

Eighteenth-Century British Periodicals LC 63: 1-123
rise of periodicals, 2-31
impact and influence of periodicals, 31-64
periodicals and society, 64-122

Eighteenth Century Children's Books CLR 152: 111-86
overviews and general studies, 114-29
eighteenth-century criticism of period children's books, 129-44
eighteenth-century British children's books, 144-66
eighteenth-century American children's books, 166-86

Eighteenth-Century Travel Narratives LC 77: 252-355
overviews and general studies, 254-79
eighteenth-century European travel narratives, 279-334
non-European eighteenth-century travel narratives, 334-55

Ekphrasis CLC 521: 1-304

Electronic "Books": Hypertext and Hyperfiction CLC 86: 367-404
- books vs. CD-ROMS, 367-76
- hypertext and hyperfiction, 376-95
- implications for publishing, libraries, and the public, 395-403

Eliot, T. S., Centenary of Birth CLC 55: 345-75

Elizabethan Drama LC 22: 140-240
- origins and influences, 142-67
- characteristics and conventions, 167-83
- theatrical production, 184-200
- histories, 200-12
- comedy, 213-20
- tragedy, 220-30

Elizabethan Prose Fiction LC 41: 1-70
- overviews and general studies, 1-15
- origins and influences, 15-43
- style and structure, 43-69

The Emergence of the Short Story in the Nineteenth Century NCLC 140: 169-279
- overviews, 171-74
- the American short story, 174-214
- the short story in Great Britain and Ireland, 214-235
- stories by women in English, 235-45
- the short story in France and Russia, 245-66
- the Latin American short story, 266-77

Enclosure of the English Common NCLC 88: 1-57
- overviews and general studies, 1-12
- early reaction to enclosure, 12-23
- nineteenth-century reaction to enclosure, 23-56

The Encyclopedists LC 26: 172-253
- overviews and general studies, 173-210
- intellectual background, 210-32
- views on esthetics, 232-41
- views on women, 241-52

English Abolitionist Literature of the Nineteenth Century NCLC 136: 111-235
- overview, 112-35
- origins and development, 135-42
- poetry, 142-58
- prose, 158-80
- sociopolitical concerns, 180-95
- English abolitionist literature and feminism, 195-233

English Caroline Literature LC 13: 221-307
- background, 222-41
- evolution and varieties, 241-62
- the Cavalier mode, 262-75
- court and society, 275-91
- politics and religion, 291-306

English Decadent Literature of the 1890s NCLC 28: 104-200
- fin de siècle: the Decadent period, 105-19
- definitions, 120-37
- major figures: "the tragic generation," 137-50
- French literature and English literary Decadence, 150-7
- themes, 157-61
- poetry, 161-82
- periodicals, 182-96

English Emblem Books LC 125: 1-99
- overviews, 2-27
- background and contexts, 27-63
- major emblem writers, 63-83
- religion and emblem books, 83-99

English Essay, Rise of the LC 18: 238-308
- definitions and origins, 236-54
- influence on the essay, 254-69
- historical background, 269-78
- the essay in the seventeenth century, 279-93
- the essay in the eighteenth century, 293-307

English-Irish Relations from Spenser to Swift LC 160: 1-172
- historical and political background, 3-38
- Spenser and Ireland, 39-71
- Ireland and English drama, 71-117
- Ireland in the age of Swift, 117-72

English Literary Criticism in the Later Seventeenth and Eighteenth Centuries LC 203: 1-121
- overviews, 3-58
- the critics, 58-121

English Mystery Cycle Dramas LC 34: 1-88
- overviews and general studies, 1-27
- the nature of dramatic performances, 27-42
- the medieval worldview and the mystery cycles, 43-67
- the doctrine of repentance and the mystery cycles, 67-76
- the fall from grace in the mystery cycles, 76-88

The English Realist Novel, 1740-1771 LC 51: 102-98
- overviews and general studies, 103-22
- from romanticism to realism, 123-58
- women and the novel, 159-175
- the novel and other literary forms, 176-197

English Renaissance Literary Criticism LC 201: 1-178
- overviews, 3-123
- the critics, 123-78

English Revolution, Literature of the LC 43: 1-58
- overviews and general studies, 2-24
- pamphlets of the English Revolution, 24-38
- political sermons of the English Revolution, 38-48
- poetry of the English Revolution, 48-57

English Romantic Hellenism NCLC 68: 143-250
- overviews and general studies, 144-69
- historical development of English Romantic Hellenism, 169-91
- influence of Greek mythology on the Romantics, 191-229
- influence of Greek literature, art, and culture on the Romantics, 229-50

English Romantic Poetry NCLC 28: 201-327
- overviews and reputation, 202-37
- major subjects and themes, 237-67
- forms of Romantic poetry, 267-78
- politics, society, and Romantic poetry, 278-99
- philosophy, religion, and Romantic poetry, 299-324

The Epiphany in Short Fiction SSC 334: 1-163

Epistolary Fiction TCLC 230: 87-208
- overviews, 88-105
- major authors, 105-46
- the epistolatory novel in Hispanic literature, 146-77
- other epistolary genres, 177-207

The Epistolary Novel LC 59: 71-170
- overviews and general studies, 72-96
- women and the Epistolary novel, 96-138
- principal figures: Britain, 138-53
- principal figures: France, 153-69

Epithalamia: Poems Celebrating Marriages PC 171: 77-200
- epithalamia of the classical period, 80-8
- epithalamia of the English Renaissance, 88-167
- epithalamia of the nineteenth and twentieth centuries, 167-98

Espionage Literature TCLC 50: 95-159
- overviews and general studies, 96-113
- espionage fiction/formula fiction, 113-26
- spies in fact and fiction, 126-38
- the female spy, 138-44
- social and psychological perspectives, 144-58

Euro-American Literary Representations of Native Americans, Nineteenth-Century NCLC 104: 132-264
- overviews and general studies, 134-53
- Native American history, 153-72
- the Indians of the Northeast, 172-93
- the Indians of the Southeast, 193-212
- the Indians of the West, 212-27
- Indian-hater fiction, 227-43
- the Indian as exhibit, 243-63

European Debates on the Conquest of the Americas LC 67: 1-129
- overviews and general studies, 3-56
- major Spanish figures, 56-98
- English perceptions of Native Americans, 98-129

European Romanticism NCLC 36: 149-284
- definitions, 149-77
- origins of the movement, 177-82
- Romantic theory, 182-200
- themes and techniques, 200-23
- romanticism in Germany, 223-39
- romanticism in France, 240-61
- romanticism in Italy, 261-4
- romanticism in Spain, 264-8
- impact and legacy, 268-82

Evolution of Fairy Tales CLR 106: 89-164
- overviews and general studies, 93-102
- the value of fairy tales for children, 102-19
- contemporary adaptations of classic fairy tales, 119-45
- characteristics of twentieth-century fairy tales, 145-63

Exile in Literature TCLC 122: 1-129
- overviews and general studies, 2-33
- exile in fiction, 33-92
- German literature in exile, 92-129

Exile in Nineteenth-Century European and American Literature NCLC 172: 141-248
- overview, 143-51
- exile in French literature, 151-81
- exile in British literature, 181-202
- exile in American literature, 202-27
- women and exile, 227-47

Exile in Short Fiction SSC 145: 1-138
- Metaphorical/Internal Exile, 4-51
- Exile in Slavic/Eastern European Culture, 51-78
- Exile to and from Africa, 78-97
- Exile in Hispanic Short Fiction, 97-137

Existentialism and Literature TCLC 42: 197-268
- overviews and definitions, 198-209
- history and influences, 209-19
- Existentialism critiqued and defended, 220-35
- philosophical and religious perspectives, 235-41
- Existentialist fiction and drama, 241-67

Ezra Pound Controversy TCLC 150: 1-132
- politics of Ezra Pound, 3-42
- anti-semitism of Ezra Pound, 42-57
- the Bollingen Award controversy, 57-76
- Pound's later writing, 76-104
- criticism of *The Pisan Cantos,* 104-32

Fabian Literature TCLC 190: 118-217
- overviews 119-143
- Shaw and Fabianism 143-69
- other major figures 169-216

Fables SSC 124: 173-360
   overviews 174-282
   major authors and works 282-358

Fairy Tales and Nineteenth-Century Literature NCLC 212: 149-268
   overview, 151-65
   The Brothers Grimm, 165-86
   Charles Dickens, 186-217
   Oscar Wilde, 217-45
   women authors, 245-67

Familiar Essay NCLC 48: 96-211
   definitions and origins, 97-130
   overview of the genre, 130-43
   elements of form and style, 143-59
   elements of content, 159-73
   the Cockneys: Hazlitt, Lamb, and Hunt, 173-91
   status of the genre, 191-210

Fantasy in Contemporary Literature CLC 193: 137-250
   overviews and general studies, 139-57
   language, form, and theory, 157-91
   major writers, 191-230
   women writers and fantasy, 230-50

Fashion in Nineteenth-Century Literature NCLC 128: 104-93
   overviews and general studies, 105-38
   fashion and American literature, 138-46
   fashion and English literature, 146-74
   fashion and French literature, 174-92

The Faust Legend LC 47: 1-117

The Faust Legend in Twentieth-Century Literature TCLC 182: 96-238
   overviews, 97-121
   Faust in the modern world, 121-74
   major works, 174-208
   comparative studies, 208-38

Fear in Literature TCLC 74: 81-258
   overviews and general studies, 81
   pre-twentieth-century literature, 123
   twentieth-century literature, 182

The Federalist Papers LC 80: 71-198
   overviews and general studies: 72-9
   influences and origins: 79-104
   political themes: 104-45
   Publius and the narrative voice: 145-73
   Anti-Federalists, then and now: 173-98
LC 256: 1-83
   historical context of *The Federalist Papers*, 3-7
   pedagogical approaches to *The Federalist Papers*, 7-39
   The Federalist Papers and political philosophy, 39-48
   contrasting views of federalism, 48-51
   authorship attribution, 51-81

Female Dramatists of the Restoration and Eighteenth Century LC 163: 1-137
   overviews, 4-55
   The Female Wits (1696), 55-80
   major plawrights, 80-113
   transforming gender, 113-121
   minor playwrights, 121-37

Feminism in the 1990s: Commentary on Works by Naomi Wolf, Susan Faludi, and Camille Paglia CLC 76: 377-415

Feminism in Children's Literature CLR 146: 18-111
   overviews and general studies, 21-38
   feminism in classic girls' stories, 38-61
   feminism in series fiction, 61-89
   feminism in young adult poetry, 89-111

Feminist Criticism, Contemporary CLC 180: 1-103
   overviews and general studies, 2-59
   modern French feminist theory, 59-102

Feminist Criticism in 1990 CLC 65: 312-60

Feminism in Literature FL 1: 1-279; 2: 1-295; 4: 1-626
   women and women's writings from antiquity through the middle ages, 1:1-99
   primary sources, 1:4-12
   women in the ancient world, 1:12-34
   women in the medieval world, 1:34-56
   women in classical art and literature, 1:56-74
   classical and medieval women writers, 1:74-96
   women in the 16th, 17th, and 18th centuries: an overview, 1:101-91
   primary sources, 1:104-11
   overviews, 1:112-32
   society, 1:132-64
   politics, 1:164-77
   women in literature, 1:177-90
   women's literature in the 16th, 17th, and 18th centuries 1:193-279
   primary sources, 1:195-201
   overviews, 1:202-39
   women's literature in the 16th, 17th, and 18th centuries, 1:239-78
   women in the 19th century: an overview, 2:1-88
   primary sources, 2:3-15
   overviews, 2:15-50
   early feminists, 2:50-67
   representations of women in literature and art in the 19th century, 2:67-86
   women's literature in the 19th century, 2:89-206
   primary sources, 2:91-9
   overviews, 2:99-140
   American women writers, 2:141-77
   British women writers, 2:177-204
   United States suffrage movement in the 19th century, 2:207-95
   primary sources, 2:209-29
   overviews, 2:229-39
   the civil war and its effect on suffrage, 2:239-53
   suffrage: issues and individuals, 2:253-94
   women in the early to mid-20th century (1900-1960): an overview, 4:1-126
   primary sources, 4:1-14
   overviews, 4:14-48
   social and economic conditions, 4:48-67
   women and the arts, 4:67-125
   suffrage in the 20th century, 4:127-234
   primary sources, 4:129-36
   overviews, 4:136-77
   major figures and organizations, 4:177-214
   women and law, 4:214-32
   women's literature from 1900 to 1960, 4:235-344
   primary sources, 4:238-41
   overviews, 4:241-61
   impact of the world wars, 4:261-304
   women and the dramatic tradition, 4:304-39
   Asian American influences, 4:339-42
   the feminist movement in the 20th century, 4:345-443
   primary sources, 4:347-58
   overviews, 4:358-403
   feminist legal battles, 4:403-34
   third-wave feminism, 4:434-42
   women's literature from 1960 to the present, 4:445-536
   primary sources, 4:448-60
   overviews, 4:460-83
   women authors of color, 4:483-97
   feminist literary theory, 4:497-511
   modern lesbian literature, 4:511-534

Feminism in Nineteenth-Century Literature NCLC 236: 1-104
   overview, 3-6
   feminist readings of fiction by women, 6-44
   women author activists, 44-78
   male authors, 78-103

Fifteenth-Century Spanish Poetry LC 100:82-173
   overviews and general studies, 83-101
   the Cancioneros, 101-57
   major figures, 157-72

The Figure of La Malinche in Mexican Literature LC 127: 91-172
   overview, 92-108
   the historical Malinche, 108-33
   Malinche reinvented, 133-72

Film and Literature TCLC 38: 97-226
   overviews and general studies, 97-119
   film and theater, 119-34
   film and the novel, 134-45
   the art of the screenplay, 145-66
   genre literature/genre film, 167-79
   the writer and the film industry, 179-90
   authors on film adaptations of their works, 190-200
   fiction into film: comparative essays, 200-23

Fin de siècle **Literature** TCLC 250: 1-107
   overviews, 2-24
   fin de siècle poetry, 24-57
   fin de siècle fiction and drama, 57-91
   fin de siècle writers, 91-107

Finance and Money as Represented in Nineteenth-Century Literature NCLC 76: 1-69
   historical perspectives, 2-20
   the image of money, 20-37
   the dangers of money, 37-50
   women and money, 50-69

Folk Literature See Early Modern Folk Literature

Folklore and Literature TCLC 86: 116-293
   overviews and general studies, 118-144
   Native American literature, 144-67
   African-American literature, 167-238
   folklore and the American West, 238-57
   modern and postmodern literature, 257-91

Food in Literature TCLC 114: 1-133
   food and children's literature, 2-14
   food as a literary device, 14-32
   rituals invloving food, 33-45
   food and social and ethnic identity, 45-90
   women's relationship with food, 91-132

Food in Nineteenth-Century Literature NCLC 108: 134-288
   overviews, 136-74
   food and social class, 174-85
   food and gender, 185-219
   food and love, 219-31
   food and sex, 231-48
   eating disorders, 248-70
   vegetarians, carnivores, and cannibals, 270-87

Food in Short Fiction SSC 154: 1-122
   food in the short fiction of Europe, 2-42
   food in the short fiction of Asia, 42-78
   food in the short fiction of the Americas, 78-122

French Drama in the Age of Louis XIV LC 28: 94-185

overview, 95-127
tragedy, 127-46
comedy, 146-66
tragicomedy, 166-84

French Enlightenment LC 14: 81-145
the question of definition, 82-9
le siècle des lumières, 89-94
women and the salons, 94-105
censorship, 105-15
the philosophy of reason, 115-31
influence and legacy, 131-44

French Literature TCLC 262: 1-94
major works of French literature, 3-93

French New Novel TCLC 98: 158-234
overviews and general studies, 158-92
influences, 192-213
themes, 213-33

French Realism NCLC 52: 136-216
origins and definitions, 137-70
issues and influence, 170-98
realism and representation, 198-215

French Revolution and English Literature
NCLC 40: 96-195
history and theory, 96-123
romantic poetry, 123-50
the novel, 150-81
drama, 181-92
children's literature, 192-5

French Symbolist Poetry NCLC 144: 1-107
overviews, 2-14
Symbolist aesthetics, 14-47
the Symbolist lyric, 47-60
history and influence, 60-105

Friendship in Nineteenth-Century Literature
NCLC 196: 1-97
spiritual and personal fulfillment, 3-31
friendships between men, 31-64
friendships between women, 64-96

The Fronde LC 200:124-230
background and history, 125-49
mazarinades, 149-72
memoirs, 172-229

Frontiersmen in American Literature
NCLC 208: 1-102
overview, 3-31
masculinity and the frontiersman, 31-54
frontier heroines, 54-101

The Fugitives and Their Poetry TCLC 290: 1-114
overviews and general studies, 3-67
Donald Davidson, 67-73
John Crowe Ransom, 73-90
Allen Tate, 90-8
Robert Penn Warren, 98-112

Futurism TCLC 166: 199-338
overviews, 200-10
poetry, 210-23
theater, 223-32
music, 232-46
Futurism and Fascism, 246-312
women Futurist writers, 312-37

Futurism, Italian TCLC 42: 269-354
principles and formative influences, 271-9
manifestos, 279-88
literature, 288-303
theater, 303-19
art, 320-30
music, 330-6
architecture, 336-9
and politics, 339-46
reputation and significance, 346-51

Gaelic Revival See Irish Literary Renaissance

Gates, Henry Louis, Jr., and African-American Literary Criticism CLC 65: 361-405

Gaucho Literature TCLC 158: 99-195
overviews and general studies, 101-43
major works, 143-95

Gambling in Nineteenth-Century Literature
NCLC 168: 1-84
overview, 2-7
gambling in American literature, 7-39
gambling in British literature, 39-57
gambling in Russian literature, 57-84

Gangsta Fiction See Street Lit

Gay and Lesbian Literature CLC 76: 416-39

Gay and Lesbian Literature, Contemporary
CLC 171: 1-130
overviews and general studies, 2-43
contemporary gay literature, 44-95
lesbianism in contemporary literature, 95-129

Gay and Lesbian Literature in the Twentieth Century TCLC 218: 114-59
overviews and general studies, 115-38
major authors and works, 138-60
homosexuality and race, 161-93
lesbian literature, 193-258

Gender and Sexuality in Disney Films CLR 223: 119-86
Disney's portrayal of women, 123-66
transgender studies of Disney, 166-77
Disney and boyhood, 177-85

Gender and Sexuality in Early Seventeenth-Century English Literature
LC 149: 1-159
overview, 3-7
crossdressing, 7-70
sexual practices, 70-92
sexual difference, 92-114
homoerotic desire, 114-58

Gender and Sexuality in Eighteenth-Century British Literature LC 155: 85-224
desire and the body, 87-115
sexual difference, 115-75
societal norms, 175-203
gender and politics, 203-23

Gender and Sexuality in Eighteenth-Century European Literature LC 175: 142-242
representations of sexuality, 144-76
notions of gender, 176-200
erotic and pornographic works, 200-23
sexuality and non-Europeans, 223-42

Gender and Sexuality in Fifteenth-Century Literature LC 145: 1-147
gender and sexuality in English literature, 3-83
gender and sexuality in European literature, 83-119
the sexuality of the "other" 119-46

Gender and Sexuality in Seventeenth-Century European Literature LC 153: 219-362
overviews, 221-30
cross-dressing, 230-71
gender identification and difference, 271-337
sexual liberation, 337-61

Gender and Sexuality in Sixteenth-Century Literature LC 147: 90-248
overviews, 92-123
gender conformation and construction, 123-53
visions and constructions of sexuality, 153-72
sex, gender, and power, 172-205
female representation and self-representation, 205-47

Gender in Nineteenth-Century Literature
NCLC 168: 192-352
overviews, 195-256
gender and race, 256-83
gender and men, 283-309
gender and class, 309-20
gender and the text, 320-51

The Generation of 1898 TCLC 198: 138-235
overviews and general studies, 139-71
formation and history, 171-201
literary criticism and the generation of 1898, 201-18
the generation of 1898 and the development of the novel, 218-34

Generation of 1898 Short Fiction SSC 75: 182-287
overviews and general studies, 182-210
major short story writers of the Generation of 1898, 210-86
Azorín, 210-16
Emilia Pardo Bazán, 216-34
Vicente Blasco Ibáñez, 234-36
Gabriel Miró, 236-43
Miguel de Unamuno, 243-68
Ramon del Valle-Inclán, 268-86

The Generation of 1927 TCLC 178: 1-109
overviews 2-17
literary and thematic assessments 17-59
major authors 59-108

The Genteel Tradition NCLC 188: 1-89
overviews, 3-43
women and the Genteel Tradition, 43-61
works in the Genteel Tradition, 61-89

Georgian Poetry TCLC 174:1-103
overviews, 2-28
cultural and literary context, 28-74
World War I and Georgian poetry, 74-103

German Baroque Novelists LC 225: 1-184
Anton Ulrich, Duke of Brunswick-Lüneberg (later Brunswick-Wolfenbüttel), 25-9
Johann Beer, 29-52
August Bohse, 53-79
Johann Christoph Ettner, 79-87
Johann Jakob Christoffel von Grimmelshausen, 87-122
Eberhard Werner Happel, 122-31
Johann Kuhnau, 132-42
Daniel Casper von Lohenstein, 142-60
Wolfgang Caspar Printz, 160-64
Christian Weise, 164-82

German *Bildungsroman* NCLC 378: 91-294
overviews and general studies, 94-120
Goethe and the *bildungsroman,* 120-229
comparative studies, 230-42
title commentary, 242-93

German Courtly Epic CMLC 132: 1-156
sources and influences, 4-21
historical context, 21-45
conventions of the courtly epic, 45-101
analyses of central texts and authors, 101-27
love and gender in the courtly epic, 128-55

German Exile Literature TCLC 30: 1-58
the writer and the Nazi state, 1-10
definition of, 10-4
life in exile, 14-32
surveys, 32-50
Austrian literature in exile, 50-2
German publishing in the United States, 52-7

German Expressionism TCLC 34: 74-160
history and major figures, 76-85
aesthetic theories, 85-109
drama, 109-26
poetry, 126-38
film, 138-42

painting, 142-7
music, 147-53
and politics, 153-8

German Humanists LC 234: 71-210
Desiderius Erasmus, 74-126
Martin Luther, 126-157
the humanistic tradition: Fischart, Wyle, and others, 157-208

German Images of America in the Nineteenth Century NCLC 254: 71-241
theory and context, 74-90
America and the German imagination, 90-147
race: German portrayals of Black and Native Americans, 147-194
German women and America, 194-201
regional perspectives, 201-239

German Naturalism TCLC 302: 1-111
literary context of German Naturalism, 3-41
sociohistorical context of German Naturalism, 41-64
specific themes and motifs in German Naturalist literature, 64-95
German Naturalism and other literary modes, 95-109

The German Volksbuch LC 251: 1-124
intellectual and social context of the Volksbuch, 4-59
comparative analyses: the Volksbuch across the centuries, 59-69
Fortunatus as a case study, 70-84
Till Eulenspiegel as a case study, 84-102
other case studies from the Volksbuch, 102-22

Ghetto Fiction See Street Lit

The Ghost Story SSC 58: 1-142
overviews and general studies, 1-21
the ghost story in American literature, 21-49
the ghost story in Asian literature, 49-53
the ghost story in European and English literature, 54-89
major figures, 89-141

The Gilded Age NCLC 84: 169-271
popular themes, 170-90
realism, 190-208
Aestheticism, 208-26
socio-political concerns, 226-70

Glasnost **and Contemporary Soviet Literature** CLC 59: 355-97

Golden Age of Children's Illustrated Books CLR 113: 93-156
overviews and general studies, 96-114
Victorian masters of the Golden Age, 115-34
the Brandywine School of children's illustration, 134-56

Gone with the Wind **as Cultural Phenomenon** TCLC 170: 1-103
overviews, 2-60
race, gender, and class in *Gone with the Wind*, 60-102

The Gospels CMLC 243: 1-293

Gothic Drama NCLC 132: 95-198
overviews, 97-125
sociopolitical contexts, 125-58
Gothic playwrights, 158-97

Gothic Literature GL 1: 1-577
Gothic Literature: an overview, 1-106
primary sources, 4-16
overviews, 16-40
origins of the Gothic, 40-57
American Gothic, 57-74
European Gothic, 74-104
society, culture, and the Gothic, 107-229
primary sources, 110-27
overviews, 127-80
race and the Gothic, 180-210
women and the Gothic, 210-28
gothic themes, settings, and figures, 231-387
primary sources, 236-49
overviews, 249-64
haunted dwellings and the supernatural, 264-301
psychology and the Gothic, 301-42
vampires, 342-85
performing arts and the Gothic, 389-474
primary sources, 394-401
drama, 401-15
film, 415-52
television, 452-60
music, 461-73
visual arts and the Gothic, 475-526
primary sources, 477-80
overviews, 480-86
architecture, 486-506
art, 506-525

Gothic Literature TCLC 202: 90-220
overviews and general studies 91-111
evolution of Gothic style 111-33
gender and the Gothic imagination 133-74
literary and thematic connections 174-95
race, society, and politics 195-219

Gothic Novel NCLC 28: 328-402
development and major works, 328-34
definitions, 334-50
themes and techniques, 350-78
in America, 378-85
in Scotland, 385-91
influence and legacy, 391-400

The Governess in Nineteenth-Century Literature NCLC 104: 1-131
overviews and general studies, 3-28
social roles and economic conditions, 28-86
fictional governesses, 86-131

The Grail Theme in Twentieth-Century Literature TCLC 142: 1-89
overviews and general studies, 2-20
major works, 20-89

Graphic Narratives CLC 86: 405-32
history and overviews, 406-21
the "Classics Illustrated" series, 421-2
reviews of recent works, 422-32

Graphic Novels CLC 177: 163-299
overviews and general studies, 165-198
critical readings of major works, 198-286
reviews of recent graphic novels, 286-299

Graphic Novels CLR 165: 1-79
overviews and general studies, 4-10
literary elements in graphic novels, 10-42
coming-of-age and immigrant perspectives in graphic novels, 42-59
Jewish graphic novels, 59-79

Graveyard Poets LC 67: 131-212
origins and development, 131-52
major figures, 152-75
major works, 175-212

The Great War, Literature of the See **Literature of the Great War**

Greek Historiography CMLC 17: 1-49

Greek Lyric Poetry, The Rise of CMLC 77: 226-329
overviews, 229-46
literary history, 246-72
themes and style, 272-302
representative authors, 302-28

Greek Mythology CMLC 26: 193-320
overviews and general studies, 194-209
origins and development of Greek mythology, 209-29
cosmogonies and divinities in Greek mythology, 229-54
heroes and heroines in Greek mythology, 254-80
women in Greek mythology, 280-320

Greek Theater CMLC 51: 1-58
criticism, 2-58

Haiku in English PC 263: 87-289

Hard-Boiled Crime Novels TCLC 317: 1-199
overviews and general studies, 5-41
what is hard-boiled fiction?, 41-87
feminism and hard-boiled crime novels, 87-176
the African American perspective in hard-boiled fiction, 176-94
the lasting influence of the hard-boiled tradition, 194-98

Hard-Boiled Detective Stories SSC 212: 93-230
overview and general study, 95-108
pulp magazines, 108-46
hard-boiled short fiction, 146-228

Hard-Boiled Fiction TCLC 118: 1-109
overviews and general studies, 2-39
major authors, 39-76
women and hard-boiled fiction, 76-109

The Harlem Renaissance HR 1: 1-563
overviews and general studies of the Harlem Renaissance, 1-137
primary sources, 3-12
overviews, 12-38
background and sources of the Harlem Renaissance, 38-56
the New Negro aesthetic, 56-91
patrons, promoters, and the New York Public Library, 91-121
women of the Harlem Renaissance, 121-37
social, economic, and political factors that influenced the Harlem Renaissance, 139-240
primary sources, 141-53
overviews, 153-87
social and economic factors, 187-213
Black intellectual and political thought, 213-40
publishing and periodicals during the Harlem Renaissance, 243-339
primary sources, 246-52
overviews, 252-68
African American writers and mainstream publishers, 268-91
anthologies: *The New Negro* and others, 291-309
African American periodicals and the Harlem Renaissance, 309-39
performing arts during the Harlem Renaissance, 341-465
primary sources, 343-48
overviews, 348-64
drama of the Harlem Renaissance, 364-92
influence of music on Harlem Renaissance writing, 437-65
visual arts during the Harlem Renaissance, 467-563
primary sources, 470-71
overviews, 471-517
painters, 517-36
sculptors, 536-58
photographers, 558-63

The Harlem Renaissance TCLC 26: 49-125
principal issues and figures, 50-67
the literature and its audience, 67-74
theme and technique in poetry, fiction, and drama, 74-115
and American society, 115-21
achievement and influence, 121-2

The Harlem Renaissance See Literature of the Harlem Renaissance

Havel, Václav, Playwright and President CLC 65: 406-63

Hawaiian Children's Literature CLR 125: 40-85
- overviews and general studies, 43-9
- depictions of Hawaiians in children's literature, 49-70
- fantasy and myth in Hawaiian children's literature, 70-85

Hellenistic Age, The CMLC 87: 98-267
- overviews, 101-48
- library at Alexandria, 148-67
- Hellenistic literature, 167-241
- Hellenistic science and culture, 242-65

Heroic Drama LC 91: 249-373
- definitions and overviews, 251-78
- politics and heroic drama, 278-303
- early plays: Dryden and Orrery, 303-51
- later plays: Lee and Otway, 351-73

Hero's Journey in the Ancient Epic, The CMLC 148: 171-340
- the journeys: incidents and themes, 173-217
- the hero and the journey, 217-253
- mythic elements of the journeys, 253-299
- *katabasis* and *nostos* in the epics, 299-338

Hillarian Circle, The LC 223: 227-340
- overviews, 230-69
- Eliza Haywood, 269-310
- Aaron Hill, 310-16
- Martha Fowke Sansom, 316-39

Hip-hop Fiction See Street Lit

Historical Fiction in Children's Literature CLR 124: 121-92
- overviews and general studies, 124-48
- race, war, and genocide in historical fiction for children, 148-68
- critical issues in historical fiction for children, 168-77
- individual works of juvenile historical fiction, 177-91

Historical Fiction, Nineteenth-Century NCLC 48: 212-307
- definitions and characteristics, 213-36
- Victorian historical fiction, 236-65
- American historical fiction, 265-88
- realism in historical fiction, 288-306

Hollywood and Literature TCLC 118: 110-251
- overviews and general studies, 111-20
- adaptations, 120-65
- socio-historical and cultural impact, 165-206
- theater and hollywood, 206-51

Holocaust and the Atomic Bomb: Fifty Years Later CLC 91: 331-82
- the Holocaust remembered, 333-52
- Anne Frank revisited, 352-62
- the atomic bomb and American memory, 362-81

Holocaust, Contemporary Literature of the CLC 252: 60-217
- general overviews, 63-106
- literary models of Holocaust representation, 106-36
- the generation after, 136-201
- post-Holocaust philosophy, theology, and ethics, 201-06
- the Binjamin Wilkomirski affair, 206-16

Holocaust Denial Literature TCLC 58: 1-110
- overviews and general studies, 1-30
- Robert Faurisson and Noam Chomsky, 30-52
- Holocaust denial literature in America, 52-71
- library access to Holocaust denial literature, 72-5
- the authenticity of Anne Frank's diary, 76-90
- David Irving and the "normalization" of Hitler, 90-109

Holocaust in Children's Literature, Representations of the CLR 110: 104-75
- overviews and general studies, 107-36
- fictional accounts of the Holocaust for children, 136-68
- Holocaust diaries written by children and young adults, 168-74

The Holocaust in Short Fiction SSC 231: 95-288
- first-generation survivors, witnesses, and others, 100-54
- second-generation authors and others, 154-287

Holocaust, Literature of the TCLC 42: 355-450
- historical overview, 357-61
- critical overview, 361-70
- diaries and memoirs, 370-95
- novels and short stories, 395-425
- poetry, 425-41
- drama, 441-8

Homosexuality in Children's Literature CLR 119: 101-69
- overviews and general studies, 104-12
- portrayals of gay and lesbian adolescence, 112-53
- presentations of gay and lesbian families in children's literature, 153-68

Homosexuality in Nineteenth-Century Literature NCLC 56: 78-182
- defining homosexuality, 80-111
- Greek love, 111-44
- trial and danger, 144-81
NCLC 180: 246-358
- defining homosexuality, 249-84
- treatment by women writers, 284-327
- treatment in works by Henry James, Nathaniel Hawthorne, and Fitz-Greene Halleck, 327-58

Humanism NCLC 228: 60-145
- criticism, 61-145

Humor in Children's Literature CLR 147: 65-133
- overviews and general studies, 68-78
- analyses of humor in individual and series works for children, 78-109
- authorial perspectives on writing humor for children, 109-18
- cultural humor in children's literature, 118-32

Humors Comedy LC 85: 194-324
- overviews, 195-251
- major figures: Ben Jonson, 251-93
- major figures: William Shakespeare, 293-324

Hungarian Literature of the Twentieth Century TCLC 26: 126-88
- surveys of, 126-47
- *Nyugat* and early twentieth-century literature, 147-56
- mid-century literature, 156-68
- and politics, 168-78
- since the 1956 revolt, 178-87

Hysteria in Nineteenth-Century Literature NCLC 64: 59-184
- the history of hysteria, 60-75
- the gender of hysteria, 75-103
- hysteria and women's narratives, 103-57
- hysteria in nineteenth-century poetry, 157-83

Image of the Noble Savage in Literature LC 79: 136-252
- overviews and development, 136-76
- the Noble Savage in the New World, 176-221
- Rousseau and the French Enlightenment's view of the noble savage, 221-51

Imagism TCLC 74: 259-454
- history and development, 260
- major figures, 288
- sources and influences, 352
- Imagism and other movements, 397
- influence and legacy, 431

Immigrants in Nineteenth-Century Literature, Representation of NCLC 112: 188-298
- overview, 189-99
- immigrants in America, 199-223
- immigrants and labor, 223-60
- immigrants in England, 260-97

Imperialism NCLC 208: 103-277
- overview, 106-31
- British Imperialism in Africa, 131-43
- Imperialism in juvenile literature, 143-203
- British Imperialism in India, 203-39
- Imperialism and adventure literature, 240-62
- British Imperialism in Scotland, 262-75

Imperialism in Short Fiction SSC 216: 1-121
- Imperialism as a social force, 4-50
- Imperialism, violence, and corruption, 50-91
- lasting effects of Imperialism, 92-119

Incest in Nineteenth-Century American Literature NCLC 76: 70-141
- overview, 71-88
- the concern for social order, 88-117
- authority and authorship, 117-40

Incest in Victorian Literature NCLC 92: 172-318
- overviews and general studies, 173-85
- novels, 185-276
- plays, 276-84
- poetry, 284-318

India, Representations of, in Early Modern Literature See Representations of India in Early Modern Literature

Indian Literature, Contemporary CLC 247: 218-90
- overviews, 221-36
- Indian writing in English, 236-63
- trends and themes, 263-90

Indian Literature in English TCLC 54: 308-406
- overview, 309-13
- origins and major figures, 313-25
- the Indo-English novel, 325-55
- Indo-English poetry, 355-67
- Indo-English drama, 367-72
- critical perspectives on Indo-English literature, 372-80
- modern Indo-English literature, 380-9
- Indo-English authors on their work, 389-404

Indian Literature in English TCLC 226: 1-164
- overviews, 2-24
- major authors, 24-81
- female Indian authors writing in English, 81-97
- postcolonialism and disapora, 97-117
- Indian poetry written in English, 117-163

Indigenous Voices in American Literature NCLC 443: 1-309

The Industrial Revolution in Literature NCLC 56: 183-273
- historical and cultural perspectives, 184-201
- contemporary reactions to the machine, 201-21
- themes and symbols in literature, 221-73

The Influence of Disney on Children's Literature CLR 143: 20-102
overviews and general studies, 24-39
Disney's adaptation of A. A. Milne's *Winnie-the-Pooh*, 39-52
other adaptations of children's literature by Disney, 52-72
approaches to feminist themes in Disney films, 72-86
depictions of colonialism and animal rights in Disney films, 86-101

The Influence of Ernest Hemingway TCLC 162: 122-259
overviews, 123-43
writers on Hemingway, 143-58
Hemingway's evocation of place, 158-84
gender and identity, 184-229
Hemingway and the quest for meaning, 229-58

The Influence of William Faulkner TCLC 170: 104-255
overviews, 105-16
Faulkner and narrative, 116-60
Faulkner and psychology, 160-80
Faulkner and race, 180-219
impact on contemporary culture, 219-43
Faulkner and women, 243-54

The Inklings TCLC 258: 205-313
overview, 207-14
group dynamics, 214-65
major authors, 266-313

International Children's Literature CLR 114: 55-120
overviews and general studies, 57-64
cultural and political influences on international children's literature, 64-105
examinations of regional and national children's literature, 105-120

Interregnum Literature See Literature of the Interregnum

Intersectionality in Global Anglophone Literature CLC 506: 3-273

Iranian Diaspora, Writers of See Writers of the Iranian Diaspora

Iraq War Literature CLC 346: 118-201
politics and media in the Iraq War, 120-50
combat trauma, 150-56
gendering the Iraq War, 156-71
writing the enemy, 171-200

Irish Children's Literature CLR 123: 77-127
overviews and general studies, 81-93
mythology in Irish children's literature, 93-100
history in Irish children's literature, 100-119
studies of children's works by Irish authors, 119-127

The Irish Famine as Represented in Nineteenth-Century Literature NCLC 64: 185-261
overviews and general studies, 187-98
historical background, 198-212
famine novels, 212-34
famine poetry, 234-44
famine letters and eye-witness accounts, 245-61

Irish Literary Renaissance TCLC 46: 172-287
overview, 173-83
development and major figures, 184-202
influence of Irish folklore and mythology, 202-22
Irish poetry, 222-34
Irish drama and the Abbey Theatre, 234-56
Irish fiction, 256-86

The Irish Literary Renaissance TCLC 222: 130-245
overviews, 131-88
influences, 188-218
genres and styles, 218-44

Irish Nationalism and Literature NCLC 44: 203-73
the Celtic element in literature, 203-19
anti-Irish sentiment and the Celtic response, 219-34
literary ideals in Ireland, 234-45
literary expressions, 245-73

The Irish Novel NCLC 80: 1-130
overviews and general studies, 3-9
principal figures, 9-22
peasant and middle class Irish novelists, 22-76
aristocratic Irish and Anglo-Irish novelists, 76-129

Irish Short Fiction Writers SSC 226: 1-173
overviews and general studies, 5-35
the Irish Literary Renaissance and the revolutionary generation, 35-81
Irish short fiction by women writers, 81-130
contemporary Irish short-fiction writers, 130-172

Irony in Renaissance Love Poetry LC 247: 1-66
origins of irony in Renaissance love poetry, 3-23
irony in early-Renaissance sonnets and sonnet sequences, 23-35
irony in mid- to late-Renaissance love poetry, 35-64

Islam in Contemporary Literature CLC 301: 107-235
Islam in Anglophone Literature or English Translation, 109-149
Islam in Francophone Literature, 149-182
Islam in African Literature, 182-202
Women and Islam, 202-234

Islam in Western Nineteenth-Century Life and Literature NCLC 188: 90-173
Islam in European literature and thought, 92-154
Islam in Russian life and literature, 154-73

Islamic Literature in English TCLC 238: 142-255
overviews and general studies, 143-78
major authors, 178-213
africa and Islam, 213-24
women and Islamic literature, 225-54

Israeli Literature TCLC 94: 1-137
overviews and general studies, 2-18
Israeli fiction, 18-33
Israeli poetry, 33-62
Israeli drama, 62-91
women and Israeli literature, 91-112
Arab characters in Israeli literature, 112-36

Israeli Literature, Contemporary CLC 240: 152-278
overviews and general studies, 156-86
major authors and representative works, 186-268
poets, 268-77

Italian Epic Poetry PC 186: 1-161
Giovanni Boccaccio's *Book of Theseus*, 5-10
Luigi Pulci's *Morgante*, 10-43
Matteo Maria Boiardo's *Orlando innamorato*, 43-52
Ludovico Ariosto's *Orlando furioso*, 52-128
Torquato Tasso's *Jerusalem Delivered*, 128-58

Italian Futurism See Futurism, Italian

Italian Humanism LC 12: 205-77
origins and early development, 206-18
revival of classical letters, 218-23
humanism and other philosophies, 224-39
humanism and humanists, 239-46
the plastic arts, 246-57
achievement and significance, 258-76

The Italian Novella SSC 164: 230-318
overviews and general studies, 231-272
major authors in the Italian novella tradition, 272-318

Italian Romanticism NCLC 60: 85-145
origins and overviews, 86-101
Italian Romantic theory, 101-25
the language of romanticism, 125-45

Jacobean Drama LC 33: 1-37
the Jacobean worldview: an era of transition, 2-14
the moral vision of Jacobean drama, 14-22
Jacobean tragedy, 22-3
the Jacobean masque, 23-36

Jamaican Literature TCLC 246: 198-309
overviews and general studies, 201-34
major Jamaican writers, 234-62
Jamaican fiction, 262-74
Jamaican poetry, 274-308

Japanese Women Short-Fiction Writers SSC 221: 55-143
challenges to the Japanese literary tradition 60-67
gender discourse 67-89
bodies, sexuality, and pregnancy 89-141

Jazz and Literature TCLC 102: 3-124

Jewish American Fiction TCLC 62: 1-181
overviews and general studies, 2-24
major figures, 24-48
Jewish writers and American life, 48-78
Jewish characters in American fiction, 78-108
themes in Jewish-American fiction, 108-43
Jewish-American women writers, 143-59
the Holocaust and Jewish-American fiction, 159-81

Jewish American Literature TCLC 250: 108-240
the immigrant experience, 131-75
major authors, 175-200
Holocaust literature, 200-39

Jewish American Poetry CLC 323: 151-250
the identity of the Jewish American poet, 153-87
major themes, 187-227
a voice for women, 227-35
major poets, 235-50

Jewish Children's Literature CLR 154: 1-49
Jewish characters in children's literature, 19-40
Jewish culture in children's literature, 40-5
reviews of Jewish children's literature, 45-9

Jews in Literature TCLC 118: 252-417
overviews and general studies, 253-97
representing the Jew in literature, 297-351
the Holocaust in literature, 351-416

The Journals of Lewis and Clark NCLC 100: 1-88
overviews and general studies, 4-30
journal-keeping methods, 30-46
Fort Mandan, 46-51
the Clark journal, 51-65
the journals as literary texts, 65-87

Judaism in Nineteenth-Century Literature NCLC 176: 1-89
contemporary commentary, 3-7
Judaism in German theory and culture, 7-63
treatment of Zionism, 63-88

Juvenile and Young Adult Science Fiction CLR 116: 135-89
    overviews and general studies, 139-61
    appeal of science fiction to young readers, 161-68
    futurism in young adult science fiction, 168-89

Juvenile Detective Fiction CLR 158: 62-130
    overviews and general studies, 65-78
    cultural and national juvenile detective literatures, 78-107
    juvenile detective series fiction, 107-30

Kabuki DC 42: 217-312
    overviews and general studies, 219-36
    significant works, 236-64
    Kabuki conventions and techniques, 264-311

Kabuki LC 73: 118-232
    overviews and general studies, 120-40
    the development of Kabuki, 140-65
    major works, 165-95
    Kabuki and society, 195-231

King Alfred the Great, The Age of See **The Age of King Alfred the Great**

The Kit-Kat Club LC 71: 66-112
    overviews and general studies, 67-88
    major figures, 88-107
    attacks on the Kit-Kat Club, 107-12

The Knickerbocker Group NCLC 56: 274-341
    overviews and general studies, 276-314
    Knickerbocker periodicals, 314-26
    writers and artists, 326-40

Künstlerroman TCLC 150: 133-260
    overviews and general studies, 135-51
    major works, 151-212
    feminism in the *Künstlerroman*, 212-49
    minority *Künstlerroman*, 249-59

The Lake Poets NCLC 52: 217-304
    characteristics of the Lake Poets and their works, 218-27
    literary influences and collaborations, 227-66
    defining and developing Romantic ideals, 266-84
    embracing Conservatism, 284-303

Language Poets TCLC 126: 66-172
    overviews and general studies, 67-122
    selected major figures in language poetry, 122-72

Larkin, Philip, Controversy CLC 81: 417-64

Latin American Literature, Twentieth-Century TCLC 58: 111-98
    historical and critical perspectives, 112-36
    the novel, 136-45
    the short story, 145-9
    drama, 149-60
    poetry, 160-7
    the writer and society, 167-86
    Native Americans in Latin American literature, 186-97

Law and Literature TCLC 126: 173-347
    overviews and general studies, 174-253
    fiction critiquing the law, 253-88
    literary responses to the law, 289-346

Lebanese Writers, Contemporary See **Contemporary Lebanese Writers**

The Legend of El Dorado LC 74: 248-350
    overviews, 249-308
    major explorations for El Dorado, 308-50

The Legend of Pope Joan LC 123: 1-88
    overviews and general studies, 3-87

Lesbian Literature, Contemporary CLC 320: 215-328
    groundbreaking books and authors: the pulps and beyond, 217-29
    patriarchal cultures: reclaiming female history and identity, 229-58
    genre fiction, 258-89
    more margins: the immigrant lesbian experience, 289-94
    the publishing and marketing of lesbian literature, 294-327

The Levellers LC 51: 200-312
    overviews and general studies, 201-29
    principal figures, 230-86
    religion, political philosophy, and pamphleteering, 287-311

The Lilith Legend in Modern Literature TCLC 170: 256-319
    overviews, 257-67
    historical and literary background, 267-89
    the Lilith legend in twentieth-century literature, 289-319

Literary Criticism in the Nineteenth Century, American NCLC 128: 1-103
    overviews and general studies, 2-44
    the transcendentalists, 44-65
    "young America," 65-71
    James Russell Lowell, 71-9
    Edgar Allan Poe, 79-97
    Walt Whitman, 97-102

Literary Darwinism CLC 385: 131-323
    overviews and general studies, 133-252
    Literary Darwinism's critique of post-structuralism, 252-79
    criticism of Literary Darwinism, 279-82
    Darwinian analysis of literature, 282-322

Literary Expressionism TCLC 142: 90-185
    overviews and general studies, 91-138
    themes in literary expressionism, 138-61
    expressionism in Germany, 161-84

The Literary Fragment TCLC 433: 1-293
    primary sources, 7-16
    predecessors to the twentieth-century fragment, 16-73
    the fragment as draft or unfinished manuscript, 73-103
    fragmentation as a narrative strategy, 103-70
    the genre of the fragment, 170-205
    fragmentation as literary theme, 205-66
    literary fragments and the visual arts, 266-91

The Literary Marketplace Nineteenth-Century NCLC 128: 194-368
    overviews and general studies, 197-228
    British literary marketplace, 228-66
    French literary marketplace, 266-82
    American literary marketplace, 282-323
    women in the literary marketplace, 323-67

Literary Patronage in the Elizabethan Age LC 60-147
    overviews 61-80
    the patrons 80-92
    the poets 92-130
    theatrical patronage 130-145

Literary Prizes TCLC 122: 130-203
    overviews and general studies, 131-34
    the Nobel Prize in Literature, 135-83
    the Pulitzer Prize, 183-203

Literature and Millenial Lists CLC 119: 431-67
    the Modern Library list, 433
    the Waterstone list, 438-439

Literature in Response to the September 11 Attacks CLC 174: 1-46
    major works about September 11, 2001, 2-22
    critical, artistic, and journalistic responses, 22-45

Literature of the American Cowboy NCLC 96: 1-60
    overview, 3-20
    cowboy fiction, 20-36
    cowboy poetry and songs, 36-59

Literature of the California Gold Rush NCLC 92: 320-85
    overviews and general studies, 322-24
    early California Gold Rush fiction, 324-44
    Gold Rush folklore and legend, 344-51
    the rise of Western local color, 351-60
    social relations and social change, 360-385

Literature of the Counter-Reformation LC 109: 213-56
    overviews and general studies, 214-33
    influential figures, 233-56

Literature of the Great War TCLC 226: 165-273
    overviews, 165-95
    the great war's impact on writers, 195-244
    poetry of the great war, 244-73

Literature of the Great War TCLC 230: 209-380
    women writers and the great war, 211-68
    World War I and modernism, 268-330
    propaganda and World War I literature, 330-79

Literature of the Harlem Renaissance TCLC 218: 260-376
    overviews and general studies, 261-78
    major figures, 279-318
    poetry of the Harlem Renaissance, 318-47
    women of the Harlem Renaissance, 347-75

Literature of the Interregnum LC 159: 219-301
    Interregnum views on theater, 221-39
    poetry of the Interregnum, 239-59
    prose of the Interregnum, 259-301

Little Magazines TCLC 194: 126-240
    overviews, 127-46
    little magazines and African American literature, 146-84
    little magazines and literary trends, 184-227
    little magazines and poetry, 227-39

The Living Theatre DC 16: 154-214

The Lost Generation SSC 340: 1-296

The Lost Generation See **Writers of the Lost Generation**

Luddism in Nineteenth-Century Literature NCLC 140: 280-365
    overviews, 281-322
    the literary response, 322-65

Ludwig Wittgenstein's Philosophy of Language TCLC 454: 67-292
    early Wittgenstein, 72-94
    late Wittgenstein, 94-164
    comprehensive readings, 164-221
    implications in additional fields, 221-54
    biographical studies, 254-89

Lynching in Nineteenth-Century Literature NCLC 148: 162-247
    lynching in literature and music, 163-92
    Ida B. Wells-Barnett and the anti-lynching movement, 192-221
    resistance to lynching in society and the press, 221-46

Machiavellism LC 167: 160-259
    overview, 161-73
    Machiavellism in literature, 173-212
    Machiavellism in philosophy, politics, and religion, 212-58

MAD Magazine CLR 109: 156-208
    overviews and general studies, 158-74

Harvey Kurtzman and the founding of MAD Magazine, 174-84
critical commentary on MAD Magazine, 184-203
the evolving role of MAD Magazine in modern society, 203-07

Madness in Nineteenth-Century Literature NCLC 76: 142-284
overview, 143-54
autobiography, 154-68
poetry, 168-215
fiction, 215-83
NCLC 228: 146-310
British fiction writers: Stevenson, Dickens, Collins, and Hardy, 148-83
English poets: Shelley, Byron, Hopkins, and Tennyson, 183-220
French writers, 220-48
Herman Melville, 248-58
women writers, 258-309

Madness in Twentieth-Century Literature TCLC 50: 160-225
overviews and general studies, 161-71
madness and the creative process, 171-86
suicide, 186-91
madness in American literature, 191-207
madness in German literature, 207-13
madness and feminist artists, 213-24

Magic Realism TCLC 110: 80-327
overviews and general studies, 81-94
magic realism in African literature, 95-110
magic realism in American literature, 110-32
magic realism in Canadian literature, 132-46
magic realism in European literature, 146-66
magic realism in Asian literature, 166-79
magic realism in Latin-American literature, 179-223
magic realism in Israeli literature and the novels of Salman Rushdie, 223-38
magic realism in literature written by women, 239-326

Magical Realism in Short Fiction SSC 148: 106-205
magical realism in Hispanic short fiction, 108-65
magical realism in North American short fiction, 165-84
magical realism as protest, 184-205

Major Cities in Nineteenth-Century Literature NCLC 176: 90-233
London and Paris in poetry, 93-99
London, 99-122
New York City, 122-65
Paris, 165-94
Rome, 194-217
St. Petersburg, 217-32

Marlowe and Shakespeare LC 320: 179-309

Marriage in Nineteenth-Century Life and Literature NCLC 232: 96-221
overview, 98-110
divorce, 110-32
social and literary conventions, 132-77
women writers, 177-220

Marriage in the Short Story SSC 139: 204-332
international perspectives on marriage in the short story, 206-66
feminist perspectives on marriage in the short story, 266-318
the depiction of infidelity in the short story, 318-332

The Martin Marprelate Tracts LC 101: 165-240
criticism, 166-240

Marxist Criticism TCLC 134: 127-57
overviews and general studies, 128-67
Marxist interpretations, 167-209

cultural and literary Marxist theory, 209-49
Marxism and feminist critical theory, 250-56

Masculinity in the Short Story SSC 138: 90-128
masculinity in gothic short fiction 93-128
masculinity and sexual orientation 128-76
masculinity from a feminist perspective 176-205
masculinity in modern society 205-34

The Masque LC 63: 124-265
development of the masque, 125-62
sources and structure, 162-220
race and gender in the masque, 221-64

McCarthyism and Literature TCLC 190: 218-383
overviews 220-58
poetry and fiction in the McCarthy era 258-316
theater in the McCarthy era 316-50
film and television in the McCarthy era 351-83

Medical Writing LC 55: 93-195
colonial America, 94-110
enlightenment, 110-24
medieval writing, 124-40
sexuality, 140-83
vernacular, 185-95

Memoirs of Trauma CLC 109: 419-466
overview, 420
criticism, 429

Memoirs, Truth in CLC 226: 253-88
arguments for and against fictionalization, 254-69
reaction to James Frey's *A Million Little Pieces,* 269-80
other suspected and proven memoir hoaxes, 280-88

Mental Illness in Short Fiction SSC 146: 74-232
depictions of mental illness in European and Russian short fiction, 75-127
depictions of mental illness in American short fiction, 127-75
women and mental illness in short fiction, 175-232

Mesmerism in Nineteenth-Century Literature NCLC 216: 104-264
overviews, 106-24
women authors, 125-49
Nathaniel Hawthorne, 149-204
other authors, 205-64

Metafiction CLC 486: 9-300
primary sources, 16-19
overviews and general studies, 19-98
metafictional novels and short stories, 98-224
metadrama, 224-43
metafictional movies and television, 243-89
metafictional comics and cartoons, 289-98

Metafiction TCLC 130: 43-228
overviews and general studies, 44-85
Spanish metafiction, 85-117
studies of metafictional authors and works, 118-228

Metaphysical Poets LC 24: 356-439
early definitions, 358-67
surveys and overviews, 367-92
cultural and social influences, 392-406
stylistic and thematic variations, 407-38

Metrical Psalms LC 129: 85-180
overviews, 87-180

Mexican Literature, Nineteenth-Century NCLC 200: 1-159
overviews, 2-49

national identity, 49-95
politics and reform, 96-136
race and culture, 136-59

Middle Eastern Literature TCLC 262: 95-200
overviews and general studies, 96-113
major Middle Eastern authors and works, 113-69
the role of women writers in Middle Eastern literature, 169-99

Missionaries in the Nineteenth-Century, Literature of NCLC 112: 299-392
history and development, 300-16
uses of ethnography, 316-31
sociopolitical concerns, 331-82
David Livingstone, 382-91

Modern Arabic Literature TCLC 282: 111-220
the historical context, 113-37
major authors, 137-47
women authors and gender issues, 147-89
the Arab Jew, 189-219

The Modern Essay TCLC 58: 199-273
overview, 200-7
the essay in the early twentieth century, 207-19
characteristics of the modern essay, 219-32
modern essayists, 232-45
the essay as a literary genre, 245-73

Modern French Literature TCLC 122: 205-359
overviews and general studies, 207-43
French theater, 243-77
gender issues and French women writers, 277-315
ideology and politics, 315-24
modern French poetry, 324-41
resistance literature, 341-58

Modern Irish Literature TCLC 102: 125-321
overview, 129-44
dramas, 144-70
fiction, 170-247
poetry, 247-321

Modern Japanese Literature TCLC 66: 284-389
poetry, 285-305
drama, 305-29
fiction, 329-61
western influences, 361-87

Modernism TCLC 70: 165-275
definitions, 166-84
Modernism and earlier influences, 184-200
stylistic and thematic traits, 200-29
poetry and drama, 229-42
redefining Modernism, 242-75

Modernist Lyric Poetry TCLC 270: 1-105
overviews, 2-21
major poets, 21-104

The Modernist Short Story, Part One: To 1929 SSC 320: 4-288

The Modernist Short Story, Part Two: 1930-1945 SSC 321: 4-288

Monasticism and Literature CMLC 74: 88-294
major figures, 89-132
secular influences, 132-54
monastic principles and literary practices, 154-232
women and monasticism, 232-93

Monster Literature, Contemporary CLC 330: 193-319
introduction: monsters and their meanings, 195-217
surveys of the literature, 217-51
major authors and works, 251-300
the vampire in popular culture, 300-18

Money in Nineteenth-Century Literature NCLC 236: 105-97

ethics, morality, and civilization, 106-66
women authors, 166-96

Mother Goose CLR 117: 35-123
overviews and general studies, 38-50
historical and literary origins of Mother Goose, 50-84
gender, race, and pedagogy in Mother Goose, 84-120
contemporary editions of Mother Goose nursery rhymes, 120-22

Motherhood in Caribbean, Chicana, and Latina Literature CLC 440: 23-147
general commentary, 25-32
Caribbean literature, 32-100
Chicana literature, 100-25
Latina literature, 126-46

Motherhood in Nineteenth-Century Literature NCLC 176: 234-338
overviews, 236-60
maternal archetypes: good, bad, and absent, 260-89
motherhood, patriarchy, and the social order, 289-316
motherhood and oppression, 316-338

Mothers in Short Fiction SSC 150: 108-237
the role of the mother in society, 111-50
major themes, 150-96
mothers and daughters, 196-216
mothers and sons, 216-36

Motivational Literature CLC 269: 244-373
the early positive psychology movement, 245-48
religious and spiritual inspiration, 248-80
the "Chicken Soup" phenomenon, 280-99
new age messages, 299-330
the modern motivational industry, 330-45

Mozambican Short-Fiction Writers SSC 216: 241-320
themes of political oppression, 243-253
effects of colonialism, 253-288
depictions of Mozambican life, 288-318

Muckraking Movement in American Journalism TCLC 34: 161-242
development, principles, and major figures, 162-70
publications, 170-9
social and political ideas, 179-86
targets, 186-208
fiction, 208-19
decline, 219-29
impact and accomplishments, 229-40

Multiculturalism CLC 189: 167-254
overviews and general studies, 168-93
the effects of multiculturalism on global literature, 193-213
multicultural themes in specific contemporary works, 213-53

Multiculturalism in Literature and Education CLC 70: 361-413

Music and Modern Literature TCLC 62: 182-329
overviews and general studies, 182-211
musical form/literary form, 211-32
music in literature, 232-50
the influence of music on literature, 250-73
literature and popular music, 273-303
jazz and poetry, 303-28

The Musical DC 34: 147-360
overviews and general studies, 149-78
race and the musical, 178-256
women and the musical, 256-84
Rodgers and Hammerstein, 284-319
Stephen Sondheim, 319-44
other major figures, 344-58

Mystery Story See Crime-Mystery-Detective Stories

Native American Autobiography, Nineteenth-Century NCLC 64: 262-389
overview, 263-8
problems of authorship, 268-81
the evolution of Native American autobiography, 281-304
political issues, 304-15
gender and autobiography, 316-62
autobiographical works during the turn of the century, 362-88

Native American Children's Literature CLR 130: 123-87
overviews and general studies, 127-48
critically evaluating Native American children's literature, 148-74
native versus non-native authorship of Native American children's literature, 174-87

Native American Literature CLC 76: 440-76

Native American Short Stories SSC 140: 171-340
overviews, 174-87
oral tales: literary renderings, transcriptions, and translations, 187-211
major authors and their works, 211-44
women and native american short stories, 244-338

Native North American Literature, Contemporary CLC 265: 87-209
themes of identity in Native North American Literature, 89-157
representative poetry, prose, and drama, 157-185
women and Native North American Literature, 185-208

Natural School, Russian NCLC 24: 205-40
history and characteristics, 205-25
contemporary criticism, 225-40

Naturalism NCLC 36: 285-382
definitions and theories, 286-305
critical debates on Naturalism, 305-16
Naturalism in theater, 316-32
European Naturalism, 332-61
American Naturalism, 361-72
the legacy of Naturalism, 372-81

Negritude TCLC 50: 226-361
origins and evolution, 227-56
definitions, 256-91
Negritude in literature, 291-343
Negritude reconsidered, 343-58

Negritude TCLC 158: 196-280
overviews and general studies, 197-208
major figures, 208-25
Negritude and humanism, 225-29
poetry of Negritude, 229-47
politics of Negritude, 247-68
the Negritude debate, 268-79

Neurodiversity in Medieval Studies CMLC 232: 1-126

The New Criticism TCLC 34: 243-318
development and ideas, 244-70
debate and defense, 270-99
influence and legacy, 299-315
TCLC 146: 1-108
overviews and general studies, 3-19
defining New Criticism, 19-28
place in history, 28-51
poetry and New Criticism, 51-78
major authors, 78-108
TCLC 266: 217-308
themes and applications, 218-81
the critics, 281-308

The New Humanists TCLC 162: 260-341
overviews, 261-92
major figures, 292-310
New Humanism in education and literature, 310-41

New South, Literature of the NCLC 116: 122-240
overviews, 124-66
the novel in the New South, 166-209
myth of the Old South in the New, 209-39

The New Woman in Nineteenth-Century Literature NCLC 156: 134-281
overview, 136-39
historical and social context, 139-57
contemporary descriptions of the new woman, 157-65
the new woman and popular fiction, 165-86
the new woman and the decadents, 187-207
the new woman and the theater, 207-48
Henry James, Bram Stoker, and Others, 248-80

The New World in Renaissance Literature LC 31: 1-51
overview, 1-18
utopia vs. terror, 18-31
explorers and Native Americans, 31-51

New York Intellectuals and *Partisan Review* TCLC 30: 117-98
development and major figures, 118-28
influence of Judaism, 128-39
Partisan Review, 139-57
literary philosophy and practice, 157-75
political philosophy, 175-87
achievement and significance, 187-97

The New Yorker TCLC 58: 274-357
overviews and general studies, 274-95
major figures, 295-304
New Yorker style, 304-33
fiction, journalism, and humor at *The New Yorker*, 333-48
the new *New Yorker*, 348-56

Newgate Novel NCLC 24: 166-204
development of Newgate literature, 166-73
Newgate Calendar, 173-7
Newgate fiction, 177-95
Newgate drama, 195-204

New Orleans in Nineteenth-Century Literature NCLC 216: 265-356
overview, 266-80
Kate Chopin, 280-301
Creole authors, 301-30
drama, 330-56

New Zealand Literature TCLC 134: 258-368
overviews and general studies, 260-300
Maori literature, 300-22
New Zealand drama, 322-32
New Zealand fiction, 332-51
New Zealand poetry, 351-67

Nigerian Fiction, Contemporary CLC 343: 106-205
Chinua Achebe: the progenitor of contemporary African literature, 108-31
post-independence disillusionment, 131-50
the new Nigerian novel, 150-86
market literature: the popular Romance, 186-204

Nigerian Literature of the Twentieth Century TCLC 30: 199-265
surveys of, 199-227
English language and African life, 227-45
politics and the Nigerian writer, 245-54
Nigerian writers and society, 255-62

Nihilism and Literature TCLC 110: 328-93
overviews and general studies, 328-44
European and Russian nihilism, 344-73
nihilism in the works of Albert Camus, Franz Kafka, and John Barth, 373-92

Nineteenth-Century American Women Social Activists: Emancipation NCLC 300: 1-164
overviews and general studies, 4-33
views from white writers, 33-67
views from black writers, 67-143
black oratory, 143-62

Nineteenth-Century American Women Social Activists: Indian Rights NCLC 300: 165-324
white women writers and Indian reform, 168-226
Indian rights and feminism, 226-76
Native American women writers, 276-91
tropes of Indianness in nineteenth-century American literature, 291-322

Nineteenth-Century American Women Social Activists: Labor NCLC 310: 1-76
perspectives on Lowell, 3-20
work and the "cult of true womanhood", 20-30
women's labor movements and race, 30-51
poverty and pollution, 51-75

Nineteenth-Century American Women Social Activists: Temperance NCLC 310: 77-168
temperance activism, 81-110
temperance literature, 110-131
temperance and women's rights, 131-166

Nineteenth-Century American Women Social Activists: Woman's Rights NCLC 310: 169-322
overviews and general studies, 173-270
rights for African American women, 270-300
rights in marriage and divorce, 300-304
right to vote, 304-320

Nineteenth-Century Spanish *Costumbrista* Writers NCLC 304: 239-323
Madrilenian *Costumbrista* writers, 241-77
Andalusian *Costumbrista* writers, 277-322

Noh Drama LC 103: 189-270
overviews, 190-94
origins and development, 194-214
structure, 214-28
types of plays, 228-45
masks in Noh drama, 245-57
Noh drama and the audience, 257-69

Noh Theater CMLC 109: 119-207
overviews and general studies, 120-35
history and development of Noh, 135-71
staging, characters, and themes in Noh theater, 171-207

Noh Theater DC 46: 76-200
overviews and general studies, 79-101
origins and development, 101-18
characters and conventions, 118-36
Noh in performance, 136-81
Noh and society, 182-99

Nonsense Verse CLR 140: 76-126
overviews and general studies, 79-90
Victorian nonsense verse, 90-112
contemporary nonsense verse, 112-25

Norse Mythology CMLC 26: 321-85
history and mythological tradition, 322-44
Eddic poetry, 344-74
Norse mythology and other traditions, 374-85

Norse Mythology CMLC 158: 219-340
general studies: the *Poetic Edda*, 221-45
general studies: the *Prose Edda*, 245-67
the *Eddas*: myths and themes, 267-301
Christian influences on the *Eddas*, 301-03
cross-disciplinary studies of the *Eddas*, 303-39

Northern Humanism LC 16: 281-356
background, 282-305
precursor of the Reformation, 305-14
the Brethren of the Common Life, the Devotio Moderna, and education, 314-40
the impact of printing, 340-56

The Novel of Manners NCLC 56: 342-96
social and political order, 343-53
domestic order, 353-73
depictions of gender, 373-83
the American novel of manners, 383-95

Novels of the Ming and Early Ch'ing Dynasties LC 76: 213-356
overviews and historical development, 214-45
major works—overview, 245-85
genre studies, 285-325
cultural and social themes, 325-55

Nuclear Literature: Writings and Criticism in the Nuclear Age TCLC 46: 288-390
overviews and general studies, 290-301
fiction, 301-35
poetry, 335-45
nuclear war in Russo-Japanese literature, 338-55
nuclear war and women writers, 355-67
the nuclear referent and literary criticism, 367-88

Occultism in Modern Literature TCLC 50: 362-406
influence of occultism on literature, 363-72
occultism, literature, and society, 372-87
fiction, 387-96
drama, 396-405

Opium and the Nineteenth-Century Literary Imagination NCLC 20: 250-301
original sources, 250-62
historical background, 262-71
and literary society, 271-9
and literary creativity, 279-300

Orientalism NCLC 96: 149-364
overviews and general studies, 150-98
Orientalism and imperialism, 198-229
Orientalism and gender, 229-59
Orientalism and the nineteenth-century novel, 259-321
Orientalism in nineteenth-century poetry, 321-63

Orphan Stories CLR 137: 90-167
overviews and general studies, 93-123
Dickensian orphan stories, 123-41
moral, colonialist, and naturalist themes in orphan stories, 141-67

Overpopulation in Nineteenth-Century Literature NCLC 184: 108-246
overviews, 110-34
literary representations of social and economic theories, 134-205
regulation of the body, 205-46

The Oxford Movement NCLC 72: 1-197
overviews and general studies, 2-24
background, 24-59
and education, 59-69
religious responses, 69-128
literary aspects, 128-178
political implications, 178-196

Pandemic Literature: Responses to Pestilence in the Contemporary World CLC 483: 1-311
primary sources, 6-13
engaging history in pandemic literature, 13-60
mixing genres in pandemic literature, 60-92
alterity, race, nation, and empire in pandemic literature, 92-147
public health and biopolitics, 147-82
environmental catastrophe and the post-human, 182-212
HIV/AIDS narratives as pandemic literature, 212-46
plague and pandemic as metaphor, 246-308

The Parnassian Movement NCLC 72: 198-241
overviews and general studies, 199-231
and epic form, 231-38
and positivism, 238-41

Pastoral Literature of the English Renaissance LC 59: 171-282
overviews and general studies, 172-214
principal figures of the Elizabethan period, 214-33
principal figures of the later Renaissance, 233-50
pastoral drama, 250-81

Penny Dreadfuls CLR 105: 123-93
overviews and general studies, 125-63
critical reviews of penny dreadfuls featuring Jack Sheppard, 163-80
penny dreadful authors and publishers, 180-93

Perceptions and Representations of Domestic Violence in Ancient Greek and Roman Literature CMLC 239: 97-301
primary sources, 101-06
defining domestic violence and rape: legal and rhetorical texts, 106-49
documenting rape: histories and biographies, 149-76
representing domestic violence: mythology, literature, and artifacts, 176-298

Periodicals, Nineteenth-Century American NCLC 132: 199-374
overviews, chronology, and development, 200-41
literary periodicals, 241-83
regional periodicals, 283-317
women's magazines and gender issues, 317-47
minority periodicals, 347-72

Periodicals, Nineteenth-Century British NCLC 24: 100-65
overviews and general studies, 100-30
in the Romantic Age, 130-41
in the Victorian era, 142-54
and the reviewer, 154-64

Physiognomy in Nineteenth-Century Literature NCLC 212: 269-361
overviews, 271-329
women authors, 329-40
theater, 340-60

Picaresque Literature of the Sixteenth and Seventeenth Centuries LC 78: 223-355
context and development, 224-71
genre, 271-98
the picaro, 299-326
the picara, 326-53

Picture Books CLR 142: 65-147
overviews and general studies, 68-116
multicultural picture books, 116-40
literary aspects of picture books, 140-47

Pilgrimage Literature CMLC 115: 233-393
overviews and themes, 234-300
major authors and works, 300-72
pilgrimage in travel writing, 372-91

Plath, Sylvia, and the Nature of Biography CLC 86: 433-62
the nature of biography, 433-52
reviews of *The Silent Woman*, 452-61

Poetomachia LC 193: 239-338
the quarrel, 240-55
the plays, 255-338

Policing Blackness: Contemporary American Literary Responses to Institutional Racism CLC 487:1-304
  primary sources, 5-8
  the novel, 8-67
  film, 67-145
  drama, 145-53
  poetry, 153-72
  music, 172-200
  memoir and nonfiction, 201-87
  young adult literature, 287-96
  social media, 296-303

The Political Novel TCLC 234: 1-127
  overviews, 3-30
  major authors and works, 30-63
  African American political novels, 64-92
  the political novel abroad, 92-126

Political Theory from the 15th to the 18th Century LC 36: 1-55
  overview, 1-26
  natural law, 26-42
  empiricism, 42-55

Polish Romanticism NCLC 52: 305-71
  overviews and general studies, 306-26
  major figures, 326-40
  Polish Romantic drama, 340-62
  influences, 362-71

Politics and Literature TCLC 94: 138-61
  overviews and general studies, 139-96
  Europe, 196-226
  Latin America, 226-48
  Africa and the Caribbean, 248-60

Pornography, Nineteenth-Century NCLC 144: 108-202
  nineteenth-century pornographers, 110-64
  pornography and literature, 164-91
  pornography and censorship, 191-201

The Portrayal of Mormonism NCLC 96: 61-148
  overview, 63-72
  early Mormon literature, 72-100
  Mormon periodicals and journals, 100-10
  women writers, 110-22
  Mormonism and nineteenth-century literature, 122-42
  Mormon poetry, 142-47

Post-apartheid Literature CLC 187: 284-382
  overviews and general studies, 286-318
  the post-apartheid novel, 318-65
  post-apartheid drama, 365-81

Post-Bellum, Pre-Harlem Literature TCLC 438: 1-300

Postcolonial African Literature TCLC 146: 110-239
  overviews and general studies, 111-45
  ideology and theory, 145-62
  postcolonial testimonial literature, 162-99
  major authors, 199-239

Postcolonialism TCLC 114: 134-239
  overviews and general studies, 135-53
  African postcolonial writing, 153-72
  Asian/Pacific literature, 172-78
  postcolonial literary theory, 178-213
  postcolonial women's writing, 213-38
  TCLC 254: 178-302
  overviews and postcolonial literary theory, 180-99
  major postcolonial authors, 199-279
  themes and regions in postcolonial literature, 279-302

Postcolonial Literature: Asia and Africa CLC 336: 186-271
  postcolonial literary theory, 188-223
  the postcolonial novel in Africa, 223-49
  the postcolonial novel in Asia, 249-71

Postmodernism TCLC 90:125-307
  overview, 126-166
  criticism, 166-224
  fiction, 224-282
  poetry, 282-300
  drama, 300-307

Poverty and Wealth in Eighteenth-Century English Literature LC 131:192-291
  overview, 193-99
  Defoe and the Augustans, 199-239
  the novel and sensibility, 239-67
  poetry and Pre-romanticism, 267-90

Pragmatism in Nineteenth-Century Literature NCLC 168: 85-209
  overviews, 86-133
  pragmatism and literature, 133-52
  Charles Sanders Peirce, 152-65
  William James, 165-208

Pre-Raphaelite Movement NCLC 20: 302-401
  overview, 302-4
  genesis, 304-12
  Germ and *Oxford and Cambridge Magazine*, 312-20
  Robert Buchanan and the "Fleshly School of Poetry," 320-31
  satires and parodies, 331-4
  surveys, 334-51
  aesthetics, 351-75
  sister arts of poetry and painting, 375-94
  influence, 394-9

The Pre-Raphaelites NCLC 196: 98-239
  overview, 100-24
  sources of inspiration, 124-55
  women and sexuality, 156-223
  impact on individual works, 223-39

Pre-romanticism LC 40: 1-56
  overviews and general studies, 2-14
  defining the period, 14-23
  new directions in poetry and prose, 23-45
  the focus on the self, 45-56

The Presentation of Literature in the Nineteenth Century NCLC 160: 159-226
  book design, 160-71
  gift books, 172-91
  serial novels, 191-214
  dime novels, 214-226

Presidential Memoirs, Contemporary CLC 272
  general commentary, 177-79
  Presidents' memoirs, 179-208
  First Ladies' memoirs, 208-17
  candidates' memoirs, 217-44

Pre-Socratic Philosophy CMLC 22: 1-56
  overviews and general studies, 3-24
  the Ionians and the Pythagoreans, 25-35
  Heraclitus, the Eleatics, and the Atomists, 36-47
  the Sophists, 47-55

The Prison in Nineteenth-Century Literature NCLC 116: 241-357
  overview, 242-60
  romantic prison, 260-78
  domestic prison, 278-316
  America as prison, 316-24
  physical prisons and prison authors, 324-56

Prophesy in Nineteenth-Century Literature NCLC 204: 97-165
  American literature, 98-119
  English Romantic poetry, 119-65

Prostitution in Nineteenth-Century Literature NCLC 192: 218-338
  overview, 220-32
  prostitution and women's identity, 232-79
  prostitution as a moral and social concern, 279-306
  prostitutes as "other," 306-37

Protestant Hagiography and Martyrology LC 84: 106-217
  overview, 106-37
  John Foxe's *Book of Martyrs*, 137-97
  martyrology and the feminine perspective, 198-216

Protestant Reformation, Literature of the LC 37: 1-83
  overviews and general studies, 1-49
  humanism and scholasticism, 49-69
  the reformation and literature, 69-82

Psychoanalysis and Literature TCLC 38: 227-338
  overviews and general studies, 227-46
  Freud on literature, 246-51
  psychoanalytic views of the literary process, 251-61
  psychoanalytic theories of response to literature, 261-88
  psychoanalysis and literary criticism, 288-312
  psychoanalysis as literature/literature as psychoanalysis, 313-34

Pulp Fiction TCLC 214: 135-260
  overviews and general studies, 136-61
  pulp magazines, 161-93
  gender and pulp fiction, 193-219
  science fiction and pulp, 219-40
  detective pulp fiction, 240-59

Pulp Fiction, Contemporary CLC 264: 241-367
  overviews and general studies, 242-71
  new pulp fiction, 271-98
  pulp from overseas, 298-330
  women's pulp fiction, 330-67

The Quarrel between the Ancients and the Moderns LC 63: 266-381
  overviews and general studies, 267-301
  Renaissance origins, 301-32
  Quarrel between the Ancients and the Moderns in France, 332-58
  Battle of the Books in England, 358-80

Race in American Comics CLC 508: 81-290
  theories of graphic media and form, 89-106
  cartoons and comic strips, 106-30
  graphic representations of historical events and eras, 130-224
  superheroes as reflections of race and culture, 224-64
  graphic memoirs, 264-87

Race in Early Modern English Literature LC 326: 1-298

Racism in Literature TCLC 138: 257-373
  overviews and general studies, 257-326
  racism and literature by and about African Americans, 292-326
  theme of racism in literature, 326-773

The Railroad in Nineteenth-Century Literature NCLC 184: 247-372
  overviews, 249-80
  symbolism, 280-314
  La Bête humaine and *Anna Karenina*, 314-44
  realism, sensationalism, and the railroad, 344-71

Rap Music CLC 76: 477-50

Reader-Response Criticism TCLC 146: 240-357
  overviews and general studies, 241-88
  critical approaches to reader response, 288-342
  reader-response interpretation, 342-57

Reader Response Theory TCLC 270:106-73

theories of reader response: a review of the literature, 108-24
the emotional response of the reader, 124-45
reading strategy, 145-52
empirical studies of reader response, 152-73

Realism in Children's Literature CLR 136: 45-98
overviews and general studies, 48-57
narrative voice in realistic fiction for children, 57-75
realism and historical fiction for children, 75-98

Realism in Short Fiction SSC 63: 128-57
overviews and general studies, 129-37
realist short fiction in France, 137-62
realist short fiction in Russia, 162-215
realist short fiction in England, 215-31
realist short fiction in the United States, 231-56

Regionalism and Local Color in Short Fiction SSC 65: 160-289
overviews and general studies, 163-205
regionalism/local color fiction of the west, 205-42
regionalism/local color fiction of the midwest, 242-57
regionalism/local color fiction of the south, 257-88

Regionalism and Local Color in Nineteenth-Century Literature NCLC 188: 174-339
women, regionalism, and local color, 177-225
Midwestern literature, 225-48
New England literature, 248-89
Southern literature, 289-339

Religion in Children's Literature CLR 121: 66-153
overviews and general studies, 69-103
religious values and didacticism in children's literature, 103-23
presentation of spirituality in children's literature, 123-33
religious themes in specific works of children's literature, 133-53

Renaissance Depictions of Islam LC 137: 256-362
overview, 258-70
travelers and captives, 270-85
religious contrasts, 286-342
English Renaissance views, 342-61

Renaissance Natural Philosophy LC 27: 201-87
cosmology, 201-28
astrology, 228-54
magic, 254-86

Renaissance Neoplatonism LC 181: 110-222
overview, 112-122
Neoplatonism in literature, 122-95
the Cambridge Platonists, 195-222

Renaissance Numerology PC 169: 79-166
overviews and general studies, 82-94
numerology in Edmund Spenser, 94-139
numerology in William Shakespeare, 139-148
numerology in George Herbert, 148-152
numerology in John Milton, 152-164

Renaissance Tragicomedy LC 169: 130-238
overviews, 132-50
sociopolitical context, 150-88
English tragicomedy, 188-214
European tragicomedy, 214-37

Renaissance Views of Kingship LC 133: 270-369
philosophical and historical views 272-305
literary views 305-68

Representations of Africa in Nineteenth-Century Literature NCLC 148: 248-351
overview, 251-66
Northeast and Central Africa, 266-76
South Africa, 276-301
West Africa, 301-49

Representations of India in Early Modern Literature LC 195: 193-301
overviews, 195-244
ideology and the view of India, 244-73
images of and by Women, 273-301

Representations of the Devil in Nineteenth-Century Literature NCLC 100: 89-223
overviews and general studies, 90-115
the Devil in American fiction, 116-43
English romanticism: the satanic school, 143-89
Luciferian discourse in European literature, 189-222

Republican Era Chinese Fiction TCLC 270: 174-298
overview and general studies, 175-91
major authors and works of Chinese fiction, 191-236
women Chinese fiction writers, 236-97

Responses to 9/11 in Short Fiction SSC 318: 181-296

Restoration Drama LC 21: 184-275
general overviews and general studies, 185-230
Jeremy Collier stage controversy, 230-9
other critical interpretations, 240-75

The Restoration Rake LC 140: 240-352
overviews 241-77
the philosophical and political rake 277-309
Rochester: the model rake 309-31
variations on the rake 331-51

Revenge Tragedy LC 71: 113-242
overviews and general studies, 113-51
Elizabethan attitudes toward revenge, 151-88
the morality of revenge, 188-216
reminders and remembrance, 217-41

Revising the Literary Canon CLC 81: 465-509

Revising the Literary Canon TCLC 114: 240-84
overviews and general studies, 241-85
canon change in American literature, 285-339
gender and the literary canon, 339-59
minority and third-world literature and the canon, 359-84

Revolutionary Astronomers LC 51: 314-65
overviews and general studies, 316-25
principal figures, 325-51
Revolutionary astronomical models, 352-64

Robin Hood, Legend of LC 19: 205-58
origins and development of the Robin Hood legend, 206-20
representations of Robin Hood, 220-44
Robin Hood as hero, 244-56

Roman Drama CMLC 92: 252-374
overviews, 254-85
style and characteristics, 286-310
Roman comedy, 310-44
Roman drama, 344-73

Roman Historiography CMLC 106: 189-383
overviews, 190-239
major historians, 239-340
the place of history in Rome, 340-83

Romance Fiction, Contemporary CLC 206: 178-271
overviews, 180-93
literary conventions, 193-215
opposing viewpoints, 215-20
reader response to Romance literature, 220-37
Romance literature in the world, 237-70

Romance Fiction in the Twentieth Century TCLC 198: 236-341
overviews and general studies, 237-57
literary conventions, 257-72
reading and interpretation, 272-99
social and cultural response, 299-323
"scorned literature," 323-40

Romantic Literary Criticism NCLC 144: 203-357
background and overviews, 205-30
literary reviews, 230-38
the German Romantics, 238-81
Wordsworth and Coleridge, 281-326
variations on Romantic critical theory, 326-56

Romanticism: German and British Crosscurrents NCLC 295: 1-174
two Romanticisms: a general comparison, 6-96
William Wordsworth: a case study, 96-101
Romanticism in art, science, and music, 101-17
stylistic and thematic parallels, 117-60
German reception of British works, 160-72

Rushdie, Salman, Satanic Verses Controversy CLC 55: 214-63; 59:404-56

Russian Émigré Literature TCLC 242: 169-331
overviews and general studies, 171-93
the first wave of Russian émigré literature, 193-215
the second and third waves of Russian émigré literature, 215-34
representative figures, 234-75
representative themes, 275-330

Russian Nihilism NCLC 28: 403-47
definitions and overviews, 404-17
women and Nihilism, 417-27
literature as reform: the Civic Critics, 427-33
Nihilism and the Russian novel: Turgenev and Dostoevsky, 433-47

Russian Poets of the Soviet Era TCLC 282: 221-345
overviews, 222-42
major authors, 242-300
women and gender, 300-44

Russian Thaw TCLC 26: 189-247
literary history of the period, 190-206
theoretical debate of socialist realism, 206-11
Novy Mir, 211-7
Literary Moscow, 217-24
Pasternak, *Zhivago*, and the Nobel prize, 224-7
poetry of liberation, 228-31
Brodsky trial and the end of the Thaw, 231-6
achievement and influence, 236-46

Saladin in Middle Eastern and European Literature and Film CMLC 157: 243-342
life of Saladin, 245-273
Saladin in Middle Eastern literature and film, 273-314
Saladin in western literature and film, 315-41

Salem Witch Trials LC 38: 1-145
overviews and general studies, 2-30
historical background, 30-65
judicial background, 65-78
the search for causes, 78-115
the role of women in the trials, 115-44

Salinger, J. D., Controversy Surrounding *In Search of J. D. Salinger* CLC 55: 325-44

Samizdat Literature TCLC 150: 261-342
overviews and general studies, 262-64

history and development, 264-309
politics and Samizdat, 309-22
voices of Samizdat, 322-42

San Francisco Renaissance Poetry TCLC 250: 241-323
overviews, 242-72
primary poets of the San Francisco Renaissance, 272-322

Sanitation Reform, Nineteenth-Century NCLC 124: 165-257
overviews and general studies, 166
primary texts, 186-89
social context, 189-221
public health in literature, 221-56

School Stories CLR 128: 111-73
overviews and general studies, 114-23
boys' school stories, 123-46
girls' school stories, 146-73

Science and Modern Literature TCLC 90: 308-419
overviews and general studies, 295-333
fiction, 333-95
poetry, 395-405
drama, 405-19

Science in Nineteenth-Century Literature NCLC 100: 224-366
overviews and general studies, 225-65
major figures, 265-336
sociopolitical concerns, 336-65

Science Fiction Film Adaptations TCLC 202: 221-339
overviews and general studies 223-81
major science fiction films 281-315
text and representation 315-38

Science Fiction, Nineteenth-Century NCLC 24: 241-306
background, 242-50
definitions of the genre, 251-56
representative works and writers, 256-75
themes and conventions, 276-305
NCLC 200: 160-224
creators and creation, 162-78
responses to scientific advances, 178-224

Science Fiction Short Stories SSC 127: 125-387
roots in the nineteenth century, 129-164
overviews and major themes, 164-217
major authors and works, 217-88
the magazines, 288-336
science fiction and gender, 336-86

Scottish Chaucerians LC 20: 363-412

The Scottish Enlightenment LC 179: 197-314
overview, 199-214
major figures, 214-49
theories and ideas, 249-88
influence on literature, 288-313

Scottish Novelists, Contemporary See Contemporary Scottish Novelists

Scottish Poetry, Eighteenth-Century LC 29: 95-167
overviews and general studies, 96-114
the Scottish Augustans, 114-28
the Scots Vernacular Revival, 132-63
Scottish poetry after Burns, 163-66

Scottish Renaissance TCLC 234: 128-210
overviews, 129-76
major figures, 176-210

The Sea in Literature TCLC 82: 72-191
drama, 73-9
poetry, 79-119
fiction, 119-91

The Sea in Nineteenth-Century English and American Literature NCLC 104: 265-362
overviews and general studies, 267-306
major figures in American sea fiction—Cooper and Melville, 306-29
American sea poetry and short stories, 329-45
English sea literature, 345-61

The Sensation Novel NCLC 80: 219-330
overviews and general studies, 221-46
principal figures, 246-62
nineteenth-century reaction, 262-91
feminist criticism, 291-329

Sentimental Comedy LC 192: 214-328
overviews, 215-38
theories of sentimental comedy, 238-60
early sentimental comedies, 260-99
The Conscious Lovers and later plays, 299-327

The Sentimental Novel NCLC 60: 146-245
overviews and general studies, 147-58
the politics of domestic fiction, 158-79
a literature of resistance and repression, 179-212
the reception of sentimental fiction, 213-44

September 11 Attacks See Literature in Response to the September 11 Attacks

Sex and Literature TCLC 82: 192-434
overviews and general studies, 193-216
drama, 216-63
poetry, 263-87
fiction, 287-431

Sexuality in Short Fiction SSC 152: 180-312
performing sexual identity, 181-211
male romantic relationships, 211-39
female sexual freedom, 239-76
sexuality and the national cultural ideal, 276-97
sexuality and the Victorian cultural ideal, 297-311

Sherlock Holmes Centenary TCLC 26: 248-310
Doyle's life and the composition of the Holmes stories, 248-59
life and character of Holmes, 259-78
method, 278-79
Holmes and the Victorian world, 279-92
Sherlockian scholarship, 292-301
Doyle and the development of the detective story, 301-07
Holmes's continuing popularity, 307-09

Short Fiction of World War II SSC 147: 207-325
overviews, 208-31
major authors, 231-80
themes and symbolism, 280-325

Short Science Fiction, Golden Age of, 1938-1950 SSC 73: 1-145
overviews and general studies, 3-48
publishing history of Golden Age Short Science Fiction, 48-65
major Golden Age Short Science Fiction authors and editors
Isaac Asimov, 65-77
Ray Bradbury, 77-92
John W. Campbell, 92-106
Arthur C. Clarke, 106-15
Robert A. Heinlein, 115-29
Damon Knight, 129-40
Frederik Pohl, 141-43

Short-Short Fiction SSC 61: 311-36
overviews and general studies, 312-19
major short-short fiction writers, 319-35

Short Story Cycles SSC 166: 176-343
short story cycles in American literature, 178-227
short story cycles in English literature, 227-44
Asian American and Asian Canadian short story cycles, 244-69
short story cycles in Canadian Literature, 269-304
short story cycles in South African Litterature, 304-21
short story cycles and identity, 321-42

Silver Age of Russian Poetry TCLC 302: 113-224
overview and general study, 118-27
symbolism, 127-49
acmeism, 149-70
futurism, 170-222

The Silver Fork Novel NCLC 88: 58-140
criticism, 59-139

Sixteenth-Century Spanish Poetry LC 194: 183-302
overview, 184-94
classical and humanist influences, 194-227
poetry and Spanish imperialism, 227-73
poetry and mysticism, 273-301

Skaldic Poetry PC 147: 257-340
form and style in Skaldic verse, 260-88
old Norse poetic and religious culture, 288-306
issues in modern Skaldic studies, 306-38

Slave Narratives, American NCLC 20: 1-91
background, 2-9
overviews and general studies, 9-24
contemporary responses, 24-7
language, theme, and technique, 27-70
historical authenticity, 70-5
antecedents, 75-83
role in development of Black American literature, 83-8

The Slave Trade in British and American Literature LC 59: 283-369
overviews and general studies, 284-91
depictions by white writers, 291-331
depictions by former slaves, 331-67

Social Conduct Literature LC 55: 196-298
overviews and general studies, 196-223
prescriptive ideology in other literary forms, 223-38
role of the press, 238-63
impact of conduct literature, 263-87
conduct literature and the perception of women, 287-96
women writing for women, 296-98

Social Protest Literature of Victorian England NCLC 160: 227-359
overviews: protest in Victorian literature, 229-62
woman question, 262-304
condition-of-England novel, 304-58

Social Protest Literature Outside England, Nineteenth-Century NCLC 124: 258-350
overviews and general studies, 259-72
oppression revealed, 272-306
literature to incite or prevent reform, 306-50

Social Realism TCLC 174: 104-229
overviews, 105-43
representative authors, 143-229

Socialism NCLC 88: 141-237
origins, 142-54
French socialism, 154-83
Anglo-American socialism, 183-205
Socialist-Feminism, 205-36

Southern Gothic Literature TCLC 142: 186-270
 overviews and general studies, 187-97
 major authors in southern Gothic literature, 197-230
 structure and technique in southern Gothic literature, 230-50
 themes in southern Gothic literature, 250-70

Southern Literature, Contemporary CLC 167: 1-132
 criticism, 2-131

Southern Literature of the Reconstruction NCLC 108: 289-369
 overview, 290-91
 reconstruction literature: the consequences of war, 291-321
 old south to new: continuities in southern culture, 321-68

Southwestern Humor SSC 81: 105-248
 overviews, 106-83
 Mark Twain, 183-97
 George Washington Harris, 197-208
 other major figures, 208-46

The Spanish Civil War in Literature TCLC 174: 230-374
 overviews, 231-47
 major authors, 247-73
 poetry of the Spanish Civil War, 273-302
 the literary context of the Spanish Civil War, 302-43
 literature and politics in the Spanish Civil War, 343-74

Spanish Civil War Literature TCLC 26: 311-85
 topics in, 312-33
 British and American literature, 333-59
 French literature, 359-62
 Spanish literature, 362-73
 German literature, 373-75
 political idealism and war literature, 375-83

Spanish Golden Age Literature LC 23: 262-332
 overviews and general studies, 263-81
 verse drama, 281-304
 prose fiction, 304-19
 lyric poetry, 319-31

Spanish Poetry, Fifteenth-Century See Fifteenth-Century Spanish Poetry

Spanish Poetry, Sixteenth Century See Sixteenth-Century Spanish Poetry

Spanish Romanticism NCLC 232: 222-306
 overviews, 223-87
 drama, 287-305

Sparta in Literature CMLC 70: 145-271
 overviews, 147-61
 Spartan poetry, 161-72
 the Spartan myth, 172-200
 historical background, 200-27
 Spartan society and culture, 227-69

Spasmodic School of Poetry NCLC 24: 307-52
 history and major figures, 307-21
 the Spasmodics on poetry, 321-7
 Firmilian and critical disfavor, 327-39
 theme and technique, 339-47
 influence, 347-51

The Spectator LC 258: 201-322
 formal and stylistic analyses of the *Spectator,* 203-31
 controversy in the *Spectator,* 231-49
 the legacy of the *Spectator,* 249-321

Speculative Fiction in North America, Contemporary CLC 327: 185-259

 surveys of the literature, 187-8
 major authors, 188-213
 imagining an alternative female identity, 213-230
 speculative fiction and technocapitalism, 230-51
 the debate: "popular" fiction or "literary" fiction, 251-8

Sports in Literature TCLC 86: 294-445
 overviews and general studies, 295-324
 major writers and works, 324-402
 sports, literature, and social issues, 402-45

Spy Novels in the Twentieth Century TCLC 182: 239-353
 overviews, 240-53
 major authors and themes, 253-96
 spy novels and history, 296-326
 literary techniques, 326-52

Steinbeck, John, Fiftieth Anniversary of *The Grapes of Wrath* CLC 59: 311-54

The Stream-of-Consciousness Novel TCLC 178: 110-95
 style and development 111-43
 representative authors 134-95

Street Lit CLC 267: 258-348
 overviews, 260-88
 the roots of street lit: Donald Goines and Iceberg Slim, 288-324
 the emergence of contemporary street lit: Sister Souljah, 324-47

Sturm und Drang NCLC 40: 196-276
 definitions, 197-238
 poetry and poetics, 238-58
 drama, 258-75

Struwwelpeter CLR 122: 124-90
 overviews and general studies, 128-45
 impact of "Der Struwwelpeter" on children's literature, 145-71
 alternate versions of "Der Struwwelpeter," 171-90

Suffrage Literature TCLC 214: 261-360
 overviews and general studies, 262-82
 major figures, 282-323
 suffrage on stage, 323-59

Supernatural Fiction in the Nineteenth Century NCLC 32: 207-87
 major figures and influences, 208-35
 the Victorian ghost story, 236-54
 the influence of science and occultism, 254-66
 supernatural fiction and society, 266-86

Supernatural Fiction, Modern TCLC 30: 59-116
 evolution and varieties, 60-74
 "decline" of the ghost story, 74-86
 as a literary genre, 86-92
 technique, 92-101
 nature and appeal, 101-15

Surrealism TCLC 30: 334-406
 history and formative influences, 335-43
 manifestos, 343-54
 philosophic, aesthetic, and political principles, 354-75
 poetry, 375-81
 novel, 381-6
 drama, 386-92
 film, 392-8
 painting and sculpture, 398-403
 achievement, 403-5

Surrealism in Children's Literature CLR 103: 127-200
 overviews and general studies, 130-52

 critical analysis of surrealist children's authors and works, 152-99

Sylvia Beach and Company TCLC 158: 281-370
 overviews and general studies, 282-97
 Shakespeare and Company, 297-314
 the business of publishing, 315-40
 Sylvia Beach and James Joyce, 341-70

Symbolism, Russian TCLC 30: 266-333
 doctrines and major figures, 267-92
 theories, 293-8
 and French Symbolism, 298-310
 themes in poetry, 310-4
 theater, 314-20
 and the fine arts, 320-32

Symbolist Movement, French NCLC 20: 169-249
 background and characteristics, 170-86
 principles, 186-91
 attacked and defended, 191-7
 influences and predecessors, 197-211
 and Decadence, 211-6
 theater, 216-26
 prose, 226-33
 decline and influence, 233-47

Syphilis See Writings on Syphilis in the Early Modern Period

Syrian Authors, Contemporary See Contemporary Syrian Authors

The Tatler LC 256: 247-325
 background and overview, 249-99
 composition of *The Tatler,* 299-312
 criticism in *The Tatler,* 312-24

Television and Literature TCLC 78: 283-426
 television and literacy, 283-98
 reading vs. watching, 298-341
 adaptations, 341-62
 literary genres and television, 362-90
 television genres and literature, 390-410
 children's literature/children's television, 410-25

Temperance in Nineteenth-Century Literature NCLC 196: 240-345
 influences on major literary figures, 242-304
 drama, 304-22
 women's issues, 322-44

Theater of the Absurd TCLC 38: 339-415
 "The Theater of the Absurd," 340-7
 major plays and playwrights, 347-58
 and the concept of the absurd, 358-86
 theatrical techniques, 386-94
 predecessors of, 394-402
 influence of, 402-13

Theater of the Absurd TCLC 226: 274-356
 overviews and major themes, 275-308
 major figures, 308-55

Theater of Cruelty DC 41: 146-248
 Antonin Artaud's Works and Theories, 147-200
 Other Significant Authors and Works, 200-48

Third-Wave Feminism CLC 531: 1-306

Time-Slip Novels CLR 151: 155-93
 overviews and general studies, 158-66
 Canadian and Antipodean time-slip novels, 166-80
 the time-slip novels of E. Nesbit and Rudyard Kipling, 180-92

Time Travel in Literature and Film TCLC 234: 211-358
 overviews, 215-44
 major authors and works, 244-97

H.G. Wells's *Time Machine,* 297-323
    time travel in film, 323-57

Tin Pan Alley See American Popular Song, Golden Age of

Tobacco Culture LC 55: 299-366
    social and economic attitudes toward tobacco, 299-344
    tobacco trade between the old world and the new world, 344-55
    tobacco smuggling in Great Britain, 355-66

Transcendentalism, American NCLC 24: 1-99
    overviews and general studies, 3-23
    contemporary documents, 23-41
    theological aspects of, 42-52
    and social issues, 52-74
    literature of, 74-96

Translation in Children's Literature CLR 135: 112-89
    overviews and general studies, 116-40
    ethics, challenges, and strategies for translating children's works, 140-65
    cultural factors in the translation of children's books, 165-88

Travel Narratives in Contemporary Literature CLC 204: 260-351
    overviews, 261-76
    major authors, 276-311
    modern travel writing, 311-31
    women writers and travel, 331-51

Travel Writing in the Nineteenth Century NCLC 44: 274-392
    the European grand tour, 275-303
    the Orient, 303-47
    North America, 347-91
    NCLC 168: 210-347
    overviews, 212-43
    women's travel writing, 243-311
    other notable travel writers and their works, 312-47

Travel Writing in the Twentieth Century TCLC 30: 407-56
    conventions and traditions, 407-27
    and fiction writing, 427-43
    comparative essays on travel writers, 443-54

Treatment of Death in Children's Literature CLR 101: 152-201
    overviews and general studies, 155-80
    analytical and bibliographical reviews of death in children's literature, 180-97
    death of animals in children's literature, 197-200

Tristan and Isolde Legend CMLC 42: 311-404

Troubadours CMLC 66: 244-383
    overviews, 245-91
    politics, economics, history, and the troubadours, 291-344
    troubadours and women, 344-82

True-Crime Literature CLC 99: 333-433
    history and analysis, 334-407
    reviews of true-crime publications, 407-23
    writing instruction, 424-29
    author profiles, 429-33

Turkish Literature TCLC 274: 86-217
    historical background: the literature of nation formation, 88-107
    women authors and gender issues, 107-23
    major authors, 123-63
    the East-West divide, 163-90
    rewriting the national history, 190-216

Twentieth-Century Danish Literature TCLC 142: 271-344
    major works, 272-84
    major authors, 284-344

Ulysses **and the Process of Textual Reconstruction** TCLC 26:386-416
    evaluations of the new *Ulysses,* 386-94
    editorial principles and procedures, 394-401
    theoretical issues, 401-16

Unconventional Family in Children's Literature CLR 102: 146-213
    overviews and general studies, 149-79
    analytical and bibliographical reviews, 179-97
    types of unconventional families: foster, adopted, homosexual, 197-212

University Wits LC 161: 291-351
    overviews, 293-311
    the dramatists and their works, 311-350

Urban Fantasy CLC 308: 251-320
    general overviews, 253-255
    Political, economic, and historical perspectives reflected in urban fantasy fiction, 256-284
    geographical themes and the importance of place in urban fantasy, 284-320

Urban Fiction See Street Lit

Urban Life in Nineteenth-Century Literature NCLC 172: 249-334
    overviews, 250-77
    urban poetry, 277-304
    urban life and individual identity, 304-34

Utilitarianism NCLC 84: 272-340
    J. S. Mill's Utilitarianism: liberty, equality, justice, 273-313
    Jeremy Bentham's Utilitarianism: the science of happiness, 313-39

Ut pictura poesis LC 176: 264-384
    background and overview, 266-85
    ut pictura poesis in the Renaissance, 285-336
    ut pictura poesis in the eighteenth century, 336-61
    Lessing and his contemporaries, 361-82

Utopianism NCLC 88: 238-346
    overviews: Utopian literature, 239-59
    Utopianism in American literature, 259-99
    Utopianism in British literature, 299-311
    Utopianism and feminism, 311-45

Utopian Children's Literature CLR 153: 110-211
    overviews and general studies, 113-64
    critical theory and utopian children's books, 164-87
    queer utopianism in young adult fiction, 187-211

Utopian Communities NCLC 208: 278-350
    Icaria, 280-90
    transcendental utopias: Brook Farm, Fruitlands, and Walden, 290-331
    Pantisocracy, 331-49

Utopian Literature, Nineteenth-Century NCLC 24: 353-473
    definitions, 354-74
    overviews and general studies, 374-88
    theory, 388-408
    communities, 409-26
    fiction, 426-53
    women and fiction, 454-71

Utopian Literature, Renaissance LC 32: 1-63
    overviews and general studies, 2-25
    classical background, 25-33
    utopia and the social contract, 33-9
    origins in mythology, 39-48
    utopia and the Renaissance country house, 48-52
    influence of millenarianism, 52-62

Vampire in Literature TCLC 46: 391-454
    origins and evolution, 392-412
    social and psychological perspectives, 413-44
    vampire fiction and science fiction, 445-53

The Vampire in Literature and Film TCLC 238: 256-337
    overviews and general studies, 258-76
    major thematic trends, 276-307
    women writers and vampires, 307-29
    vampires in film, 329-36

Vernacular Bibles LC 67: 214-388
    overviews and general studies, 215-59
    the English Bible, 259-355
    the German Bible, 355-88

Victorian Autobiography NCLC 40: 277-363
    development and major characteristics, 278-88
    themes and techniques, 289-313
    the autobiographical tendency in Victorian prose and poetry, 313-47
    Victorian women's autobiographies, 347-62
    NCLC 152: 230-365
    overviews and general studies, 232-61
    autobiography and the self, 261-93
    autobiography and gender, 293-307
    autobiography and class, 307-36
    autobiography and fiction, 336-64

Victorian Critical Theory NCLC 136: 236-379
    overviews and general studies, 237-86
    Matthew Arnold, 286-324
    Walter Pater and aestheticism, 324-36
    other Victorian critics, 336-78

Victorian Fantasy Literature NCLC 60: 246-384
    overviews and general studies, 247-91
    major figures, 292-366
    women in Victorian fantasy literature, 366-83

Victorian Ghost Stories NCLC 220: 103-86
    overviews, 105-25
    background: ghost stories of the early nineteenth century, 125-41
    major authors and significant works, 141-85

Victorian Hellenism NCLC 68: 251-376
    overviews and general studies, 252-78
    the meanings of Hellenism, 278-335
    the literary influence, 335-75

Victorian Illustrated Fiction NCLC 120: 247-356
    overviews and development, 128-76
    technical and material aspects of book illustration, 276-84
    Charles Dickens and his illustrators, 284-320
    William Makepeace Thackeray, 320-31
    George Eliot and Frederic Leighton, 331-51
    Lewis Carroll and John Tenniel, 351-56

Victorian Novel NCLC 32: 288-454
    development and major characteristics, 290-310
    themes and techniques, 310-58
    social criticism in the Victorian novel, 359-97
    urban and rural life in the Victorian novel, 397-406
    women in the Victorian novel, 406-25
    Mudie's Circulating Library, 425-34
    the late-Victorian novel, 434-51

Vietnamese Literature TCLC 102: 322-386

Vietnam War in Literature and Film CLC 91: 383-437
    overview, 384-8
    prose, 388-412

film and drama, 412-24
poetry, 424-35

Vietnam War, Contemporary Literature Arising from the CLC 254: 172-286
overviews, 173-202
representative authors, 202-50
Vietnam war poetry, 250-62
women in Vietnam war literature, 262-86

The Vietnam War in Short Fiction SSC 79: 83-177
overviews and general studies, 84-93
women authors of Vietnam War short fiction, 93-116
Robert Olen Butler: *A Good Scent from a Strange Mountain* (1992), 116-31
Barry Hannah: *Airships* (1978), 131-50
Tim O'Brien: *The Things They Carried* (1990), 150-65
Tobias Wolff: *Back in the World* (1985), 165-69
other authors and works, 169-76

Violence in Literature TCLC 98: 235-358
overviews and general studies, 236-74
violence in the works of modern authors, 274-358

Violence in Nineteenth-Century Literature NCLC 236: 198-326
civilization and law, 200-24
gender and sexuality, 224-53
race and ethnicity, 253-88
violence against women, 288-326

Virtue and Vice in the Middle Ages CMLC 159: 141-340
theology and philosophy of virtue and vice, 145-87
pastoral and instructional literature, 187-297
virtue and vice in poetry and romance, 297-320
medieval drama: miracle, mystery, and morality plays, 321-37

Voices of Immigrants SSC 341: 1-290

Vorticism TCLC 62: 330-426
Wyndham Lewis and Vorticism, 330-8
characteristics and principles of Vorticism, 338-65
Lewis and Pound, 365-82
Vorticist writing, 382-416
Vorticist painting, 416-26

Walt Whitman and Queer Theory NCLC 433: 1-293
early approaches to same-sex desire in Whitman, 8-74
late twentieth-century readings and visions of a gay Whitman, 74-149
twenty-first-century analyses and queer Whitman criticism, 149-291

War in Children's Literature CLR 127: 149-97
overviews and general studies, 152-70
World Wars I and II in children's literature, 170-86
other presentations of war in children's literature, 186-97

The War Novel TCLC 278: 218-330
overview, 219-28
the World War I novel, 228-64
the World War II novel, 264-324
the Vietnam War novel, 324-29

Warfare and Chivalry in the Medieval Epic CMLC 154: 127-284
overviews and general studies, 130-245
medieval epic as a record of chivalric warfare, 245-64

influence of the medieval epic on the practice of chivalry, 265-83

Watergate and Journalism TCLC 186: 283-334
overviews 284-304
anonymous sources 304-22
lessons learned 322-33

The Well-Made Play NCLC 80: 331-370
overviews and general studies, 332-45
Scribe's style, 345-56
the influence of the well-made play, 356-69

Welsh Literature TCLC 262: 201-302
overviews, 203-38
major authors, 238-301

West African Literature, Contemporary CLC 317: 234-356
contemporary West African literature: an Introduction
magical realism and the oral tradition
West African women: gender issues and female resistance in literature
themes and motifs in contemporary West African literature

Westerns, Contemporary American CLC 260: 260-382
New Westerns/Anti-Westerns, 263-309
traditional Westerns, 309-17
Native American voices, 317-64
film and television, 364-70
depictions of women in literature of the American West, 370-81

Western Literature in Japan, Nineteenth-Century NCLC 156: 282-352
overviews, 283-305
European literature in Japan, 305-28
American literature in Japan, 328-52

William Shakespeare and His Works in Nineteenth-Century Literature and Culture NCLC 204: 166-340
overviews, 168-92
English poetry, 192-231
Emily Dickinson, 231-59
Herman Melville, 259-72
Charles Dickens, 273-300
Alexander Pushkin, 300-40

Witchcraft NCLC 224: 216-304
overviews, 217-51
society and literature, 251-68
women, 268-304

Women and Medicine NCLC 220: 187-328
overviews, 190-250
the "Doctress," 251-80
major authors and significant works, 280-327

Women in Modern Literature TCLC 94: 262-425
overviews and general studies, 263-86
American literature, 286-304
other national literatures, 304-33
fiction, 333-94
poetry, 394-407
drama, 407-24

Women in Old Norse Sagas CMLC 139: 275-347
overview, 278-95
women and the transmission of saga literature, 295-302
women and christianity in the sagas, 302-28
the vengeful woman in the sagas, 328-32
the characterization of women in the sagas, 332-45

Women Philosophers of the Eighteenth Century LC 187: 184-308
the philosophers, 186-267
critiques of male thinkers, 267-308

Women Philosophers of the Seventeenth Century LC 185: 226-329
overviews, 228-42
the philosophers, 242-97
relationships with male contemporaries, 297-314
gender, philosophy, and science, 314-28

Women Playwrights, Nineteenth-Century NCLC 200: 225-334
European authors, 227-65
North American authors, 265-334

Women Writers, Seventeenth-Century LC 30: 2-58
overview, 2-15
women and education, 15-9
women and autobiography, 19-31
women's diaries, 31-9
early feminists, 39-58

Women's Autobiographical Writing TCLC 222: 246-393
overviews, 247-86
individual authors and works, 287-332
the mother in women's autobiography, 332-55
foreign autobiographies, 355-92

Women's Autobiography, Nineteenth Century NCLC 76: 285-368
overviews and general studies, 287-300
autobiographies concerned with religious and political issues, 300-15
autobiographies by women of color, 315-38
autobiographies by women pioneers, 338-51
autobiographies by women of letters, 351-68

Women's Diaries, Nineteenth-Century NCLC 48: 308-54
overview, 308-13
diary as history, 314-25
sociology of diaries, 325-34
diaries as psychological scholarship, 334-43
diary as autobiography, 343-8
diary as literature, 348-53

Women's Periodicals LC 134: 292-382
English women's periodicals: overviews, 293-307
French women's periodicals: overviews, 307-19
early imitators of Addison and Steele, 320-42
The Female Spectator, 342-70
Journal des dames, 370-80

Women's Travel Narratives NCLC 445: 1-290

World War I Literature See Literature of the Great War

World War I Literature TCLC 34: 392-486
overview, 393-403
English, 403-27
German, 427-50
American, 450-66
French, 466-74
and modern history, 474-82

World War I Short Fiction SSC 71: 187-347
overviews and general studies, 187-206
female short fiction writers of World War I, 206-36
Central Powers
Czechoslovakian writers of short fiction, 236-44
German writers of short fiction, 244-61
Entente/Allied Alliance

Australian writers of short fiction, 261-73
English writers of short fiction, 273-305
French writers of short fiction, 305-11
Associated Power: American writers of short fiction, 311-46

World War II Literature TCLC 194: 241-397
overviews, 242-99
the literary response to war and violence, 299-329
wartime propaganda, 329-45
writing from exile, 345-59
World War II drama, 359-97

World War II Women's Writing TCLC 274: 218-305
autobiographical writings, 219-53
World War II women's fiction, 253-79
women and World War II: roles and responses, 279-305

Writers of the Iranian Diaspora CLC 386: 157-322
overviews and general studies, 160-72
literary, political, and cultural context, 172-208
national and transnational identity, 208-41
Iranian diaspora in performance, 241-74
mass media and digital technology, 274-321

Writers of the Lost Generation TCLC 178: 196-369
overviews 197-225
major figures 225-98
women of the Lost Generation 298-341
expatriate writers and Paris 341-68

Writings on Syphilis in the Early Modern Period LC 144: 245-350
overview 247-56
William Clowes' *Short and Profitable Treatise* 256-57
Fracastoro's *Syphilis* 257-89
Medieval and Renaissance Literary Representations of Syphilis 289-333
Eighteenth-Century Literary Representations of Syphilis 333-48

Yellow Journalism NCLC 36: 383-456
overviews and general studies, 384-96
major figures, 396-413

Yiddish Drama DC 61: 117-307
overviews and general studies, 122-48
Yiddish theater and Jewish identity, 148-93
adaptations and cross-cultural influences, 193-279
reviews and performance studies, 279-305

Yiddish Literature TCLC 130: 229-364
overviews and general studies, 230-54
major authors, 254-305
Yiddish literature in America, 305-34
Yiddish and Judaism, 334-64

Young Adult Literature, Contemporary CLC 234: 267-341
general overviews, representative authors, and reviews, 270-83
feminism and young adult literature for young women, 283-305
interviews with YA authors, 305-14
using YA fiction in the classroom, 314-26
religious issues, sexual orientation, and alternative communities in YA lit, 326-41

Young Playwrights Festival
1988 CLC 55: 376-81
1989 CLC 59: 398-403
1990 CLC 65: 444-8

CLR Cumulative Nationality Index

AMERICAN
Aardema, Verna **17**
Aaseng, Nathan **54**
Abbott, Jacob **208**
Adams, Adrienne **73**
Adkins, Jan **7, 77**
Adler, C(arole) S(chwerdtfeger) **78**
Adler, David A. **108**
Adler, Irving **27**
Adoff, Arnold **7**
Alcott, Louisa May **1, 38, 109, 195, 196, 222**
Alda, Arlene **93**
Aldrich, Bess Streeter **70**
Alexander, Lloyd (Chudley) **1, 5, 48, 227**
Alexie, Sherman **179**
Alger, Horatio **87, 170, 221**
Aliki **9, 71**
Allard, Harry **85**
Anaya, Rudolfo **129**
Anderson, Laurie Halse **138, 213**
Anderson, Poul (William) **58**
Angelou, Maya **53, 184, 266**
Anglund, Joan Walsh **1**
Anthony, Piers **118**
Applegate, K. A. **90**
Armstrong, Jennifer **66**
Armstrong, William H(oward) **1, 117**
Arnold, Caroline **61**
Arnosky, James Edward **15, 93**
Aruego, José (Espiritu) **5**
Ashabranner, Brent (Kenneth) **28**
Asimov, Isaac **12, 79**
Atwater, Florence (Hasseltine Carroll) **19**
Atwater, Richard (Tupper) **19**
Avi **24, 68, 188**
Aylesworth, Jim **89**
Aylesworth, Thomas G(ibbons) **6**
Babbitt, Natalie (Zane Moore) **2, 53, 141**
Bacon, Martha Sherman **3**
Baldwin, James **191, 255**
Ballard, Robert D(uane) **60**
Bang, Molly Garrett **8**
Barrett, Judi **98**
Barron, T(homas) A(rchibald) **86**
Baum, L(yman) Frank **15, 107, 216**
Baylor, Byrd **3**
Beagle, Peter S. **220**
Bear, Greg **175**
Bellairs, John (Anthony) **37**
Beller, Susan Provost **106**
Bemelmans, Ludwig **6, 93**
Benary-Isbert, Margot **12**
Bendick, Jeanne **5**
Berenstain, Jan(ice) **19, 150**
Berenstain, Stan(ley) **19, 150**
Berger, Melvin H. **32**
Bess, Clayton **39**
Bethancourt, T. Ernesto **3**
Bishop, Claire Huchet **80**

Block, Francesca Lia **33, 116, 185**
Blos, Joan W(insor) **18**
Blumberg, Rhoda **21**
Blume, Judy (Sussman) **2, 15, 69, 176**
Bogart, Jo Ellen **59**
Bond, Nancy (Barbara) **11**
Bontemps, Arna(ud Wendell) **6**
Bova, Ben(jamin William) **3, 96**
Boyd, Candy Dawson **50**
Boynton, Sandra **105**
Bradbury, Ray **174**
Bradley, Marion Zimmer **158**
Brancato, Robin F(idler) **32**
Branley, Franklyn M(ansfield) **13**
Brashares, Ann **113**
Brett, Jan (Churchill) **27**
Bridgers, Sue Ellen **18, 199**
Bridwell, Norman **96**
Brink, Carol Ryrie **30, 149**
Brooks, Bruce **25**
Brooks, Gwendolyn (Elizabeth) **27**
Brown, Marcia (Joan) **12**
Brown, Marc (Tolon) **29**
Brown, Margaret Wise **10, 107**
Bruchac, Joseph III **46**
Bryan, Ashley F. **18, 66**
Buck, Pearl S. **238**
Bunting, Eve **28, 56, 82, 189**
Burch, Robert J(oseph) **63**
Burnett, Frances (Eliza) Hodgson **24, 122, 182, 215, 231**
Burroughs, Edgar Rice **157**
Burton, Virginia Lee **11**
Butler, Octavia E(stelle) **65, 186**
Byars, Betsy (Cromer) **1, 16, 72**
Cather, Willa **98**
Cabot, Meg **85**
Cadnum, Michael **78**
Caines, Jeannette (Franklin) **24**
Calhoun, Mary **42**
Cameron, Eleanor (Frances) **1, 72**
Cannon, Janell **120**
Card, Orson Scott **116**
Carle, Eric **10, 72**
Carter, Alden R(ichardson) **22**
Cassedy, Sylvia **26**
Catalanotto, Peter **68**
Charlip, Remy **8**
Childress, Alice **14**
Choi, Sook Nyul **53**
Christopher, Matt(hew Frederick) **33, 119**
Ciardi, John (Anthony) **19**
Cisneros, Sandra **123**
Clark, Ann Nolan **16**
Cleary, Beverly (Atlee Bunn) **2, 8, 72, 229**
Cleaver, Bill **6**
Cleaver, Vera (Allen) **6**
Clement, Hal **197**
Clifton, (Thelma) Lucille **5, 251**

Climo, Shirley **69**
Clowes, Daniel **198**
Coatsworth, Elizabeth (Jane) **2**
Cobb, Vicki **2**
Cohen, Daniel (E.) **3, 43**
Cole, Brock **18**
Cole, Joanna **5, 40**
Collier, Christopher **126**
Collier, James Lincoln **3, 126**
Collins, Suzanne **203**
Colum, Padraic **36**
Conford, Ellen **10, 71**
Conrad, Pam **18**
Coolidge, Susan **206**
Cooney, Barbara **23**
Cooper, Floyd **60**
Cooper, James Fenimore **105, 188**
Cooper, Susan **4, 67, 161, 253**
Corbett, Scott **1**
Corcoran, Barbara (Asenath) **50**
Cormier, Robert (Edmund) **12, 55, 167, 243**
Cox, Palmer **24**
Crane, Stephen **132, 272**
Creech, Sharon **42, 89**
Crews, Donald **7**
Cronin, Doreen **105, 136**
Crutcher, Chris(topher C.) **28, 159**
Cummings, Pat (Marie) **48**
Curry, Jane L(ouise) **31**
Curtis, Christopher Paul **68, 172**
Curtis, Jamie Lee **88**
Cushman, Karen **55**
Dalgliesh, Alice **62**
Daly, Maureen **96, 262**
Danziger, Paula **20**
Daugherty, James (Henry) **78**
d'Aulaire, Edgar Parin **21**
d'Aulaire, Ingri (Mortenson Parin) **21**
Davis, Ossie **56**
Day, Alexandra **22**
de Angeli, Marguerite (Lofft) **1**
DeClements, Barthe (Faith) **23**
DeJong, Meindert **1, 73**
Denslow, W(illiam) W(allace) **15**
dePaola, Tomie **4, 24, 81**
Dessen, Sarah **192**
Diaz, David **65**
DiCamillo, Kate **117, 216**
Dillon, Diane (Claire) **44**
Dillon, Leo **44**
Disch, Thomas M(ichael) **18**
Disney, Walt **223**
Dixon, Franklin W. **61**
Dodge, Mary (Elizabeth) Mapes **62**
Domanska, Janina **40**
Donovan, John **3, 183**
Dorris, Michael (Anthony) **58**
Dorros, Arthur (M.) **42**
Draper, Sharon M(ills) **57**

Dr. Seuss **1, 9, 53, 100, 211**
Duke, Kate **51**
Duncan, Lois **29, 129**
Duvoisin, Roger (Antoine) **23**
Eager, Edward (McMaken) **43**
Eastman, Charles Alexander **214**
Ehlert, Lois (Jane) **28**
Ellison, Ralph **197**
Emberley, Barbara A(nne) **5**
Emberley, Ed(ward Randolph) **5, 81**
Engdahl, Sylvia Louise **2**
Enright, Elizabeth (Wright) **4**
Epstein, Beryl (M. Williams) **26**
Epstein, Samuel **26**
Estes, Eleanor (Ruth) **2, 70**
Ets, Marie Hall **33**
Falconer, Ian **90, 146**
Farmer, Philip José **201**
Feelings, Muriel (Lavita Grey) **5**
Feelings, Tom **5, 58**
Ferry, Charles **34**
Field, Rachel (Lyman) **21**
Finley, Martha **148**
Fisher, Aileen (Lucia) **49**
Fisher, Dorothy (Frances) Canfield **71,**
Fisher, Leonard Everett **18**
Fitzgerald, F. Scott **176, 269**
Fitzgerald, John D(ennis) **1**
Fitzhugh, Louise (Perkins) **1, 72, 187**
Flack, Marjorie **28**
Fleischman, (Albert) Sid(ney) **1, 15**
Fleischman, Paul **20, 66**
Fletcher, Ralph **104**
Forbes, Esther **27, 147**
Foster, Genevieve (Stump) **7**
Fox, Paula **1, 44, 96**
Frank, Pat **193**
Freedman, Russell (Bruce) **20, 71**
Freeman, Don **30, 90**
Fritz, Jean (Guttery) **2, 14, 96**
Frost, Robert (Lee) **67**
Fujikawa, Gyo **25**
Gaberman, Judie Angell **33**
Gág, Wanda (Hazel) **4, 150**
Gaiman, Neil **109, 177, 205, 207**
Gaines, Ernest J(ames) **62**
Galdone, Paul **16**
Gallant, Roy A(rthur) **30**
Gammell, Stephen **83**
Gantos, Jack **18, 85**
Garden, Nancy **51, 199**
Gauch, Patricia Lee **56**
Geisel, Theodor Seuss **1, 9, 53, 100, 211**
Geisert, Arthur **87**
George, Jean Craighead **1, 80, 136**
Gerstein, Mordicai **102**
Gibbons, Gail (Gretchen) **8**
Giblin, James Cross **29**
Giovanni, Nikki **6, 73**
Glenn, Mel **51**
Glubok, Shirley (Astor) **1**
Goble, Paul **21**
Goffstein, M(arilyn) B(rooke) **3**
Goodrich, Samuel Griswold **212**
Gordon, Sheila **27**
Gorey, Edward (St. John) **36, 246**
Graham, Lorenz (Bell) **10**
Gramatky, Hardie **22**
Green, John **204**
Greene, Bette **2, 140**
Greene, Constance C(larke) **62**
Greenfield, Eloise **4, 38**
Grifalconi, Ann **35**
Griffin, John Howard **211**
Grimes, Nikki **42**
Gruelle, Johnny **34**
Guy, Rosa (Cuthbert) **13, 137**

Hadley, Lee **40**
Hale, Lucretia Peabody **105**
Haley, Alex **192, 256**
Haley, Gail E(inhart) **21**
Hamilton, Virginia (Esther) **1, 11, 40, 127**
Handler, Daniel **79, 182**
Hansberry, Lorraine **265**
Hansen, Joyce (Viola) **21**
Harris, Joel Chandler **49, 128, 237**
Haskins, James S. **3, 39**
Haugaard, Erik Christian **11, 173**
Hausman, Gerald **89**
Hautman, Pete **176**
Hautzig, Esther Rudomin **22**
Hawthorne, Nathaniel **103, 163, 267**
Haynes, Betsy **90**
Hays, Wilma Pitchford **59**
Haywood, Carolyn **22**
Heide, Florence Parry **60**
Heinlein, Robert A(nson) **75**
Hemingway, Ernest **168, 201**
Henkes, Kevin **23, 108**
Henry, Marguerite **4**
Hentoff, Nat(han Irving) **1, 52**
Hesse, Karen **54, 141**
Highwater, Jamake (Mamake) **17**
Hinton, S(usan) E(loise) **3, 23**
Hitz, Demi **58**
Hoban, Lillian **67**
Hoban, Russell (Conwell) **3, 69, 139, 242**
Hoban, Tana **13, 76**
Hobbie, Holly **88**
Hobbs, Valerie **148**
Hobbs, Will(iam Carl) **59**
Hoberman, Mary Ann **22**
Hoff, Syd(ney) **83**
Hogrogian, Nonny **2, 95**
Holland, Isabelle **57**
Holling, Holling C(lancy) **50**
Hopkins, Lee Bennett **44**
Hopkinson, Deborah **118**
Horvath, Polly **90**
Howe, James **9**
Hughes, Dean **76**
Hughes, (James) Langston **17**
Hunt, Irene **1**
Hurd, Clement (G.) **49**
Hurd, Edith Thacher **49**
Hurmence, Belinda **25**
Hurston, Zora Neale **177**
Hyde, Margaret O(ldroyd) **23**
Hyman, Trina Schart **50**
Irving, Washington **97**
Irwin, Ann(abelle Bowen) **40**
Isadora, Rachel **7**
Jackson, Jesse **28**
James, Henry **189, 255**
Janeczko, Paul B(ryan) **47**
Jarrell, Randall **6, 111**
Jeffers, Susan **30**
Johnson, Angela **33**
Johnson, Crockett **98**
Johnson, James Weldon **32, 247**
Jonas, Ann **12, 74**
Jordan, June **10**
Joyce, William **26**
Juster, Norton **112**
Kadohata, Cynthia **121**
Kalman, Maira **32**
Keats, Ezra Jack **1, 35**
Keller, Holly **45**
Kellogg, Steven (Castle) **6**
Kennedy, X. J. **27**
Kerr, M. E. **29**
Kesey, Ken **170**
Khalsa, Dayal Kaur **30**
Kherdian, David **24**

Kincaid, Jamaica **63**
Kindl, Patrice **132**
King, Martin Luther, Jr. **206**
King, Stephen **124, 194**
Kjelgaard, James Arthur **81**
Klein, Norma **2, 19, 162**
Klevin, Elisa **85**
Knight, David C(arpenter) **38**
Knowles, John **98**
Koller, Jackie French **68**
Konigsburg, E(laine) L(obl) **1, 47, 81**
Kotzwinkle, William **6**
Krauss, Ruth (Ida) **42**
Krasilovsky, Phyllis **83**
Krementz, Jill **5**
Krull, Kathleen **44**
Kuklin, Susan **51**
Kurtz, Jane **123**
Kurtzman, Harvey **209**
Kushner, Donn (J.) **55**
Kuskin, Karla (Seidman) **4**
Lackey, Mercedes **193**
Langstaff, John (Meredith) **3**
Langton, Jane (Gillson) **33**
Lasky, Kathryn **11, 140**
Latham, Jean Lee **50**
Lattany, Kristin (Elaine Eggleston) Hunter **3**
Lauber, Patricia (Grace) **16**
Lavine, Sigmund Arnold **35**
Lawson, Robert **2, 73**
Leaf, (Wilbur) Munro **25**
Lee, Harper **169**
Lee, Stan **207**
Le Guin, Ursula K(roeber) **3, 28, 91, 173**
Leinster, Murray **192**
L'Engle, Madeline (Camp Franklin) **1, 14, 57, 172, 261**
Lenski, Lois **26**
Lerner, Carol **34**
LeShan, Eda J(oan) **6**
Lester, Julius (Bernard) **2, 41, 143**
Levine, Gail Carson **85**
Levithan, David **181**
Levitin, Sonia (Wolff) **53**
Lionni, Leo(nard) **7, 71**
Lipsyte, Robert (Michael) **23, 76**
Livingston, Myra Cohn **7**
Lobel, Arnold (Stark) **5**
Locker, Thomas **14**
London, Jack **108**
Longfellow, Henry Wadsworth **99**
Lovelace, Maud Hart **231**
Lynch, Chris **58**
MacLachlan, Patricia **14**
Maestro, Betsy (Crippen) **45**
Maestro, Giulio **45**
Manley, Seon **3**
Marciano, John Bemelmans **93**
Marrin, Albert **53**
Marshall, James (Edward) **21**
Martin, Ann M(atthews) **32**
Martin, Bill Jr. **97**
Mathers, Petra **76**
Mathis, Sharon Bell **3, 147**
Mayer, Mercer **11**
Mazer, Harry **16**
Mazer, Norma Fox **23**
McCaffrey, Anne (Inez) **49, 130**
McCloskey, (John) Robert **7**
McClung, Robert M(arshall) **11**
McCord, David (Thompson Watson) **9**
McCully, Emily Arnold **46**
McDermott, Gerald (Edward) **9**
McGovern, Ann **50**
McHargue, Georgess **2**
McKillip, Patricia A. **213**
McKinley, (Jennifer Carolyn) Robin **10, 81, 127**

McKissack, Fredrick L(emuel) 55
McKissack, Patricia (L'Ann) C(arwell) 23, 55, 129
McMillan, Bruce 47
Means, Florence Crannell 56
Meigs, Cornelia Lynde 55
Meltzer, Milton 13
Merriam, Eve 14
Merrill, Jean (Fairbanks) 52
Meyer, Stephenie 142, 180
Miller, Arthur 195, 269
Milne, Lorus J. 22
Milne, Margery 22
Minarik, Else Holmelund 33
Mitchell, Margaret 190
Mohr, Nicholasa 22, 209
Monjo, F(erdinand) N(icholas III) 2
Moore, Lilian 15
Mora, Pat(ricia) 58
Morrison, Toni 99, 190, 258
Moser, Barry (A.) 49
Moss, Marissa 134
Mowry, Jess 65
Mukerji, Dhan Gopal 10
Muñoz, Elías Miguel 218
Munsch, Robert (Norman) 19
Murphy, Jim 53
Myers, Christopher 97
Myers, Walter Dean 4, 16, 35, 110, 185, 206, 267
Namioka, Lensey 48
Napoli, Donna Jo 51
Naylor, Gloria 202
Naylor, Phyllis Reynolds 17, 135
Ness, Evaline (Michelow) 6
Neufeld, John (Arthur) 52
Nixon, Joan Lowery 24
Norton, Andre 50, 184
Nourse, Alan E(dward) 33
Numeroff, Laura Joffe 85
Nye, Naomi Shihab 59, 193
O'Brien, Robert C. 2
O'Dell, Scott 1, 16, 126
Oneal, Zibby 13, 169
Orgel, Doris 48
Osborne, Mary Pope 88
Paolini, Christopher 102
Parish, Peggy 22
Park, Barbara 34
Park, Linda Sue 84
Pascal, Francine 25
Patent, Dorothy Hinshaw 19
Paterson, Katherine (Womeldorf) 7, 50, 127, 218
Paulsen, Gary 19, 54, 82
Peck, Richard (Wayne) 15, 142
Peck, Robert Newton 45, 163
Peet, Bill 12
Pene du Bois, William (Sherman) 1
Petersham, Maud (Sylvia Fuller) 24
Petersham, Miska 24
Petry, Ann (Lane) 12, 214
Pfeffer, Susan Beth 11
Pierce, Meredith Ann 20
Pilkey, Dav(id Murray Jr.) 48, 160
Pinkney, Jerry 43
Pinkney, (Jerry) Brian 54
Pinkwater, Daniel Manus 4, 175
Polacco, Patricia Ann 40
Politi, Leo 29
Porter, Eleanor H. 110, 217
Potok, Chaim 92
Prelutsky, Jack 13, 115
Pringle, Laurence P(atrick) 4, 57
Provensen, Alice 11
Provensen, Martin (Elias) 11
Pyle, Howard 22, 117
Quackenbush, Robert 122

Rael, Elsa Okon 84
Ransome, James E. 86
Raskin, Ellen 1, 12
Rathmann, Peggy 77
Rau, Margaret 8
Rawlings, Marjorie Kinnan 63
Rawls, (Woodrow) Wilson 81
Reeder, Carolyn 69
Reiss, Johanna (de Leeuw) 19
Rey, H(ans) A(ugusto) 5, 93
Rey, Margret (Elisabeth) 5, 93
Richards, Laura E(lizabeth Howe) 54
Rinaldi, Ann 46
Ringgold, Faith 30, 174
Riordan, Rick 190
Roberts, Elizabeth Madox 100
Roberts, Willo Davis 95
Robinet, Harriette Gillem 64
Rockwell, Thomas 6
Rodgers, Mary 20
Rohmann, Eric 100
Ryder, Joanne (Rose) 37
Rylant, Cynthia 15, 86, 187
Sachar, Louis 28, 79, 161, 200
Sachs, Marilyn (Stickle) 2
Salinger, J(erome) D(avid) 18, 181
Sanchez, Alex 181
Sanchez, Sonia 18
Sandburg, Carl (August) 67
San Souci, Robert D. 43
Sattler, Helen Roney 24
Sawyer, Ruth 36
Say, Allen 22, 135
Scarry, Richard (McClure) 3, 41
Schlein, Miriam 41
Schulz, Charles M. 188
Schwartz, Alvin 3, 89
Schwartz, Amy 25
Scieszka, Jon 27, 107
Scott, Jack Denton 20
Sebestyen, Ouida 17
Selden, George 8
Selsam, Millicent E(llis) 1
Sendak, Maurice (Bernard) 1, 17, 74, 131, 196
Seredy, Kate 10
Shannon, David 87
Shaw, Janet 96
Shearer, John 34
Shippen, Katherine B(inney) 36
Showers, Paul C. 6
Silverberg, Robert 59
Silverstein, Alvin 25
Silverstein, Shel(don Allan) 5, 96, 232
Silverstein, Virginia B(arbara Opshelor) 25
Simon, Hilda Rita 39
Simon, Seymour 9, 63
Singer, Isaac Bashevis 1
Singer, Marilyn 48
Sleator, William (Warner III) 29, 128
Slote, Alfred 4
Small, David 53
Smalls, Irene 103
Smith, Betty 202
Smith, Jessie Willcox 59
Smith, Lane 47
Smucker, Barbara (Claassen) 10
Sneve, Virginia Driving Hawk 2
Snyder, Zilpha Keatley 31, 121
Sobol, Donald J. 4
Sonnenblick, Jordan 144
Soto, Gary 38
Sparks, Beatrice 139
Speare, Elizabeth George 8
Spier, Peter (Edward) 5
Spinelli, Jerry 26, 82, 200
Spykman, E(lizabeth) C(hoate) 35
Stanley, Diane 46

Staples, Suzanne Fisher 60, 137
Starbird, Kaye 60
Steig, William (H.) 2, 15, 103
Steinbeck, John 172, 194, 195, 251
Steptoe, John (Lewis) 2, 12
Sterling, Dorothy 1
Stevenson, James 17
St. George, Judith 57
Stine, R(obert) L(awrence) 37, 111
St. John, Nicole 46
Stowe, Harriet Beecher 131
Strasser, Todd 11
Stratemeyer, Edward L. 166
Stratton-Porter, Gene 87, 220
Suhl, Yuri (Menachem) 2
Taback, Simms 100
Tafuri, Nancy (E.) 74
Tarkington, Booth 241
Tarry, Ellen 26
Tate, Eleanora E(laine) 37
Taylor, Mildred D(elois) 9, 59, 90, 144, 241
Taylor, Sidney 178
Taylor, Theodore 30
Thomas, Angie 259
Thomas, Ianthe 8
Thomas, Joyce Carol 19
Thompson, Julian F(rancis) 24
Thompson, Kay 22, 98
Tobias, Tobi 4
Tresselt, Alvin 30
Tudor, Tasha 13
Tunis, Edwin (Burdett) 2
Twain, Mark 58, 60, 66, 156, 187, 245, 254, 266
Uchida, Yoshiko 6, 56
Van Allsburg, Chris 5, 13, 113
Vande Velde, Vivian 145
Viorst, Judith 3, 90
Voigt, Cynthia 13, 48, 141
von Ziegesar, Cecily 239
Vonnegut, Kurt 265
Waber, Bernard 55
Walker, Alice 198, 256
Wallace, Barbara Brooks 150
Walter, Mildred Pitts 15, 61
Ward, Jesmyn 222
Ware, Chris 191
Warner, Susan 179, 219
Watkins, Yoko Kawashima 182
Watson, Clyde 3
Weiss, Harvey 4
Wells, Rosemary 16, 69
Wersba, Barbara 3, 78
Westerfeld, Scott 225
Wharton, Edith 136
Whelan, Gloria 90
White, E(lwyn) B(rooks) 1, 21, 107, 238, 272
White, Robb 3
Whitney, Phyllis A(yame) 59
Wibberley, Leonard (Patrick O'Connor) 3
Wiese, Kurt 86
Wiesel, Elie 192
Wiesner, David 43, 84
Wiggin (Riggs), Kate Douglas (Smith) 52, 179
Wilder, Laura (Elizabeth) Ingalls 2, 111, 229
Wilkinson, Brenda 20
Willard, Nancy 5
Willems, Mo 114
Williams, Barbara 48
Williams, Garth (Montgomery) 57
Williams, Jay 8
Williams, Vera B. 9
Williams-Garcia, Rita 36
Willis, Connie 66
Winthrop, Elizabeth 89
Wisniewski, David 51
Wojciechowska, Maia (Teresa) 1

Wolff, Virginia Euwer 62
Wood, Audrey 26
Wood, Don 26
Woodson, Jacqueline (Amanda) 49, 260
Wood, Juen Rae 82
Worth, Valerie 21
Wyeth, N. C. 106
Yang, Gene Luen 178, 246
Yarbrough, Camille 29
Yashima, Taro 4
Yep, Laurence Michael 3, 17, 54, 132
Yolen, Jane (Hyatt) 4, 44, 149, 248
Yorinks, Arthur 20
Young, Ed (Tse-chun) 27
Zalben, Jane Breskin 84
Zelinsky, Paul O. 55
Zim, Herbert S(pencer) 2
Zindel, Paul 3, 45, 85, 186
Zolotow, Charlotte S(hapiro) 2, 77

ANTIGUAN

Kincaid, Jamaica 63

AUSTRALIAN

Baillie, Allan (Stuart) 49
Baker, Jeannie 28
Base, Graeme (Rowland) 22
Brinsmead, H(esba) F(ay) 47
Chapman, Jean 65
Chauncy, Nan(cen Beryl Masterman) 6
Clark, Margaret 99
Clark, Mavis Thorpe 30
Clarke, Judith 61
Crew, Gary 42
Fox, Mem 80
Gleitzman, Morris
Graham, Bob 31
Hathorn, Libby 81
Hilton, Nette 25
Jennings, Paul 40
Kelleher, Victor (Michael Kitchener) 36
Klein, Robin 21
Lindsay, Norman Alfred William 8
Marsden, John 34
Mattingley, Christobel (Rosemary) 24
Nix, Garth 68, 187
Ormerod, Jan(ette Louise) 20
Ottley, Reginald Leslie 16
Phipson, Joan 5
Rodda, Emily 32
Roughsey, Dick 41
Rubinstein, Gillian (Margaret) 35
Southall, Ivan (Francis) 2, 165
Spence, Eleanor (Rachel) 26
Tan, Shaun 184
Thiele, Colin (Milton) 27
Travers, P(amela) L(yndon) 2, 93, 262
Trezise, Percy (James) 41
Vogel, Ilse-Margret 170
Wrightson, (Alice) Patricia 4, 14, 154
Zusak, Markus 250

AUSTRIAN

Bemelmans, Ludwig 6
Donnelly, Elfie 104
Kafka, Franz 193
Noestlinger, Christine 12
Orgel, Doris 48
Salten, Felix 215
Zwerger, Lisbeth 46

BELGIAN

Hergé 6, 114, 241
Vincent, Gabrielle 13

CANADIAN

Bedard, Michael (John) 35
Bell, William 91
Blades, Ann (Sager) 15
Bogart, Jo Ellen 59
Buffie, Margaret 39
Burnford, Sheila (Philip Cochrane Every) 2
Cameron, Eleanor (Frances) 1, 72
Cleaver, Elizabeth (Ann Mrazik) 13
Cox, Palmer 24
Doctorow, Cory 194
Doyle, Brian 22
Ellis, Sarah 42
Gal, Laszlo 61
Gay, Marie-Louise 27
Godfrey, Martyn N. 57
Grey Owl 32, 227
Haig-Brown, Roderick (Langmere) 31
Harris, Christie (Lucy) Irwin 47
Houston, James A(rchibald) 3
Hudson, Jan 40
Hughes, Monica (Ince) 9, 60
Johnston, Julie 41
Katz, Welwyn Wilton 45
Khalsa, Dayal Kaur 30
Korman, Gordon (Richard) 25
Kovalski, Maryann 34
Kropp, Paul 96
Kurelek, William 2, 210
Kushner, Donn (J.) 55
Lawson, Julie 89
Lee, Dennis (Beynon) 3
Little, (Flora) Jean 4
Lunn, Janet (Louise Swoboda) 18
Mackay, Claire 43
Major, Kevin (Gerald) 11
Markoosie 23
Matas, Carol 52
McNicoll, Sylvia 99
Milne, Lorus J. 22
Montgomery, L(ucy) M(aud) 8, 91, 145, 270
Mowat, Farley (McGill) 20, 248
Munsch, Robert (Norman) 19
Nichols, Ruth 149
Oberman, Sheldon 54
o huigin, sean 75
Pearson, Kit 26
Poulin, Stéphane 28
Reid, Barbara (Jane) 64
Richler, Mordecai 17
Roberts, Charles G(eorge) D(ouglas) 33
Seton, Ernest (Evan) Thompson 59
Smucker, Barbara (Claassen) 10
Stren, Patti 5
Taylor, Cora (Lorraine) 63
Wallace, Ian 37
Wynne-Jones, Tim(othy) 21, 58
Yee, Paul (R.) 44

CHILEAN

Allende, Isabel 99, 171
Krahn, Fernando 3

CHINESE

Lord, Bette Bao 151
Namioka, Lensey 48
Young, Ed (Tse-chun) 27

CUBAN

Ada, Alma Flor 62
Muñoz, Elías Miguel 218

CZECH

Comenius, John Amos 191
Kafka, Franz 193
Sasek, Miroslav 4
Sis, Peter 45, 110

DANISH

Andersen, Hans Christian 6, 113
Bodker, Cecil 23
Drescher, Henrik 20
Haugaard, Erik Christian 11, 173
Holm, (Else) Anne (Lise) 75
Michaëlis, Karin 237
Minarik, Else Holmelund 33
Nielsen, Kay (Rasmus) 16

DUTCH

Biegel, Paul 27
Bruna, Dick 7
DeJong, Meindert 1, 73
Haar, Jaap ter 15
Lionni, Leo(nard) 7, 71
Reiss, Johanna (de Leeuw) 19
Schmidt, Annie M. G. 22
Spier, Peter (Edward) 5
Vos, Ida 85

ENGLISH

Adams, Richard (George) 20, 121
Ahlberg, Allan 18, 233
Ahlberg, Janet 18
Aiken, Joan (Delano) 1, 19, 90
Alcock, Vivien 26
Aldiss, Brian W. 197
Allan, Mabel Esther 43
Almond, David 85, 168, 258
Andrews, Julie 85
Ardizzone, Edward (Jeffrey Irving) 3
Arundel, Honor (Morfydd) 35
Ashley, Bernard 4, 189
Awdry, Wilbert Vere 23
Baker, Jeannie 28
Banks, Lynne Reid 86
Banner, Angela 24
Barbauld, Anna Laetitia 160
Barker, Cicely Mary 88
Barklem, Jill 31
Base, Graeme (Rowland) 22
Bawden, Nina (Mary Mabey) 2, 51
Belloc, Hilaire 102, 224
Bianco, Margery Williams 19, 146
Biro, Val 28
Blake, Quentin (Saxby) 31
Blake, William 52
Blyton, Enid (Mary) 31, 204
Bond, (Thomas) Michael 1, 95
Bond, Ruskin 171
Boston, L(ucy) M(aria Wood) 3
Brazil, Angela 157
Breinburg, Petronella 31
Briggs, Raymond (Redvers) 10, 168
Brooke, L(eonard) Leslie 20
Brooks, Kevin 201
Browne, Anthony (Edward Tudor) 19, 156, 254
Browning, Robert 97
Bunyan, John 124
Burnett, Frances (Eliza) Hodgson 24, 122, 182, 215, 231
Burningham, John (Mackintosh) 9
Burton, Hester (Wood-Hill) 1
Caldecott, Randolph (J.) 14, 110
Carroll, Lewis 2, 18, 108, 230
Causley, Charles (Stanley) 30
Chauncy, Nan(cen Beryl Masterman) 6
Chambers, Aidan 151
Clarke, Arthur C. 119
Clarke, Pauline 28
Cooper, Susan (Mary) 4, 67, 161, 253
Corbett, W(illiam) J(esse) 19
Crane, Walter 56
Creech, Sharon 164
Cresswell, Helen 18

Cross, Gillian (Clare) **28**
Crossley-Holland, Kevin (John William) **47, 84**
Cruikshank, George **63**
Dahl, Roald **1, 7, 41, 111, 224**
Defoe, Daniel **61, 164**
de la Mare, Walter (John) **23, 148**
Dhondy, Farrukh **41, 234**
Dickens, Charles **95, 162, 271**
Dickinson, Peter (Malcolm) **29, 125**
Doctorow, Cory **194**
Dodgson, Charles L(utwidge) **2, 18, 108**
Doherty, Berlie **21**
Edgeworth, Maria **153**
Ewing, Juliana (Horatia Gatty) **78**
Farjeon, Eleanor **34**
Farmer, Penelope (Jane) **8**
Fielding, Sarah **253**
Fine, Anne **25, 180**
Foreman, Michael **32**
French, Fiona **37**
Gaiman, Neil **109, 177, 205, 207**
Gardam, Jane (Mary) **12**
Garfield, Leon **21, 166**
Garner, Alan **20, 130**
Gerrard, Roy **23**
Goble, Paul **21**
Godden, (Margaret) Rumer **20**
Godfrey, Martyn N. **57**
Golding, William **94, 130**
Goodall, John S(trickland) **25**
Greenaway, Kate **6, 111**
Grey Owl **32, 227**
Griffiths, Helen **75**
Haddon, Mark **188**
Haig-Brown, Roderick (Langmere) **31**
Hamley, Dennis **47**
Handford, Martin (John) **22**
Harris, Rosemary (Jeanne) **30**
Henty, G(eorge) A(lfred) **76, 249**
Herriot, James **80**
Hill, Eric **13**
Howker, Janni **14**
Hughes, Monica (Ince) **9, 60**
Hughes, Shirley **15**
Hughes, Ted **3, 131**
Hughes, Thomas **160**
Hutchins, Pat **20**
Huxley, Aldous (Leonard) **151**
Jacques, Brian **21**
Jefferies, Richard **217**
Jones, Diana Wynne **23, 120**
Keeping, Charles (William James) **34**
Kelleher, Victor (Michael Kitchener) **36**
Kemp, Gene **29**
Kingsley, Charles **77, 167, 234**
King-Smith, Dick **40**
Kipling, (Joseph) Rudyard **39, 65, 83, 199, 212, 257, 259**
Klause, Annette Curtis **104**
Laird, Elizabeth (Mary Risk) **65**
Lear, Edward **1, 75, 169**
Lewis, C(live) S(taples) **3, 27, 109, 173, 242**
Lively, Penelope (Margaret) **7, 159**
Lofting, Hugh (John) **19, 143**
Macaulay, David (Alexander) **3, 14**
Mark, Jan(et Marjorie) **11**
Masefield, John **164**
Mayne, William (James Carter) **25, 123**
McBratney, Sam **44**
McCaughrean, Geraldine **38**
McKean, Dave **186**
McKee, David (John) **38**
McNaughton, Colin **54**
Milligan, Spike **92**
Milne, A(lan) A(lexander) **1, 26, 108, 226, 270**
Mole, John **61**
Molesworth, Mary Louisa **102, 166**
Moorcock, Michael **203**
Moore, Alan **209**
Morpurgo, Michael **51**
Murphy, Jill (Frances) **39**
Naidoo, Beverley **29**
Needle, Jan **43**
Nesbit, E(dith) **3, 70, 252**
Newbery, John **147**
Nicholson, William **76**
Nimmo, Jenny **44**
Norton, Mary **6, 140**
Oakley, Graham **7**
Orwell, George **68, 171, 196**
Ottley, Reginald Leslie **16**
Ouida **208**
Owen, Gareth **31**
Oxenbury, Helen **22, 70**
Paton Walsh, Gillian (Jill) **2, 65, 128**
Peyton, K. M. **3**
Pienkowski, Jan (Michal) **6**
Potter, (Helen) Beatrix **1, 19, 73, 165, 213**
Pratchett, Terry **64, 225**
Pullman, Philip (Nicholas) **20, 62, 84, 202**
Rackham, Arthur **57**
Ransome, Arthur (Michell) **8, 215**
Rayner, Mary **41**
Reed, Talbot Baines **76**
Reid Banks, Lynne **24**
Rosen, Michael (Wayne) **45**
Rossetti, Christina **115**
Rowling, J(oanne) K(athleen) **66, 80, 112, 183, 235**
Rushdie, Salman **125**
Serraillier, Ian (Lucien) **2**
Sewell, Anna **17, 219**
Sharp, Margery **27**
Shelley, Mary Wollstonecraft **133**
Shepard, Ernest Howard **27**
Simmonds, Posy **23**
Streatfeild, (Mary) Noel **17, 83**
Stroud, Jonathan **134**
Sutcliff, Rosemary **1, 37, 138**
Swift, Jonathan **53, 161**
Tenniel, John **18, 146, 243**
Tolkien, J(ohn) R(onald) R(euel) **56, 152, 236**
Tomlinson, Theresa **60**
Townsend, John Rowe **2**
Travers, P(amela) L(yndon) **2, 93, 262**
Trease, (Robert) Geoffrey **42**
Treece, Henry **2**
Turner, Philip **89**
Ure, Jean **34**
Walsh, Jill Paton **2, 65**
Wells, H(erbert) G(eorge) **64, 133, 200, 250**
Westall, Robert (Atkinson) **13, 177**
White, T(erence) H(anbury) **139**
Wildsmith, Brian **2, 52**
Willard, Barbara (Mary) **2**
Williams, Kit **4**
Wyndham, John **190**
Yeoman, John **46**
Yonge, Charlotte Mary **210**
Zephaniah, Benjamin **220**

FILIPINO

Aruego, José (Espiritu) **5**

FINNISH

Jansson, Tove Marika **2, 125**
Unnerstad, Edith (Totterman) **36**

FRENCH

Aymé, Marcel (Andre) **25**
Belloc, Hilaire **102, 224**
Berna, Paul **19**
Billout, Guy (Rene) **33**
Boutet de Monvel, (Louis) M(aurice) **32**
Brunhoff, Jean de **4, 116**
Brunhoff, Laurent de **4, 116**
Dumas, Alexandre (père) **134, 205, 257, 271**
Goscinny, René **37, 198**
Guillot, Rene **22**
Perrault, Charles **79, 134, 203**
Saint-Exupéry, Antoine (Jean Baptiste Marie Roger) de **10, 142, 229**
Uderzo, Albert **37**
Ungerer, Tomi **3, 77**
Verne, Jules **88, 212, 232**

GERMAN

Baumann, Hans **35**
Benary-Isbert, Margot **12**
d'Aulaire, Edgar Parin **21**
Ende, Michael (Andreas Helmuth) **14, 138**
Frank, Anne **101, 189**
Funke, Cornelia **145**
Grimm, Jacob **112**
Grimm, Wilhelm **112**
Haenel, Wolfram **64**
Hartling, Peter **29**
Hauff, Wilhelm **155**
Heine, Helme **18**
Hoffmann, E. T. A. **133**
Hoffmann, Heinrich **70**
Janosch **26**
Kaestner, Erich **4, 153**
Kruess, James **9**
Levitin, Sonia (Wolff) **53**
Remarque, Erich Maria **159**
Rey, H(ans) A(ugusto) **5**
Rey, Margret (Elisabeth) **5**
Richter, Hans Peter **21**
Vogel, Ilse-Margret **170**
Wilhelm, Hans **46**
Zimnik, Reiner **3**

GREEK

Aesop **14, 115**
Zei, Alki **6**

HUNGARIAN

Biro, Val **28**
Gal, Laszlo **61**
Galdone, Paul **16**
Seredy, Kate **10**

INDIAN

Bond, Ruskin **171**
Desai, Anita **249**
Dhondy, Farrukh **41, 234**
Mukerji, Dhan Gopal **10**

IRANIAN

Satrapi, Marjane **185**

IRISH

Colfer, Eoin **112**
Colum, Padraic **36**
Daly, Maureen **96, 262**
Dillon, Eilis **26**
Doyle, Malachy **83**
Goldsmith, Oliver **208**
Lewis, C(live) S(taples) **3, 27, 109, 173, 242**
Lynch, Patricia **167**
Meade, L.T. **163, 236**
O'Shea, (Catherine) Pat(ricia Shiels) **18**
Shaw, George Bernard **252**
Stoker, Bram **178**
Swift, Jonathan **53, 161**
Wilde, Oscar **114, 264**

ISRAELI

Ofek, Uriel **28**
Orlev, Uri **30, 191**
Shulevitz, Uri **5, 61**

ITALIAN
Collodi, Carlo **5, 120**
Innocenti, Roberto **56, 126**
Munari, Bruno **9**
Rodari, Gianni **24**
Ventura, Piero (Luigi) **16**

JAMAICAN
Berry, James **22, 143**

JAPANESE
Anno, Mitsumasa **2, 14, 122**
Gomi, Taro **57**
Ichikawa, Satomi **62**
Iwasaki (Matsumoto), Chihiro **18**
Kitamura, Satoshi **60**
Kuratomi, Chizuko **32**
Maruki, Toshi **19**
Mori, Kyoko **64**
Nakatani, Chiyoko **30**
Say, Allen **22**
Tejima **20**
Watanabe, Shigeo **8**
Watkins, Yoko Kawashima **182**
Whitney, Phyllis A(yame) **59**
Yashima, Taro **4**

KOREAN
Choi, Sook Nyul **53**

MYANMARI
Rayner, Mary **41**

NEW ZEALANDER
Allen, Pamela **44**
Cowley, (Cassia) Joy **55**
de Roo, Anne Louise **63**
Dodd, Lynley (Stuart) **62**
Duder, Tessa **43**
Gee, Maurice (Gough) **56**
Gordon, Gaelyn **75**
Laird, Elizabeth (Mary Risk) **65**
Macdonald, Caroline **60**
Mahy, Margaret (May) **7, 78, 155, 240**
Park, (Rosina) Ruth (Lucia) **51**
Taylor, William **63**

NIGERIAN
Achebe, (Albert) Chinua(lumogu) **20, 156**
Emecheta, Buchi **158**
Nwapa, Flora (Nwanzuruaha) **162**

NORTHERN IRISH
Bunting, Eve **28, 56, 189**
Waddell, Martin **31**

NORWEGIAN
Asbjørnsen, Peter **104**
d'Aulaire, Ingri (Mortenson Parin) **21**
Moe, Jørgen **104**
Proeysen, Alf **24**
Vestly, Anne-Cath **99**

POLISH
Domanska, Janina **40**
Hautzig, Esther Rudomin **22**
Janosch **26**
Korczak, Janusz **152**
Orlev, Uri **30**
Pienkowski, Jan (Michal) **6**
Shulevitz, Uri **5, 61**
Singer, Isaac Bashevis **1**
Suhl, Yuri (Menachem) **2**
Vogel, Ilse-Margret **170**
Wojciechowska, Maia (Teresa) **1**

ROMANIAN
Wiesel, Elie **192**

RUSSIAN
Asimov, Isaac **12, 79**
Chukovsky, Kornei Ivanovich **239**
Ginsburg, Mirra **45**
Korinetz, Yuri (Iosifovich) **4**
Spirin, Gennady **88**

SCOTTISH
Baillie, Allan (Stuart) **49**
Ballantyne, R(obert) M(ichael) **137, 228**
Bannerman, Helen (Brodie Cowan Watson) **21, 144**
Barrie, J(ames) M(atthew) **16, 124, 244**
Burnford, Sheila (Philip Cochrane Every) **2**
Doyle, Sir Arthur Conan **106**
Grahame, Kenneth **5, 135, 211, 226**
Hunter, Mollie **25**
Lang, Andrew **101, 174, 227**
Lingard, Joan **89**
MacDonald, George **67, 233**
Scott, Sir Walter **154**
Sinclair, Catherine **183**
Stevenson, Robert Louis (Balfour) **10, 11, 107, 180, 204, 210, 221**

SOUTH AFRICAN
Daly, Nicholas **41**
Gordon, Sheila **27**
Lewin, Hugh **9**
Naidoo, Beverley **29**
Seed, Jenny **76**
Tolkien, J(ohn) R(onald) R(euel) **56**

SPANISH
Sánchez-Silva, José Maria **12**

SWEDISH
Beckman, Gunnel **25**
Beskow, Elsa (Maartman) **17**
Bjoerk, Christina **22**
Gripe, Maria (Kristina) **5**
Lagerlof, Selma (Ottiliana Lovisa) **7**
Lindgren, Astrid (Ericsson) **1, 39, 119, 260**
Lindgren, Barbro **20, 86**
Unnerstad, Edith (Totterman) **36**

SWISS
Carigiet, Alois **38**
Delessert, Etienne **81**
Duvoisin, Roger (Antoine) **23**
Gallaz, Christophe **126**
Glenn, Mel **51**
Mueller, Jörg **43**
Pfister, Marcus **42**
Spyri, Johanna (Heusser) **13, 115**
Von Wyss, Johann David **92**

THAI
Ho, Minfong **28**

TRINIDADIAN
Guy, Rosa (Cuthbert) **13, 137**

WELSH
Arundel, Honor (Morfydd) **35**
Dahl, Roald **1, 7, 41, 111, 224**

ZIMBABWEAN
Paul, Korky **87**

CLR-272 Title Index

The Black Riders and Other Lines (Crane) **272**:14, 61-52
Charlotte's Web (White) **272**:124-72
The Correspondence of Stephen Crane (Crane) **272**:89
"Death of a Pig" (White) **272**:143, 162, 167, 171

Essays of E. B. White (White) **272**:143, 167
George's Mother (Crane) **272**:62, 83
Letters of E. B. White (White) **272**:148, 168, 170
Maggie: A Girl of the Streets (Crane) **272**:34, 56, 61-63, 68, 83

The Red Badge of Courage: An Episode of the American Civil War (Crane) **272**:4-118
Stuart Little (White) **272**:162
The Third Violet (Crane) **272**:62, 95